AOI HOUSE

OMNIBUS COLLECTION I

art by
SHIEI

story by
ADAM ARNOLD

AOI HOUSE

OMNIBUS COLLECTION I

story by Adam Arnold   art by Carmela "Shiei" Doneza

STAFF CREDITS

toning	**Jon Zamar, Armand Roy Canlas**
lettering	**Jon Zamar, Nate Legaspi, Gabe dela Cruz**
graphic design	**Jon Zamar, Cheese, Nate Legaspi, Adam Arnold**
cover design	**Nicky Lim**
assistant editor	**Adam Arnold**
editor	**Jason DeAngelis**

Visit us online at www.gomanga.com

ISBN: 978-1-933164-73-1

Printed in Canada

First printing: March 2008

10 9 8 7 6 5 4 3 2 1

Seven Seas

SEASON ONE

EXTRAS

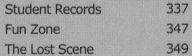

AOI HOUSE

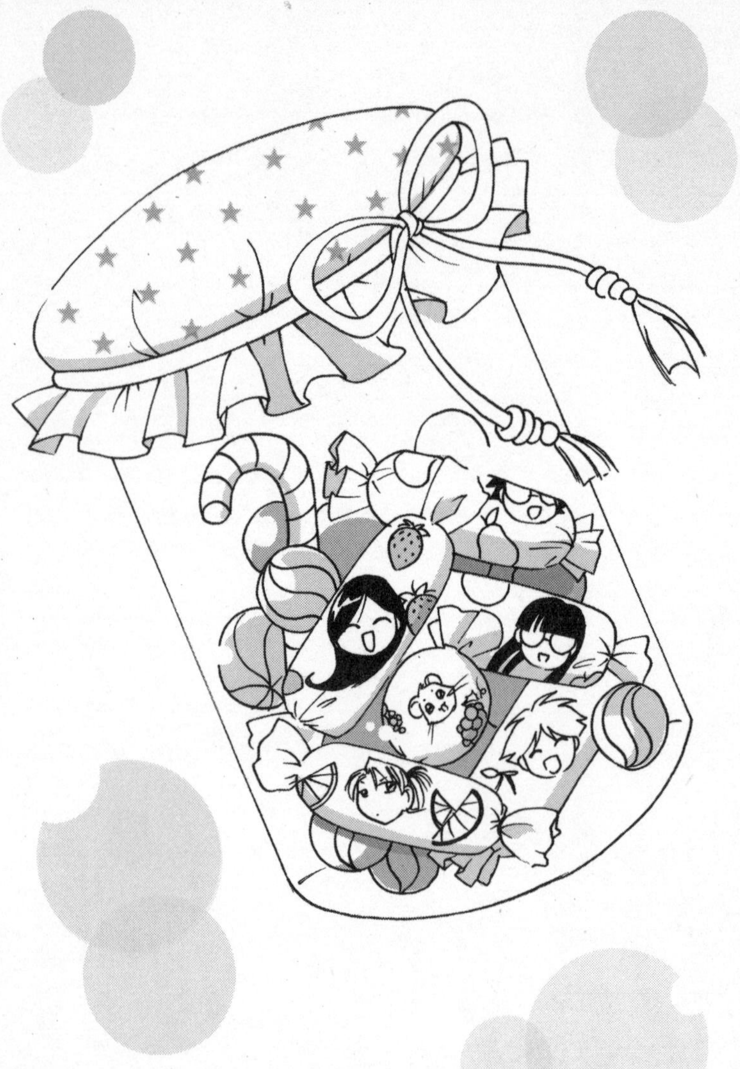

EPISODE 1: ARRIVAL

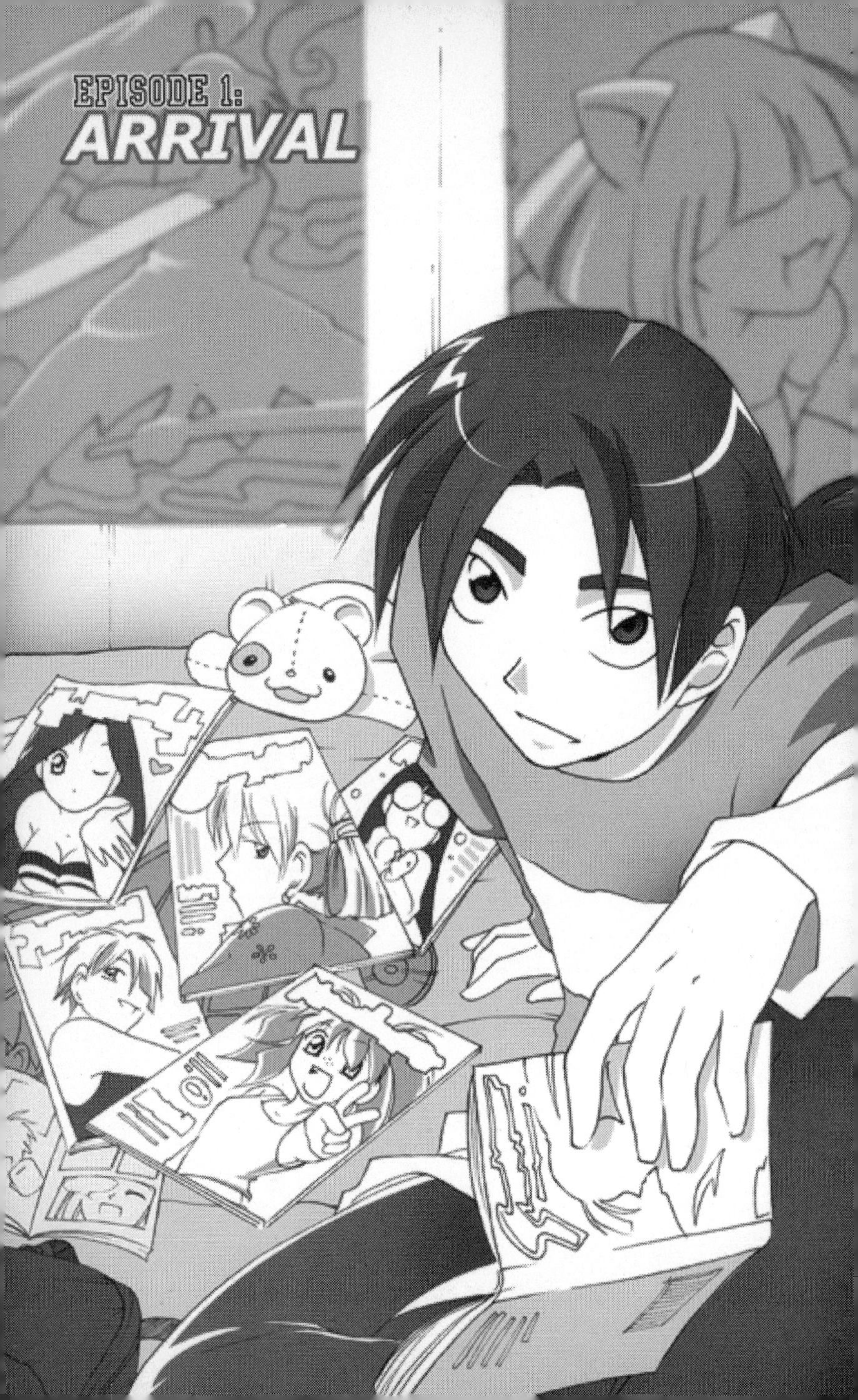

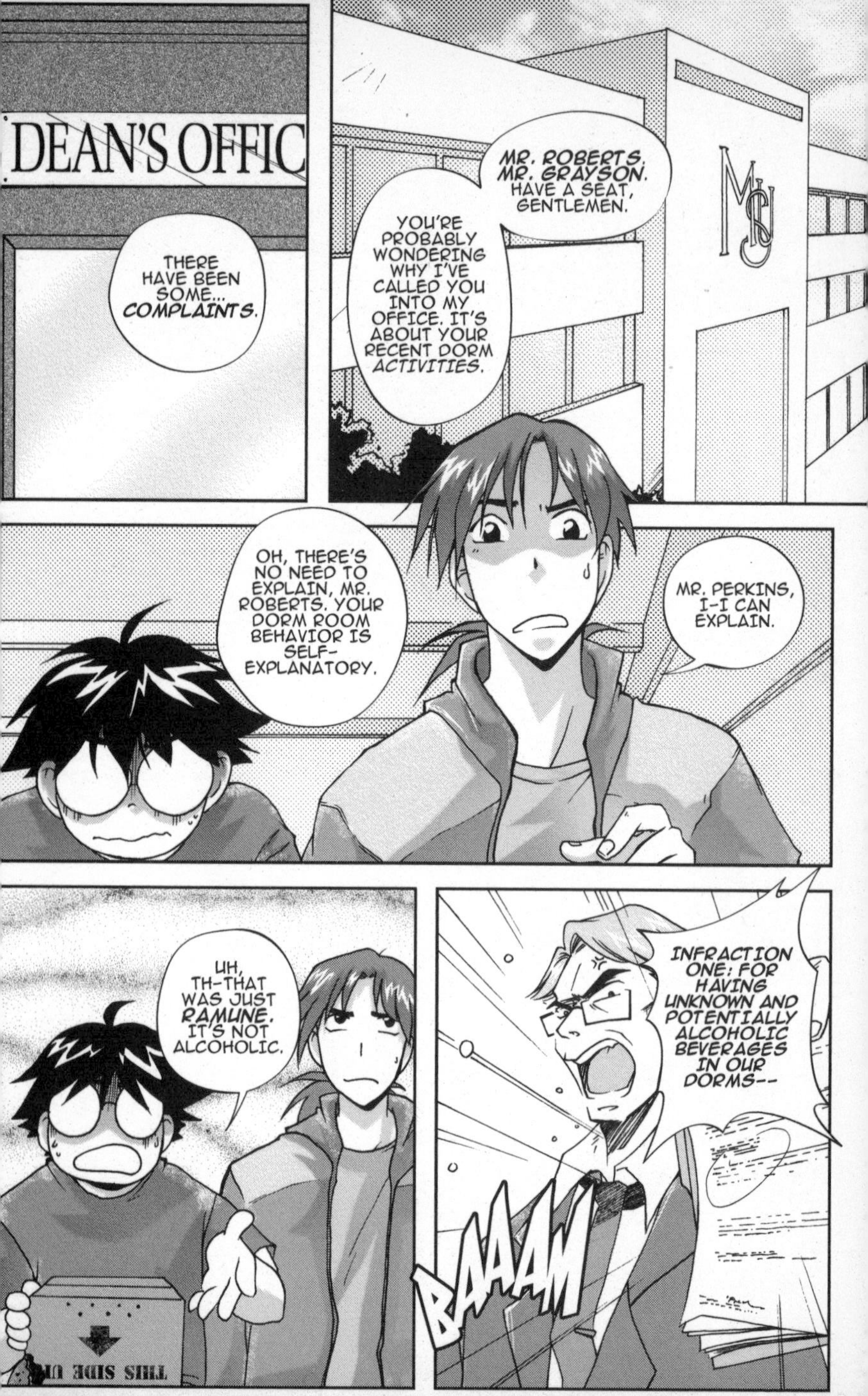
MR. ROBERTS. MR. GRAYSON. HAVE A SEAT, GENTLEMEN.
YOU'RE PROBABLY WONDERING WHY I'VE CALLED YOU INTO MY OFFICE. IT'S ABOUT YOUR RECENT DORM ACTIVITIES.
MSU
DEAN'S OFFIC
THERE HAVE BEEN SOME... COMPLAINTS.
MR. PERKINS, I-I CAN EXPLAIN.
OH, THERE'S NO NEED TO EXPLAIN, MR. ROBERTS. YOUR DORM ROOM BEHAVIOR IS SELF-EXPLANATORY.
INFRACTION ONE: FOR HAVING UNKNOWN AND POTENTIALLY ALCOHOLIC BEVERAGES IN OUR DORMS--
BAAAM
UH, TH-THAT WAS JUST RAMUNE. IT'S NOT ALCOHOLIC.

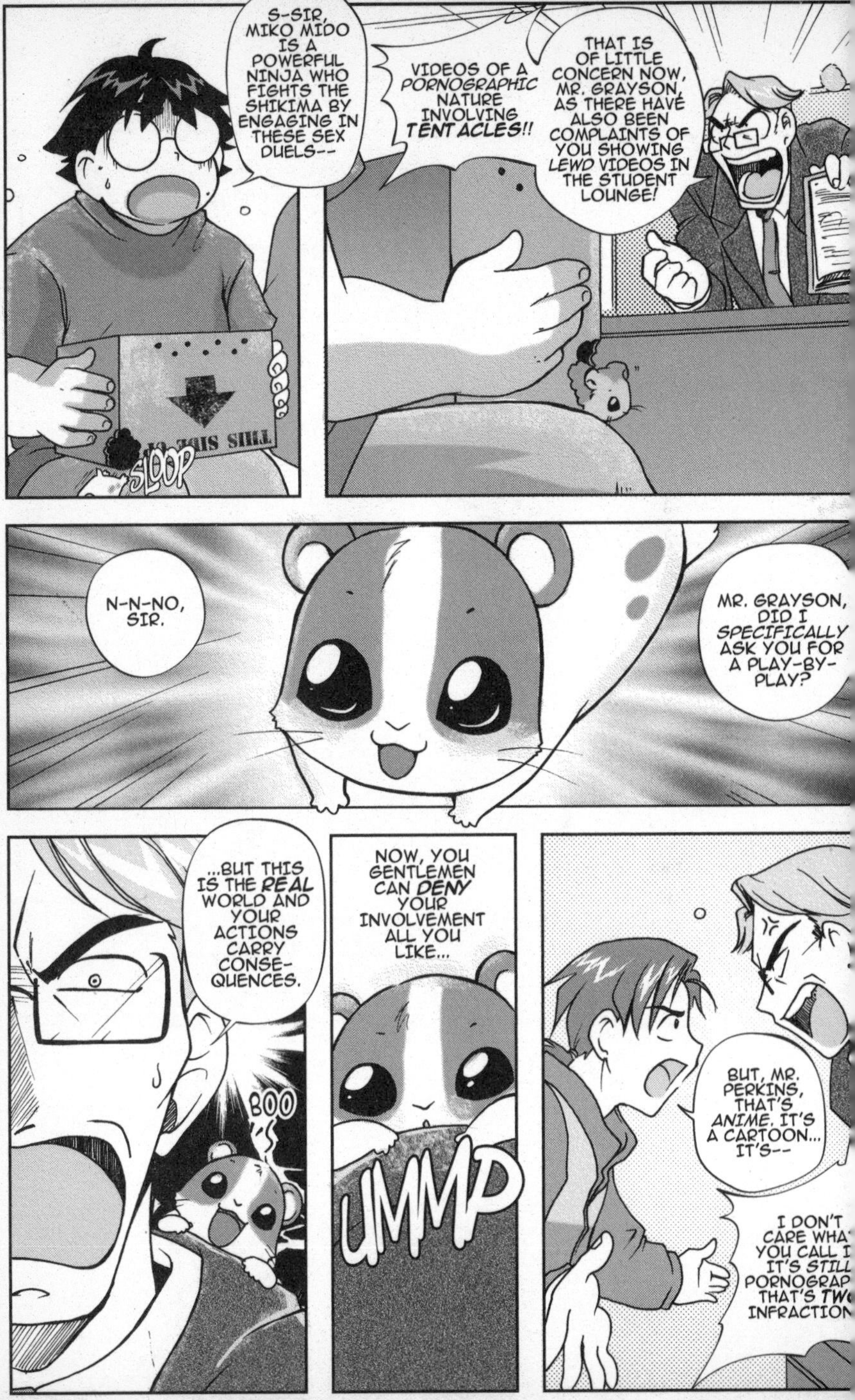
THAT IS OF LITTLE CONCERN NOW, MR. GRAYSON, AS THERE HAVE ALSO BEEN COMPLAINTS OF YOU SHOWING *LEWD* VIDEOS IN THE STUDENT LOUNGE!
VIDEOS OF A *PORNOGRAPHIC* NATURE INVOLVING ***TENTACLES***!!
S-SIR, MIKO MIDO IS A POWERFUL NINJA WHO FIGHTS THE SHIKIMA BY ENGAGING IN THESE SEX DUELS--
SLOOP
MR. GRAYSON, DID I *SPECIFICALLY* ASK YOU FOR A PLAY-BY-PLAY?
N-N-NO, SIR.
BUT, MR. PERKINS, THAT'S *ANIME*. IT'S A CARTOON... IT'S--
I DON'T CARE WHA YOU CALL I IT'S *STILL* PORNOGRAP THAT'S *TW* INFRACTION
NOW, YOU GENTLEMEN CAN ***DENY*** YOUR INVOLVEMENT ALL YOU LIKE...
UMMP
...BUT THIS IS THE ***REAL*** WORLD AND YOUR ACTIONS CARRY CONSE-QUENCES.
BOO

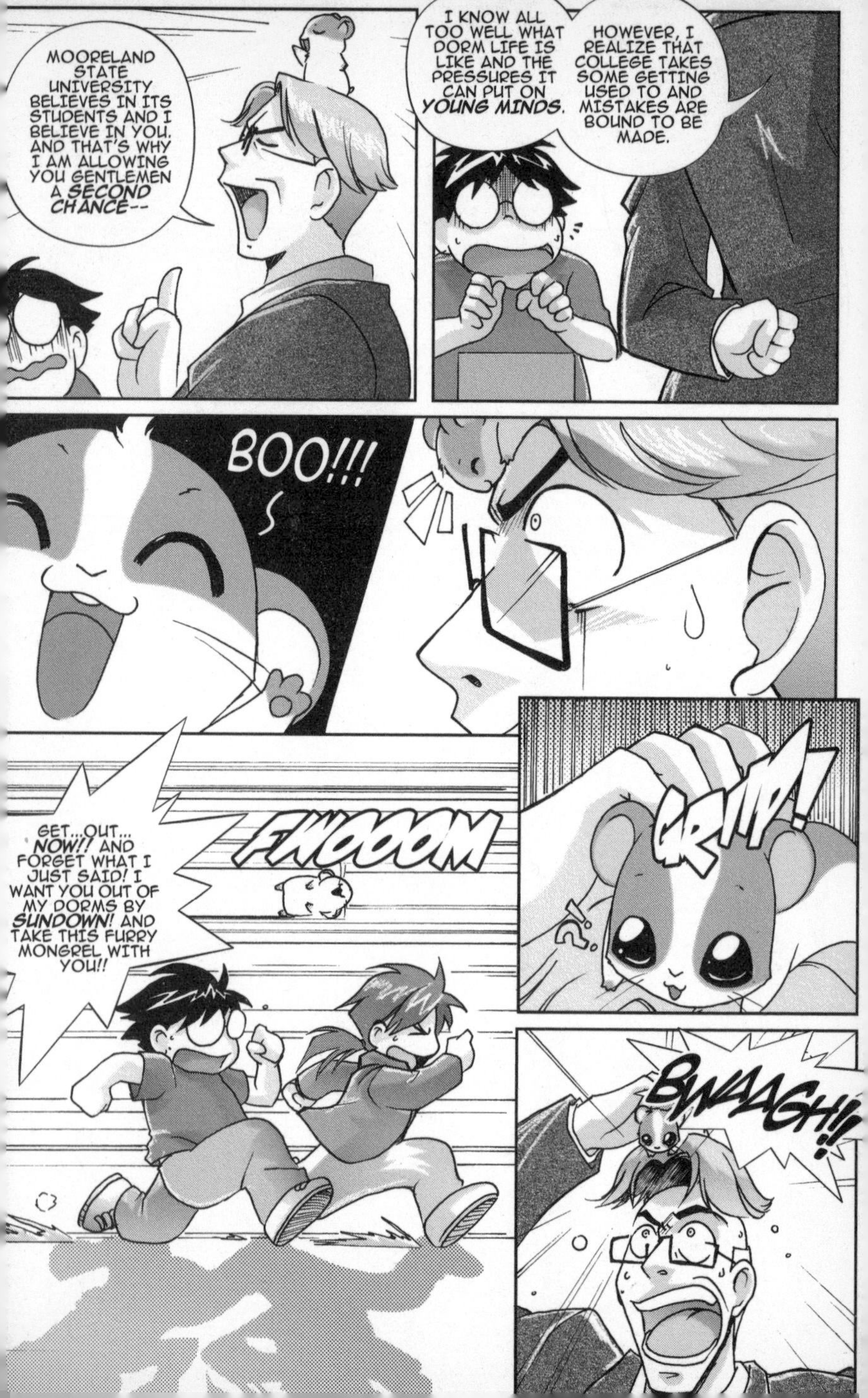
MOORELAND STATE UNIVERSITY BELIEVES IN ITS STUDENTS AND I BELIEVE IN YOU, AND THAT'S WHY I AM ALLOWING YOU GENTLEMEN A SECOND CHANCE--
I KNOW ALL TOO WELL WHAT DORM LIFE IS LIKE AND THE PRESSURES IT CAN PUT ON YOUNG MINDS.
HOWEVER, I REALIZE THAT COLLEGE TAKES SOME GETTING USED TO AND MISTAKES ARE BOUND TO BE MADE.
BOO!!!
GRIP!
BWAAGH!!
GET...OUT... NOW!! AND FORGET WHAT I JUST SAID! I WANT YOU OUT OF MY DORMS BY SUNDOWN! AND TAKE THIS FURRY MONGREL WITH YOU!!
FWOOOM

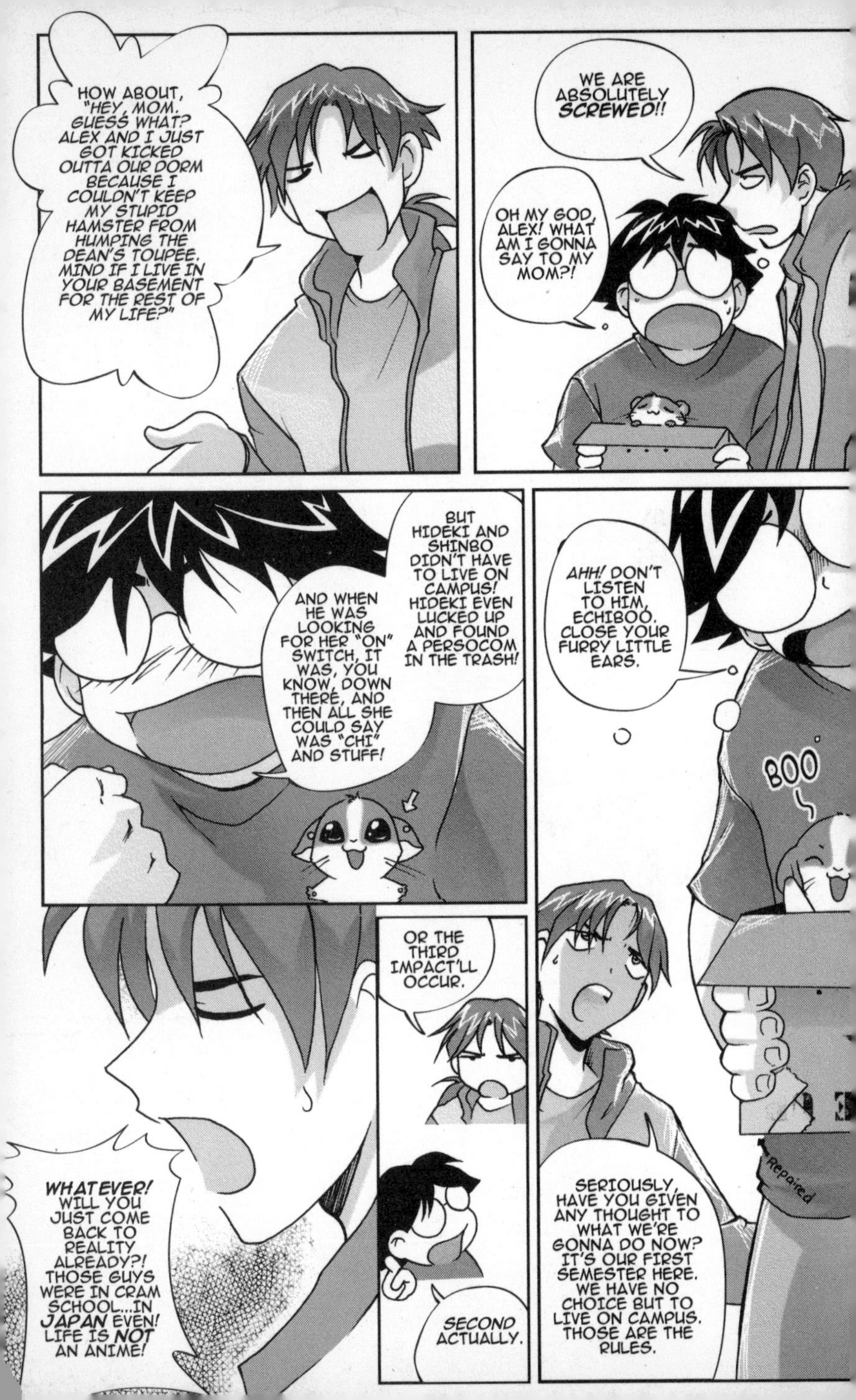

WE ARE ABSOLUTELY SCREWED!!
OH MY GOD, ALEX! WHAT AM I GONNA SAY TO MY MOM?!
HOW ABOUT, "HEY, MOM. GUESS WHAT? ALEX AND I JUST GOT KICKED OUTTA OUR DORM BECAUSE I COULDN'T KEEP MY STUPID HAMSTER FROM HUMPING THE DEAN'S TOUPEE. MIND IF I LIVE IN YOUR BASEMENT FOR THE REST OF MY LIFE?"
AHH! DON'T LISTEN TO HIM, ECHIBOO. CLOSE YOUR FURRY LITTLE EARS.
BOO
BUT HIDEKI AND SHINBO DIDN'T HAVE TO LIVE ON CAMPUS! HIDEKI EVEN LUCKED UP AND FOUND A PERSOCOM IN THE TRASH!
AND WHEN HE WAS LOOKING FOR HER "ON" SWITCH, IT WAS, YOU KNOW, DOWN THERE, AND THEN ALL SHE COULD SAY WAS "CHI" AND STUFF!
Repaired
SERIOUSLY, HAVE YOU GIVEN ANY THOUGHT TO WHAT WE'RE GONNA DO NOW? IT'S OUR FIRST SEMESTER HERE. WE HAVE NO CHOICE BUT TO LIVE ON CAMPUS. THOSE ARE THE RULES.
OR THE THIRD IMPACT'LL OCCUR.
SECOND ACTUALLY.
WHATEVER! WILL YOU JUST COME BACK TO REALITY ALREADY?! THOSE GUYS WERE IN CRAM SCHOOL...IN JAPAN EVEN! LIFE IS NOT AN ANIME!

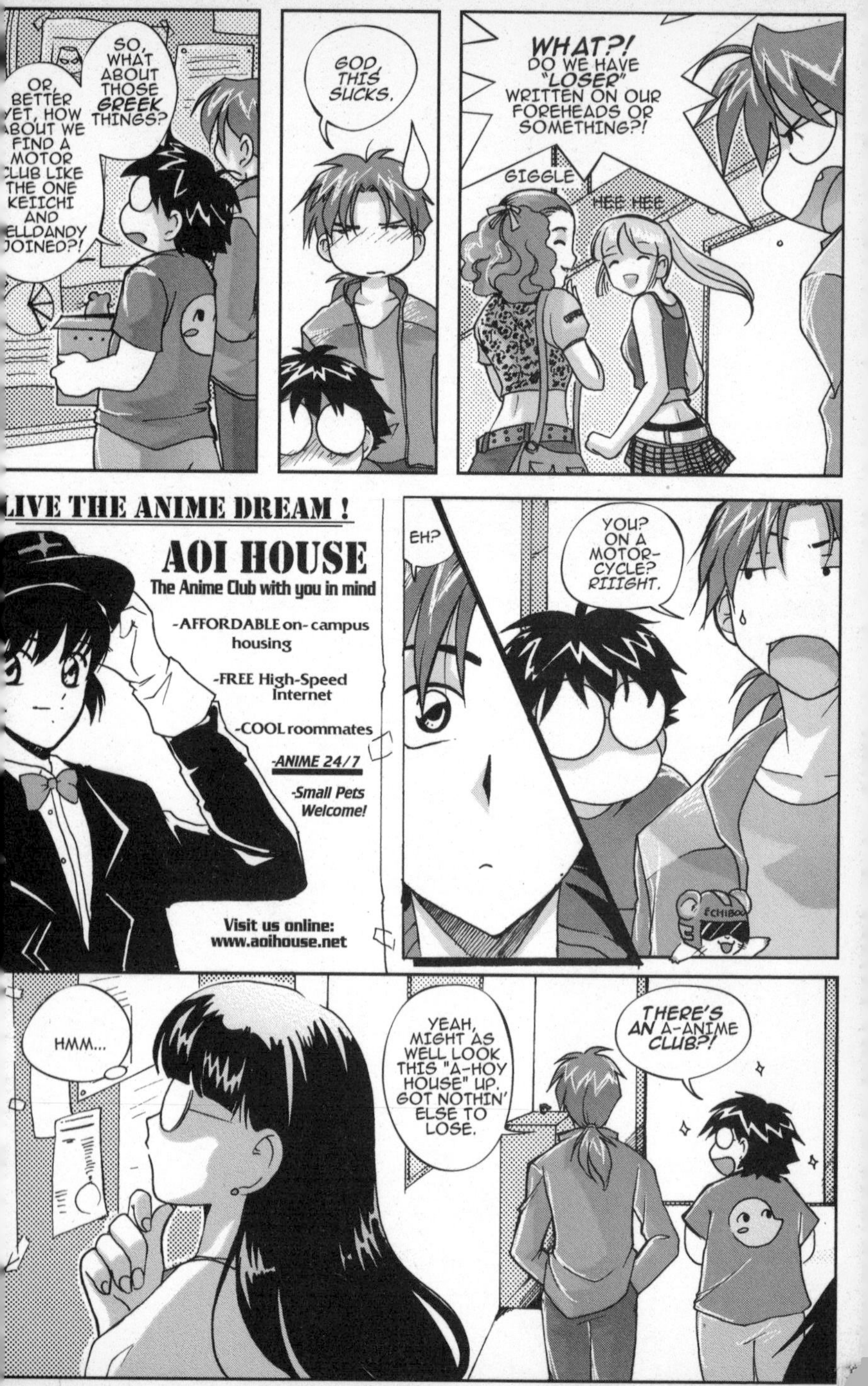
WHAT?! DO WE HAVE "LOSER" WRITTEN ON OUR FOREHEADS OR SOMETHING?!
GIGGLE
HEE HEE
GOD, THIS SUCKS.
SO, WHAT ABOUT THOSE GREEK THINGS?
OR, BETTER YET, HOW ABOUT WE FIND A MOTOR CLUB LIKE THE ONE KEIICHI AND BELLDANDY JOINED?!
YOU? ON A MOTOR-CYCLE? RIIIGHT.
EH?
ECHIBOO
LIVE THE ANIME DREAM !
AOI HOUSE
The Anime Club with you in mind
-AFFORDABLE on- campus housing
-FREE High-Speed Internet
-COOL roommates
-ANIME 24/7
-Small Pets Welcome!
Visit us online: www.aoihouse.net
THERE'S AN A-ANIME CLUB?!
YEAH, MIGHT AS WELL LOOK THIS "A-HOY HOUSE" UP. GOT NOTHIN' ELSE TO LOSE.
HMM...

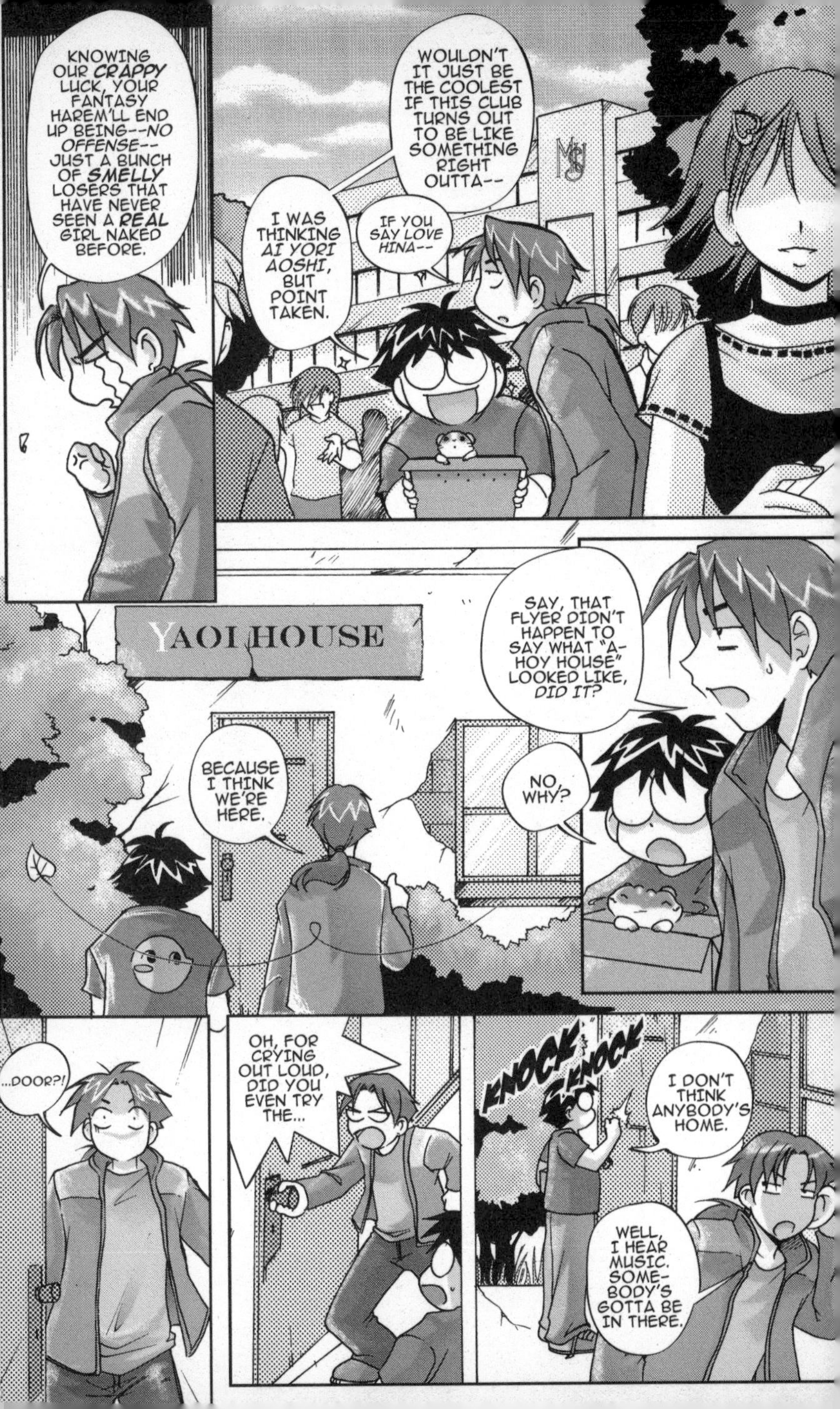
WOULDN'T IT JUST BE THE COOLEST IF THIS CLUB TURNS OUT TO BE LIKE SOMETHING RIGHT OUTTA--
IF YOU SAY LOVE HINA--
I WAS THINKING AI YORI AOSHI, BUT POINT TAKEN.
KNOWING OUR CRAPPY LUCK, YOUR FANTASY HAREM'LL END UP BEING--NO OFFENSE--JUST A BUNCH OF SMELLY LOSERS THAT HAVE NEVER SEEN A REAL GIRL NAKED BEFORE.
SAY, THAT FLYER DIDN'T HAPPEN TO SAY WHAT "A-HOY HOUSE" LOOKED LIKE, DID IT?
NO, WHY?
YAOI HOUSE
BECAUSE I THINK WE'RE HERE.
KNOCK KNOCK
I DON'T THINK ANYBODY'S HOME.
WELL, I HEAR MUSIC. SOME-BODY'S GOTTA BE IN THERE.
OH, FOR CRYING OUT LOUD, DID YOU EVEN TRY THE...
...DOOR?!

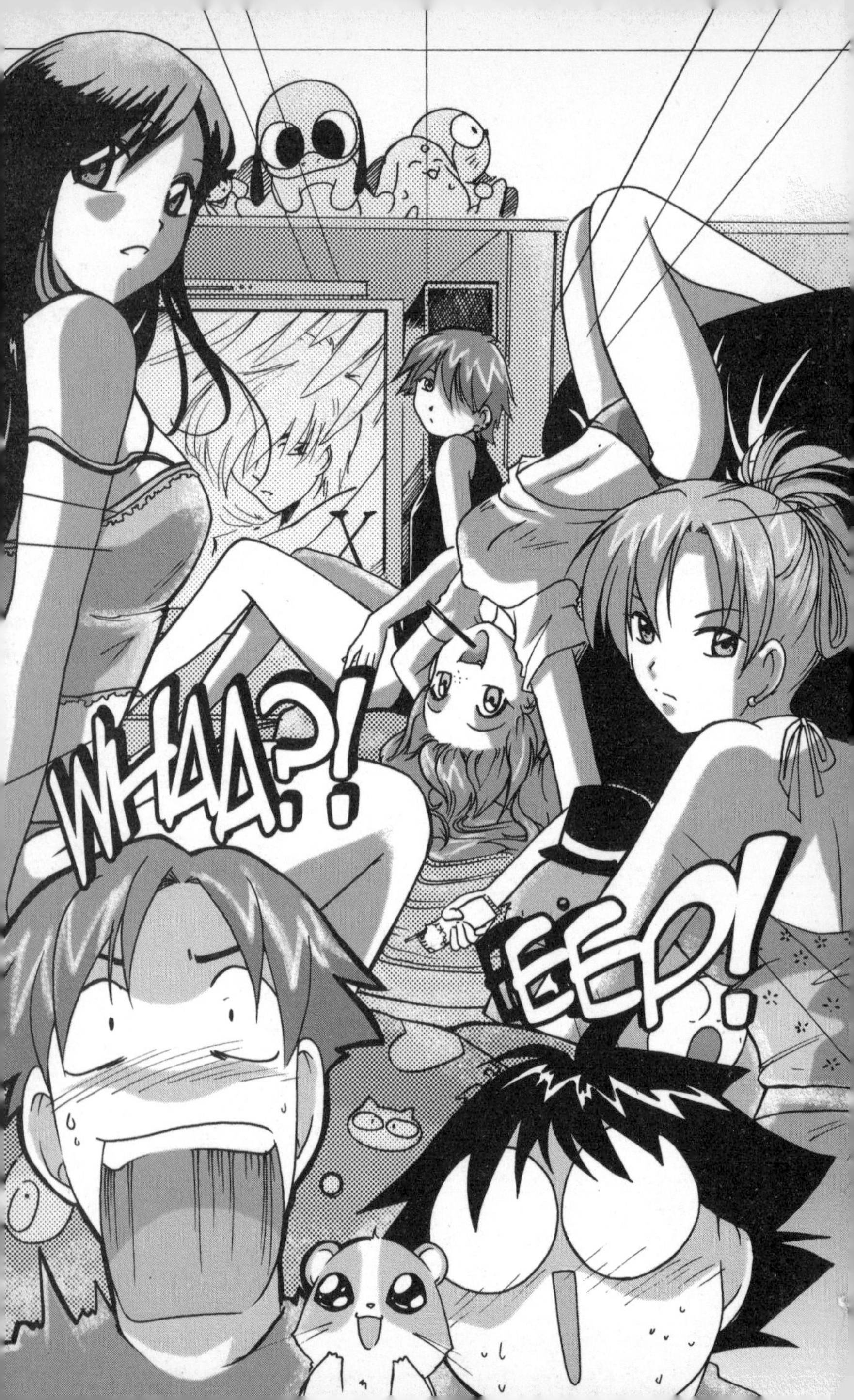
EEP!
WHAA?!

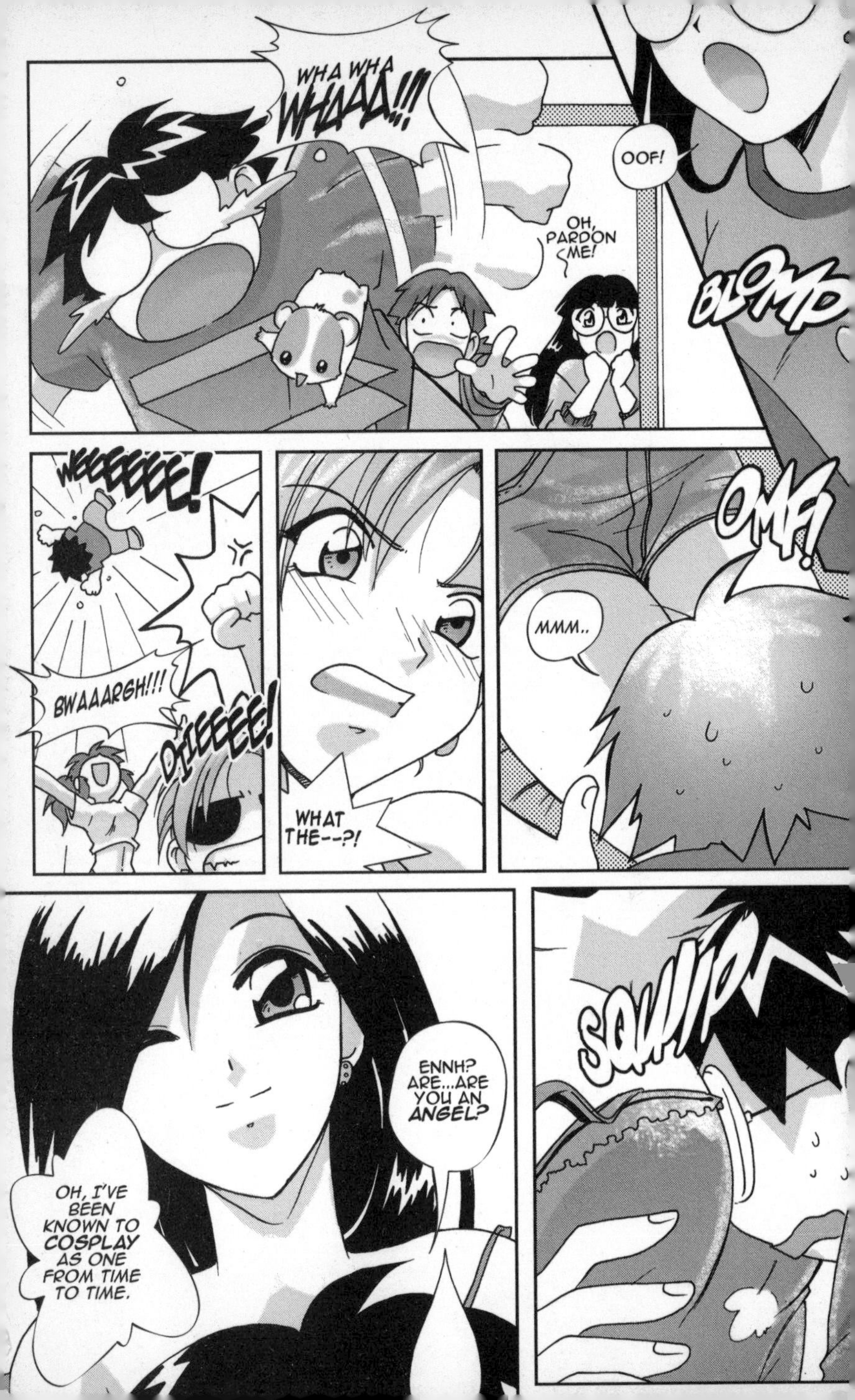
OOF!
BLOMP
WHA WHA WHAAA!!!
OH, PARDON ME!
OMF!
MMM..
WHAT THE--?!
WEEEEEEE!
BWAAARGH!!!!
DIEEEEE!
SQUIP
ENNH? ARE...ARE YOU AN ANGEL?
OH, I'VE BEEN KNOWN TO COSPLAY AS ONE FROM TIME TO TIME.

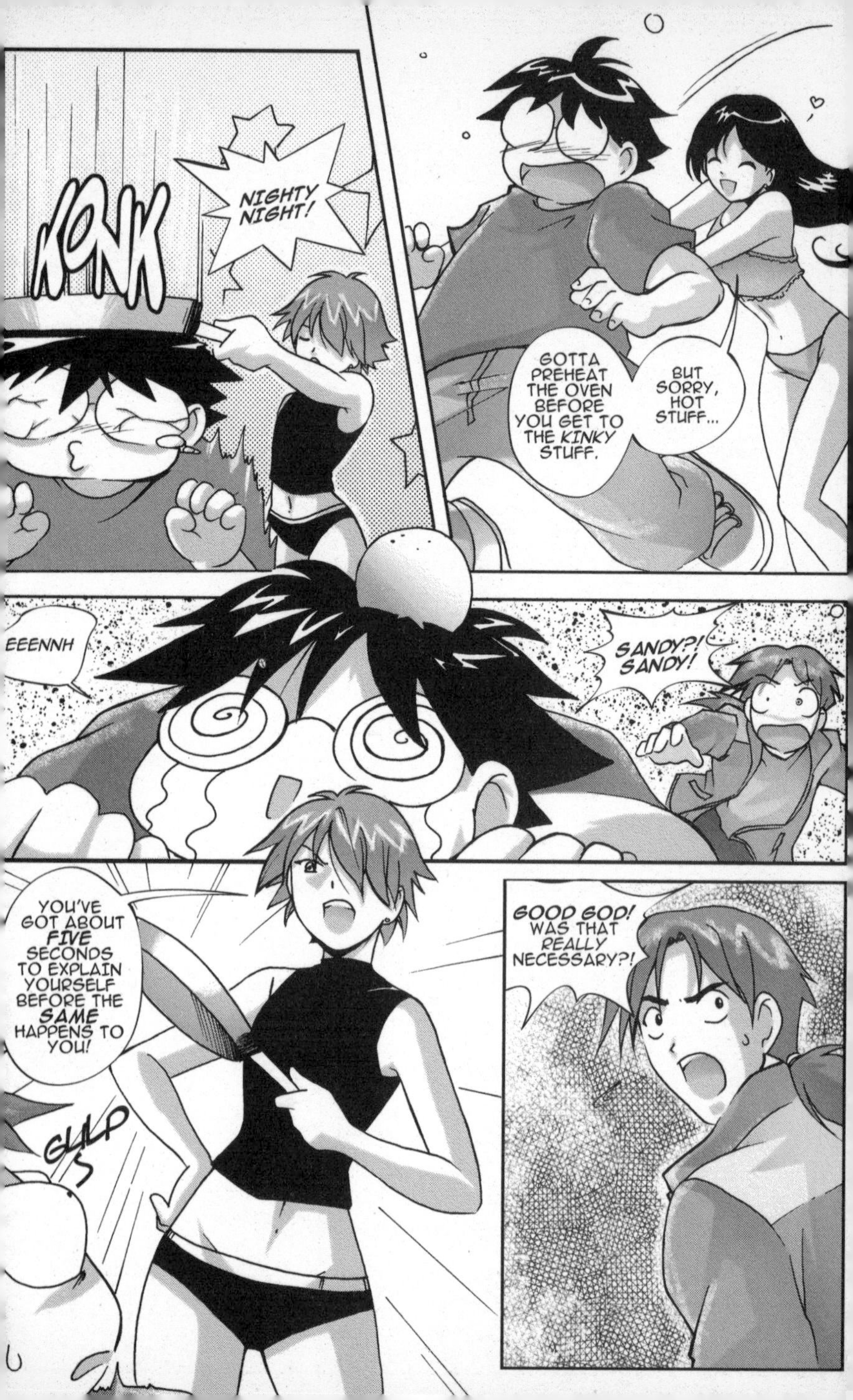
BUT SORRY, HOT STUFF...
GOTTA PREHEAT THE OVEN BEFORE YOU GET TO THE KINKY STUFF.
NIGHTY NIGHT!
KONK
SANDY?! SANDY!
EEENNH
GOOD GOD! WAS THAT REALLY NECESSARY?!
YOU'VE GOT ABOUT FIVE SECONDS TO EXPLAIN YOURSELF BEFORE THE SAME HAPPENS TO YOU!
GULP

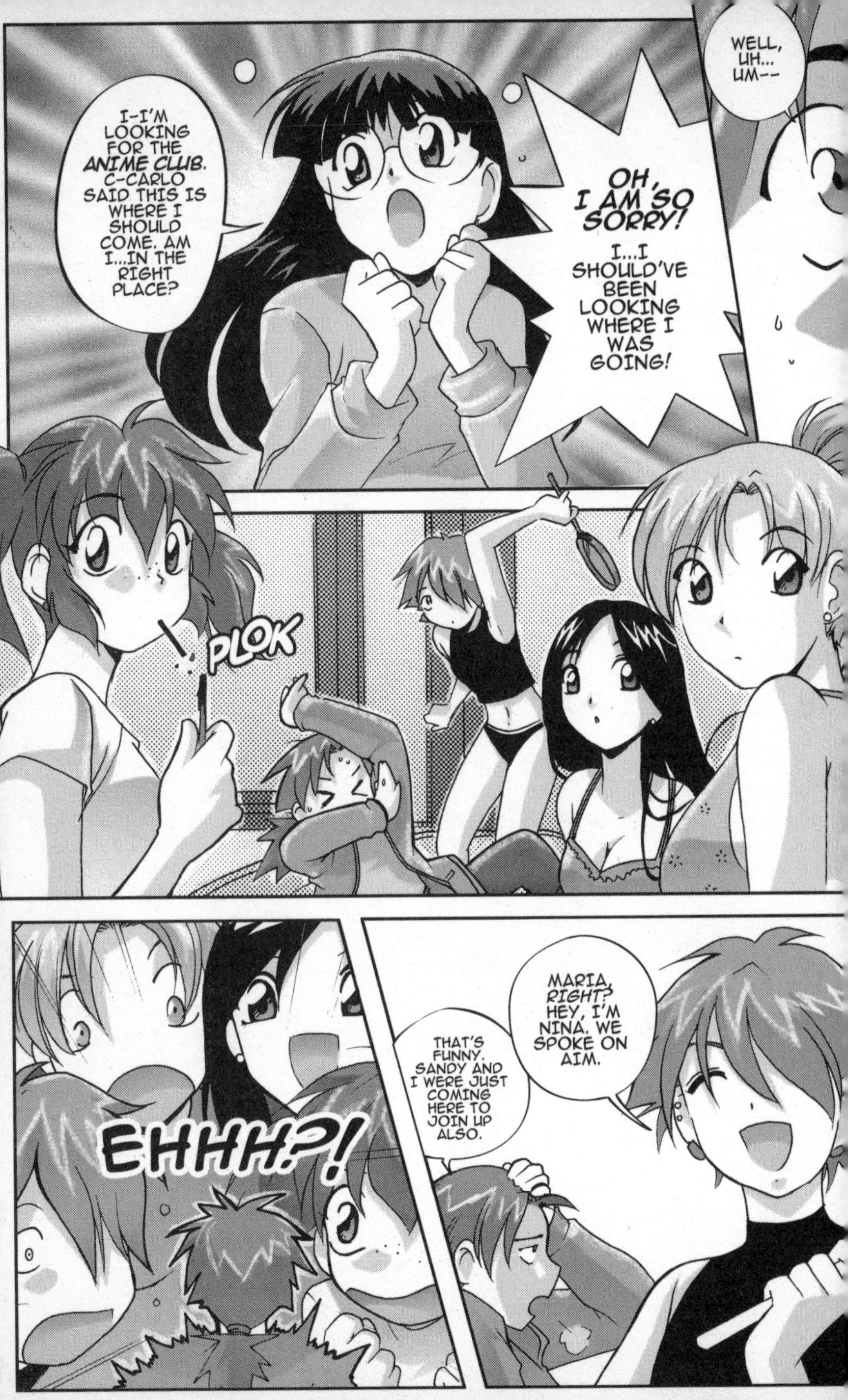
WELL, UH... UM--
OH, I AM SO SORRY!
I...I SHOULD'VE BEEN LOOKING WHERE I WAS GOING!
I-I'M LOOKING FOR THE ANIME CLUB. C-CARLO SAID THIS IS WHERE I SHOULD COME. AM I...IN THE RIGHT PLACE?
PLOK
MARIA, RIGHT? HEY, I'M NINA. WE SPOKE ON AIM.
THAT'S FUNNY. SANDY AND I WERE JUST COMING HERE TO JOIN UP ALSO.
EHHH?!

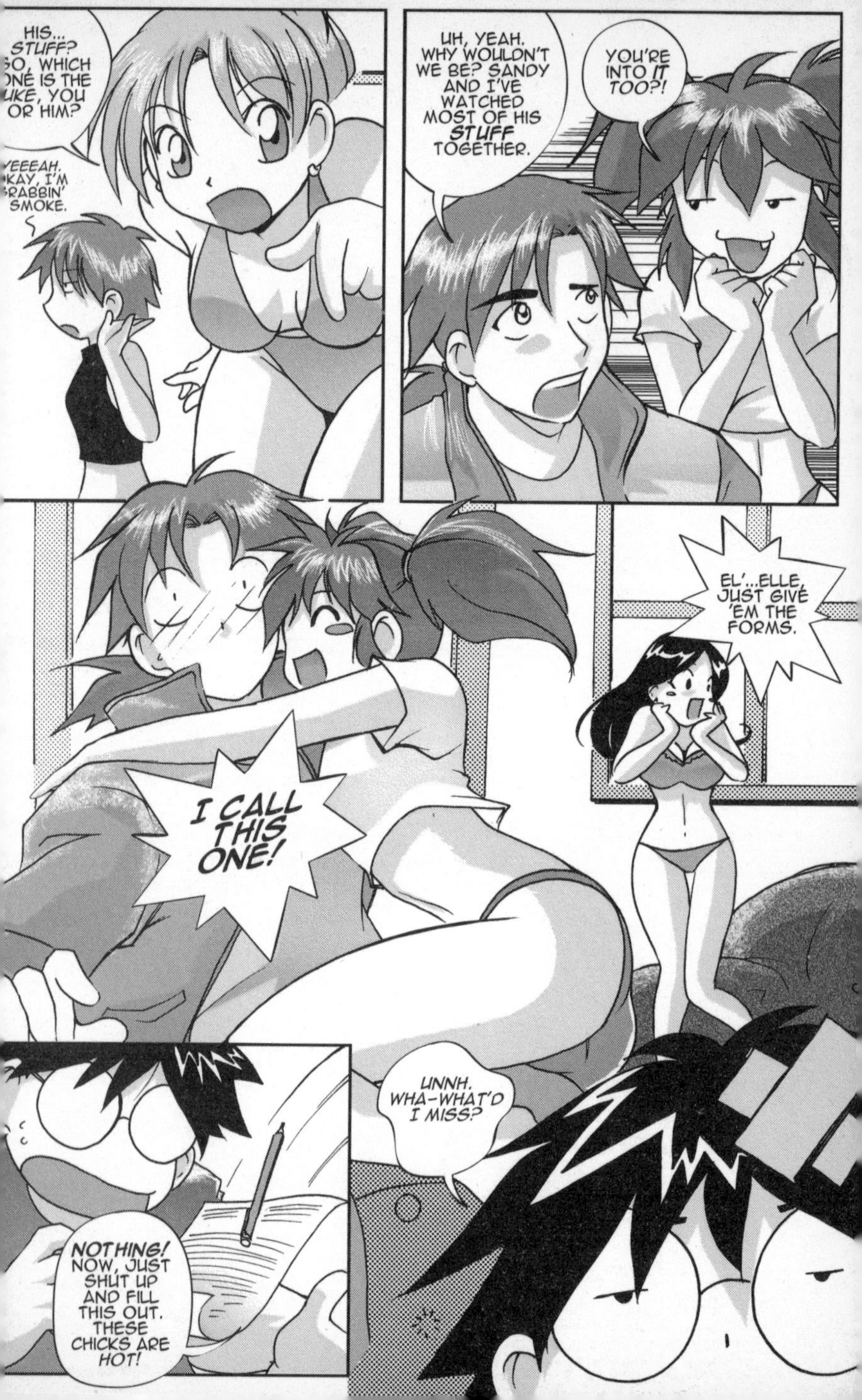
YOU'RE INTO IT TOO?!
UH, YEAH. WHY WOULDN'T WE BE? SANDY AND I'VE WATCHED MOST OF HIS STUFF TOGETHER.
HIS... STUFF? SO, WHICH ONE IS THE UKE, YOU OR HIM?
YEEEAH. OKAY, I'M GRABBIN' SMOKE.
EL'...ELLE, JUST GIVE 'EM THE FORMS.
I CALL THIS ONE!
UNNH. WHA-WHAT'D I MISS?
NOTHING! NOW, JUST SHUT UP AND FILL THIS OUT. THESE CHICKS ARE HOT!

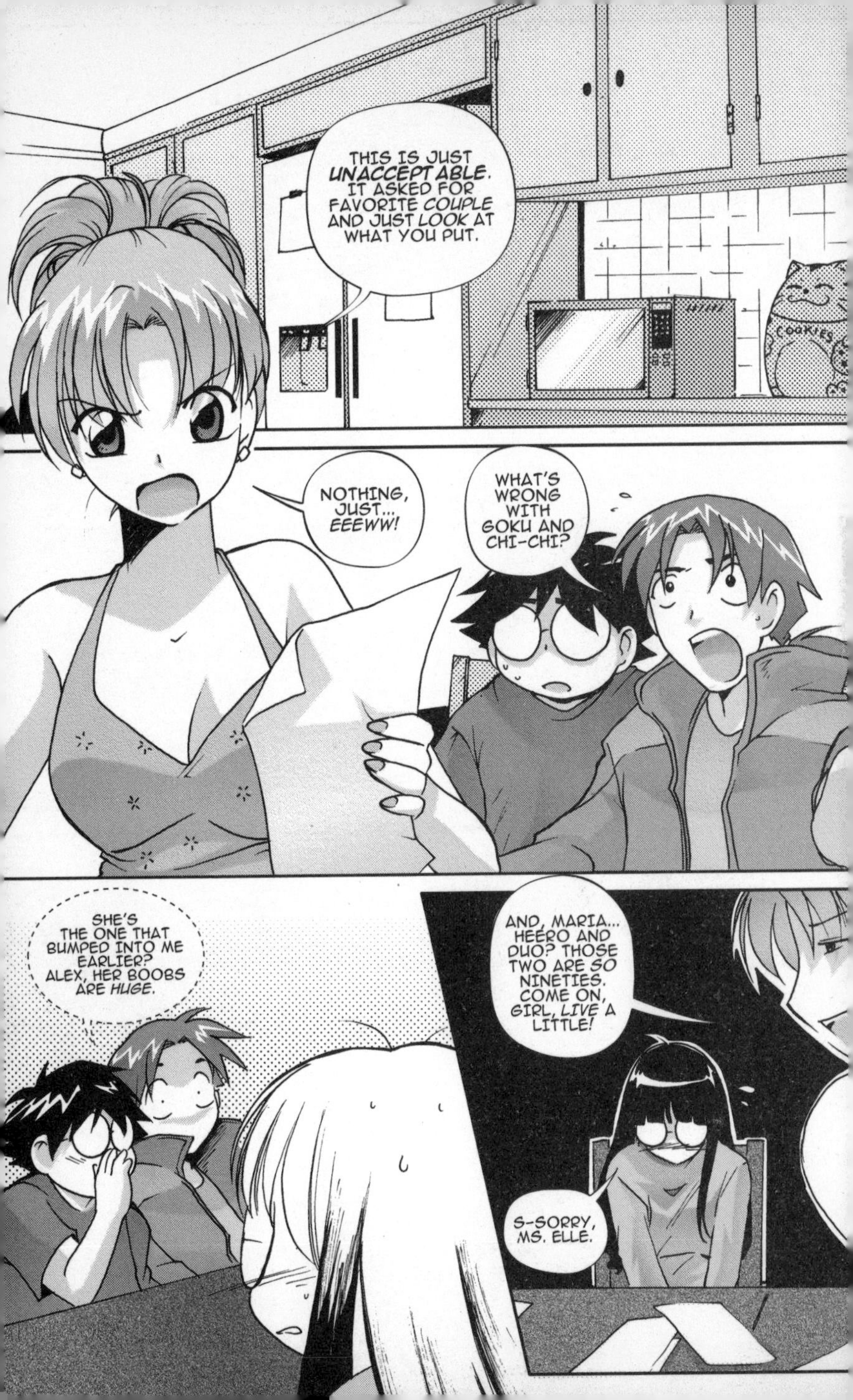
THIS IS JUST UNACCEPTABLE. IT ASKED FOR FAVORITE COUPLE AND JUST LOOK AT WHAT YOU PUT.
COOKIES
WHAT'S WRONG WITH GOKU AND CHI-CHI?
NOTHING, JUST... EEEWW!
AND, MARIA... HEERO AND DUO? THOSE TWO ARE SO NINETIES. COME ON, GIRL, LIVE A LITTLE!
S-SORRY, MS. ELLE.
SHE'S THE ONE THAT BUMPED INTO ME EARLIER? ALEX, HER BOOBS ARE HUGE.

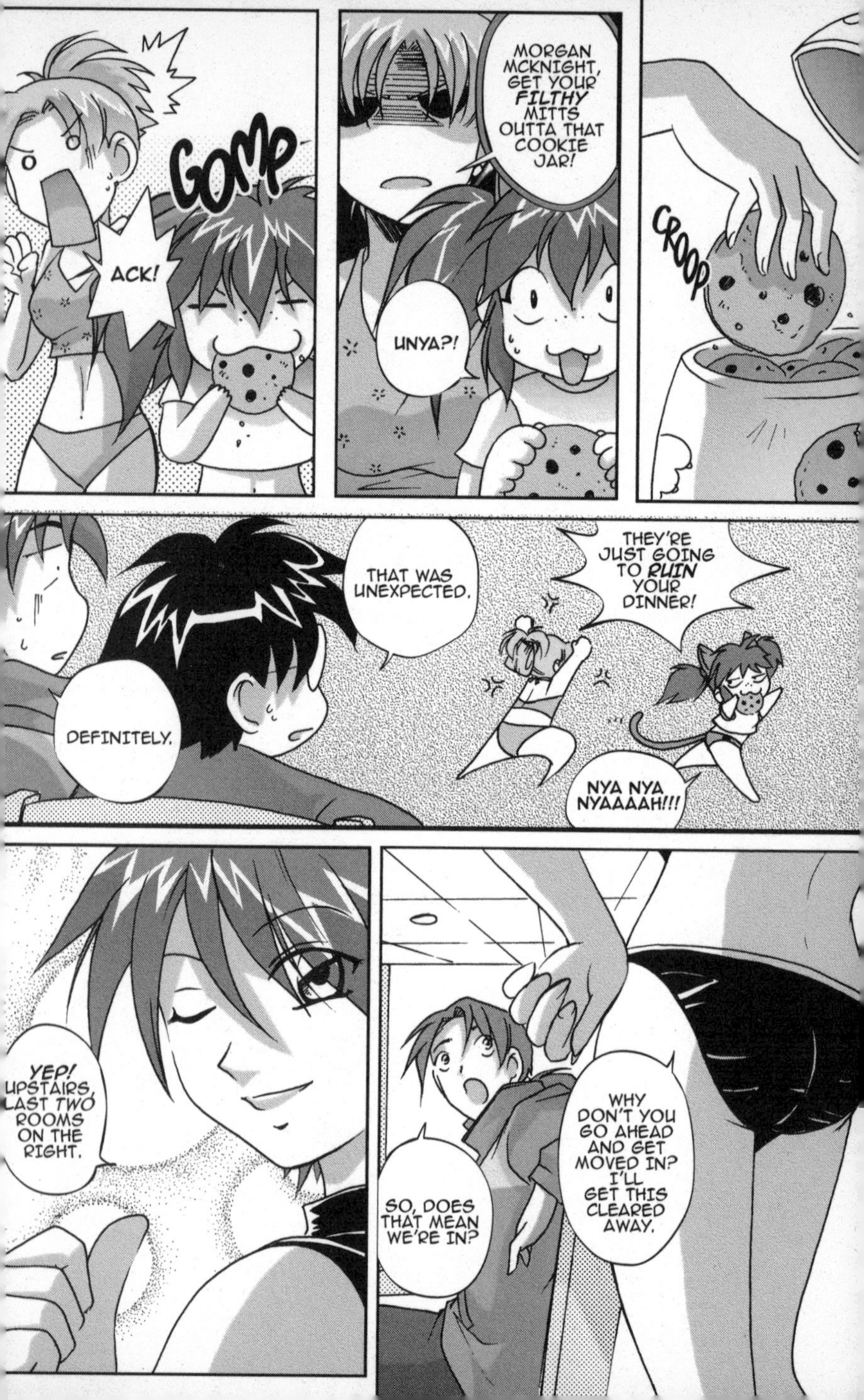
CROOP
MORGAN MCKNIGHT, GET YOUR *FILTHY* MITTS OUTTA THAT COOKIE JAR!
UNYA?!
M
GOMP
ACK!
THEY'RE JUST GOING TO *RUIN* YOUR DINNER!
THAT WAS UNEXPECTED.
NYA NYA NYAAAAH!!!
DEFINITELY.
WHY DON'T YOU GO AHEAD AND GET MOVED IN? I'LL GET THIS CLEARED AWAY.
SO, DOES THAT MEAN WE'RE IN?
YEP! UPSTAIRS, LAST *TWO* ROOMS ON THE RIGHT.

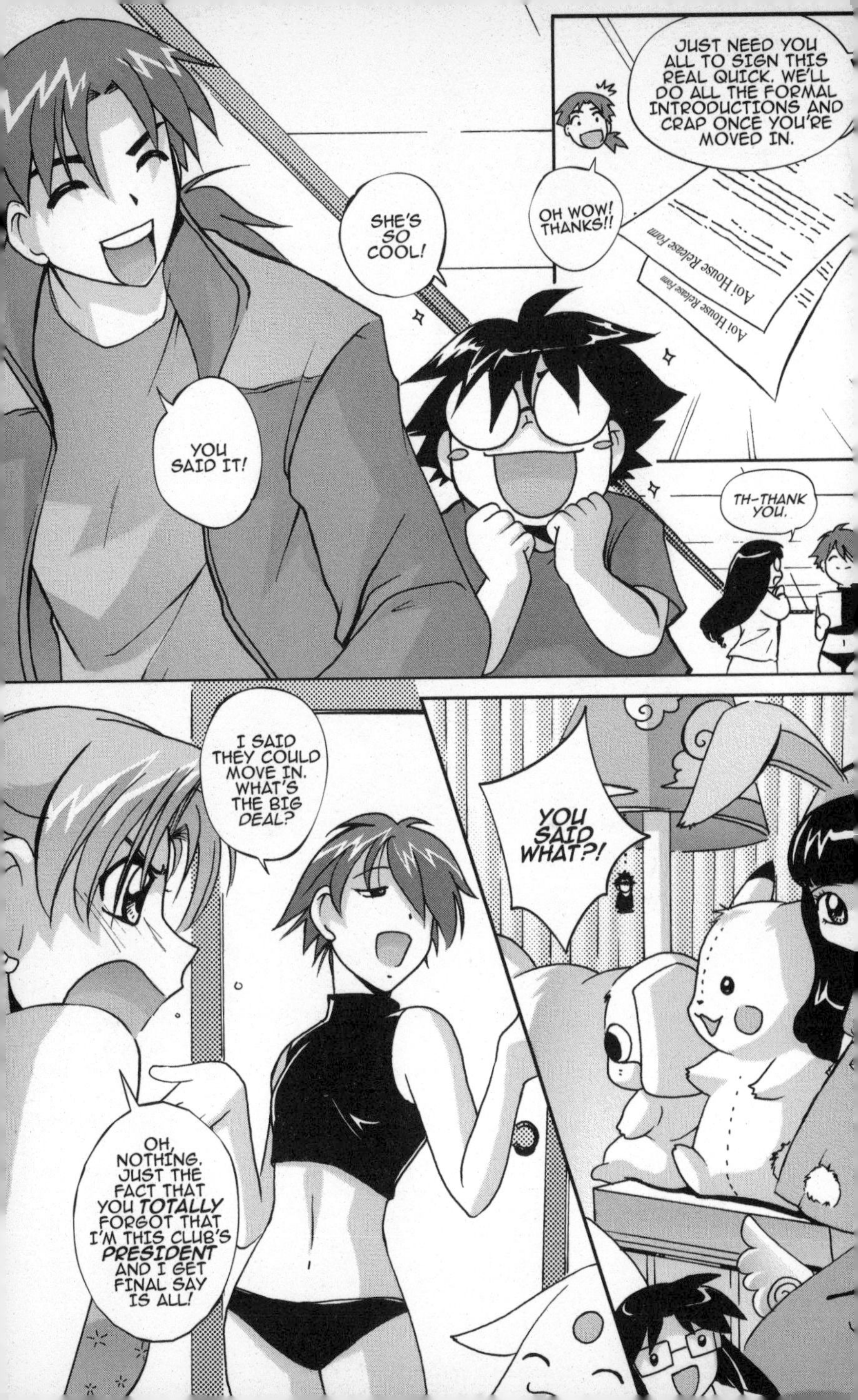
JUST NEED YOU ALL TO SIGN THIS REAL QUICK. WE'LL DO ALL THE FORMAL INTRODUCTIONS AND CRAP ONCE YOU'RE MOVED IN.
Aoi House Release Form
Aoi House Release Form
OH WOW! THANKS!!
SHE'S SO COOL!
TH-THANK YOU.
YOU SAID IT!
YOU SAID WHAT?!
I SAID THEY COULD MOVE IN. WHAT'S THE BIG DEAL?
OH, NOTHING. JUST THE FACT THAT YOU TOTALLY FORGOT THAT I'M THIS CLUB'S PRESIDENT AND I GET FINAL SAY IS ALL!

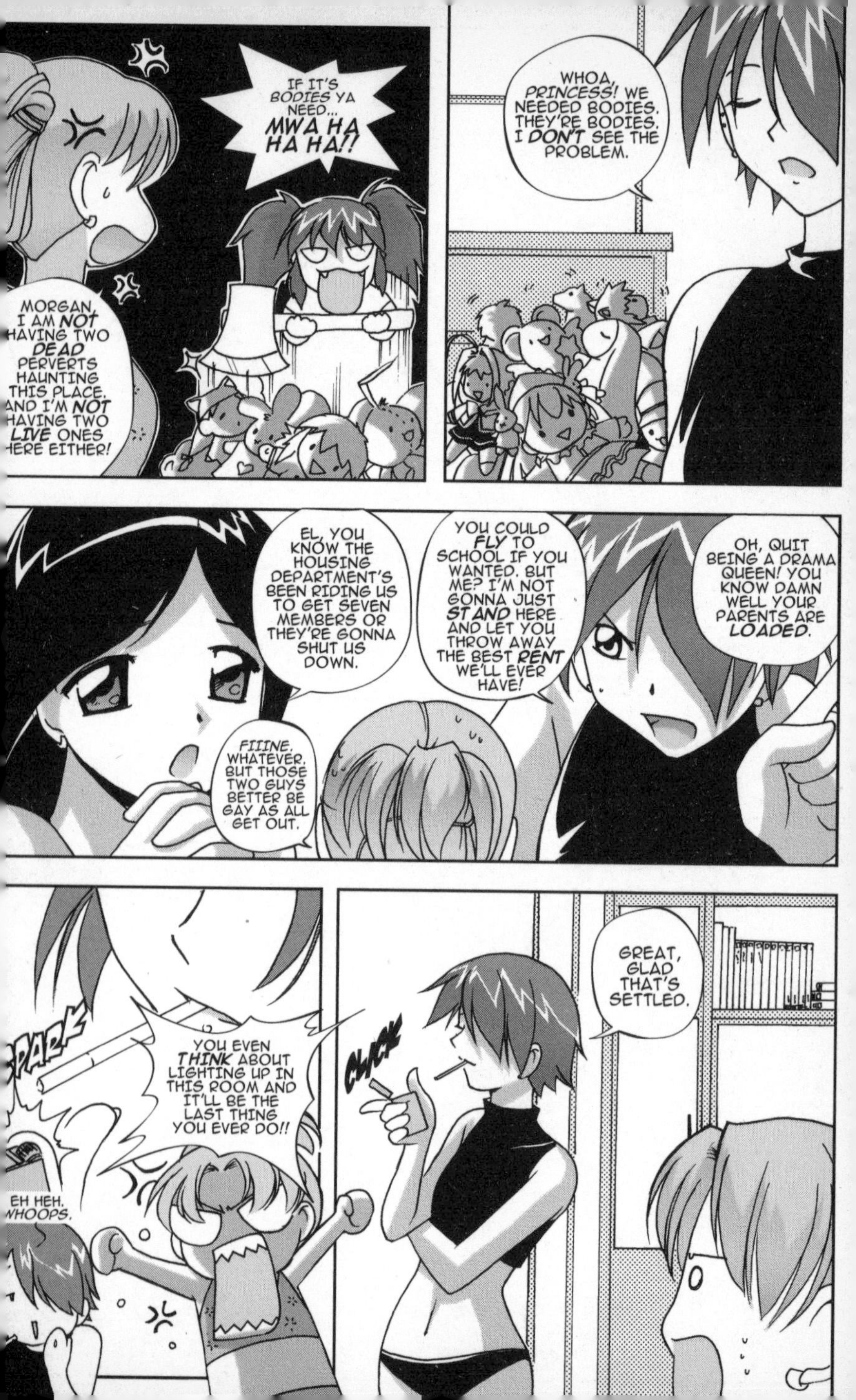
WHOA, PRINCESS! WE NEEDED BODIES. THEY'RE BODIES. I DON'T SEE THE PROBLEM.
IF IT'S BODIES YA NEED... MWA HA HA HA!!
MORGAN, I AM NOT HAVING TWO DEAD PERVERTS HAUNTING THIS PLACE. AND I'M NOT HAVING TWO LIVE ONES HERE EITHER!
OH, QUIT BEING A DRAMA QUEEN! YOU KNOW DAMN WELL YOUR PARENTS ARE LOADED.
YOU COULD FLY TO SCHOOL IF YOU WANTED. BUT ME? I'M NOT GONNA JUST STAND HERE AND LET YOU THROW AWAY THE BEST RENT WE'LL EVER HAVE!
EL, YOU KNOW THE HOUSING DEPARTMENT'S BEEN RIDING US TO GET SEVEN MEMBERS OR THEY'RE GONNA SHUT US DOWN.
FIIINE. WHATEVER. BUT THOSE TWO GUYS BETTER BE GAY AS ALL GET OUT.
GREAT, GLAD THAT'S SETTLED.
CLICK
SPARK
YOU EVEN THINK ABOUT LIGHTING UP IN THIS ROOM AND IT'LL BE THE LAST THING YOU EVER DO!!
EH HEH. WHOOPS.

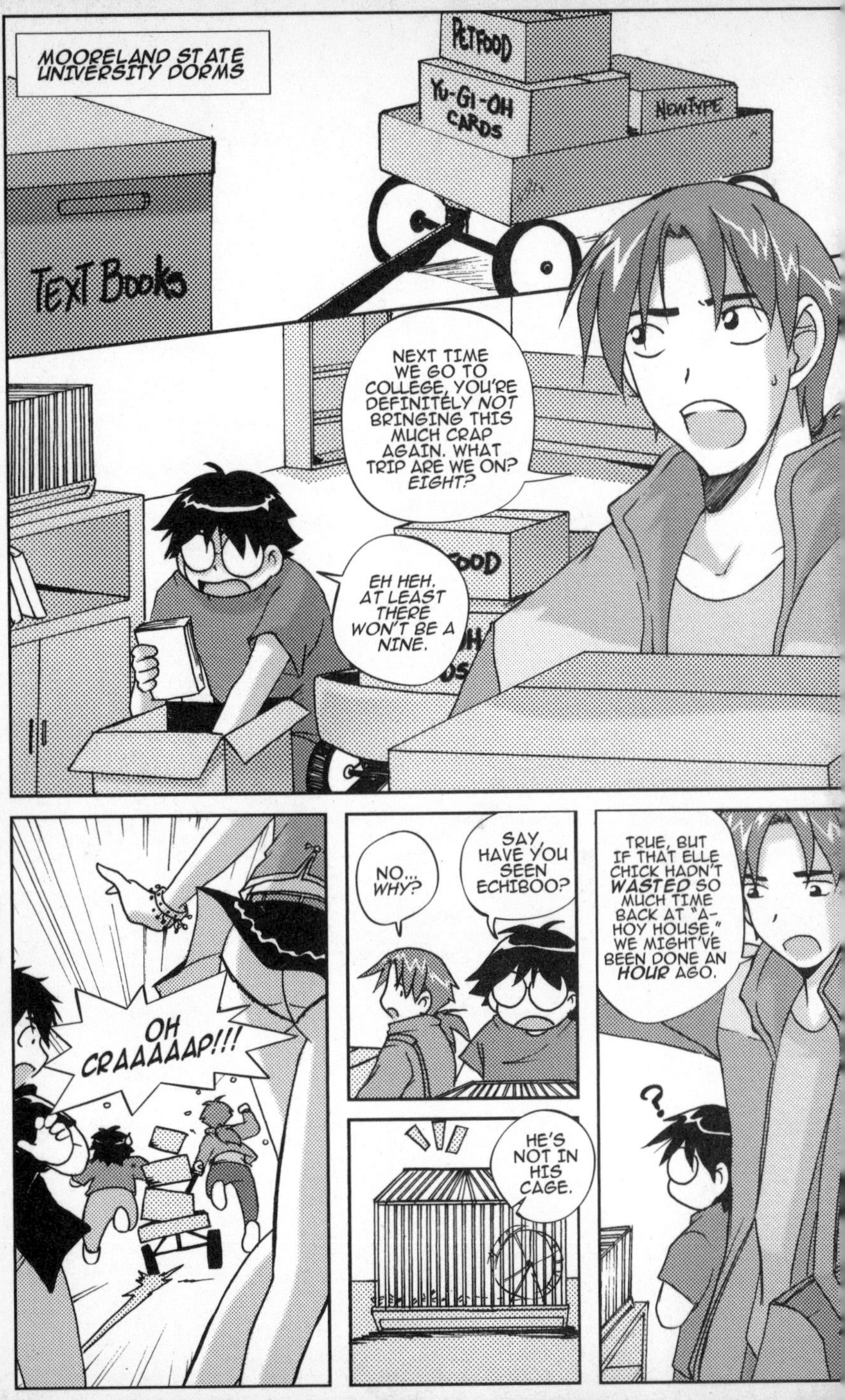
MOORELAND STATE UNIVERSITY DORMS
PETFOOD
YU-GI-OH CARDS
NEWTYPE
TEXT BOOKS
NEXT TIME WE GO TO COLLEGE, YOU'RE DEFINITELY *NOT* BRINGING THIS MUCH CRAP AGAIN. WHAT TRIP ARE WE ON? *EIGHT?*
EH HEH. AT LEAST THERE WON'T BE A NINE.
TRUE, BUT IF THAT ELLE CHICK HADN'T *WASTED* SO MUCH TIME BACK AT "A-HOY HOUSE," WE MIGHT'VE BEEN DONE AN *HOUR* AGO.
?
SAY, HAVE YOU SEEN ECHIBOO?
NO... *WHY?*
HE'S NOT IN HIS CAGE.
OH CRAAAAAP!!!

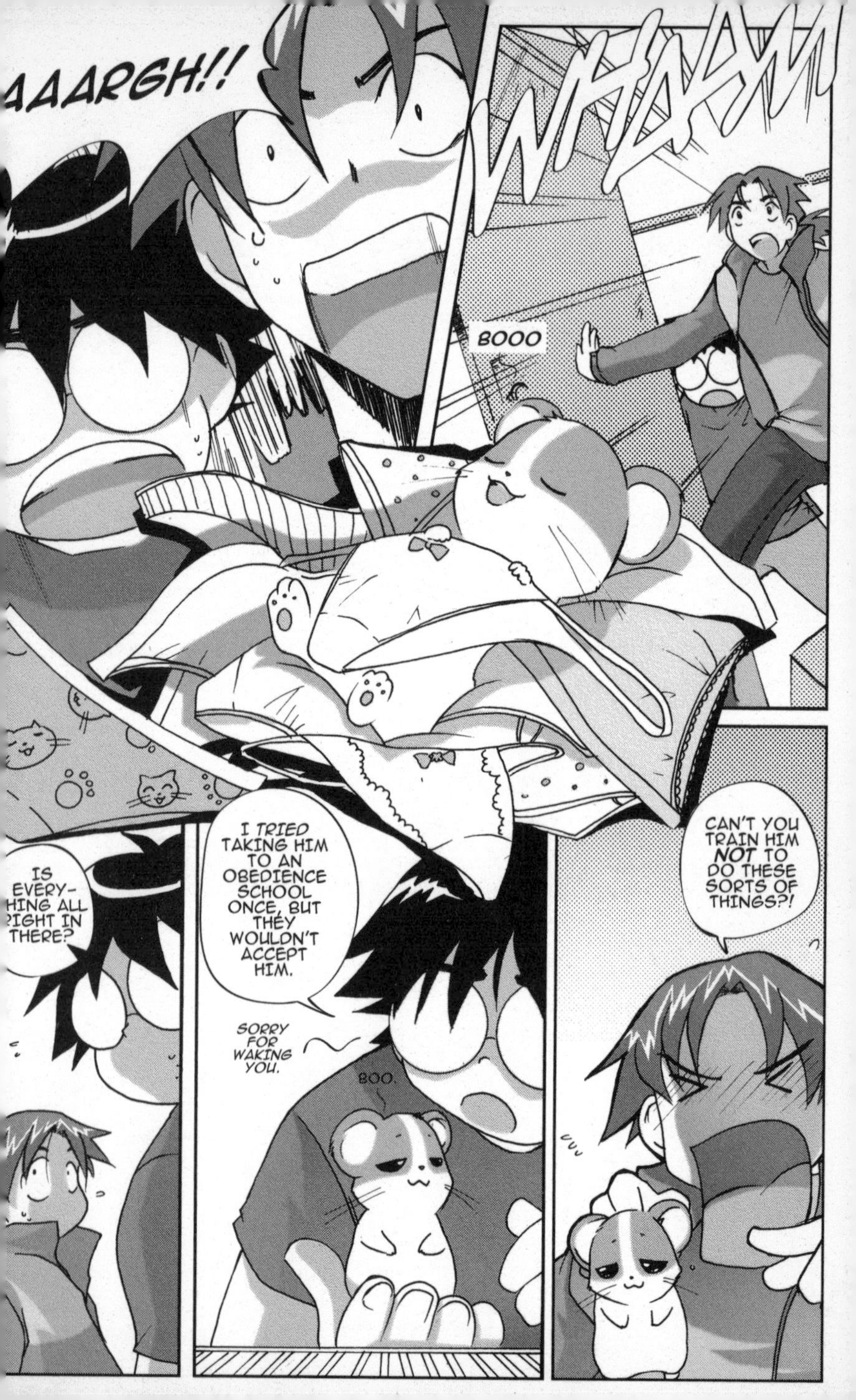
WHAM
BOOO
AAARGH!!
CAN'T YOU TRAIN HIM NOT TO DO THESE SORTS OF THINGS?!
I TRIED TAKING HIM TO AN OBEDIENCE SCHOOL ONCE, BUT THEY WOULDN'T ACCEPT HIM.
SORRY FOR WAKING YOU.
BOO.
IS EVERY-HING ALL RIGHT IN THERE?

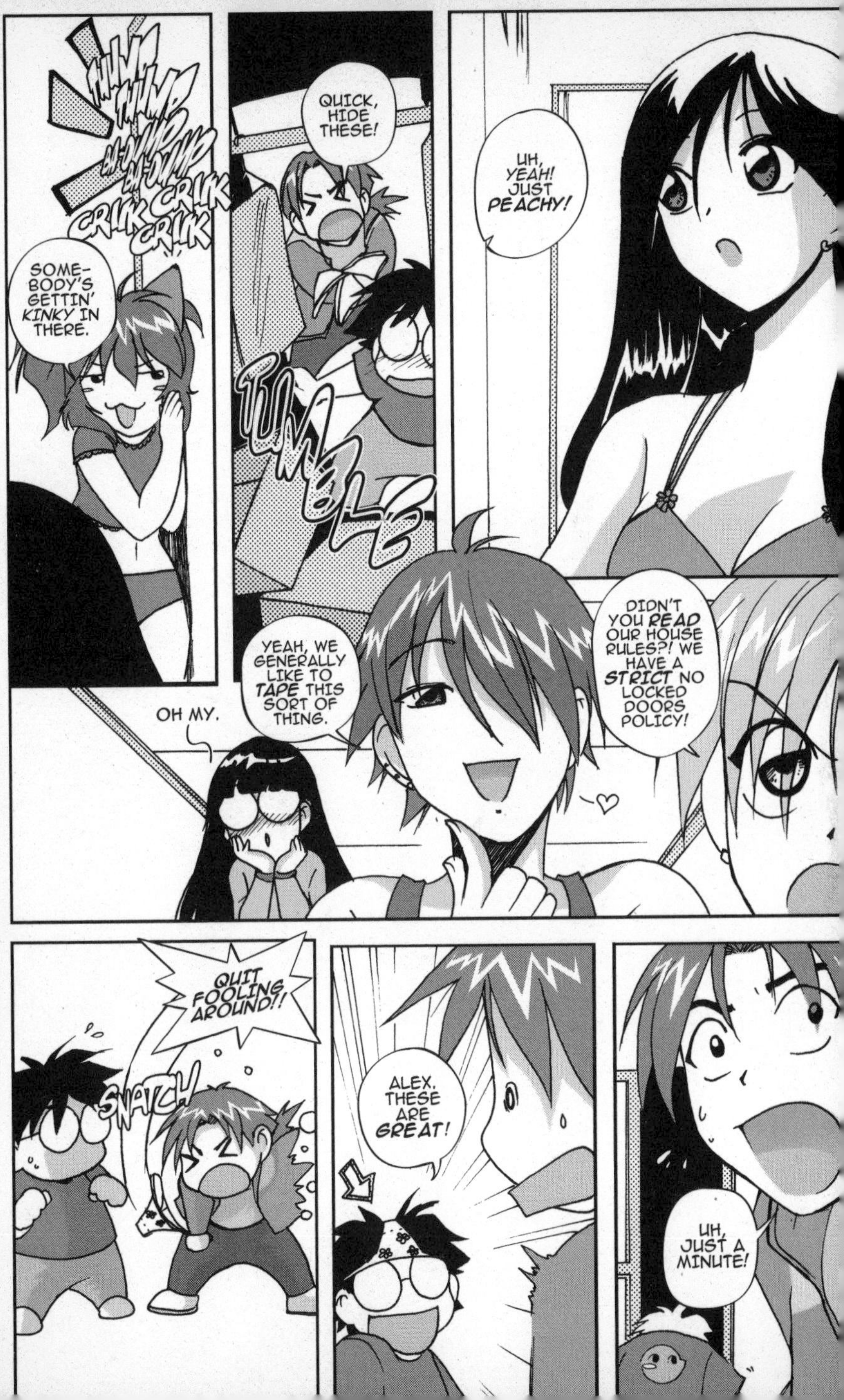
UH, YEAH! JUST PEACHY!
QUICK, HIDE THESE!
TUMBLE
THUMP THUMP BA-DUMP BA-DUMP
CRIK CRIK CRIK
SOME-BODY'S GETTIN' KINKY IN THERE.
DIDN'T YOU READ OUR HOUSE RULES?! WE HAVE A STRICT NO LOCKED DOORS POLICY!
YEAH, WE GENERALLY LIKE TO TAPE THIS SORT OF THING.
OH MY.
UH, JUST A MINUTE!
ALEX. THESE ARE GREAT!
QUIT FOOLING AROUND!!
SNATCH

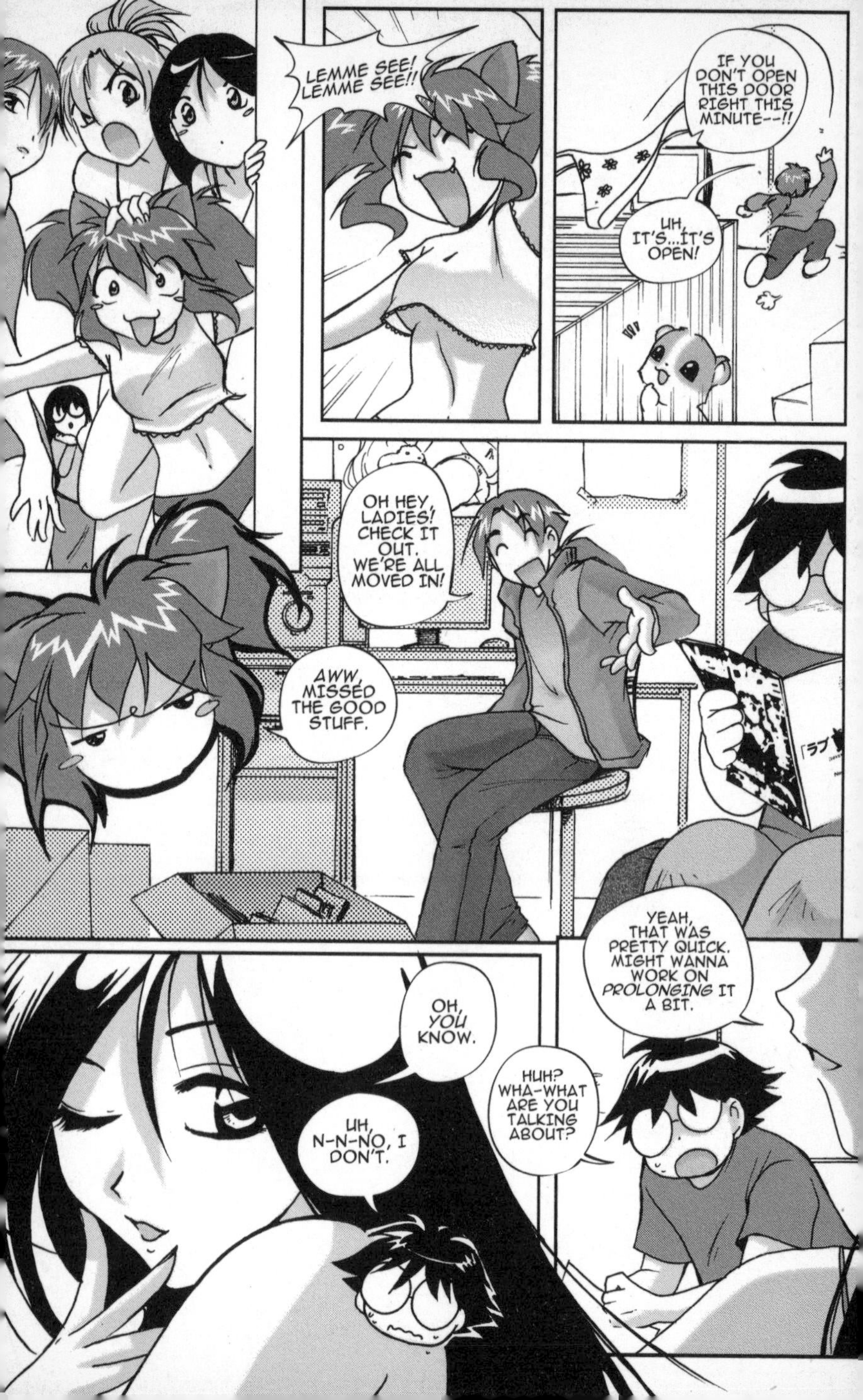
IF YOU DON'T OPEN THIS DOOR RIGHT THIS MINUTE--!!
UH, IT'S...IT'S OPEN!
LEMME SEE! LEMME SEE!!
OH HEY, LADIES! CHECK IT OUT. WE'RE ALL MOVED IN!
AWW, MISSED THE GOOD STUFF.
YEAH, THAT WAS PRETTY QUICK. MIGHT WANNA WORK ON *PROLONGING* IT A BIT.
HUH? WHA-WHAT ARE YOU TALKING ABOUT?
OH, *YOU* KNOW.
UH, N-N-NO, I DON'T.

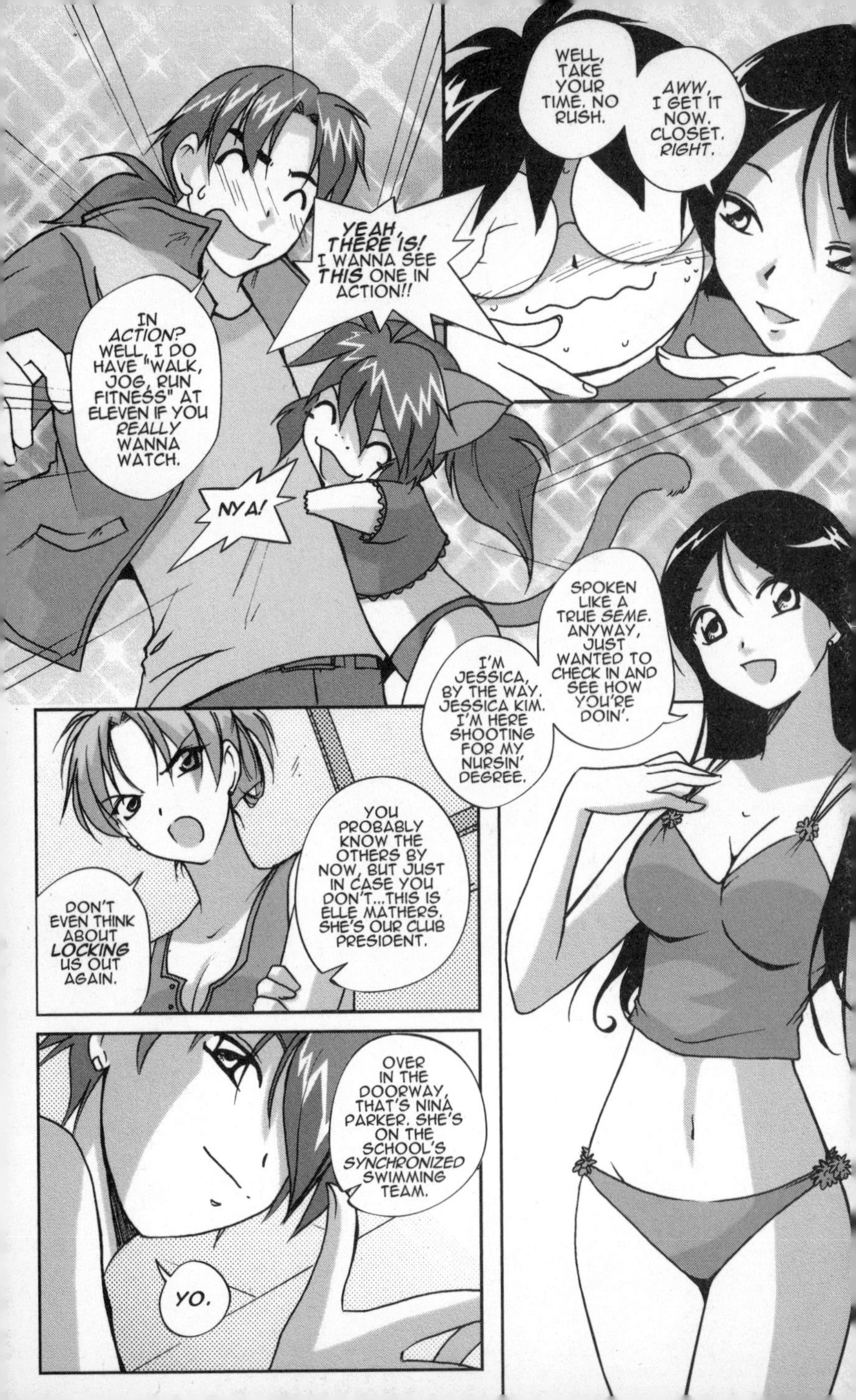
AWW, I GET IT NOW. CLOSET. *RIGHT*.
WELL, TAKE YOUR TIME. NO RUSH.
YEAH, THERE IS! I WANNA SEE **THIS** ONE IN ACTION!!
IN *ACTION?* WELL, I DO HAVE "WALK, JOG, RUN FITNESS" AT ELEVEN IF YOU *REALLY* WANNA WATCH.
NYA!
SPOKEN LIKE A TRUE *SEME*. ANYWAY, JUST WANTED TO CHECK IN AND SEE HOW YOU'RE DOIN'.
I'M JESSICA, BY THE WAY. JESSICA KIM. I'M HERE SHOOTING FOR MY NURSIN' DEGREE.
YOU PROBABLY KNOW THE OTHERS BY NOW, BUT JUST IN CASE YOU DON'T...THIS IS ELLE MATHERS. SHE'S OUR CLUB PRESIDENT.
DON'T EVEN THINK ABOUT ***LOCKING*** US OUT AGAIN.
OVER IN THE DOORWAY, THAT'S NINA PARKER. SHE'S ON THE SCHOOL'S *SYNCHRONIZED* SWIMMING TEAM.
YO.

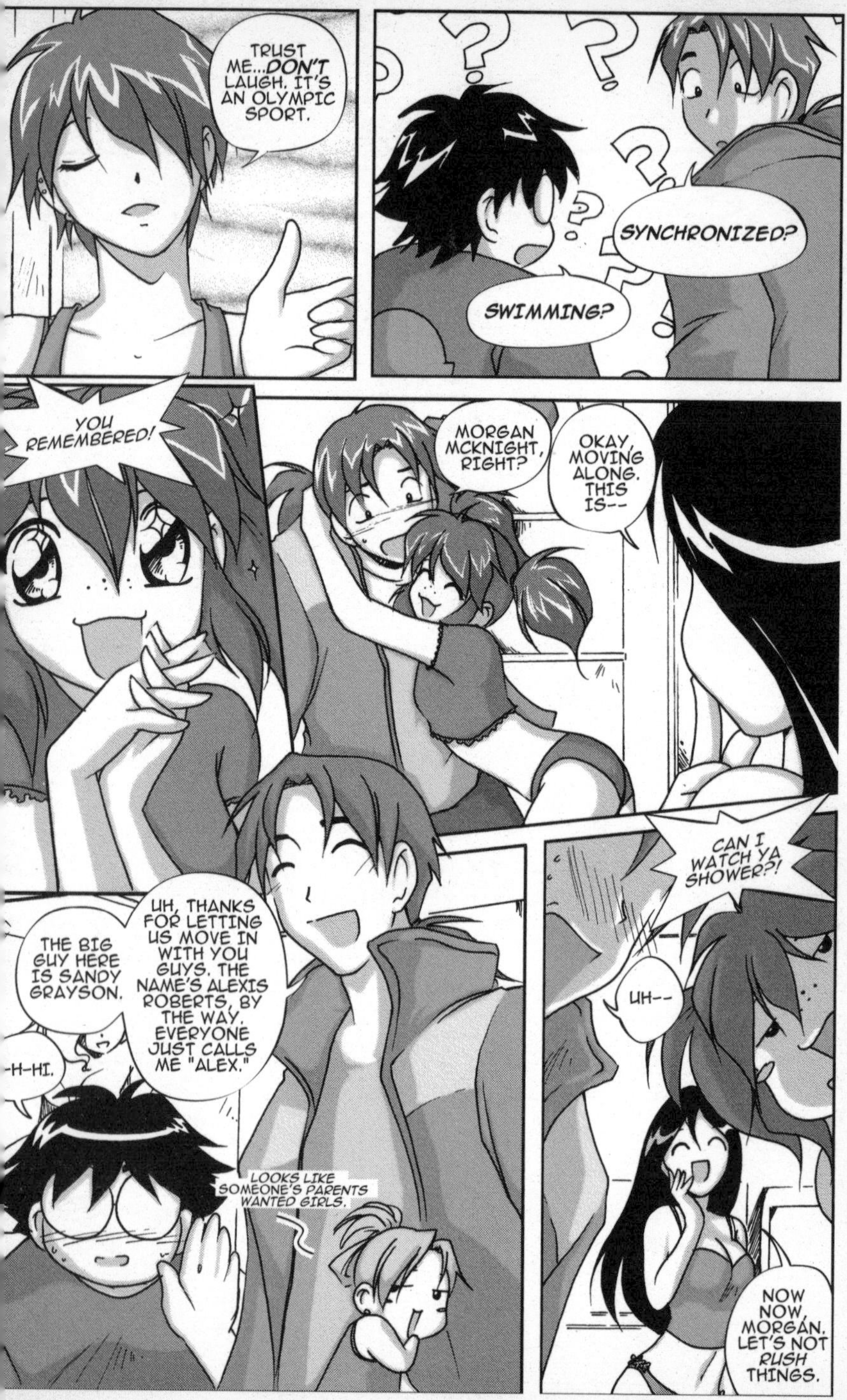
SYNCHRONIZED?
SWIMMING?
TRUST ME...DON'T LAUGH. IT'S AN OLYMPIC SPORT.
MORGAN MCKNIGHT, RIGHT?
OKAY, MOVING ALONG. THIS IS--
YOU REMEMBERED!
CAN I WATCH YA SHOWER?!
UH--
NOW NOW, MORGAN. LET'S NOT RUSH THINGS.
UH, THANKS FOR LETTING US MOVE IN WITH YOU GUYS. THE NAME'S ALEXIS ROBERTS, BY THE WAY. EVERYONE JUST CALLS ME "ALEX."
THE BIG GUY HERE IS SANDY GRAYSON.
-H-HI.
LOOKS LIKE SOMEONE'S PARENTS WANTED GIRLS.

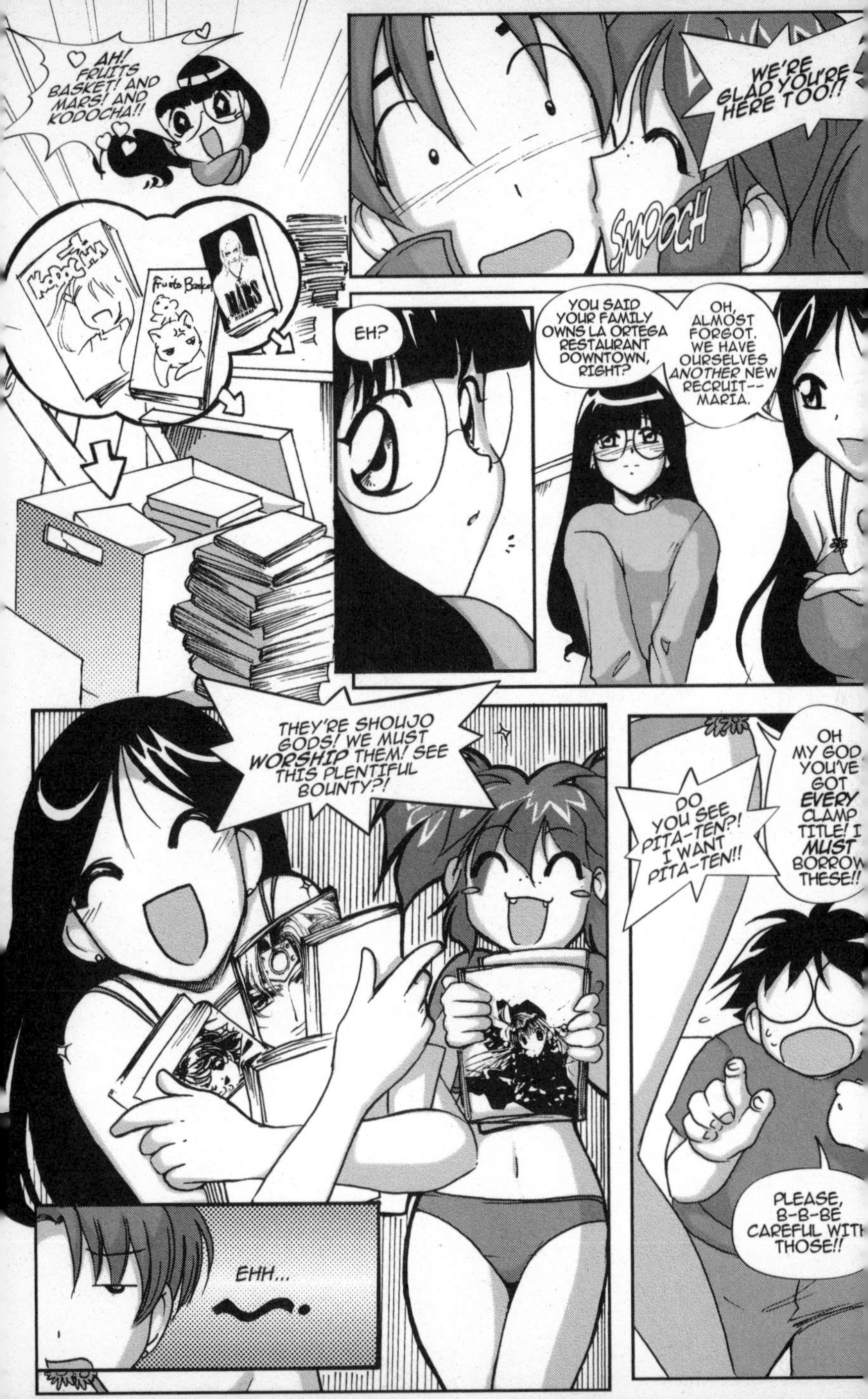
WE'RE GLAD YOU'RE HERE TOO!!
SMOOCH
AH! FRUITS BASKET! AND MARS! AND KODOCHA!!
MARS
OH, ALMOST FORGOT. WE HAVE OURSELVES ANOTHER NEW RECRUIT--MARIA.
YOU SAID YOUR FAMILY OWNS LA ORTEGA RESTAURANT DOWNTOWN, RIGHT?
EH?
OH MY GOD, YOU'VE GOT EVERY CLAMP TITLE! I MUST BORROW THESE!!
DO YOU SEE PITA-TEN?! I WANT PITA-TEN!!
PLEASE, B-B-BE CAREFUL WITH THOSE!!
THEY'RE SHOUJO GODS! WE MUST WORSHIP THEM! SEE THIS PLENTIFUL BOUNTY?!
EHH...

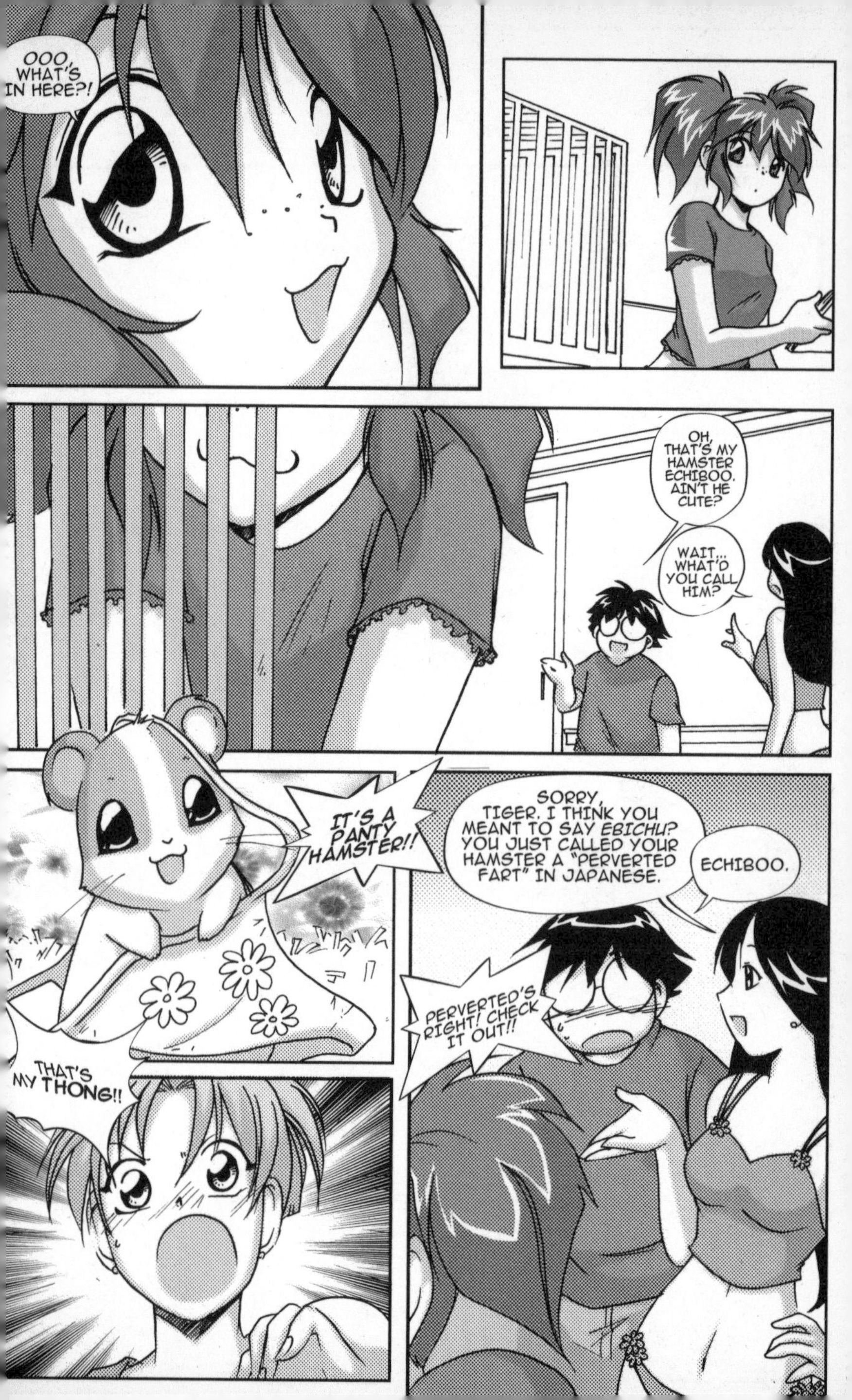
OOO, WHAT'S IN HERE?!
OH, THAT'S MY HAMSTER ECHIBOO. AIN'T HE CUTE?
WAIT... WHAT'D YOU CALL HIM?
ECHIBOO.
SORRY, TIGER. I THINK YOU MEANT TO SAY EBICHU? YOU JUST CALLED YOUR HAMSTER A "PERVERTED FART" IN JAPANESE.
PERVERTED'S RIGHT! CHECK IT OUT!!
IT'S A PANTY HAMSTER!!
THAT'S MY THONG!!

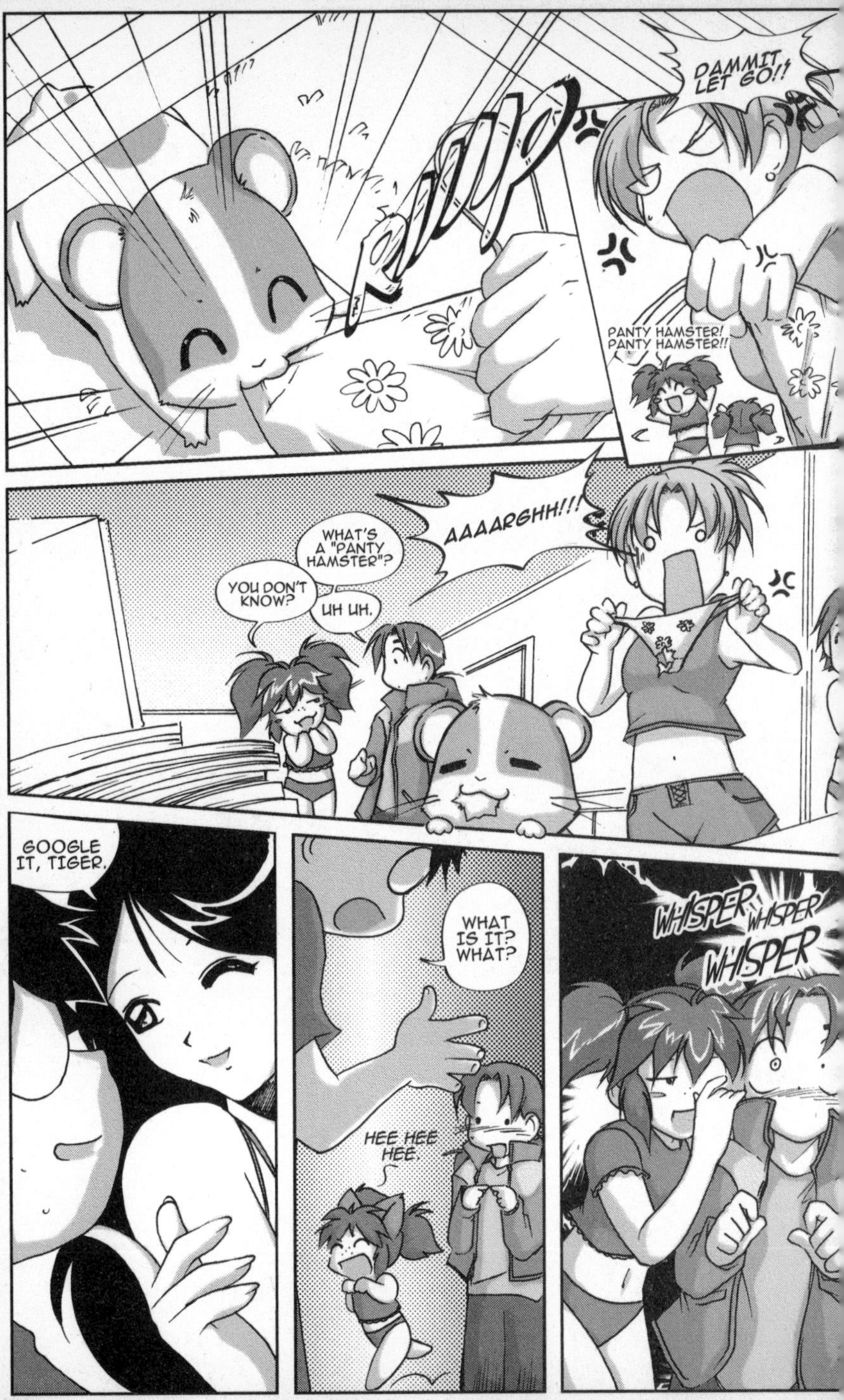
DAMMIT LET GO!!
PANTY HAMSTER! PANTY HAMSTER!!
AAAARGHH!!!
WHAT'S A "PANTY HAMSTER"?
YOU DON'T KNOW?
UH UH.
WHISPER WHISPER WHISPER
WHAT IS IT? WHAT?
HEE HEE HEE.
GOOGLE IT, TIGER.

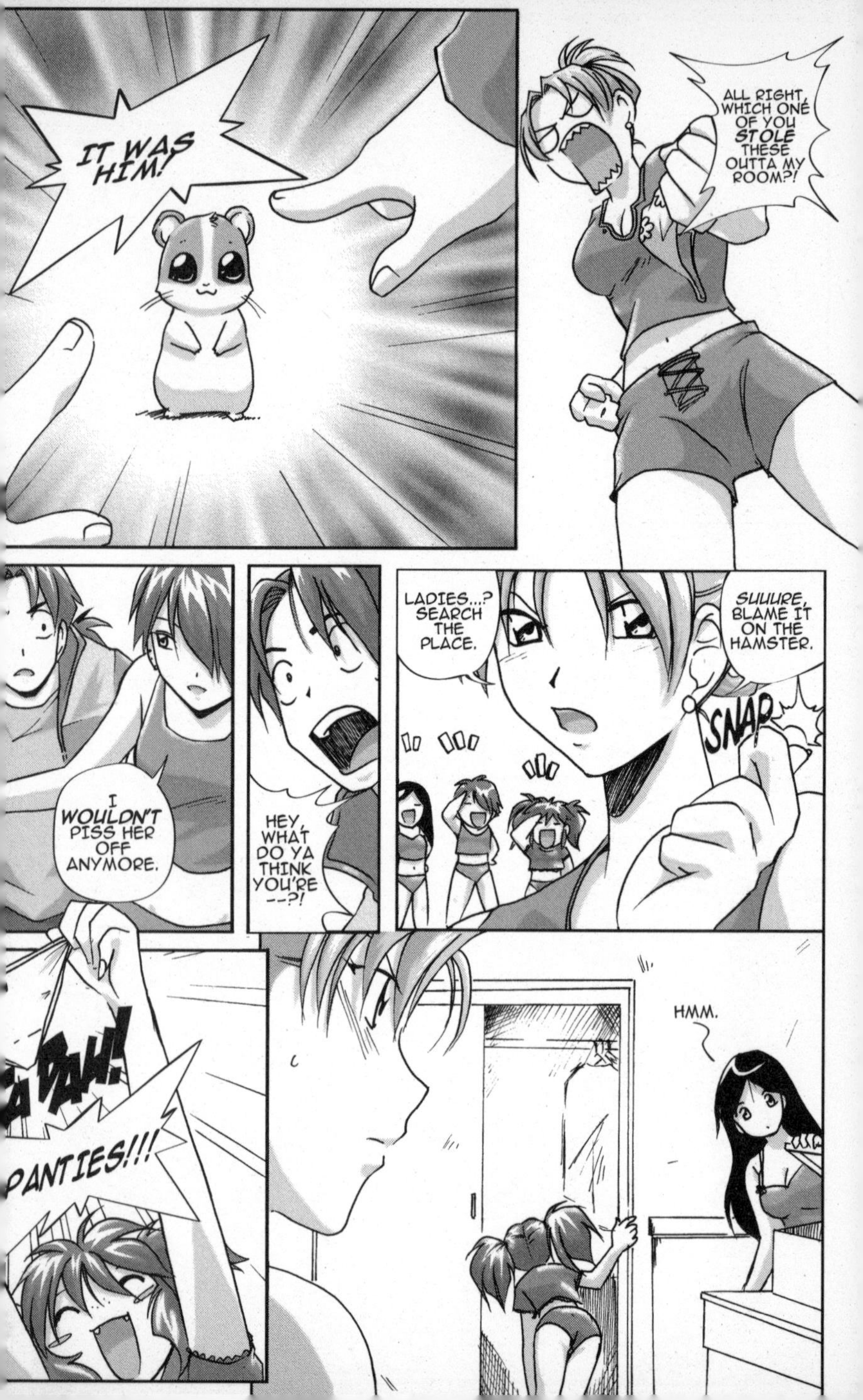
ALL RIGHT, WHICH ONE OF YOU STOLE THESE OUTTA MY ROOM?!
IT WAS HIM!
SUUURE, BLAME IT ON THE HAMSTER.
SNAP
LADIES...? SEARCH THE PLACE.
HEY, WHAT DO YA THINK YOU'RE --?!
I WOULDN'T PISS HER OFF ANYMORE.
HMM.
BAH!
PANTIES!!!

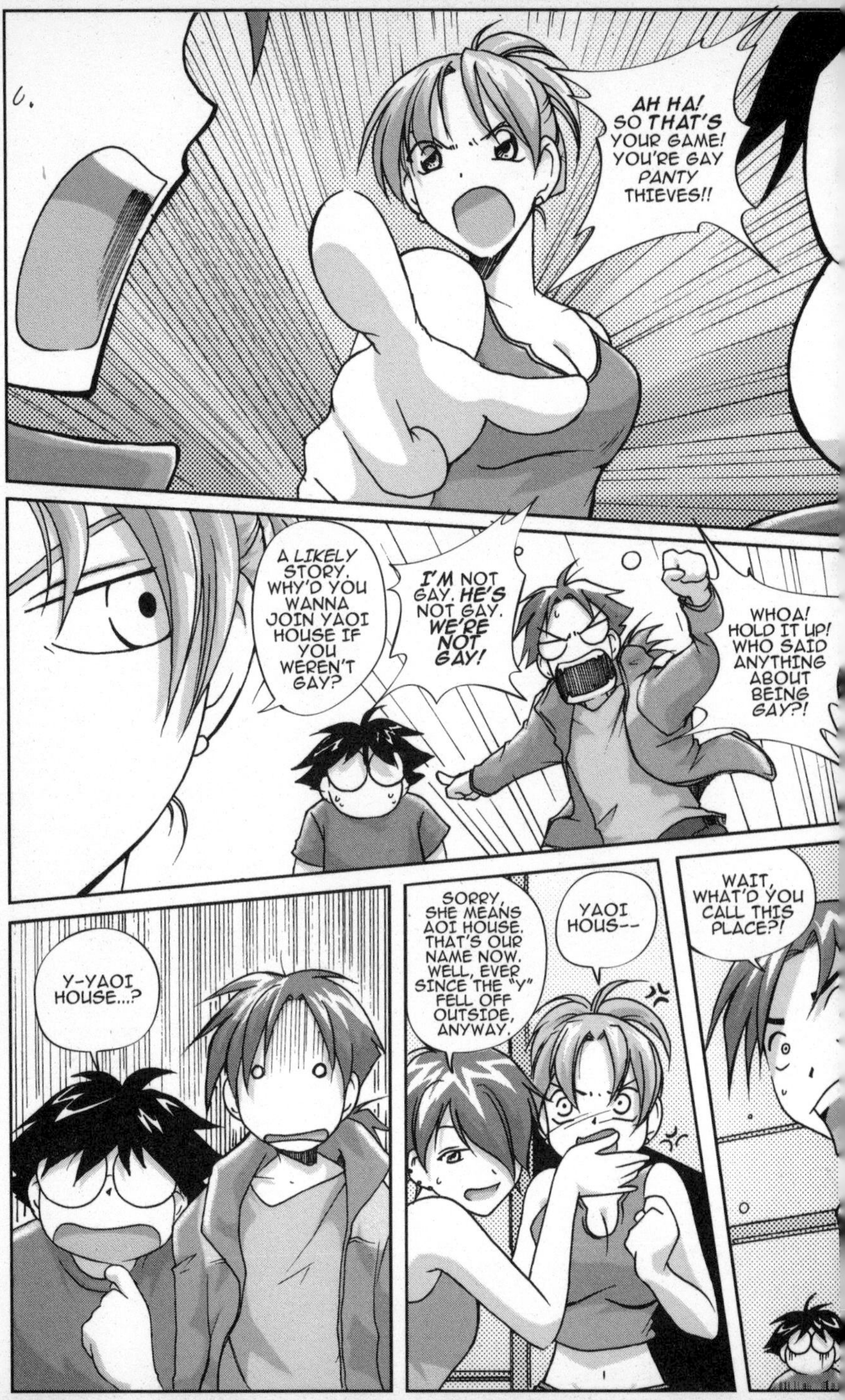
AH HA! SO THAT'S YOUR GAME! YOU'RE GAY PANTY THIEVES!!
WHOA! HOLD IT UP! WHO SAID ANYTHING ABOUT BEING GAY?!
I'M NOT GAY. HE'S NOT GAY. WE'RE NOT GAY!
A LIKELY STORY. WHY'D YOU WANNA JOIN YAOI HOUSE IF YOU WEREN'T GAY?
WAIT, WHAT'D YOU CALL THIS PLACE?!
YAOI HOUS--
SORRY, SHE MEANS AOI HOUSE. THAT'S OUR NAME NOW. WELL, EVER SINCE THE "Y" FELL OFF OUTSIDE, ANYWAY.
Y-YAOI HOUSE...?

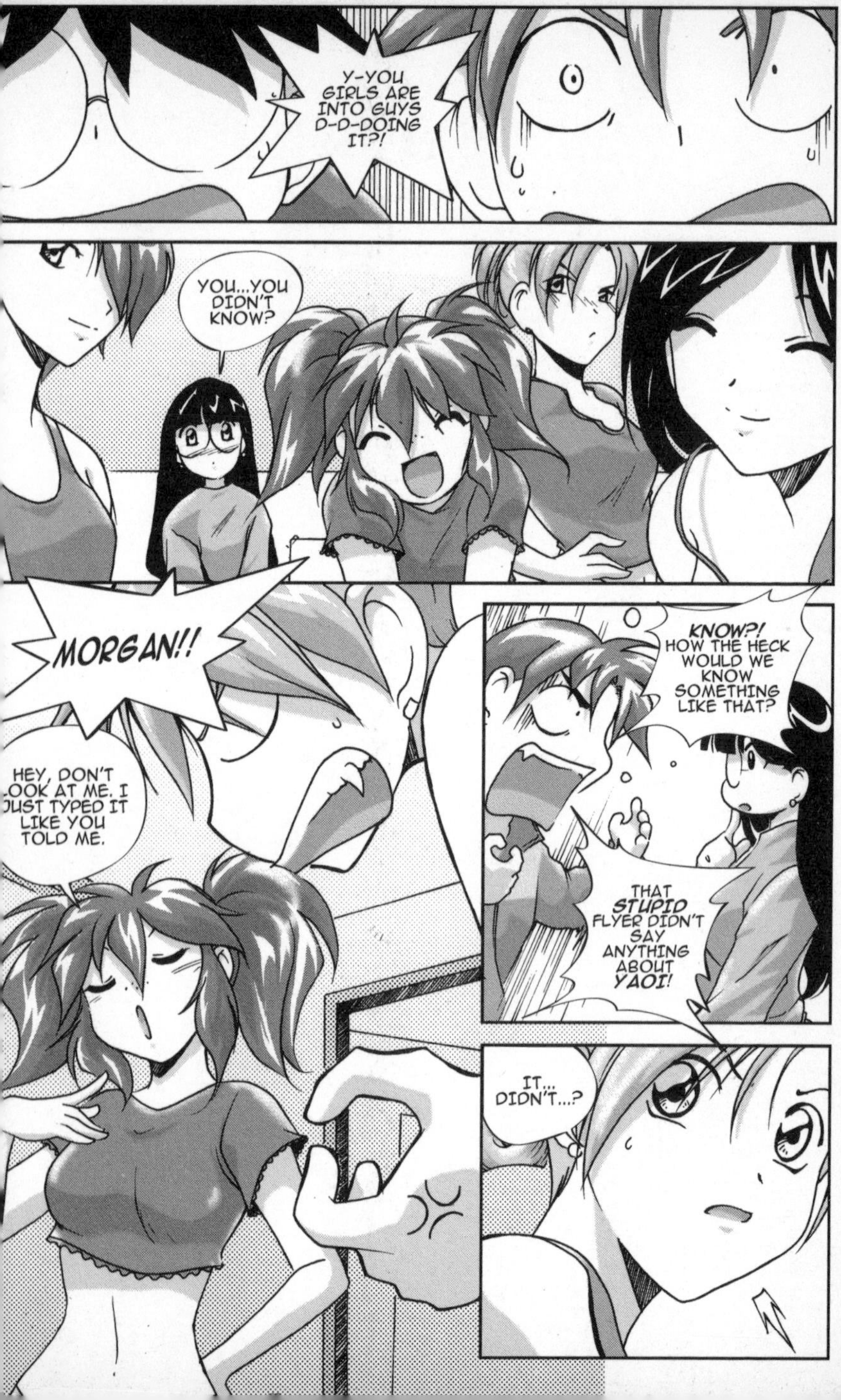
Y-YOU GIRLS ARE INTO GUYS D-D-DOING IT?!
YOU...YOU DIDN'T KNOW?
KNOW?! HOW THE HECK WOULD WE KNOW SOMETHING LIKE THAT?
THAT STUPID FLYER DIDN'T SAY ANYTHING ABOUT YAOI!
IT... DIDN'T...?
MORGAN!!
HEY, DON'T LOOK AT ME. I JUST TYPED IT LIKE YOU TOLD ME.

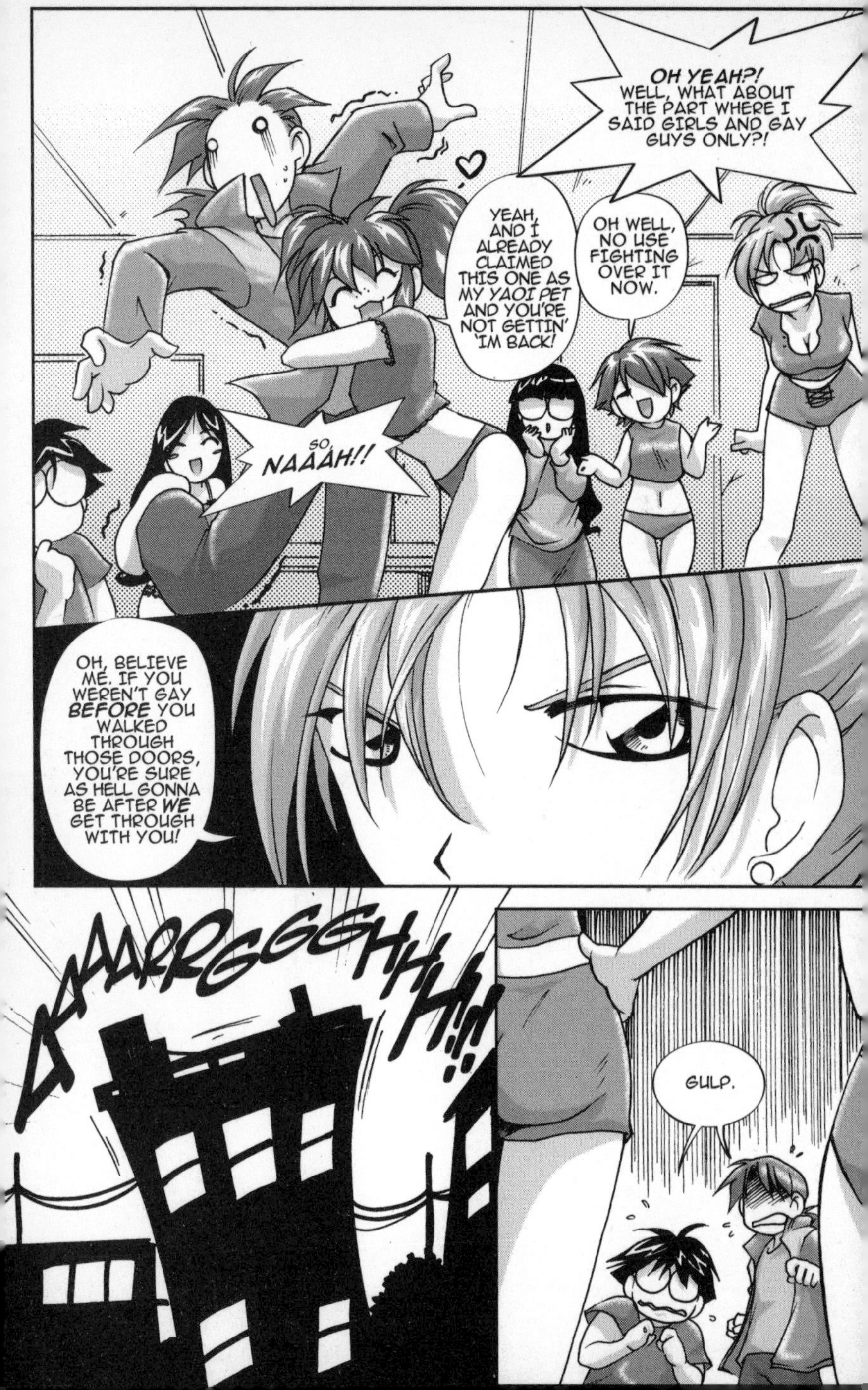
OH YEAH?! WELL, WHAT ABOUT THE PART WHERE I SAID GIRLS AND GAY GUYS ONLY?!
OH WELL, NO USE FIGHTING OVER IT NOW.
YEAH, AND I ALREADY CLAIMED THIS ONE AS MY YAOI PET AND YOU'RE NOT GETTIN' 'IM BACK!
SO, NAAAH!!
OH, BELIEVE ME. IF YOU WEREN'T GAY BEFORE YOU WALKED THROUGH THOSE DOORS, YOU'RE SURE AS HELL GONNA BE AFTER WE GET THROUGH WITH YOU!
GULP.
AAARRGGGHHH!!!

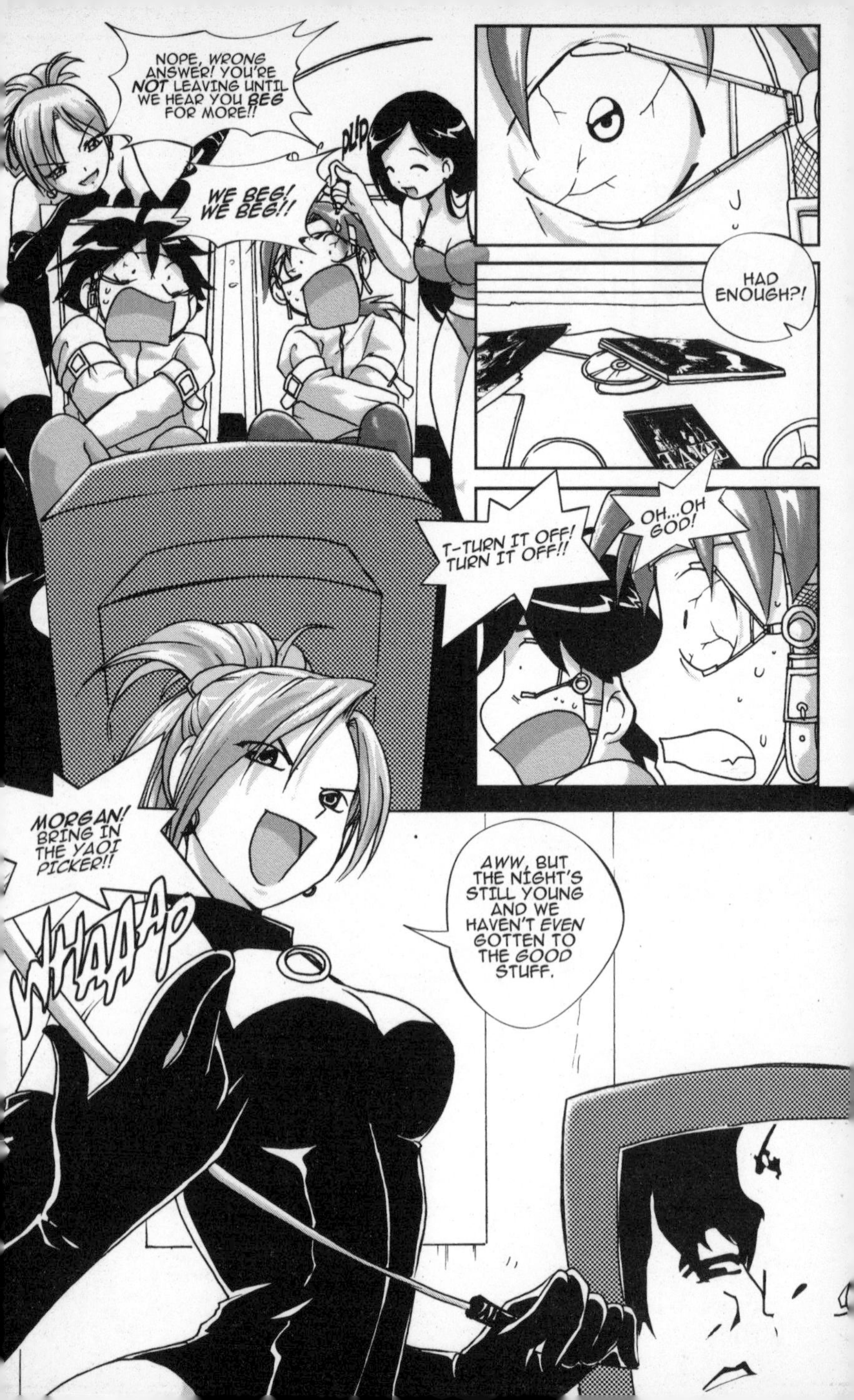
HAD ENOUGH?!
OH...OH GOD!
T-TURN IT OFF! TURN IT OFF!!
NOPE, WRONG ANSWER! YOU'RE NOT LEAVING UNTIL WE HEAR YOU BEG FOR MORE!!
PLIP
WE BEG! WE BEG!!
AWW, BUT THE NIGHT'S STILL YOUNG AND WE HAVEN'T EVEN GOTTEN TO THE GOOD STUFF.
MORGAN! BRING IN THE YAOI PICKER!!
WHAAP

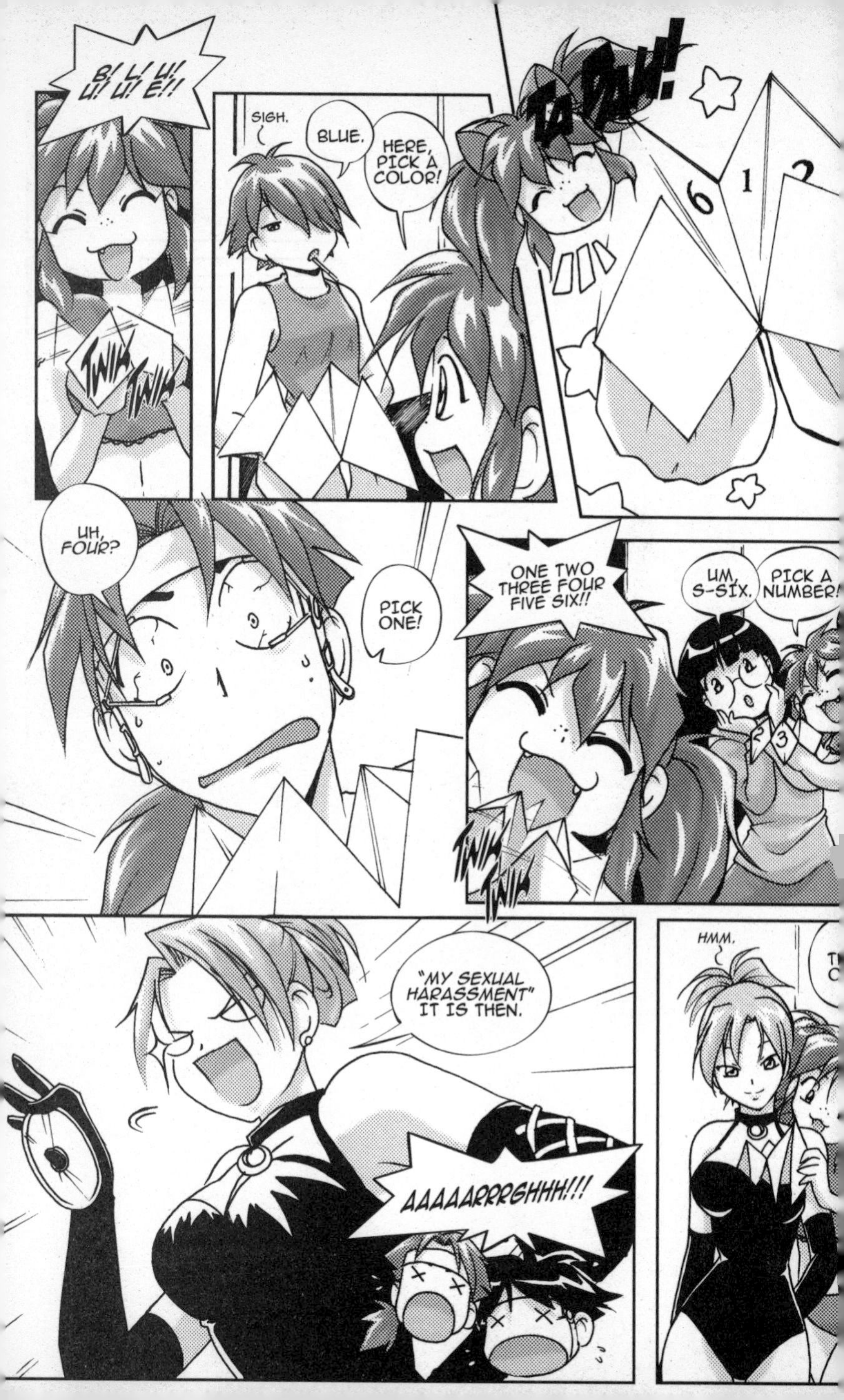
TA DAH!
HERE, PICK A COLOR!
SIGH.
BLUE.
B! L! U! U! U! E!!
TWIK TWIK
PICK A NUMBER!
UM, S-SIX.
ONE TWO THREE FOUR FIVE SIX!!
TWIK TWIK
PICK ONE!
UH, FOUR?
HMM.
"MY SEXUAL HARASSMENT" IT IS THEN.
AAAAARRRGHHH!!!

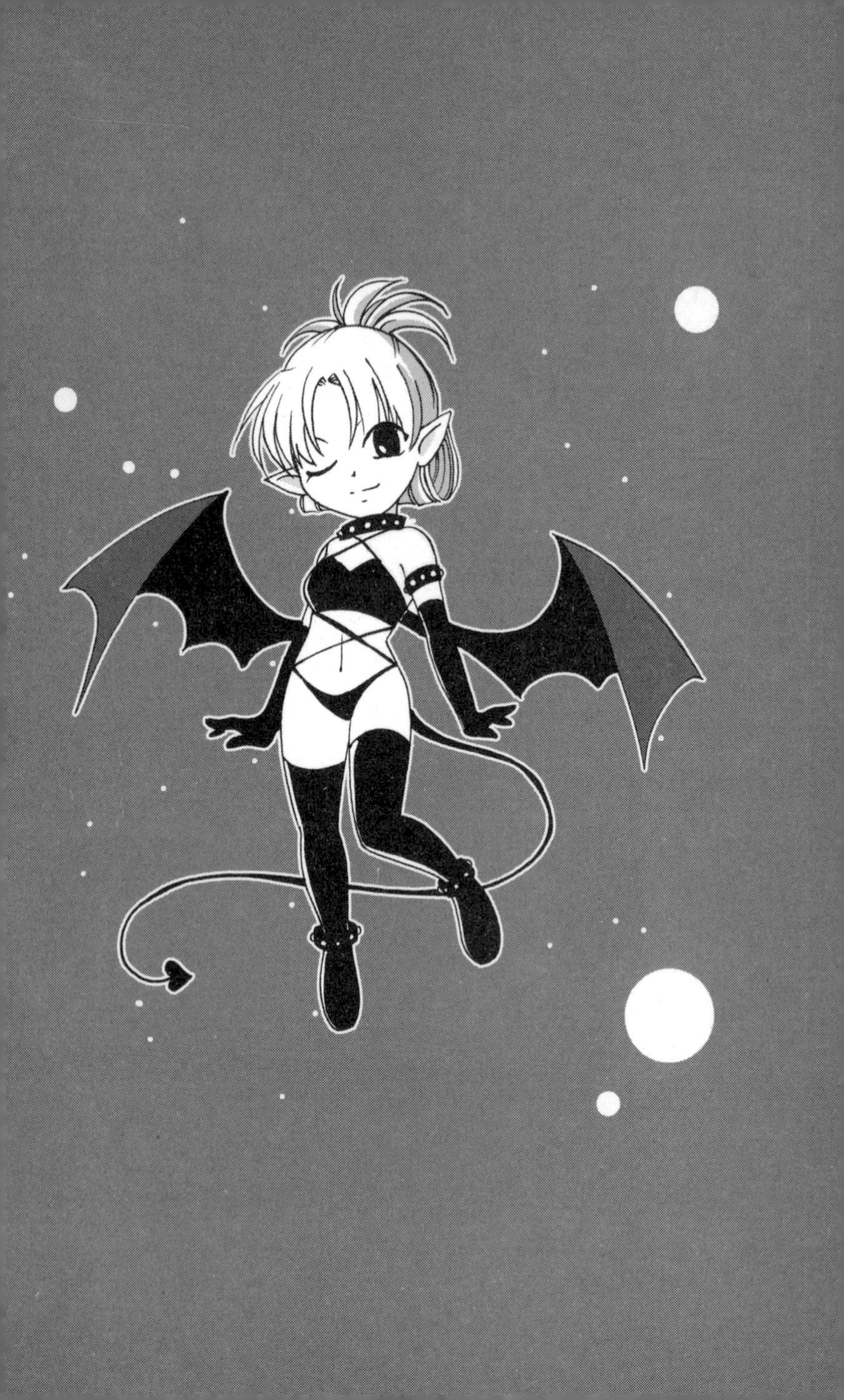

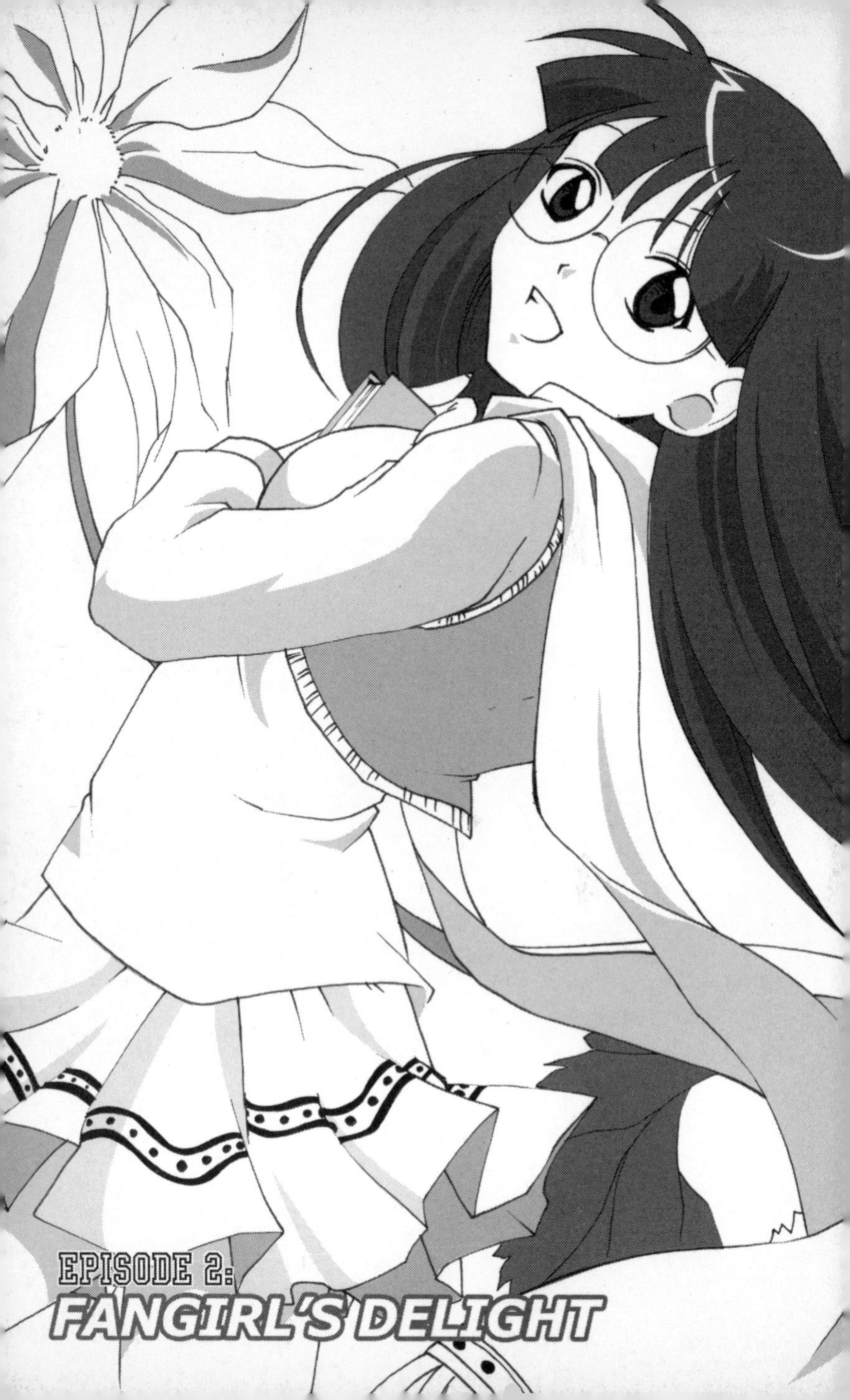

EPISODE 2: FANGIRL'S DELIGHT

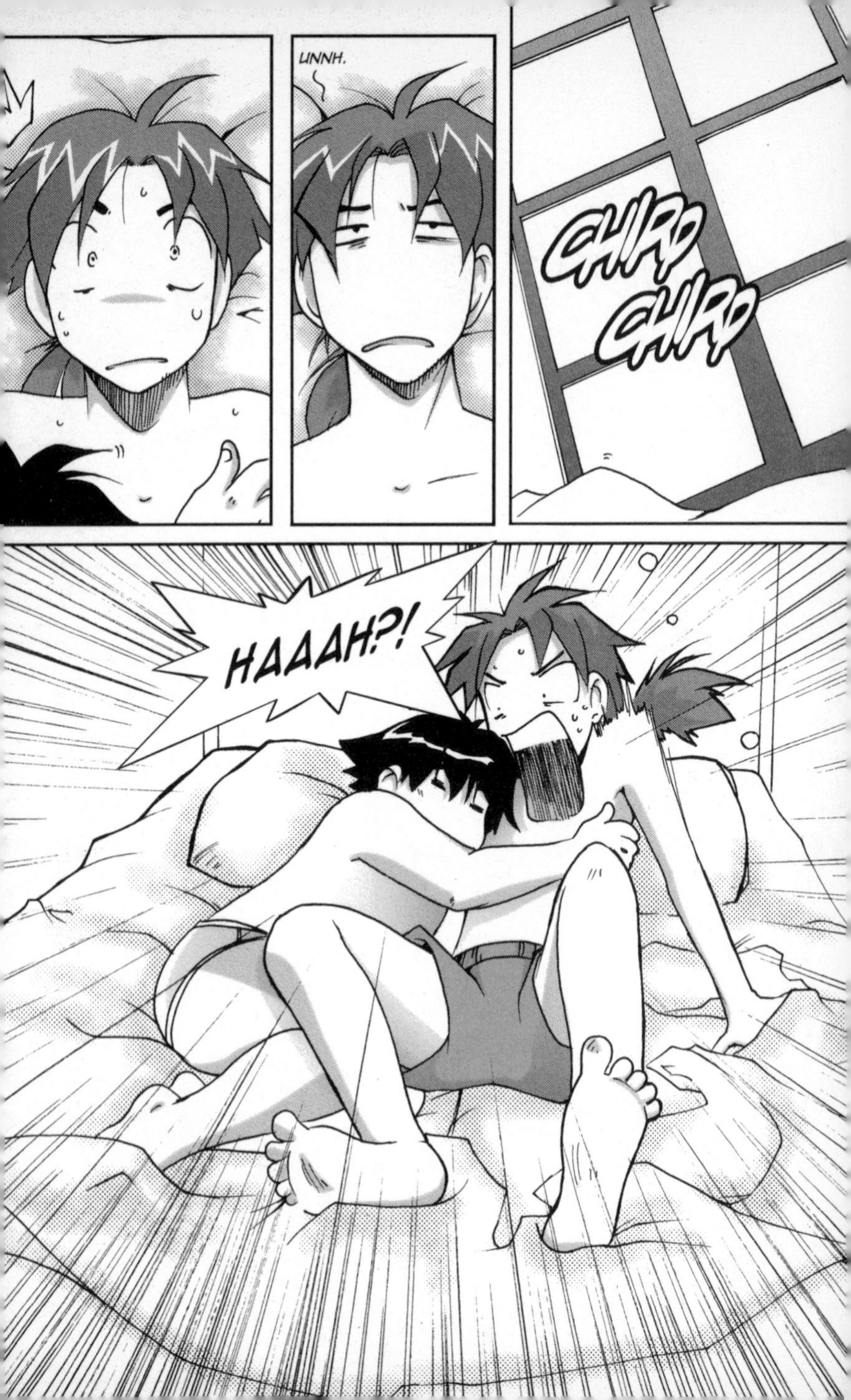
CHIRP CHIRP
UNNH.
HAAAH?!

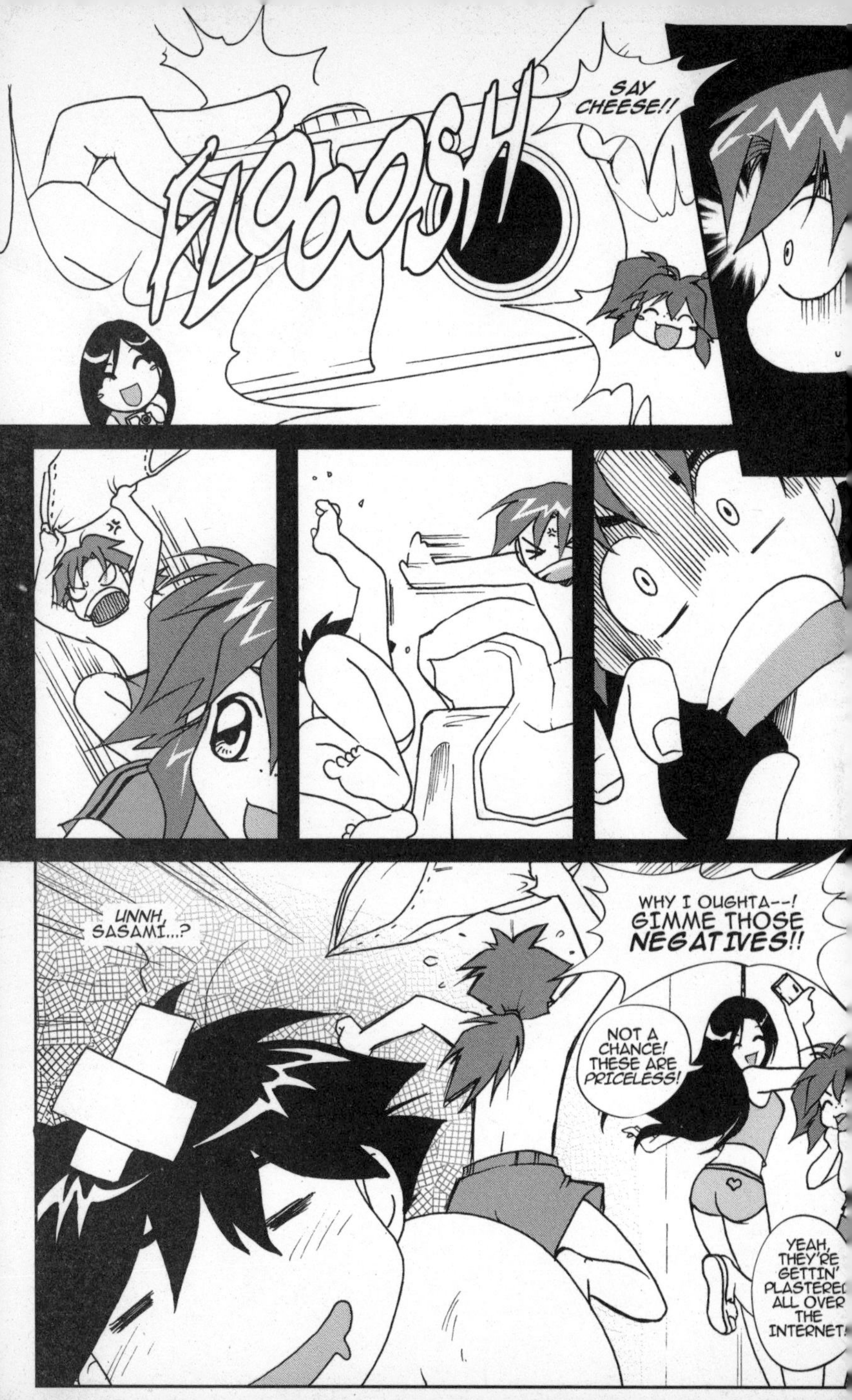
SAY CHEESE!!
FLOOOSH
WHY I OUGHTA--! GIMME THOSE NEGATIVES!!
NOT A CHANCE! THESE ARE PRICELESS!
YEAH, THEY'RE GETTIN' PLASTERED ALL OVER THE INTERNET!
UNNH, SASAMI...?

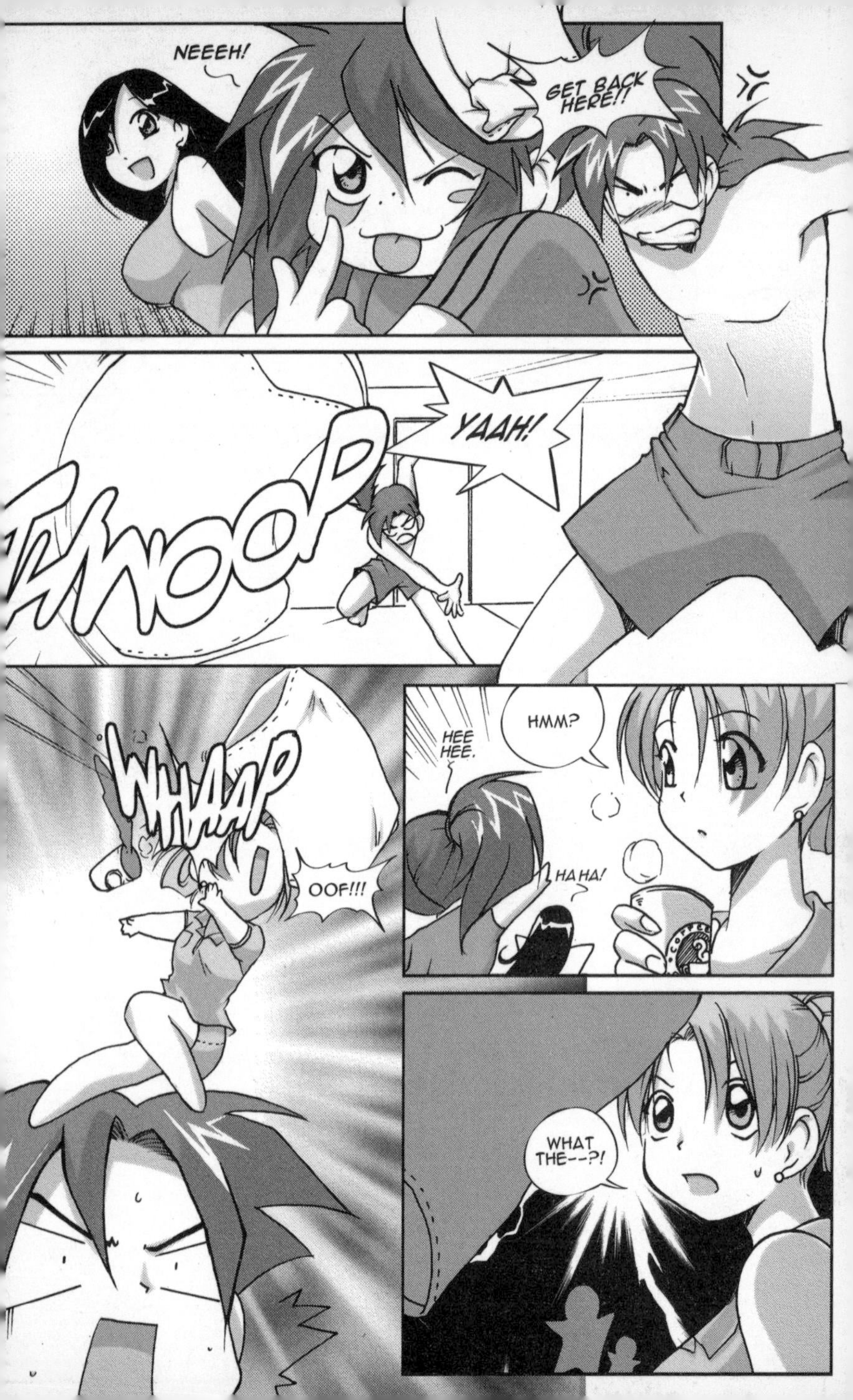
GET BACK HERE!!
NEEEH!
YAAH!
THWOOP
HMM?
HEE HEE.
HA HA!
WHAT THE--?!
WHAAP
OOF!!!

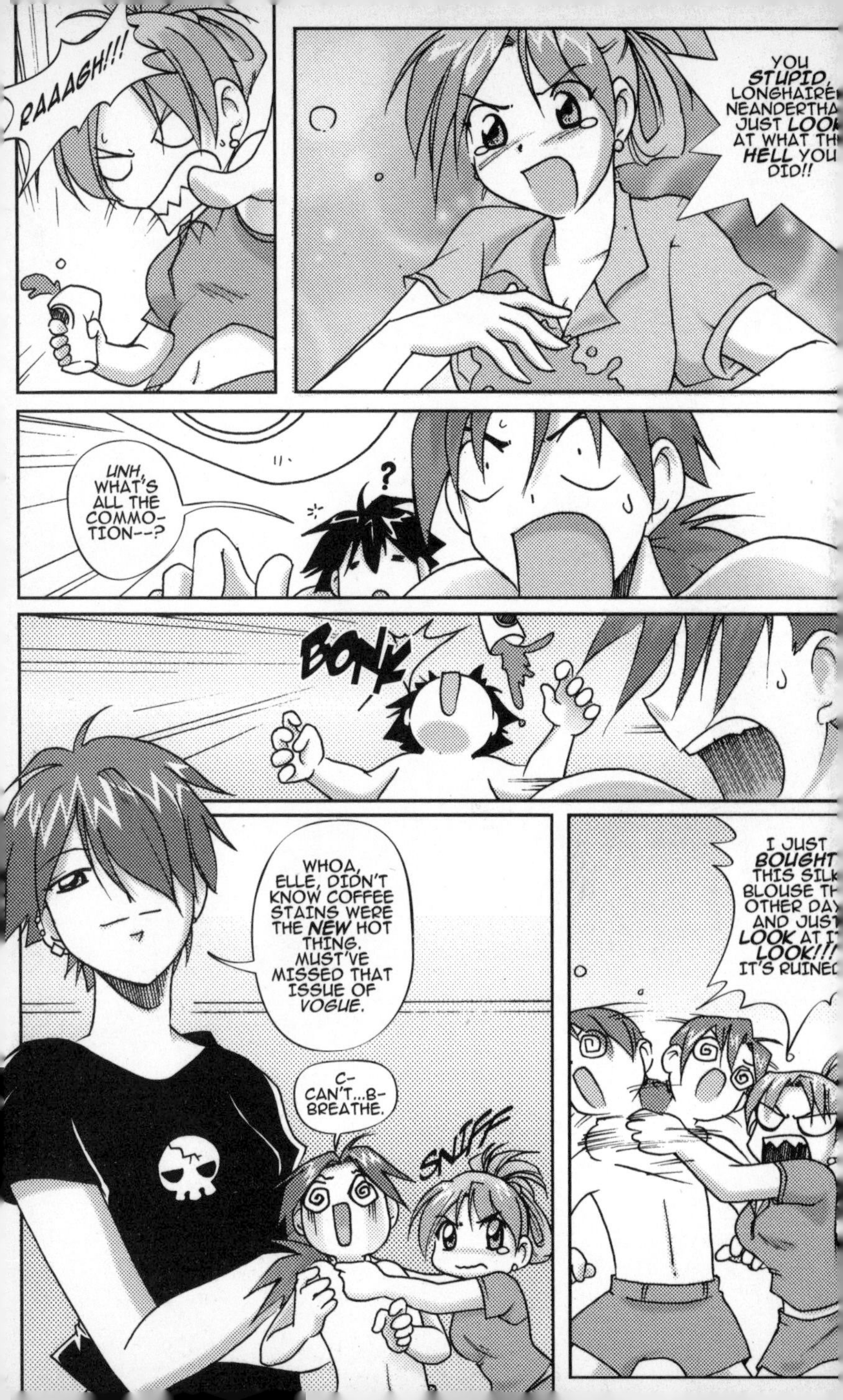

YOU STUPID, LONGHAIRE NEANDERTHA JUST LOOK AT WHAT TH HELL YOU DID!!
RAAAGH!!!
UNH, WHAT'S ALL THE COMMO-TION--?
BONK
I JUST BOUGHT THIS SILK BLOUSE TH OTHER DAY AND JUST LOOK AT I LOOK!!! IT'S RUINEC
WHOA, ELLE, DIDN'T KNOW COFFEE STAINS WERE THE NEW HOT THING. MUST'VE MISSED THAT ISSUE OF VOGUE.
C- CAN'T...B- BREATHE.
SNIFF

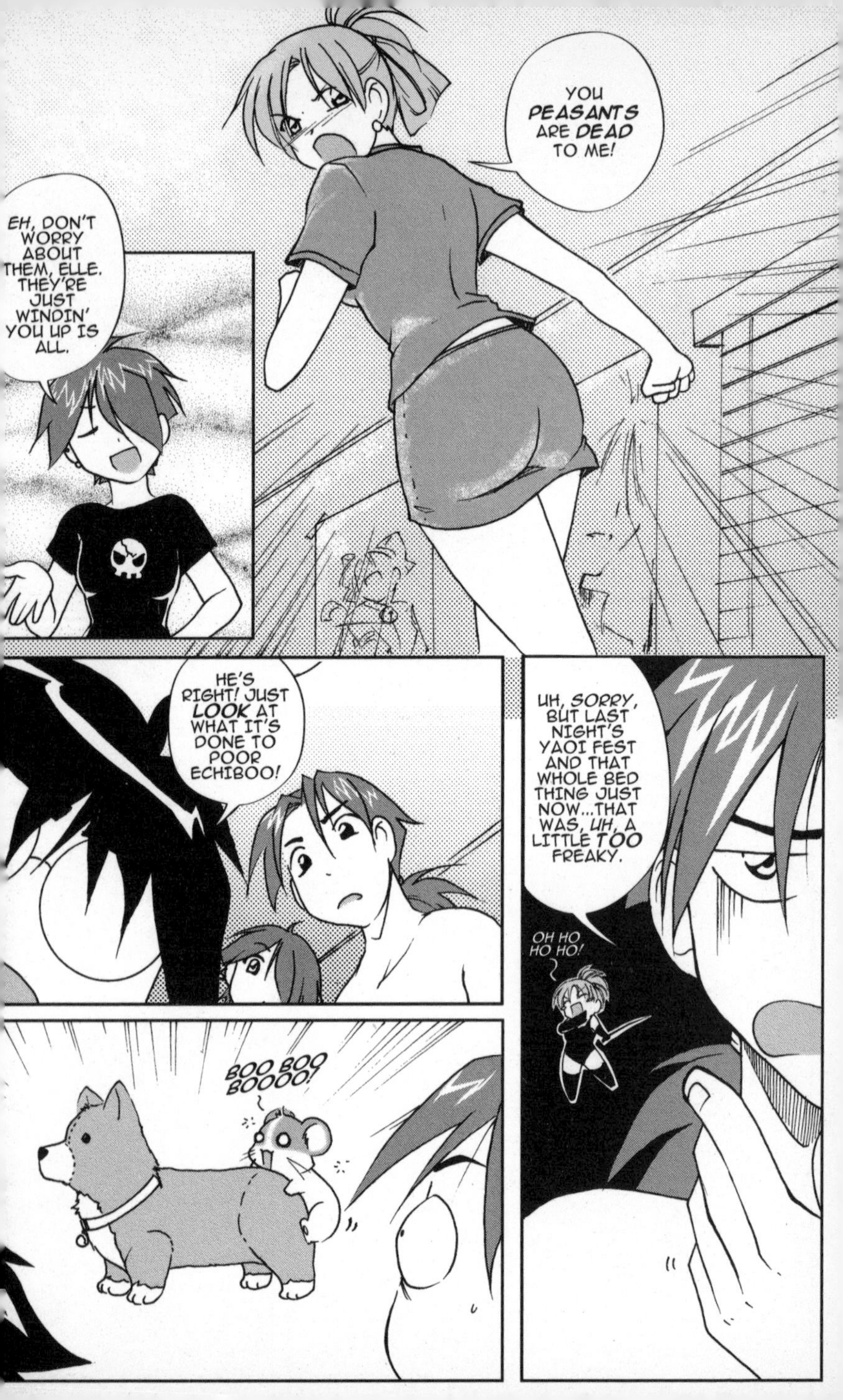
YOU PEASANTS ARE DEAD TO ME!
EH, DON'T WORRY ABOUT THEM, ELLE. THEY'RE JUST WINDIN' YOU UP IS ALL.
UH, SORRY, BUT LAST NIGHT'S YAOI FEST AND THAT WHOLE BED THING JUST NOW...THAT WAS, UH, A LITTLE TOO FREAKY.
OH HO HO HO!
HE'S RIGHT! JUST LOOK AT WHAT IT'S DONE TO POOR ECHIBOO!
BOO BOO BOOOO!

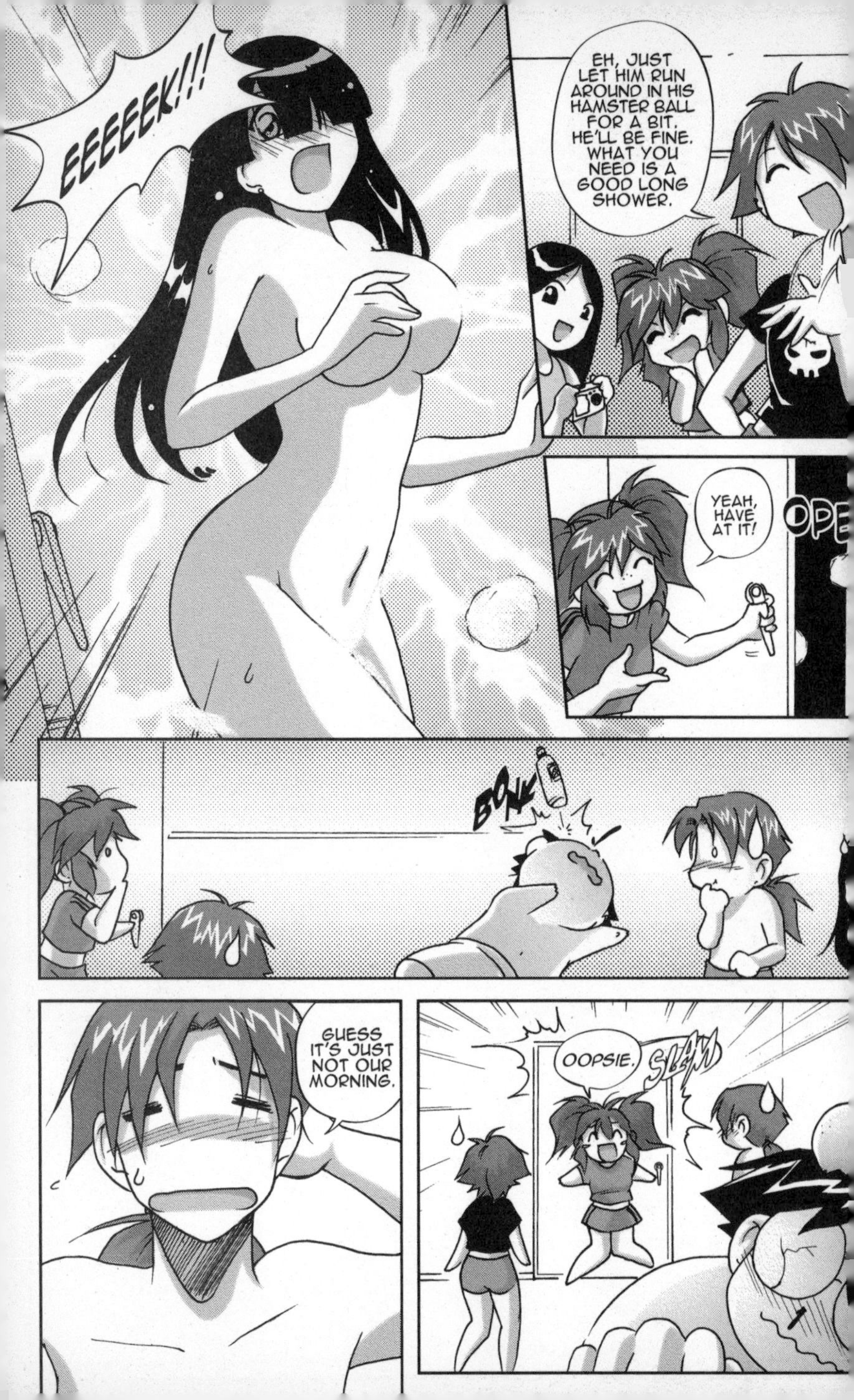
EH, JUST LET HIM RUN AROUND IN HIS HAMSTER BALL FOR A BIT. HE'LL BE FINE. WHAT YOU NEED IS A GOOD LONG SHOWER.
YEAH, HAVE AT IT!
OPE
EEEEEK!!!
BONK
OOPSIE.
SLAM
GUESS IT'S JUST NOT OUR MORNING.

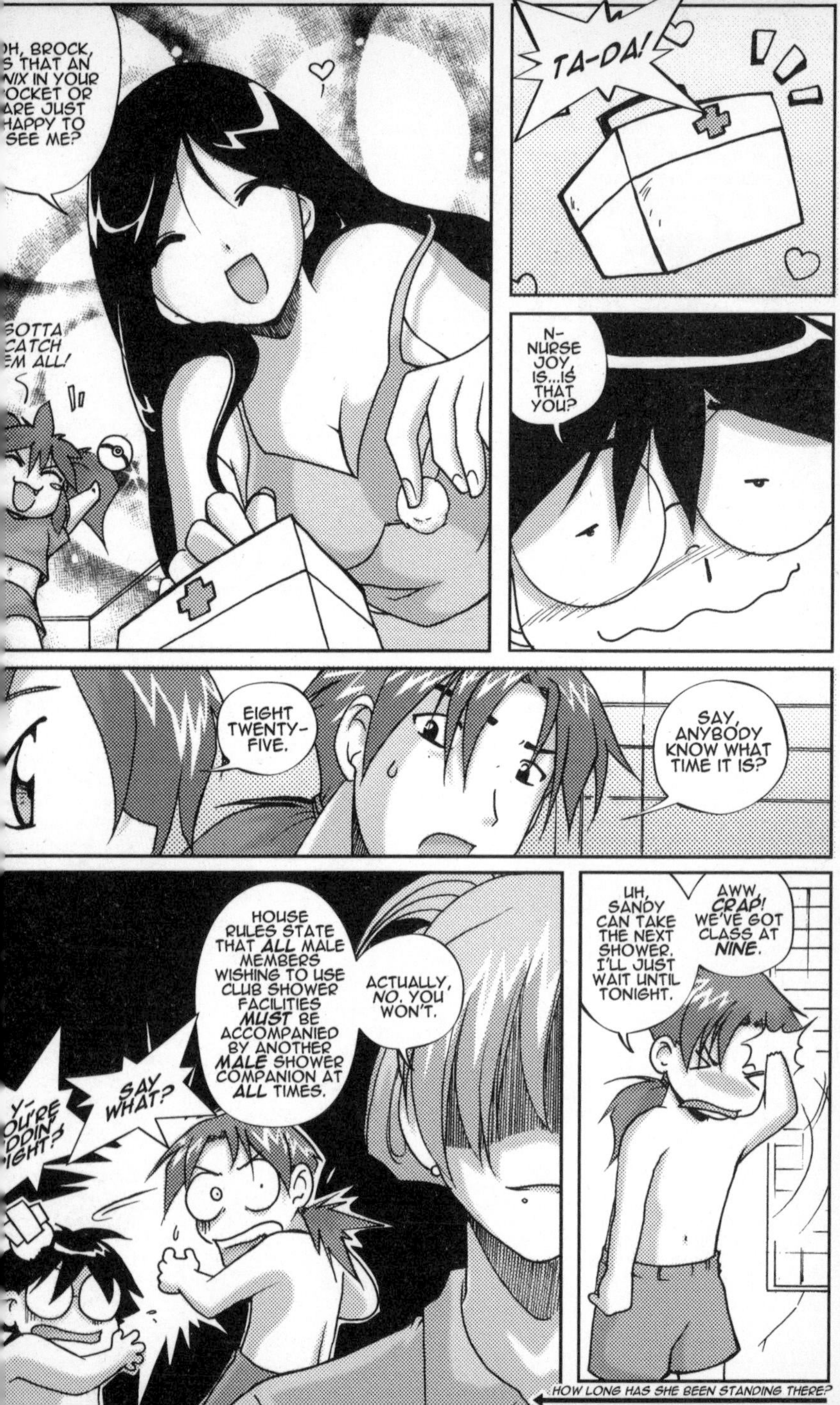
TA-DA!
N-NURSE JOY, IS...IS THAT YOU?
)H, BROCK, S THAT AN NIX IN YOUR OCKET OR ARE JUST HAPPY TO SEE ME?
SOTTA CATCH EM ALL!
SAY, ANYBODY KNOW WHAT TIME IT IS?
EIGHT TWENTY-FIVE.
AWW, CRAP! WE'VE GOT CLASS AT NINE.
UH, SANDY CAN TAKE THE NEXT SHOWER. I'LL JUST WAIT UNTIL TONIGHT.
ACTUALLY, NO. YOU WON'T.
HOUSE RULES STATE THAT ALL MALE MEMBERS WISHING TO USE CLUB SHOWER FACILITIES MUST BE ACCOMPANIED BY ANOTHER MALE SHOWER COMPANION AT ALL TIMES.
SAY WHAT?
Y-OU'RE DDIN' IGHT?!
HOW LONG HAS SHE BEEN STANDING THERE?

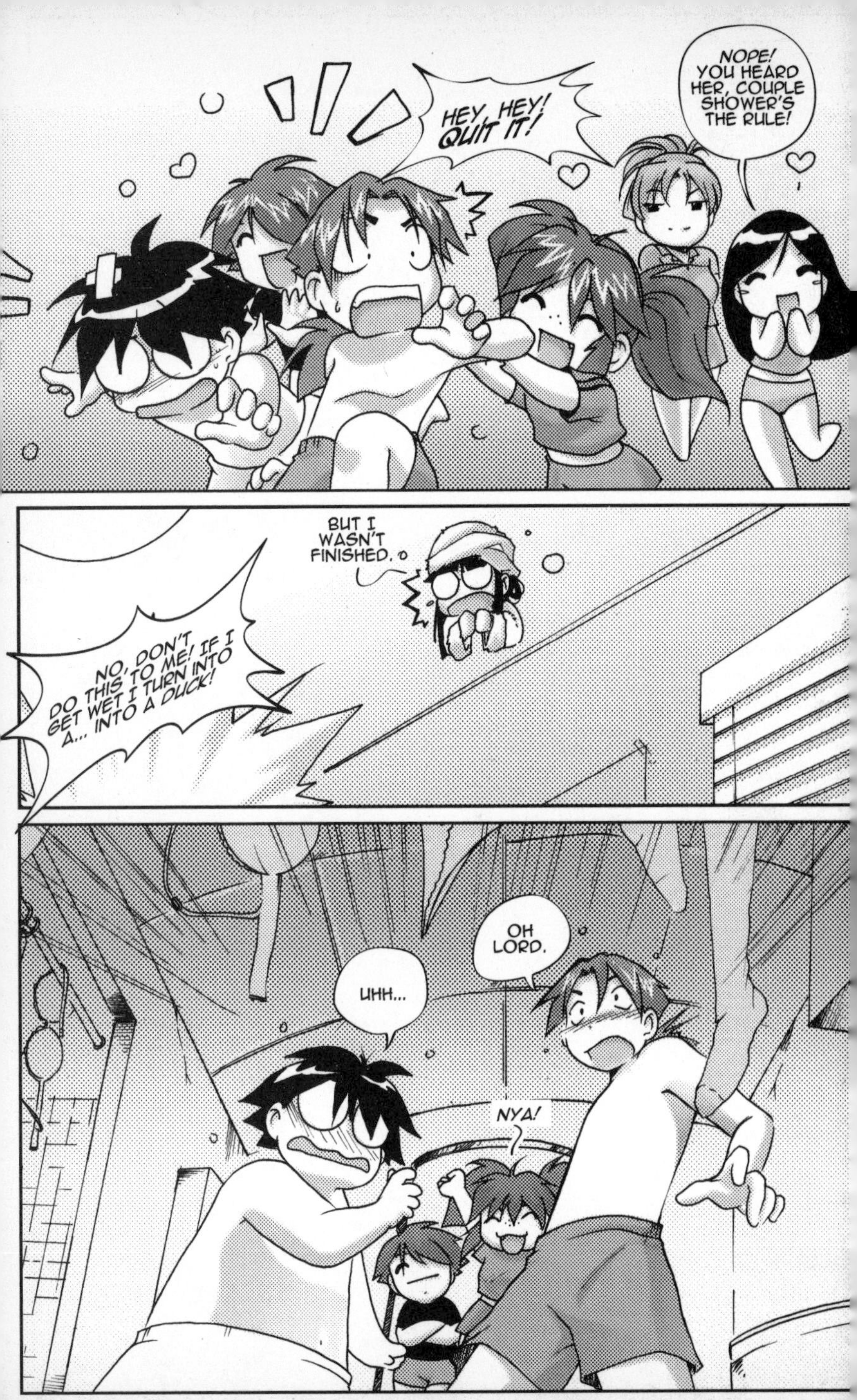
NOPE! YOU HEARD HER, COUPLE SHOWER'S THE RULE!
HEY, HEY! QUIT IT!
BUT I WASN'T FINISHED.
NO, DON'T DO THIS TO ME! IF I GET WET I TURN INTO A... INTO A DUCK!
OH LORD.
UHH...
NYA!

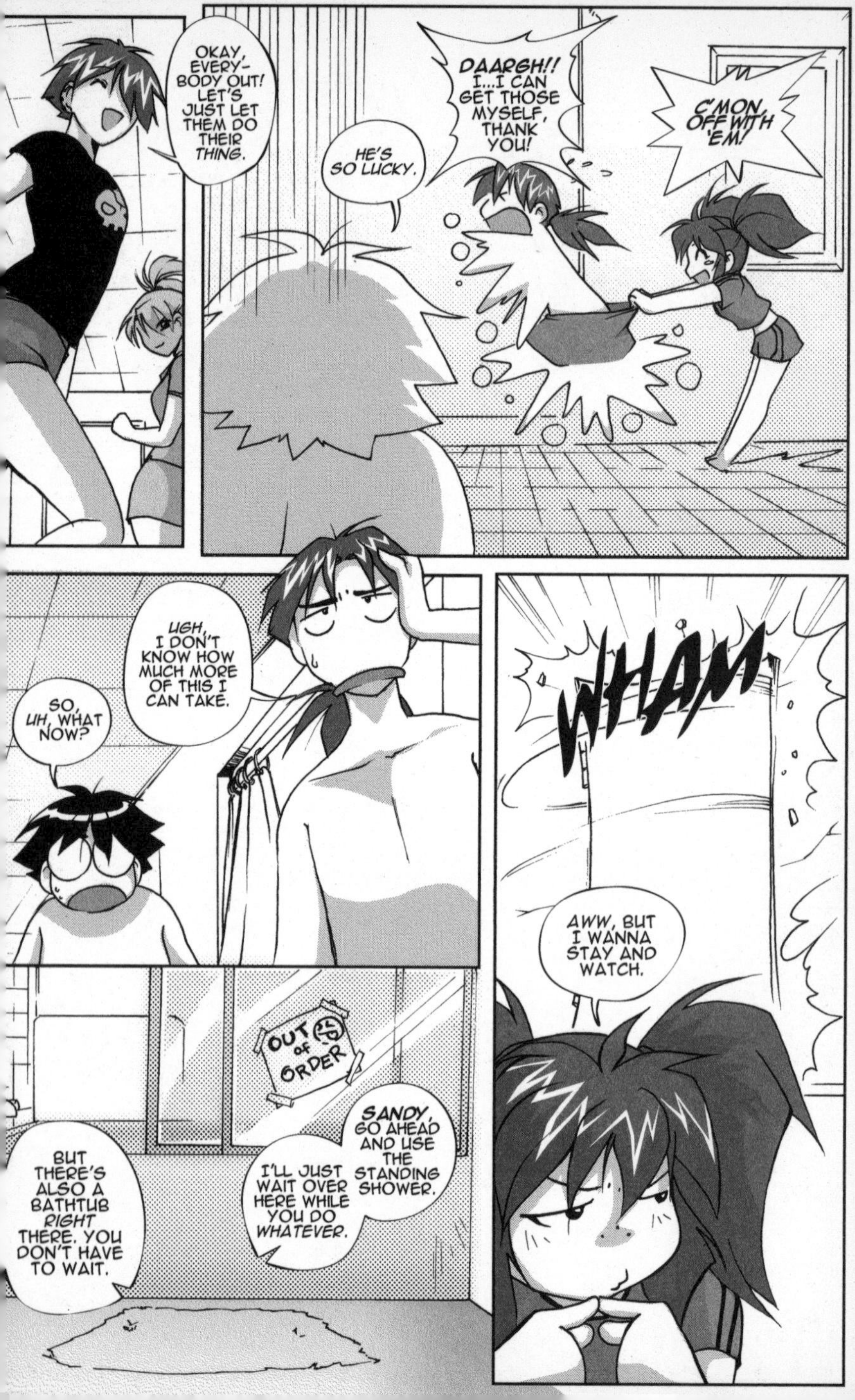
C'MON, OFF WITH 'EM!
DAARGH!! I...I CAN GET THOSE MYSELF, THANK YOU!
HE'S SO LUCKY.
OKAY, EVERY-BODY OUT! LET'S JUST LET THEM DO THEIR THING.
WHAM
AWW, BUT I WANNA STAY AND WATCH.
UGH, I DON'T KNOW HOW MUCH MORE OF THIS I CAN TAKE.
SO, UH, WHAT NOW?
OUT of ORDER
SANDY, GO AHEAD AND USE THE STANDING SHOWER.
I'LL JUST WAIT OVER HERE WHILE YOU DO WHATEVER.
BUT THERE'S ALSO A BATHTUB RIGHT THERE. YOU DON'T HAVE TO WAIT.

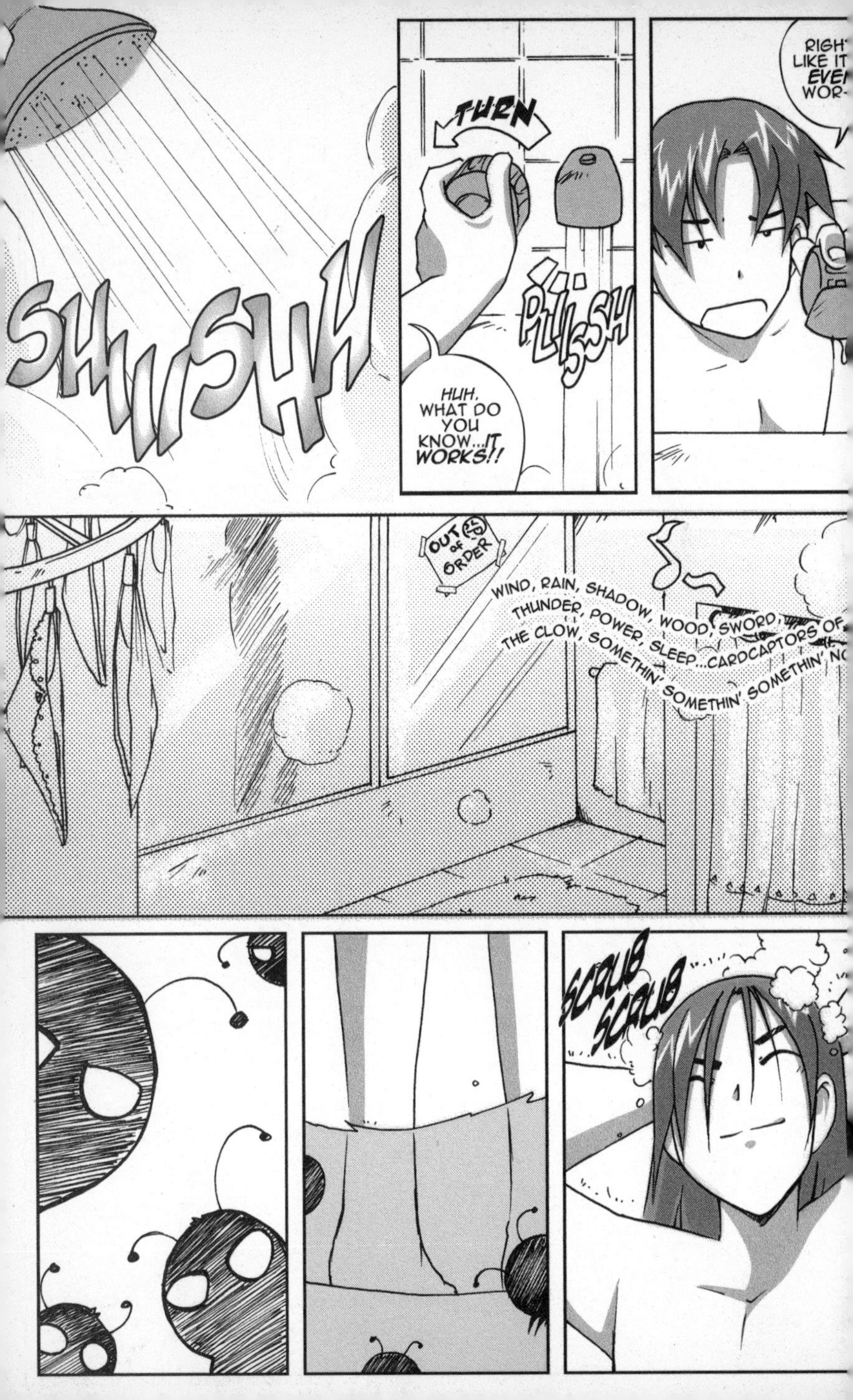
RIGHT LIKE IT EVEN WOR-
TURN
PLISSH
HUH, WHAT DO YOU KNOW...IT WORKS!!
SHHSHH
OUT OF ORDER
WIND, RAIN, SHADOW, WOOD, SWORD, THUNDER, POWER, SLEEP...CARDCAPTORS OF THE CLOW, SOMETHIN' SOMETHIN' SOMETHIN' NO
SCRUB SCRUB

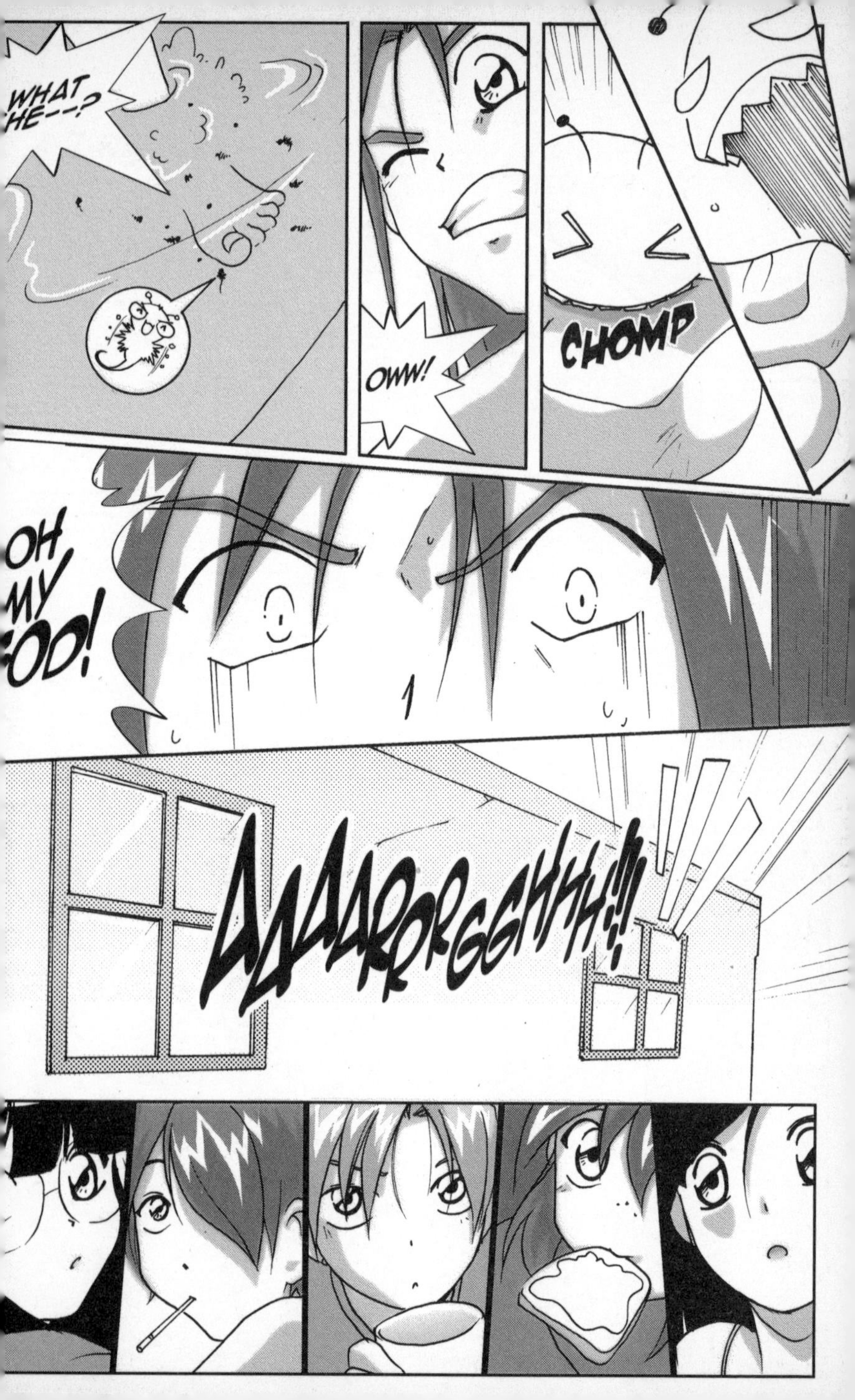
CHOMP
OWW!
WHAT HE--?
OH MY GOD!
AAAARRRGGHHH!!!

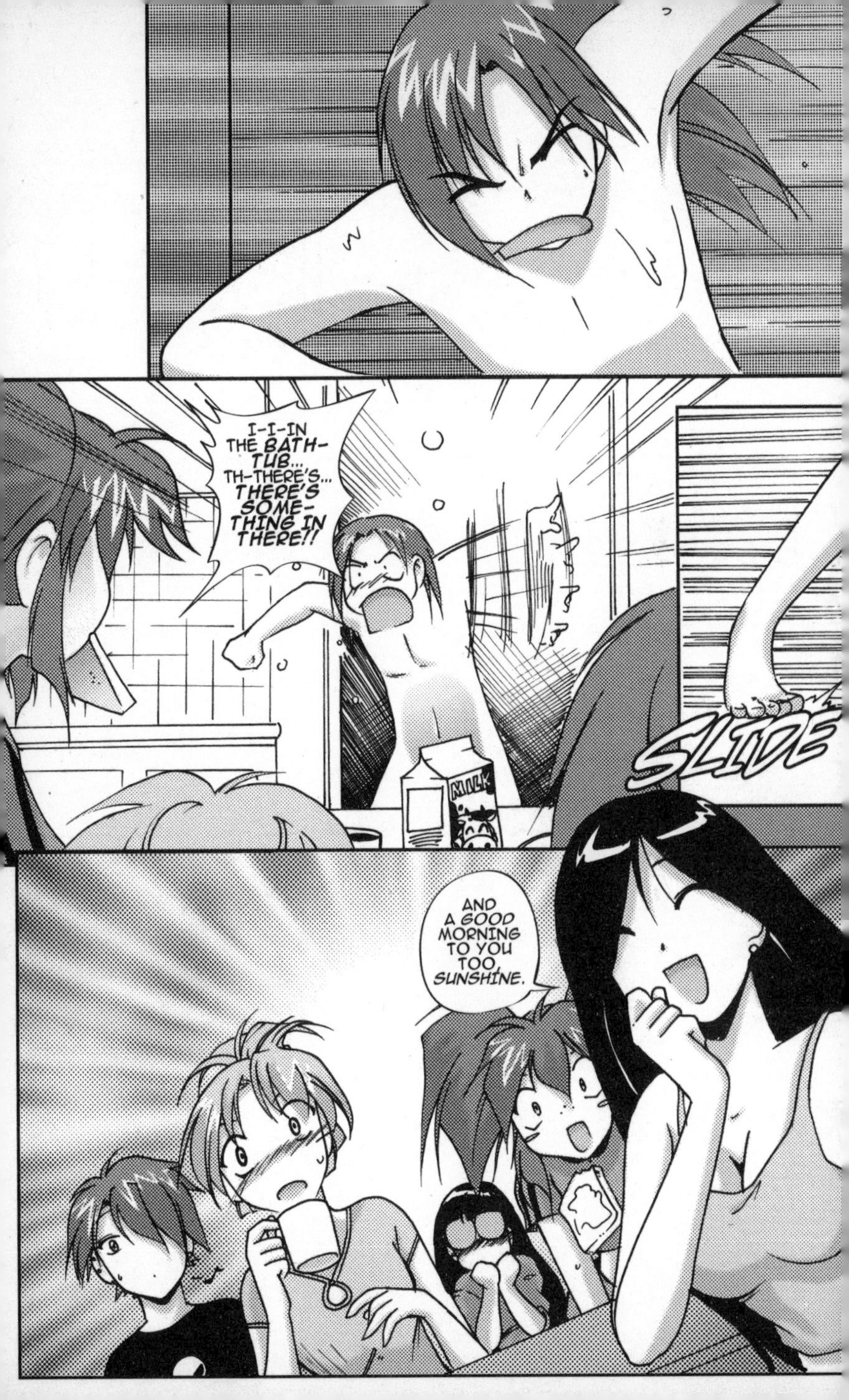
I-I-IN THE BATH-TUB... TH-THERE'S... THERE'S SOME-THING IN THERE!!
SLIDE
AND A GOOD MORNING TO YOU TOO, SUNSHINE.
MILK

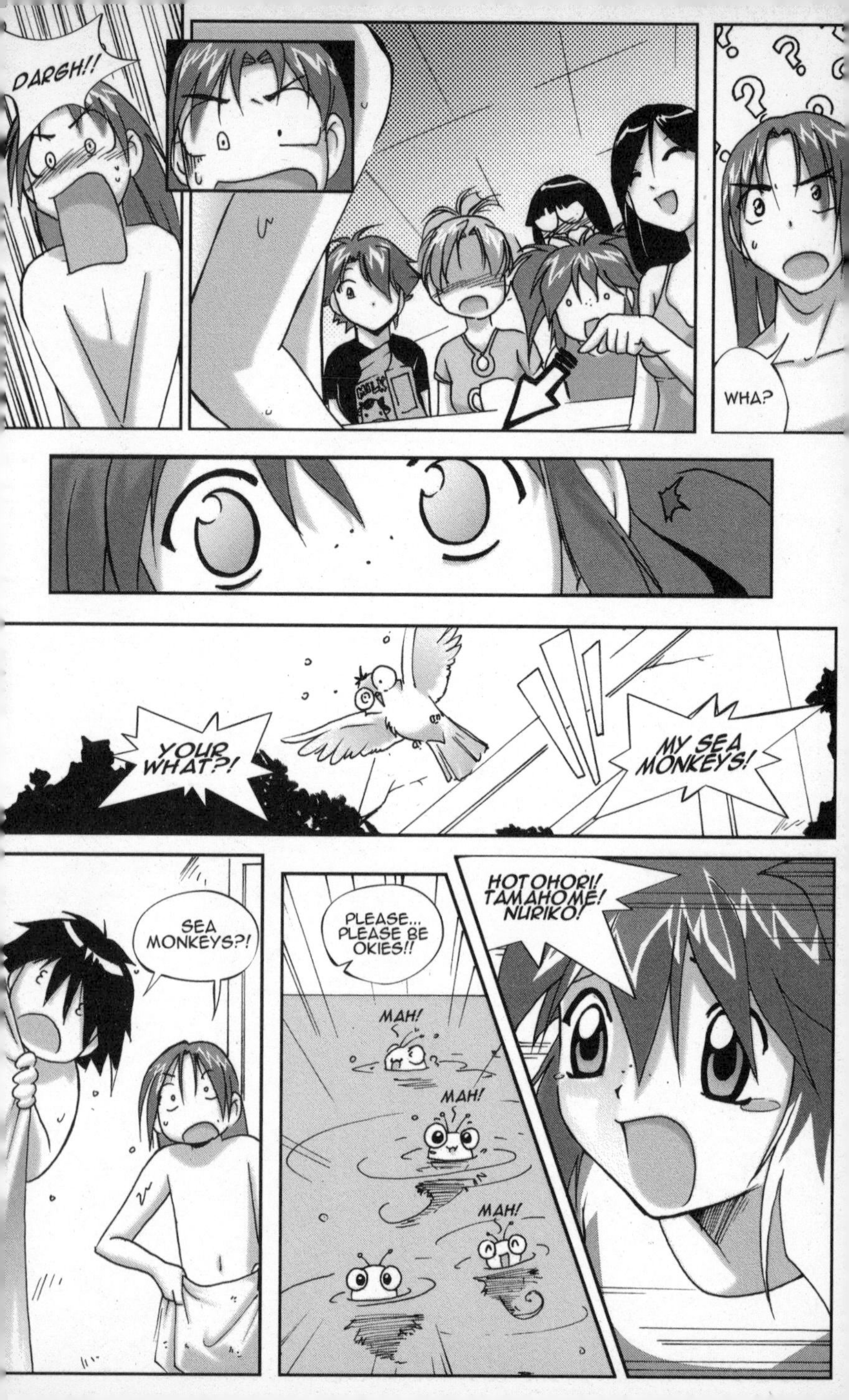
WHA?
DARGH!!
MY SEA MONKEYS!
YOUR WHAT?!
HOTOHORI! TAMAHOME! NURIKO!
PLEASE... PLEASE BE OKIES!!
MAH!
MAH!
MAH!
SEA MONKEYS?!

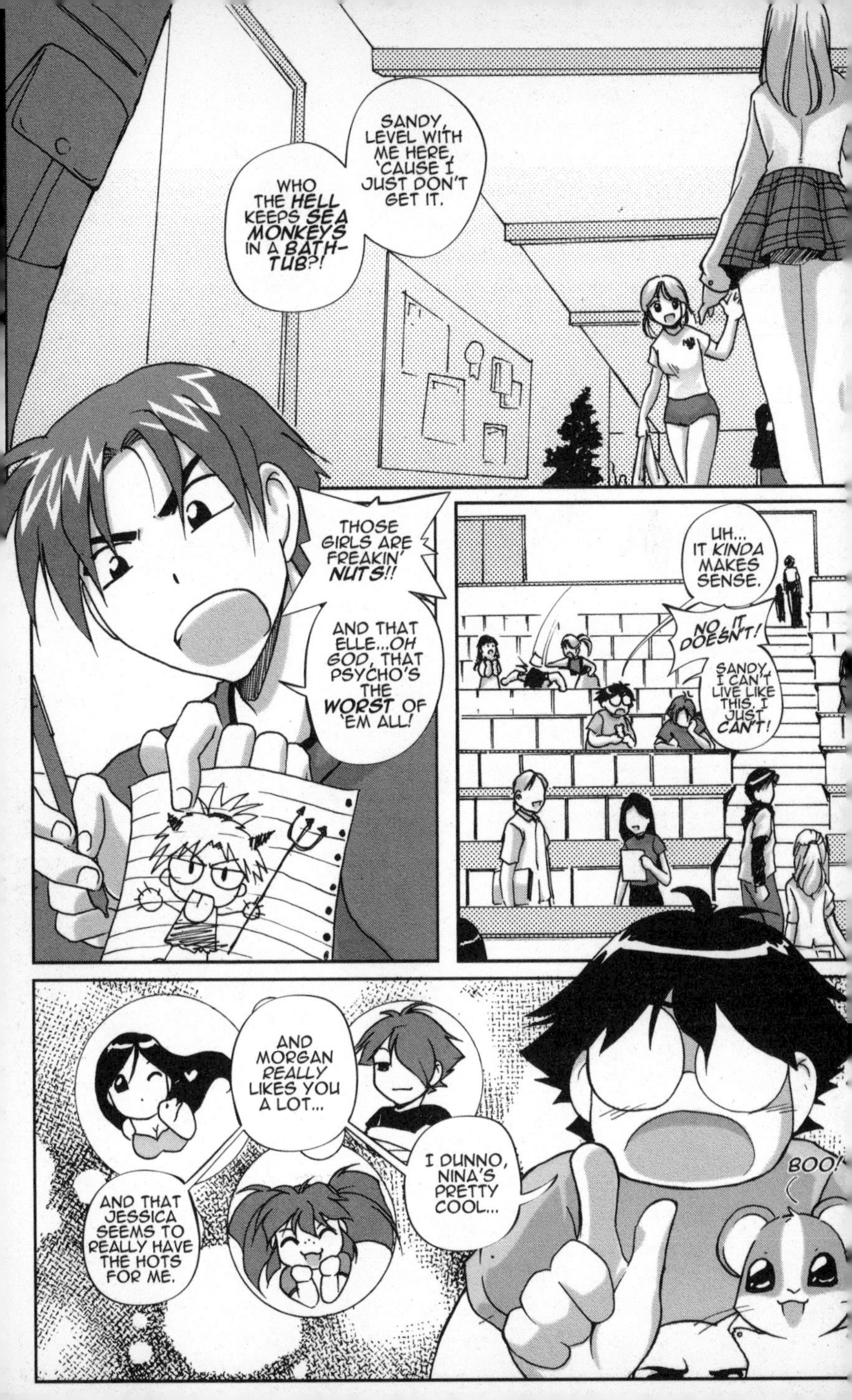
SANDY, LEVEL WITH ME HERE, 'CAUSE I JUST DON'T GET IT.
WHO THE HELL KEEPS SEA MONKEYS IN A BATH-TUB?!
UH... IT KINDA MAKES SENSE.
NO, IT DOESN'T!
SANDY, I CAN'T LIVE LIKE THIS. I JUST CAN'T!
THOSE GIRLS ARE FREAKIN' NUTS!!
AND THAT ELLE...OH GOD, THAT PSYCHO'S THE WORST OF 'EM ALL!
BOO!
I DUNNO, NINA'S PRETTY COOL...
AND MORGAN REALLY LIKES YOU A LOT...
AND THAT JESSICA SEEMS TO REALLY HAVE THE HOTS FOR ME.

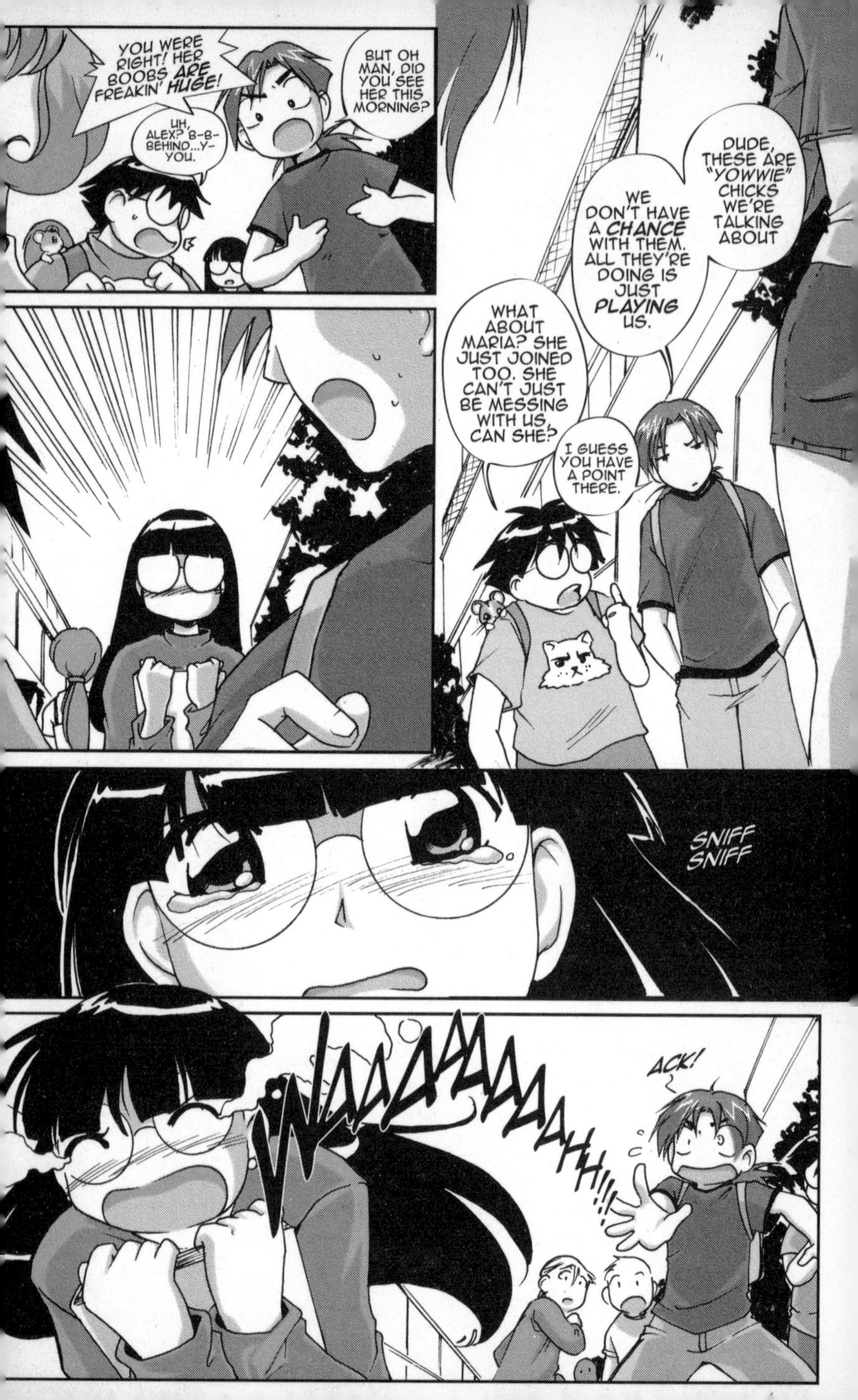
DUDE, THESE ARE "YOWWIE" CHICKS WE'RE TALKING ABOUT
WE DON'T HAVE A CHANCE WITH THEM. ALL THEY'RE DOING IS JUST PLAYING US.
WHAT ABOUT MARIA? SHE JUST JOINED TOO. SHE CAN'T JUST BE MESSING WITH US, CAN SHE?
I GUESS YOU HAVE A POINT THERE.
BUT OH MAN, DID YOU SEE HER THIS MORNING?
YOU WERE RIGHT! HER BOOBS ARE FREAKIN' HUGE!
UH, ALEX? B-B-BEHIND...Y-YOU.
SNIFF SNIFF
ACK!
WAAAAAAAAAAHH!!!

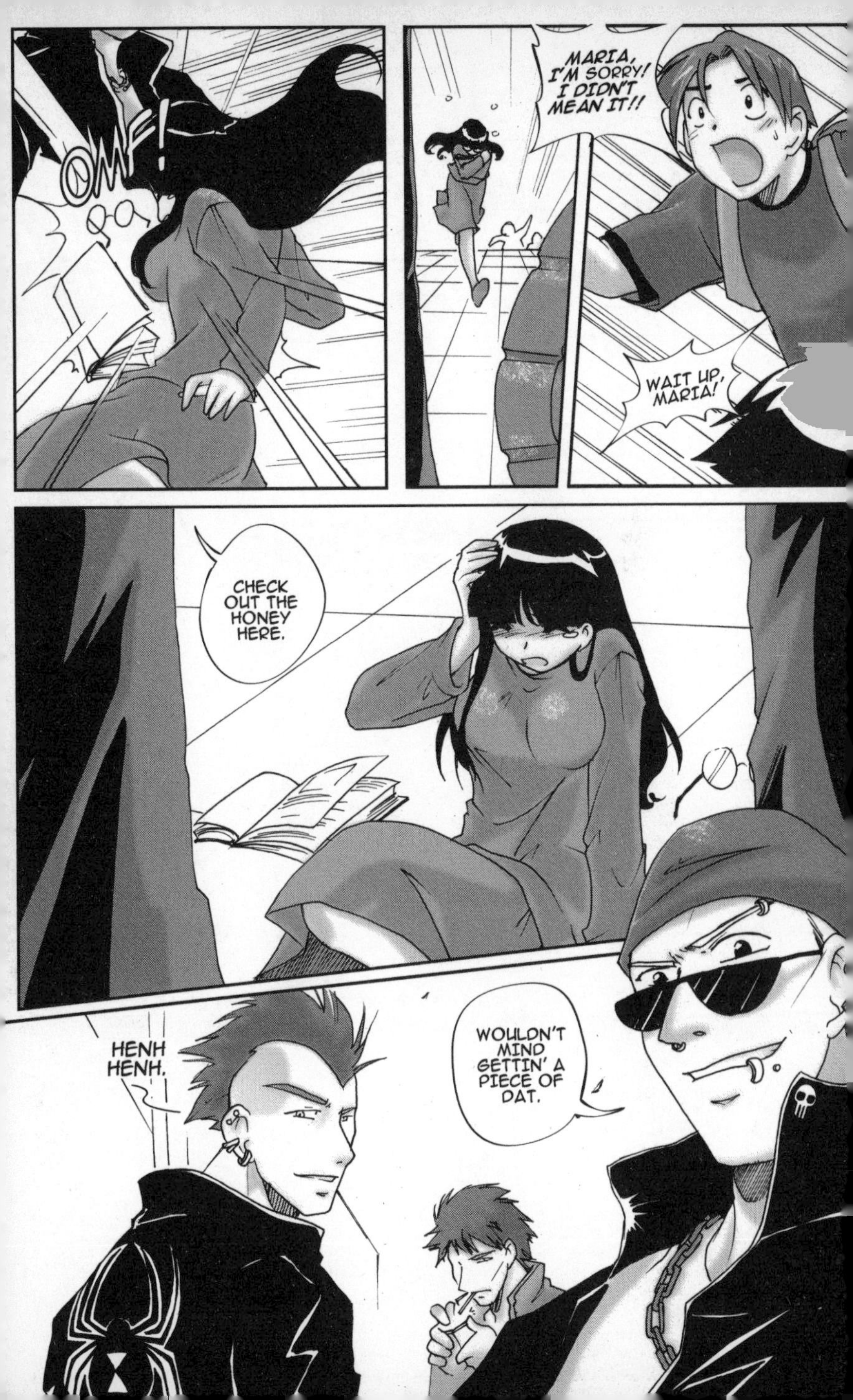
MARIA, I'M SORRY! I DIDN'T MEAN IT!!
WAIT UP, MARIA!
OMF!
CHECK OUT THE HONEY HERE.
WOULDN'T MIND GETTIN' A PIECE OF DAT.
HENH HENH.

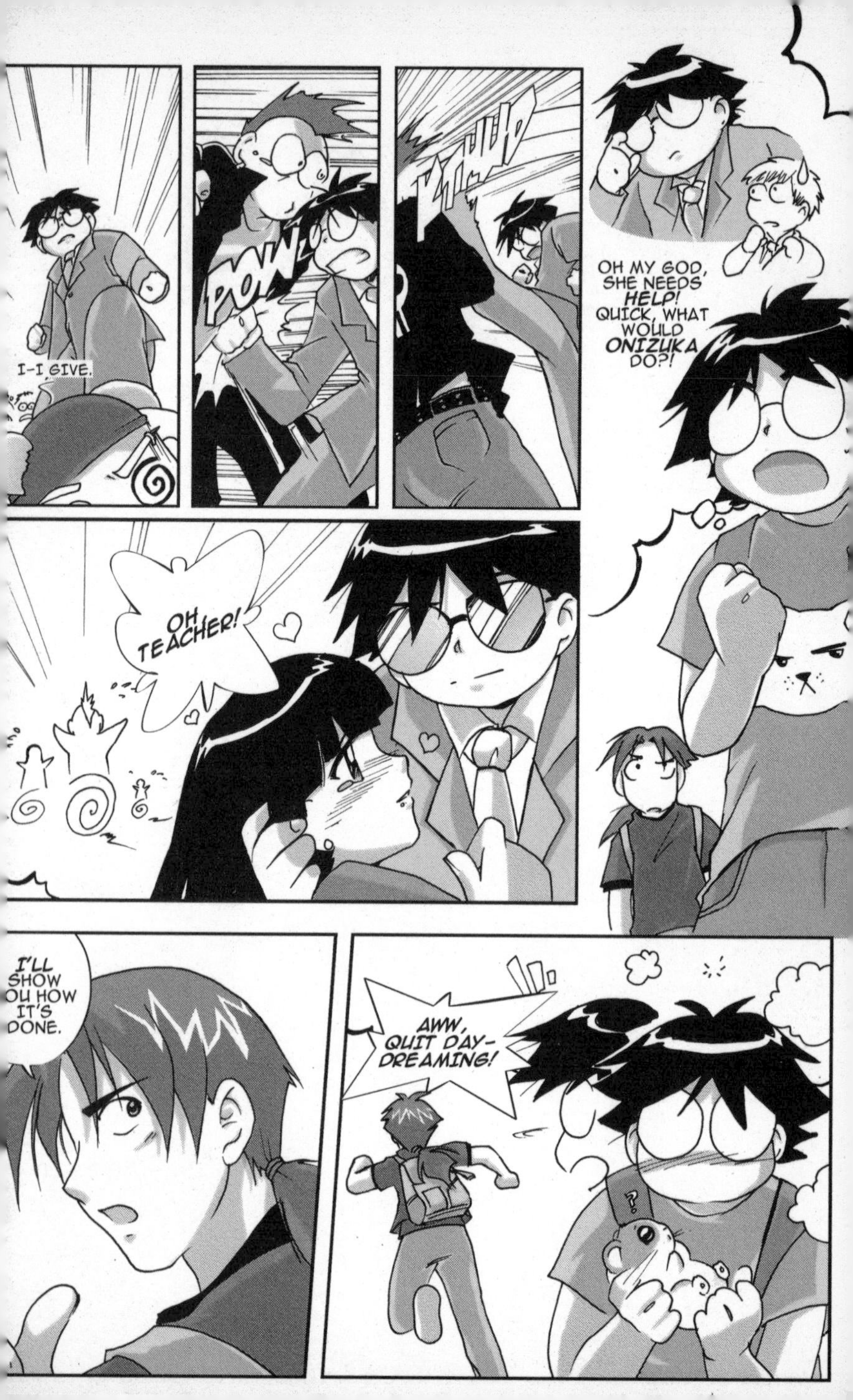
OH MY GOD, SHE NEEDS HELP! QUICK, WHAT WOULD ONIZUKA DO?!
POW!
I-I GIVE.
OH TEACHER!
AWW, QUIT DAY-DREAMING!
I'LL SHOW OU HOW IT'S DONE.

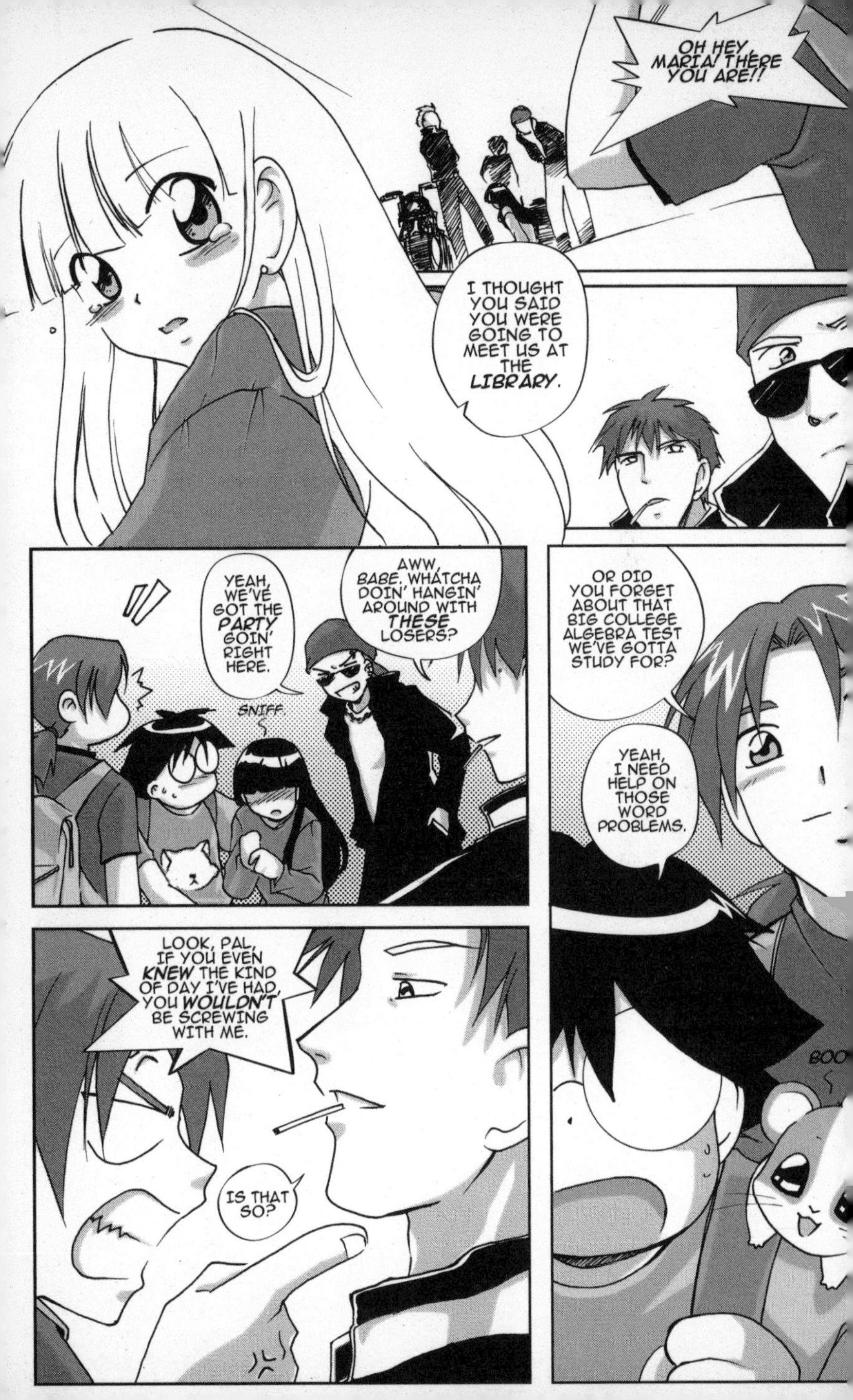
OH HEY, MARIA! THERE YOU ARE!!
I THOUGHT YOU SAID YOU WERE GOING TO MEET US AT THE LIBRARY.
OR DID YOU FORGET ABOUT THAT BIG COLLEGE ALGEBRA TEST WE'VE GOTTA STUDY FOR?
YEAH, I NEED HELP ON THOSE WORD PROBLEMS.
AWW, BABE. WHÁTCHA DOIN' HANGIN' AROUND WITH THESE LOSERS?
YEAH, WE'VE GOT THE PARTY GOIN' RIGHT HERE.
SNIFF
BOO
LOOK, PAL, IF YOU EVEN KNEW THE KIND OF DAY I'VE HAD, YOU WOULDN'T BE SCREWING WITH ME.
IS THAT SO?

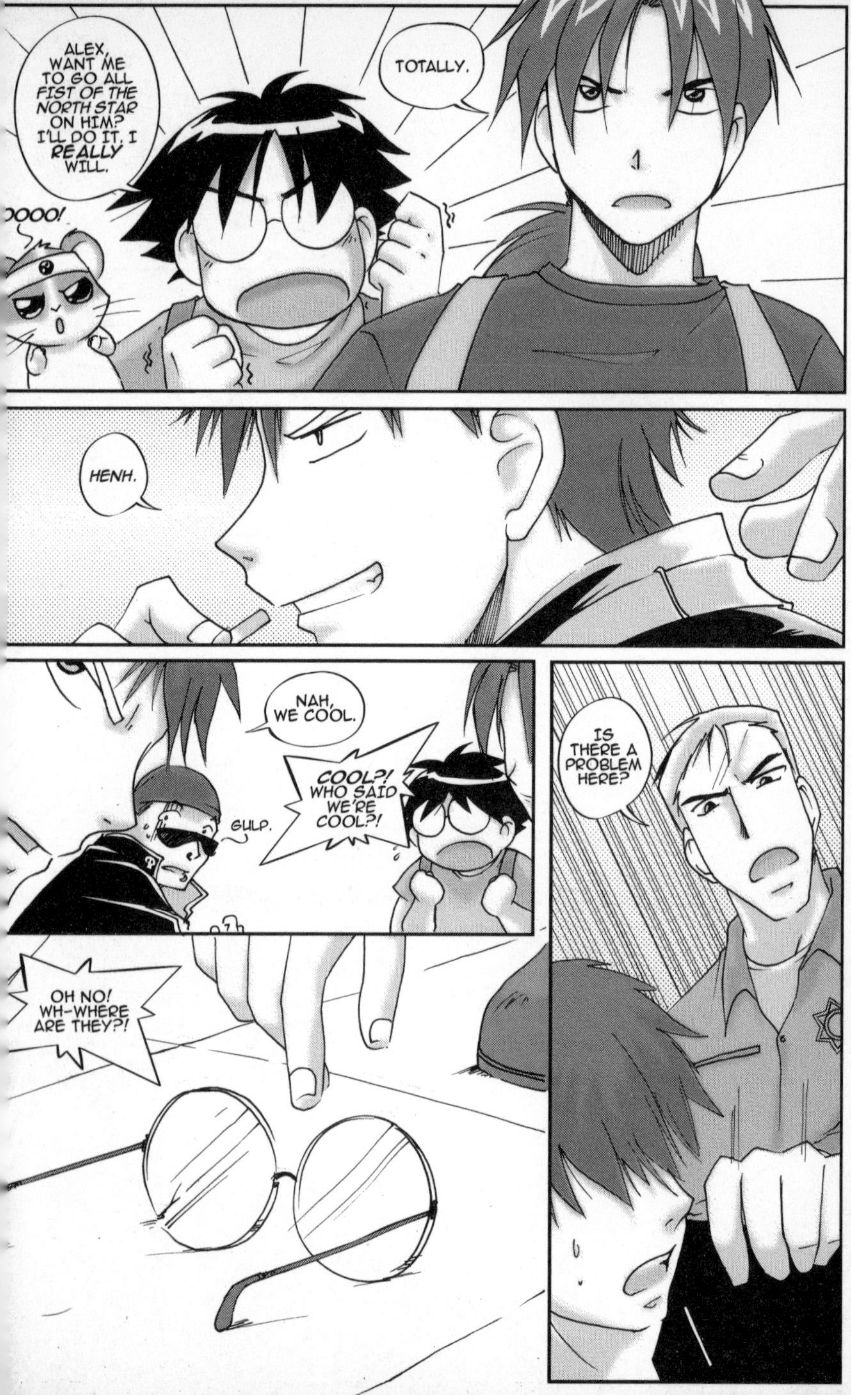
TOTALLY.
ALEX, WANT ME TO GO ALL FIST OF THE NORTH STAR ON HIM? I'LL DO IT. I REALLY WILL.
OOOO!
HENH.
IS THERE A PROBLEM HERE?
NAH, WE COOL.
COOL?! WHO SAID WE'RE COOL?!
GULP.
OH NO! WH-WHERE ARE THEY?!

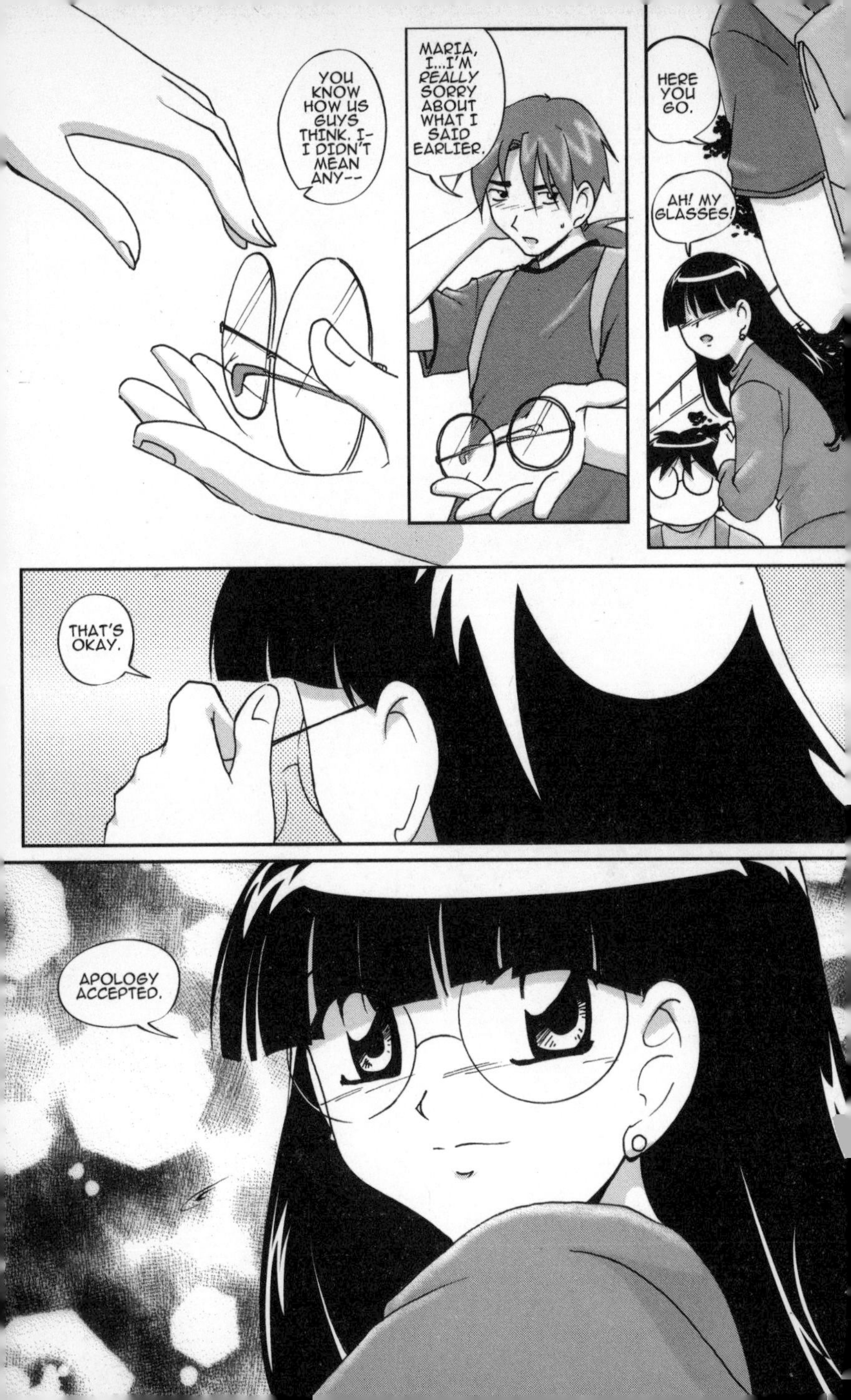
HERE YOU GO.
AH! MY GLASSES!
MARIA, I...I'M REALLY SORRY ABOUT WHAT I SAID EARLIER.
YOU KNOW HOW US GUYS THINK. I-I DIDN'T MEAN ANY--
THAT'S OKAY.
APOLOGY ACCEPTED.

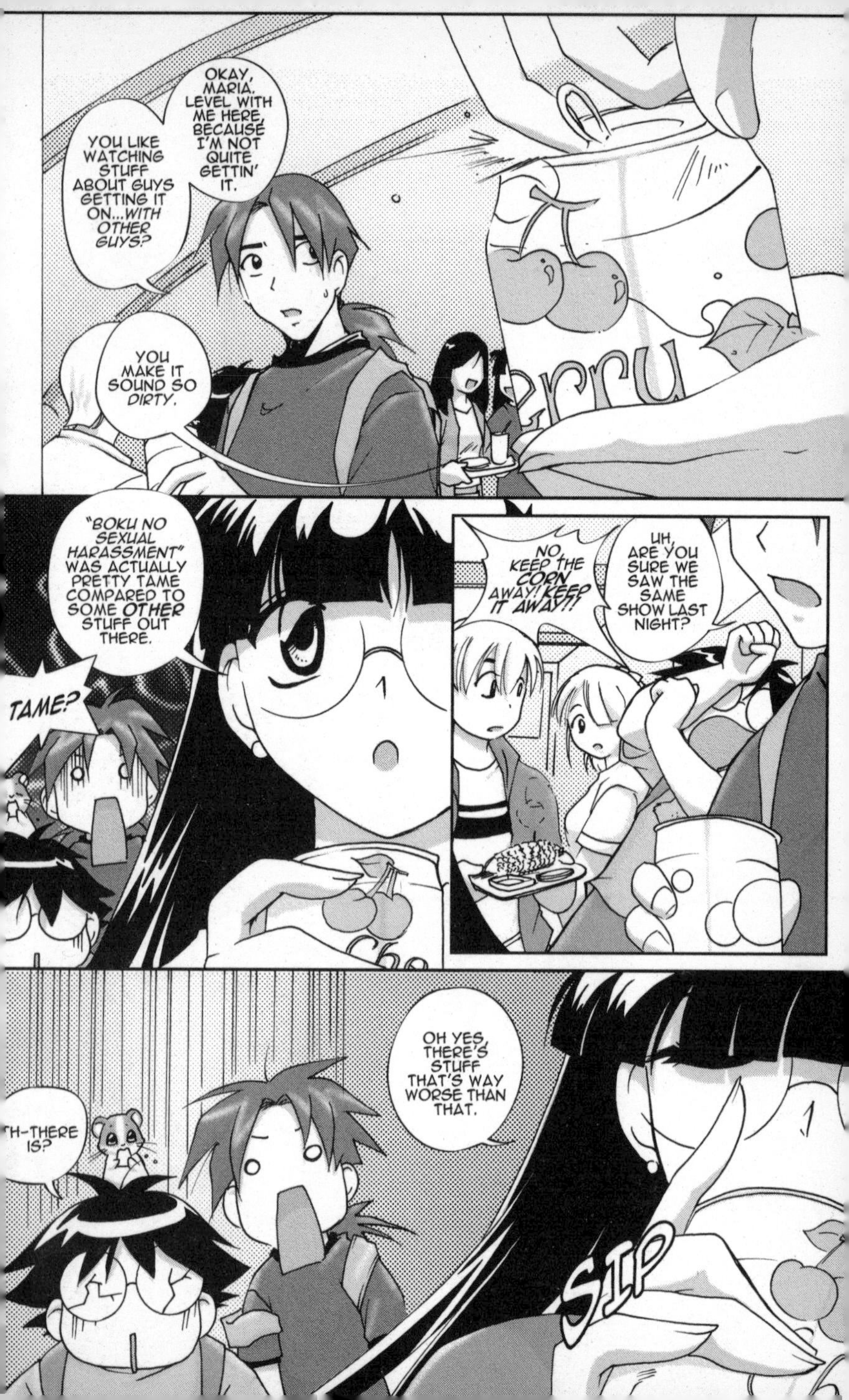
OKAY, MARIA. LEVEL WITH ME HERE, BECAUSE I'M NOT QUITE GETTIN' IT.
YOU LIKE WATCHING STUFF ABOUT GUYS GETTING IT ON...*WITH OTHER GUYS*?
YOU MAKE IT SOUND SO *DIRTY*.
UH, ARE YOU SURE WE SAW THE SAME SHOW LAST NIGHT?
NO, KEEP THE **CORN** AWAY! ***KEEP IT AWAY!!***
"*BOKU NO SEXUAL HARASSMENT*" WAS ACTUALLY PRETTY TAME COMPARED TO SOME ***OTHER*** STUFF OUT THERE.
TAME?
OH YES, THERE'S STUFF THAT'S WAY WORSE THAN THAT.
TH-THERE IS?
SIP

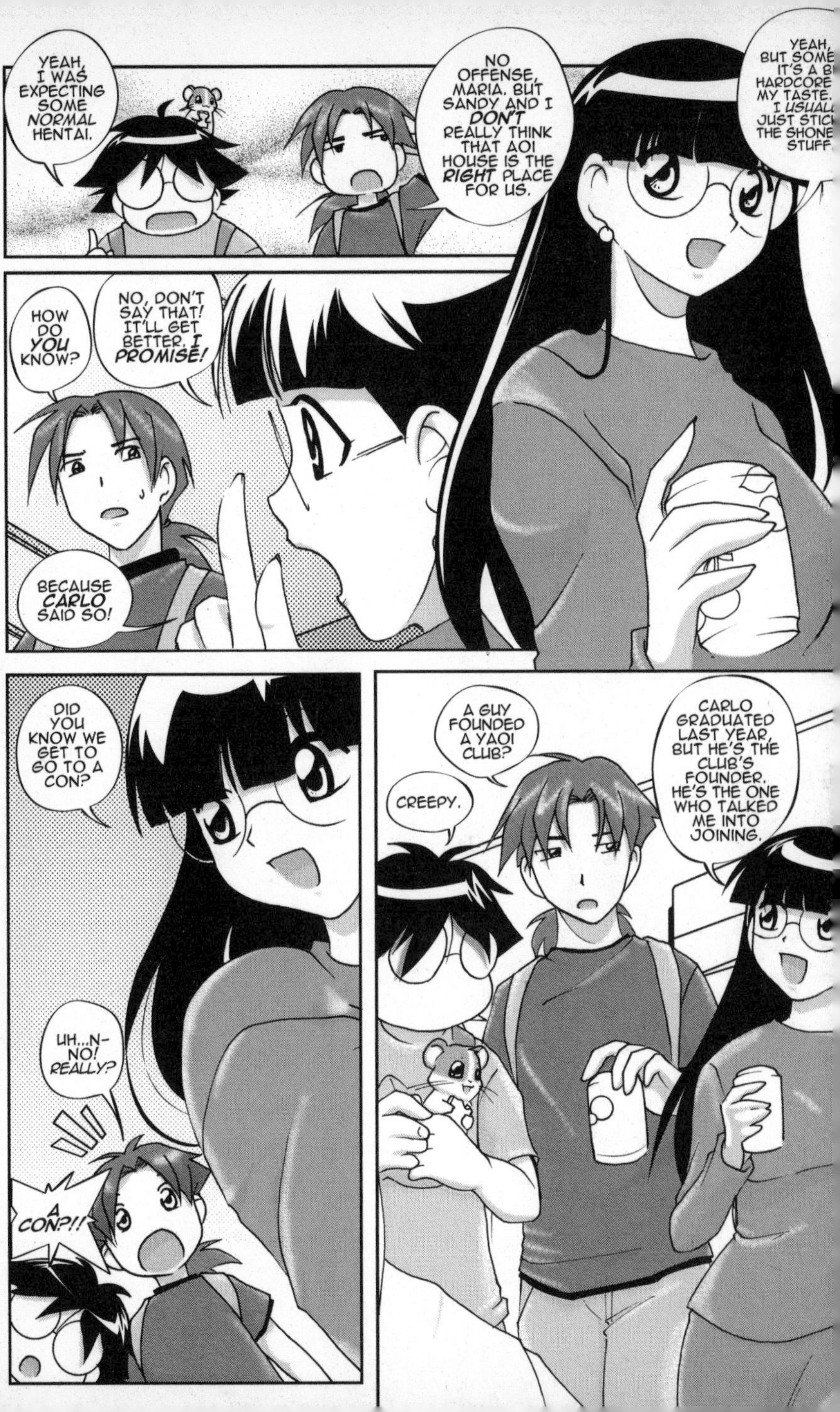
YEAH, BUT SOME IT'S A BI HARDCORE MY TASTE. I USUALL JUST STICK THE SHONE STUFF.
NO OFFENSE, MARIA. BUT SANDY AND I DON'T REALLY THINK THAT AOI HOUSE IS THE RIGHT PLACE FOR US.
YEAH, I WAS EXPECTING SOME NORMAL HENTAI.
NO, DON'T SAY THAT! IT'LL GET BETTER. I PROMISE!
HOW DO YOU KNOW?
BECAUSE CARLO SAID SO!
CARLO GRADUATED LAST YEAR, BUT HE'S THE CLUB'S FOUNDER. HE'S THE ONE WHO TALKED ME INTO JOINING.
A GUY FOUNDED A YAOI CLUB?
CREEPY.
DID YOU KNOW WE GET TO GO TO A CON?
UH...N-NO! REALLY?
A CON?!!

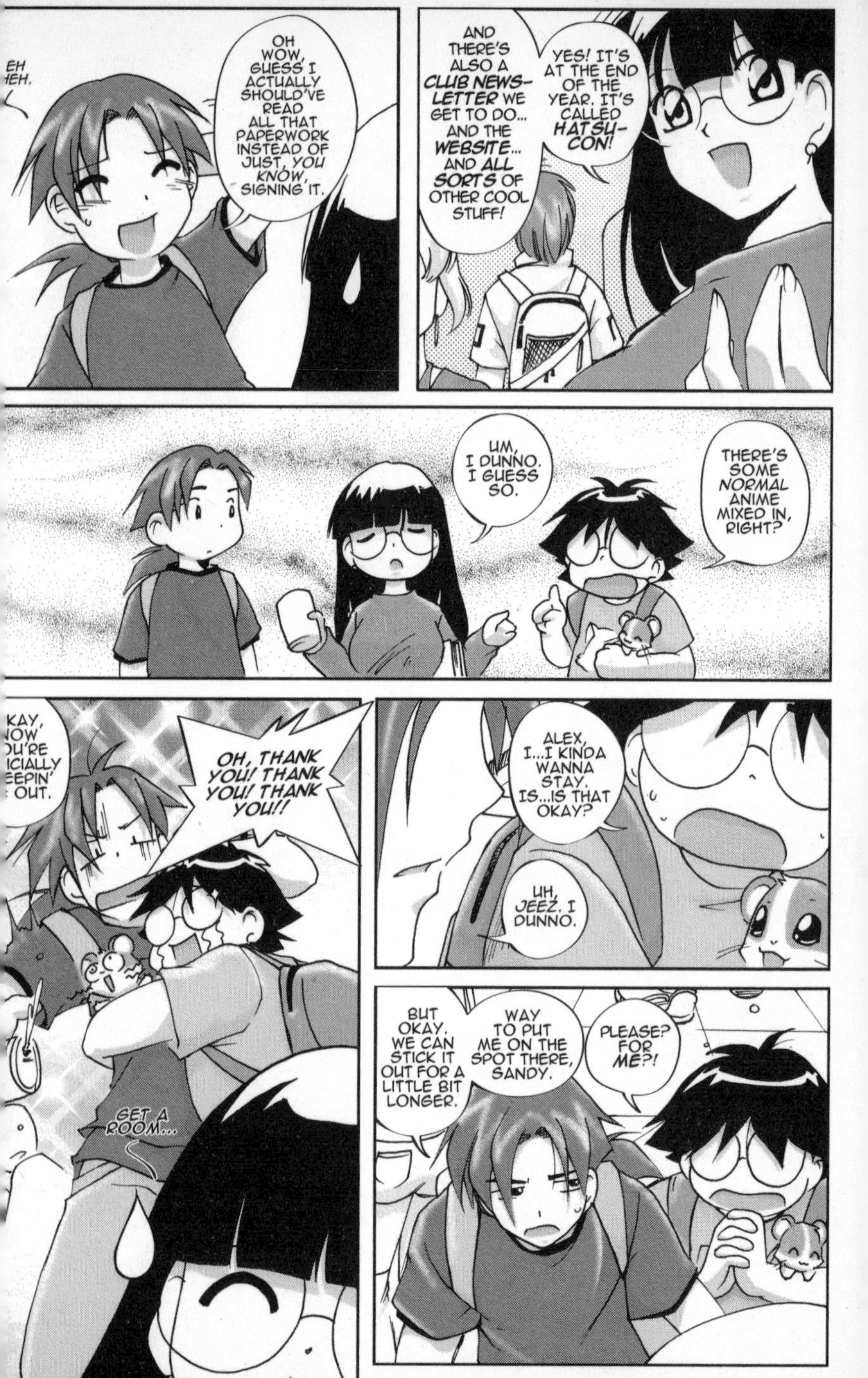
YES! IT'S AT THE END OF THE YEAR. IT'S CALLED HATSU-CON!
AND THERE'S ALSO A CLUB NEWSLETTER WE GET TO DO... AND THE WEBSITE... AND ALL SORTS OF OTHER COOL STUFF!
OH WOW, GUESS I ACTUALLY SHOULD'VE READ ALL THAT PAPERWORK INSTEAD OF JUST, YOU KNOW, SIGNING IT.
EH HEH.
THERE'S SOME NORMAL ANIME MIXED IN, RIGHT?
UM, I DUNNO. I GUESS SO.
ALEX, I...I KINDA WANNA STAY. IS...IS THAT OKAY?
UH, JEEZ. I DUNNO.
PLEASE? FOR ME?!
WAY TO PUT ME ON THE SPOT THERE, SANDY.
BUT OKAY, WE CAN STICK IT OUT FOR A LITTLE BIT LONGER.
OH, THANK YOU! THANK YOU! THANK YOU!!
KAY, NOW YOU'RE ICIALLY EEPIN' OUT.
GET A ROOM...

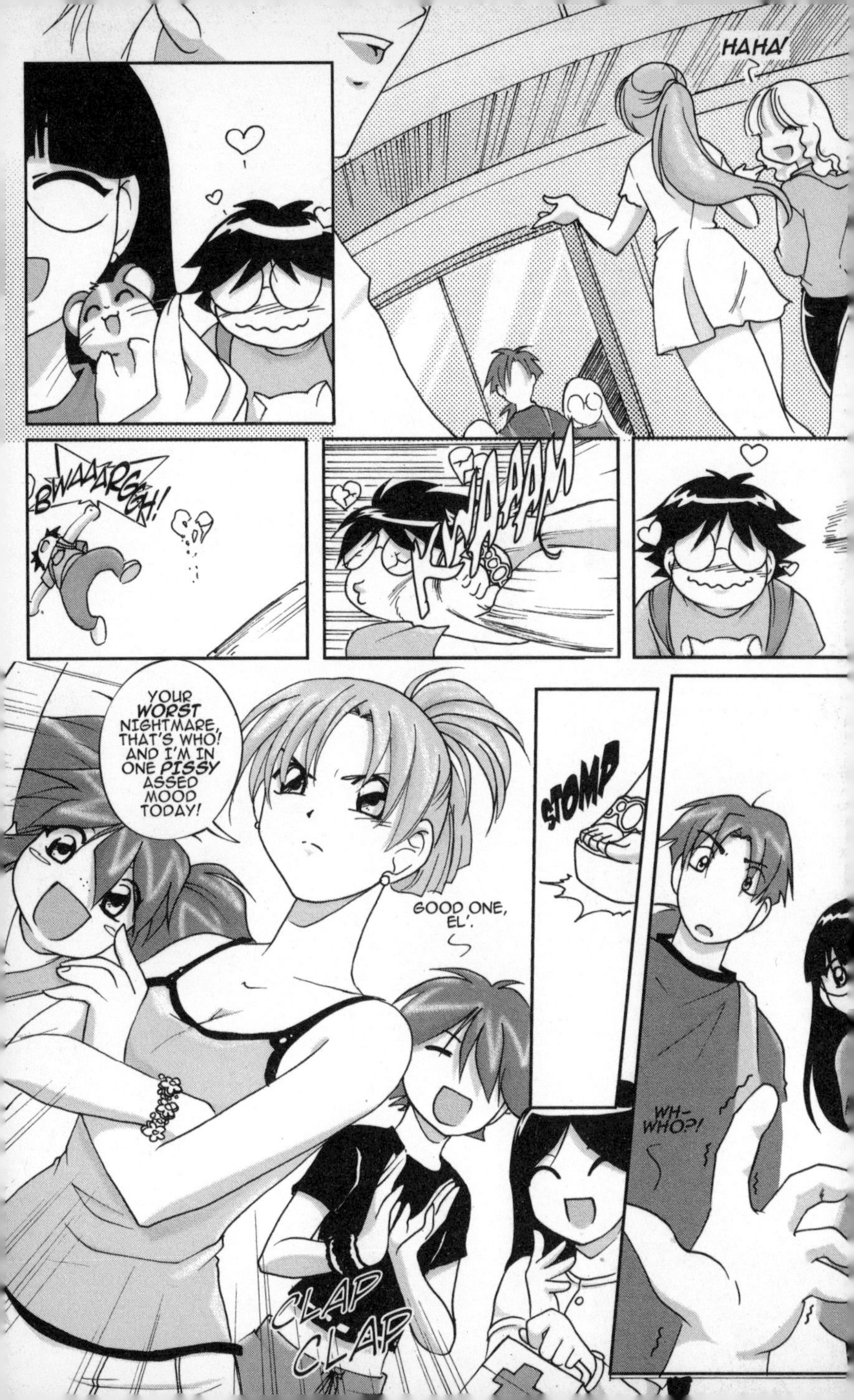
HAHA!
BWAAARGGH!
KWAAAM
WH-WHO?!
STOMP
YOUR WORST NIGHTMARE, THAT'S WHO! AND I'M IN ONE PISSY ASSED MOOD TODAY!
GOOD ONE, EL'.
CLAP CLAP

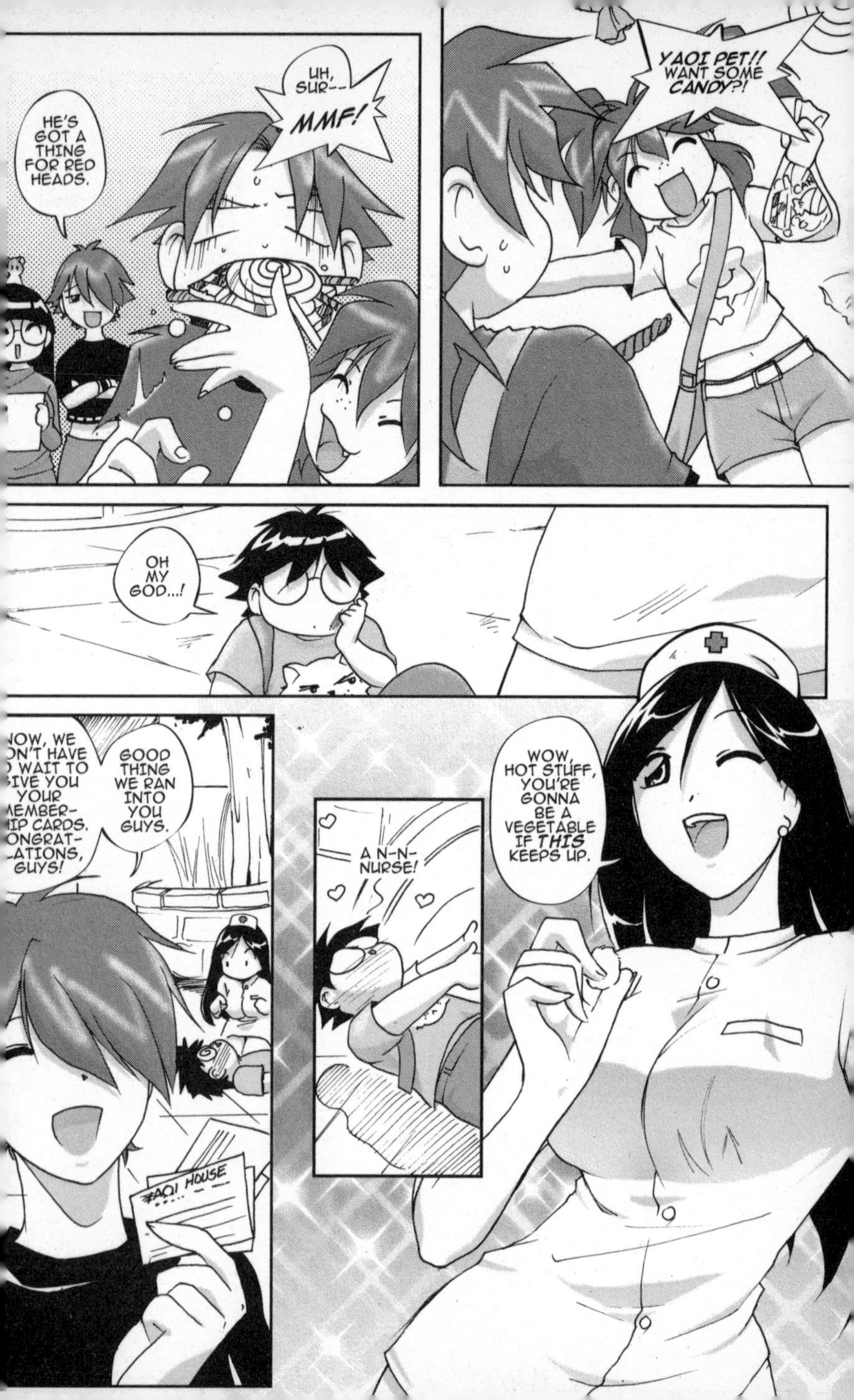
YAOI PET!! WANT SOME CANDY?!
UH, SUR--
MMF!
HE'S GOT A THING FOR RED HEADS.
OH MY GOD...!
WOW, HOT STUFF, YOU'RE GONNA BE A VEGETABLE IF THIS KEEPS UP.
A N-N-NURSE!
GOOD THING WE RAN INTO YOU GUYS.
NOW, WE ON'T HAVE O WAIT TO IVE YOU YOUR MEMBER-IP CARDS. ONGRAT-LATIONS, GUYS!
AOI HOUSE

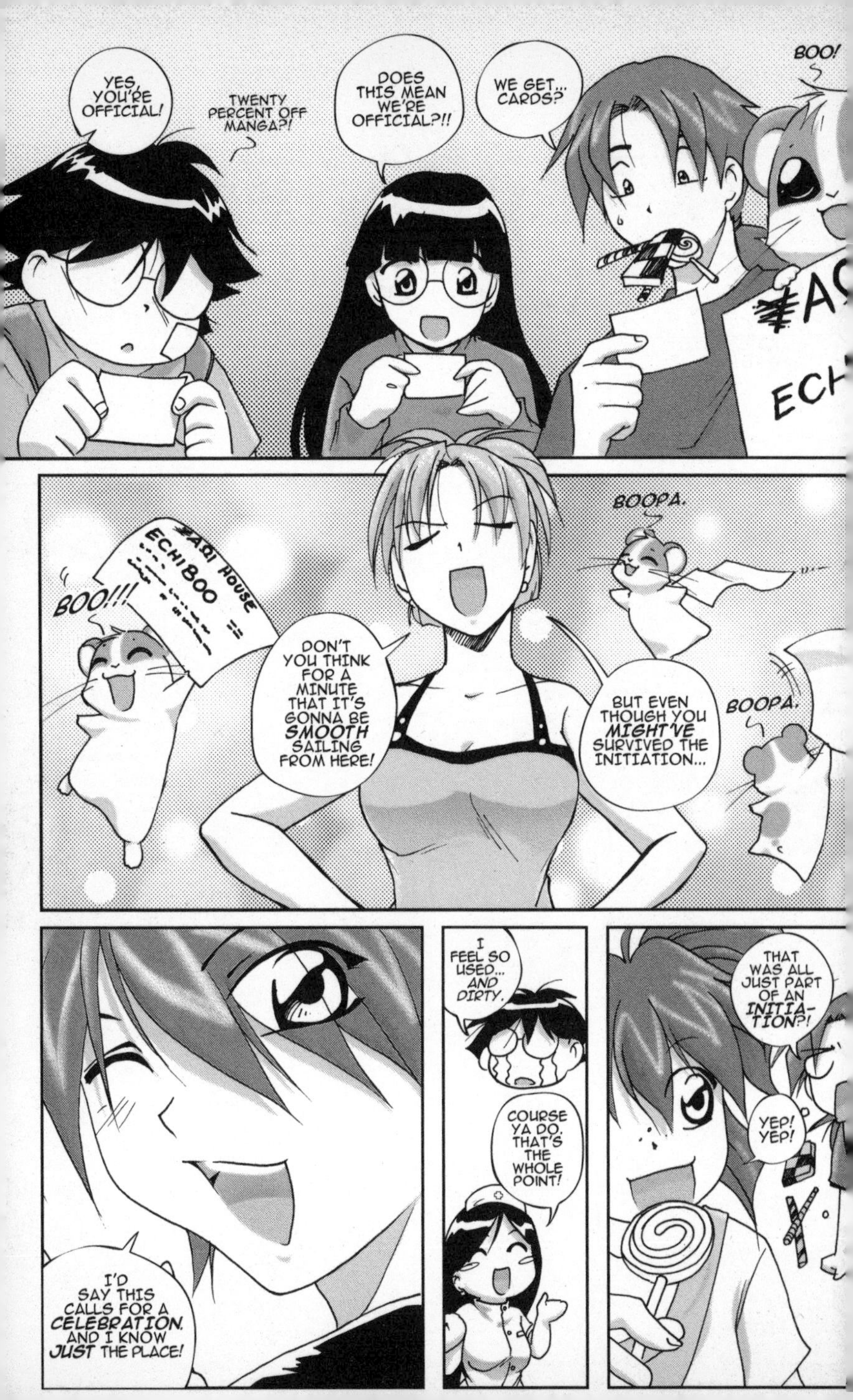
BOO!
WE GET... CARDS?
DOES THIS MEAN WE'RE OFFICIAL?!!
TWENTY PERCENT OFF MANGA?!
YES, YOU'RE OFFICIAL!
BOOPA.
BOOPA.
BUT EVEN THOUGH YOU MIGHT'VE SURVIVED THE INITIATION...
DON'T YOU THINK FOR A MINUTE THAT IT'S GONNA BE SMOOTH SAILING FROM HERE!
ECHIBOO
BOO!!!
THAT WAS ALL JUST PART OF AN INITIATION?!
YEP! YEP!
I FEEL SO USED... AND DIRTY.
COURSE YA DO. THAT'S THE WHOLE POINT!
I'D SAY THIS CALLS FOR A CELEBRATION, AND I KNOW JUST THE PLACE!

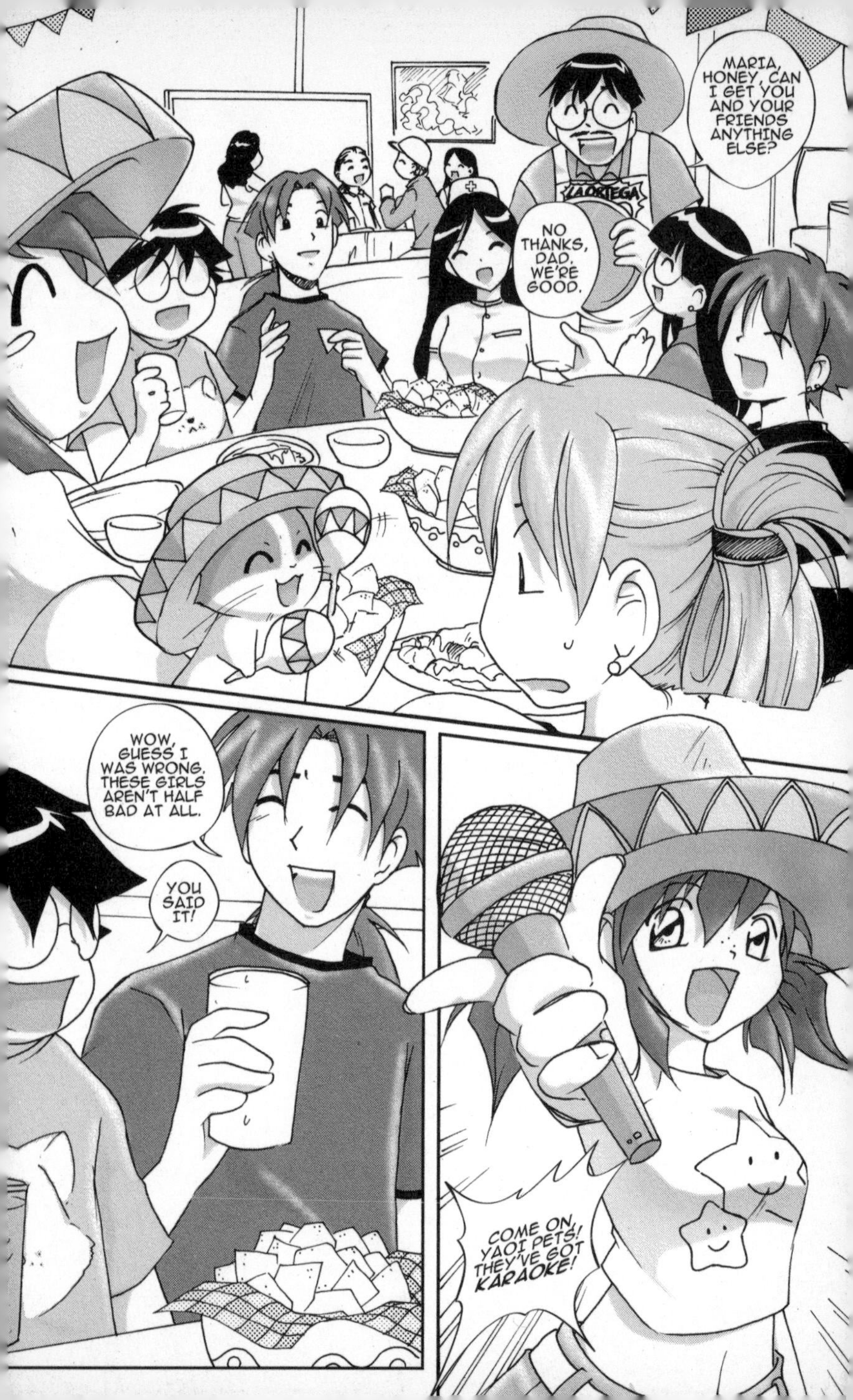
MARIA, HONEY, CAN I GET YOU AND YOUR FRIENDS ANYTHING ELSE?
NO THANKS, DAD. WE'RE GOOD.
LA ORTEGA
COME ON, YAOI PETS! THEY'VE GOT *KARAOKE*!
WOW, GUESS I WAS WRONG. THESE GIRLS AREN'T HALF BAD AT ALL.
YOU SAID IT!

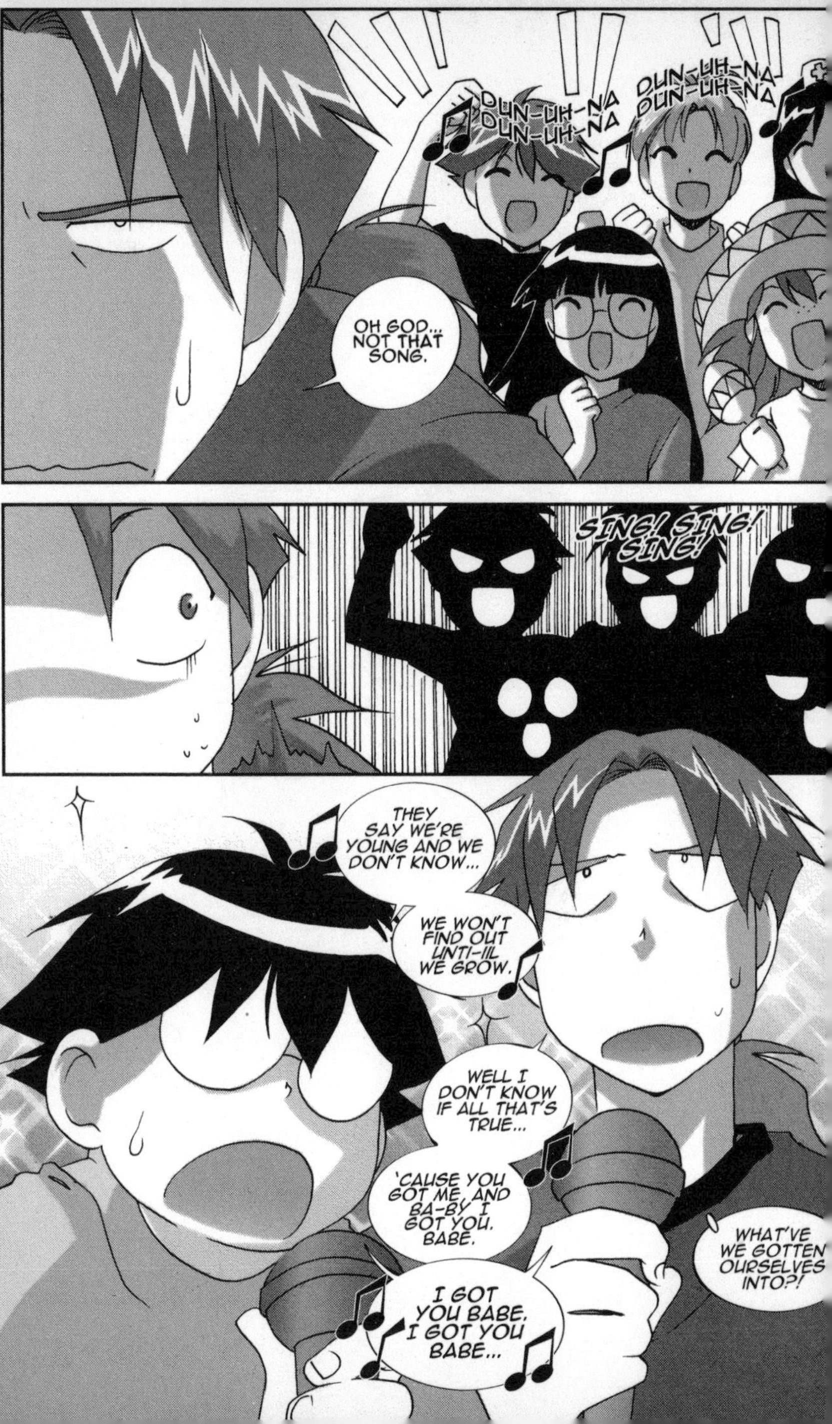
DUN-UH-NA DUN-UH-NA
DUN-UH-NA DUN-UH-NA
OH GOD... NOT THAT SONG.
SING! SING! SING!
THEY SAY WE'RE YOUNG AND WE DON'T KNOW...
WE WON'T FIND OUT UNTI-IIL WE GROW.
WELL I DON'T KNOW IF ALL THAT'S TRUE...
'CAUSE YOU GOT ME, AND BA-BY I GOT YOU. BABE.
WHAT'VE WE GOTTEN OURSELVES INTO?!
I GOT YOU BABE, I GOT YOU BABE...

BOOPA

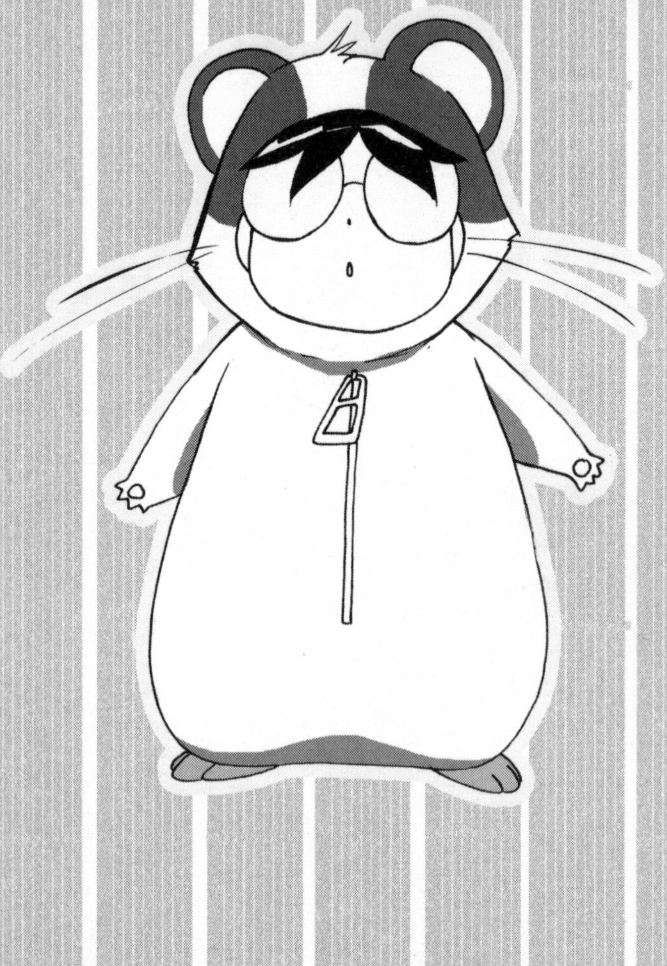

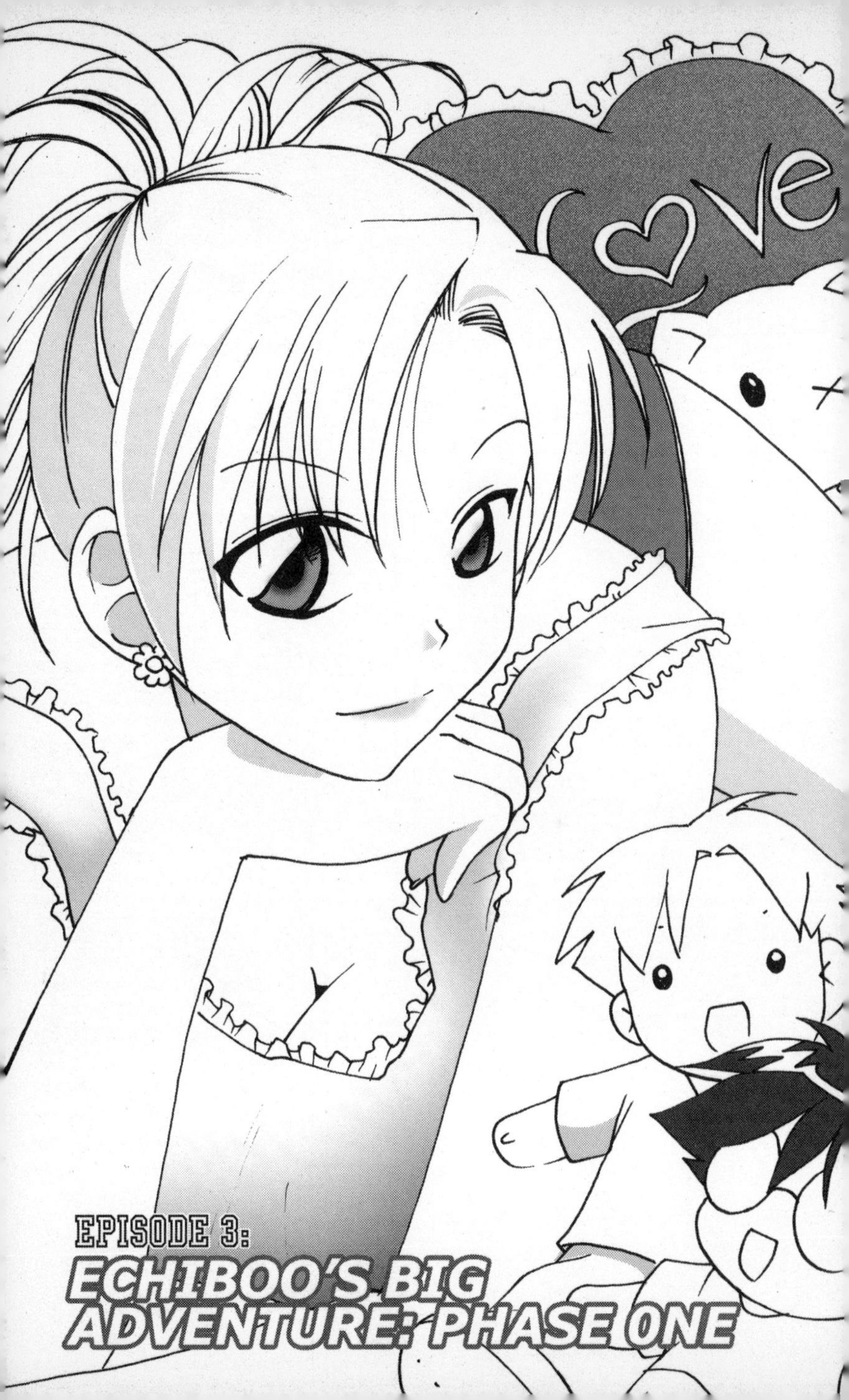

EPISODE 3:
ECHIBOO'S BIG ADVENTURE: PHASE ONE

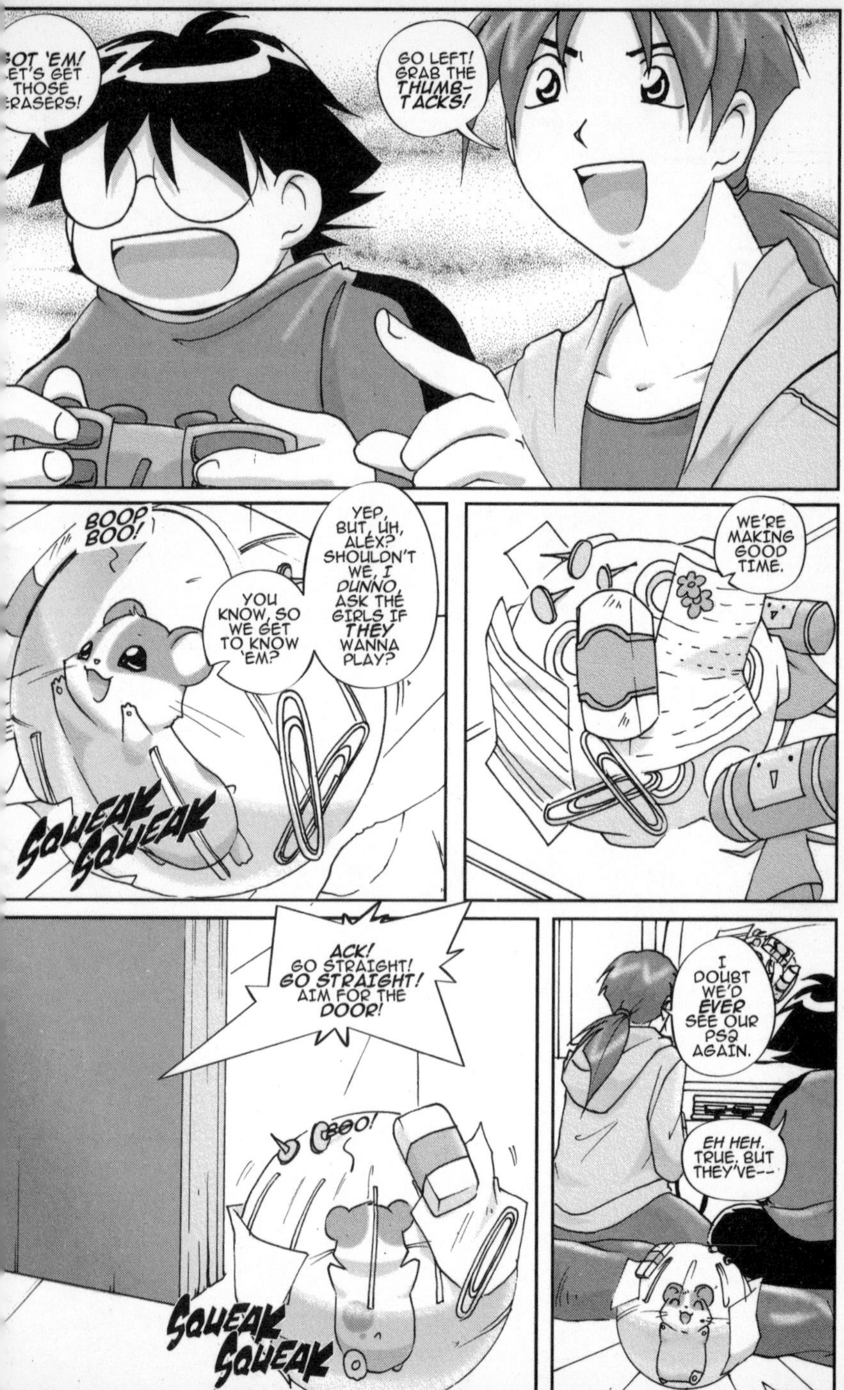
GO LEFT! GRAB THE THUMB-TACKS!
GOT 'EM! ET'S GET THOSE ERASERS!
WE'RE MAKING GOOD TIME.
YEP, BUT, UH, ALEX? SHOULDN'T WE, I DUNNO, ASK THE GIRLS IF THEY WANNA PLAY?
YOU KNOW, SO WE GET TO KNOW 'EM?
BOOP BOO!
SQUEAK SQUEAK
I DOUBT WE'D EVER SEE OUR PS2 AGAIN.
EH HEH. TRUE, BUT THEY'VE--
ACK! GO STRAIGHT! GO STRAIGHT! AIM FOR THE DOOR!
BOO!
SQUEAK SQUEAK

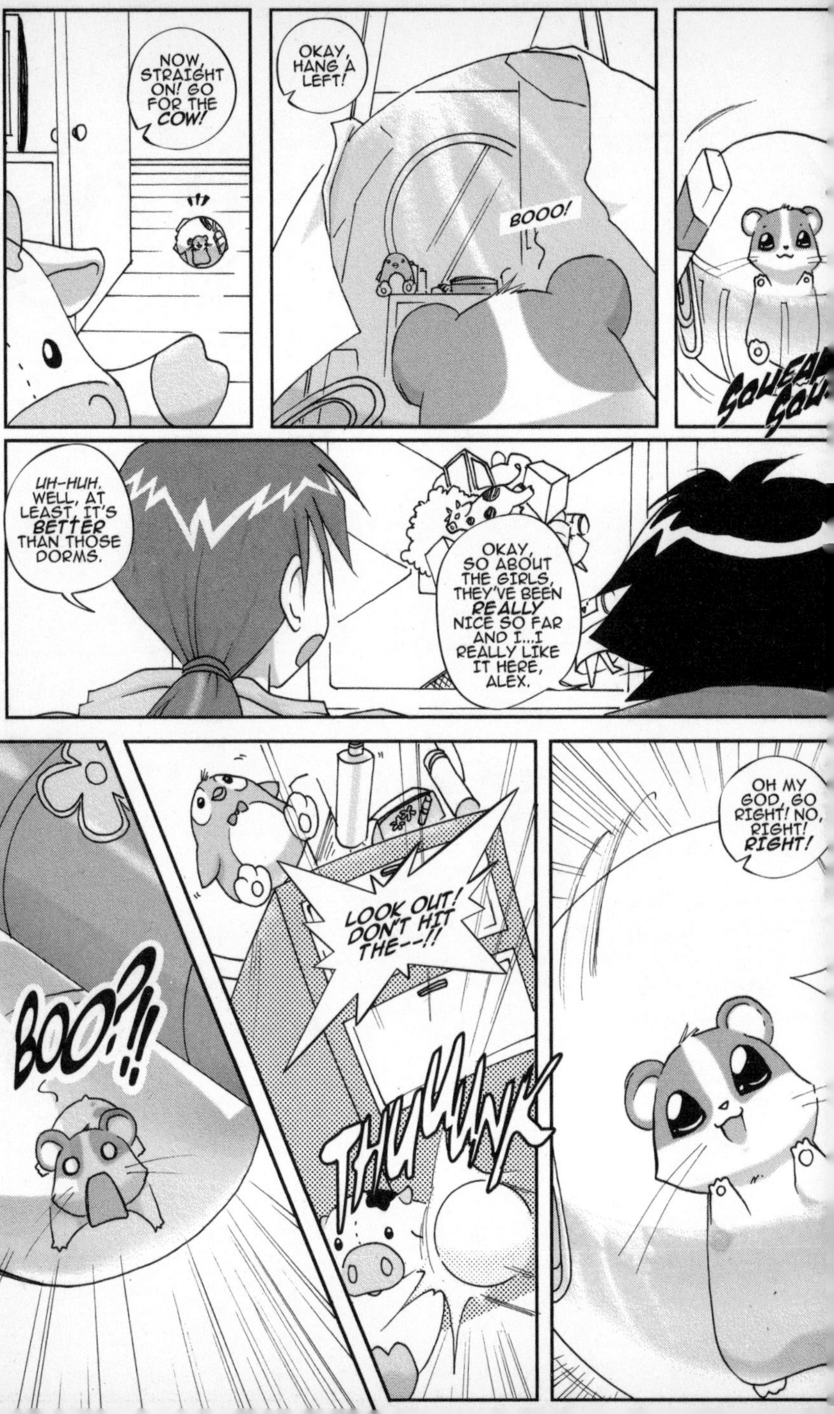
SQUEA
SQU
OKAY, HANG A LEFT!
BOOO!
NOW, STRAIGHT ON! GO FOR THE *COW!*
OKAY, SO ABOUT THE GIRLS, THEY'VE BEEN ***REALLY*** NICE SO FAR AND I...I REALLY LIKE IT HERE, ALEX.
UH-HUH. WELL, AT LEAST, IT'S ***BETTER*** THAN THOSE DORMS.
OH MY GOD, GO RIGHT! NO, RIGHT! ***RIGHT!***
LOOK OUT! DON'T HIT THE--!!
THUUNK
BOO?!!

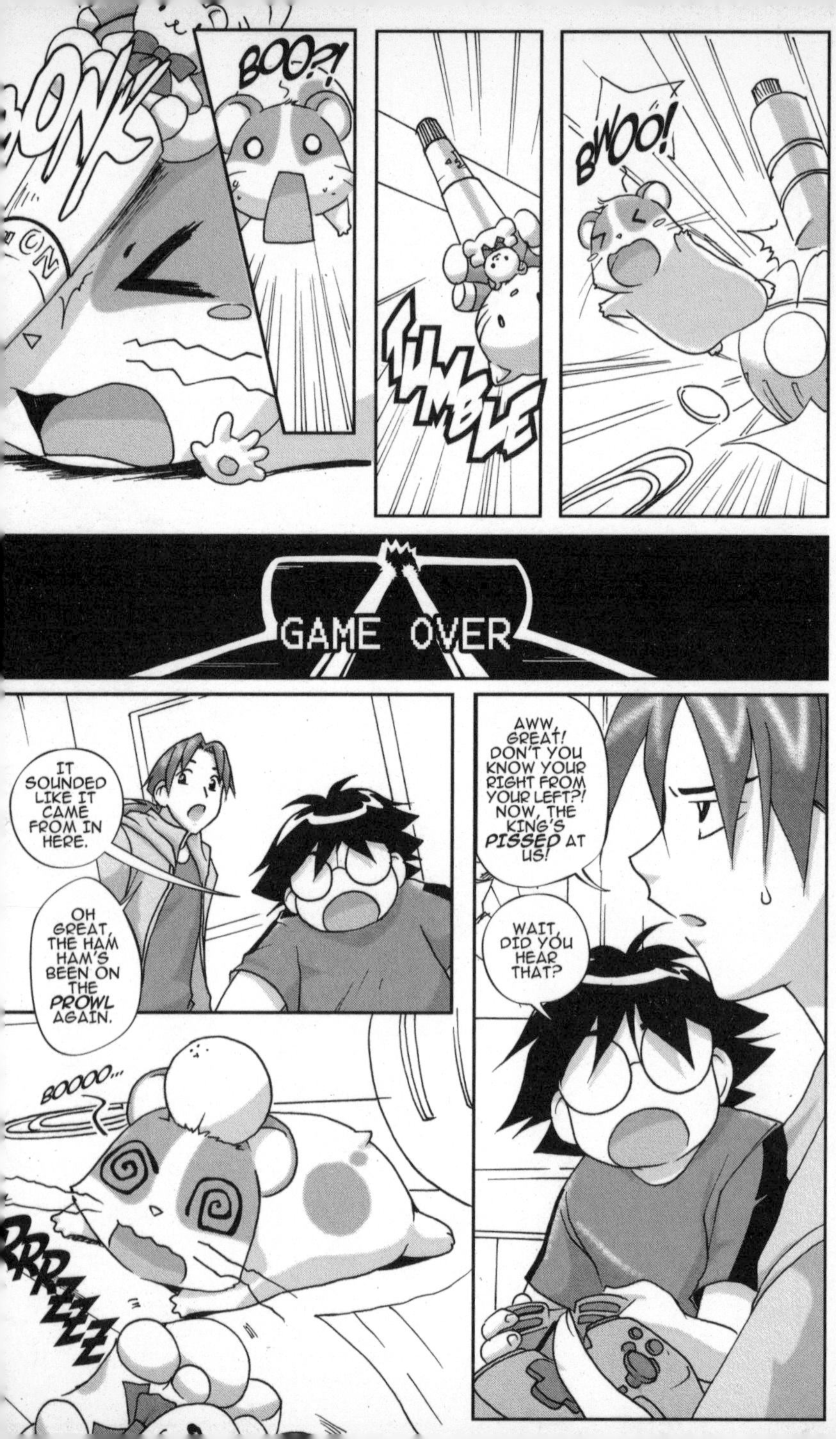
BWOO!
TUMBLE
BOO?!
ONK
GAME OVER
AWW, GREAT! DON'T YOU KNOW YOUR RIGHT FROM YOUR LEFT?! NOW, THE KING'S *PISSED* AT US!
WAIT, DID YOU HEAR THAT?
IT SOUNDED LIKE IT CAME FROM IN HERE.
OH GREAT, THE HAM HAM'S BEEN ON THE *PROWL* AGAIN.
BOOOO...
RRRZZZZ

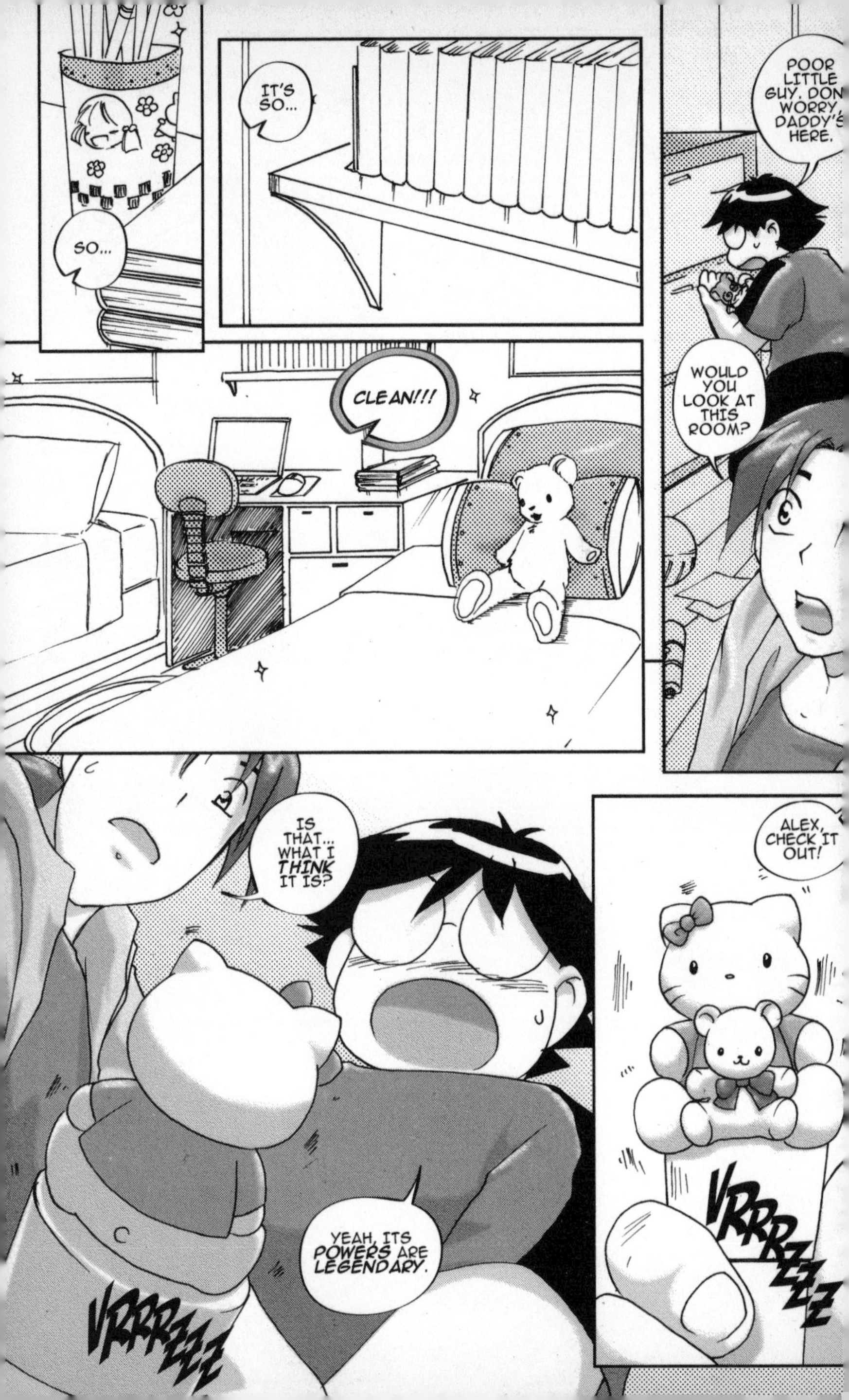
POOR LITTLE GUY. DON WORRY, DADDY'S HERE.
WOULD YOU LOOK AT THIS ROOM?
IT'S SO...
SO...
CLEAN!!!
ALEX, CHECK IT OUT!
VRRRZZZZ
IS THAT... WHAT I *THINK* IT IS?
YEAH, ITS *POWERS* ARE *LEGENDARY*.
VRRRZZZZ

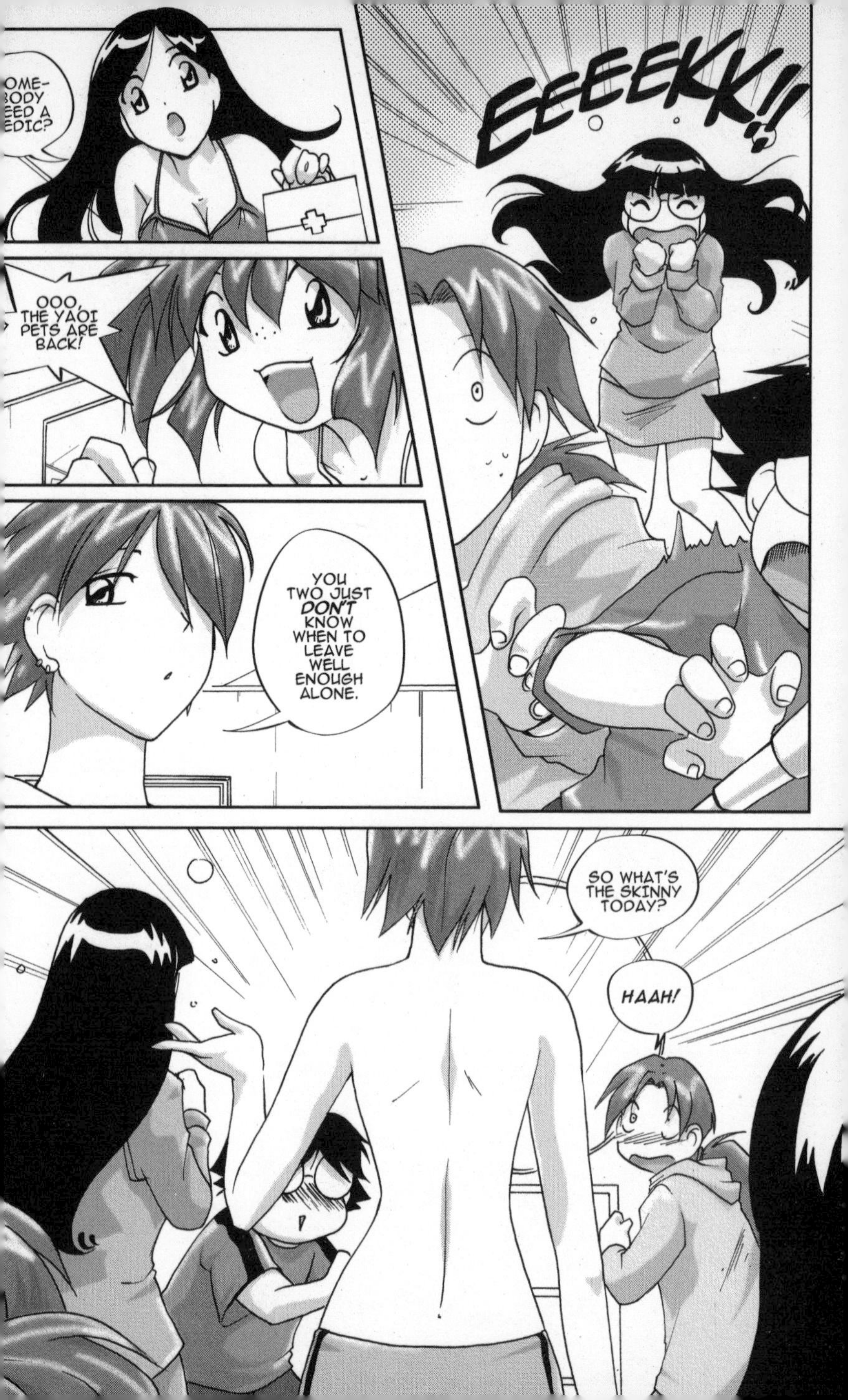
EEEEKK!!
OME- BODY EED A EDIC?
OOO, THE YAOI PETS ARE BACK!
YOU TWO JUST **DON'T** KNOW WHEN TO LEAVE WELL ENOUGH ALONE.
SO WHAT'S THE SKINNY TODAY?
HAAH!

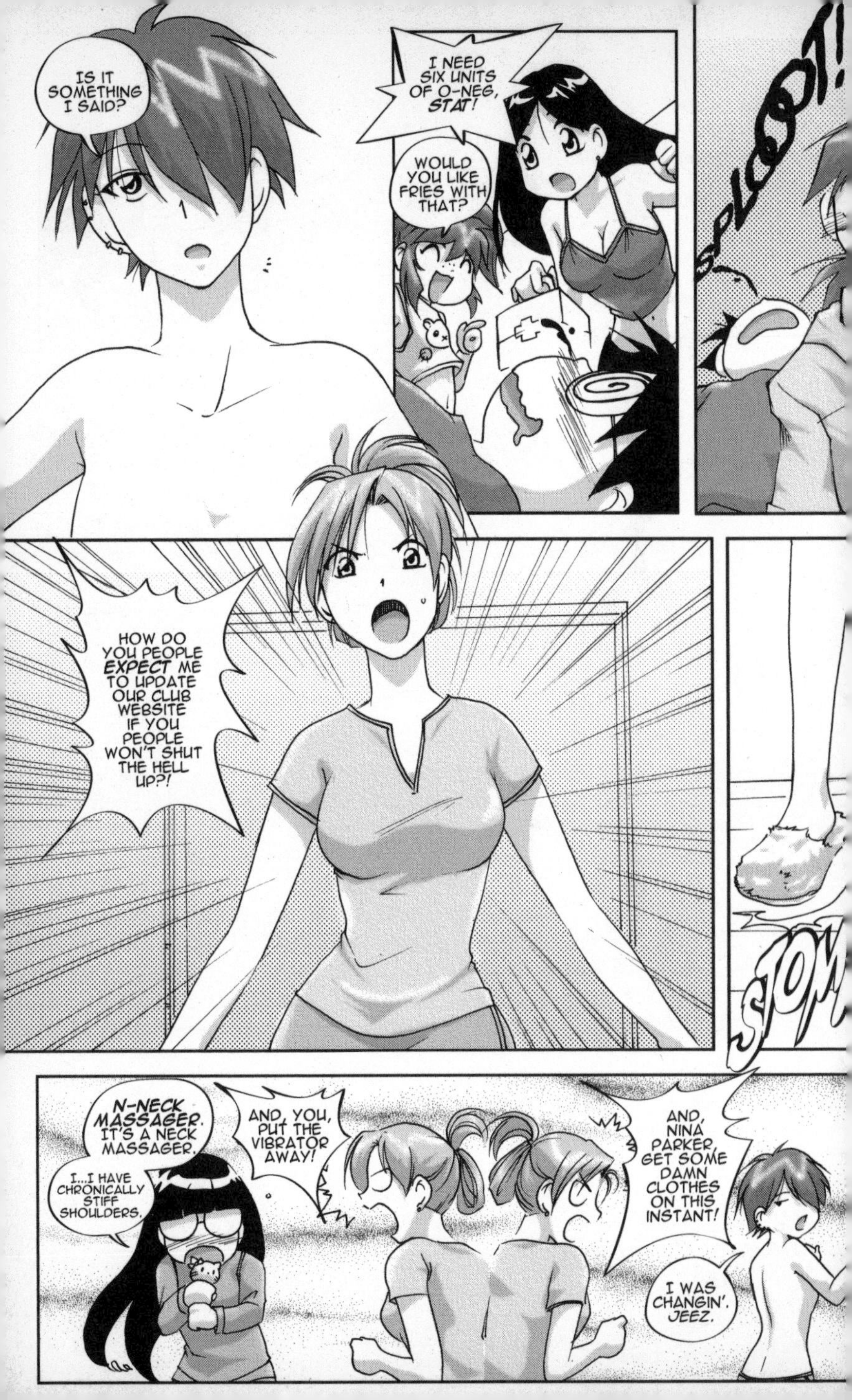
SPLOOOT!
I NEED SIX UNITS OF O-NEG, STAT!
WOULD YOU LIKE FRIES WITH THAT?
IS IT SOMETHING I SAID?
STOM
HOW DO YOU PEOPLE EXPECT ME TO UPDATE OUR CLUB WEBSITE IF YOU PEOPLE WON'T SHUT THE HELL UP?!
AND, NINA PARKER, GET SOME DAMN CLOTHES ON THIS INSTANT!
I WAS CHANGIN'. JEEZ.
AND, YOU, PUT THE VIBRATOR AWAY!
N-NECK MASSAGER. IT'S A NECK MASSAGER.
I...I HAVE CHRONICALLY STIFF SHOULDERS.

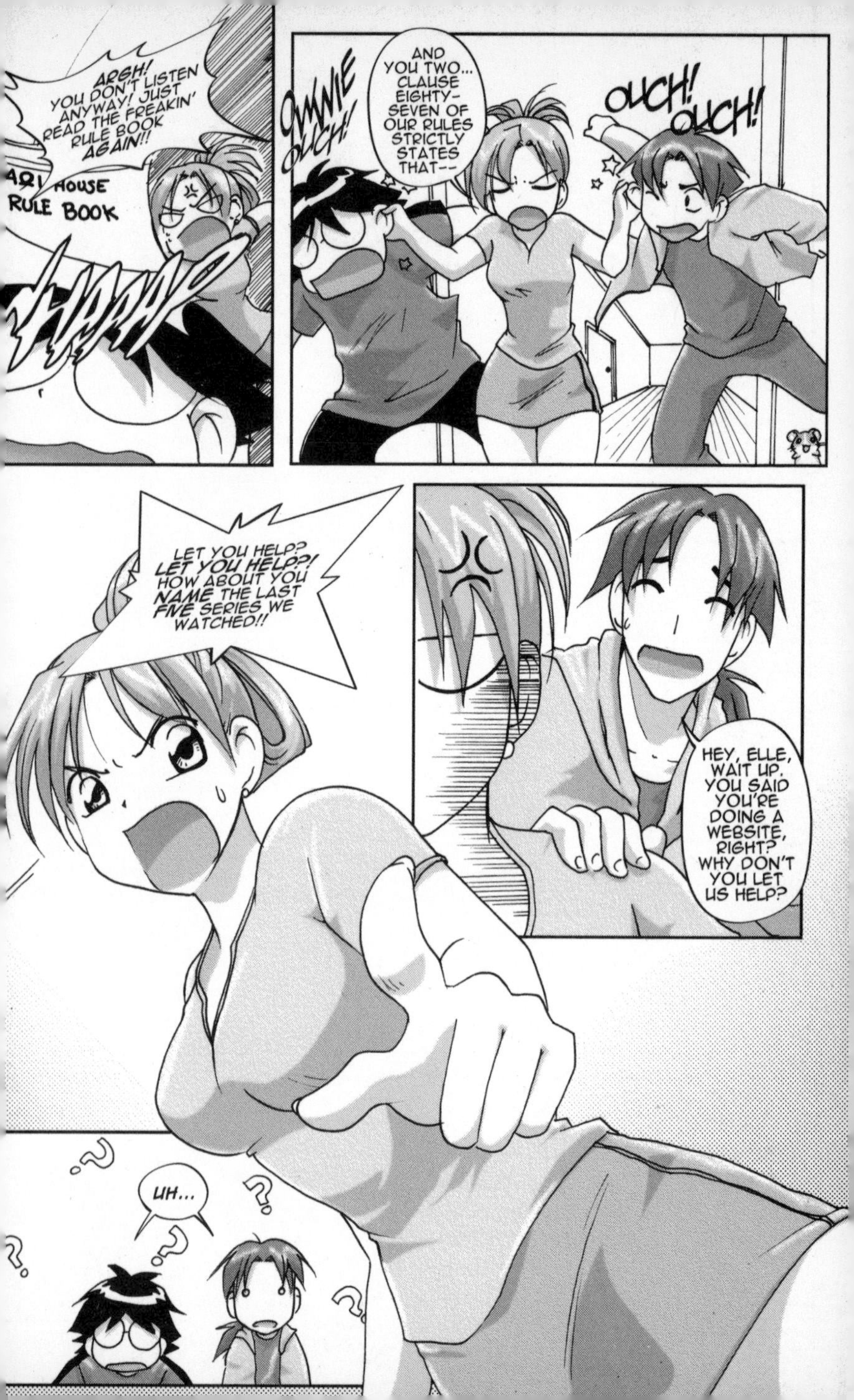
OUCH! OUCH!
AND YOU TWO... CLAUSE EIGHTY-SEVEN OF OUR RULES STRICTLY STATES THAT--
OWWIE OUCH!
ARGH! YOU DON'T LISTEN ANYWAY! JUST READ THE FREAKIN' RULE BOOK AGAIN!!
HOUSE RULE BOOK
HEY, ELLE, WAIT UP. YOU SAID YOU'RE DOING A WEBSITE, RIGHT? WHY DON'T YOU LET US HELP?
LET YOU HELP? LET YOU HELP?! HOW ABOUT YOU NAME THE LAST FIVE SERIES WE WATCHED!!
UH...

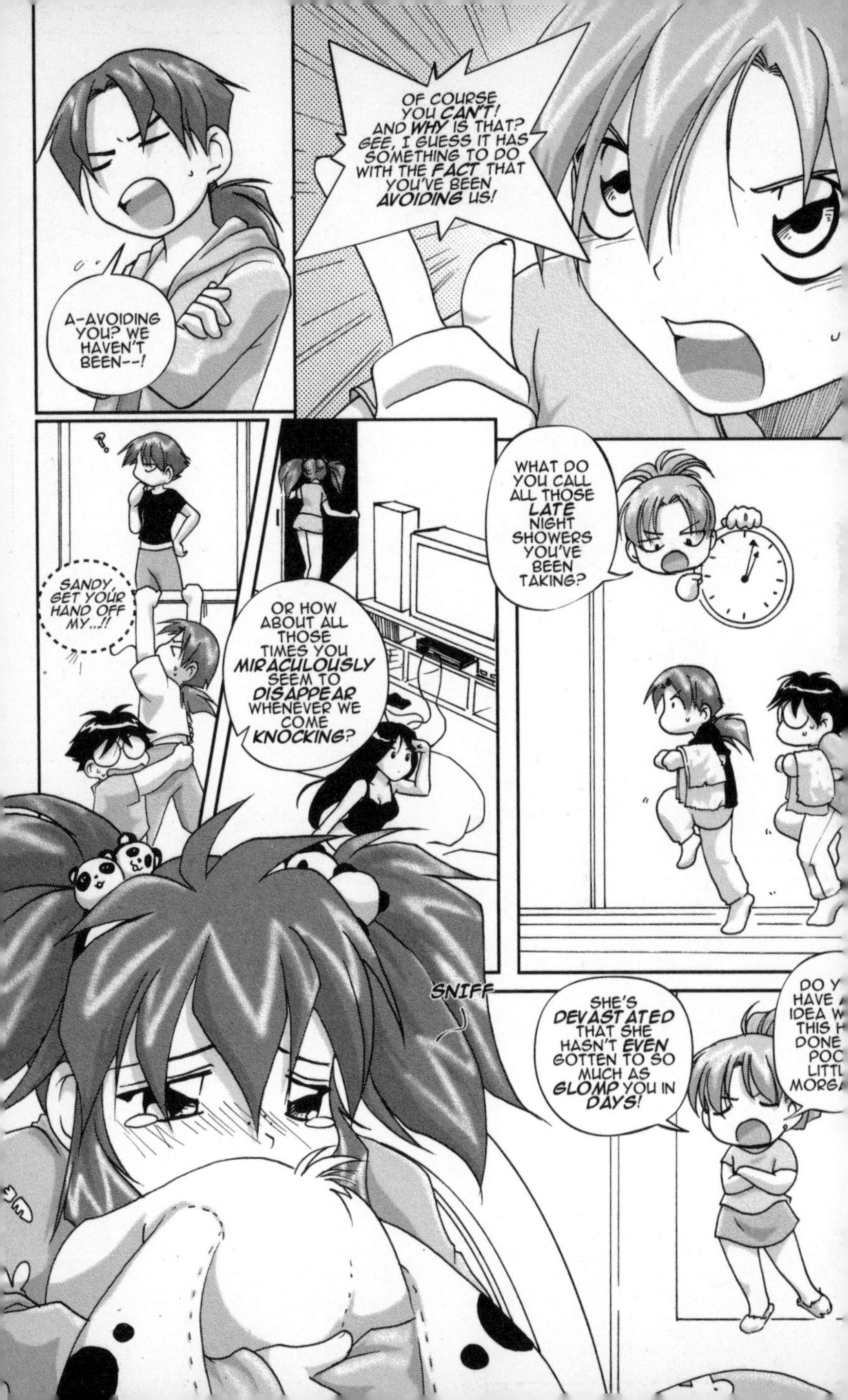

OF COURSE YOU CAN'T! AND WHY IS THAT? GEE, I GUESS IT HAS SOMETHING TO DO WITH THE FACT THAT YOU'VE BEEN AVOIDING US!
A-AVOIDING YOU? WE HAVEN'T BEEN--!
WHAT DO YOU CALL ALL THOSE LATE NIGHT SHOWERS YOU'VE BEEN TAKING?
OR HOW ABOUT ALL THOSE TIMES YOU MIRACULOUSLY SEEM TO DISAPPEAR WHENEVER WE COME KNOCKING?
SANDY, GET YOUR HAND OFF MY...!!
SHE'S DEVASTATED THAT SHE HASN'T EVEN GOTTEN TO SO MUCH AS GLOMP YOU IN DAYS!
SNIFF

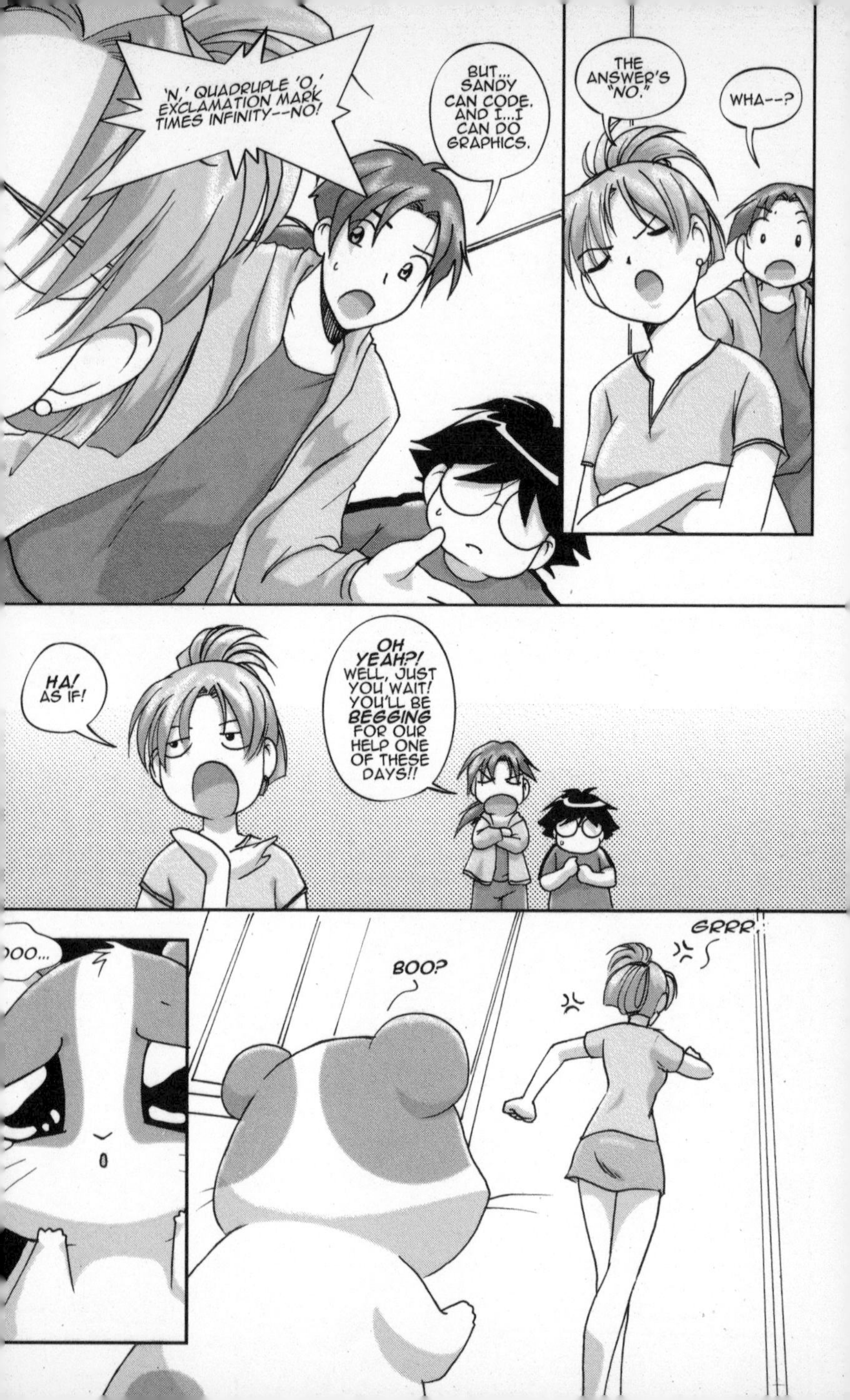
WHA--?
THE ANSWER'S "NO."
BUT... SANDY CAN CODE. AND I...I CAN DO GRAPHICS.
'N,' QUADRUPLE 'O,' EXCLAMATION MARK TIMES INFINITY--NO!
OH YEAH?! WELL, JUST YOU WAIT! YOU'LL BE BEGGING FOR OUR HELP ONE OF THESE DAYS!!
HA! AS IF!
GRRR
BOO?
OOO...

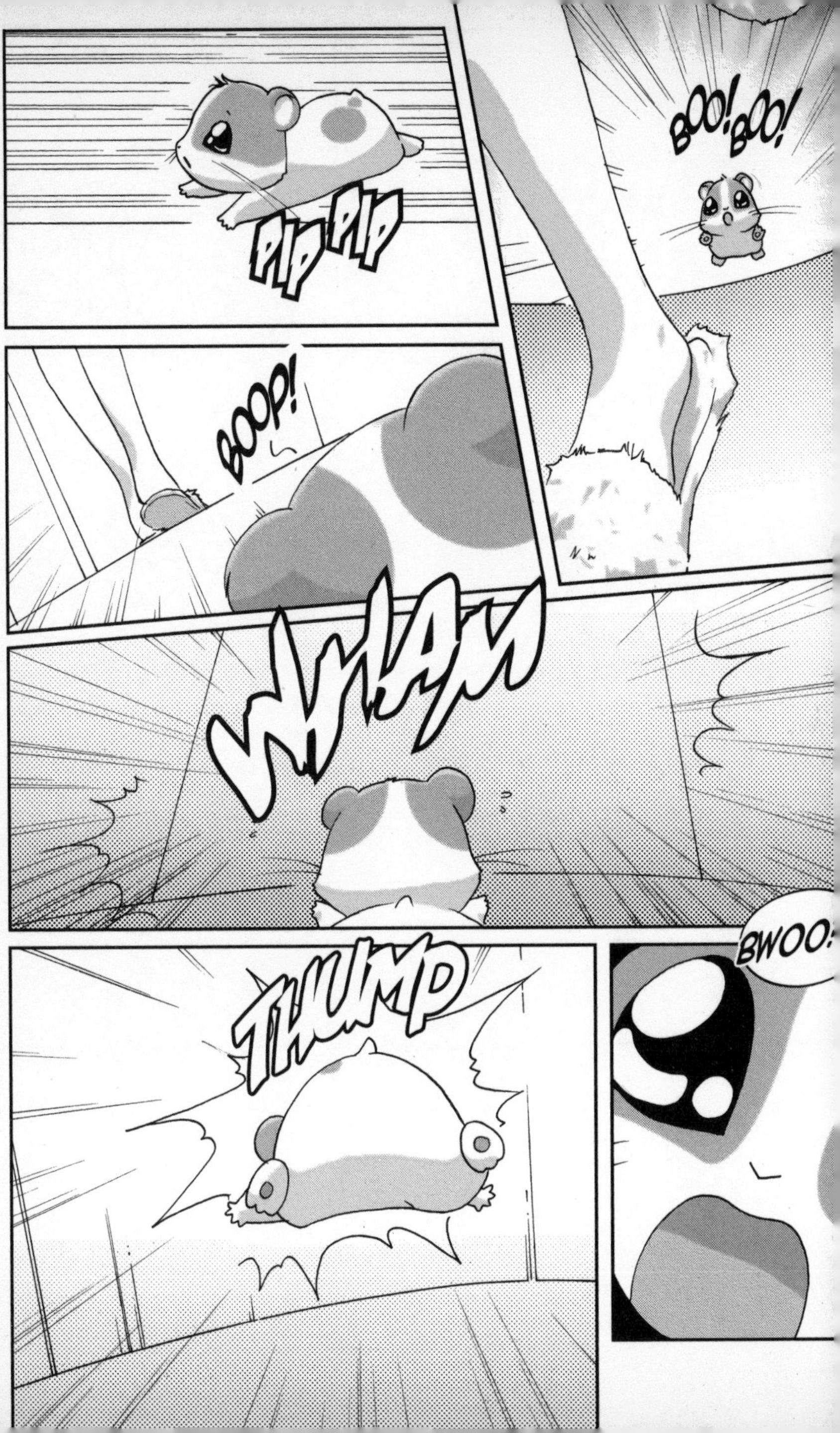
BOO! BOO!
PIP PIP
BOOP!
WHAM
BWOO
THUMP

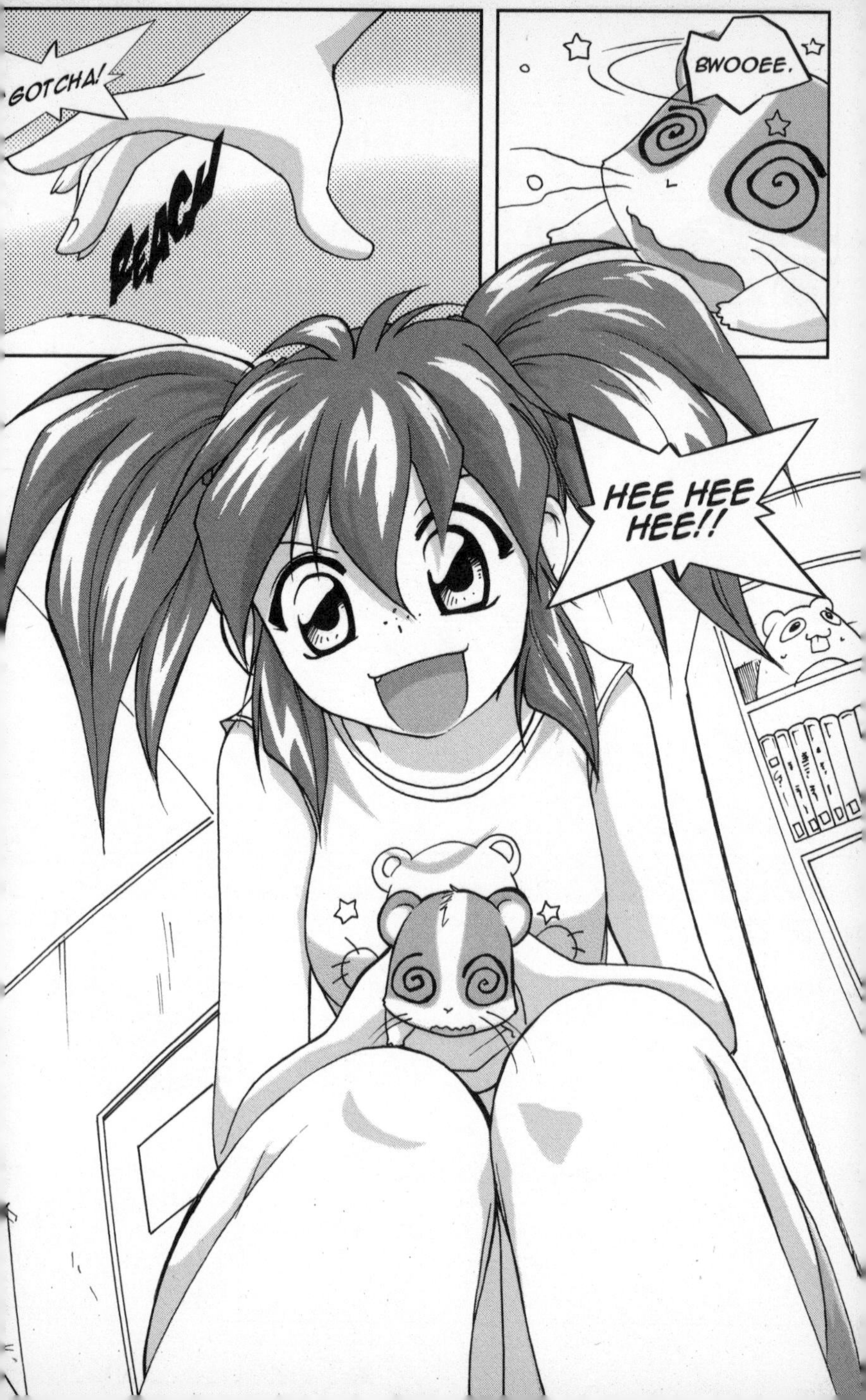
BWOOEE.
GOTCHA!
REACH
HEE HEE HEE!!

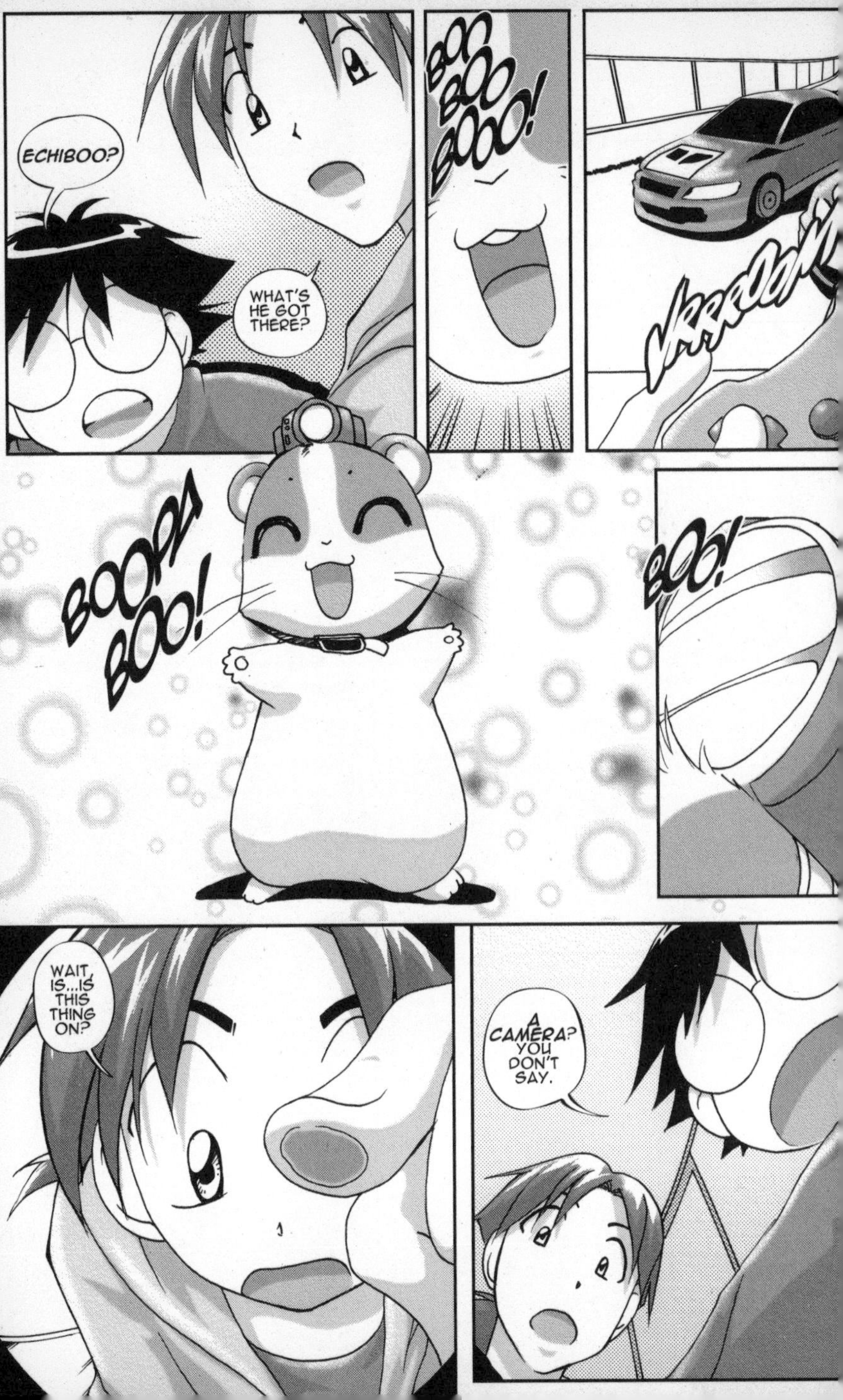
VRRROOM
BOO BOO BOOO!
ECHIBOO?
WHAT'S HE GOT THERE?
BOO!
BOOP♪ BOO!
A CAMERA? YOU DON'T SAY.
WAIT, IS...IS THIS THING ON?

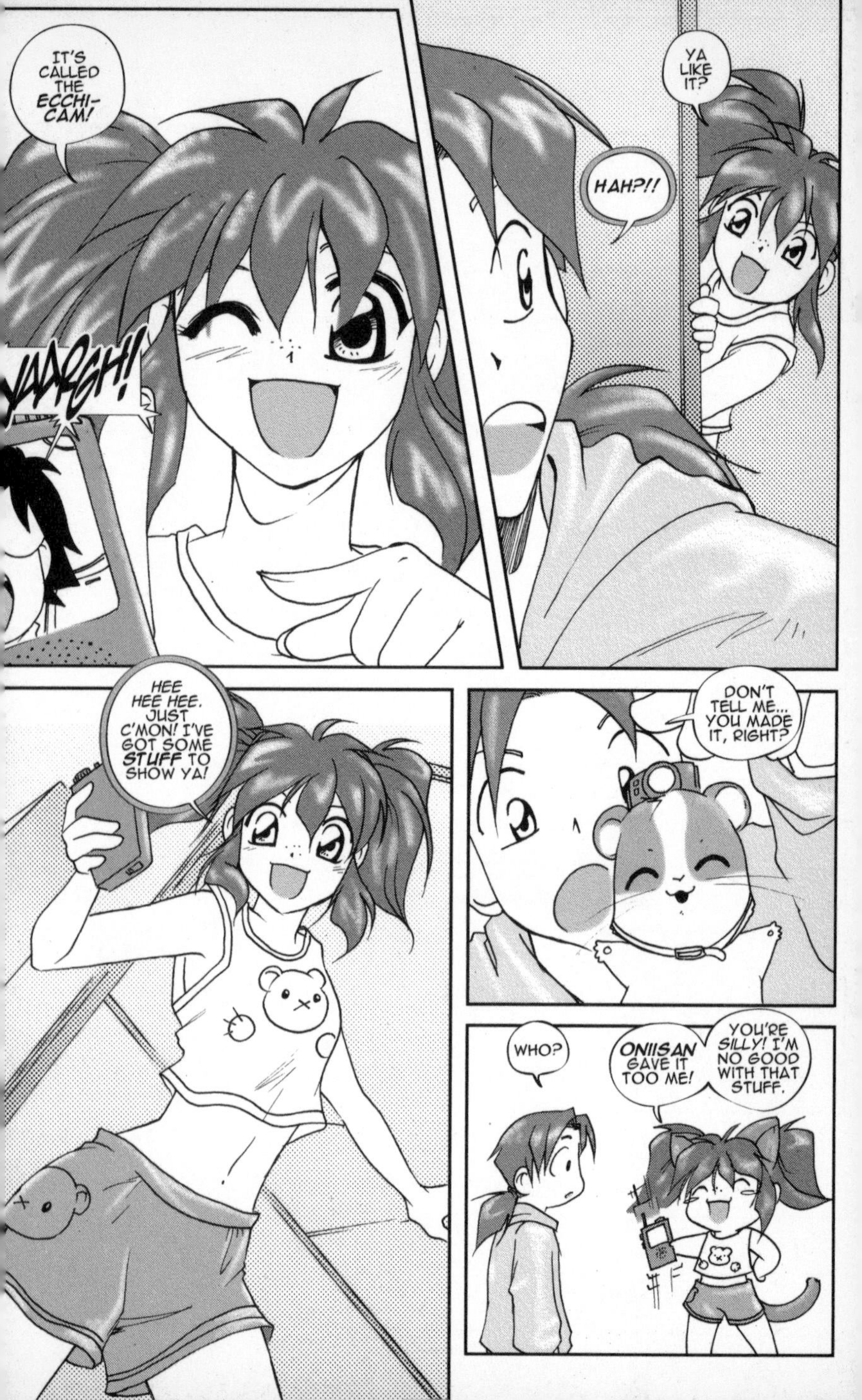
YA LIKE IT?
HAH?!!
IT'S CALLED THE ECCHI-CAM!
YAARGH!
DON'T TELL ME... YOU MADE IT, RIGHT?
YOU'RE SILLY! I'M NO GOOD WITH THAT STUFF.
ONIISAN GAVE IT TOO ME!
WHO?
HEE HEE HEE. JUST C'MON! I'VE GOT SOME STUFF TO SHOW YA!

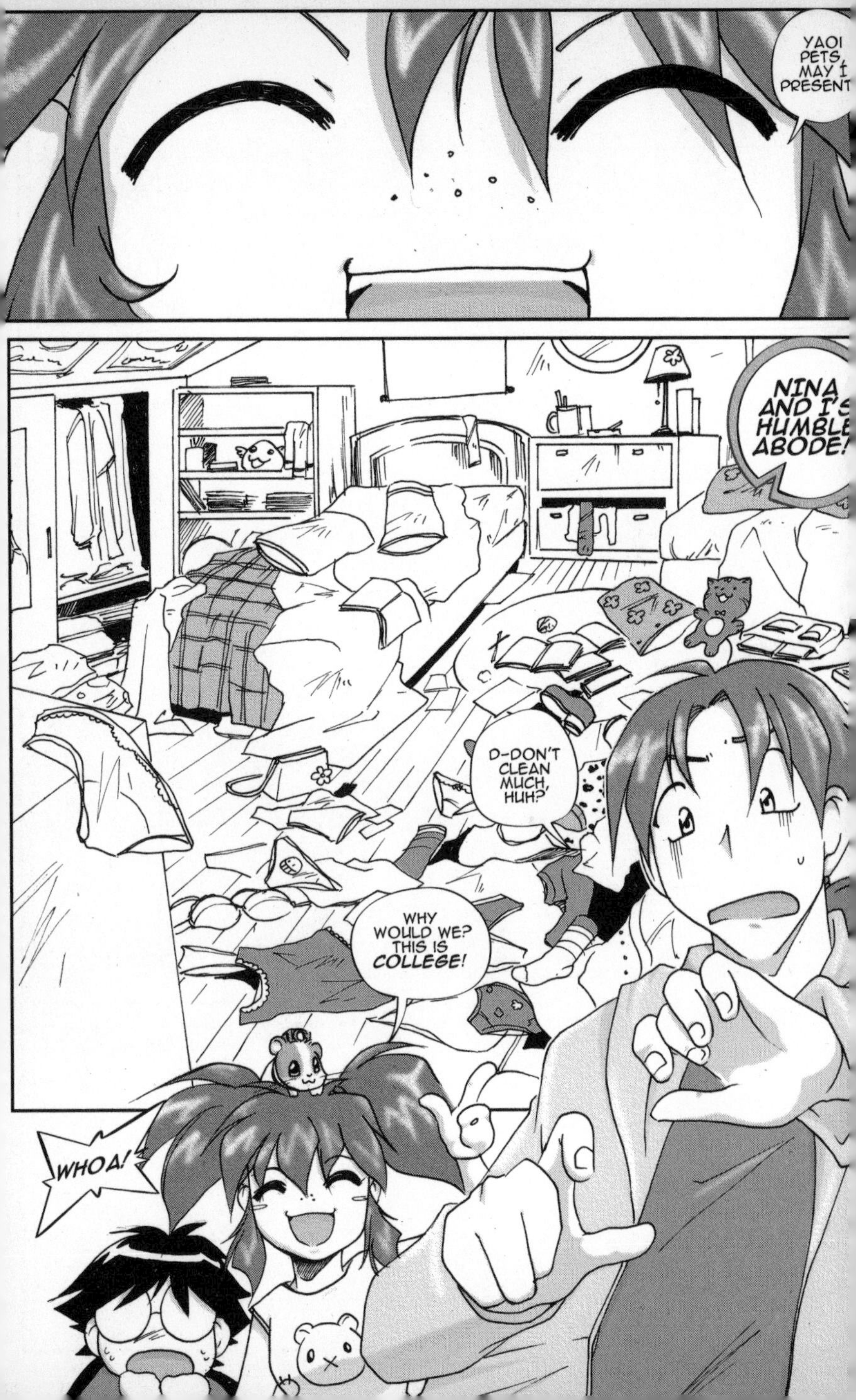
YAOI PETS, MAY I PRESENT
NINA AND I'S HUMBLE ABODE!
D-DON'T CLEAN MUCH, HUH?
WHY WOULD WE? THIS IS COLLEGE!
WHOA!

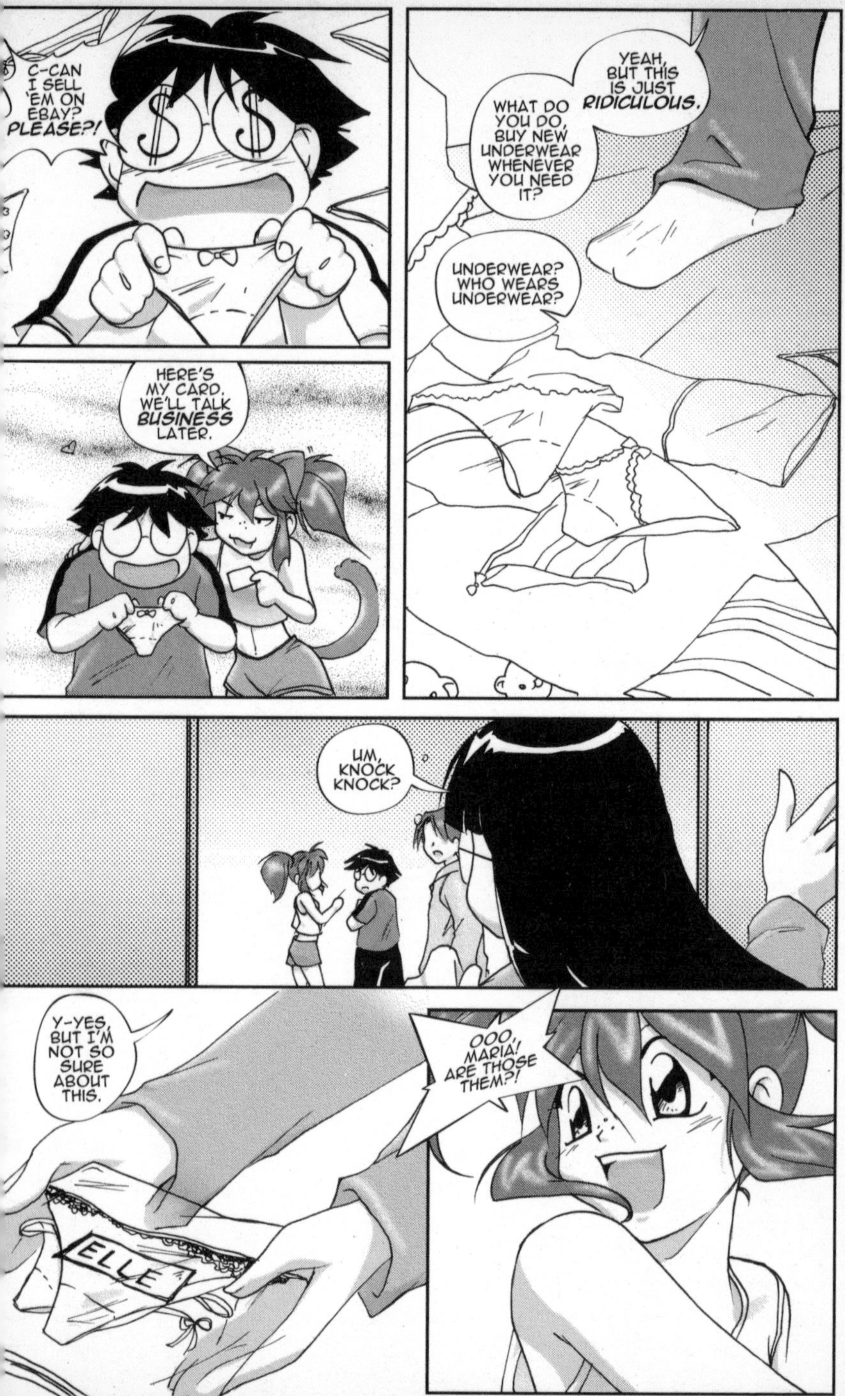

YEAH, BUT THIS IS JUST *RIDICULOUS.*
WHAT DO YOU DO, BUY NEW UNDERWEAR WHENEVER YOU NEED IT?
UNDERWEAR? WHO WEARS UNDERWEAR?
C-CAN I SELL 'EM ON EBAY? *PLEASE?!*
HERE'S MY CARD. WE'LL TALK *BUSINESS* LATER.
UM, KNOCK KNOCK?
OOO, MARIA! ARE THOSE THEM?!
Y-YES, BUT I'M NOT SO SURE ABOUT THIS.
ELLE

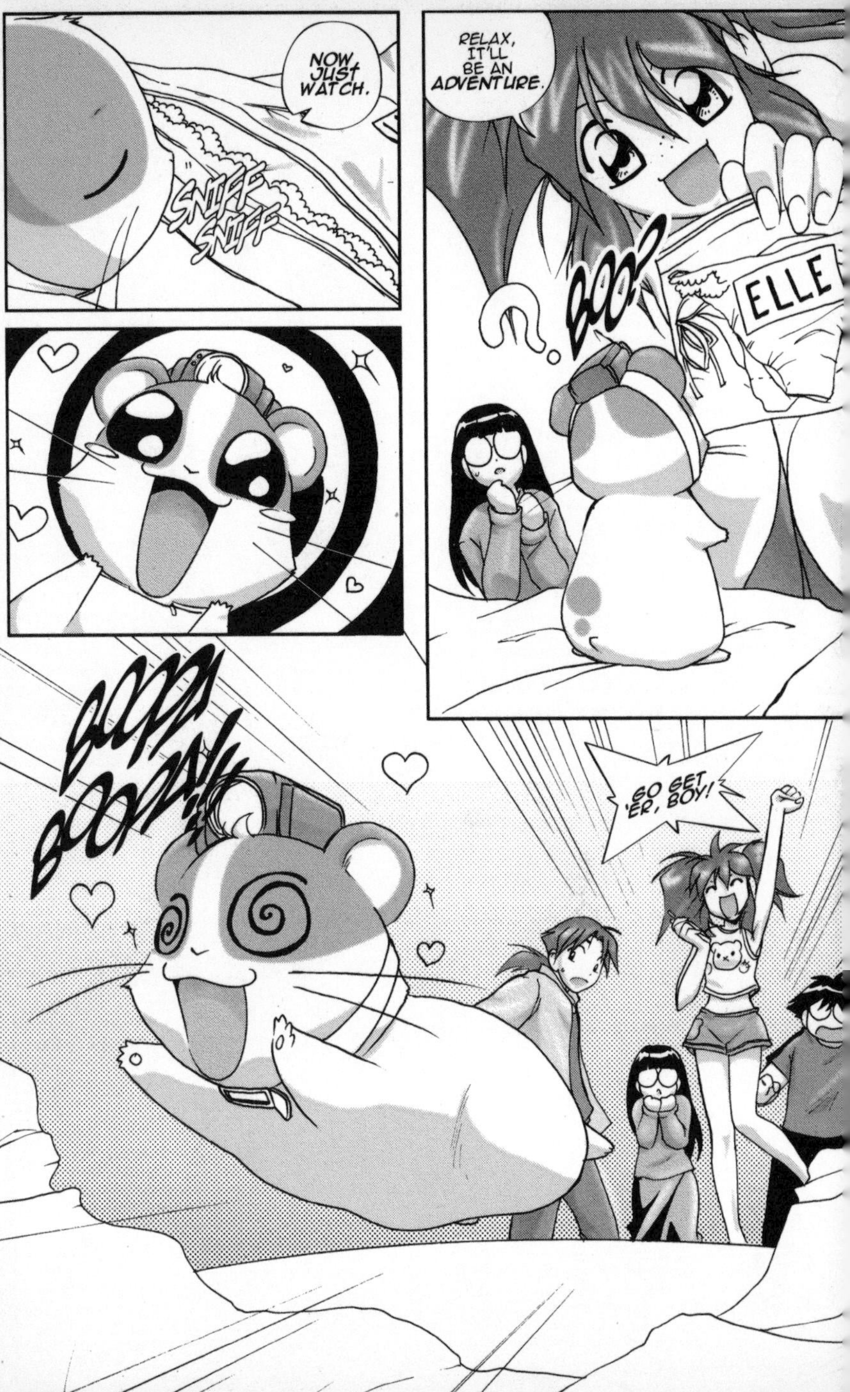
RELAX, IT'LL BE AN ADVENTURE.
BOOP
?
NOW, JUST WATCH.
SNIFF SNIFF
ELLE
GO GET 'ER, BOY!
BOOM BOOM!!

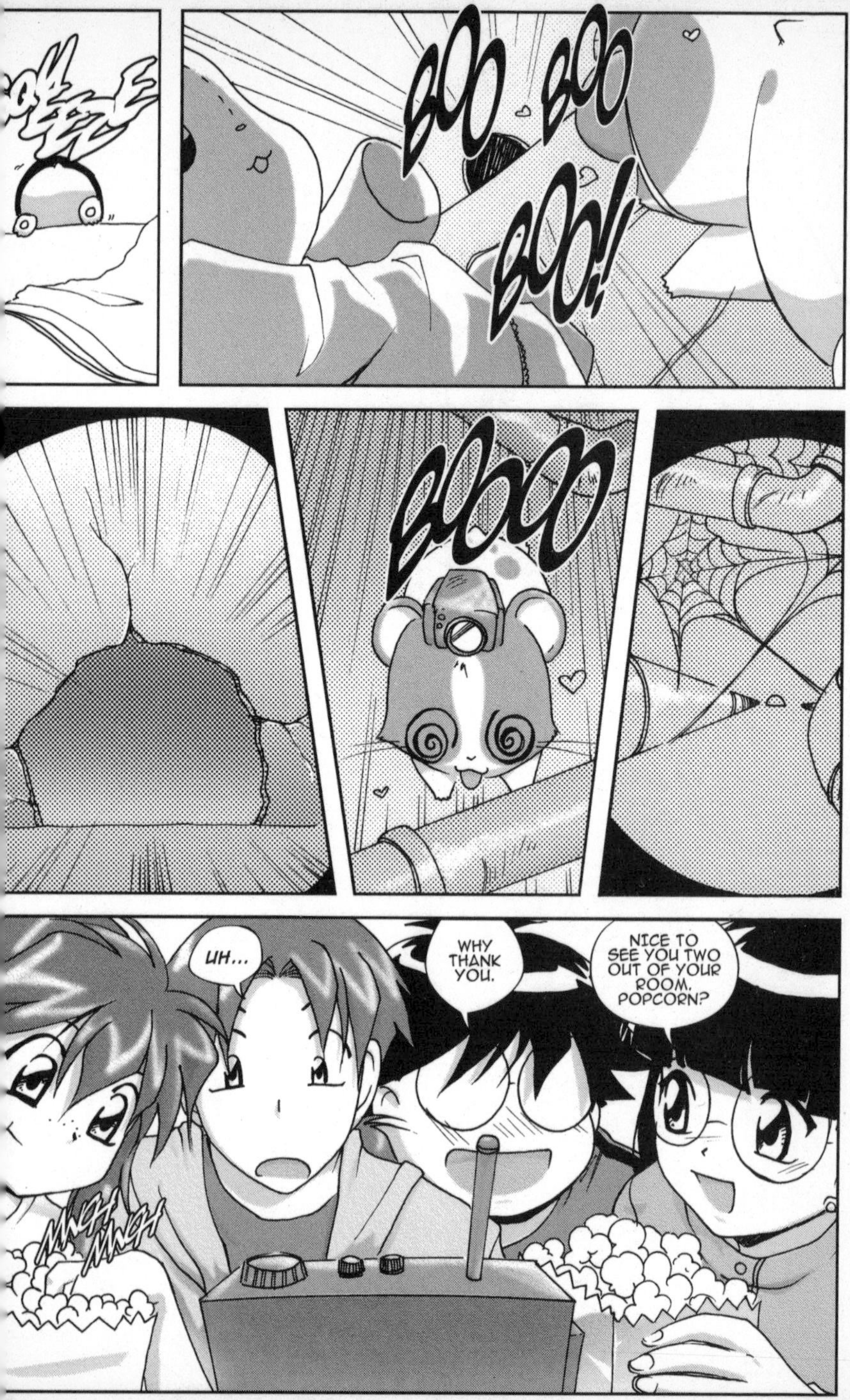
BOO BOO BOO!
BOOO
NICE TO SEE YOU TWO OUT OF YOUR ROOM. POPCORN?
WHY THANK YOU.
UH...
MNCH MNCH

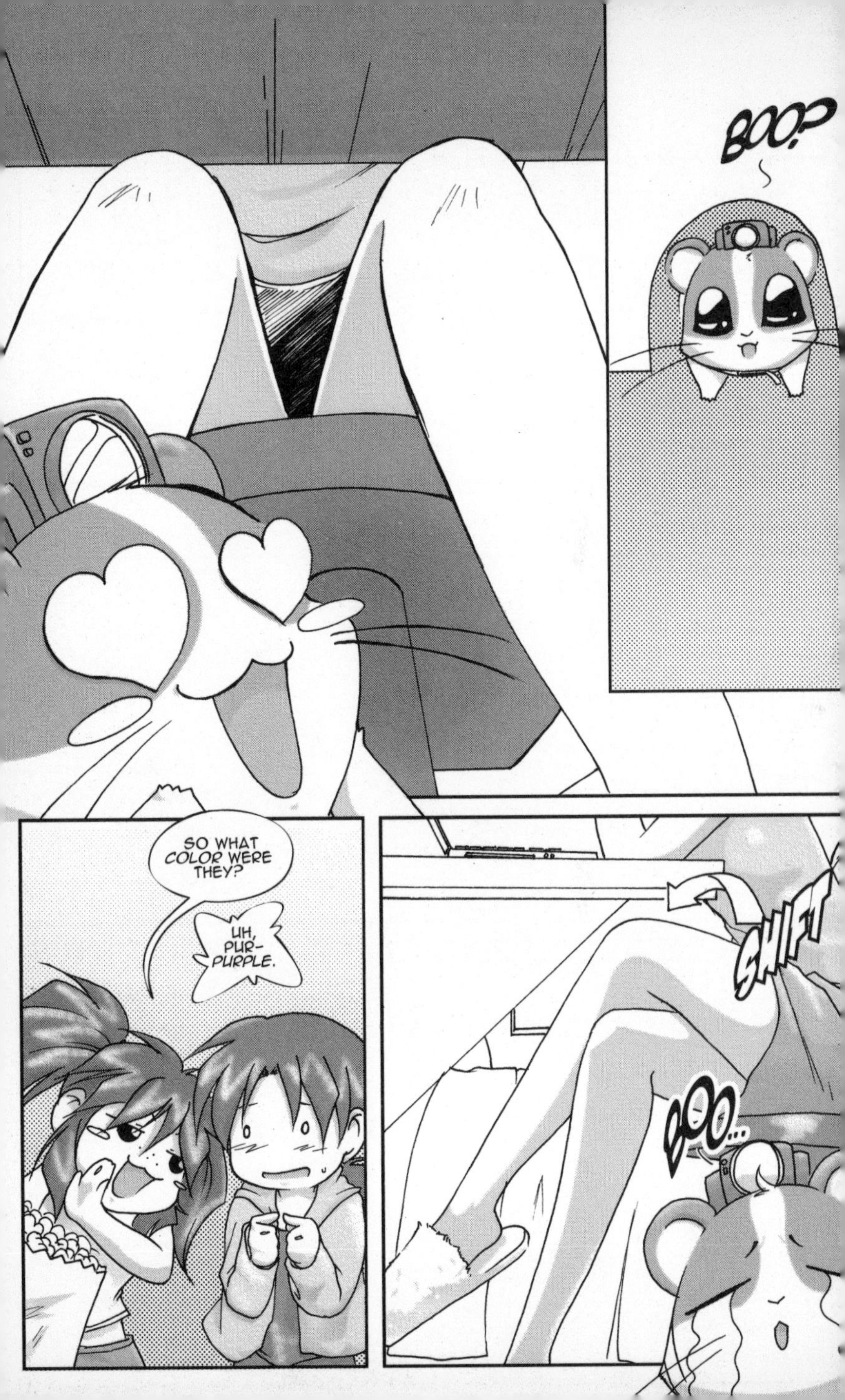
BOO?
SHIFT
BOO...
SO WHAT COLOR WERE THEY?
UH, PUR-PURPLE.

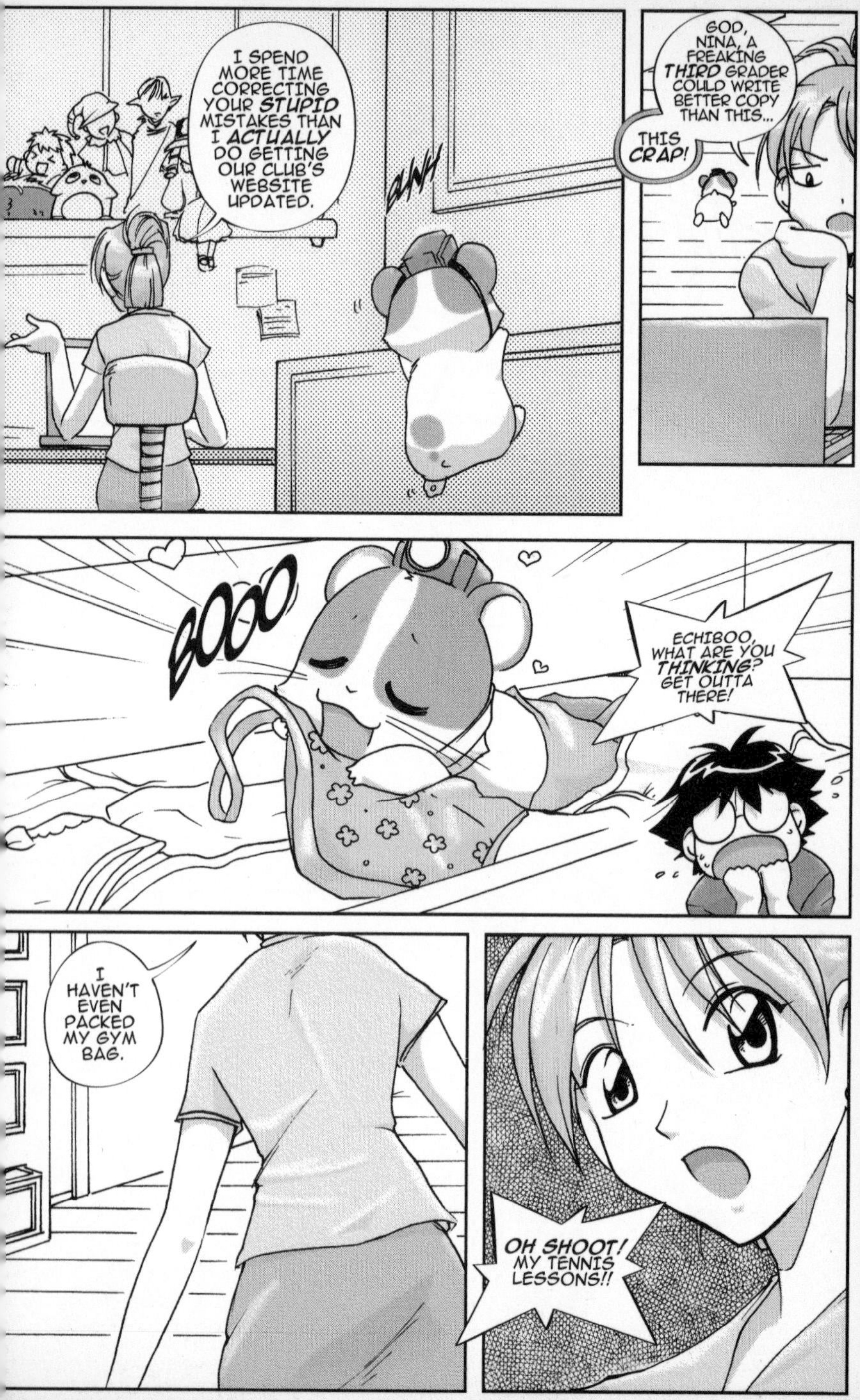
GOD, NINA, A FREAKING THIRD GRADER COULD WRITE BETTER COPY THAN THIS...
THIS CRAP!
I SPEND MORE TIME CORRECTING YOUR STUPID MISTAKES THAN I ACTUALLY DO GETTING OUR CLUB'S WEBSITE UPDATED.
ECHIBOO, WHAT ARE YOU THINKING? GET OUTTA THERE!
BOOO
OH SHOOT! MY TENNIS LESSONS!!
I HAVEN'T EVEN PACKED MY GYM BAG.

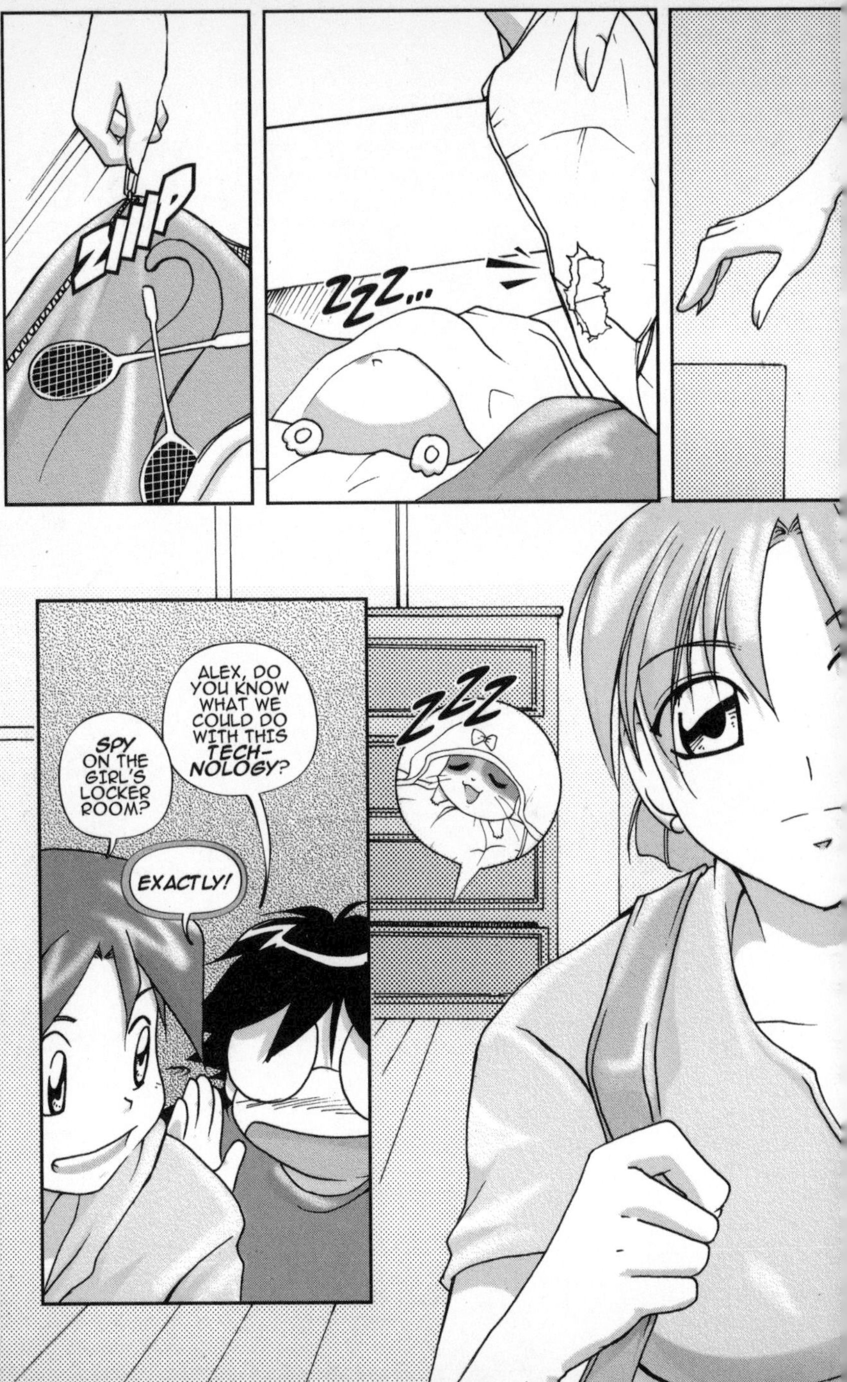
ZZZ...
ZIIIP
ZZZ
ALEX, DO YOU KNOW WHAT WE COULD DO WITH THIS *TECHNOLOGY*?
SPY ON THE GIRL'S LOCKER ROOM?
EXACTLY!

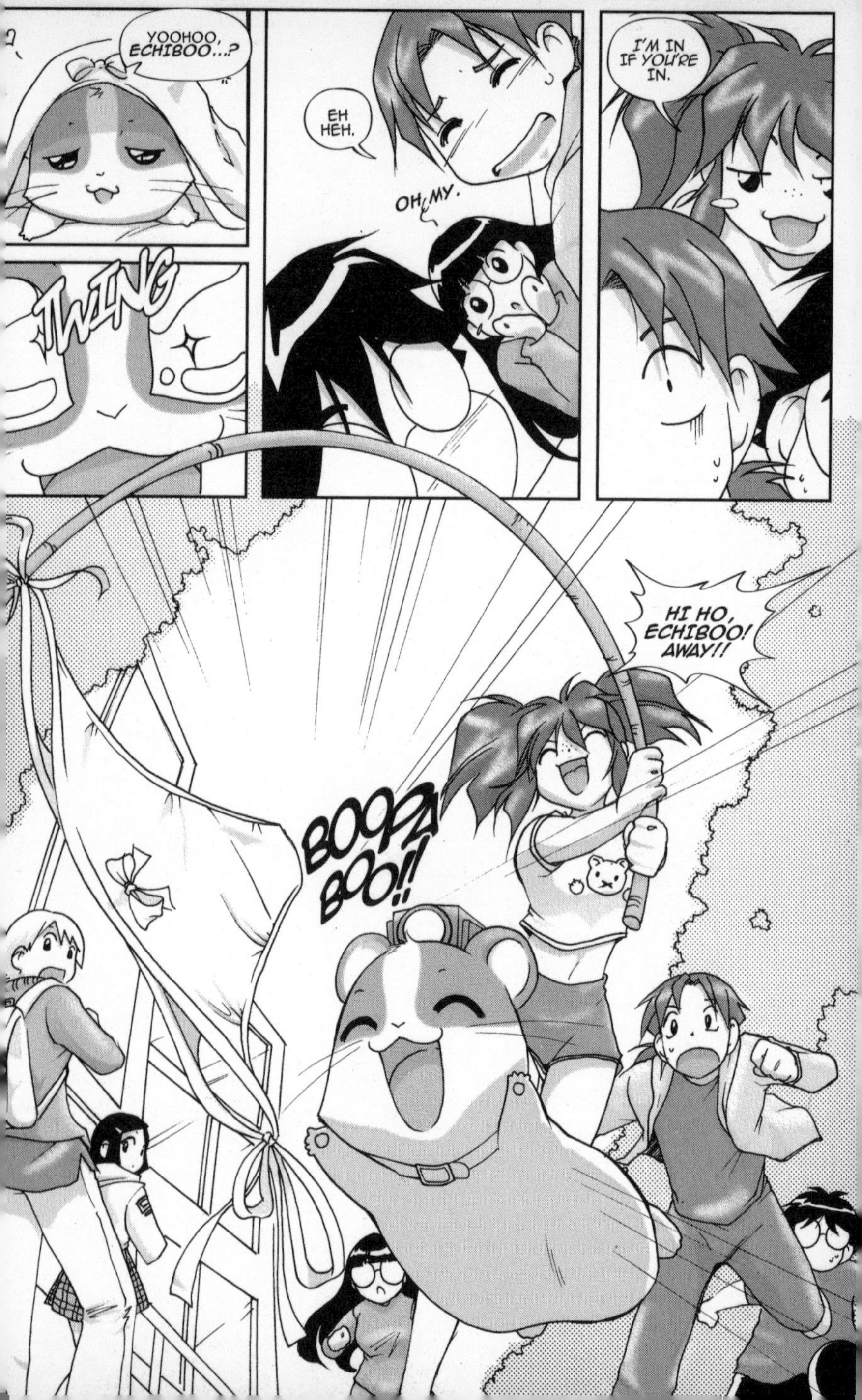
I'M IN IF YOU'RE IN.
EH HEH.
OH, MY.
YOOHOO, ECHIBOO...?
TWING
HI HO, ECHIBOO! AWAY!!
BOOPA BOO!!

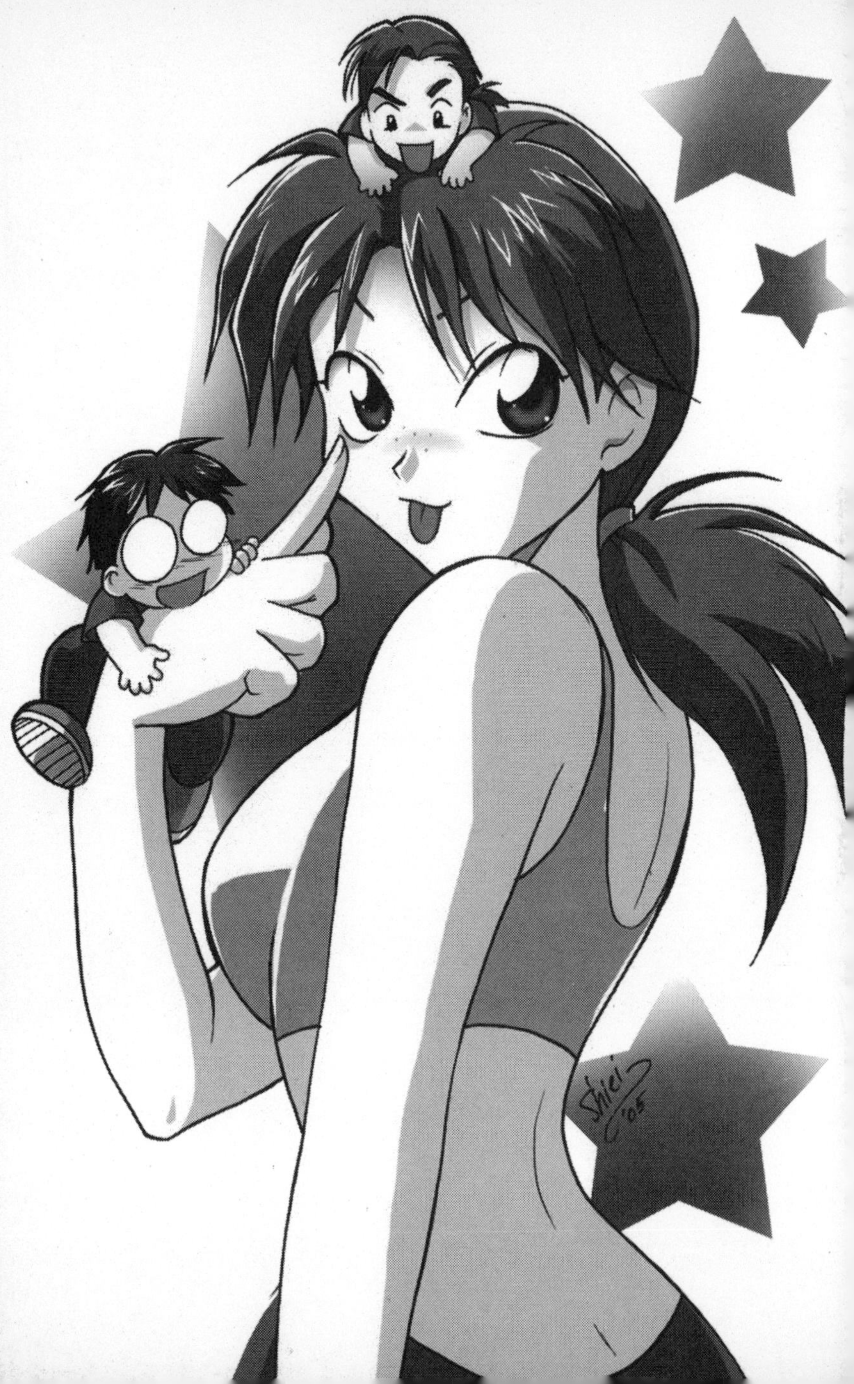

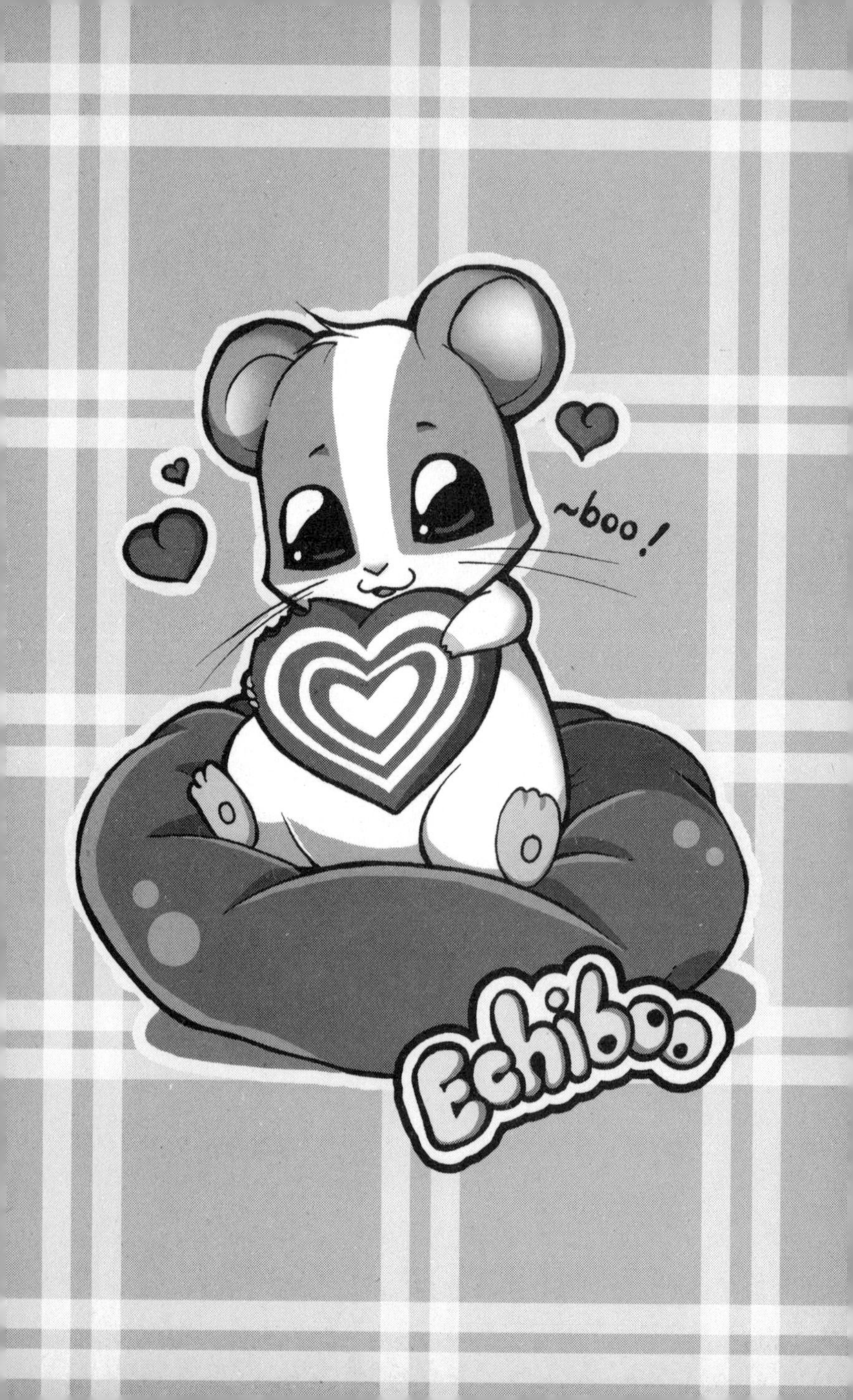
~boo!
Echiboo

EPISODE 4: ECHIBOO'S BIG ADVENTURE: PHASE TWO

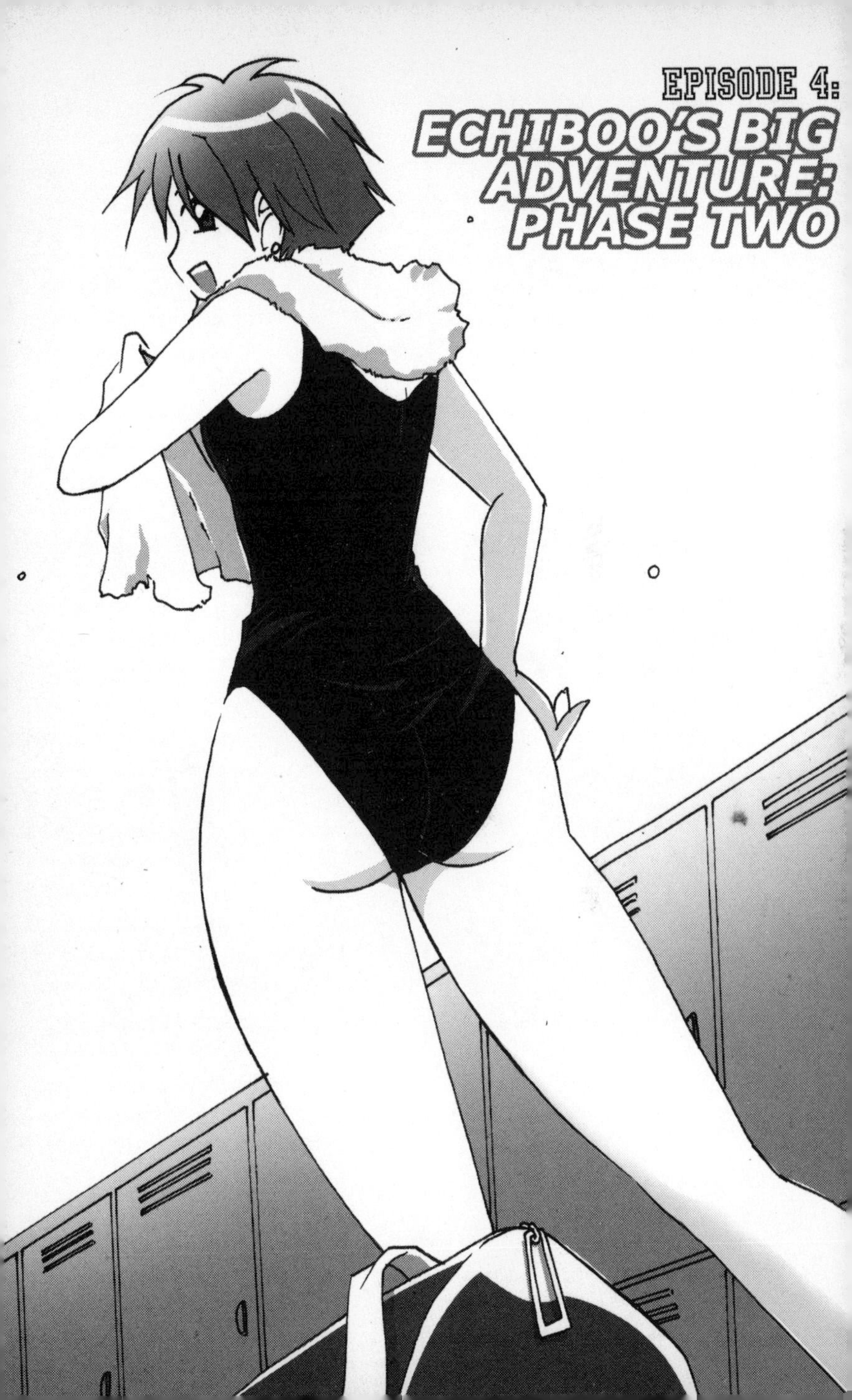

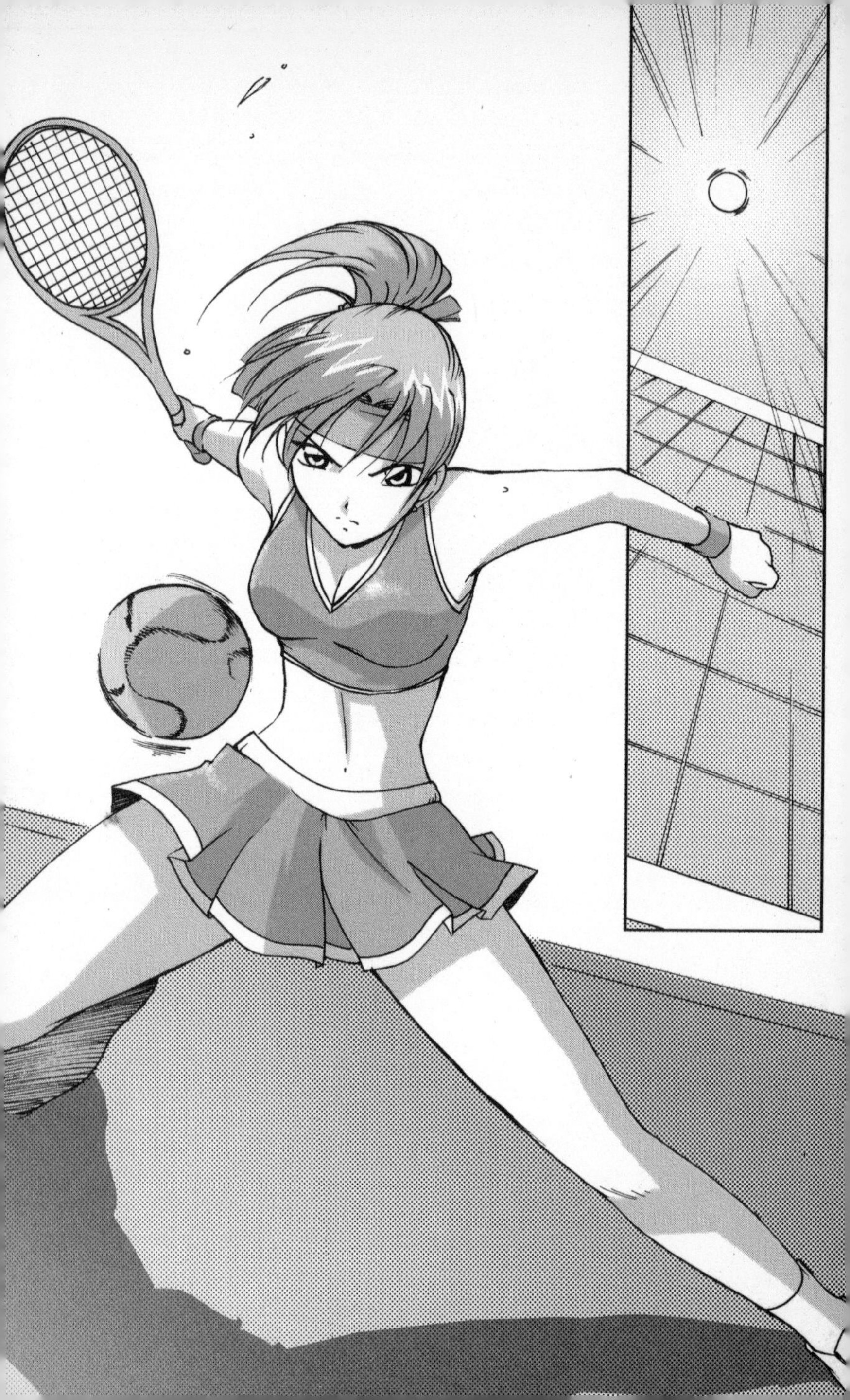

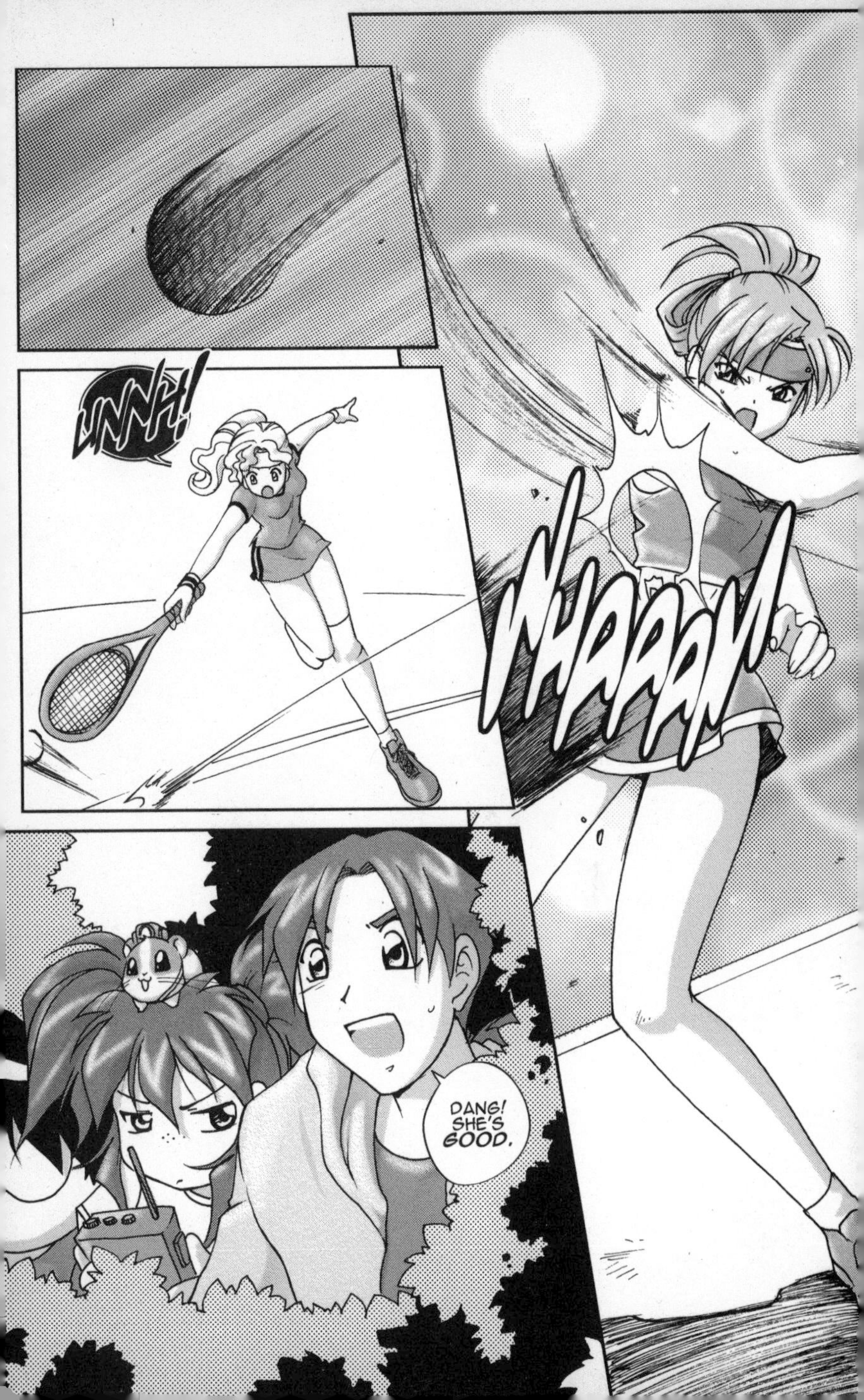
WHAAAM!
UNNH!
DANG! SHE'S GOOD.

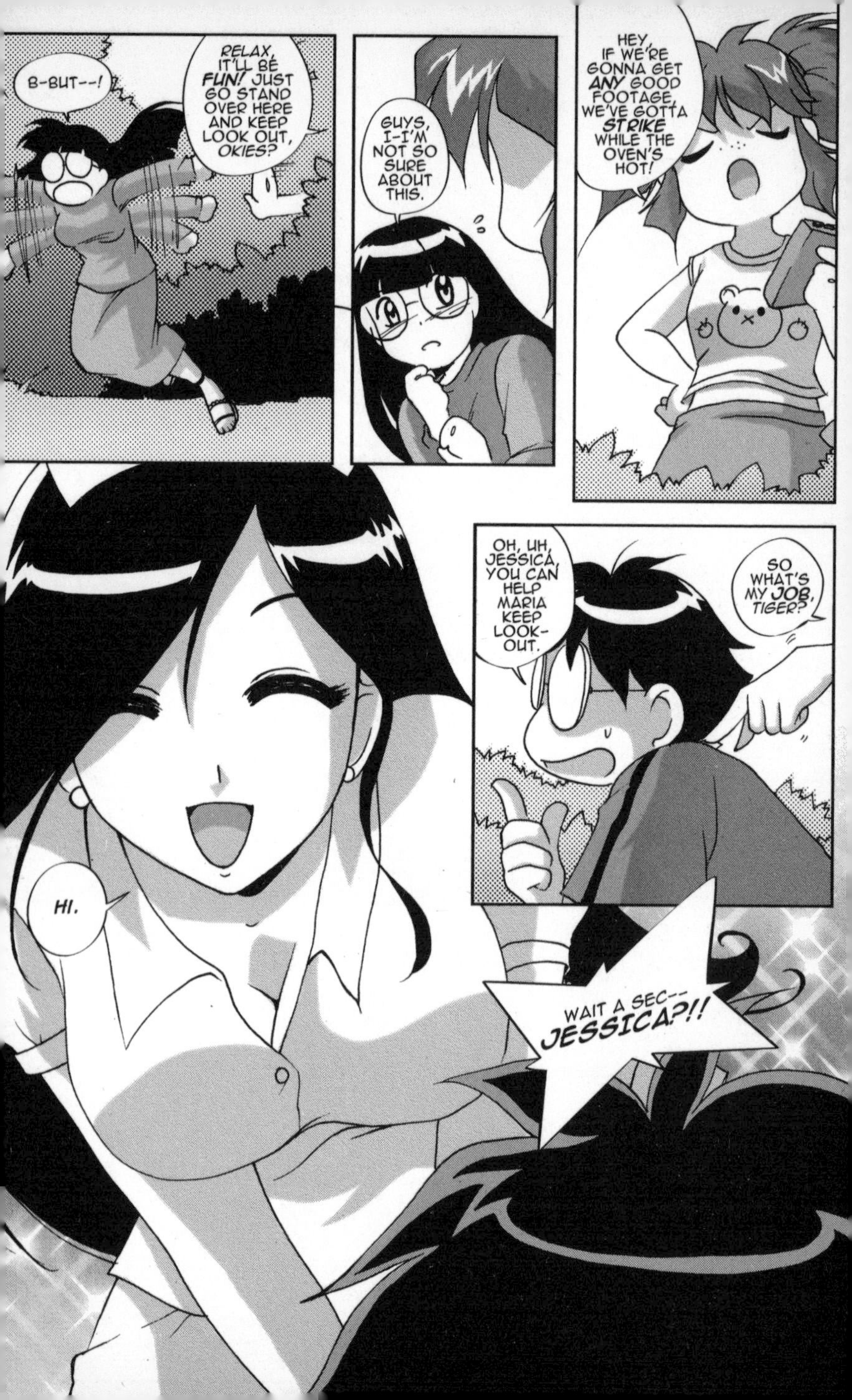
HEY, IF WE'RE GONNA GET ANY GOOD FOOTAGE, WE'VE GOTTA STRIKE WHILE THE OVEN'S HOT!
GUYS, I-I'M NOT SO SURE ABOUT THIS.
RELAX, IT'LL BE FUN! JUST GO STAND OVER HERE AND KEEP LOOK OUT, OKIES?
B-BUT--!
SO WHAT'S MY JOB, TIGER?
OH, UH, JESSICA, YOU CAN HELP MARIA KEEP LOOK-OUT.
HI.
WAIT A SEC-- JESSICA?!!

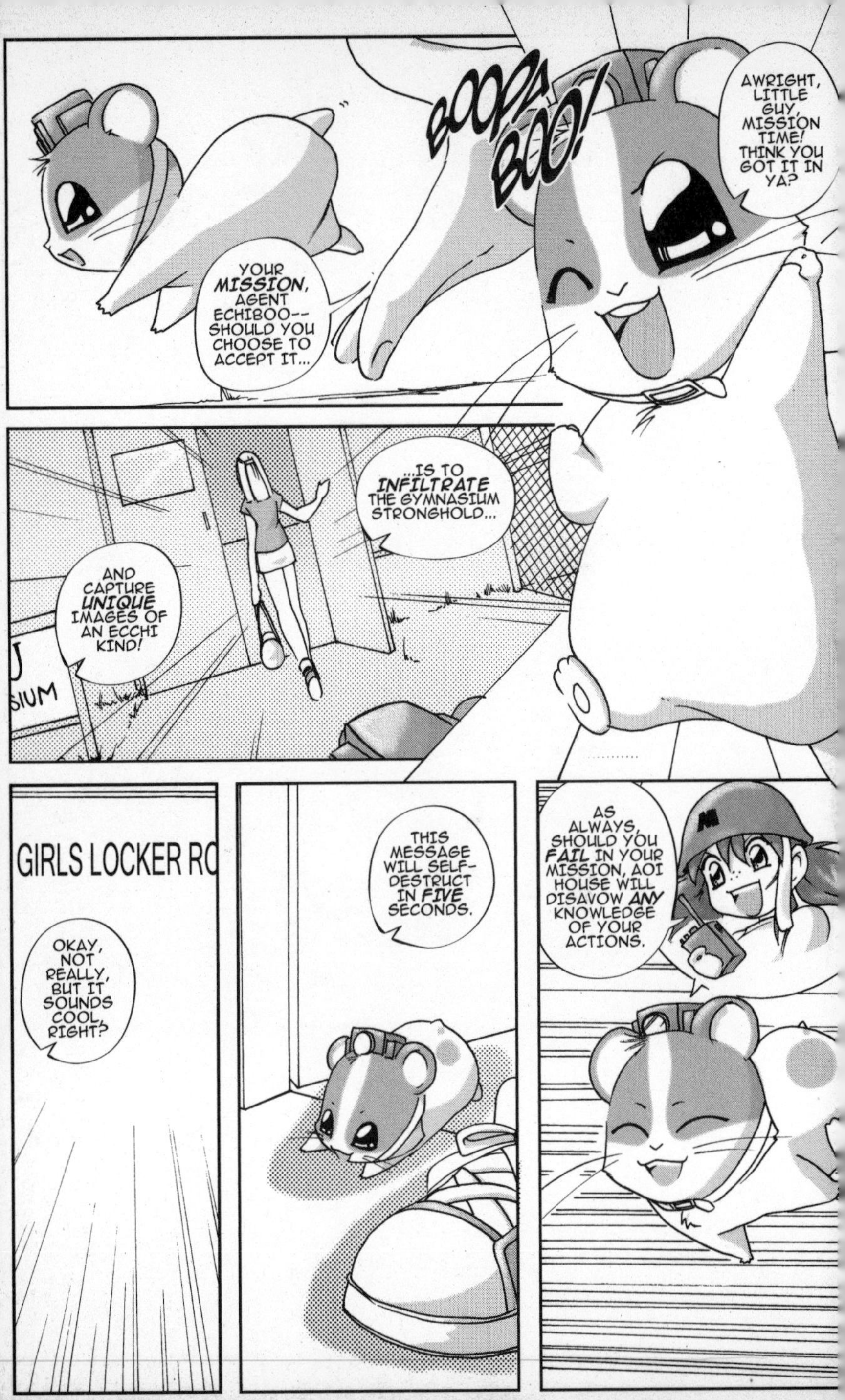
AWRIGHT, LITTLE GUY, MISSION TIME! THINK YOU GOT IT IN YA?
BOOPA BOO!
YOUR MISSION, AGENT ECHIBOO-- SHOULD YOU CHOOSE TO ACCEPT IT...
...IS TO INFILTRATE THE GYMNASIUM STRONGHOLD...
AND CAPTURE UNIQUE IMAGES OF AN ECCHI KIND!
SIUM
....
AS ALWAYS, SHOULD YOU FAIL IN YOUR MISSION, AOI HOUSE WILL DISAVOW ANY KNOWLEDGE OF YOUR ACTIONS.
THIS MESSAGE WILL SELF-DESTRUCT IN FIVE SECONDS.
GIRLS LOCKER RO
OKAY, NOT REALLY, BUT IT SOUNDS COOL, RIGHT?

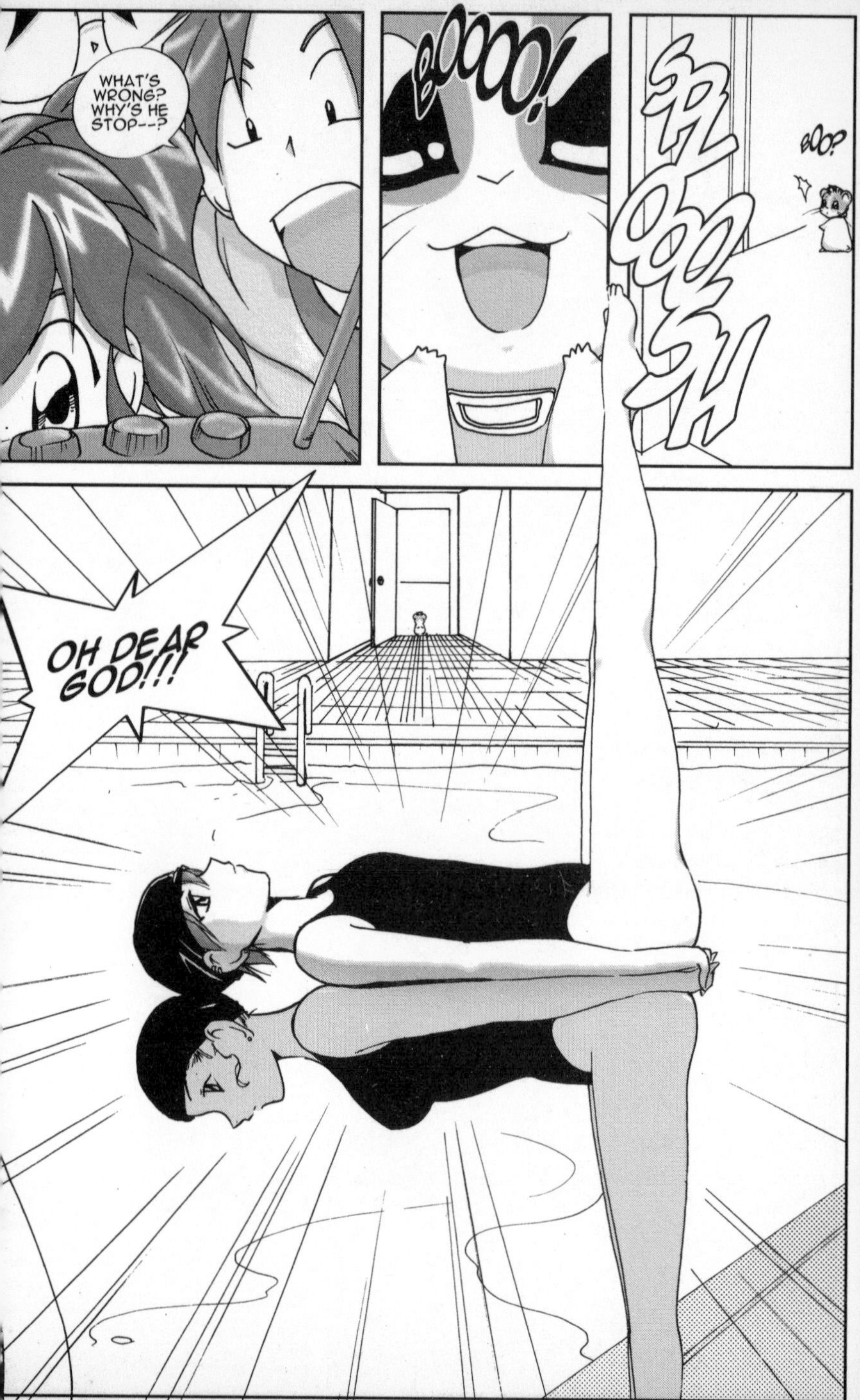
BOO?
SPLOOOOSH
BOOOO!
WHAT'S WRONG? WHY'S HE STOP--?
OH DEAR GOD!!!

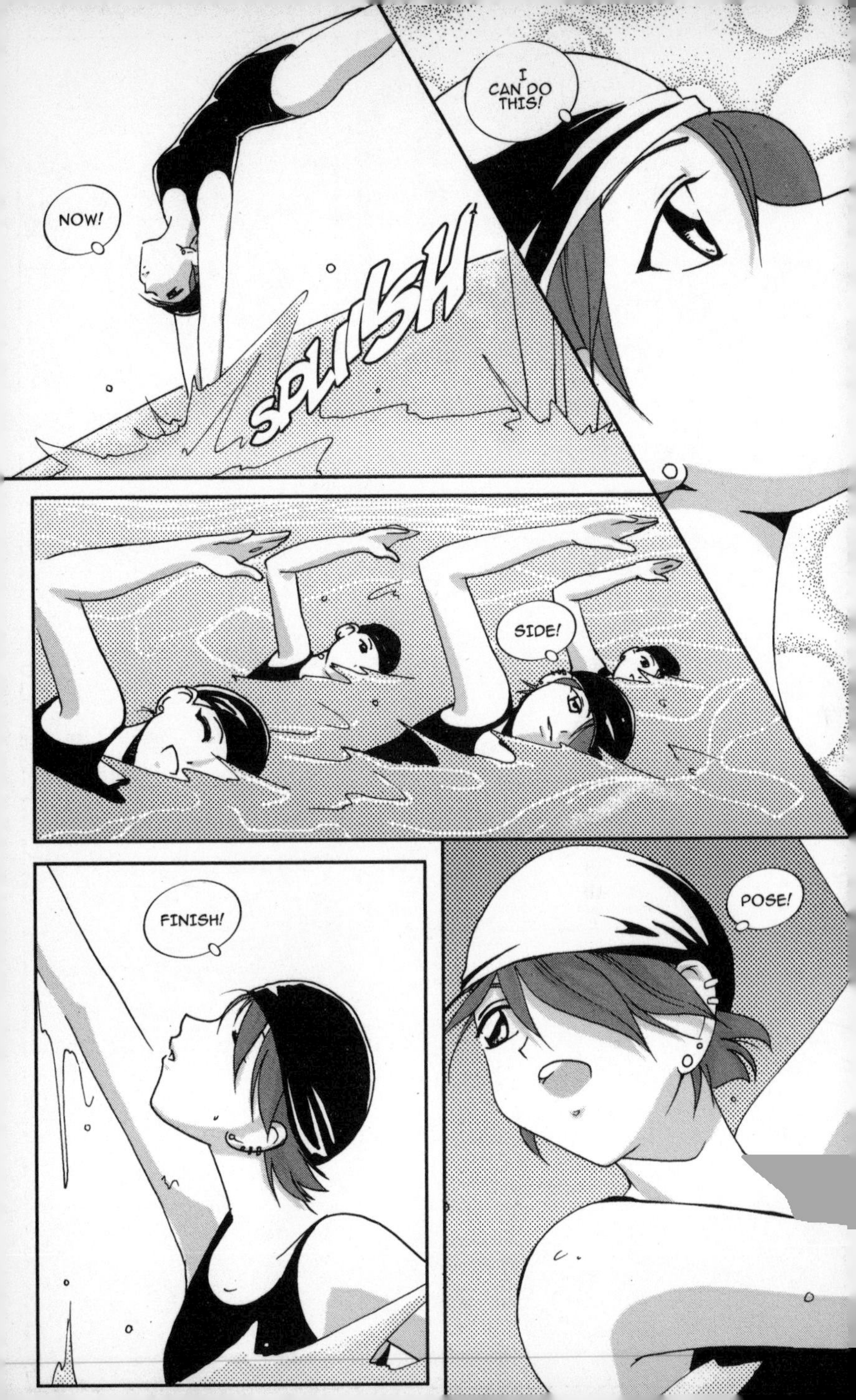
I CAN DO THIS!
NOW!
SPLISH
SIDE!
POSE!
FINISH!

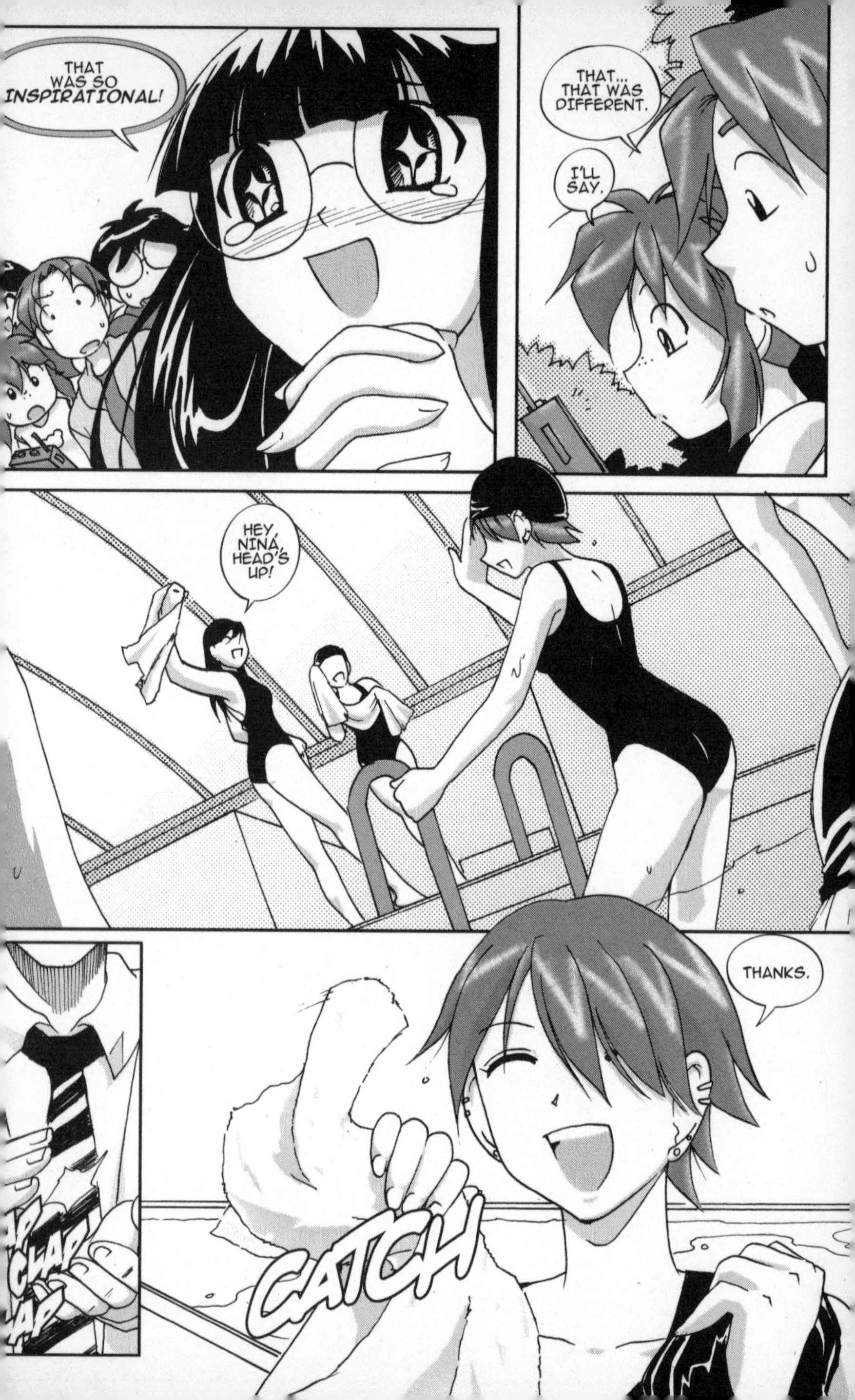

THAT... THAT WAS DIFFERENT.
I'LL SAY.
THAT WAS SO INSPIRATIONAL!
HEY, NINA, HEAD'S UP!
THANKS.
CATCH

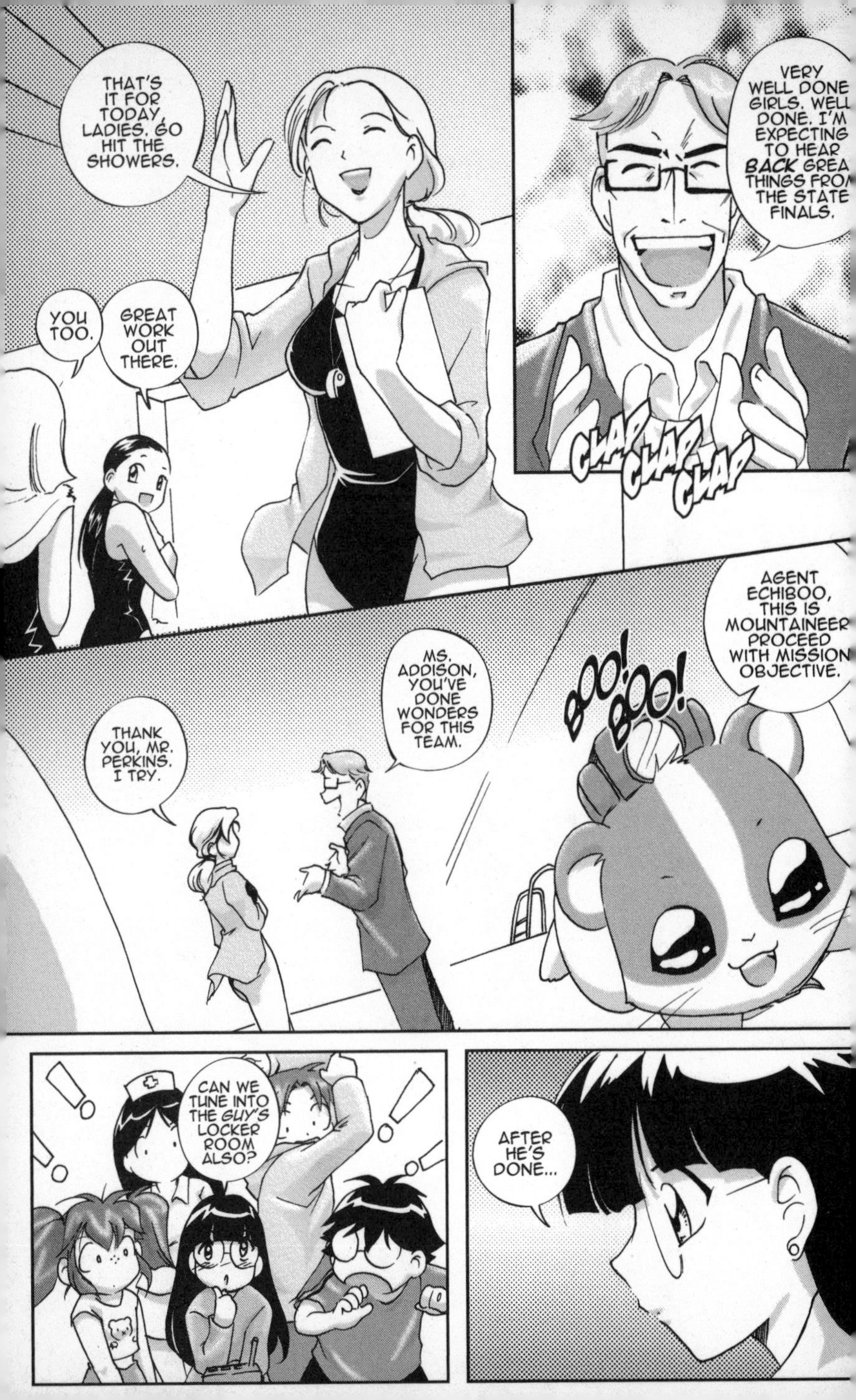
VERY WELL DONE GIRLS. WELL DONE. I'M EXPECTING TO HEAR BACK GREA THINGS FROM THE STATE FINALS.
CLAP CLAP CLAP
THAT'S IT FOR TODAY, LADIES. GO HIT THE SHOWERS.
GREAT WORK OUT THERE.
YOU TOO.
AGENT ECHIBOO, THIS IS MOUNTAINEER PROCEED WITH MISSION OBJECTIVE.
BOO! BOO!
MS. ADDISON, YOU'VE DONE WONDERS FOR THIS TEAM.
THANK YOU, MR. PERKINS. I TRY.
AFTER HE'S DONE...
CAN WE TUNE INTO THE *GUY'S* LOCKER ROOM ALSO?

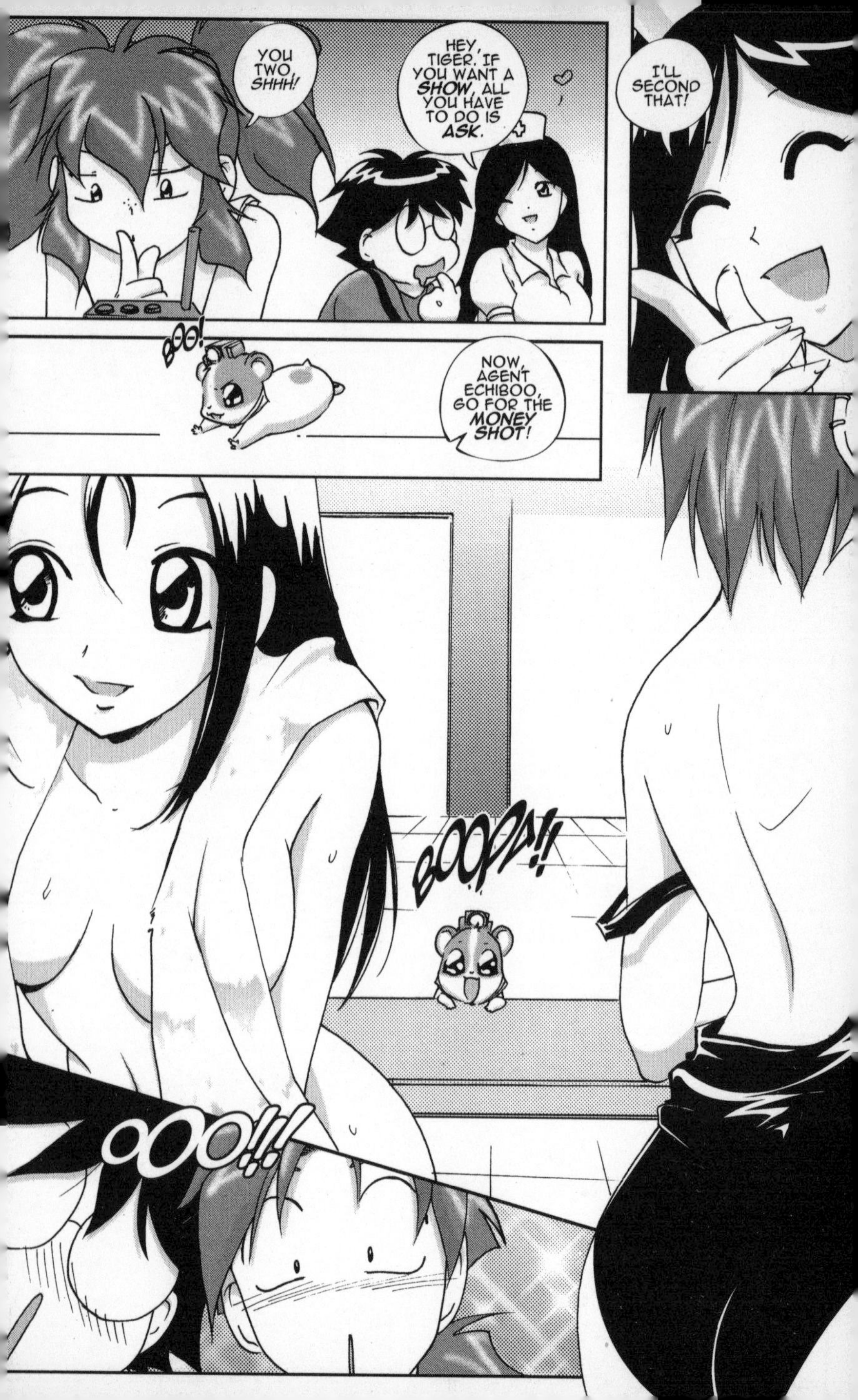
I'LL SECOND THAT!
HEY, TIGER. IF YOU WANT A SHOW, ALL YOU HAVE TO DO IS ASK.
YOU TWO, SHHH!
NOW, AGENT ECHIBOO, GO FOR THE MONEY SHOT!
BOO!
BOOP!!
OOO!!

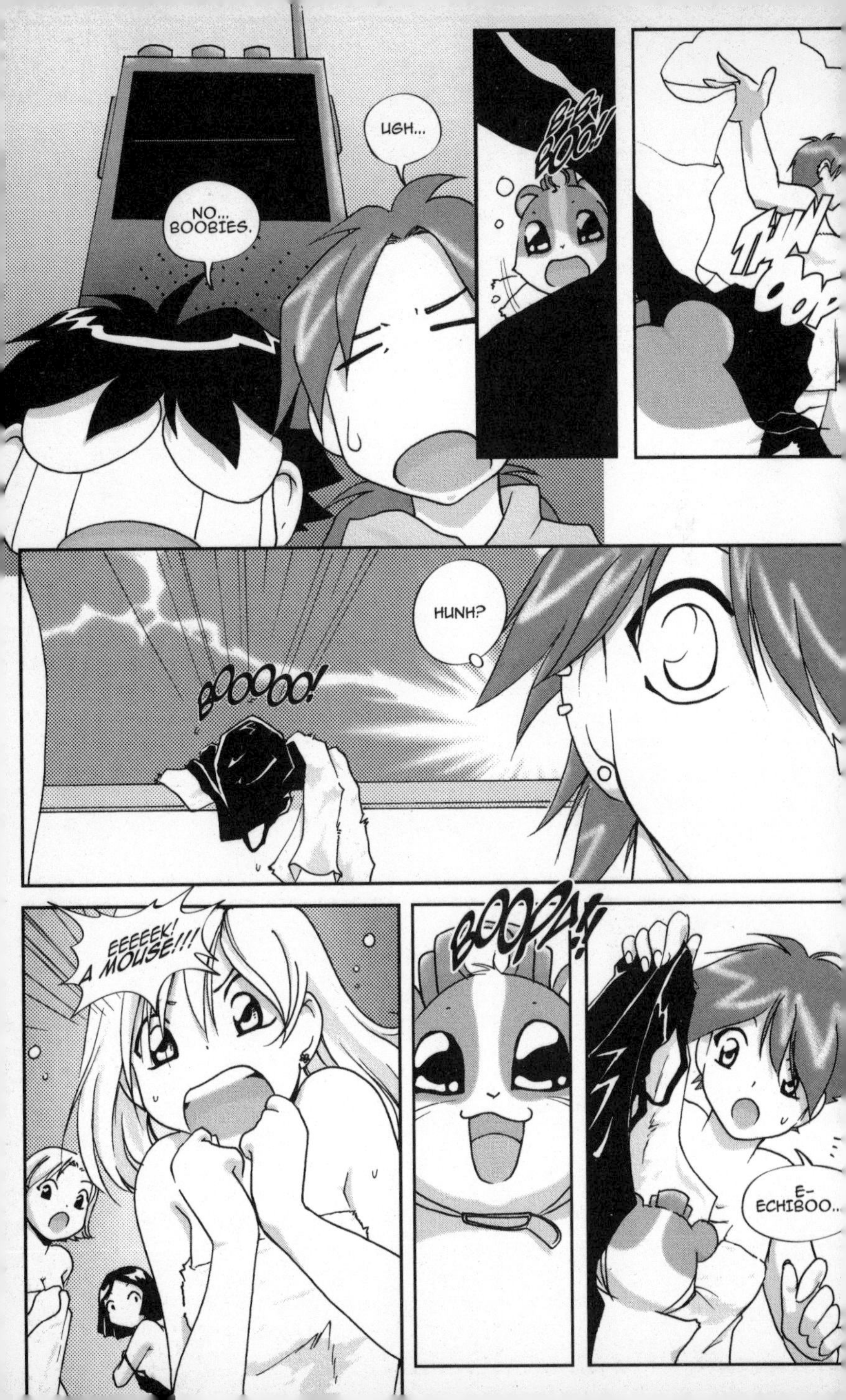
THWOOP
BEEBOO!!
UGH...
NO... BOOBIES.
HUNH?
BOOOOO!
BOOPA!!
E-ECHIBOO...
EEEEEK! A MOUSE!!!

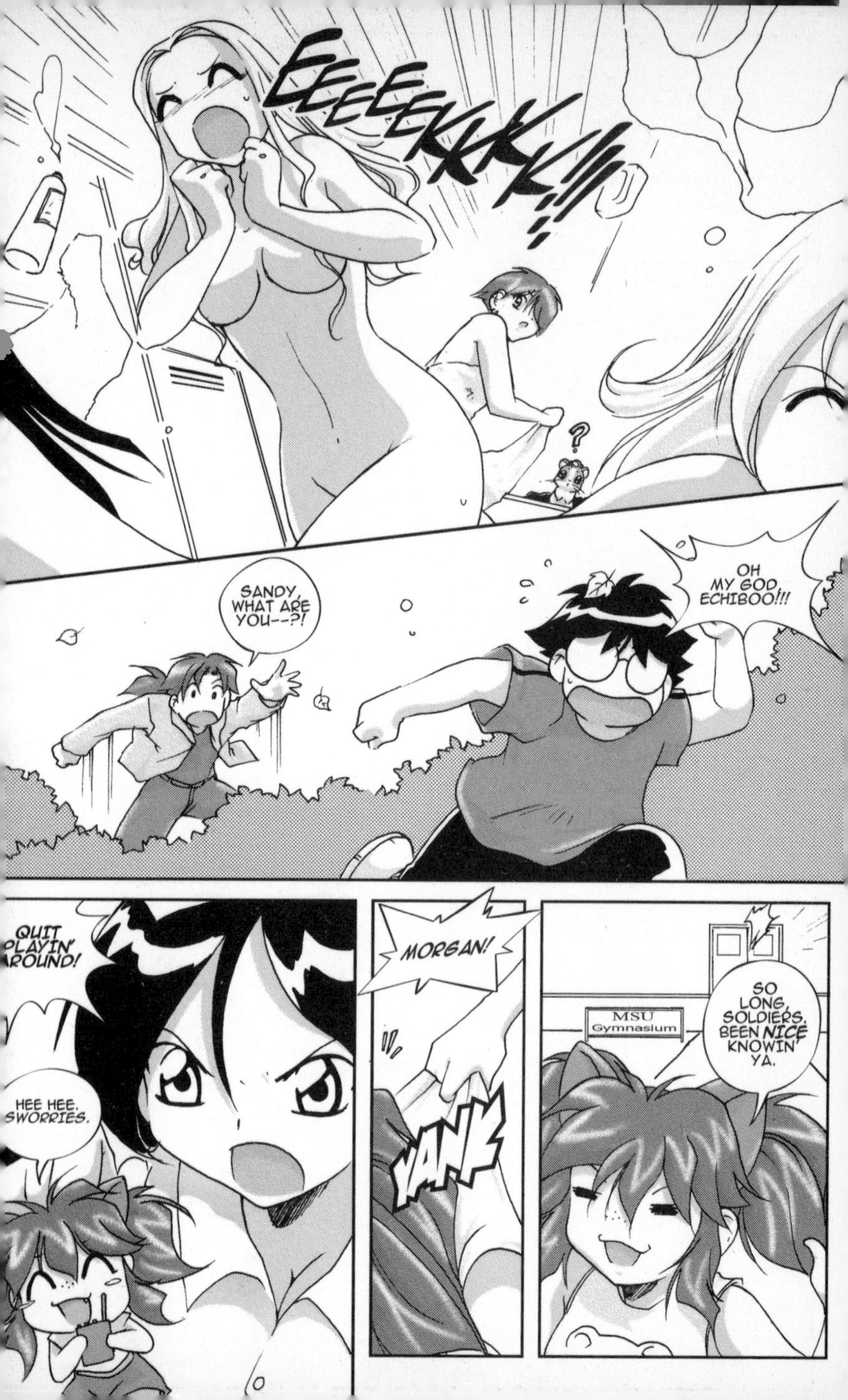
EEEEEKKK!!!!
OH MY GOD ECHIBOO!!!
SANDY, WHAT ARE YOU--?!
MSU Gymnasium
SO LONG, SOLDIERS. BEEN NICE KNOWIN' YA.
MORGAN!
YANK
QUIT PLAYIN' AROUND!
HEE HEE. SWORRIES.

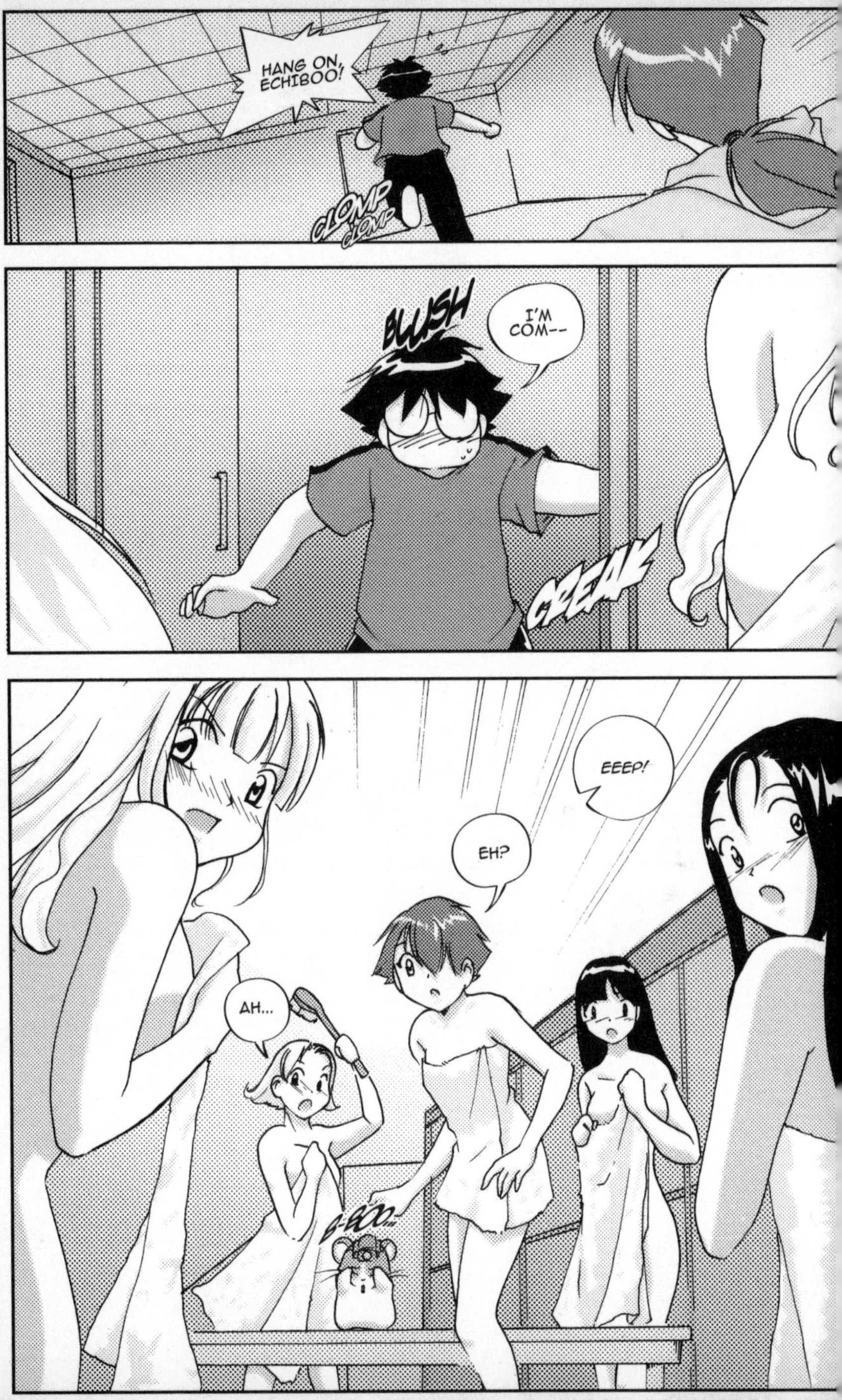
HANG ON, ECHIBOO!
CLOMP CLOMP
I'M COM--
BLUSH
CREAK
EEEP!
EH?
AH...
B-BOO...

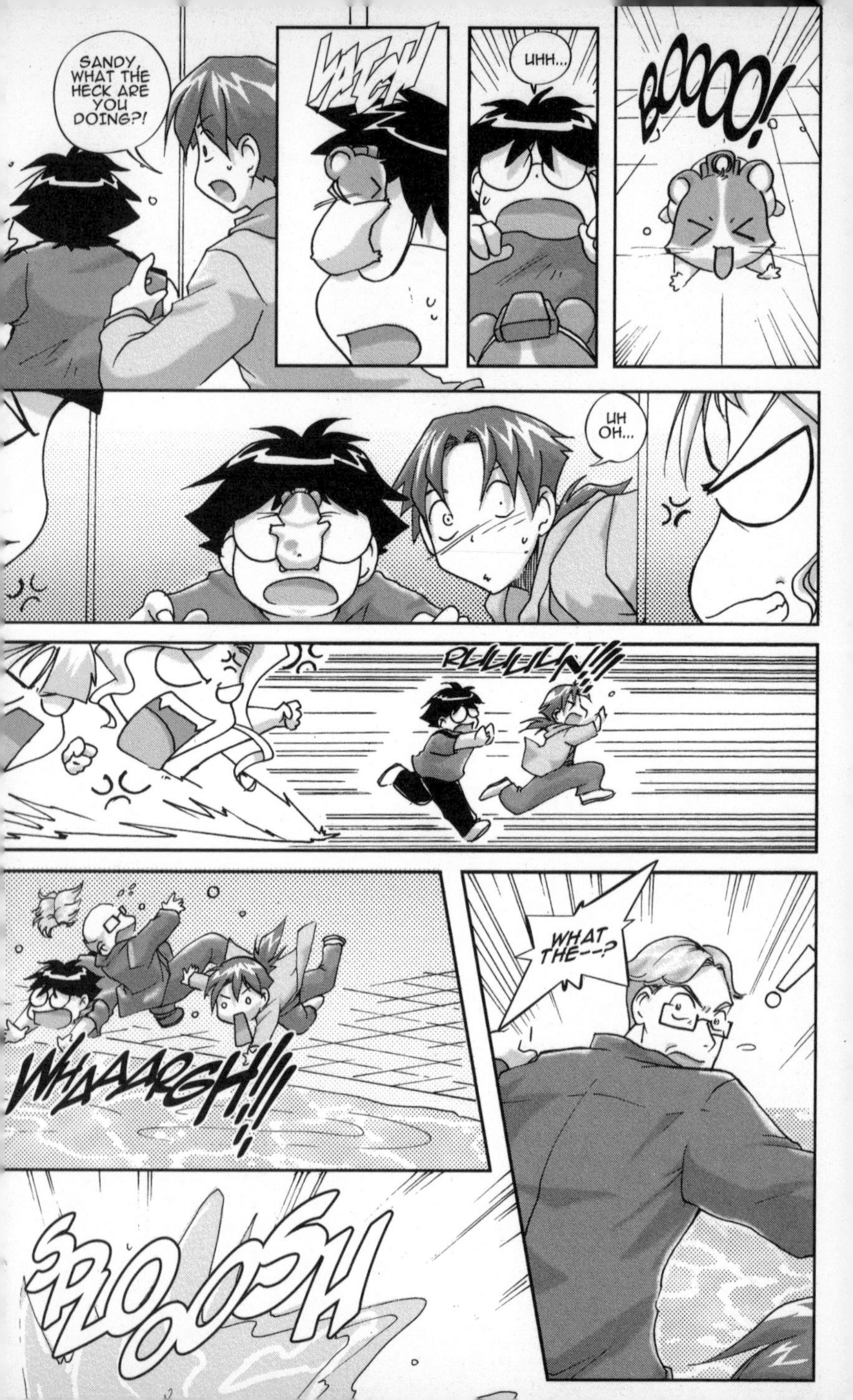
BOOOO!
UHH...
SANDY, WHAT THE HECK ARE YOU DOING?!
UH OH...
RUUUUUN!!!
WHAT THE--?
WHAAARGH!!!
SPLOOOSH

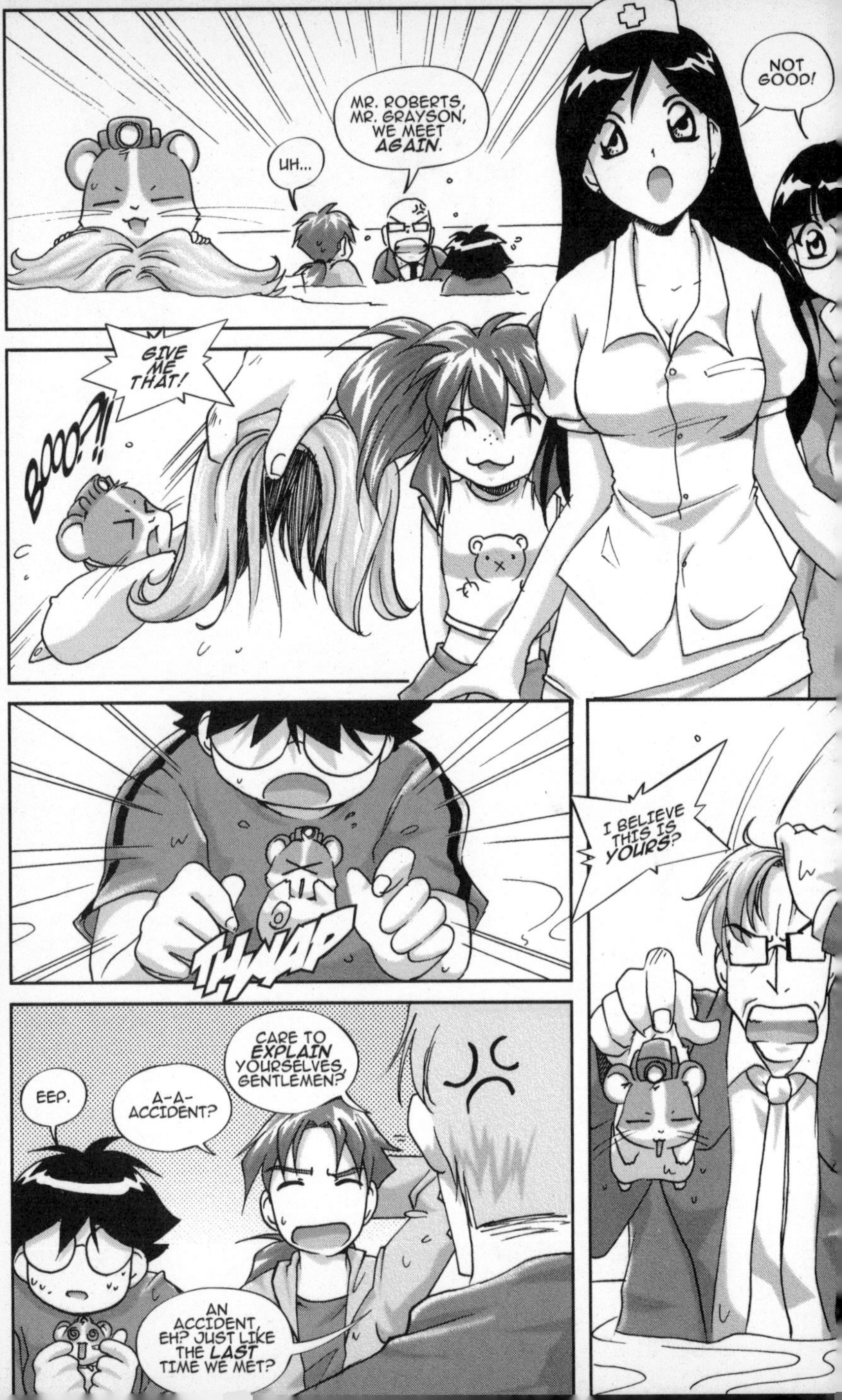
NOT GOOD!
MR. ROBERTS, MR. GRAYSON, WE MEET AGAIN.
UH...
GIVE ME THAT!
BOOO?!!
I BELIEVE THIS IS YOURS?
THWAP
CARE TO EXPLAIN YOURSELVES, GENTLEMEN?
A-A-ACCIDENT?
EEP.
AN ACCIDENT, EH? JUST LIKE THE LAST TIME WE MET?

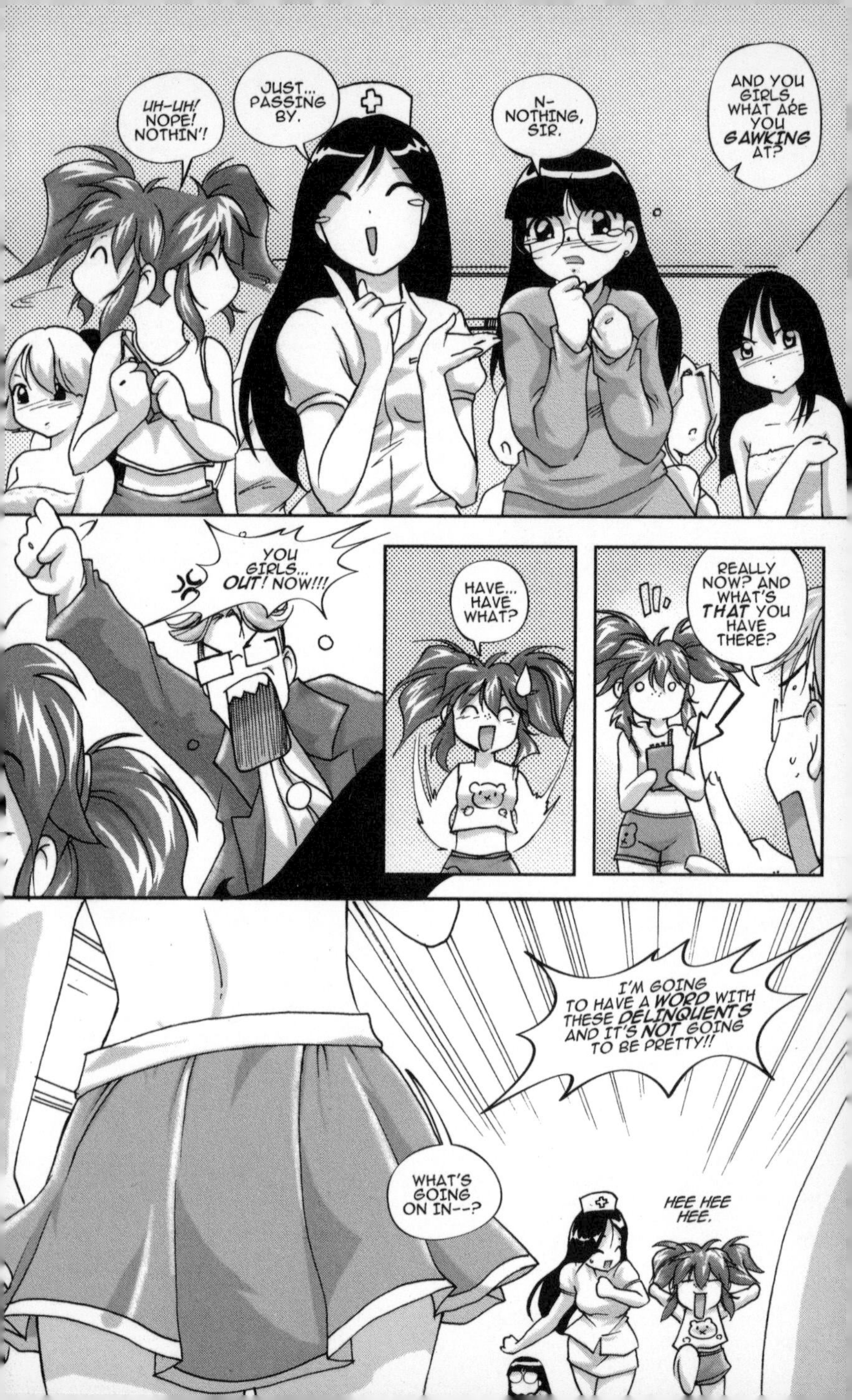
AND YOU GIRLS, WHAT ARE YOU GAWKING AT?
N-NOTHING, SIR.
JUST... PASSING BY.
UH-UH! NOPE! NOTHIN'!
REALLY NOW? AND WHAT'S THAT YOU HAVE THERE?
HAVE... HAVE WHAT?
YOU GIRLS... OUT! NOW!!!
I'M GOING TO HAVE A WORD WITH THESE DELINQUENTS AND IT'S NOT GOING TO BE PRETTY!!
HEE HEE HEE.
WHAT'S GOING ON IN--?

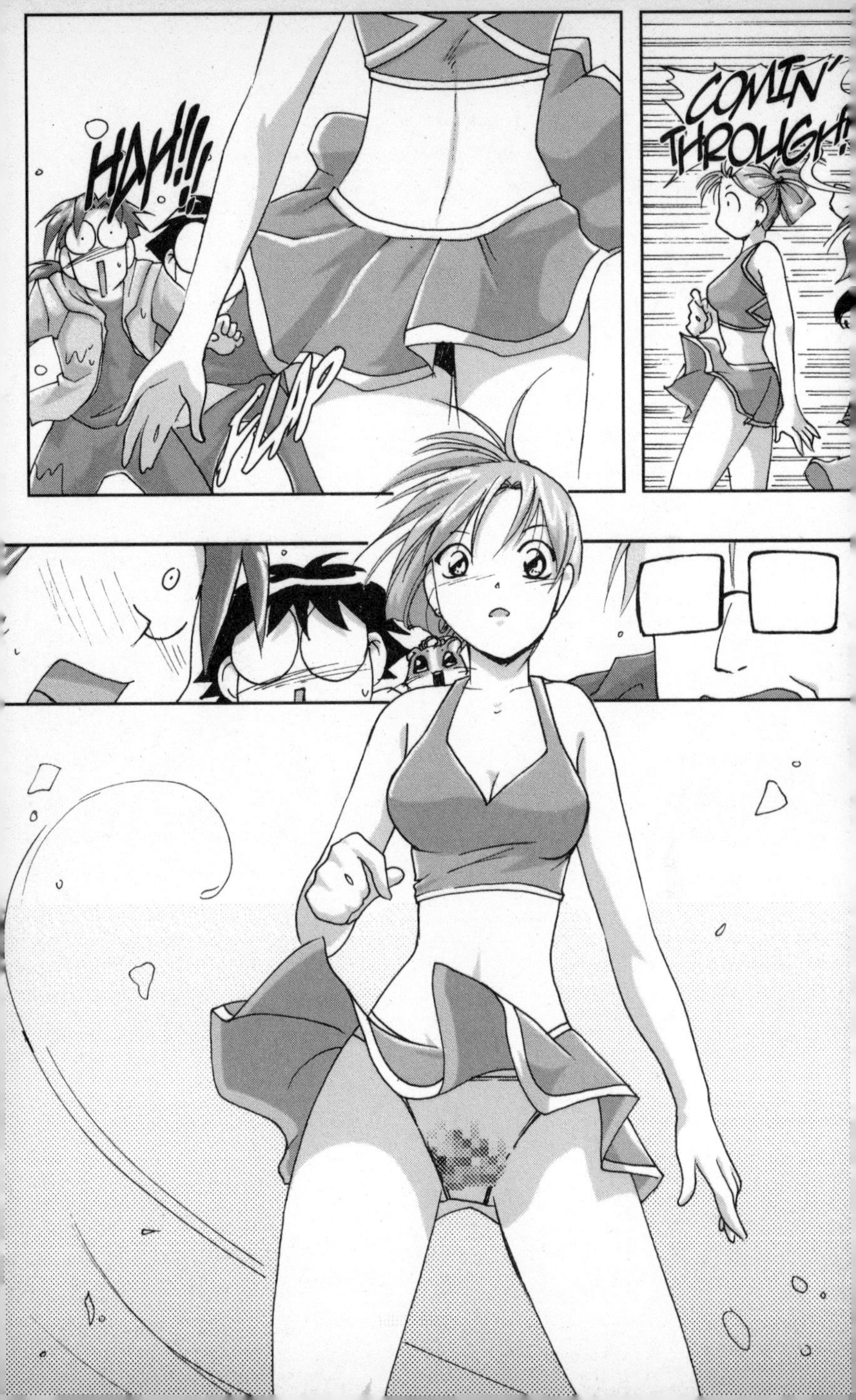
COMIN' THROUGH!!
HAH!!!
FLAP

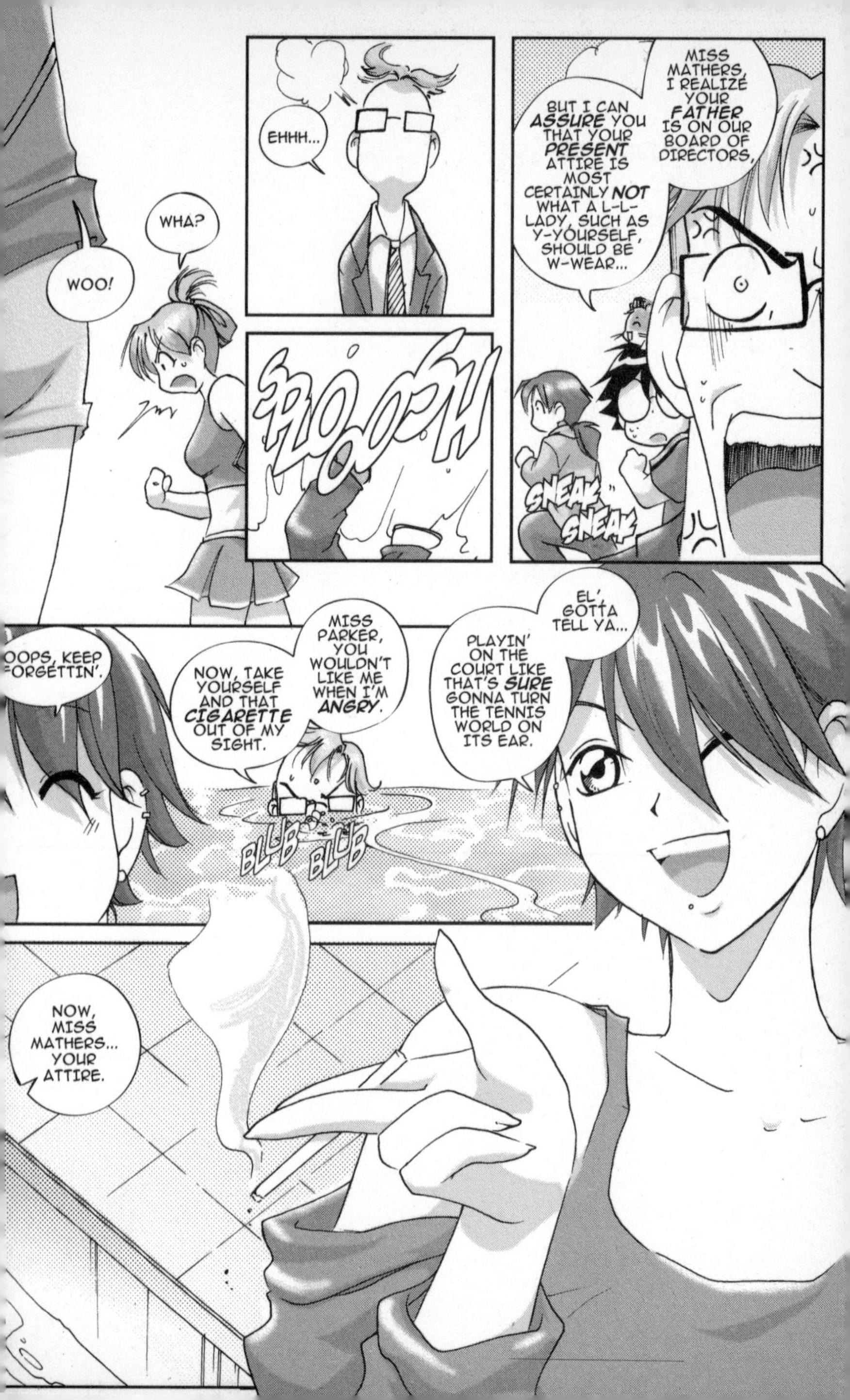
MISS MATHERS, I REALIZE YOUR FATHER IS ON OUR BOARD OF DIRECTORS,
BUT I CAN ASSURE YOU THAT YOUR PRESENT ATTIRE IS MOST CERTAINLY NOT WHAT A L-L-LADY, SUCH AS Y-YOURSELF, SHOULD BE W-WEAR...
SNEAK SNEAK
EHHH...
SPLOOOSH
WHA?
WOO!
EL', GOTTA TELL YA...
PLAYIN' ON THE COURT LIKE THAT'S SURE GONNA TURN THE TENNIS WORLD ON ITS EAR.
MISS PARKER, YOU WOULDN'T LIKE ME WHEN I'M ANGRY.
NOW, TAKE YOURSELF AND THAT CIGARETTE OUT OF MY SIGHT.
BLUB BLUB
OOPS, KEEP FORGETTIN'.
NOW, MISS MATHERS... YOUR ATTIRE.

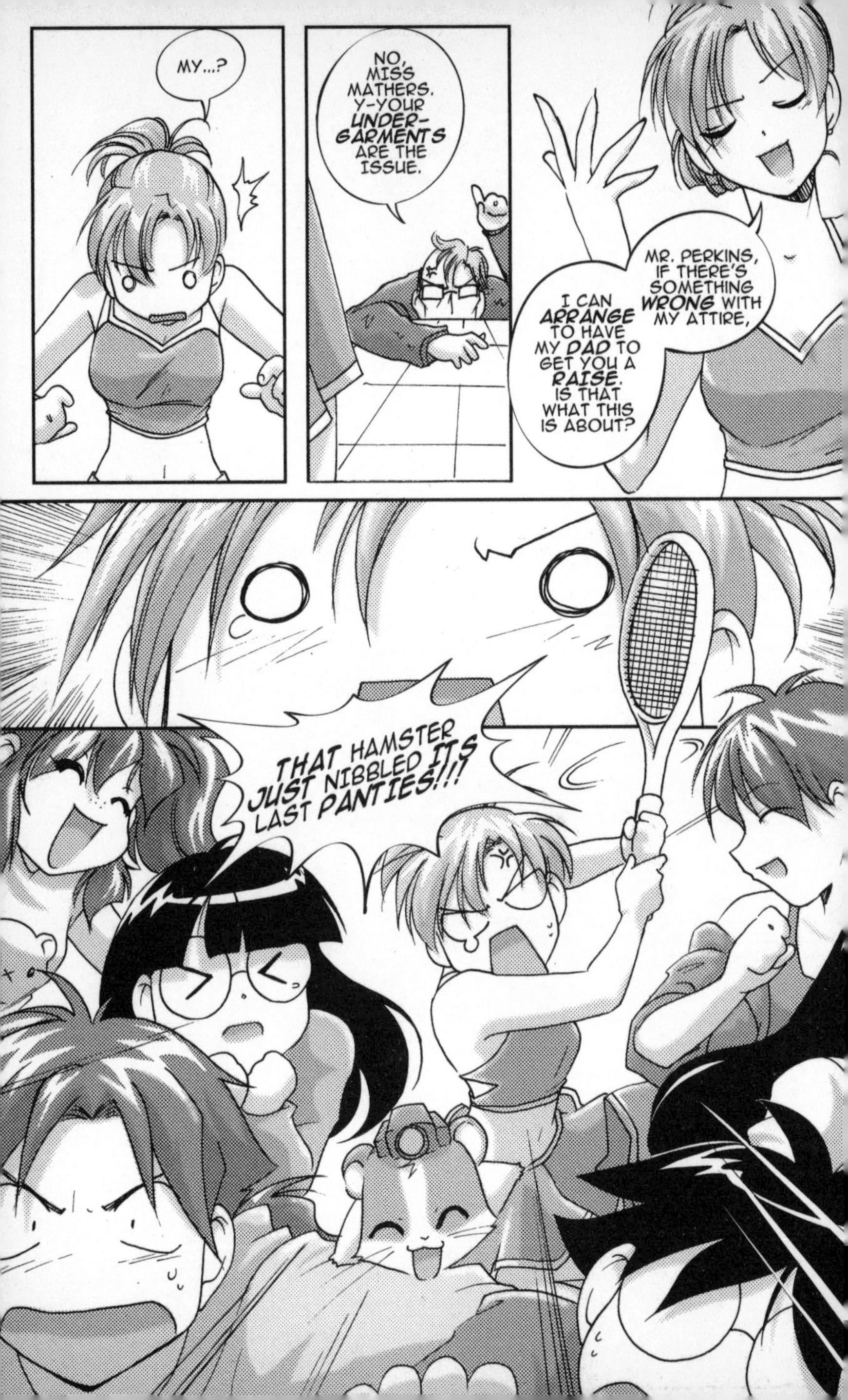
MR. PERKINS, IF THERE'S SOMETHING WRONG WITH MY ATTIRE,
I CAN ARRANGE TO HAVE MY DAD TO GET YOU A RAISE. IS THAT WHAT THIS IS ABOUT?
NO, MISS MATHERS. Y-YOUR UNDER-GARMENTS ARE THE ISSUE.
MY...?
THAT HAMSTER JUST NIBBLED ITS LAST PANTIES!!!

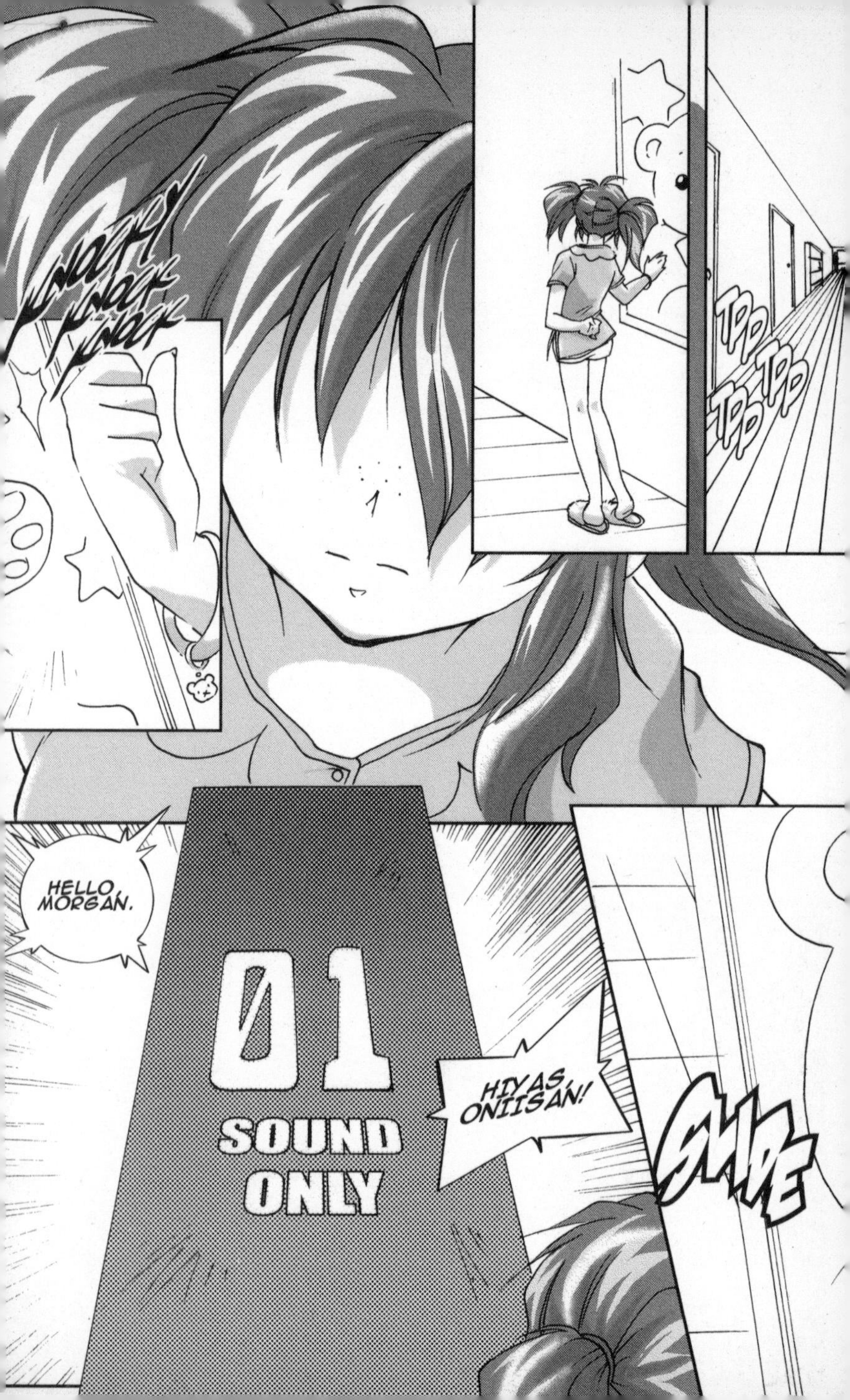
TPD TPD TPD TPD
KNOCK! KNOCK KNOCK
SLIDE
HIYAS, ONIISAN!
01
SOUND ONLY
HELLO, MORGAN.

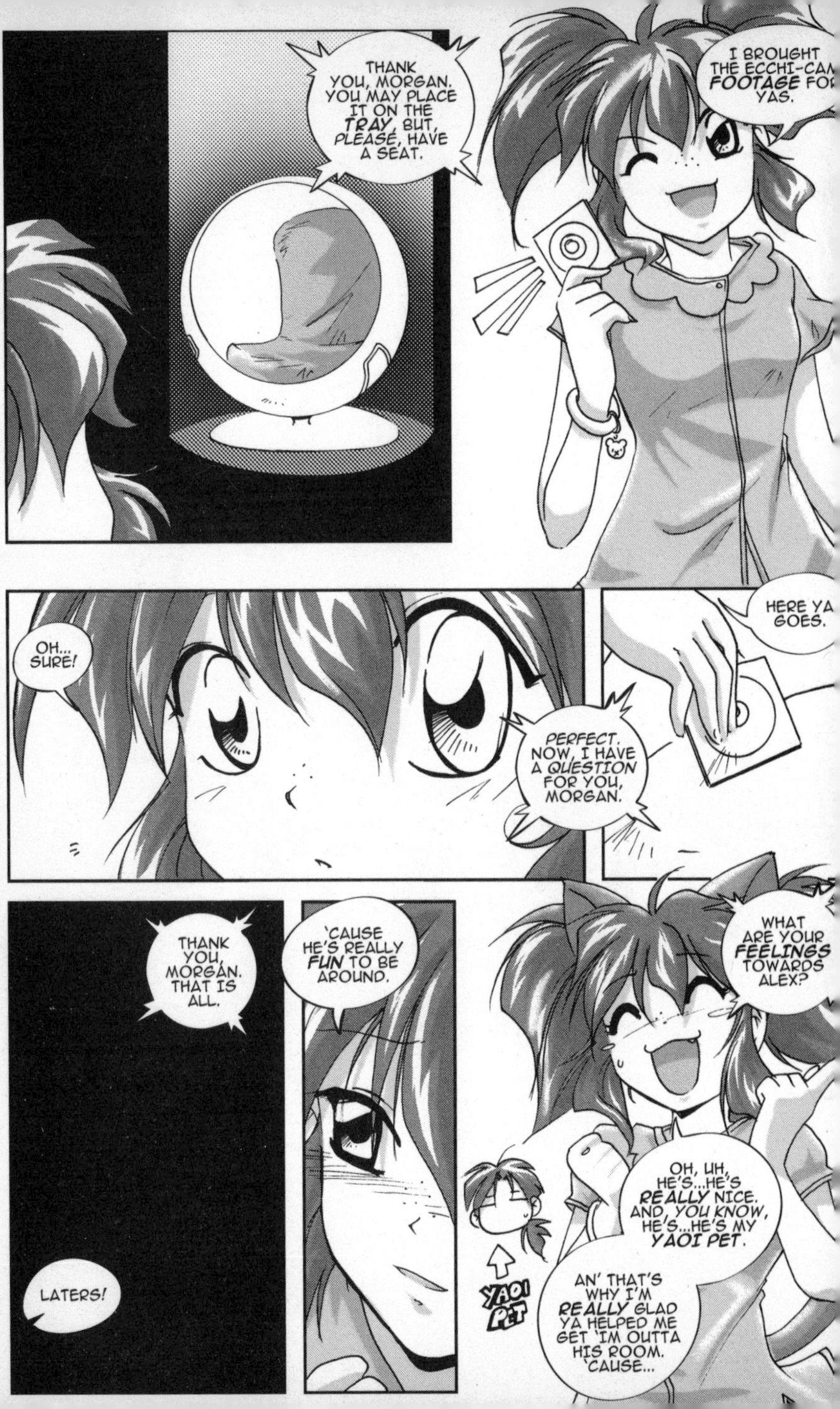

I BROUGHT THE ECCHI-CAM FOOTAGE FO YAS.
THANK YOU, MORGAN. YOU MAY PLACE IT ON THE TRAY, BUT, PLEASE, HAVE A SEAT.
HERE YA GOES.
PERFECT. NOW, I HAVE A QUESTION FOR YOU, MORGAN.
OH... SURE!
WHAT ARE YOUR FEELINGS TOWARDS ALEX?
OH, UH, HE'S...HE'S REALLY NICE. AND, YOU KNOW, HE'S...HE'S MY YAOI PET.
YAOI PET
AN' THAT'S WHY I'M REALLY GLAD YA HELPED ME GET 'IM OUTTA HIS ROOM. 'CAUSE...
'CAUSE HE'S REALLY FUN TO BE AROUND.
THANK YOU, MORGAN. THAT IS ALL.
LATERS!

AOI
House

SEAL OF APPROVAL

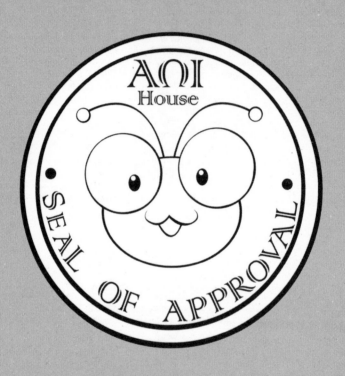

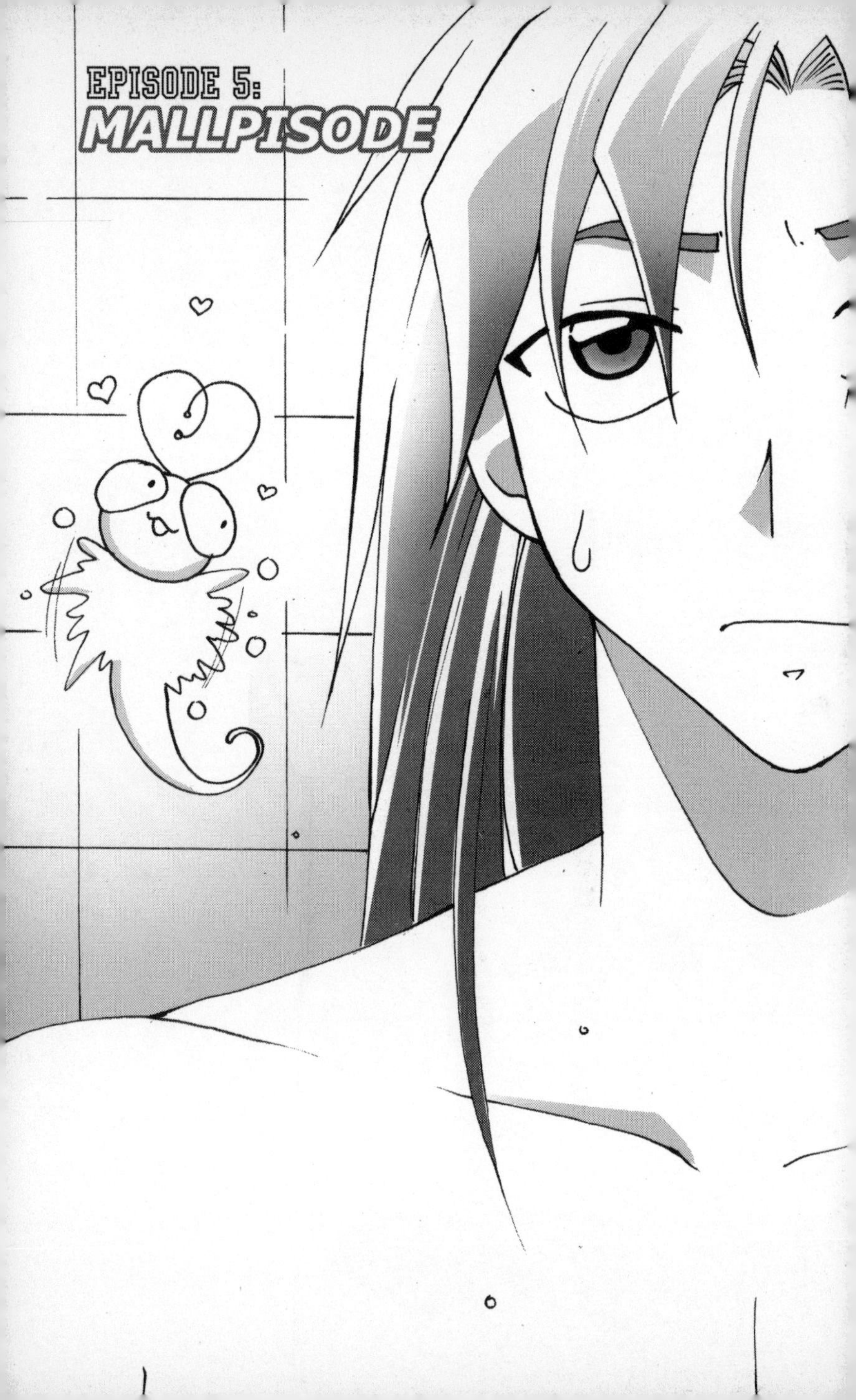
EPISODE 5:
MALLPISODE

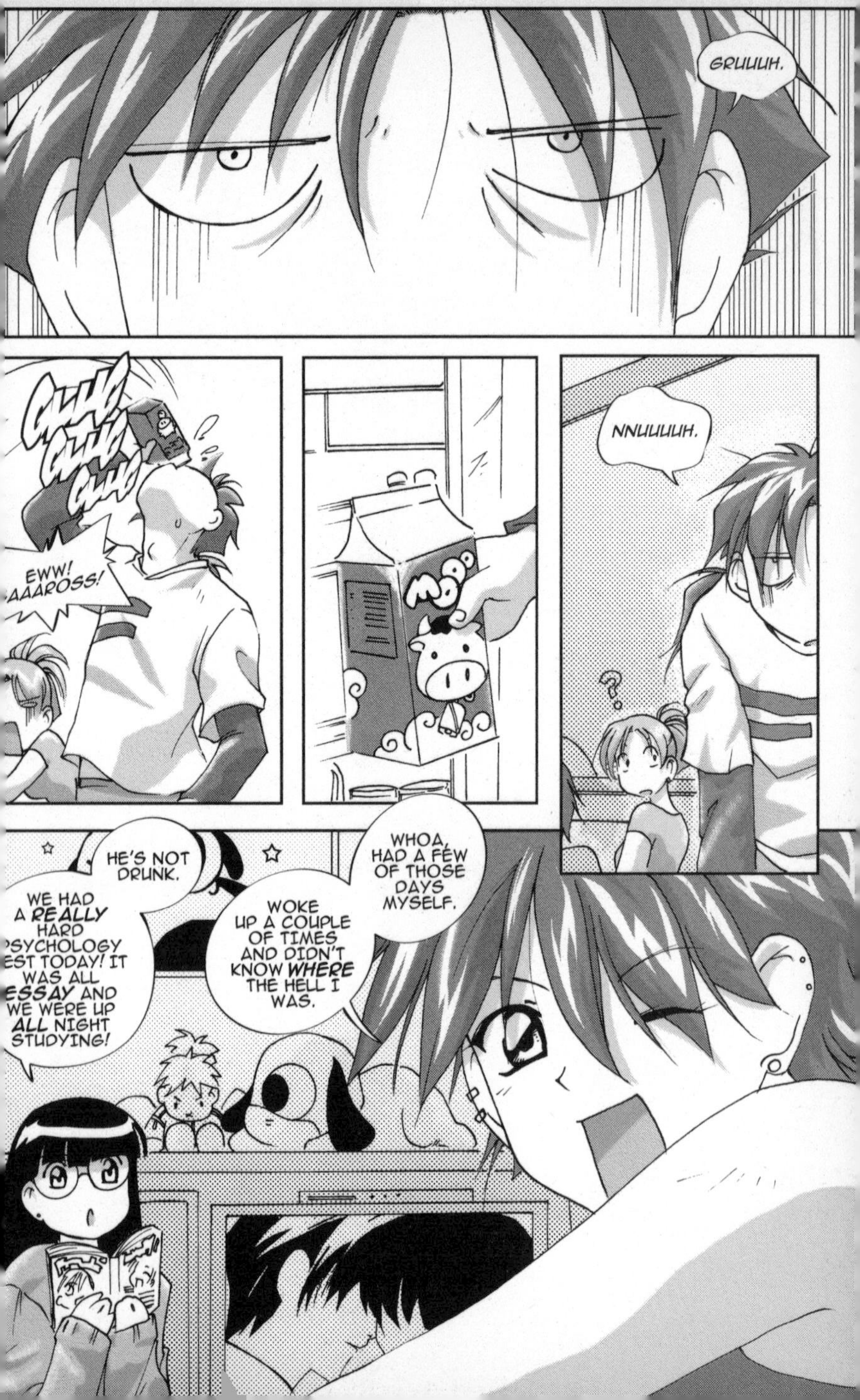
GRUUUH.
NNUUUUH.
GLUG GLUG GLUG
EWW! AAAROSS!
WHOA, HAD A FEW OF THOSE DAYS MYSELF.
WOKE UP A COUPLE OF TIMES AND DIDN'T KNOW **WHERE** THE HELL I WAS.
HE'S NOT DRUNK.
WE HAD A **REALLY** HARD PSYCHOLOGY EST TODAY! IT WAS ALL **ESSAY** AND WE WERE UP **ALL** NIGHT STUDYING!

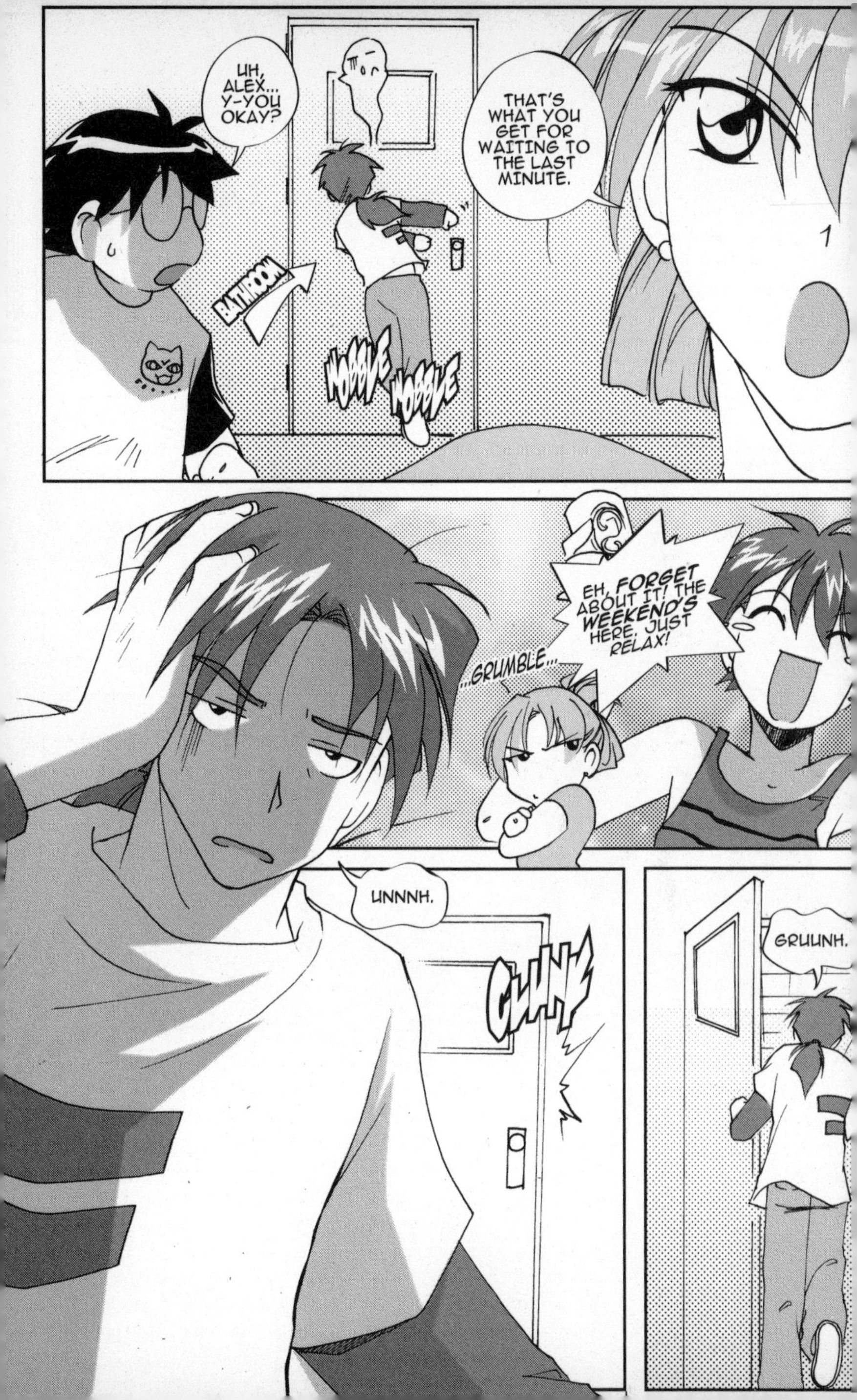
THAT'S WHAT YOU GET FOR WAITING TO THE LAST MINUTE.
UH, ALEX... Y-YOU OKAY?
BATHROOM
WOBBLE WOBBLE
EH, FORGET ABOUT IT! THE WEEKEND'S HERE. JUST RELAX!
...GRUMBLE...
GRUUNH.
UNNNH.
CLUNK

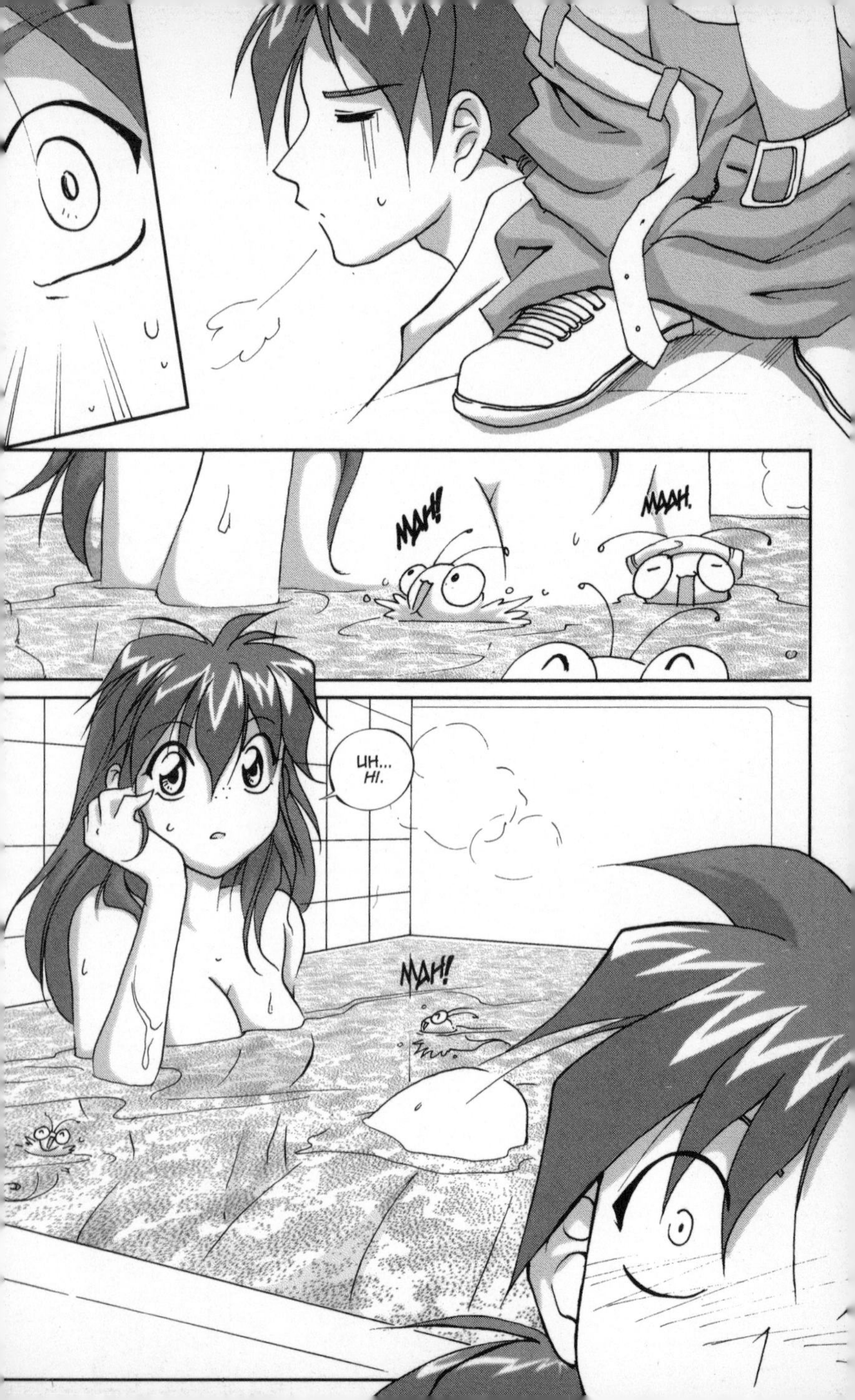
MAAH.
MAH!
UH... HI.
MAH!

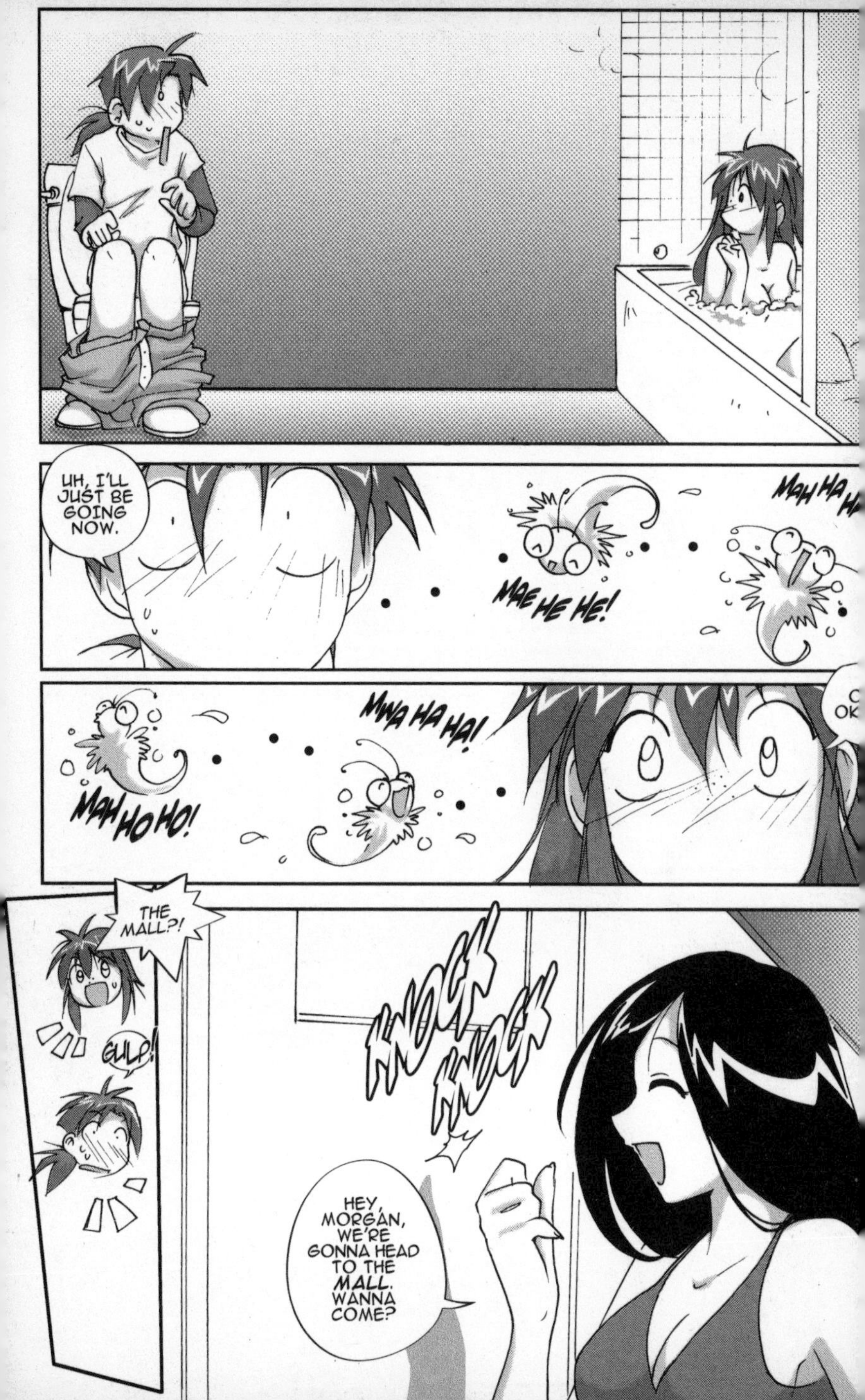
MAH HA
MAE HE HE!
UH, I'LL JUST BE GOING NOW.
MWA HA HA!
MAH HO HO!
KNOCK KNOCK
HEY, MORGAN, WE'RE GONNA HEAD TO THE MALL. WANNA COME?
THE MALL?!
GULP!

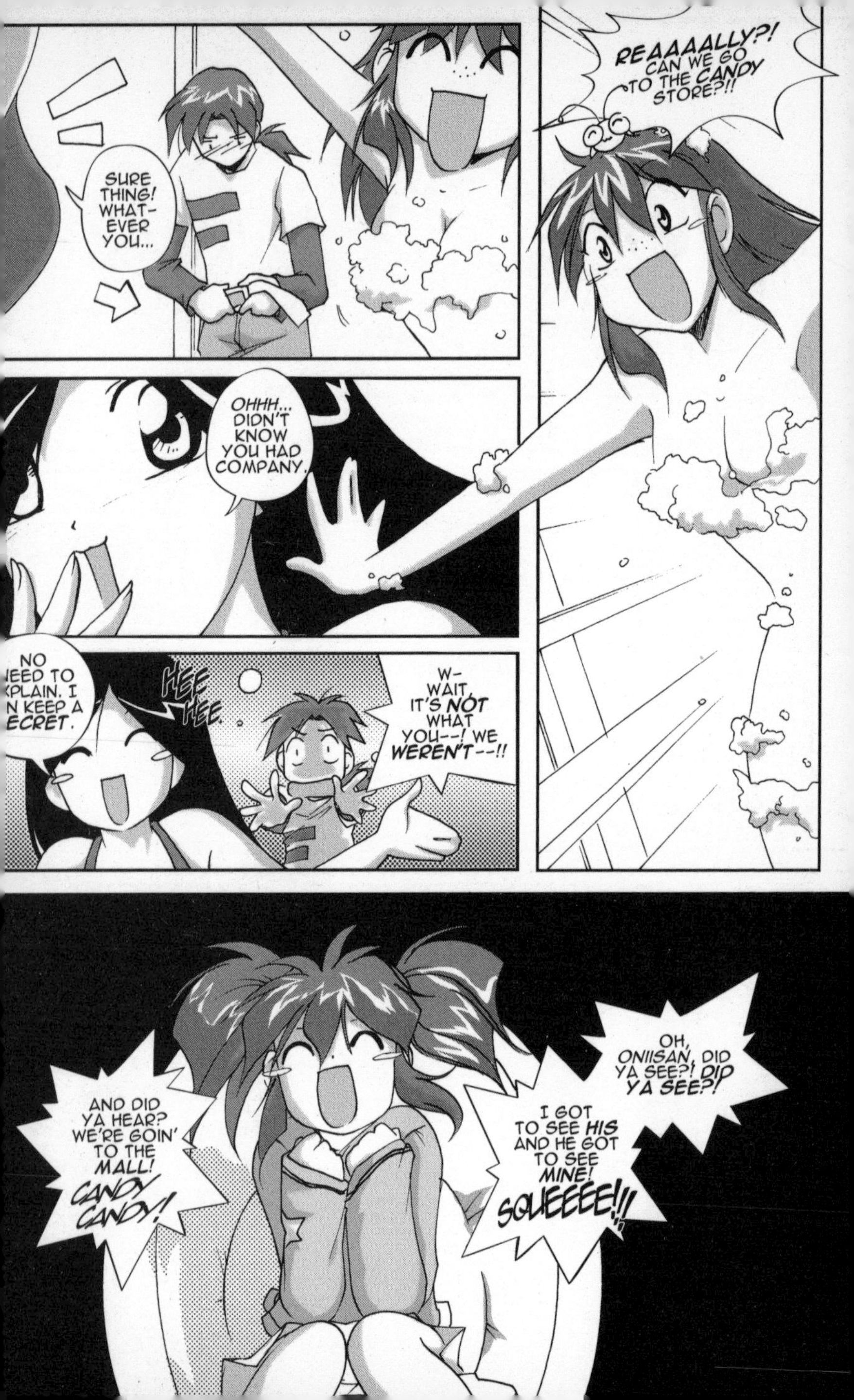
REAAAALLY?! CAN WE GO TO THE CANDY STORE?!!
SURE THING! WHAT-EVER YOU...
OHHH... DIDN'T KNOW YOU HAD COMPANY.
W-WAIT, IT'S NOT WHAT YOU--! WE WEREN'T--!!
HEE HEE
NO EED TO KPLAIN. I N KEEP A ECRET.
OH, ONIISAN, DID YA SEE?! DID YA SEE?!
I GOT TO SEE HIS AND HE GOT TO SEE MINE! SQUEEEEE!!!
AND DID YA HEAR? WE'RE GOIN' TO THE MALL! CANDY CANDY!

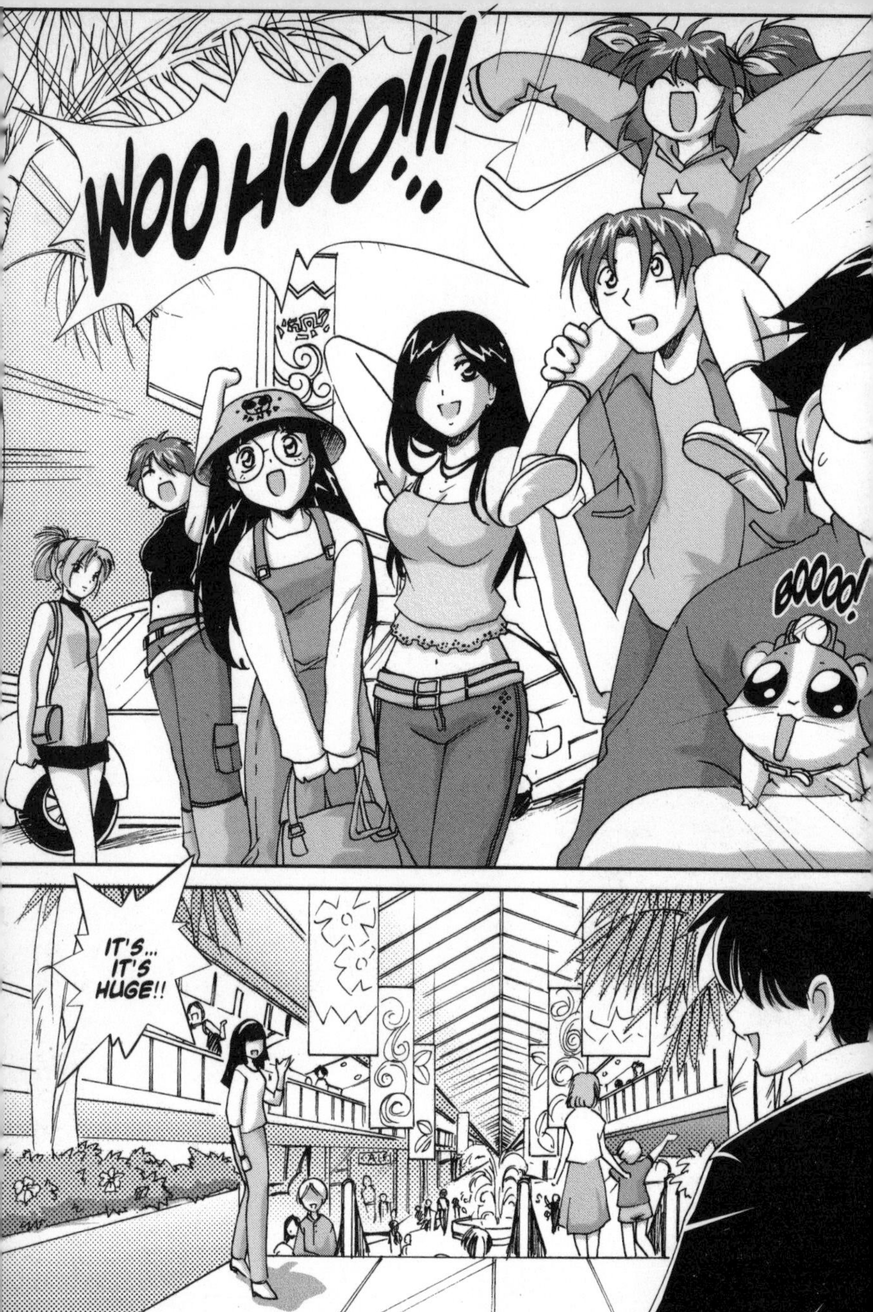
WOO HOO!!!
BOOOO!
IT'S... IT'S HUGE!!

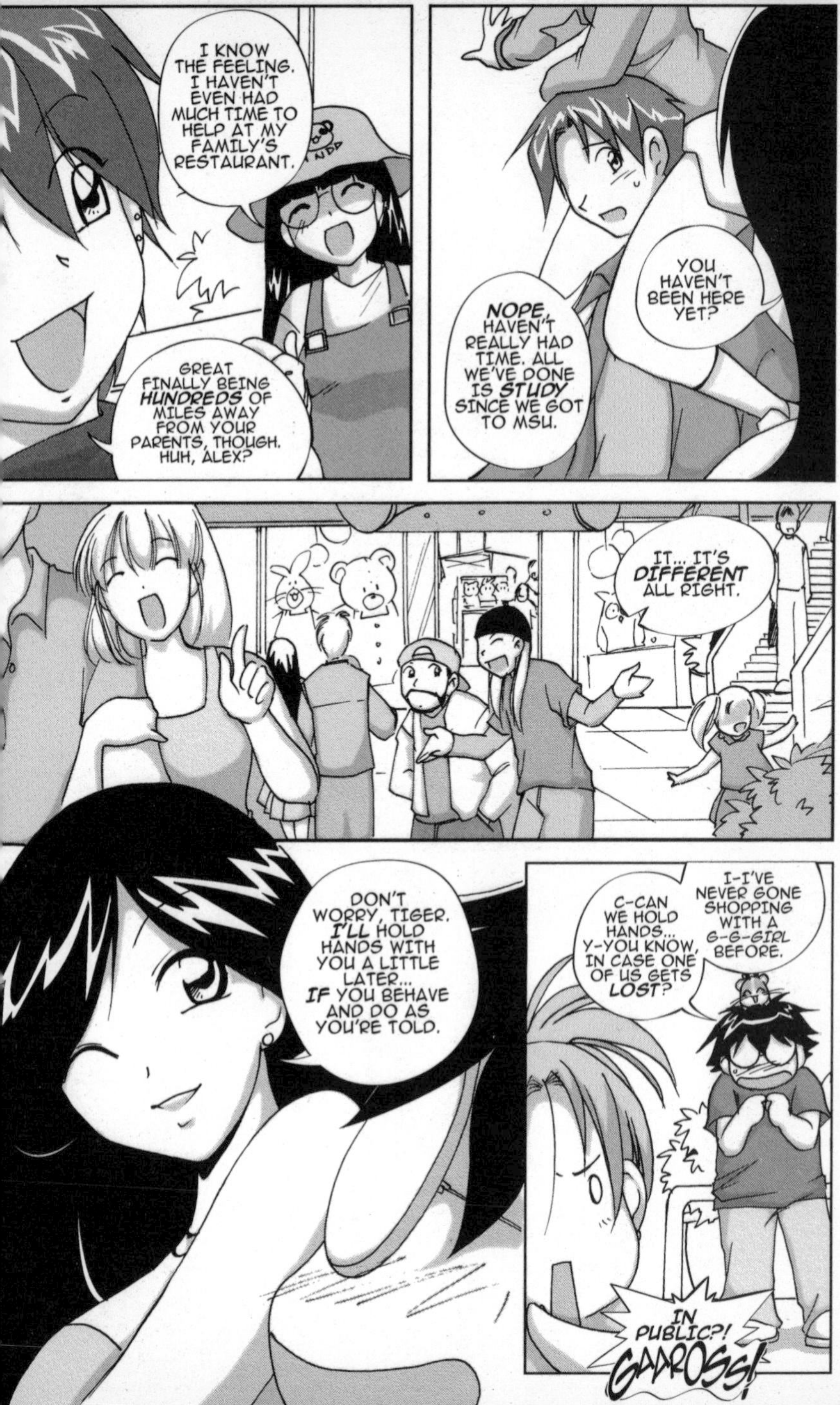
YOU HAVEN'T BEEN HERE YET?
NOPE, HAVEN'T REALLY HAD TIME. ALL WE'VE DONE IS STUDY SINCE WE GOT TO MSU.
I KNOW THE FEELING. I HAVEN'T EVEN HAD MUCH TIME TO HELP AT MY FAMILY'S RESTAURANT.
GREAT FINALLY BEING HUNDREDS OF MILES AWAY FROM YOUR PARENTS, THOUGH. HUH, ALEX?
IT... IT'S DIFFERENT ALL RIGHT.
I-I'VE NEVER GONE SHOPPING WITH A G-G-GIRL BEFORE.
C-CAN WE HOLD HANDS... Y-YOU KNOW, IN CASE ONE OF US GETS LOST?
IN PUBLIC?!
GADROSS!
DON'T WORRY, TIGER. I'LL HOLD HANDS WITH YOU A LITTLE LATER... IF YOU BEHAVE AND DO AS YOU'RE TOLD.

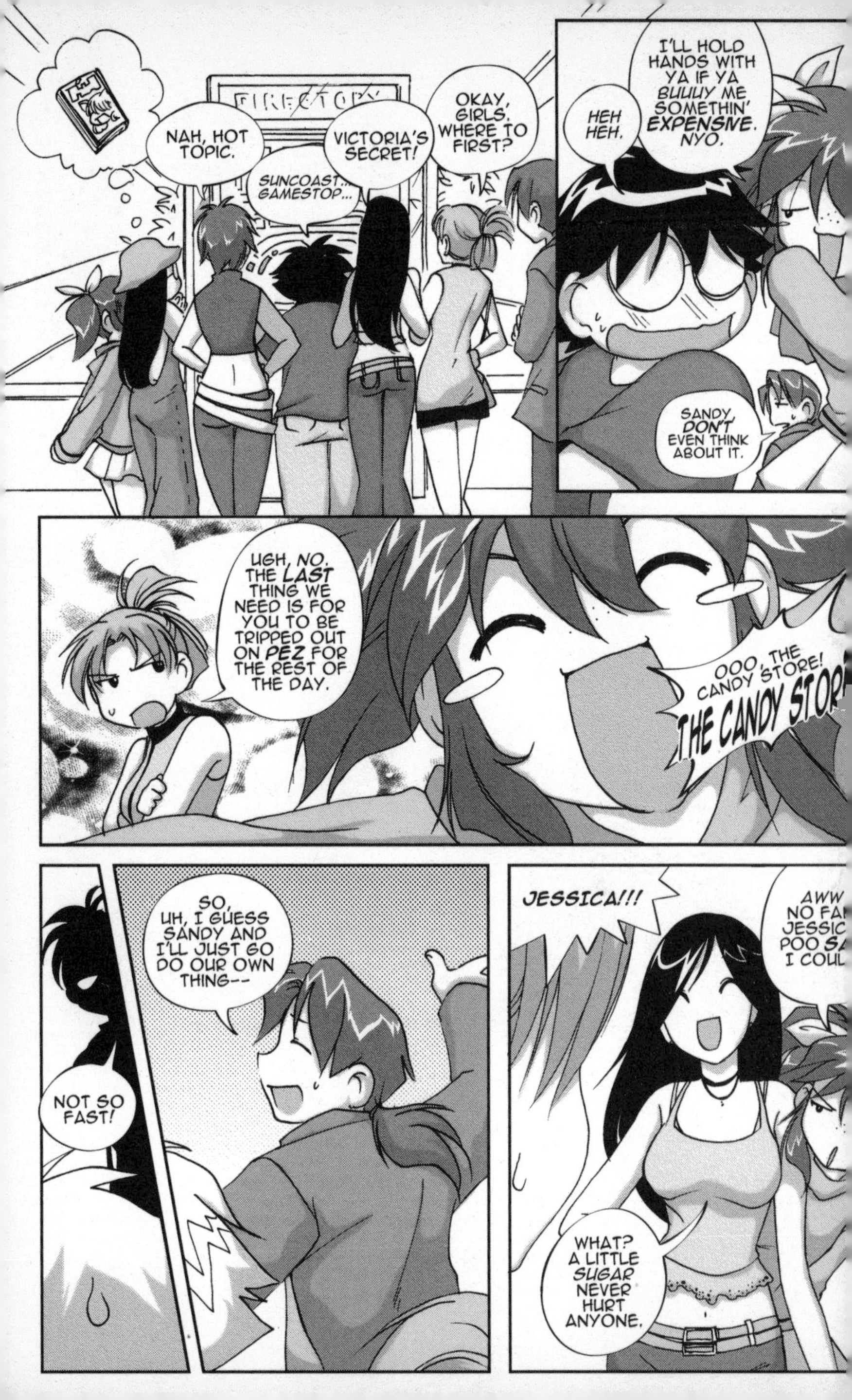
I'LL HOLD HANDS WITH YA IF YA BUUUY ME SOMETHIN' EXPENSIVE. NYO.
HEH HEH.
SANDY, DON'T EVEN THINK ABOUT IT.
OKAY, GIRLS. WHERE TO FIRST?
VICTORIA'S SECRET!
SUNCOAST... GAMESTOP...
NAH, HOT TOPIC.
OOO, THE CANDY STORE!
THE CANDY STOR
UGH, NO. THE LAST THING WE NEED IS FOR YOU TO BE TRIPPED OUT ON PEZ FOR THE REST OF THE DAY.
AWW NO FA JESSIC POO SA I COUL
JESSICA!!!
WHAT? A LITTLE SUGAR NEVER HURT ANYONE.
SO, UH, I GUESS SANDY AND I'LL JUST GO DO OUR OWN THING--
NOT SO FAST!

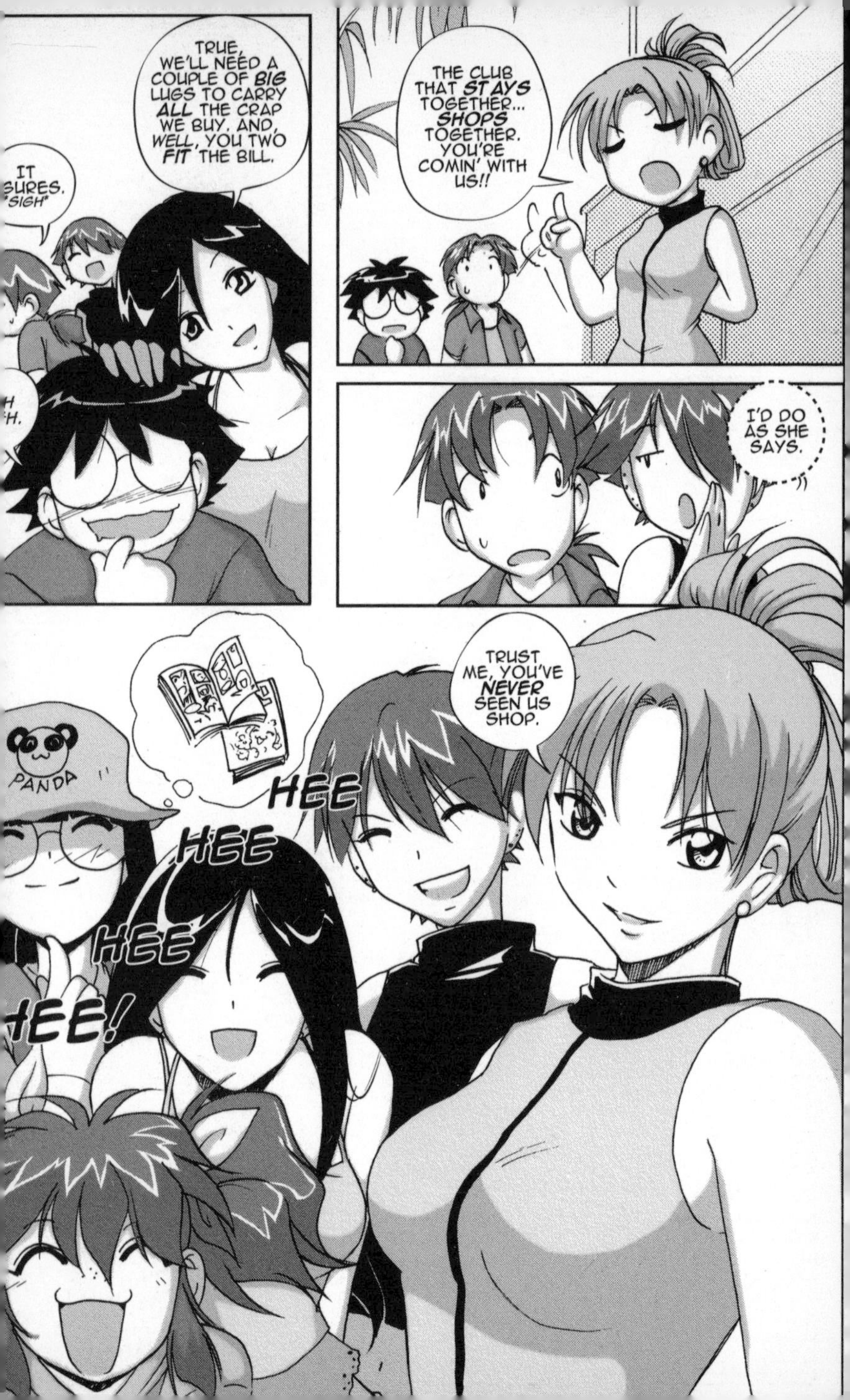
THE CLUB THAT STAYS TOGETHER... SHOPS TOGETHER. YOU'RE COMIN' WITH US!!
I'D DO AS SHE SAYS.
TRUE, WE'LL NEED A COUPLE OF BIG LUGS TO CARRY ALL THE CRAP WE BUY. AND, WELL, YOU TWO FIT THE BILL.
IT SURES. *SIGH*
TRUST ME, YOU'VE NEVER SEEN US SHOP.
PANDA
HEE
HEE
HEE
HEE!

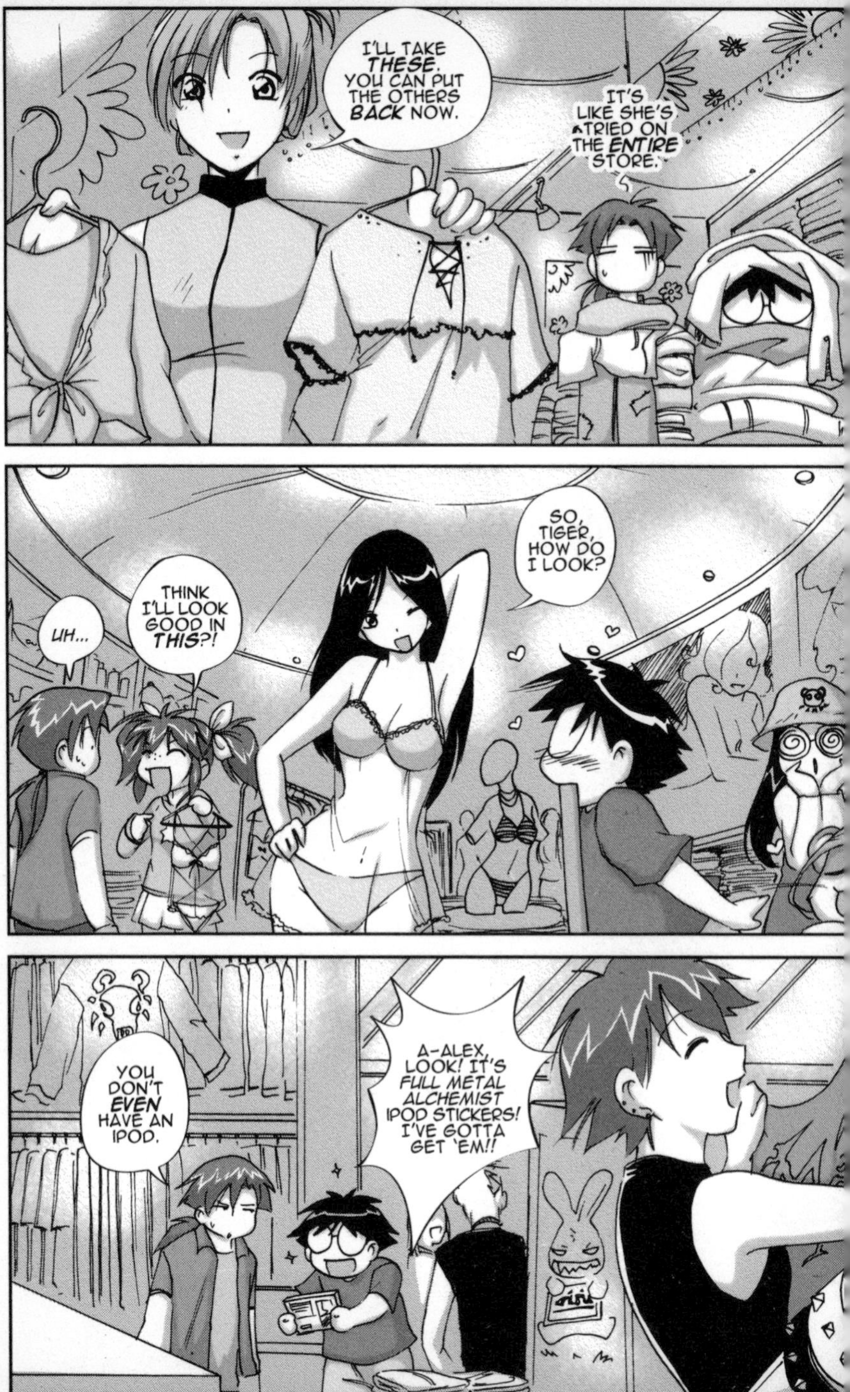
IT'S LIKE SHE'S TRIED ON THE ENTIRE STORE.
I'LL TAKE THESE. YOU CAN PUT THE OTHERS BACK NOW.
SO, TIGER, HOW DO I LOOK?
THINK I'LL LOOK GOOD IN THIS?!
UH...
A-ALEX, LOOK! IT'S FULL METAL ALCHEMIST IPOD STICKERS! I'VE GOTTA GET 'EM!!
YOU DON'T EVEN HAVE AN IPOD.

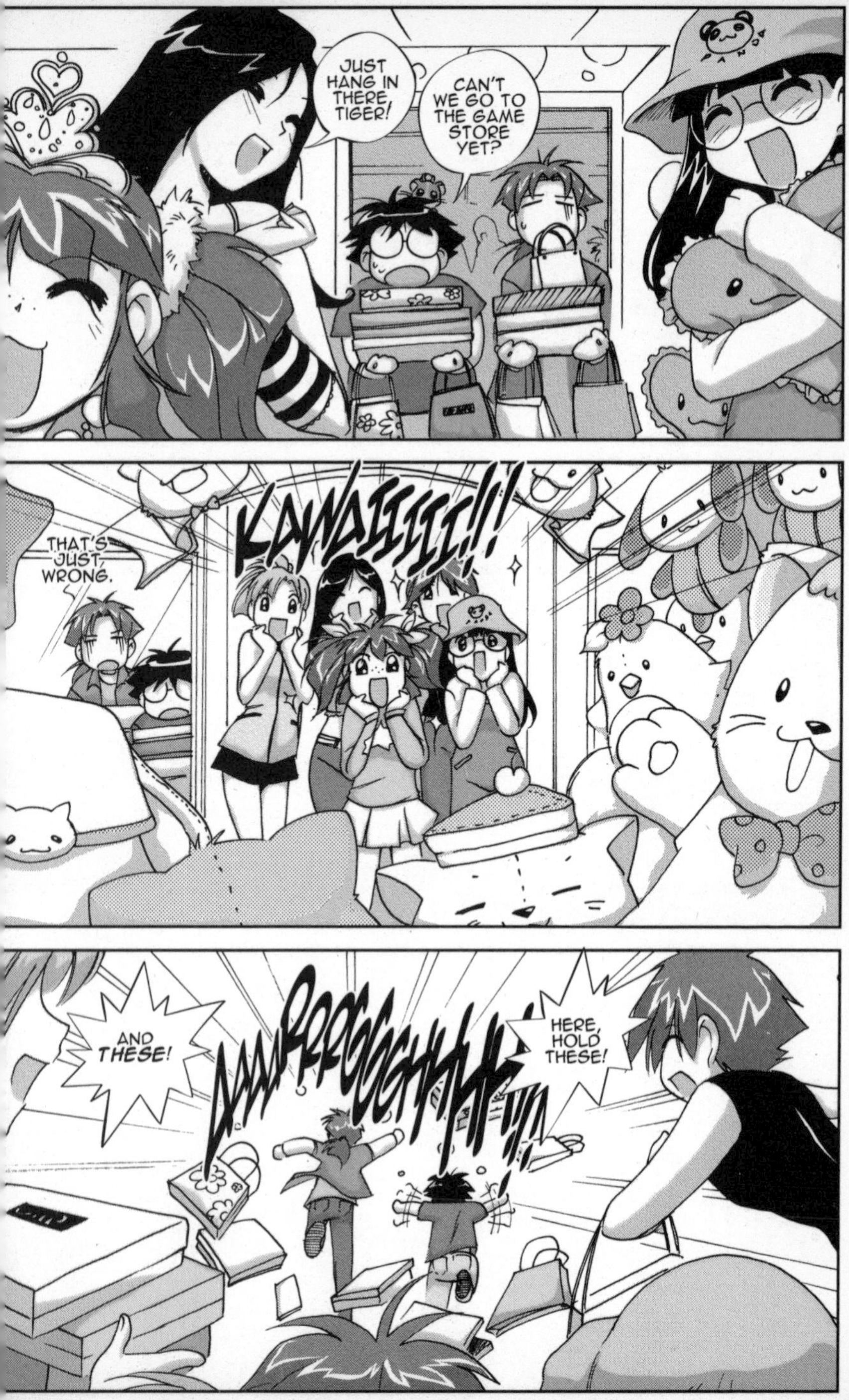
CAN'T WE GO TO THE GAME STORE YET?
JUST HANG IN THERE TIGER!
KAWAIIIIII!!!
THAT'S JUST WRONG.
HERE, HOLD THESE!
AND *THESE*!

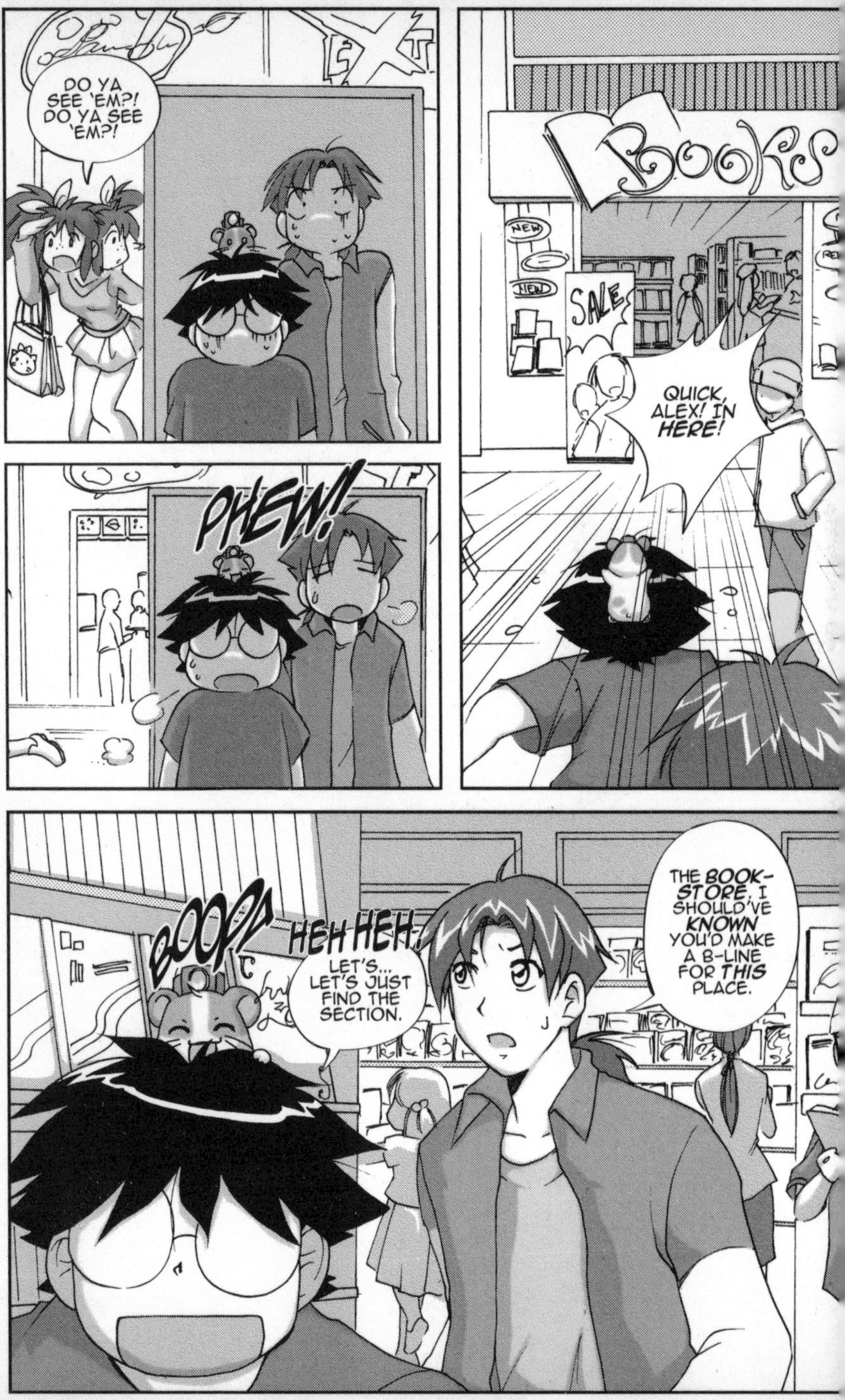
BOOKS
NEW
NEW
SALE
QUICK, ALEX! IN HERE!
DO YA SEE 'EM?! DO YA SEE 'EM?!
PHEW!
THE BOOK-STORE. I SHOULD'VE KNOWN YOU'D MAKE A B-LINE FOR THIS PLACE.
HEH HEH.
LET'S... LET'S JUST FIND THE SECTION.
BOOP

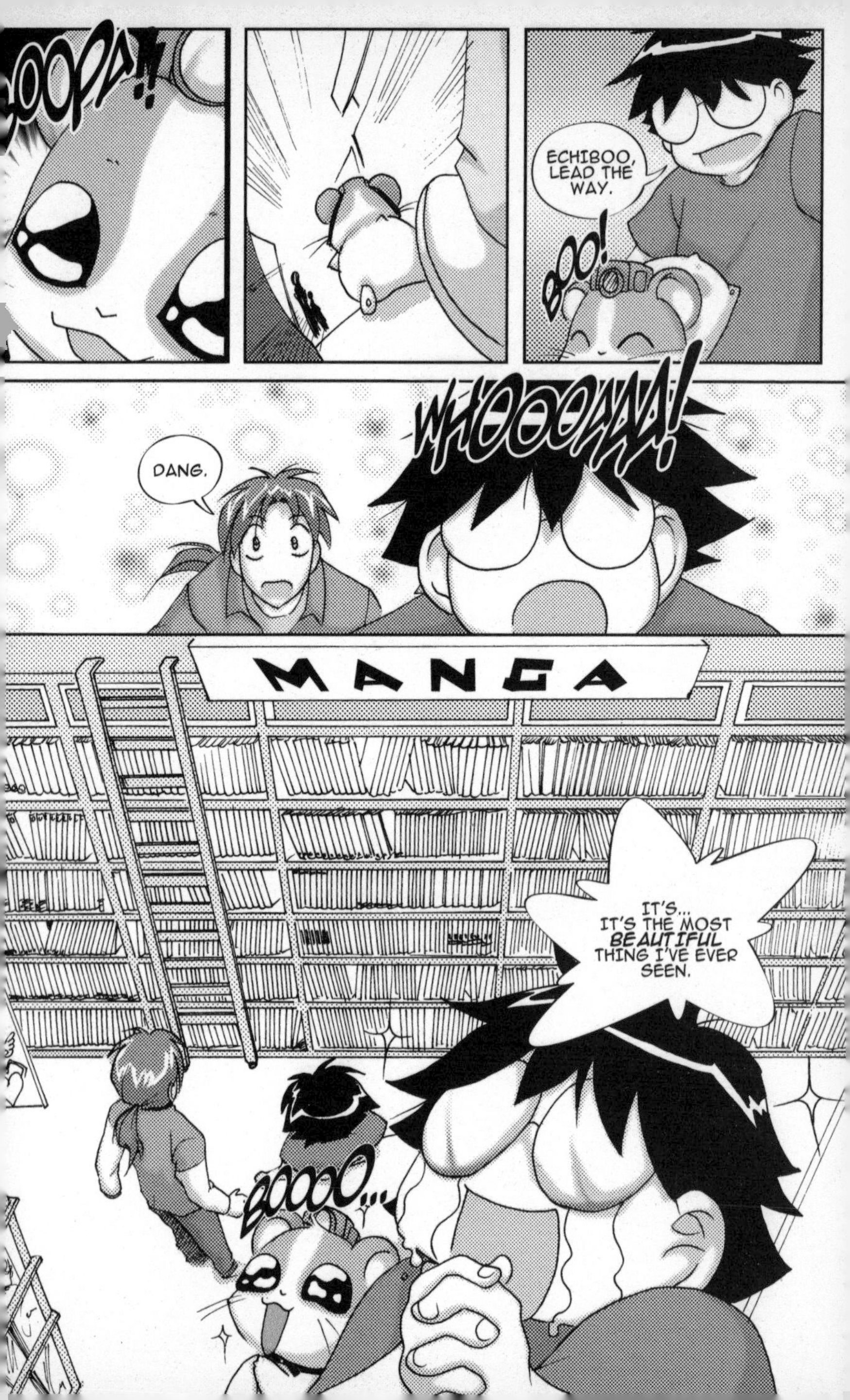
ECHIBOO, LEAD THE WAY.
BOO!
WHOOOM!
DANG.
MANGA
IT'S... IT'S THE MOST *BEAUTIFUL* THING I'VE EVER SEEN.
BOOOO...

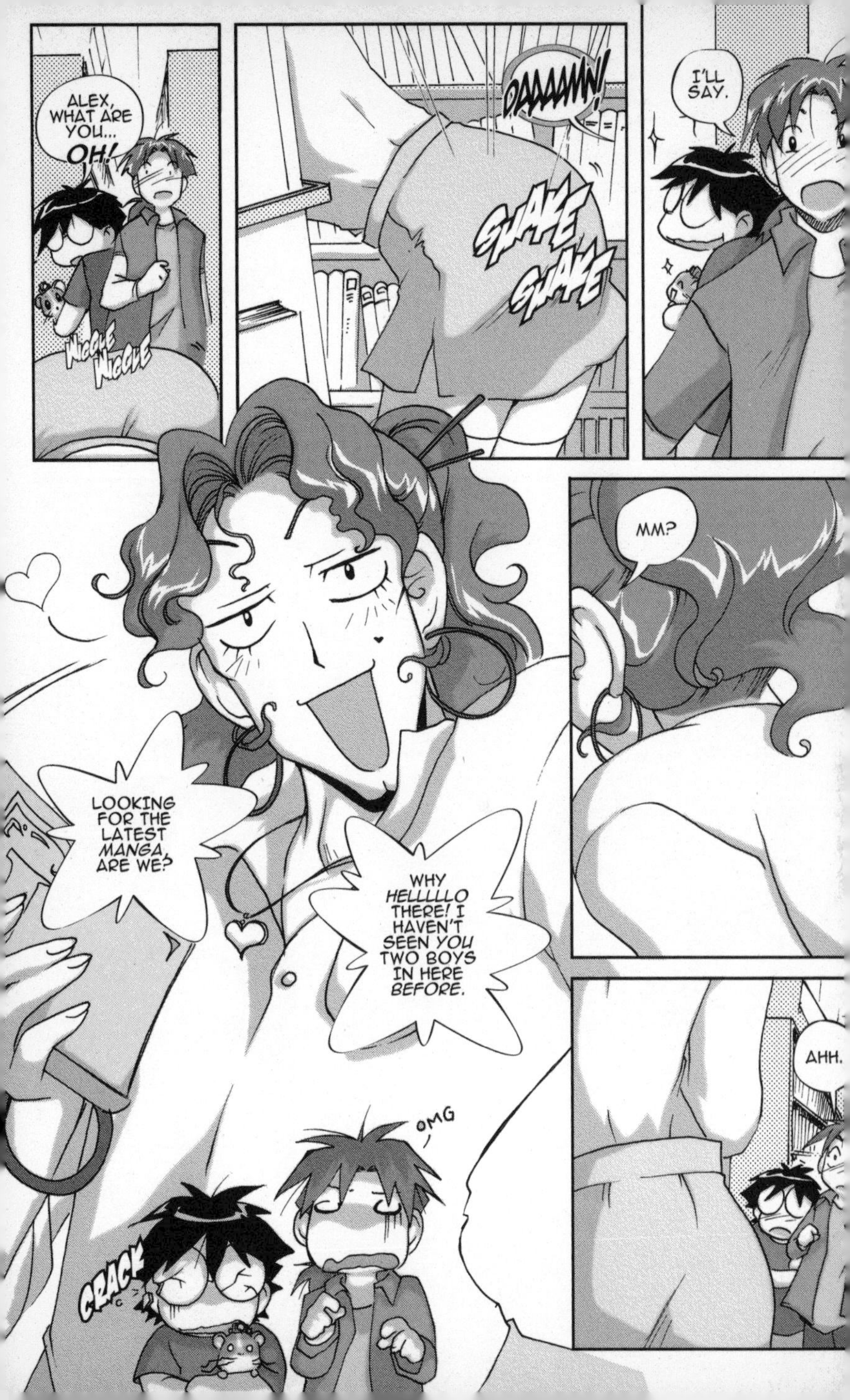
ALEX, WHAT ARE YOU... OH!
WIGGLE WIGGLE
DAAAAMN!
SHAKE SHAKE
I'LL SAY.
MM?
AHH.
WHY HELLLLLLO THERE! I HAVEN'T SEEN YOU TWO BOYS IN HERE BEFORE.
LOOKING FOR THE LATEST MANGA ARE WE?
OMG
CRACK

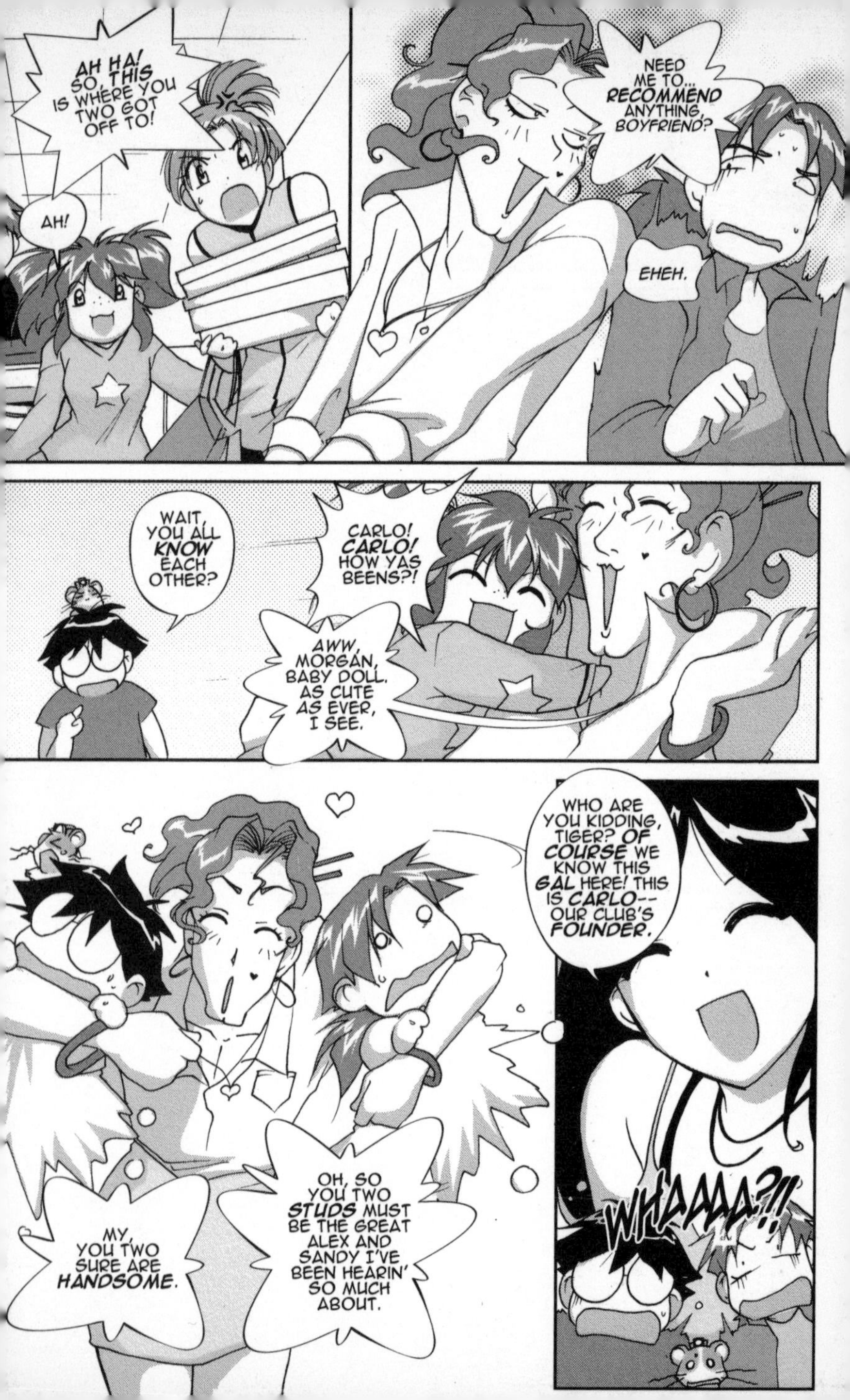
NEED ME TO... RECOMMEND ANYTHING, BOYFRIEND?
EHEH.
AH HA! SO, THIS IS WHERE YOU TWO GOT OFF TO!
AH!
CARLO! CARLO! HOW YAS BEENS?!
AWW, MORGAN, BABY DOLL. AS CUTE AS EVER, I SEE.
WAIT, YOU ALL KNOW EACH OTHER?
WHO ARE YOU KIDDING, TIGER? OF COURSE WE KNOW THIS GAL HERE! THIS IS CARLO-- OUR CLUB'S FOUNDER.
WHAAAA?!!
OH, SO YOU TWO STUDS MUST BE THE GREAT ALEX AND SANDY I'VE BEEN HEARIN' SO MUCH ABOUT.
MY, YOU TWO SURE ARE HANDSOME.

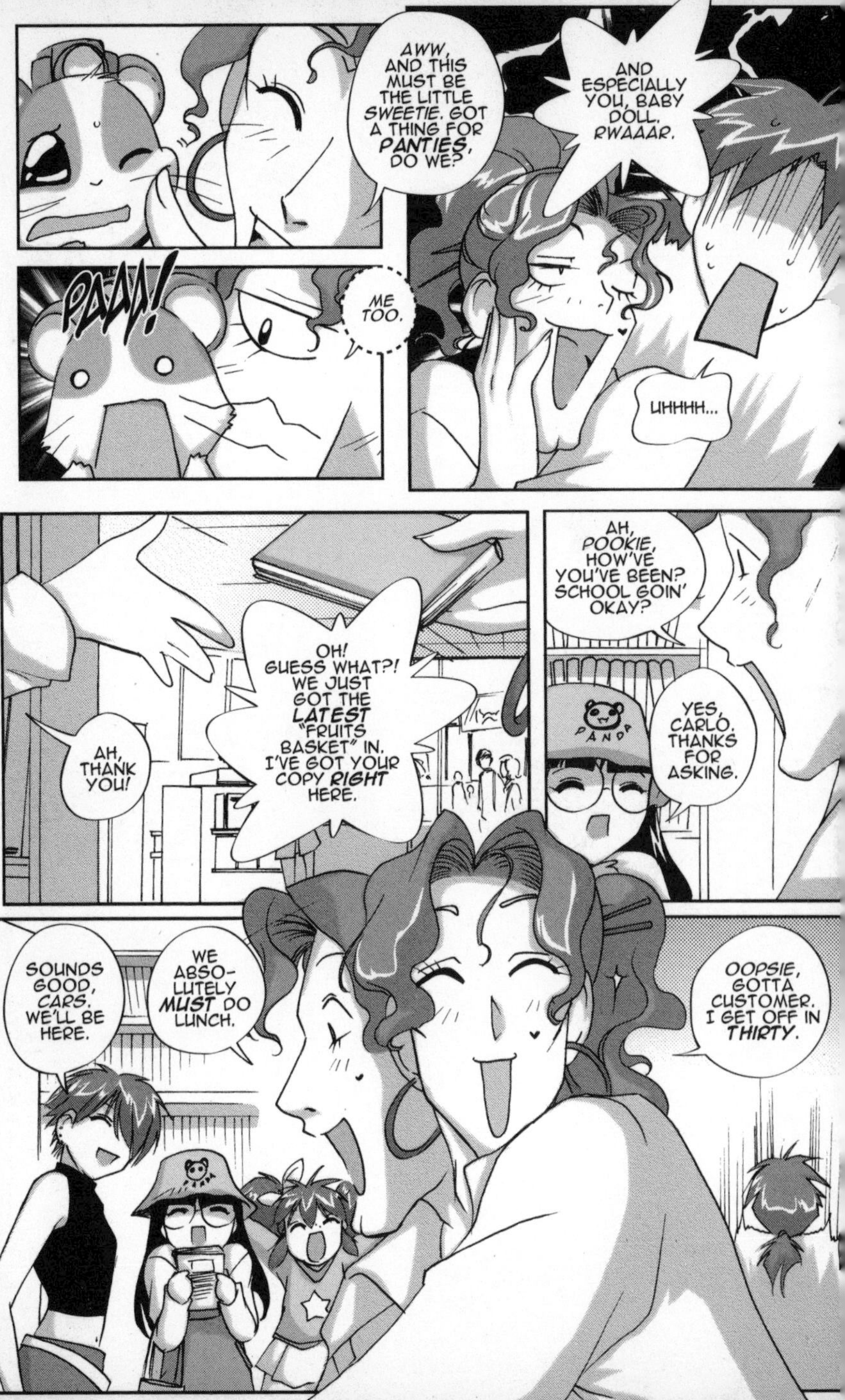
AND ESPECIALLY YOU, BABY DOLL. RWAAAR.
UHHHH...
AWW, AND THIS MUST BE THE LITTLE *SWEETIE*. GOT A THING FOR ***PANTIES***, DO WE?
PAAA!
ME TOO.
AH, *POOKIE*, HOW'VE YOU'VE BEEN? SCHOOL GOIN' OKAY?
YES, CARLO. THANKS FOR ASKING.
OH! GUESS WHAT?! WE JUST GOT THE ***LATEST*** "FRUITS BASKET" IN. I'VE GOT YOUR COPY ***RIGHT*** HERE.
AH, THANK YOU!
OOPSIE, GOTTA CUSTOMER. I GET OFF IN ***THIRTY***.
WE ABSO-LUTELY ***MUST*** DO LUNCH.
SOUNDS GOOD, CARS. WE'LL BE HERE.

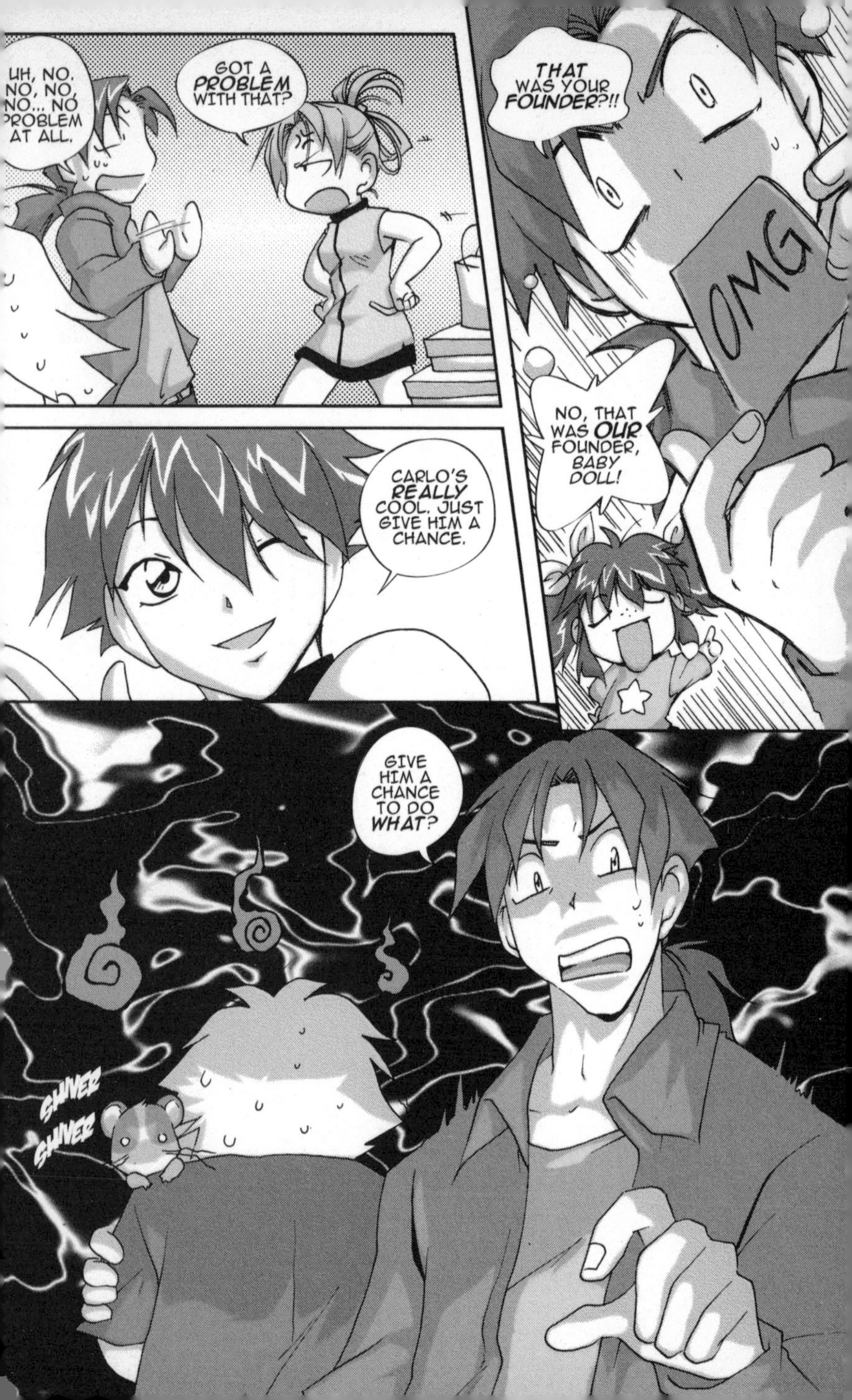
THAT WAS YOUR FOUNDER?!!
OMG
NO, THAT WAS OUR FOUNDER, BABY DOLL!
GOT A PROBLEM WITH THAT?
UH, NO. NO, NO, NO... NO PROBLEM AT ALL.
CARLO'S REALLY COOL. JUST GIVE HIM A CHANCE.
GIVE HIM A CHANCE TO DO WHAT?
SHIVER
SHIVER

EPISODE 6: FOOD COURTIN'

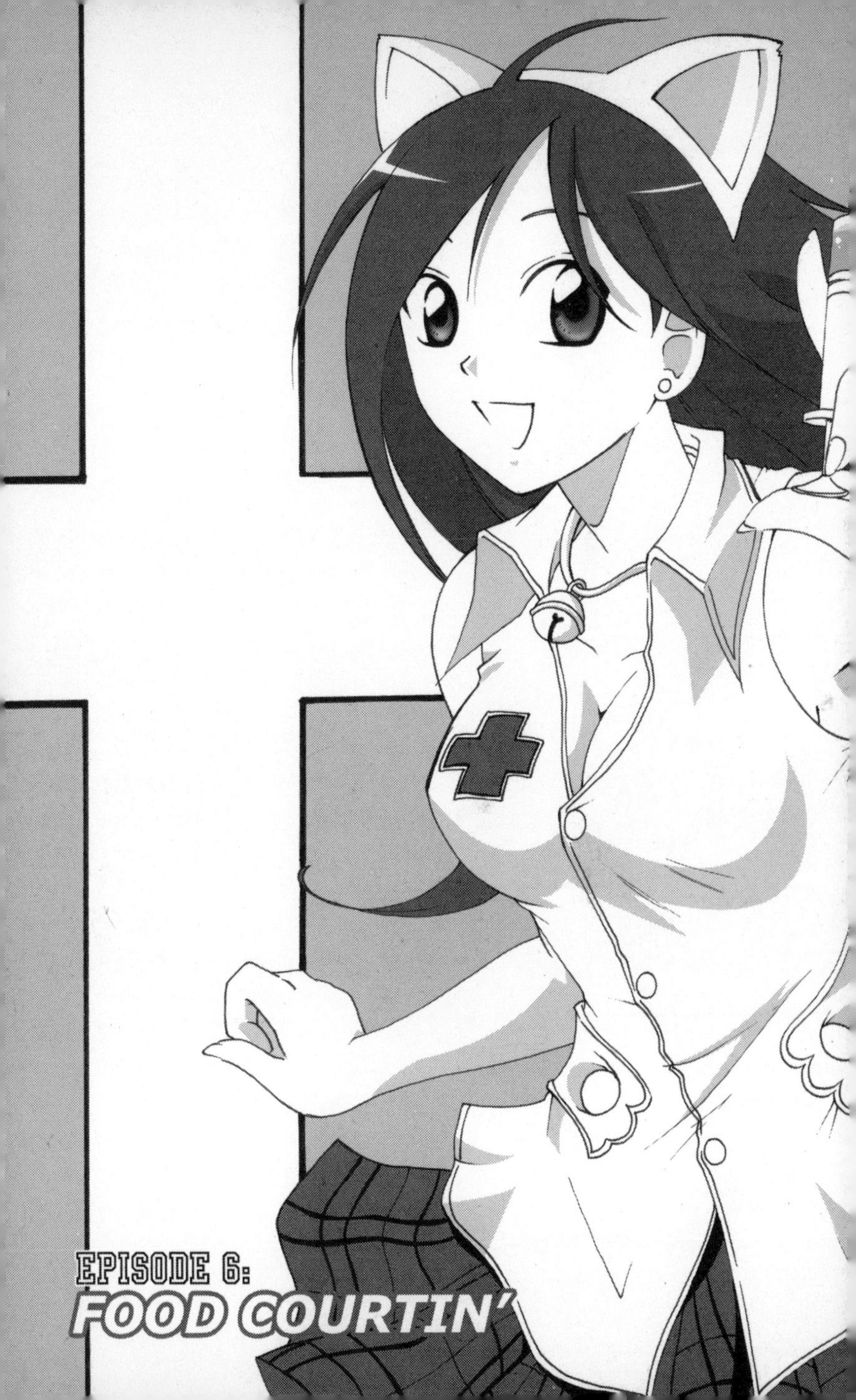

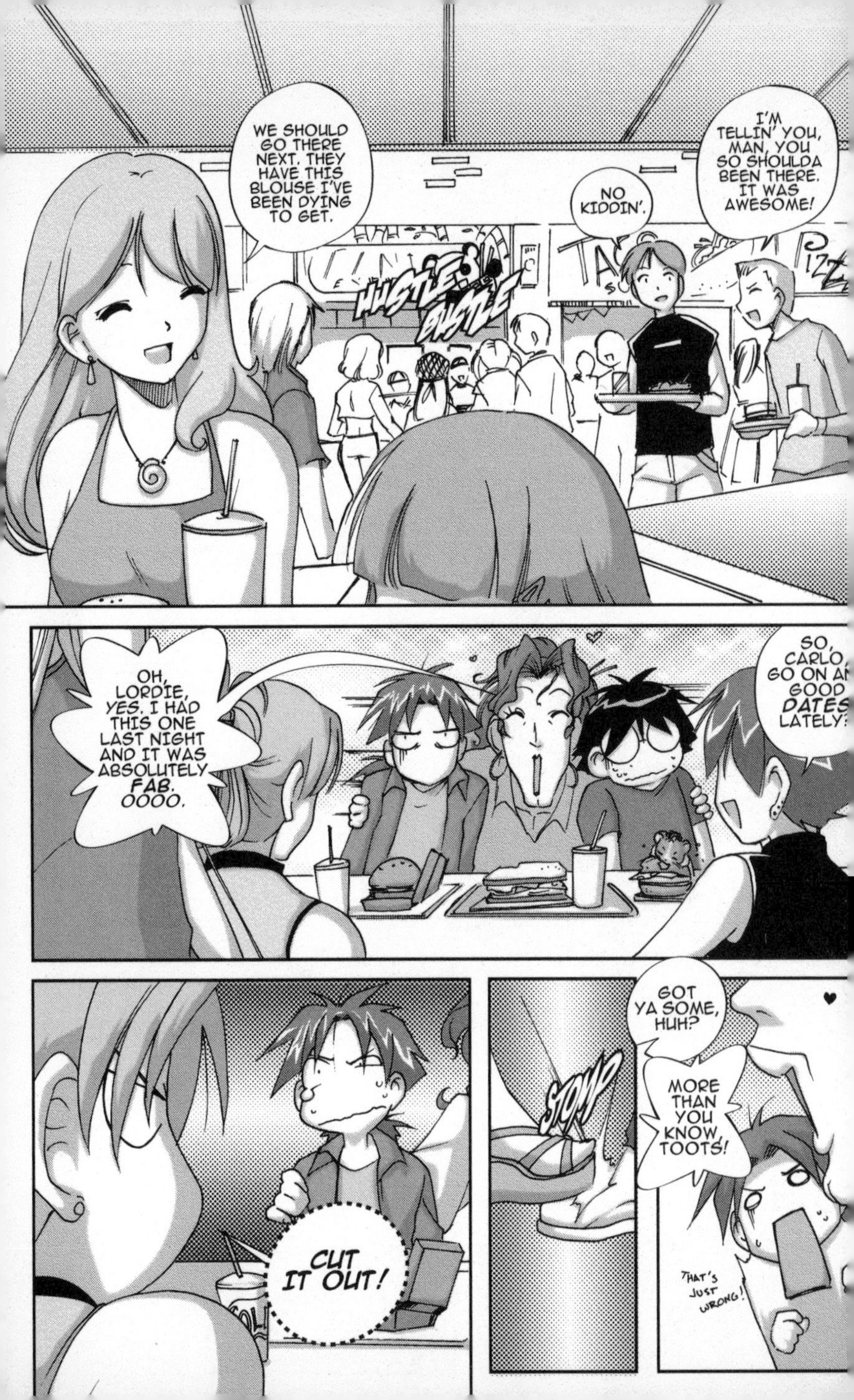
I'M TELLIN' YOU, MAN, YOU SO SHOULDA BEEN THERE. IT WAS AWESOME!
NO KIDDIN'.
WE SHOULD GO THERE NEXT. THEY HAVE THIS BLOUSE I'VE BEEN DYING TO GET.
HUSTLE BUSTLE
SO, CARLO GO ON AN GOOD DATES LATELY?
OH, LORDIE, YES. I HAD THIS ONE LAST NIGHT AND IT WAS ABSOLUTELY FAB. OOOO.
GOT YA SOME, HUH?
STOMP
MORE THAN YOU KNOW, TOOTS!
THAT'S JUST WRONG!
CUT IT OUT!

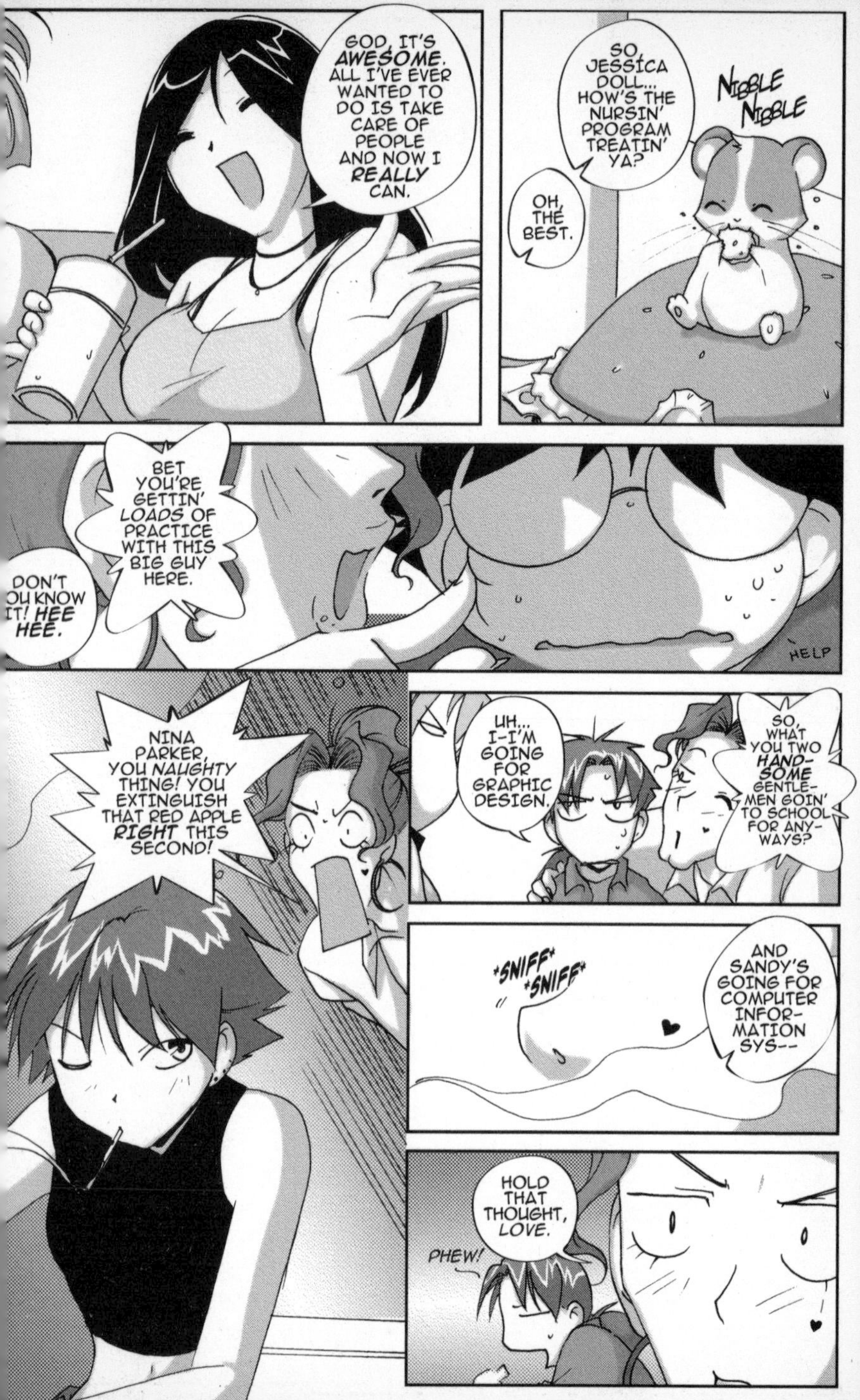

SO, JESSICA DOLL... HOW'S THE NURSIN' PROGRAM TREATIN' YA?
NIBBLE NIBBLE
OH, THE BEST.
GOD, IT'S AWESOME. ALL I'VE EVER WANTED TO DO IS TAKE CARE OF PEOPLE AND NOW I REALLY CAN.
BET YOU'RE GETTIN' LOADS OF PRACTICE WITH THIS BIG GUY HERE.
DON'T OU KNOW IT! HEE HEE.
HELP
SO, WHAT YOU TWO HANDSOME GENTLEMEN GOIN' TO SCHOOL FOR ANYWAYS?
UH... I-I'M GOING FOR GRAPHIC DESIGN.
AND SANDY'S GOING FOR COMPUTER INFORMATION SYS--
SNIFF *SNIFF*
HOLD THAT THOUGHT, LOVE.
PHEW!
NINA PARKER, YOU NAUGHTY THING! YOU EXTINGUISH THAT RED APPLE RIGHT THIS SECOND!

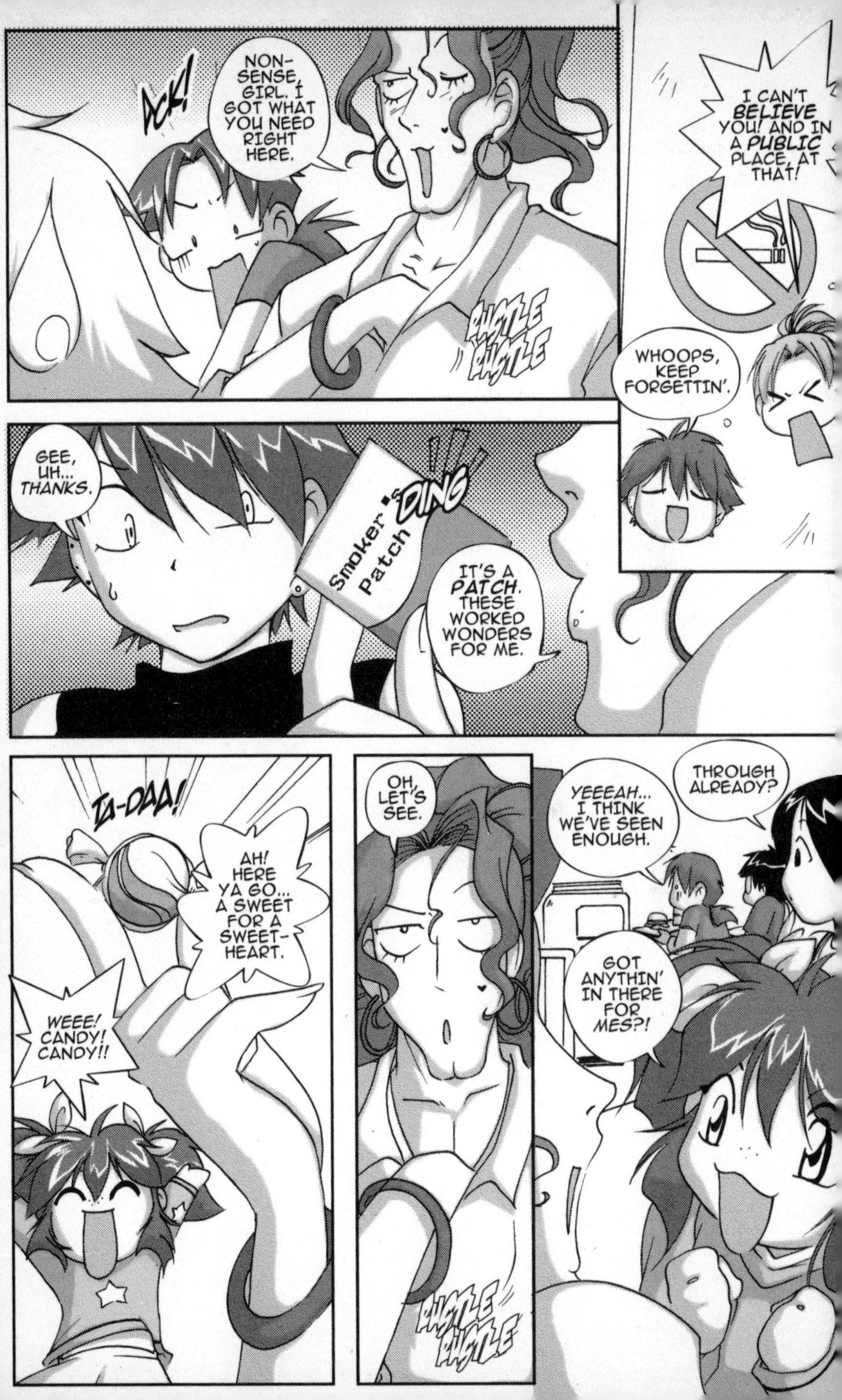
I CAN'T BELIEVE YOU! AND IN A PUBLIC PLACE, AT THAT!
WHOOPS, KEEP FORGETTIN'.
ACK!
NON-SENSE, GIRL. I GOT WHAT YOU NEED RIGHT HERE.
RUSTLE RUSTLE
DING
GEE, UH... THANKS.
Smoker's Patch
IT'S A PATCH. THESE WORKED WONDERS FOR ME.
THROUGH ALREADY?
YEEEAH... I THINK WE'VE SEEN ENOUGH.
GOT ANYTHIN' IN THERE FOR MES?!
OH, LET'S SEE.
RUSTLE RUSTLE
TA-DAA!
AH! HERE YA GO... A SWEET FOR A SWEET-HEART.
WEEE! CANDY! CANDY!!

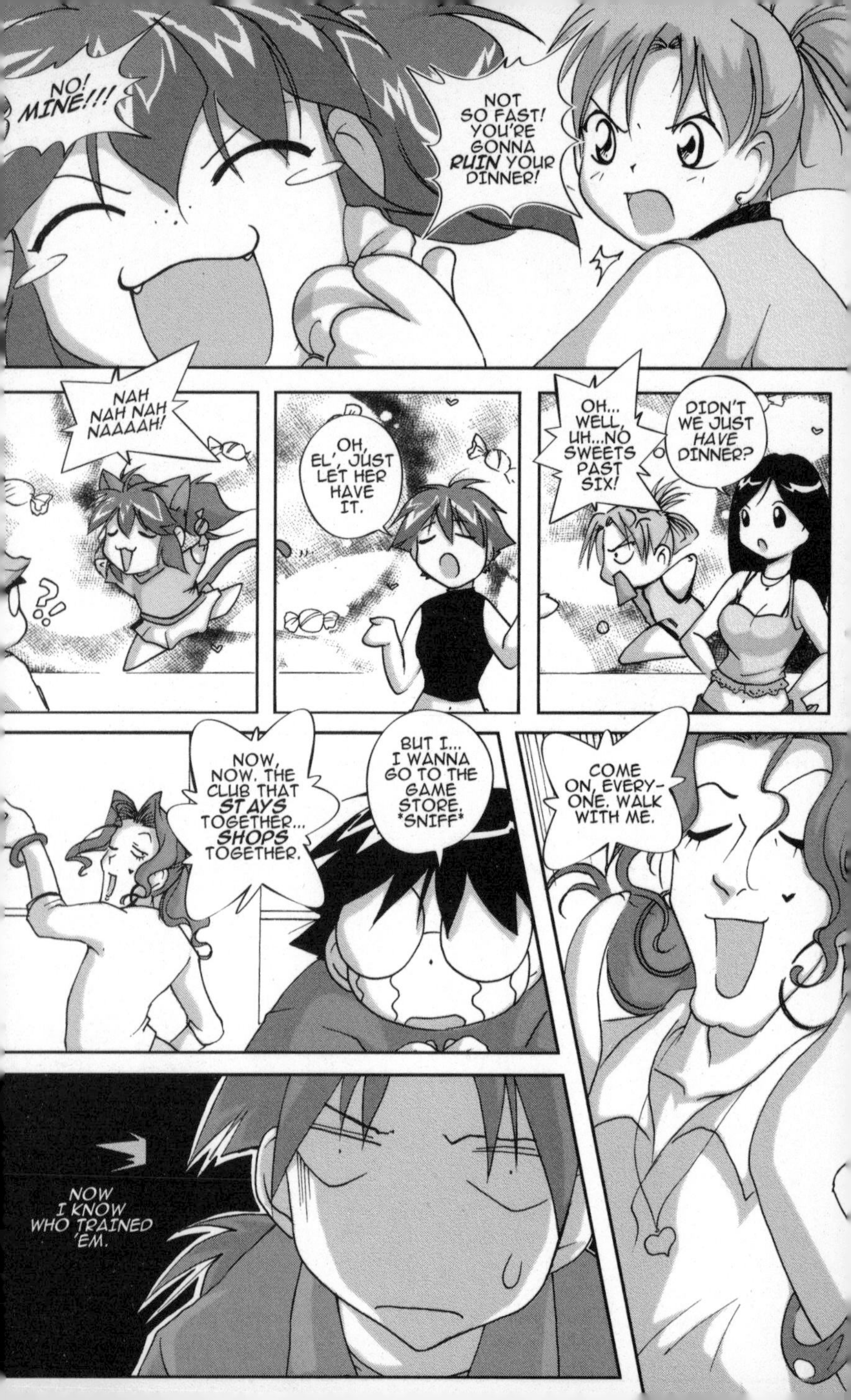
NOT SO FAST! YOU'RE GONNA *RUIN* YOUR DINNER!
NO! *MINE!!!*
DIDN'T WE JUST *HAVE* DINNER?
OH... WELL, UH...NO SWEETS PAST SIX!
OH, EL', JUST LET HER HAVE IT.
NAH NAH NAH NAAAAH!
COME ON, EVERY-ONE. WALK WITH ME.
BUT I... I WANNA GO TO THE GAME STORE. *SNIFF*
NOW, NOW. THE CLUB THAT ***STAYS*** TOGETHER... ***SHOPS*** TOGETHER.
NOW I KNOW WHO TRAINED 'EM.

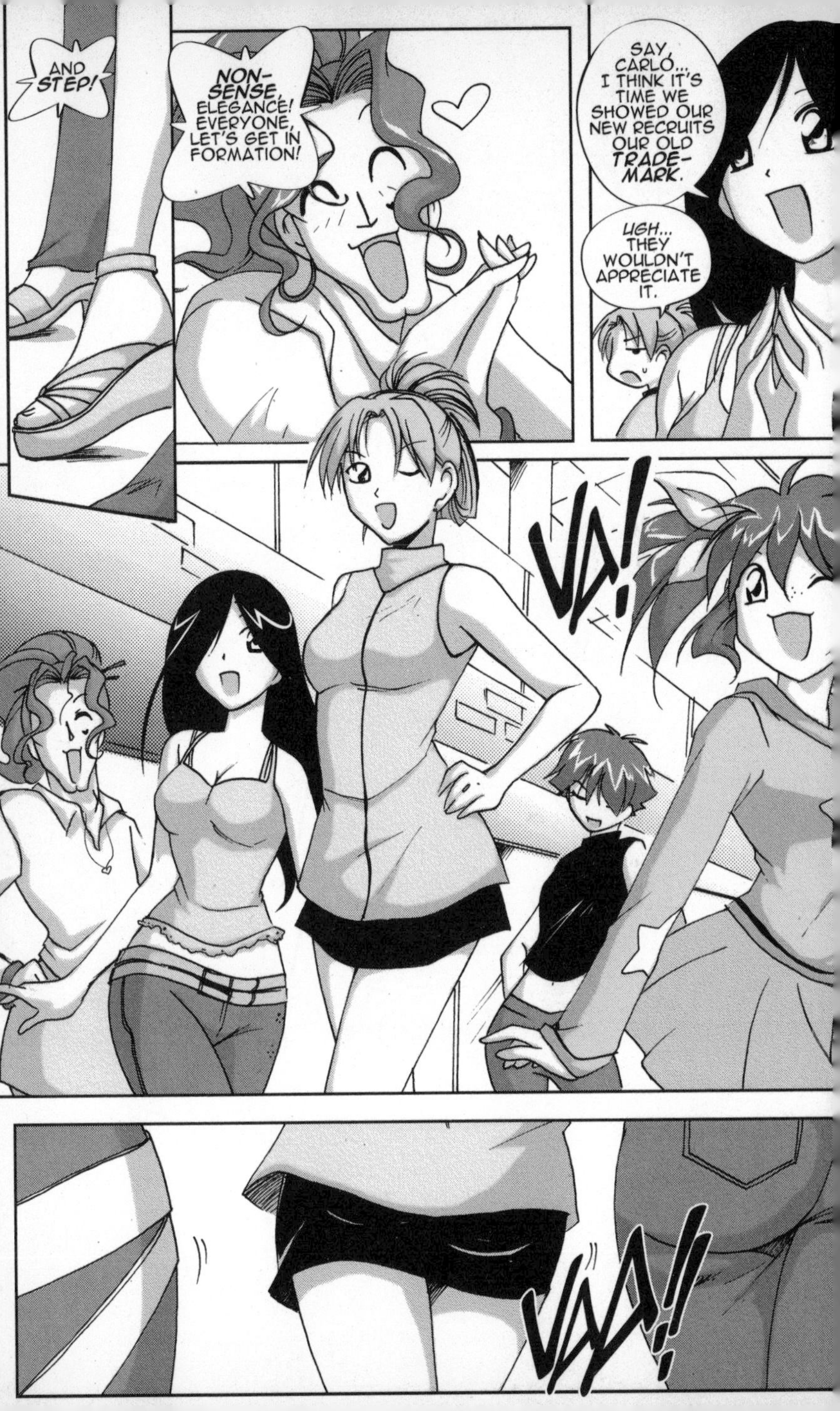
SAY, CARLO... I THINK IT'S TIME WE SHOWED OUR NEW RECRUITS OUR OLD TRADE-MARK.
UGH... THEY WOULDN'T APPRECIATE IT.
NON-SENSE, ELEGANCE! EVERYONE, LET'S GET IN FORMATION!
AND STEP!
VA!
VAA!!

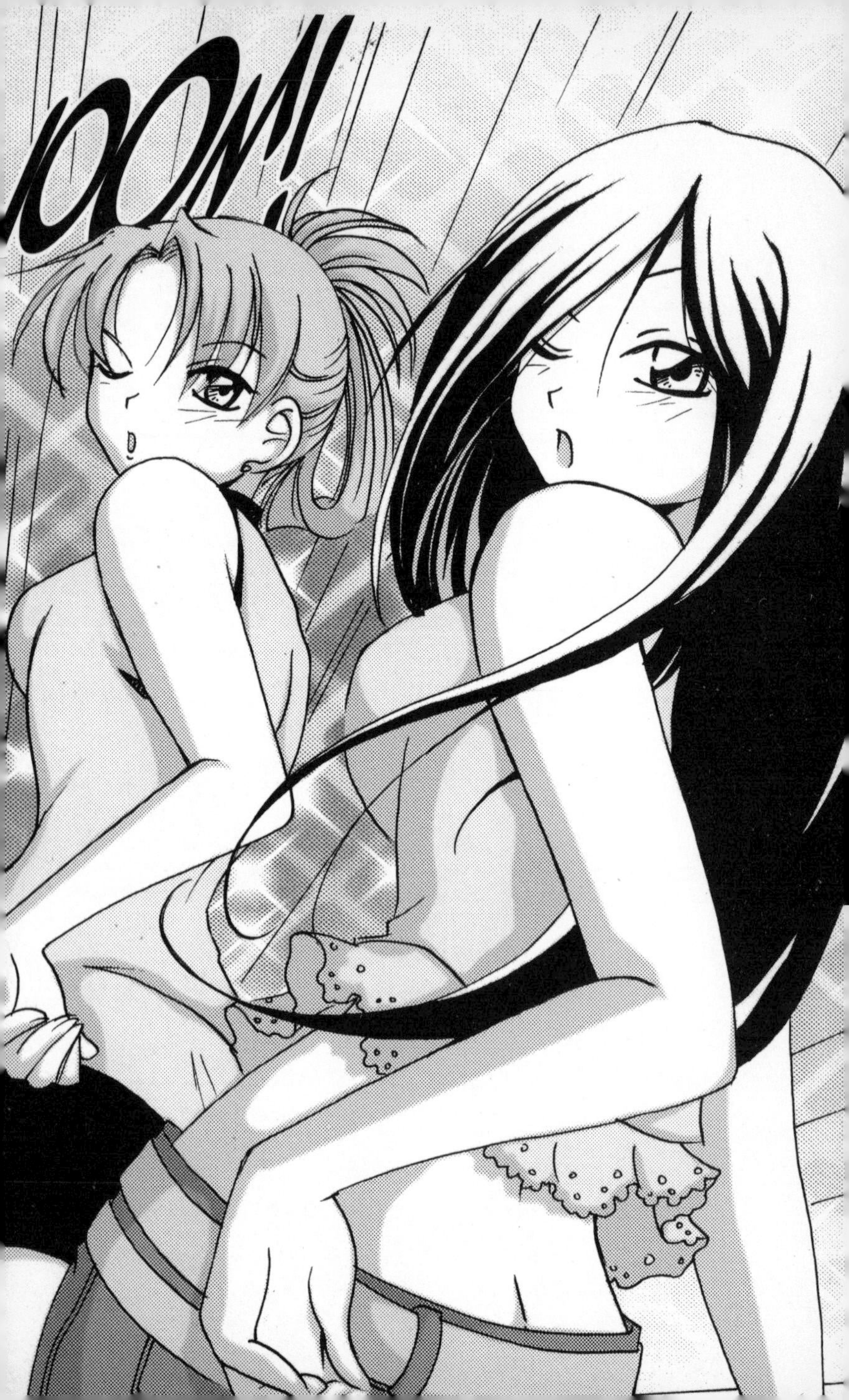
OOM!

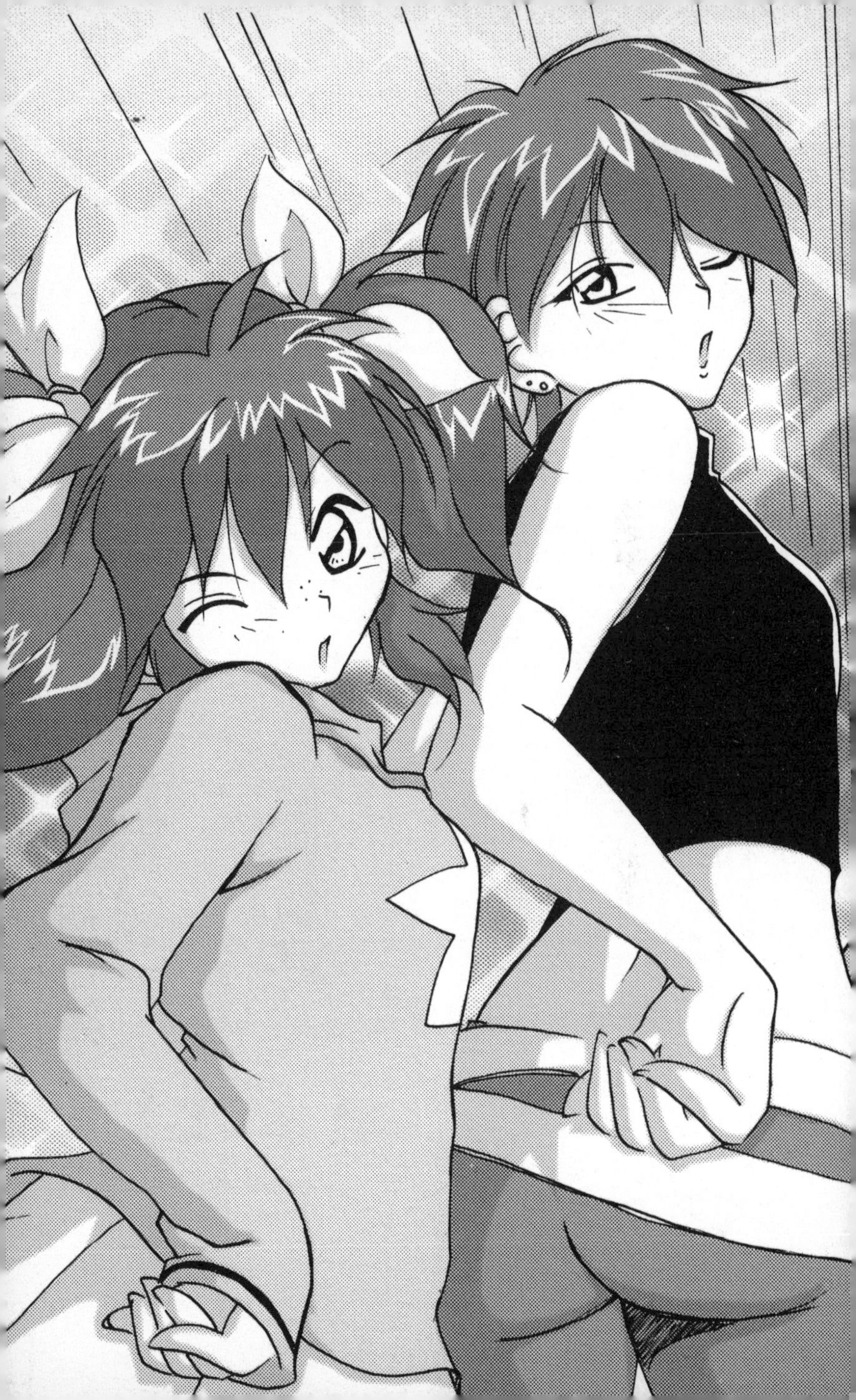

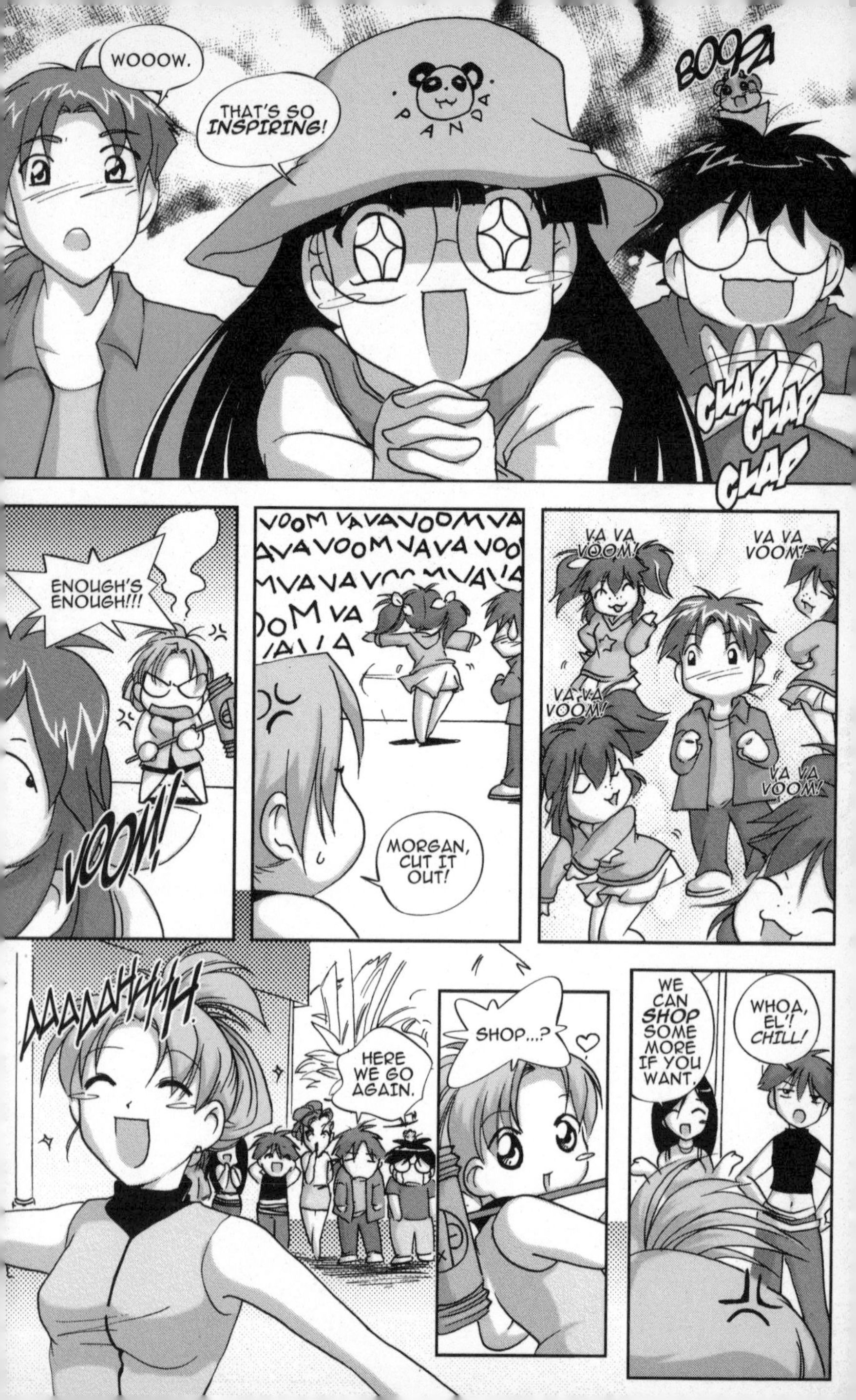
BOOP!
WOOOW.
THAT'S SO INSPIRING!
CLAP CLAP CLAP
VA VA VOOM!
VA VA VOOM!
VA VA VOOM!
VA VA VOOM!
VOOM VAVAVOOM VA
VAVAVOOM VAVA VOO
MVAVAVOOMVAVA
OOM VA
VAVA
MORGAN, CUT IT OUT!
ENOUGH'S ENOUGH!!!
VOOM!
WHOA, EL! CHILL!
WE CAN SHOP SOME MORE IF YOU WANT.
SHOP...?
HERE WE GO AGAIN.
AAAAHHHH.

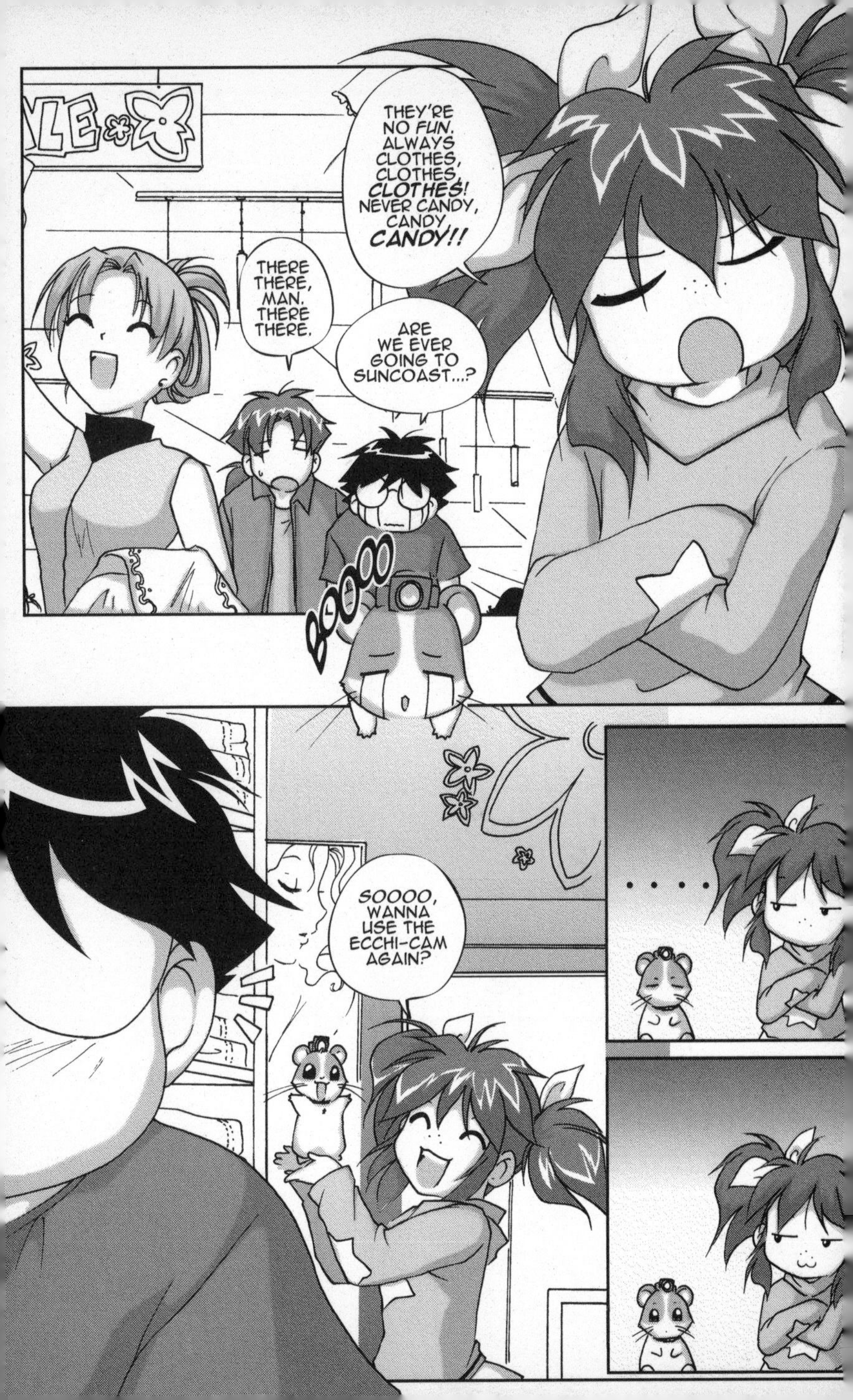
THEY'RE NO FUN. ALWAYS CLOTHES, CLOTHES, CLOTHES! NEVER CANDY, CANDY, CANDY!!
ARE WE EVER GOING TO SUNCOAST...?
THERE THERE, MAN. THERE THERE.
BOOOO
....
SOOOO, WANNA USE THE ECCHI-CAM AGAIN?

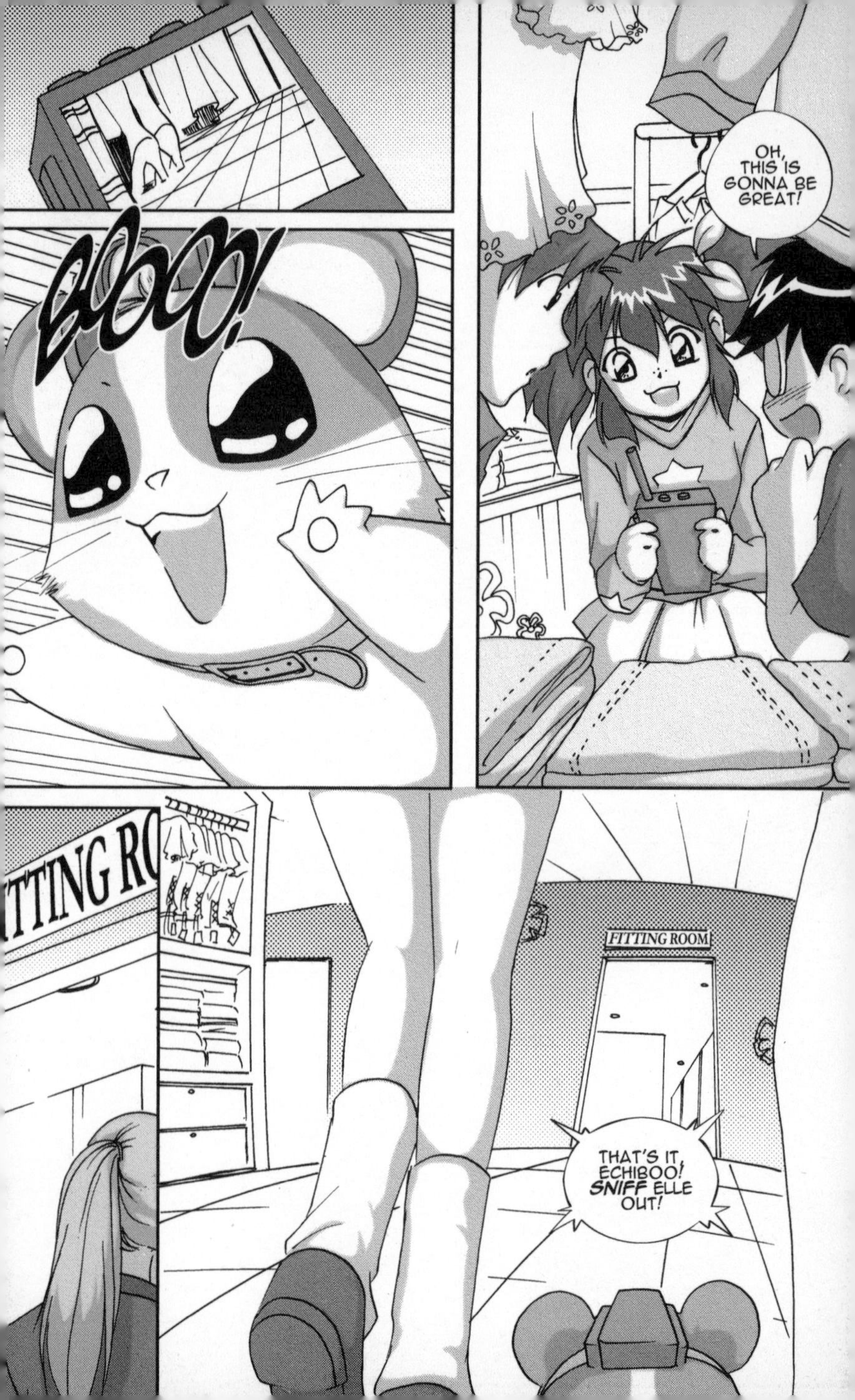
OH, THIS IS GONNA BE GREAT!
BOOO!
FITTING ROOM
THAT'S IT, ECHIBOO! SNIFF ELLE OUT!
FITTING RO

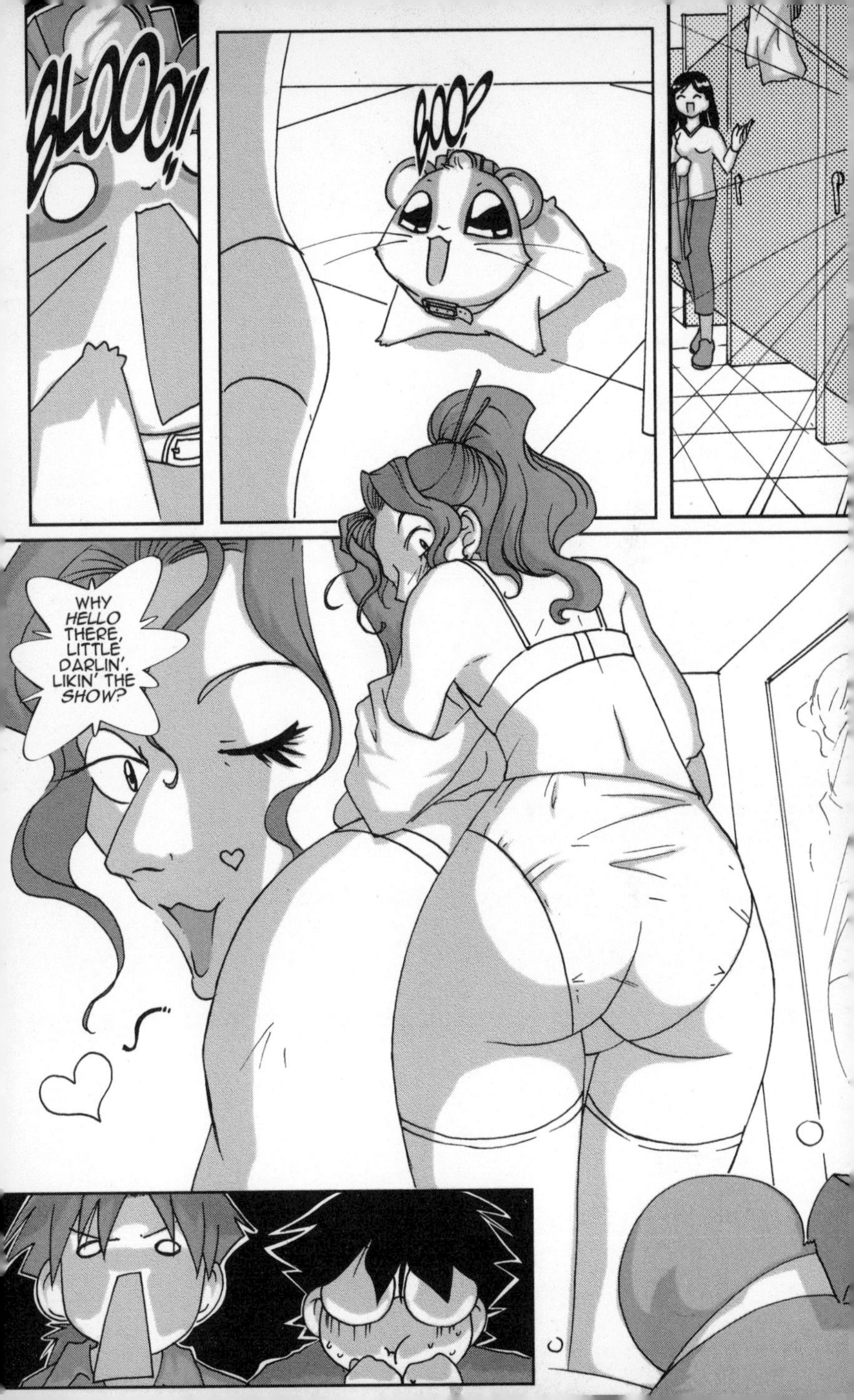
BOO?
BLOOO!!
WHY HELLO THERE, LITTLE DARLIN'. LIKIN' THE SHOW?

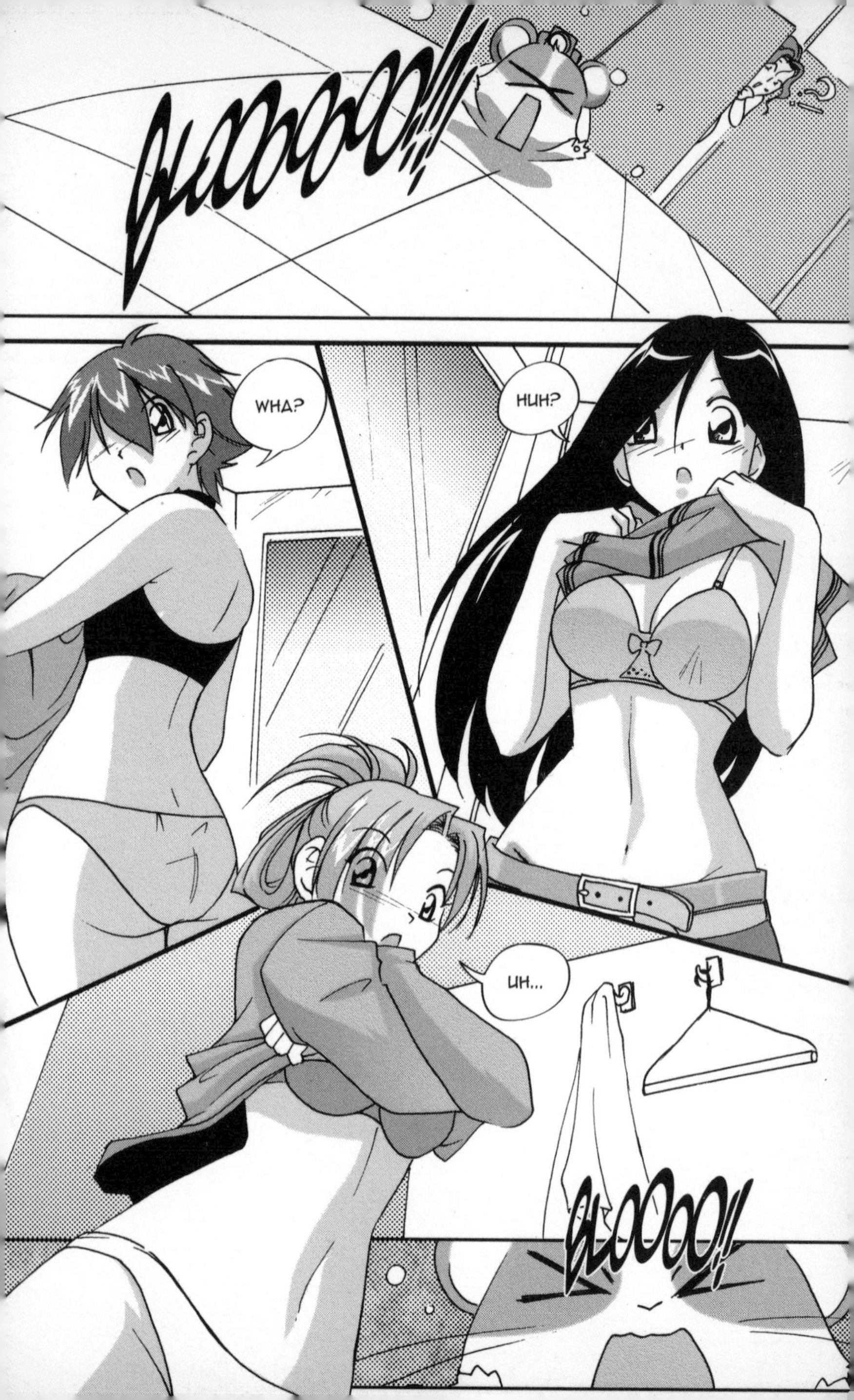
GUOOOO!!!
HUH?
WHA?
UH...
GUOOO!!

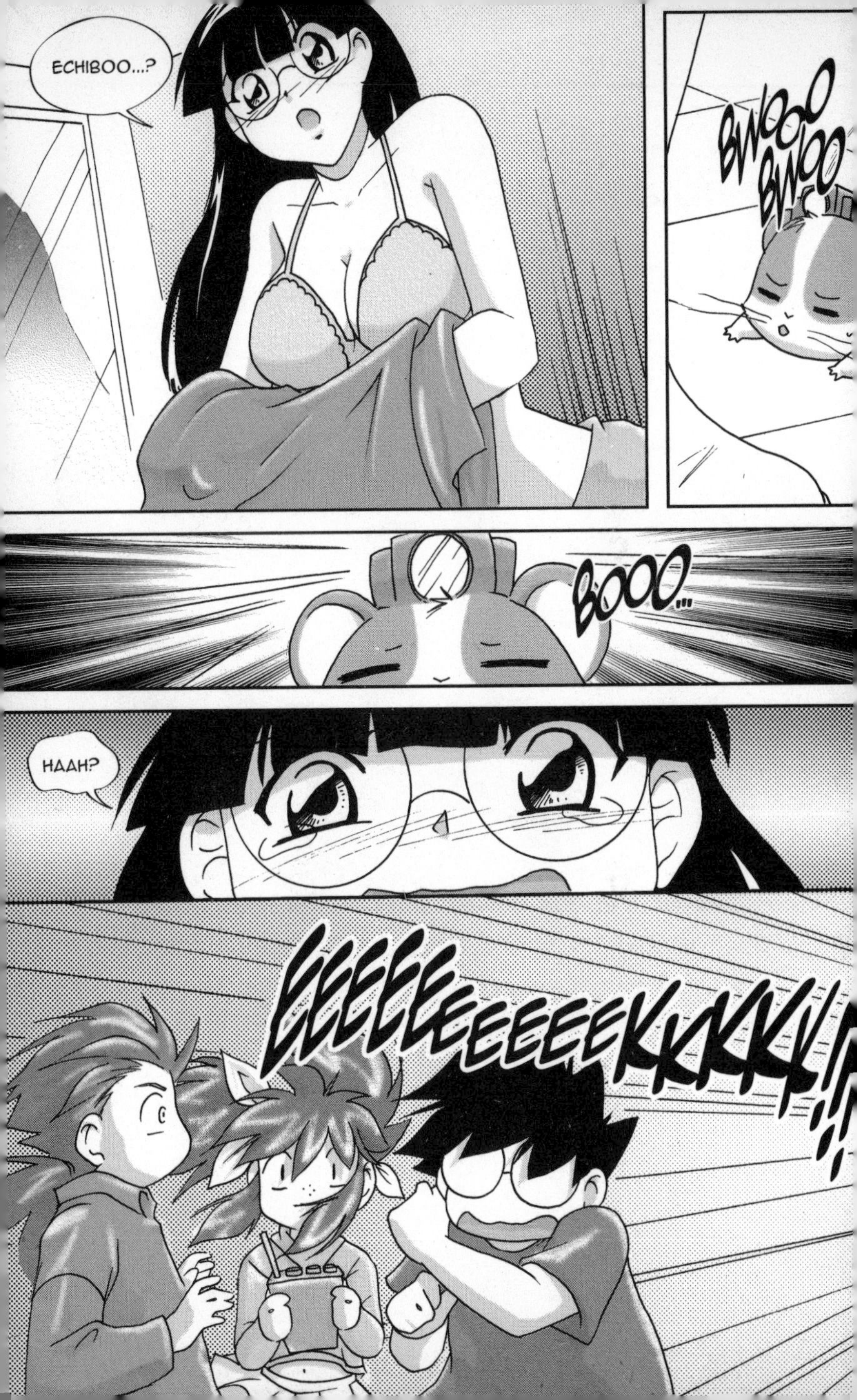
BWOOO
BWOO
BWOO
ECHIBOO...?
BOOO...
HAAH?
EEEEEEEEEEEKKKK!!!

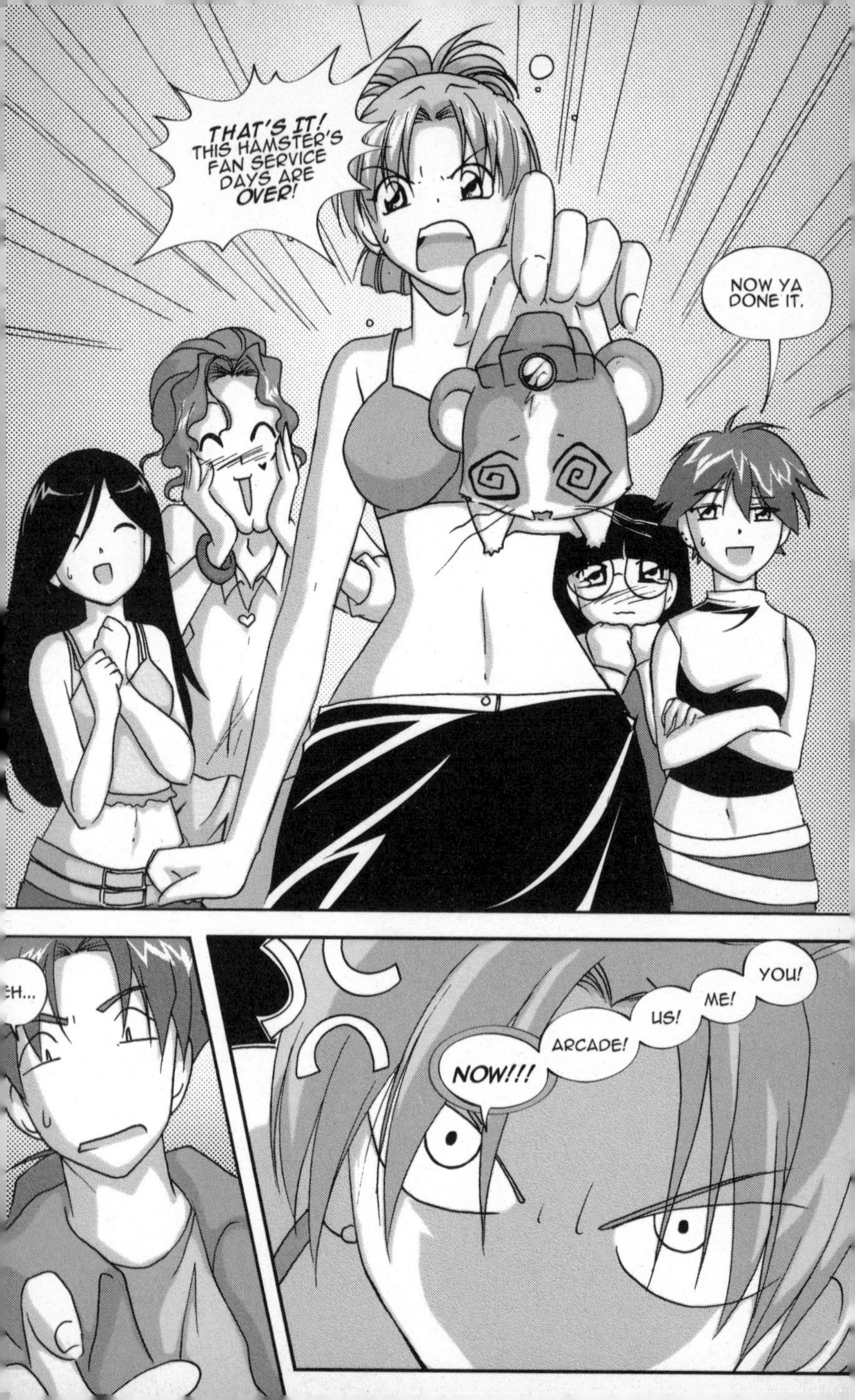
THAT'S IT! THIS HAMSTER'S FAN SERVICE DAYS ARE OVER!
NOW YA DONE IT.
YOU!
ME!
US!
ARCADE!
NOW!!!
H...

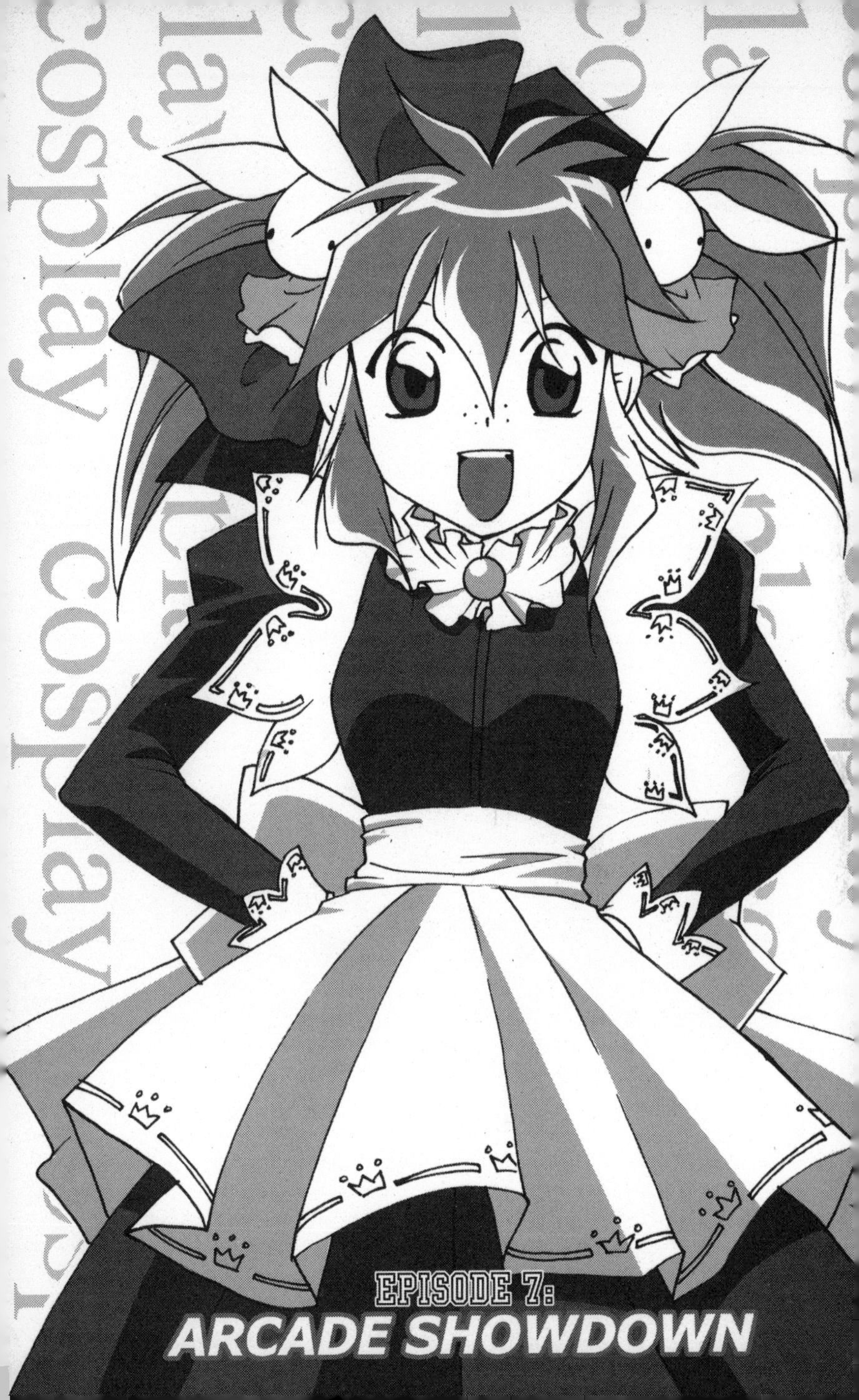

EPISODE 7: ARCADE SHOWDOWN

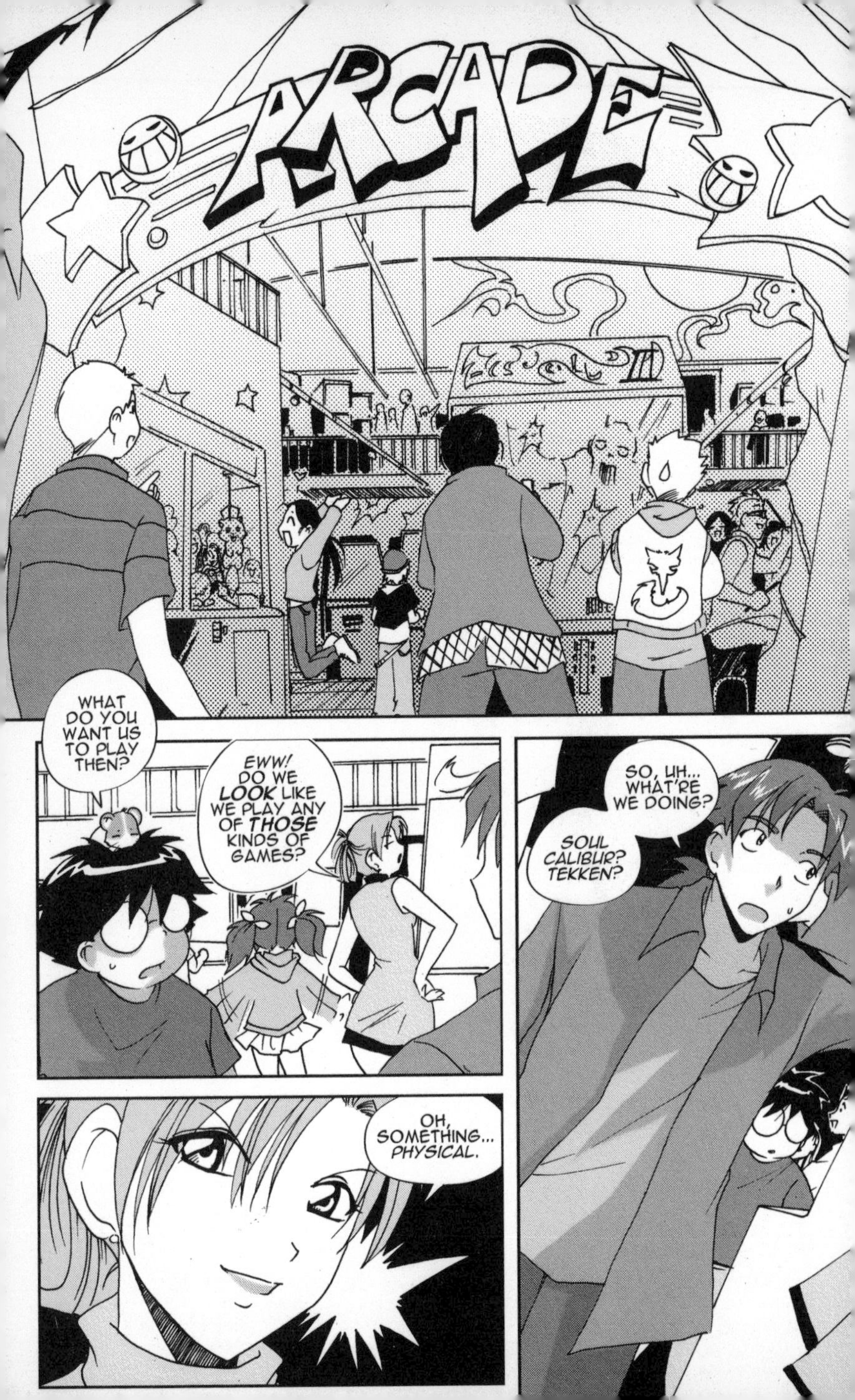
ARCADE
SO, UH... WHAT'RE WE DOING?
SOUL CALIBUR? TEKKEN?
EWW! DO WE **LOOK** LIKE WE PLAY ANY OF **THOSE** KINDS OF GAMES?
WHAT DO YOU WANT US TO PLAY THEN?
OH, SOMETHING... PHYSICAL.

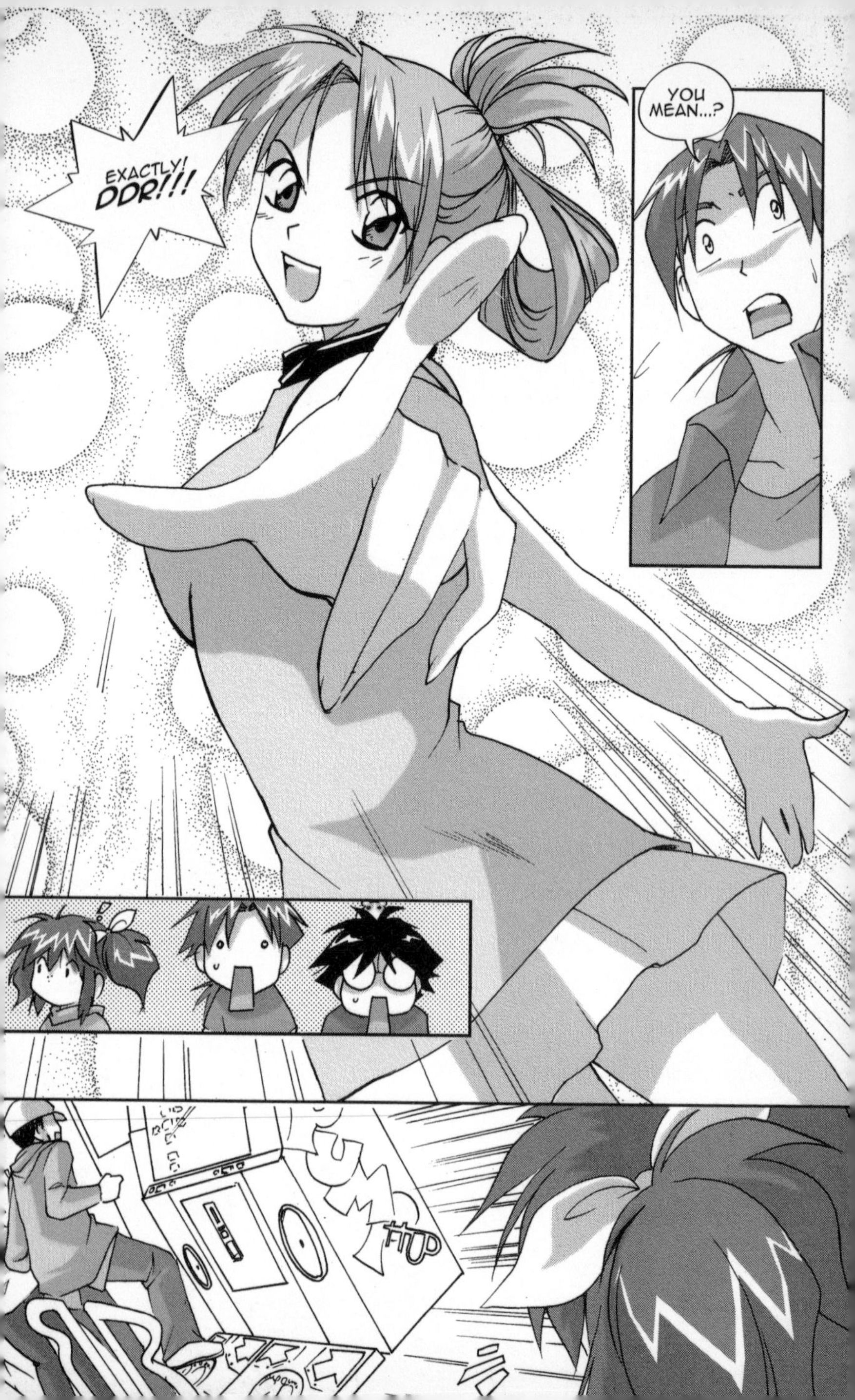
YOU MEAN...?
EXACTLY! DDR!!!

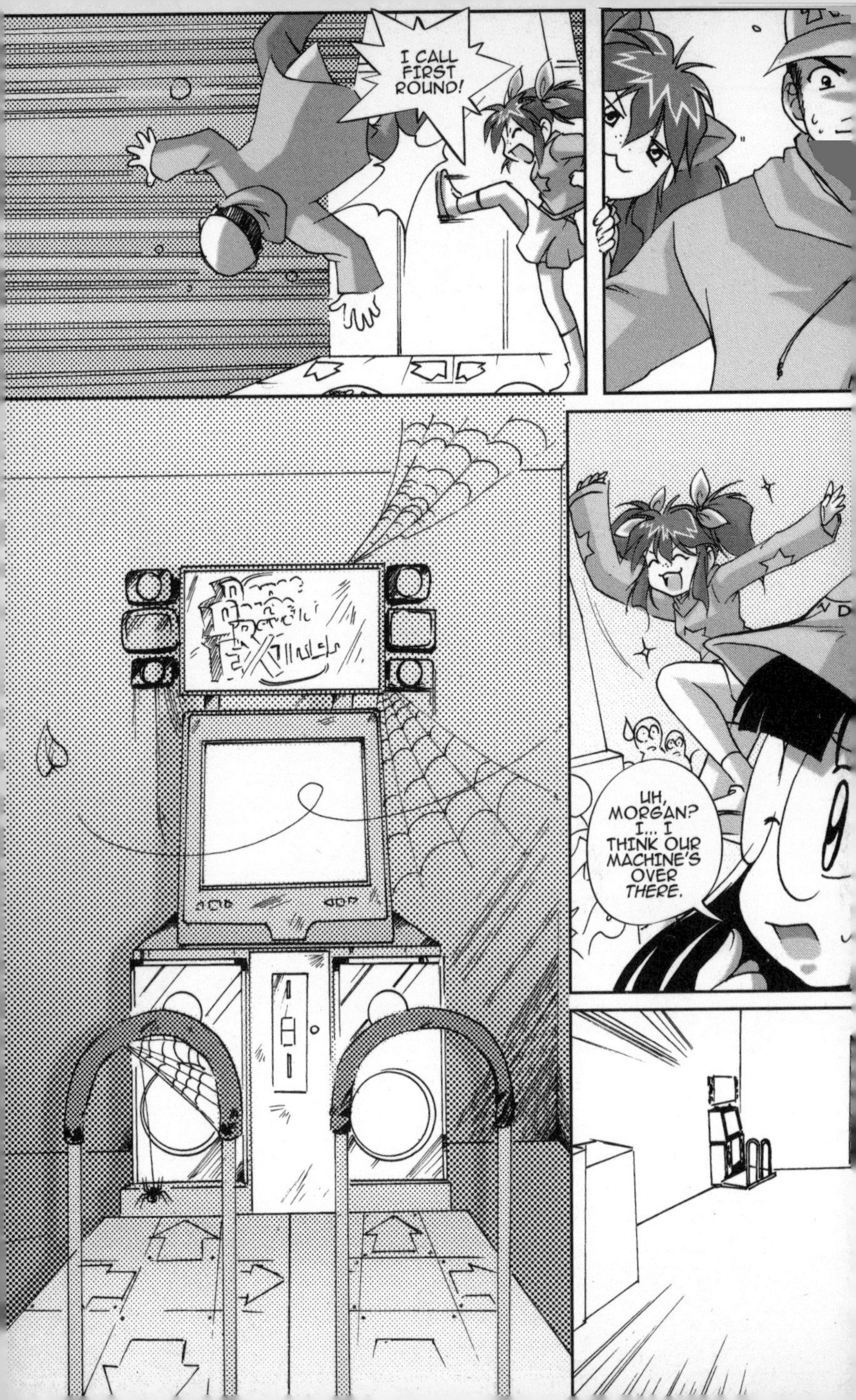
I CALL FIRST ROUND!
UH, MORGAN? I... I THINK OUR MACHINE'S OVER THERE.

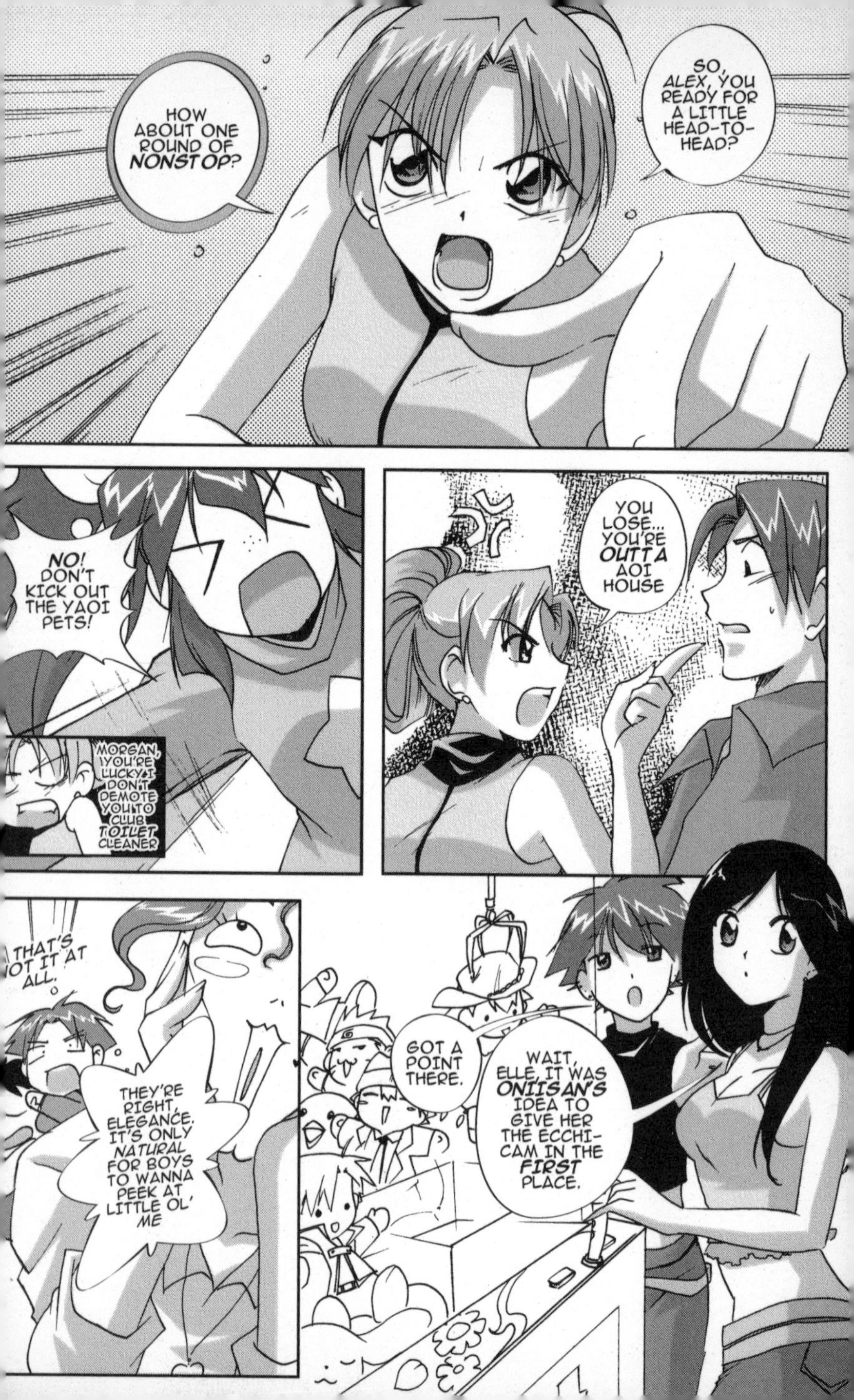
SO, *ALEX*, YOU READY FOR A LITTLE HEAD-TO-HEAD?
HOW ABOUT ONE ROUND OF ***NONSTOP***?
YOU LOSE... YOU'RE ***OUTTA*** AOI HOUSE
NO! DON'T KICK OUT THE YAOI PETS!
MORGAN, YOU'RE LUCKY I DON'T DEMOTE YOU TO CLUB *TOILET* CLEANER
WAIT, ELLE, IT WAS ***ONIISAN'S*** IDEA TO GIVE HER THE ECCHI-CAM IN THE ***FIRST*** PLACE.
GOT A POINT THERE.
THAT'S OT IT AT ALL.
THEY'RE RIGHT, ELEGANCE. IT'S ONLY *NATURAL* FOR BOYS TO WANNA PEEK AT LITTLE OL' *ME*

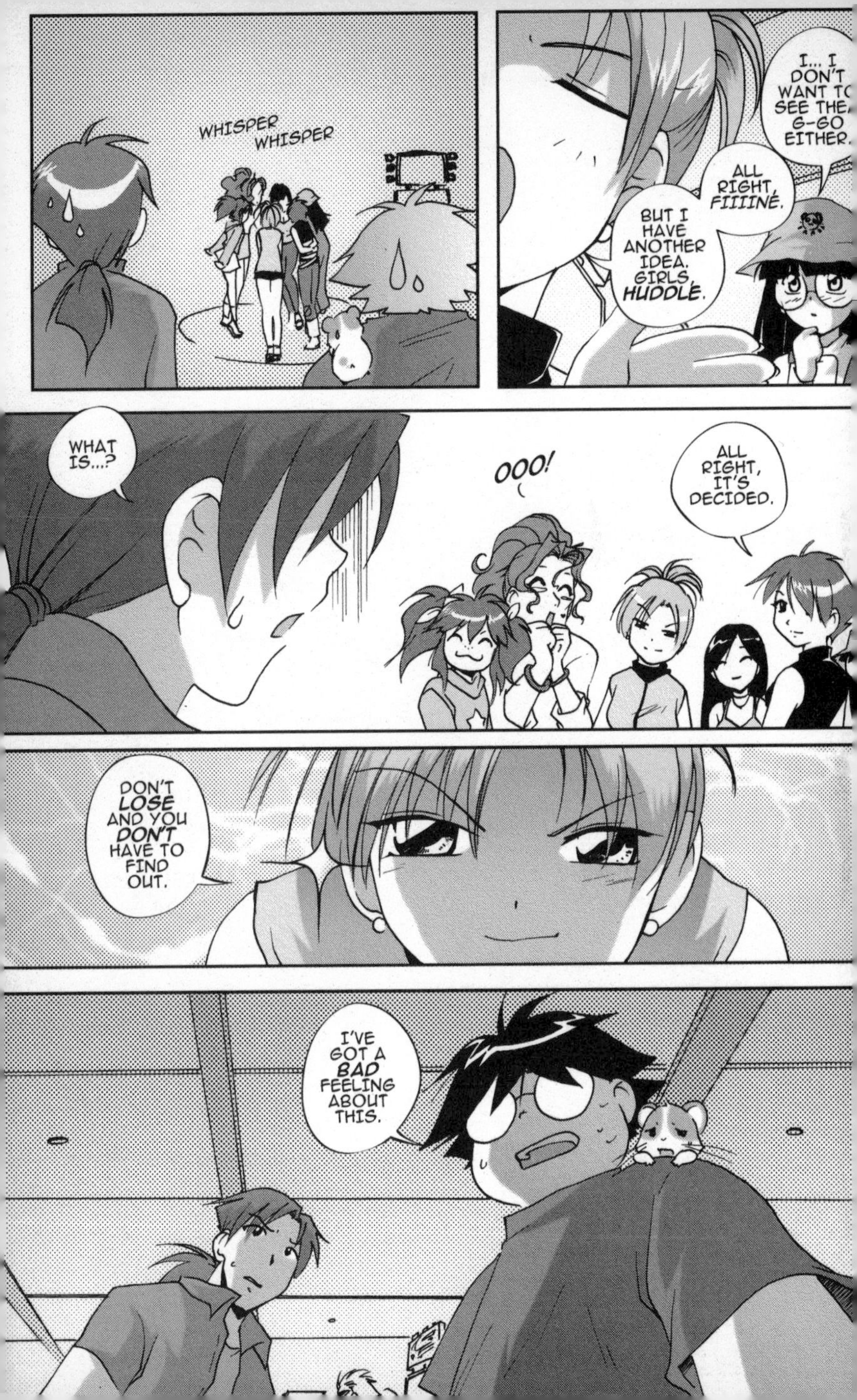

I... I DON'T WANT TO SEE THE G-GO EITHER.
ALL RIGHT, FIIIINE.
BUT I HAVE ANOTHER IDEA. GIRLS, HUDDLE.
WHISPER WHISPER
ALL RIGHT, IT'S DECIDED.
OOO!
WHAT IS...?
DON'T LOSE AND YOU DON'T HAVE TO FIND OUT.
I'VE GOT A BAD FEELING ABOUT THIS.

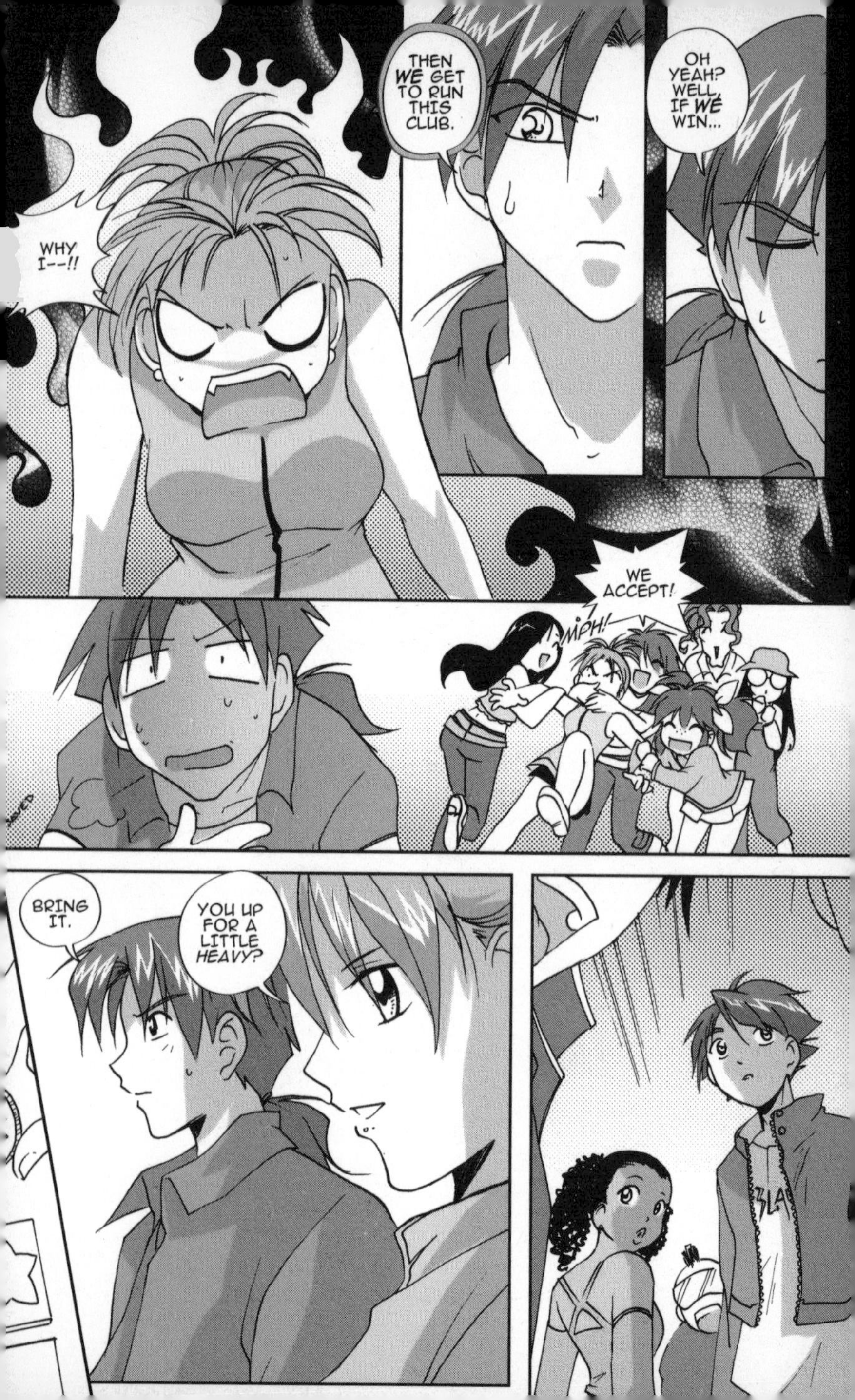
OH YEAH? WELL, IF WE WIN...
THEN WE GET TO RUN THIS CLUB.
WHY I--!!
WE ACCEPT!
MPH!
YOU UP FOR A LITTLE HEAVY?
BRING IT.

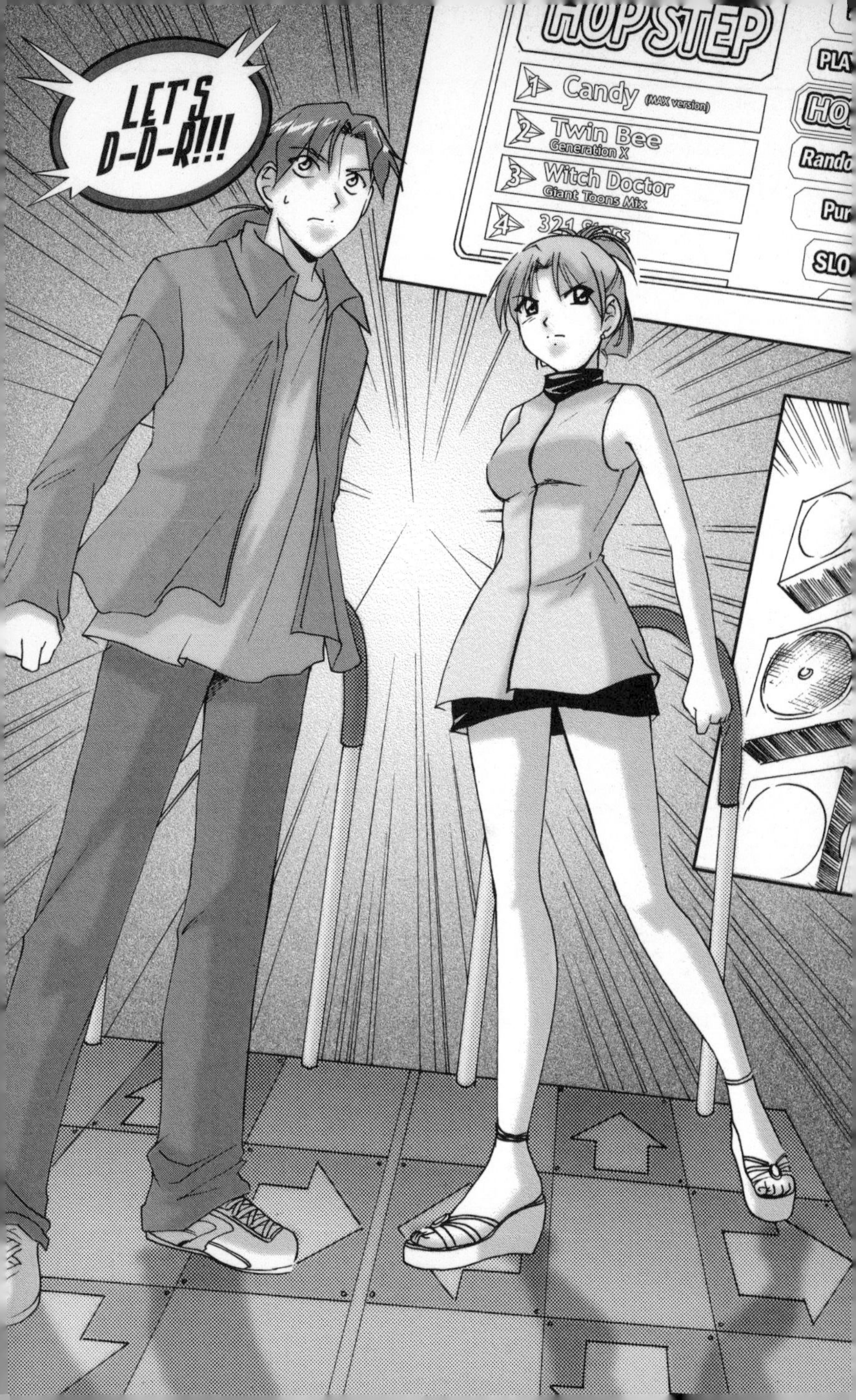
LET'S D-D-R!!!
HOP STEP
1 Candy (MAX version)
2 Twin Bee Generation X
3 Witch Doctor Giant Toons Mix

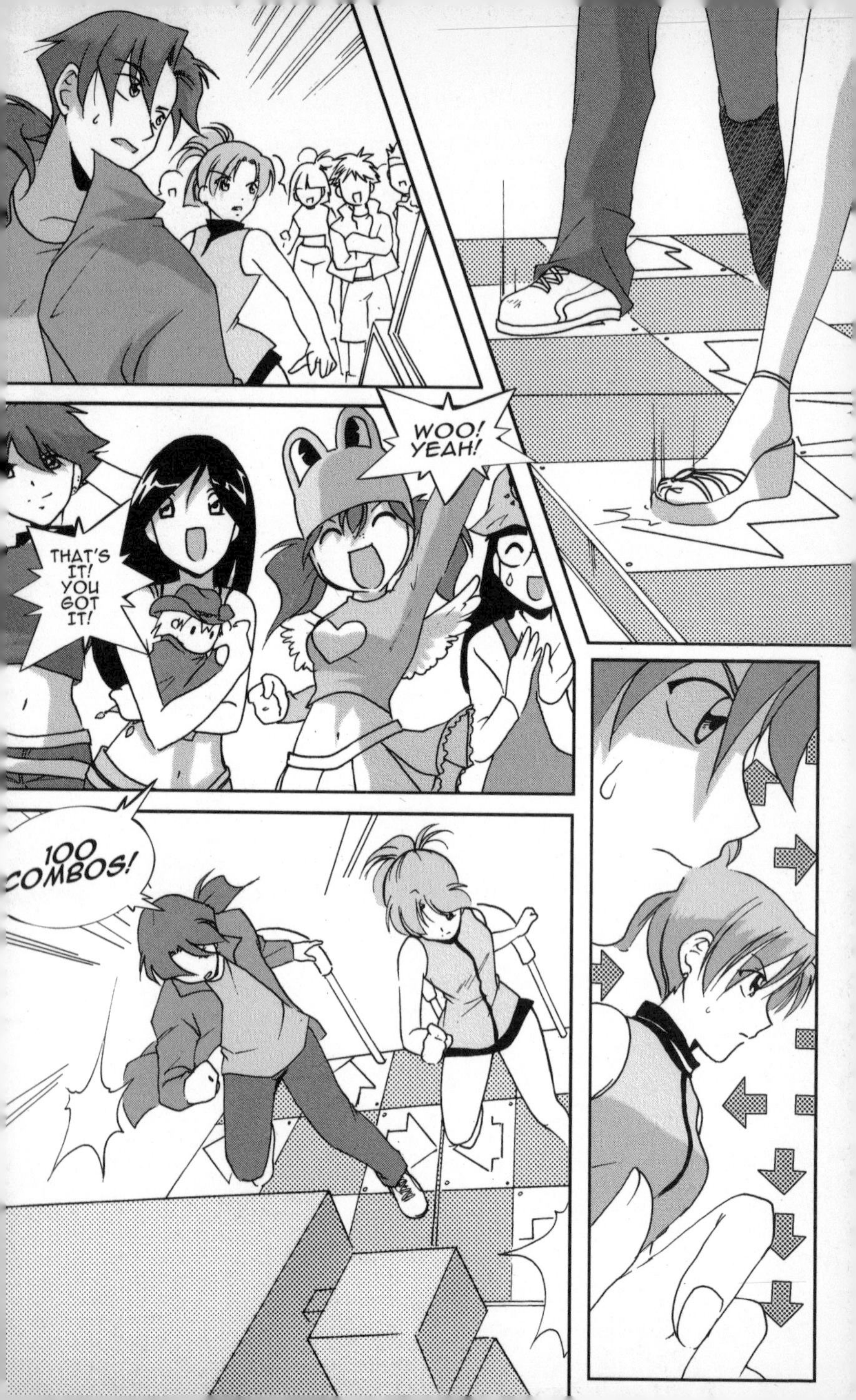
WOO! YEAH!
THAT'S IT! YOU GOT IT!
100 COMBOS!

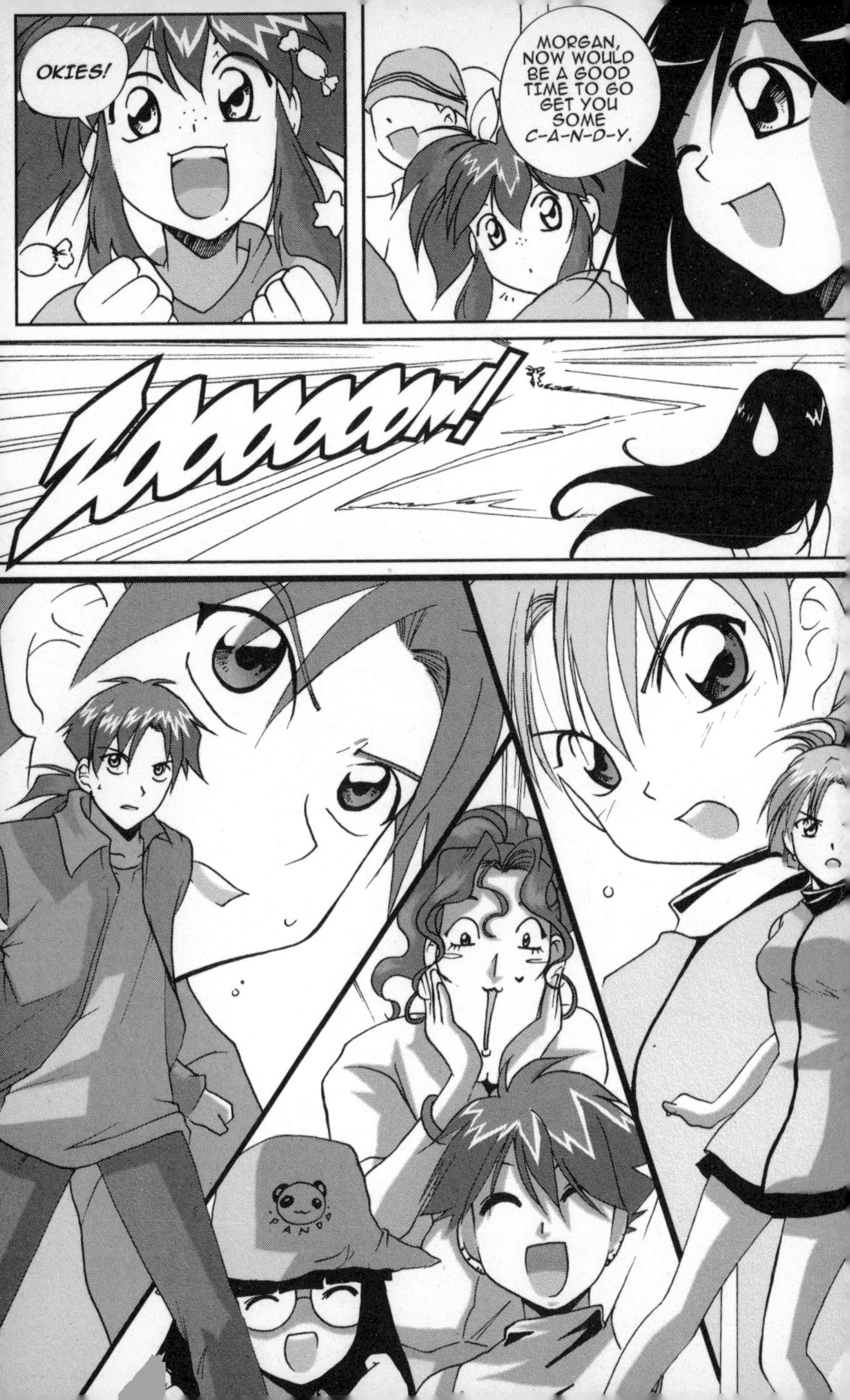
MORGAN, NOW WOULD BE A GOOD TIME TO GO GET YOU SOME C-A-N-D-Y.
OKIES!
ZOOOOOM!

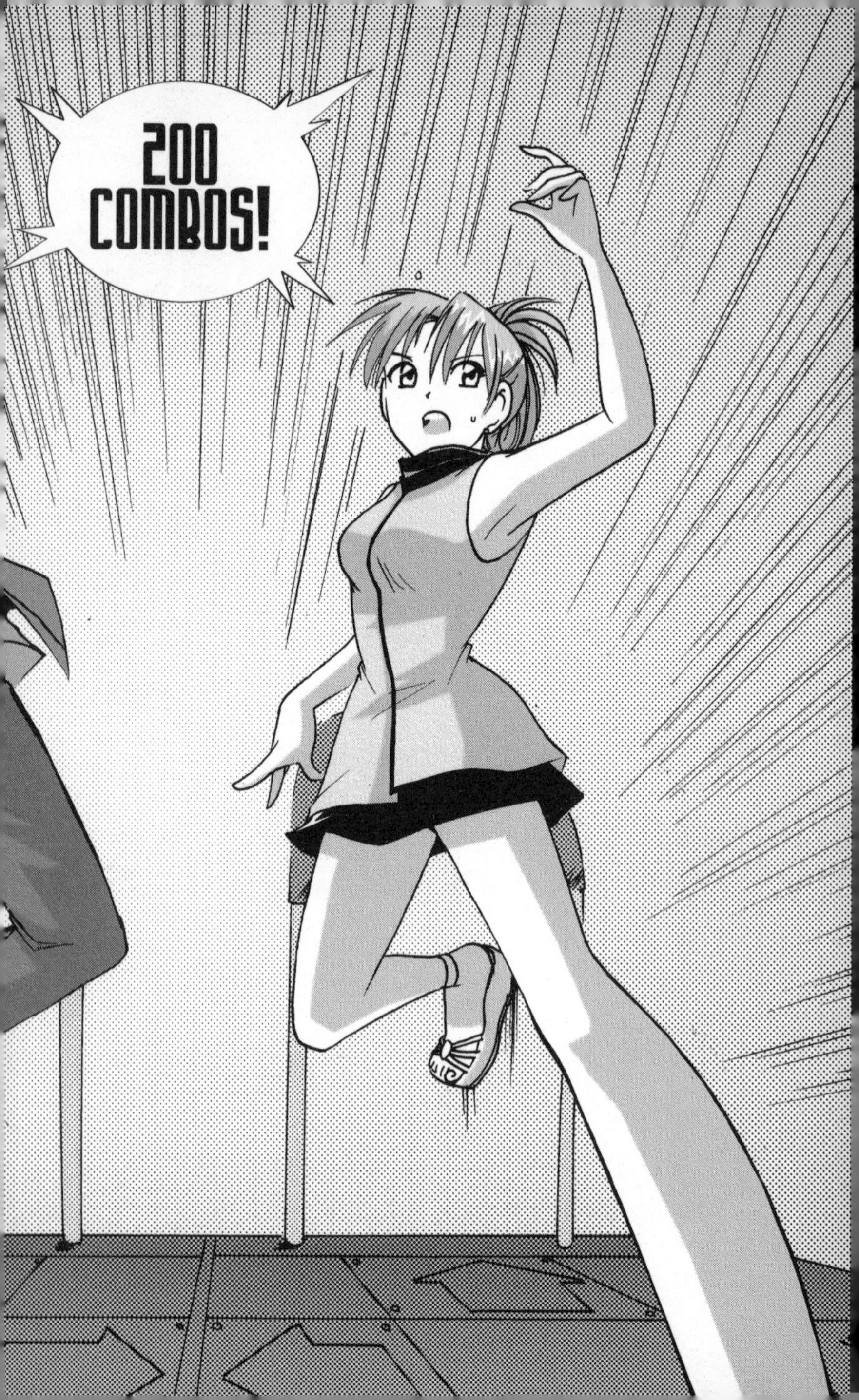
200 COMBOS!

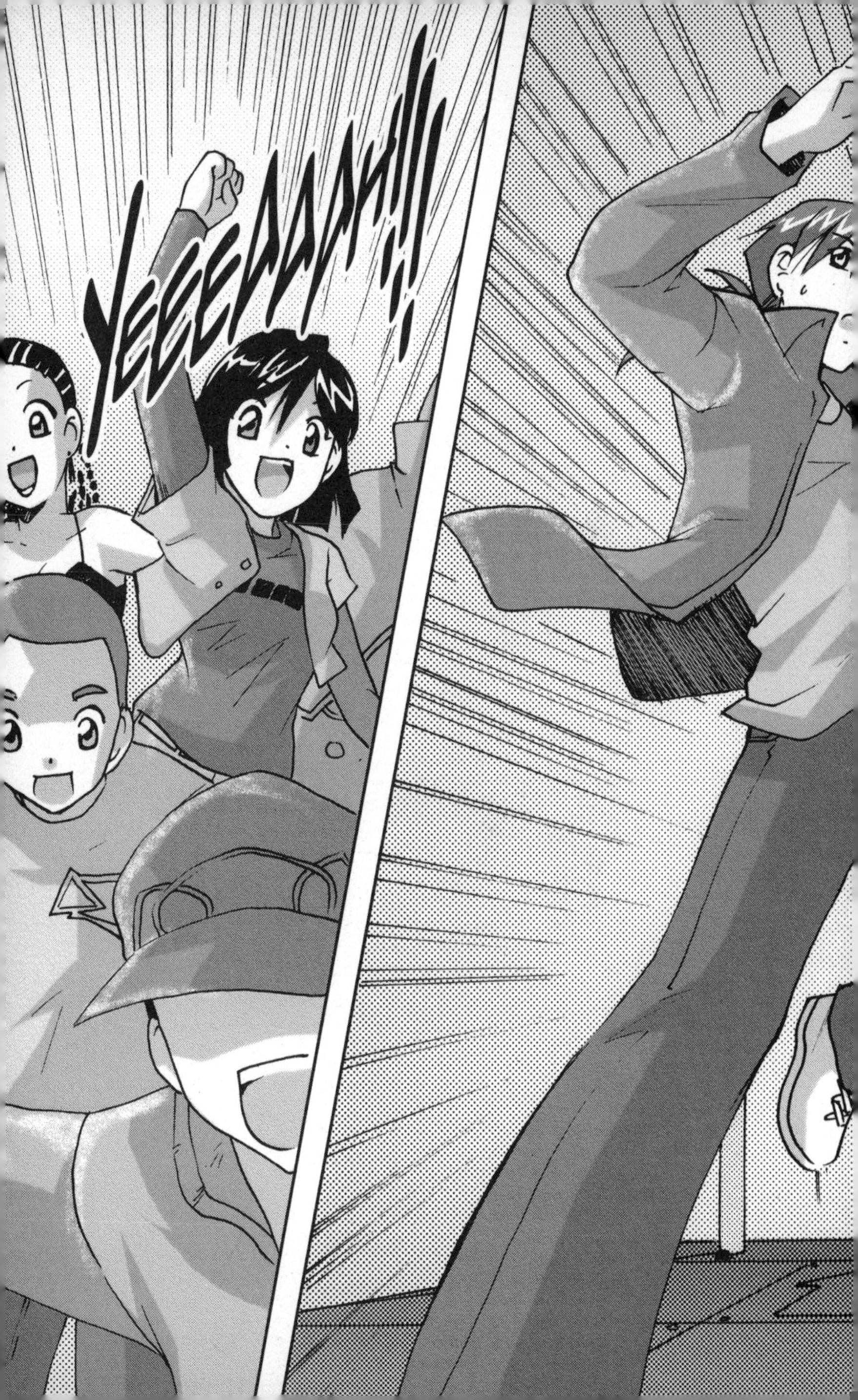
YEEEAAAH!!!

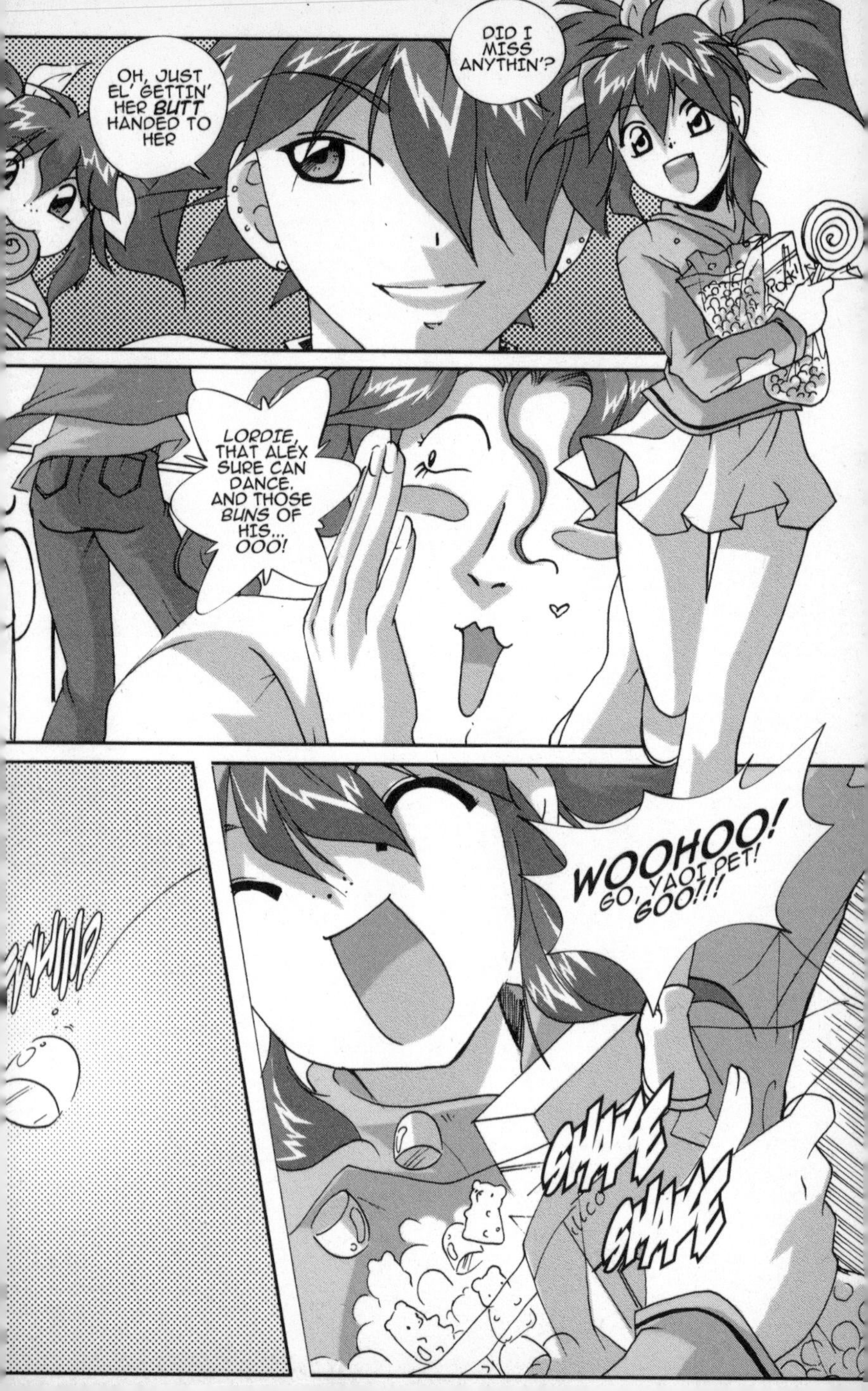
DID I MISS ANYTHIN'?
OH, JUST EL' GETTIN' HER BUTT HANDED TO HER
LORDIE, THAT ALEX SURE CAN DANCE. AND THOSE BUNS OF HIS... OOO!
WOOHOO! GO, YAOI PET! GOO!!!
SHAKE
SHAKE

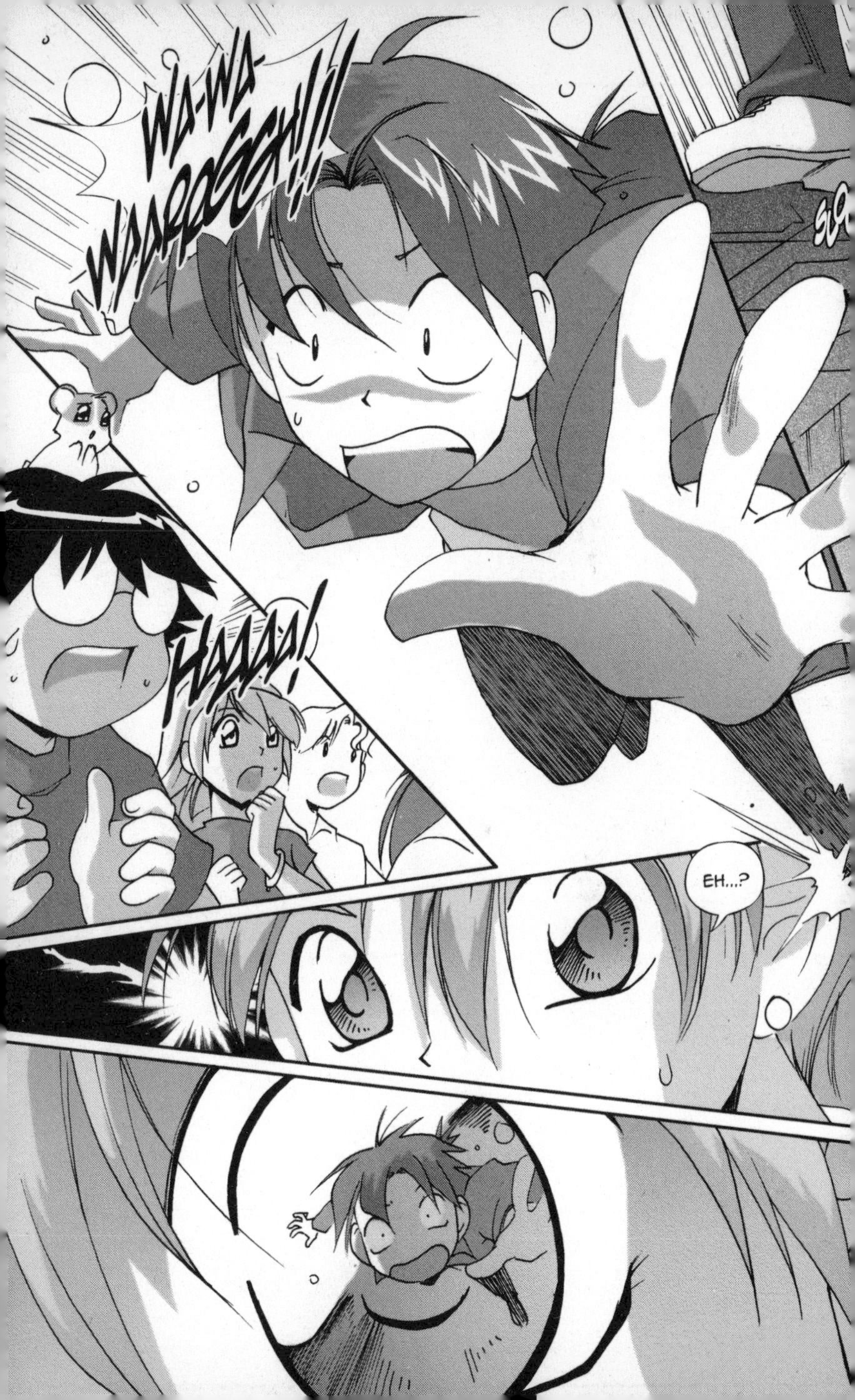
SLO
WA-WA-WAAAAGH!!!
HAAA!
EH...?

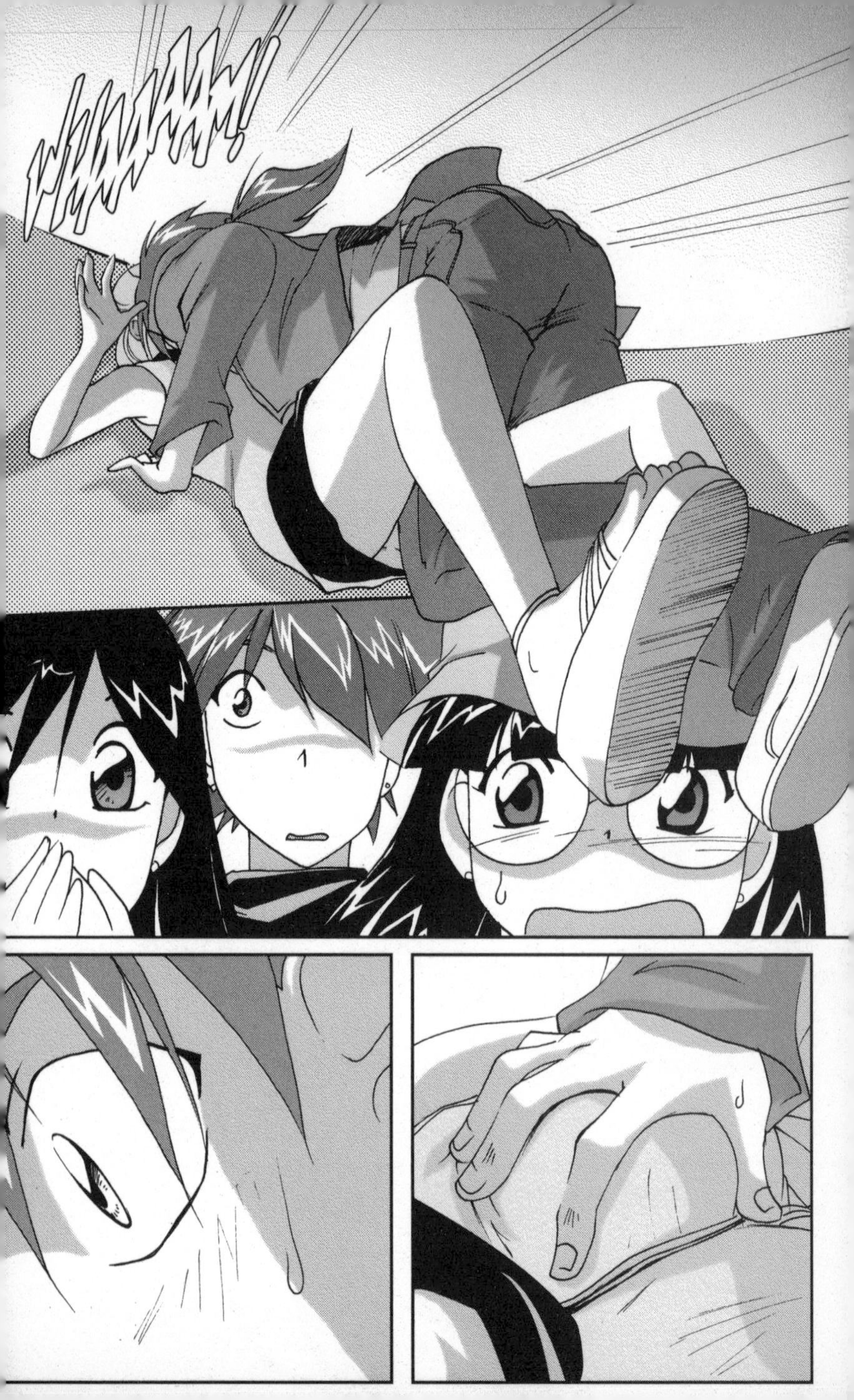
WHAAAM!

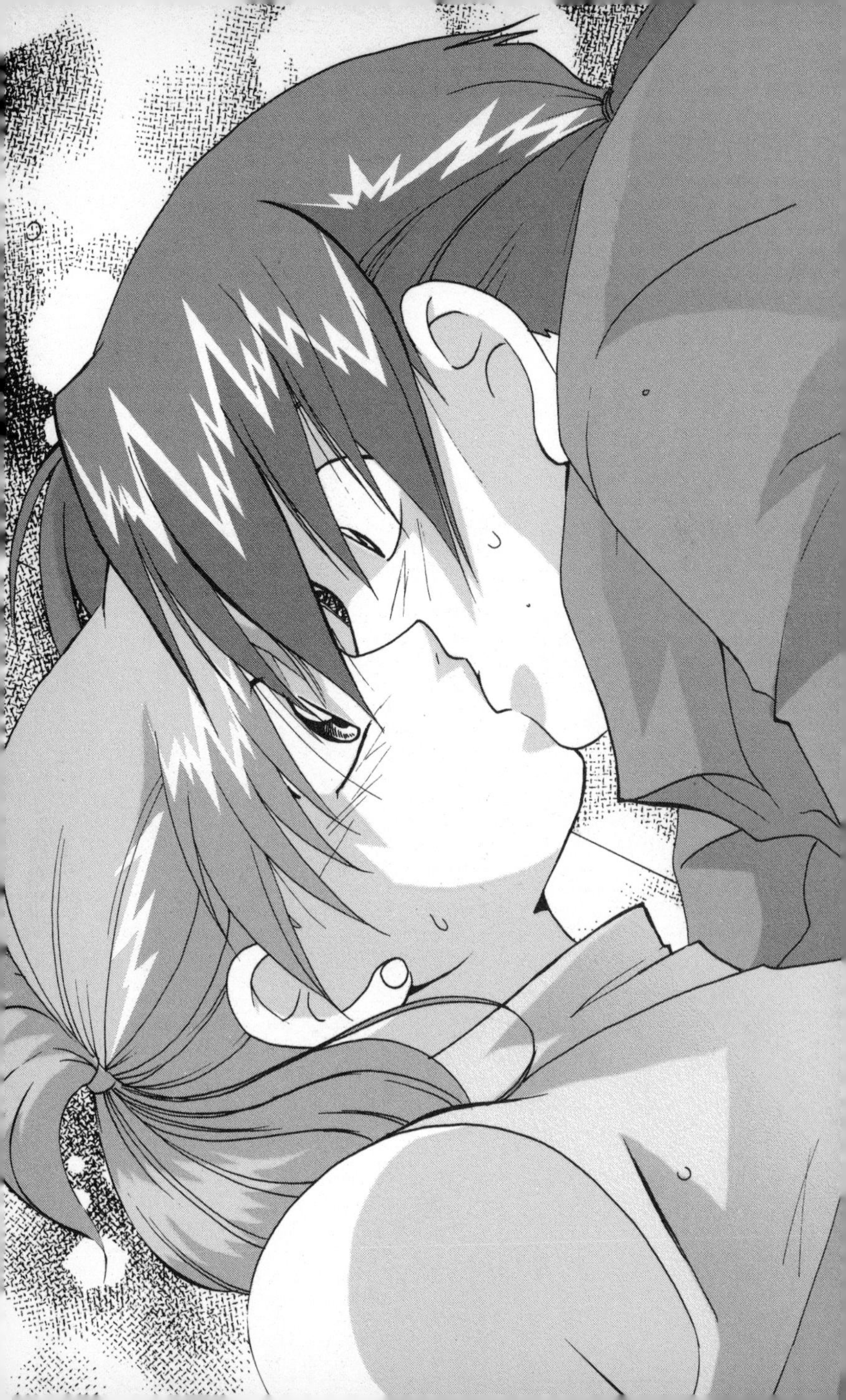

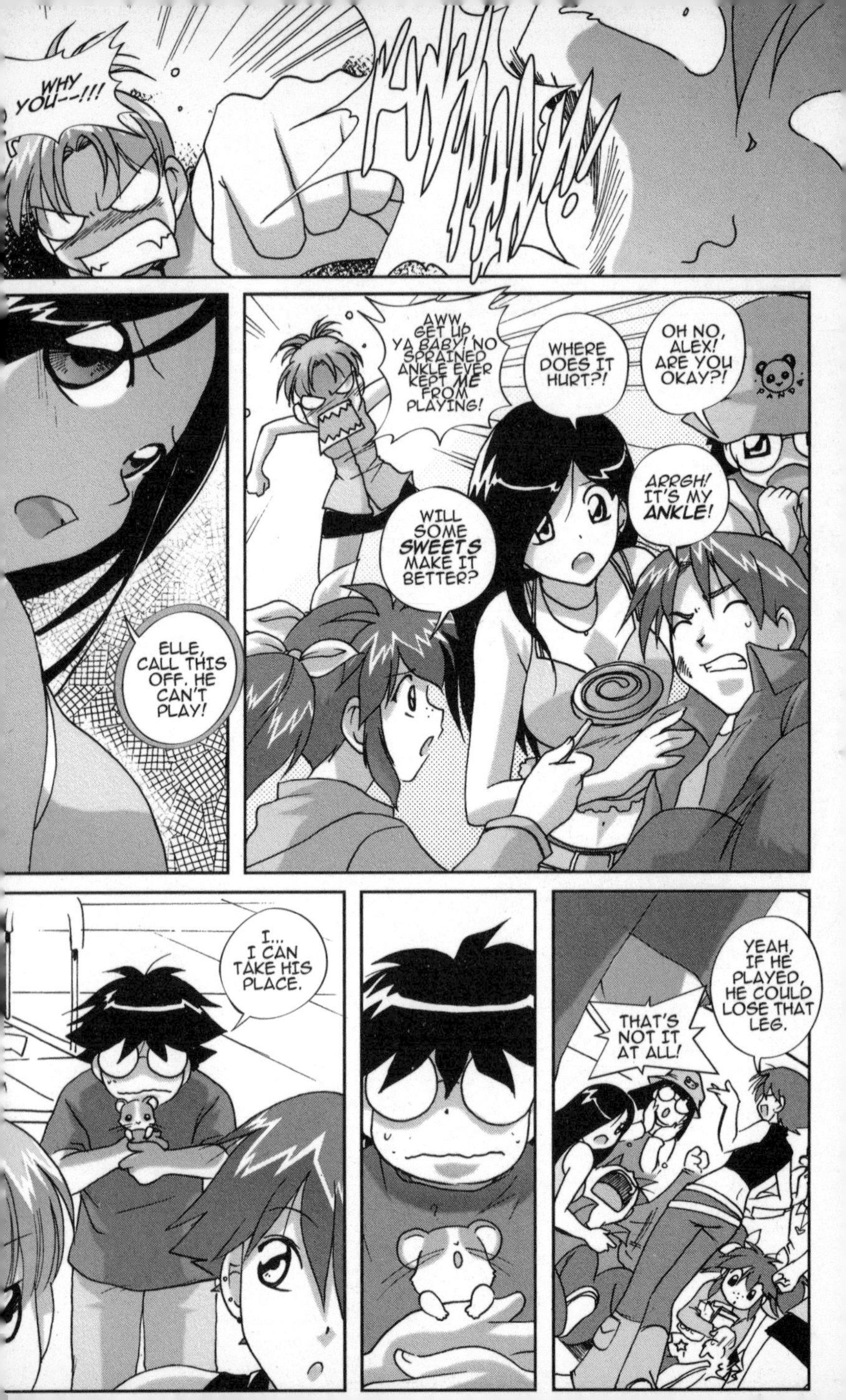
WHY YOU--!!!
OH NO, ALEX! ARE YOU OKAY?!
WHERE DOES IT HURT?!
AWW GET UP, YA BABY! NO SPRAINED ANKLE EVER KEPT ME FROM PLAYING!
ARRGH! IT'S MY ANKLE!
WILL SOME SWEETS MAKE IT BETTER?
ELLE, CALL THIS OFF. HE CAN'T PLAY!
YEAH, IF HE PLAYED, HE COULD LOSE THAT LEG.
THAT'S NOT IT AT ALL!
I... I CAN TAKE HIS PLACE.

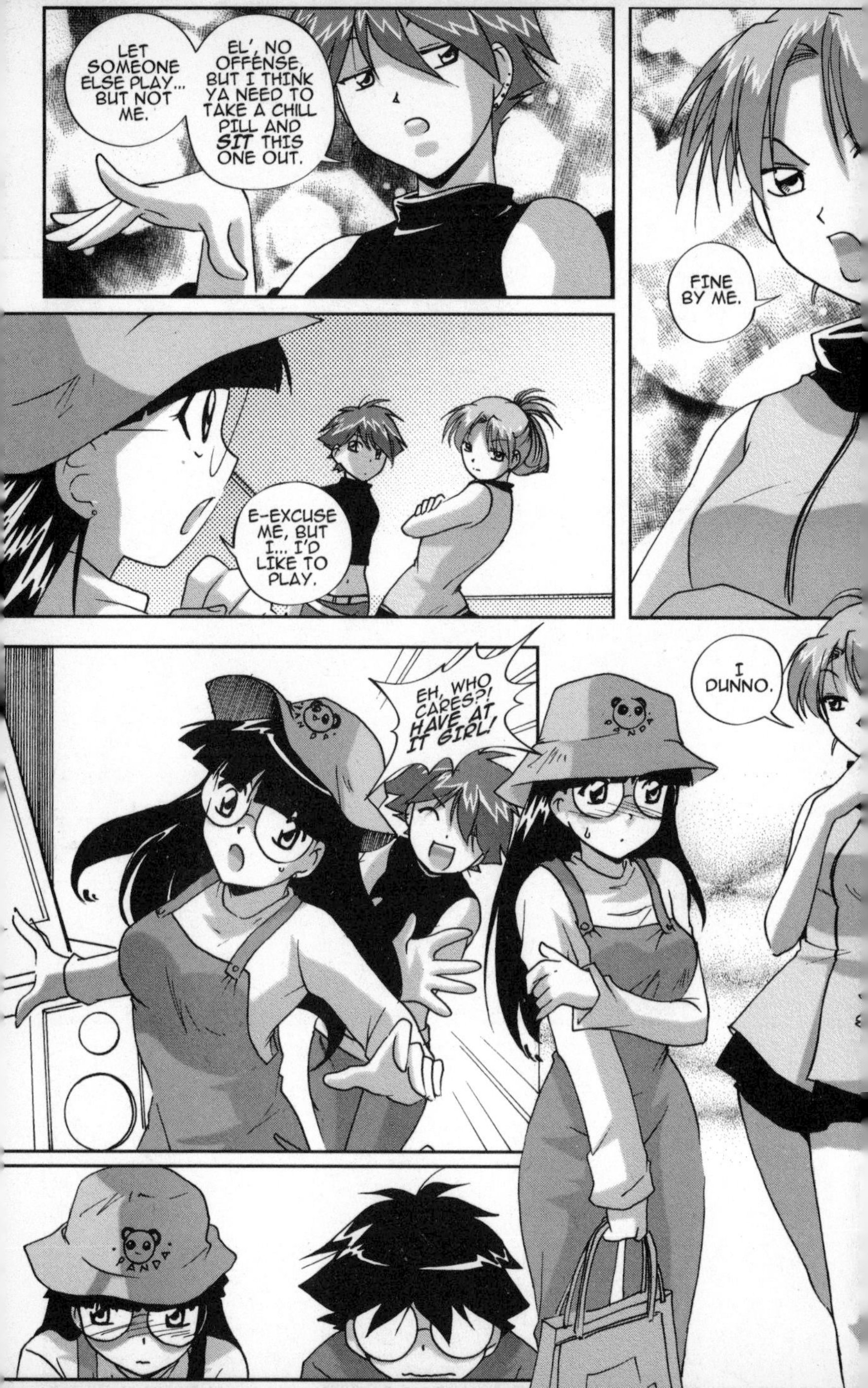
FINE BY ME.
EL', NO OFFENSE, BUT I THINK YA NEED TO TAKE A CHILL PILL AND SIT THIS ONE OUT.
LET SOMEONE ELSE PLAY... BUT NOT ME.
E-EXCUSE ME, BUT I... I'D LIKE TO PLAY.
I DUNNO.
EH, WHO CARES?! HAVE AT IT GIRL!

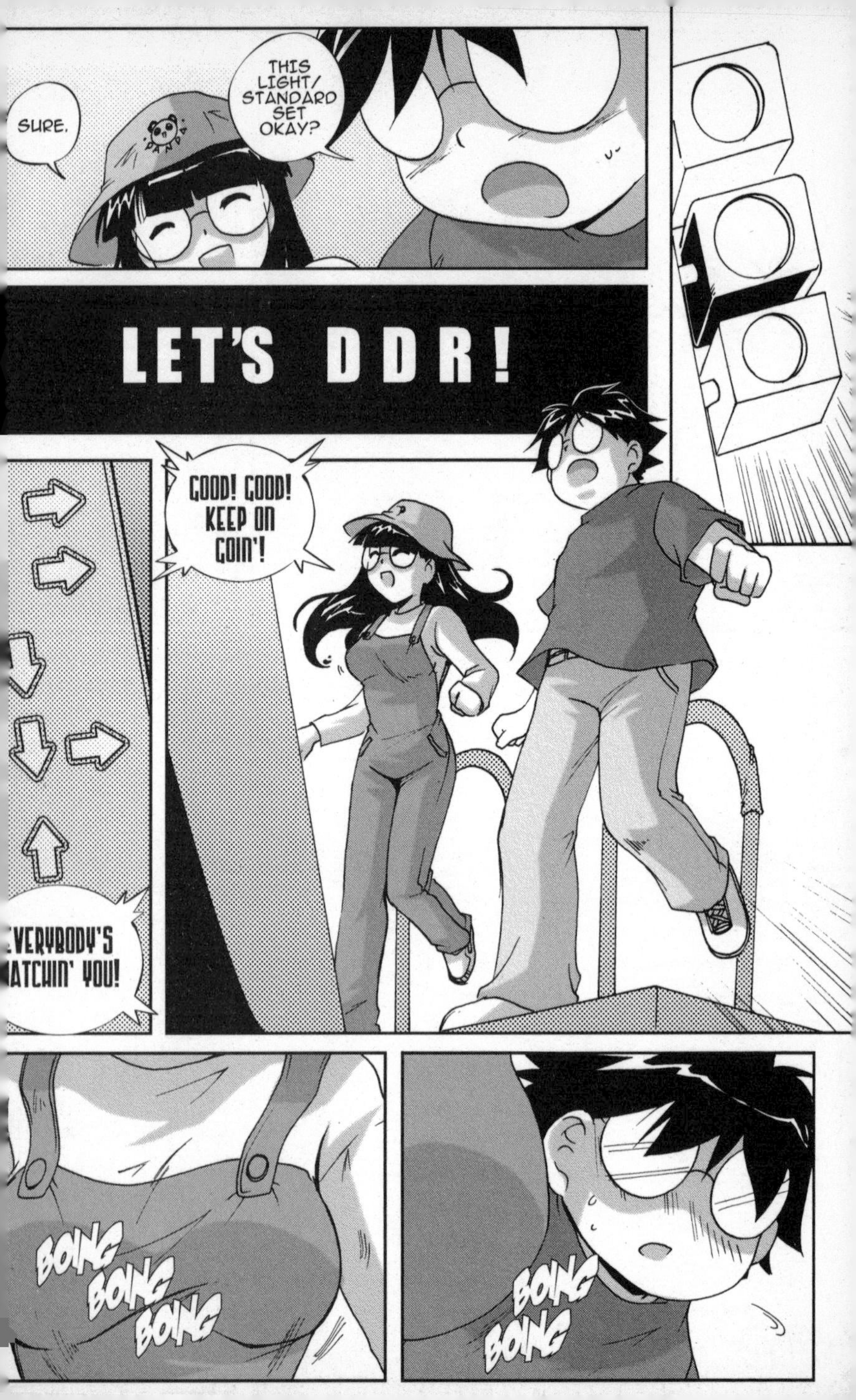
THIS LIGHT/ STANDARD SET OKAY?
SURE.
LET'S DDR!
GOOD! GOOD! KEEP ON GOIN'!
EVERYBODY'S WATCHIN' YOU!
BOING BOING
BOING BOING BOING

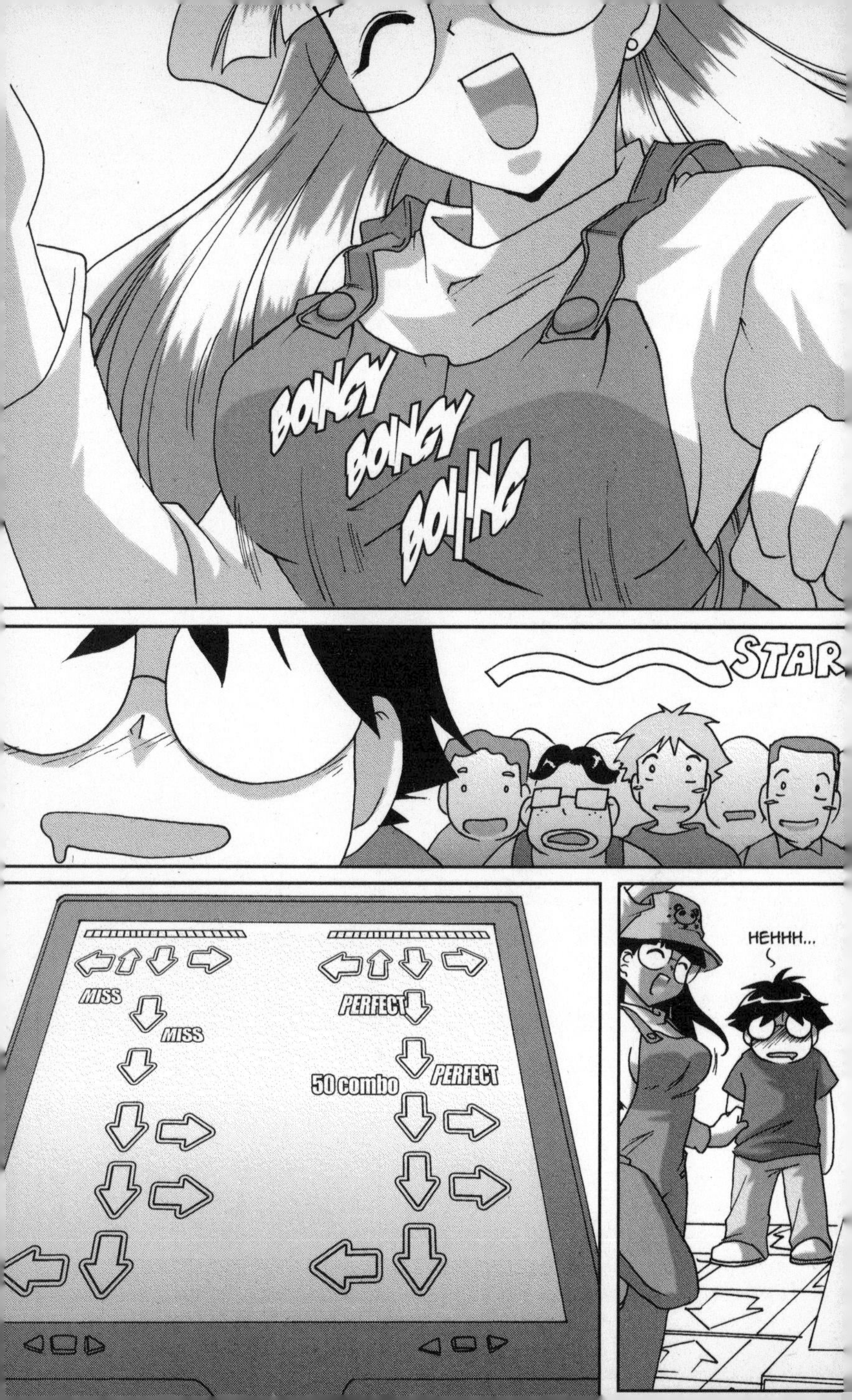
BOINGY
BOINGY
BOING
STAR
HEHHH...
PERFECT
MISS
MISS
PERFECT
50 combo

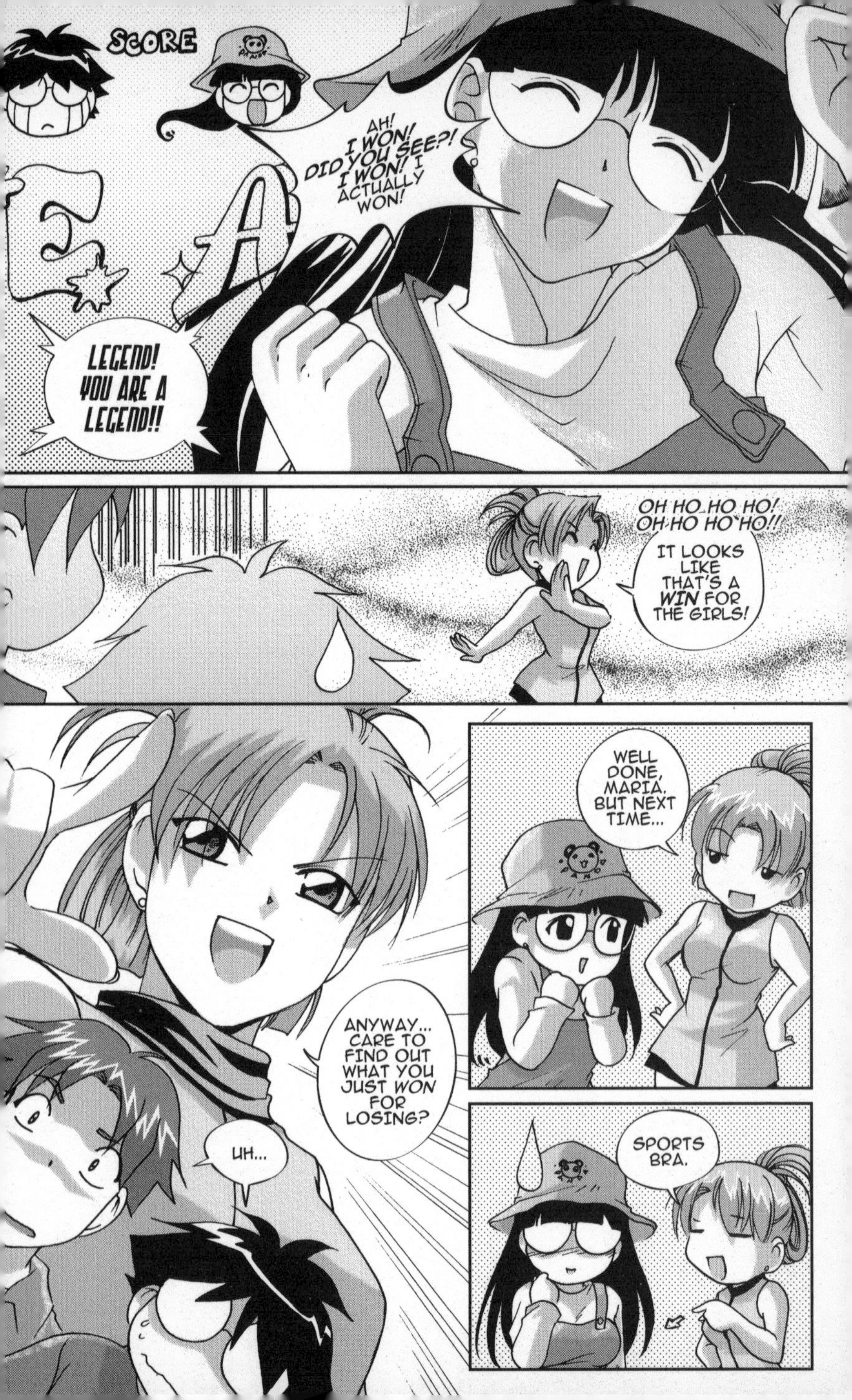
SCORE
AH! I WON! DID YOU SEE?! I WON! I ACTUALLY WON!
LEGEND! YOU ARE A LEGEND!!
OH HO HO HO! OH HO HO HO!!
IT LOOKS LIKE THAT'S A *WIN* FOR THE GIRLS!
WELL DONE, MARIA. BUT NEXT TIME...
SPORTS BRA.
ANYWAY... CARE TO FIND OUT WHAT YOU JUST *WON* FOR LOSING?
UH...

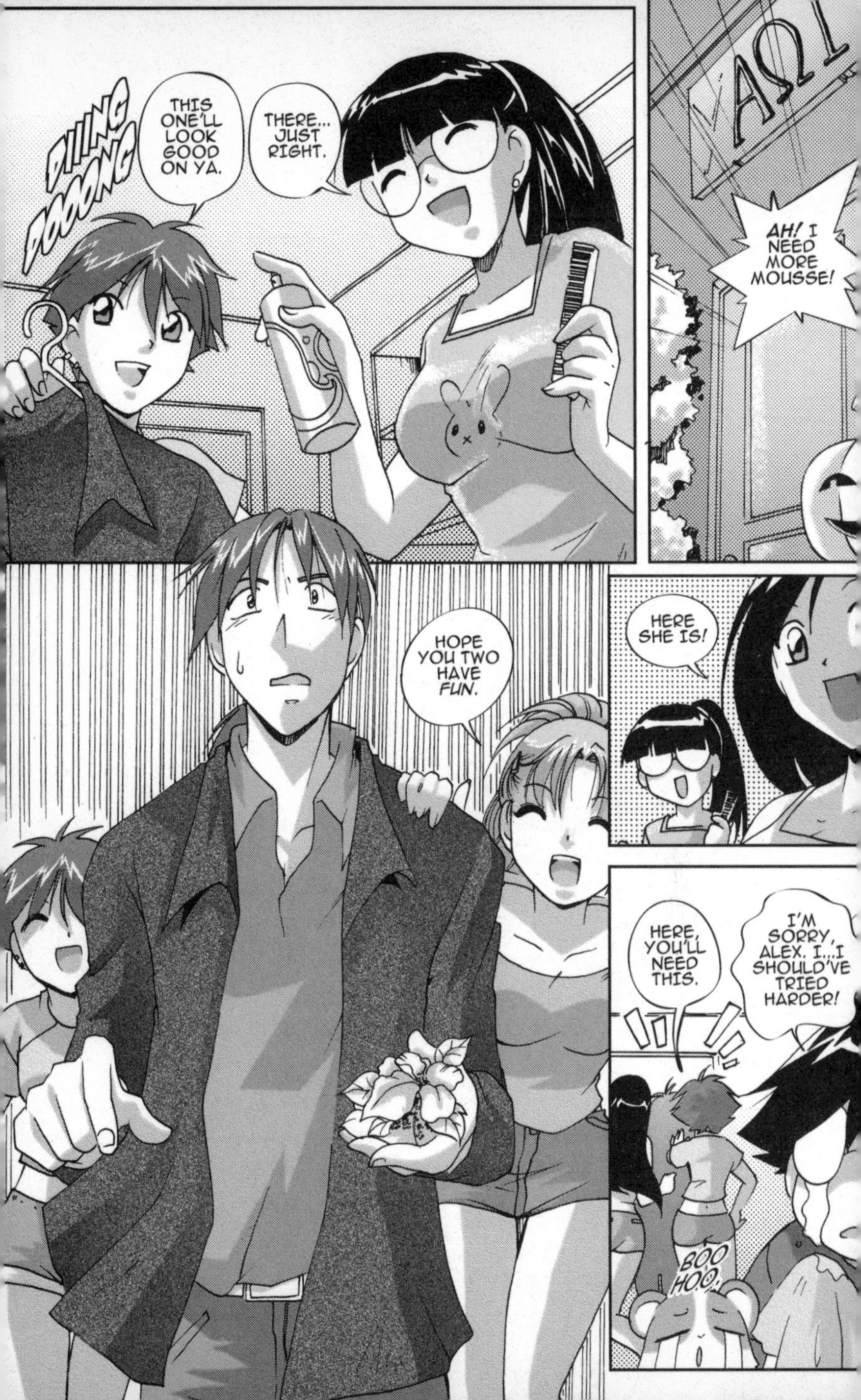
AH! I NEED MORE MOUSSE!
THERE... JUST RIGHT.
THIS ONE'LL LOOK GOOD ON YA.
DIIING DOOONG
HERE SHE IS!
I'M SORRY, ALEX. I...I SHOULD'VE TRIED HARDER!
HERE, YOU'LL NEED THIS.
BOO HOO.
HOPE YOU TWO HAVE FUN.

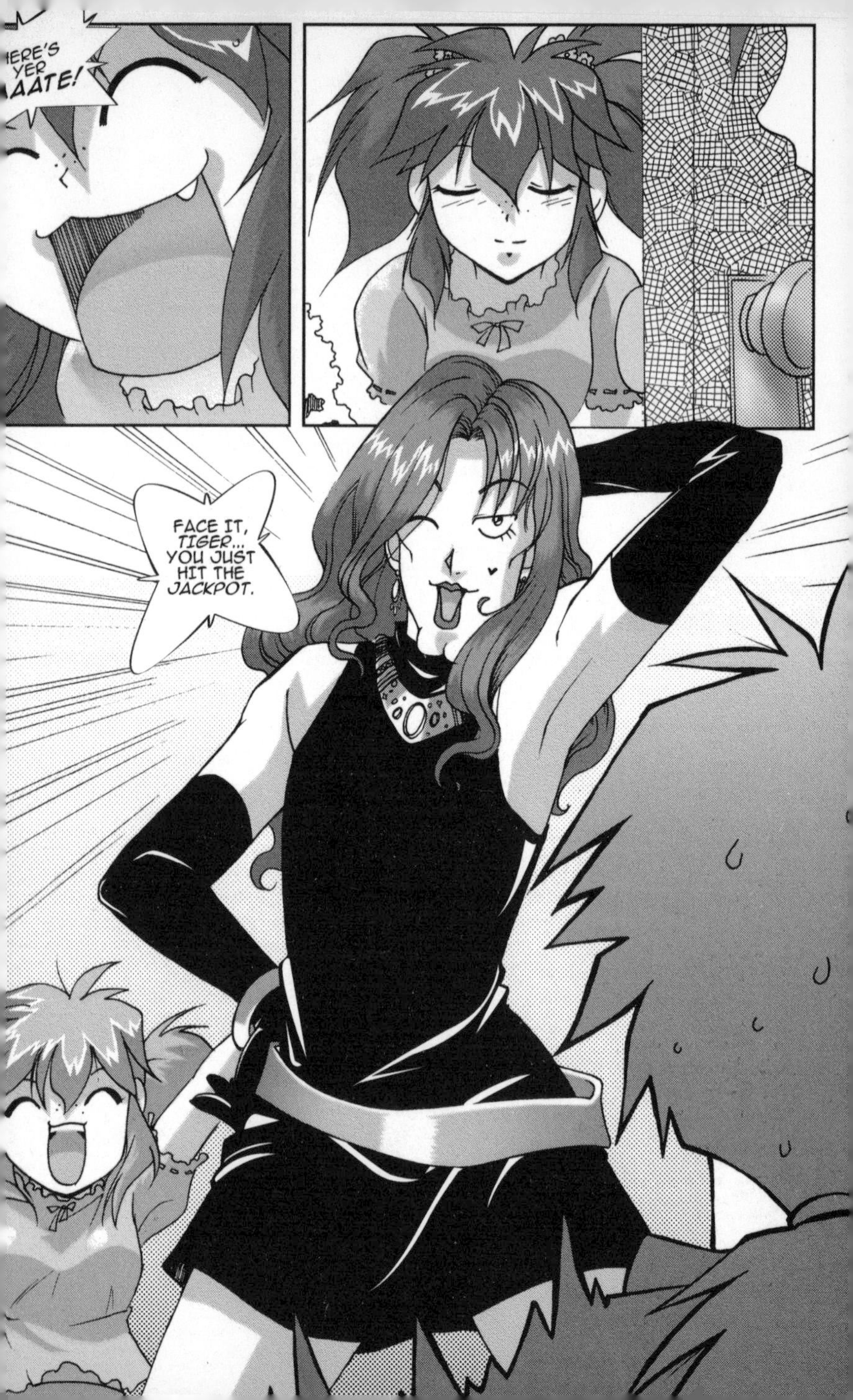
HERE'S YER AATE!
FACE IT, TIGER... YOU JUST HIT THE JACKPOT.

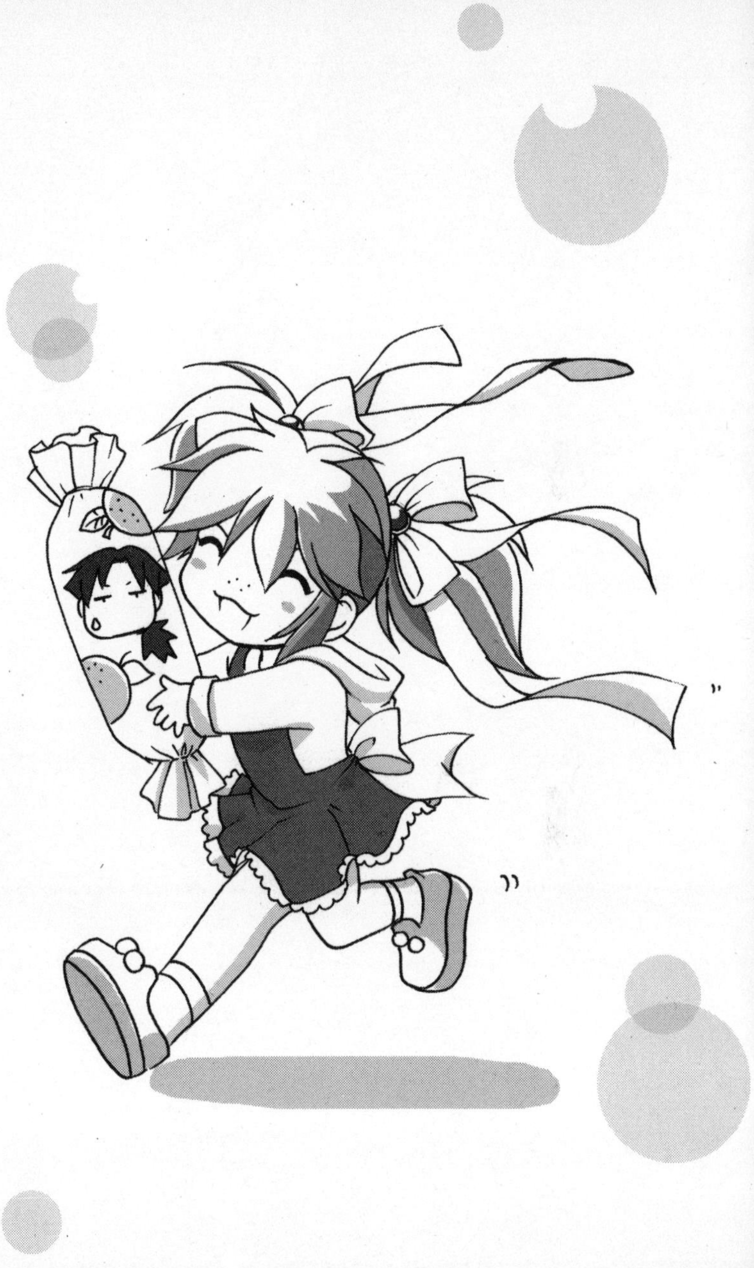

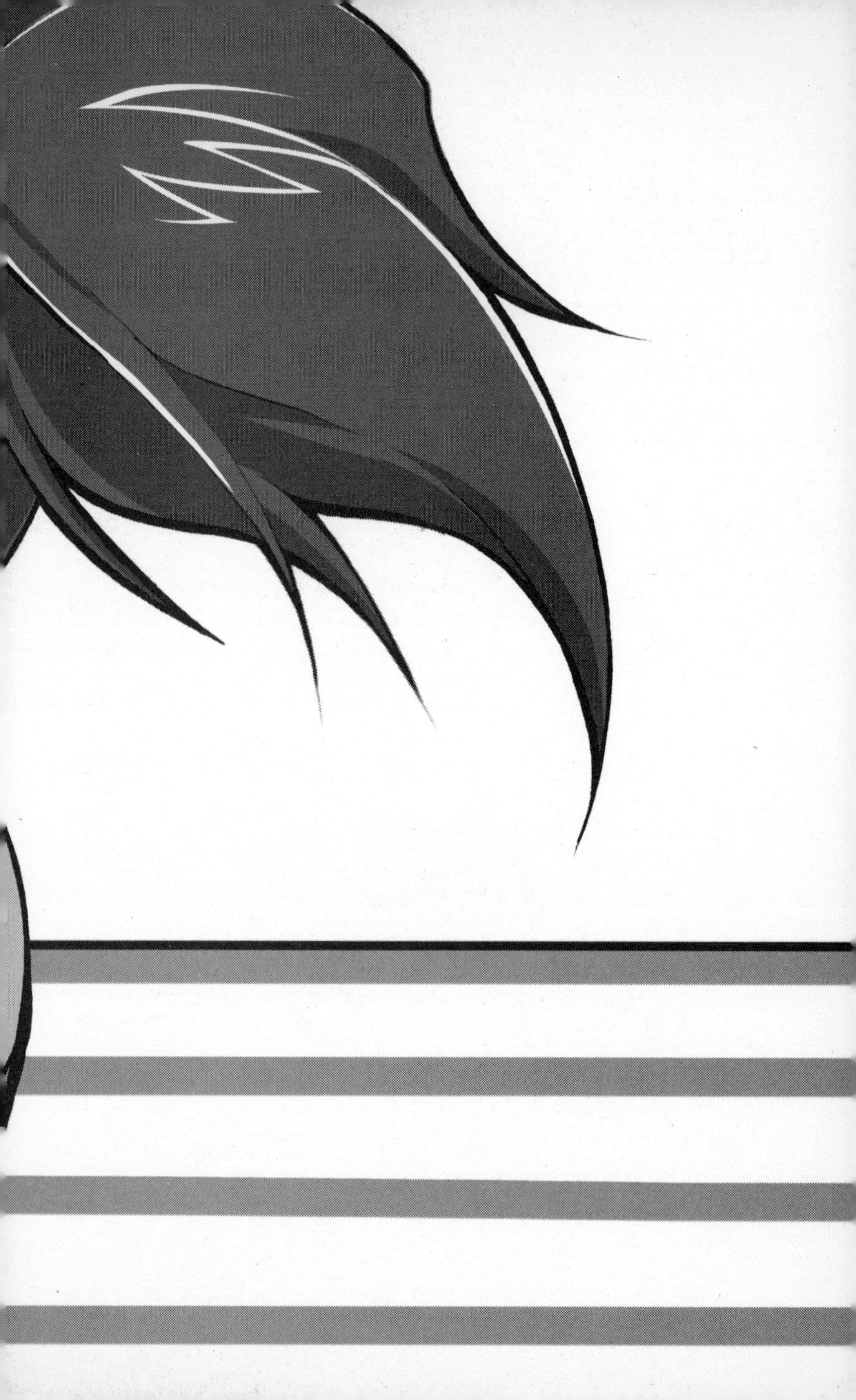

EPISODE 8: PLAYFUL SECRETS

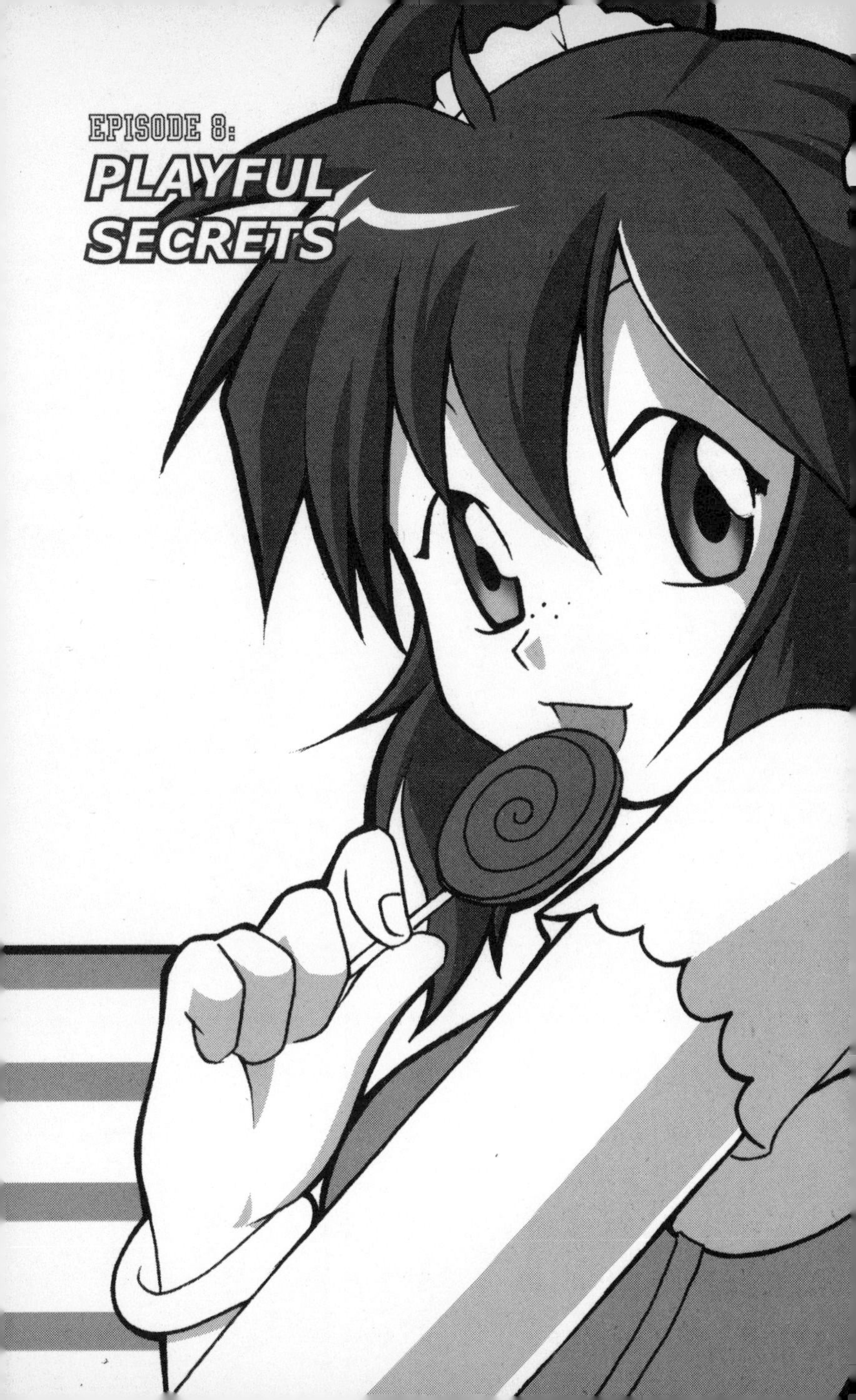

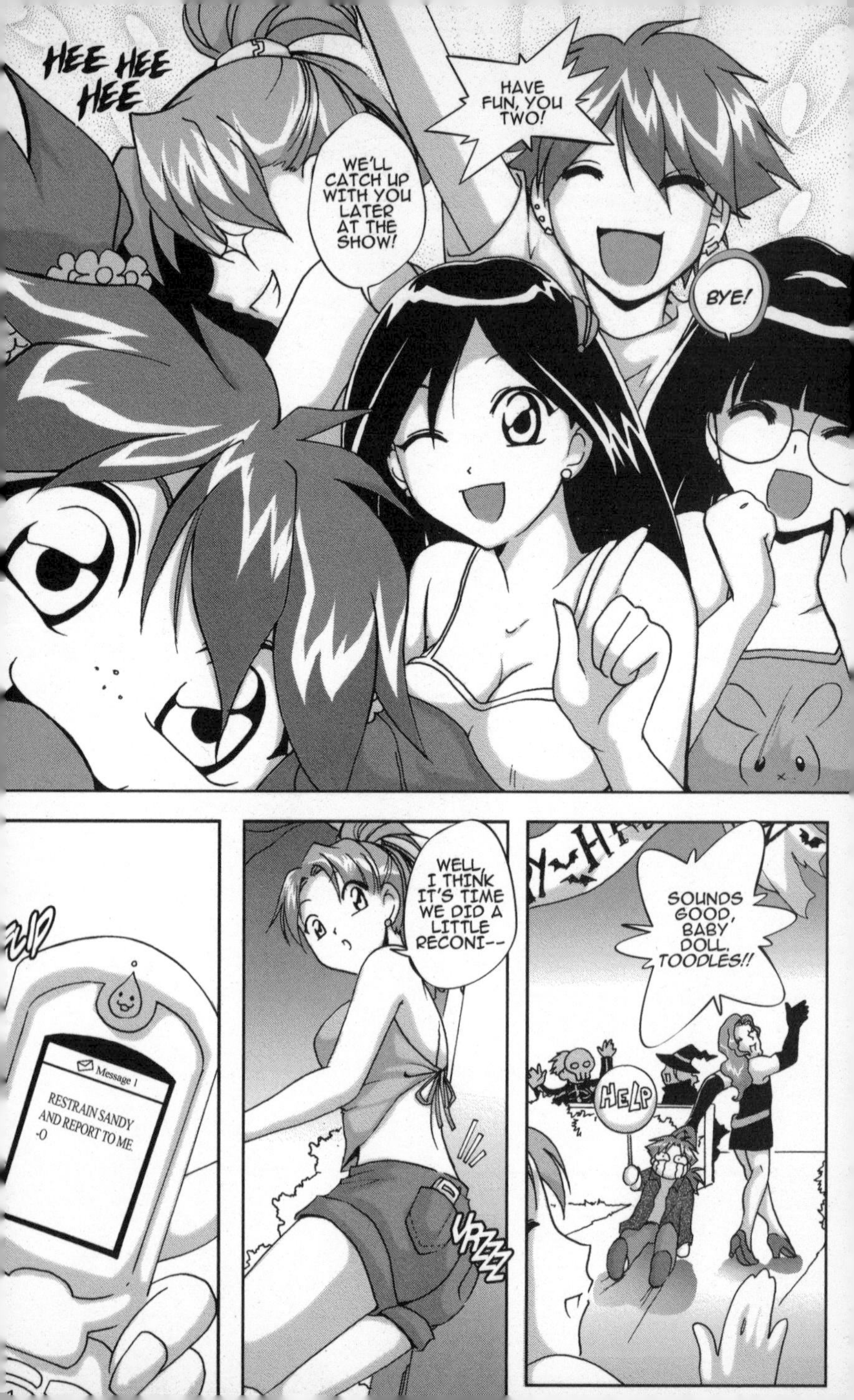
HAVE FUN, YOU TWO!
WE'LL CATCH UP WITH YOU LATER AT THE SHOW!
BYE!
HEE HEE HEE
SOUNDS GOOD, BABY DOLL. TOODLES!!
HELP
WELL, I THINK IT'S TIME WE DID A LITTLE RECONI--
VRZZZ
Message 1
RESTRAIN SANDY AND REPORT TO ME.
-O

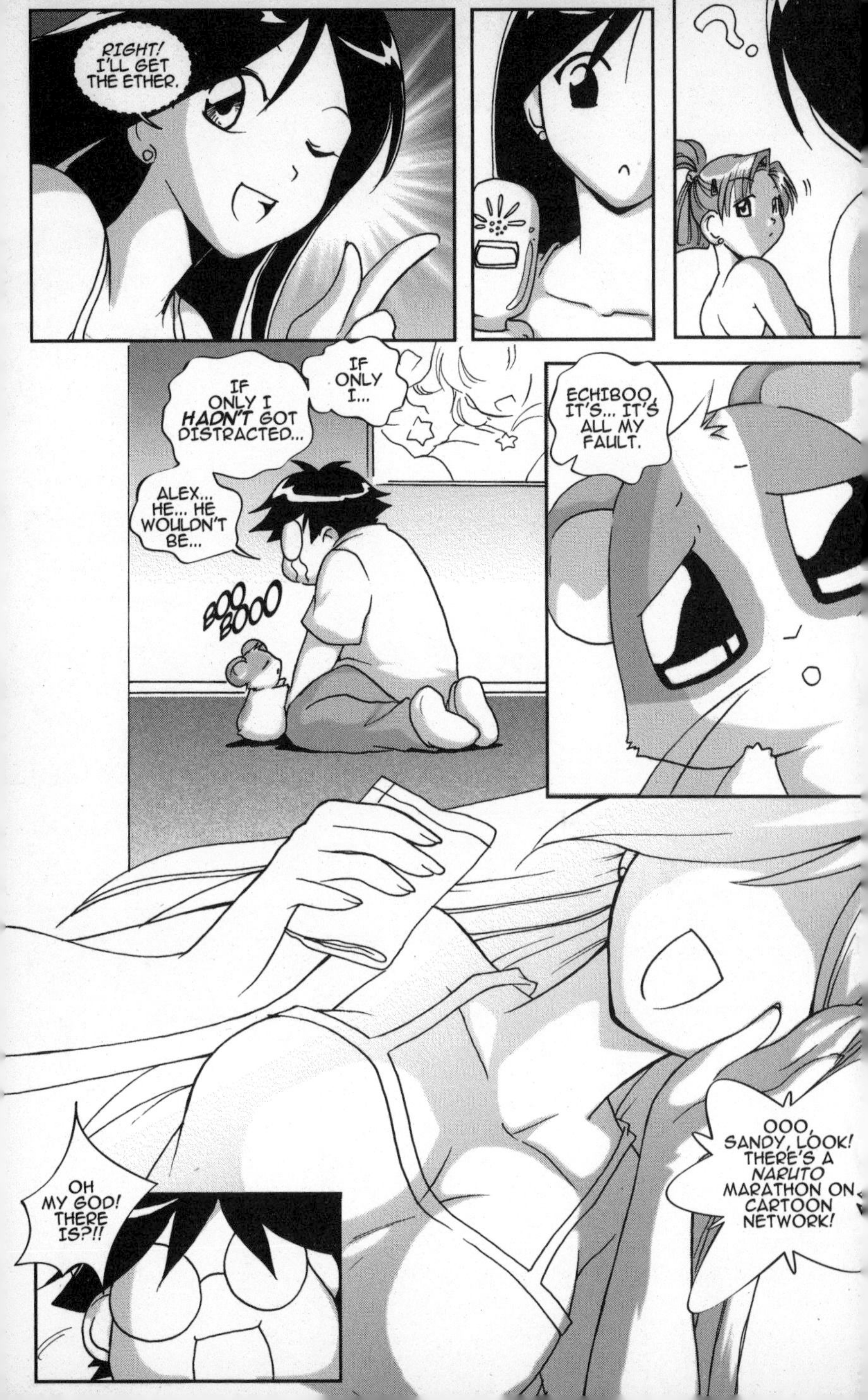
RIGHT! I'LL GET THE ETHER.
ECHIBOO, IT'S... IT'S ALL MY FAULT.
IF ONLY I...
IF ONLY I *HADN'T* GOT DISTRACTED...
ALEX... HE... HE WOULDN'T BE...
BOO BOOO
OOO, SANDY, LOOK! THERE'S A *NARUTO* MARATHON ON CARTOON NETWORK!
OH MY GOD! THERE IS?!!

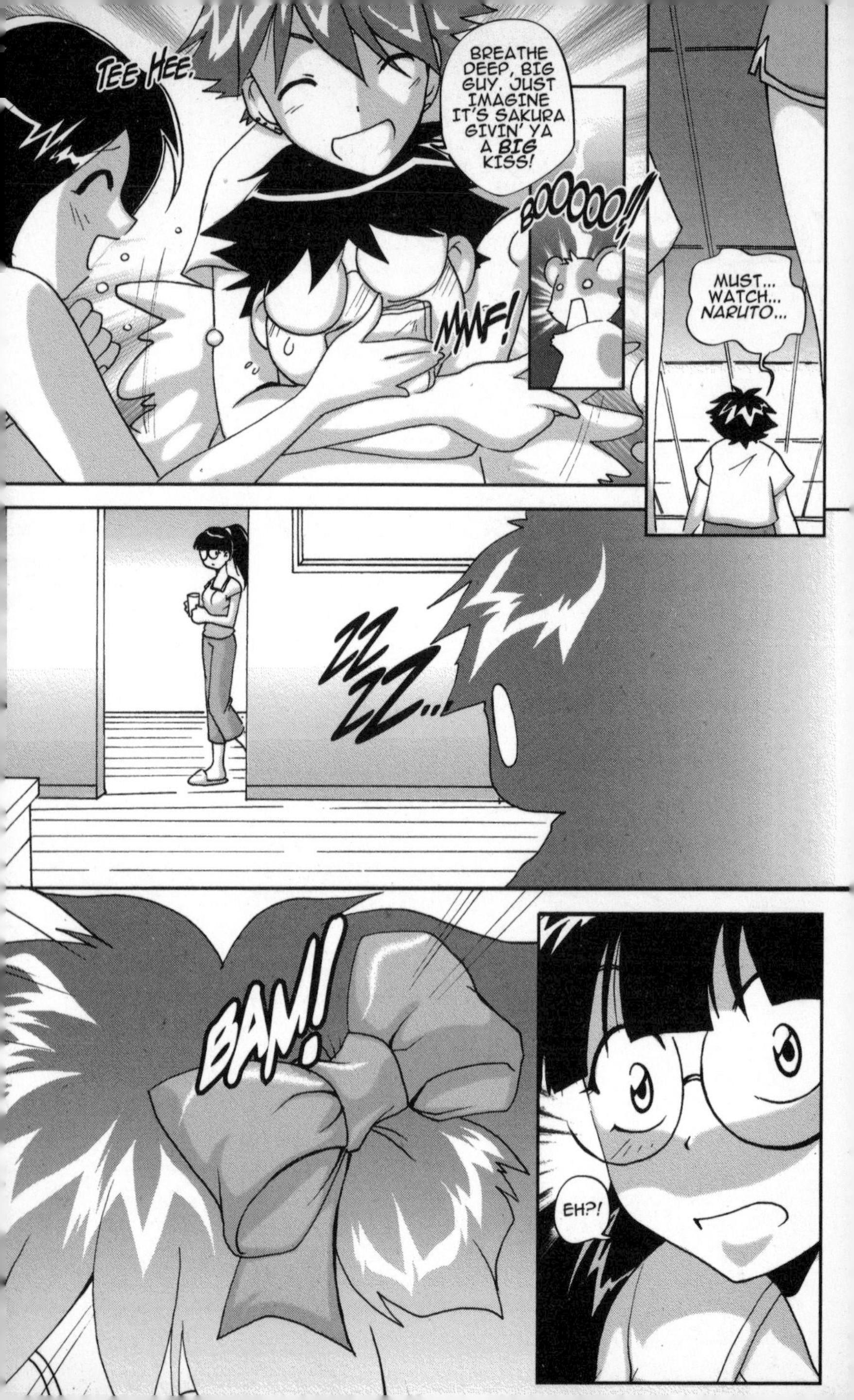
MUST... WATCH... NARUTO...
BREATHE DEEP, BIG GUY, JUST IMAGINE IT'S SAKURA GIVIN' YA A BIG KISS!
TEE HEE.
BOOOOOO!!
MMF!
ZZZZZ...
EH?!
BAM!

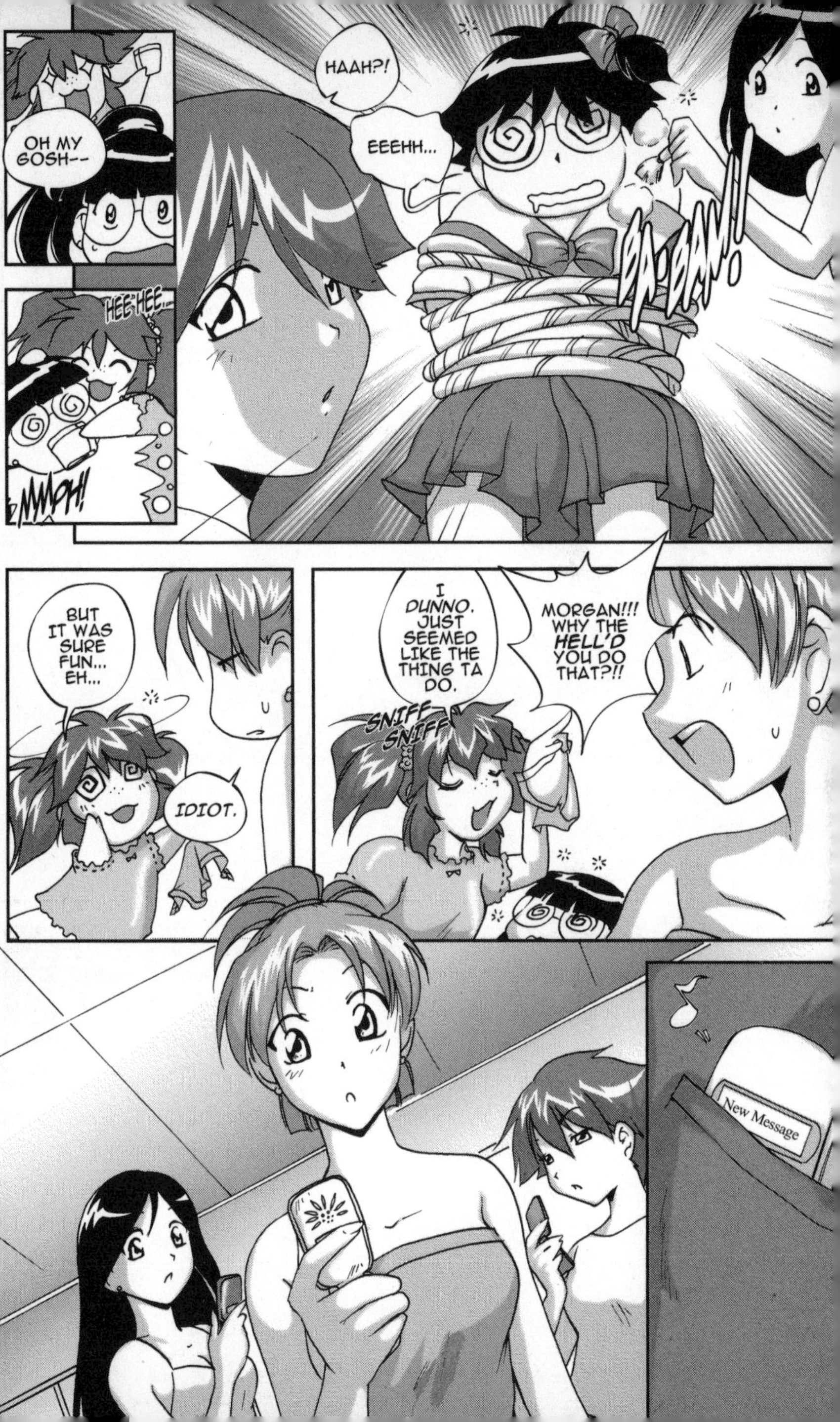
HAAH?!
EEEHH...
BA-BAM!!
OH MY GOSH--
HEE HEE...
MMMPH!
MORGAN!!! WHY THE HELL'D YOU DO THAT?!!
I DUNNO. JUST SEEMED LIKE THE THING TA DO.
SNIFF SNIFF
BUT IT WAS SURE FUN... EH...
IDIOT.
New Message

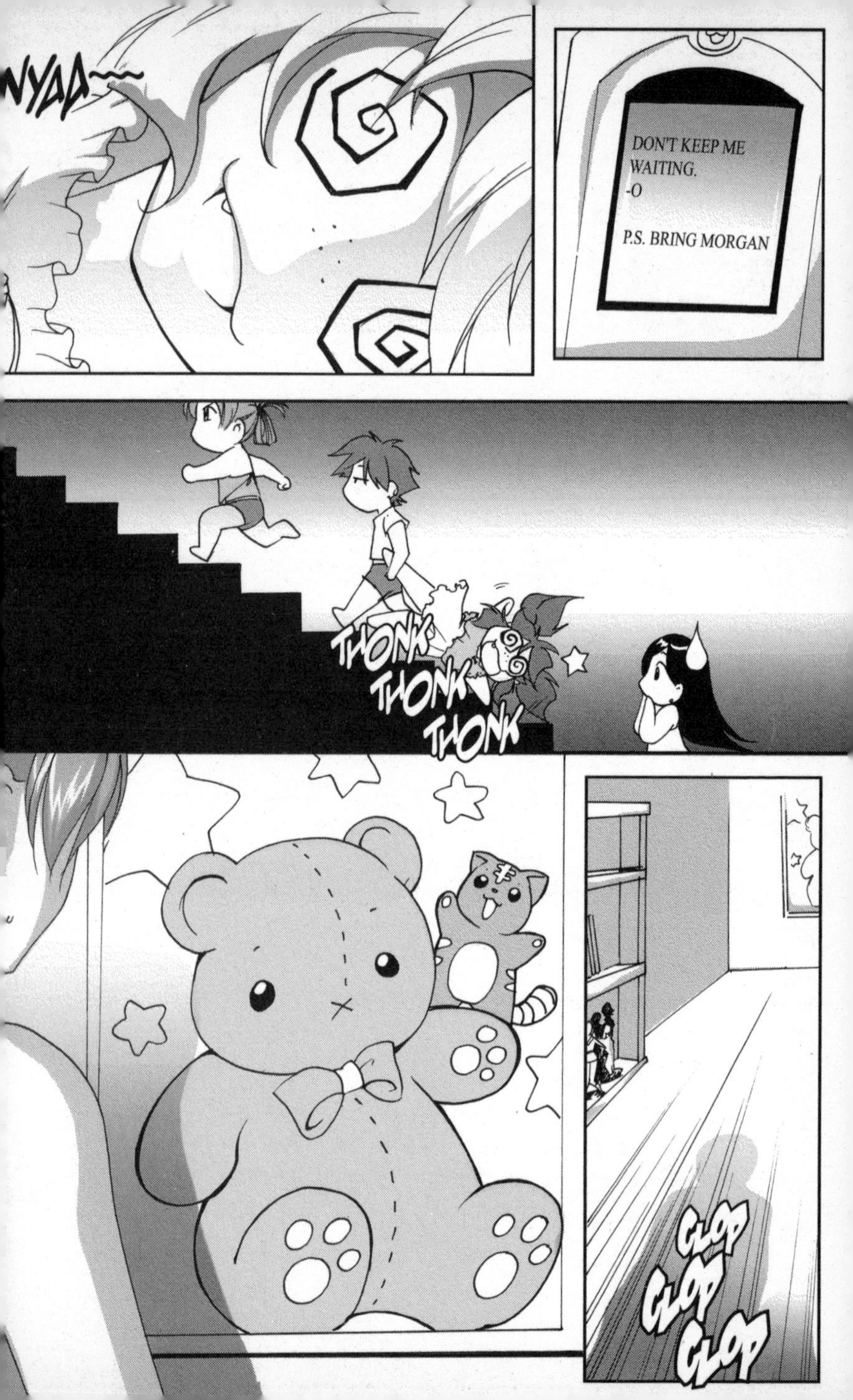
DON'T KEEP ME WAITING.
-O
P.S. BRING MORGAN
NYAA~~~
THONK
THONK
THONK
GLOP
GLOP
GLOP

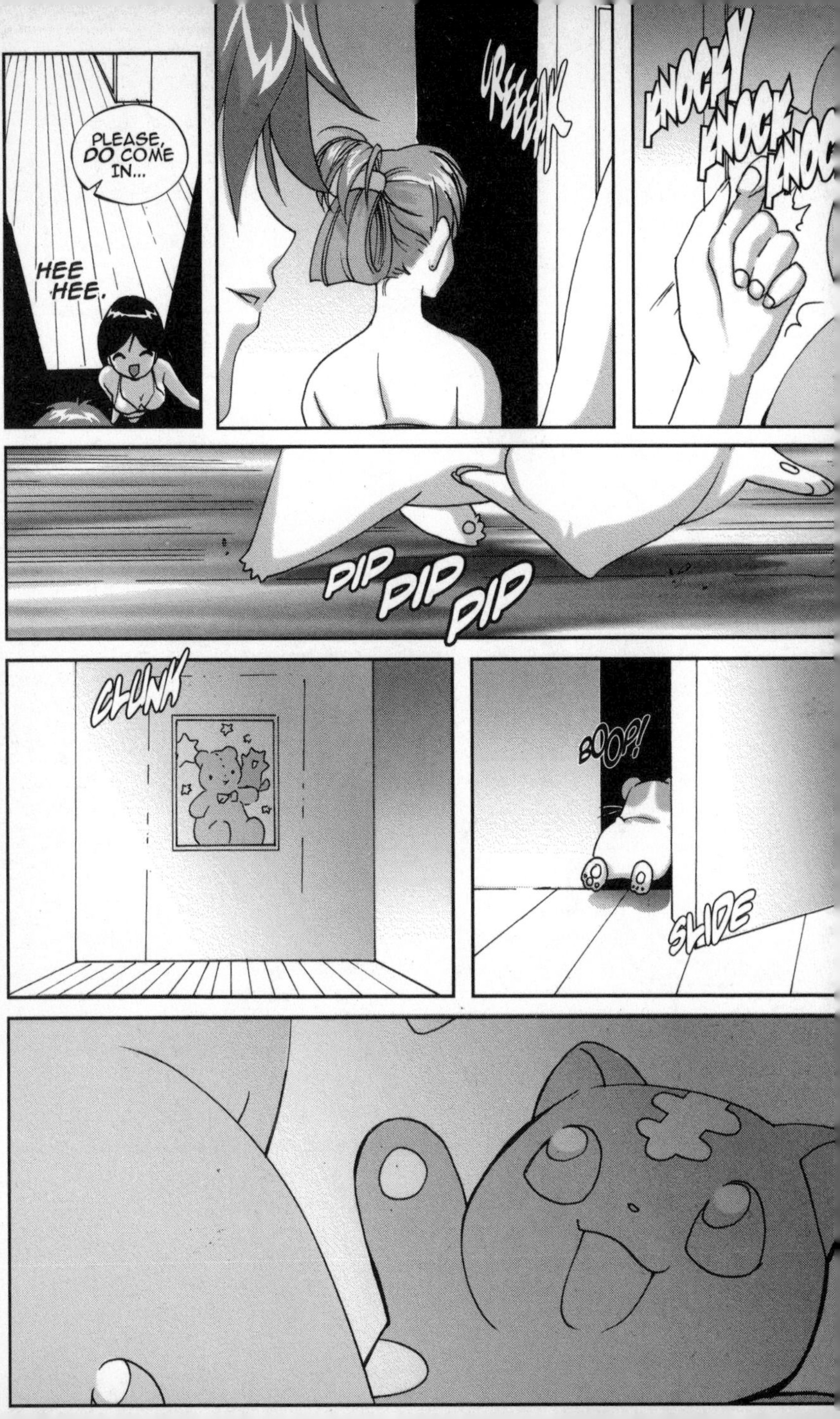
KNOCKY
KNOCK
KNOC
UREEEEAK
PLEASE, DO COME IN...
HEE HEE.
PIP PIP PIP
BOOP!
SLIDE
CHUNK

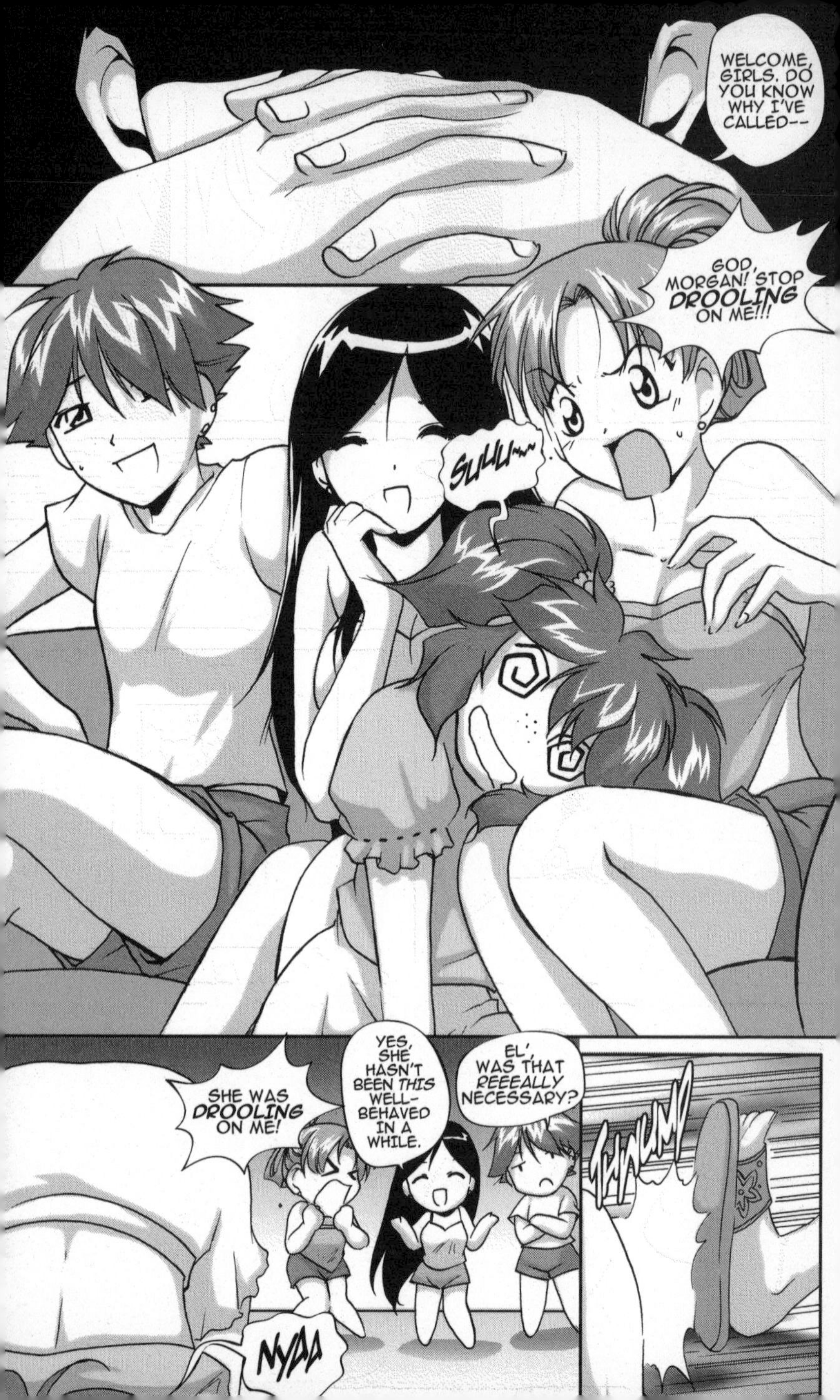
WELCOME, GIRLS. DO YOU KNOW WHY I'VE CALLED--
GOD, MORGAN! STOP DROOLING ON ME!!!
SUUU~~
EL', WAS THAT REEEALLY NECESSARY?
YES, SHE HASN'T BEEN THIS WELL-BEHAVED IN A WHILE.
SHE WAS DROOLING ON ME!
NYAA

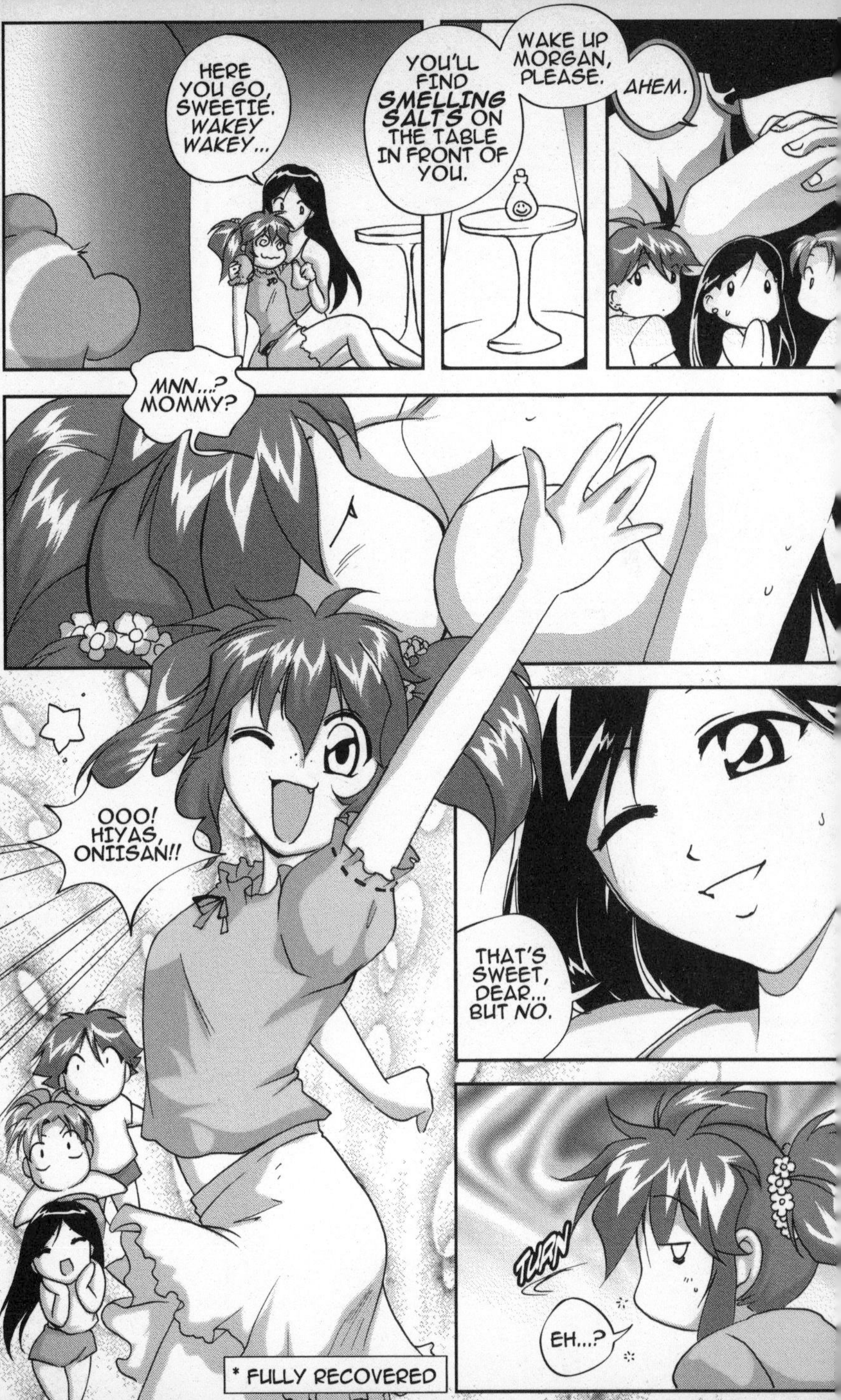
AHEM.
WAKE UP MORGAN, PLEASE.
YOU'LL FIND *SMELLING SALTS* ON THE TABLE IN FRONT OF YOU.
HERE YOU GO, SWEETIE. *WAKEY WAKEY*...
MNN...? MOMMY?
THAT'S SWEET, DEAR... BUT *NO*.
TURN
EH...?
OOO! HIYAS, ONIISAN!!
* FULLY RECOVERED

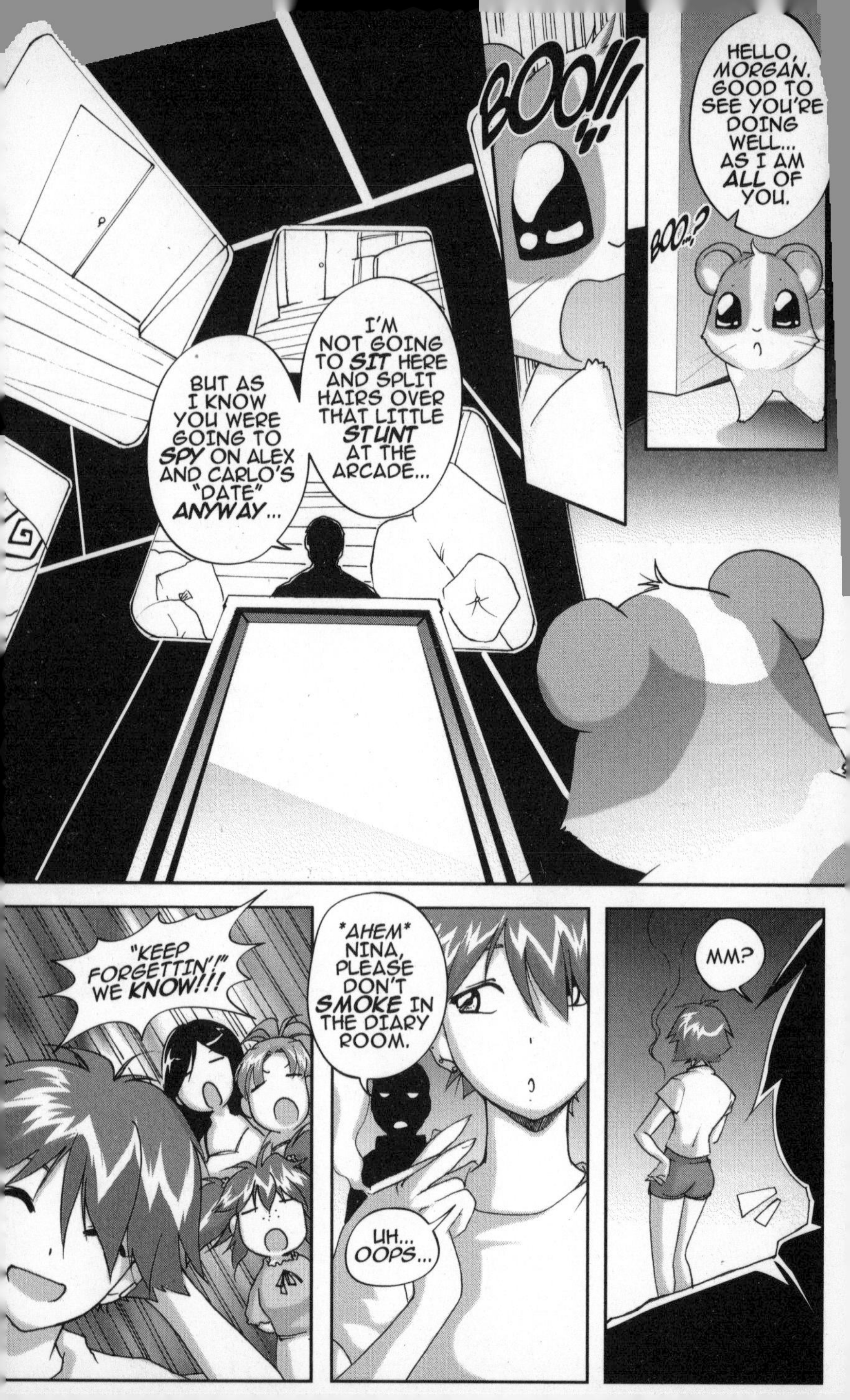
HELLO, MORGAN. GOOD TO SEE YOU'RE DOING WELL... AS I AM ALL OF YOU.
BOO...?
BOO!!
I'M NOT GOING TO SIT HERE AND SPLIT HAIRS OVER THAT LITTLE STUNT AT THE ARCADE...
BUT AS I KNOW YOU WERE GOING TO SPY ON ALEX AND CARLO'S "DATE" ANYWAY...
MM?
AHEM NINA, PLEASE DON'T SMOKE IN THE DIARY ROOM.
UH... OOPS...
"KEEP FORGETTIN'!" WE KNOW!!!

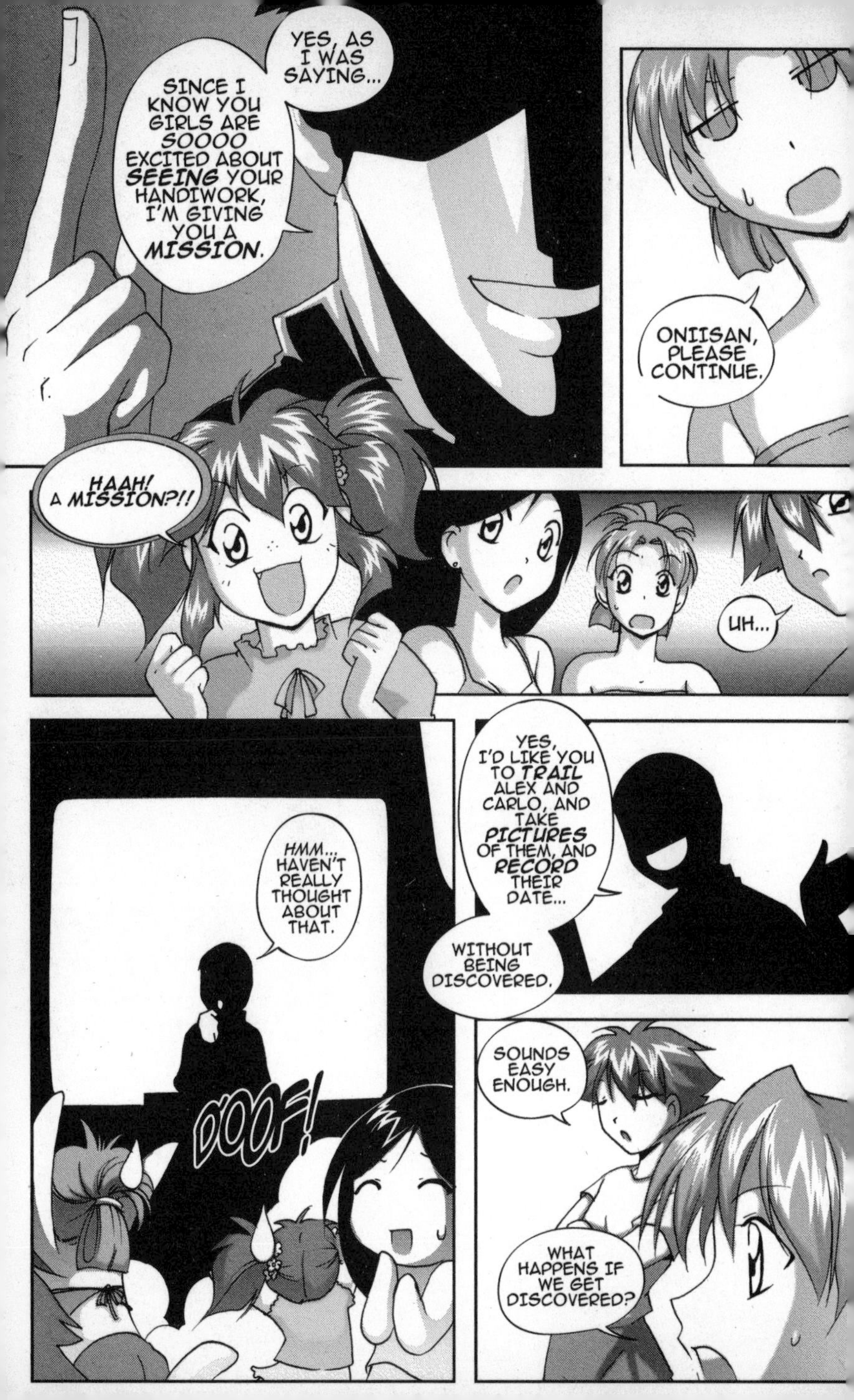
ONIISAN, PLEASE CONTINUE.
YES, AS I WAS SAYING...
SINCE I KNOW YOU GIRLS ARE SOOOO EXCITED ABOUT SEEING YOUR HANDIWORK, I'M GIVING YOU A MISSION.
HAAH! A MISSION?!!
UH...
YES, I'D LIKE YOU TO TRAIL ALEX AND CARLO, AND TAKE PICTURES OF THEM, AND RECORD THEIR DATE...
WITHOUT BEING DISCOVERED.
SOUNDS EASY ENOUGH.
WHAT HAPPENS IF WE GET DISCOVERED?
HMM... HAVEN'T REALLY THOUGHT ABOUT THAT.
DOOF!

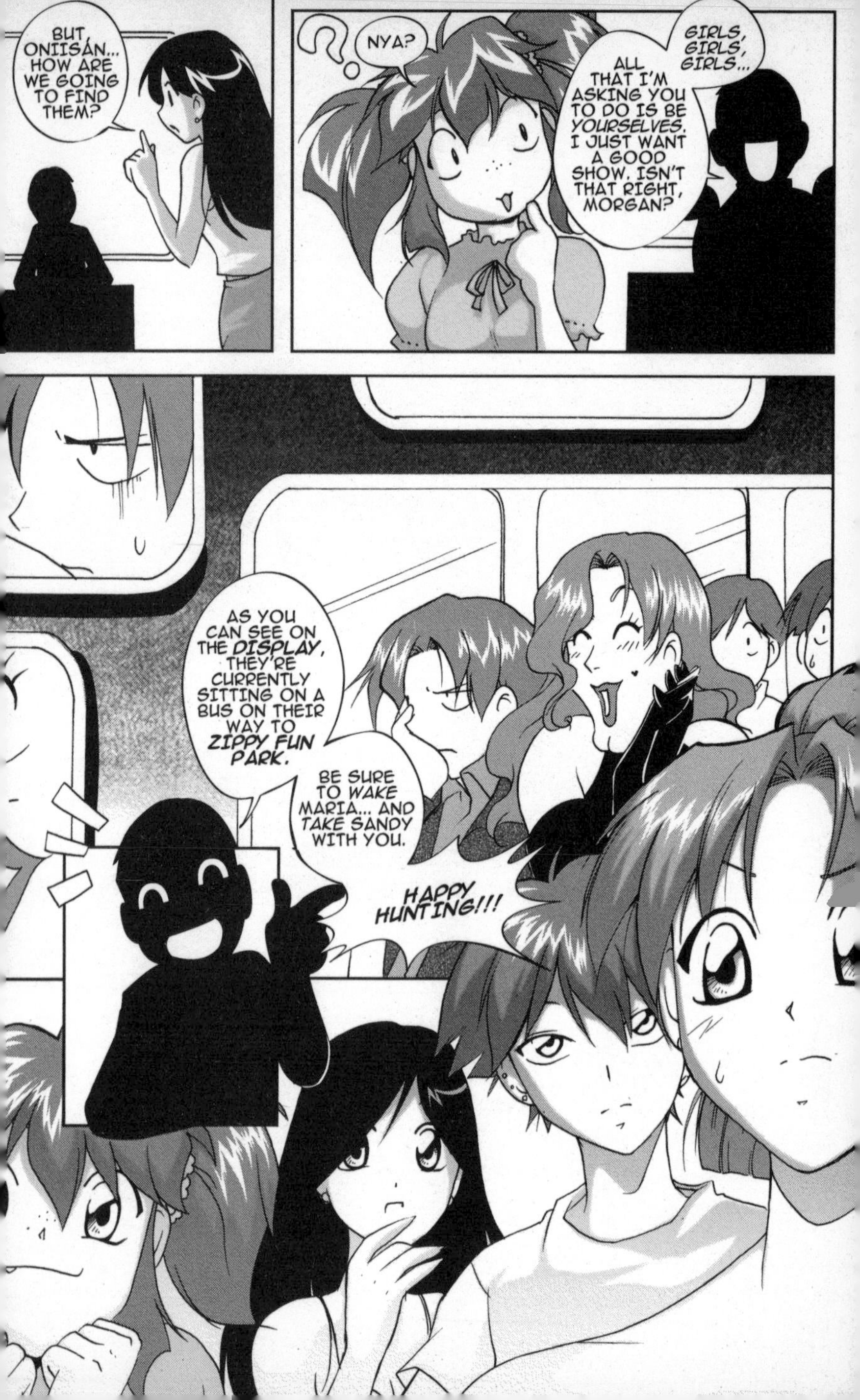
GIRLS, GIRLS, GIRLS...
ALL THAT I'M ASKING YOU TO DO IS BE *YOURSELVES*. I JUST WANT A GOOD SHOW. ISN'T THAT RIGHT, MORGAN?
NYA?
BUT, ONIISÁN... HOW ARE WE GOING TO FIND THEM?
AS YOU CAN SEE ON THE ***DISPLAY***, THEY'RE CURRENTLY SITTING ON A BUS ON THEIR WAY TO ***ZIPPY FUN PARK.***
BE SURE TO *WAKE* MARIA... AND *TAKE* SANDY WITH YOU.
HAPPY HUNTING!!!

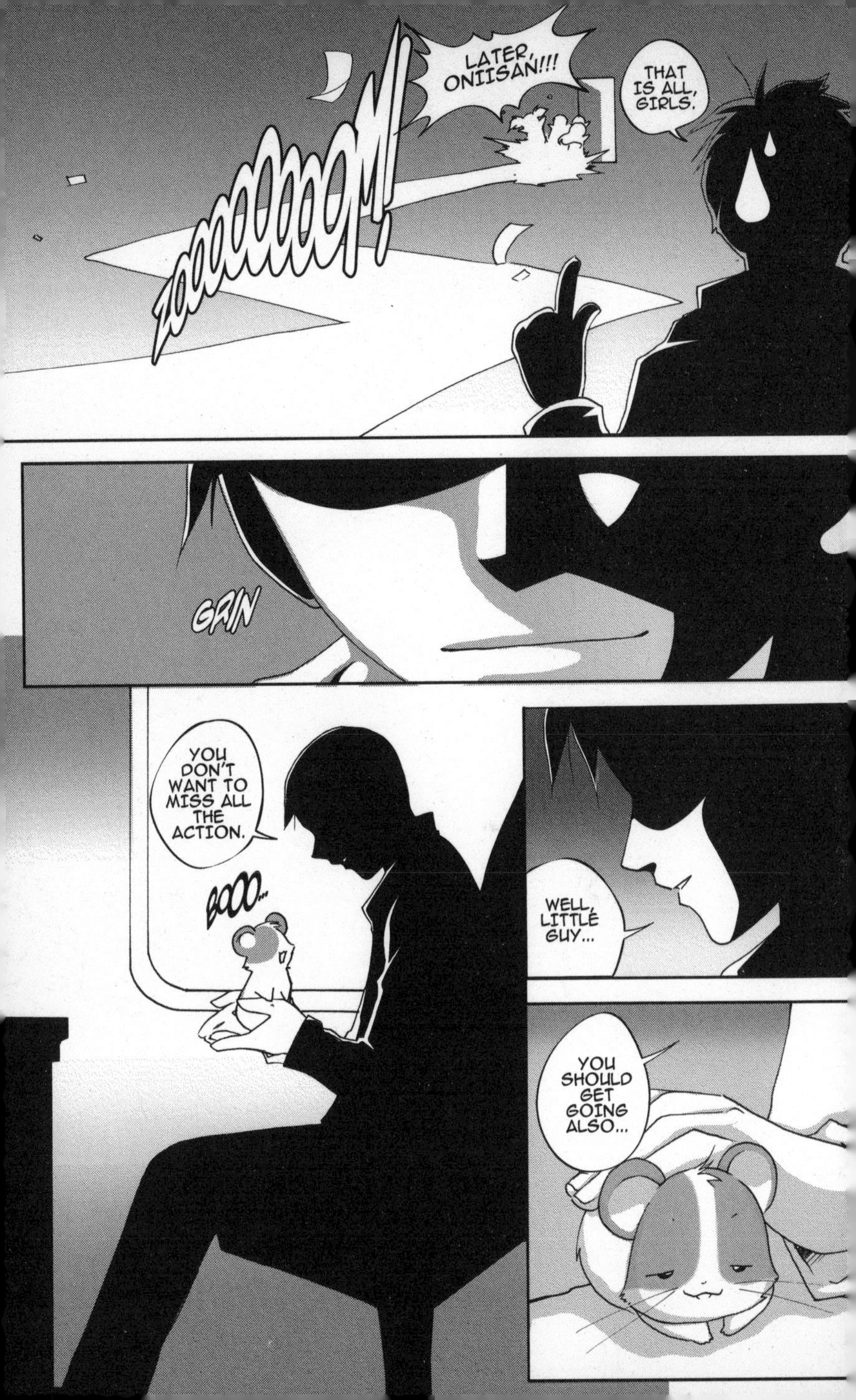
THAT IS ALL, GIRLS.
LATER, ONIISAN!!!
ZOOOOOOOOM!!
GRIN
WELL, LITTLE GUY...
YOU SHOULD GET GOING ALSO...
YOU DON'T WANT TO MISS ALL THE ACTION.
BOOO...

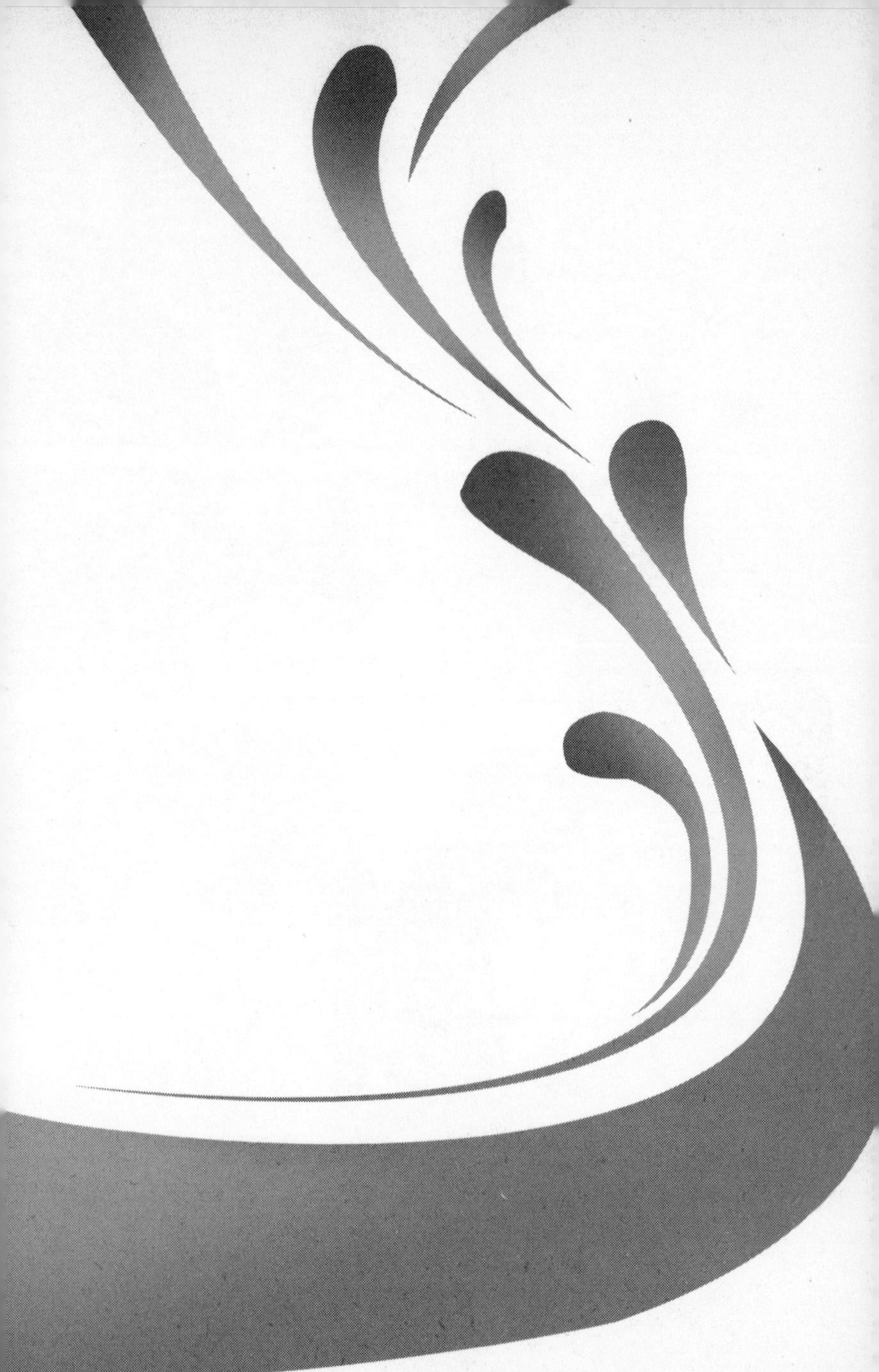

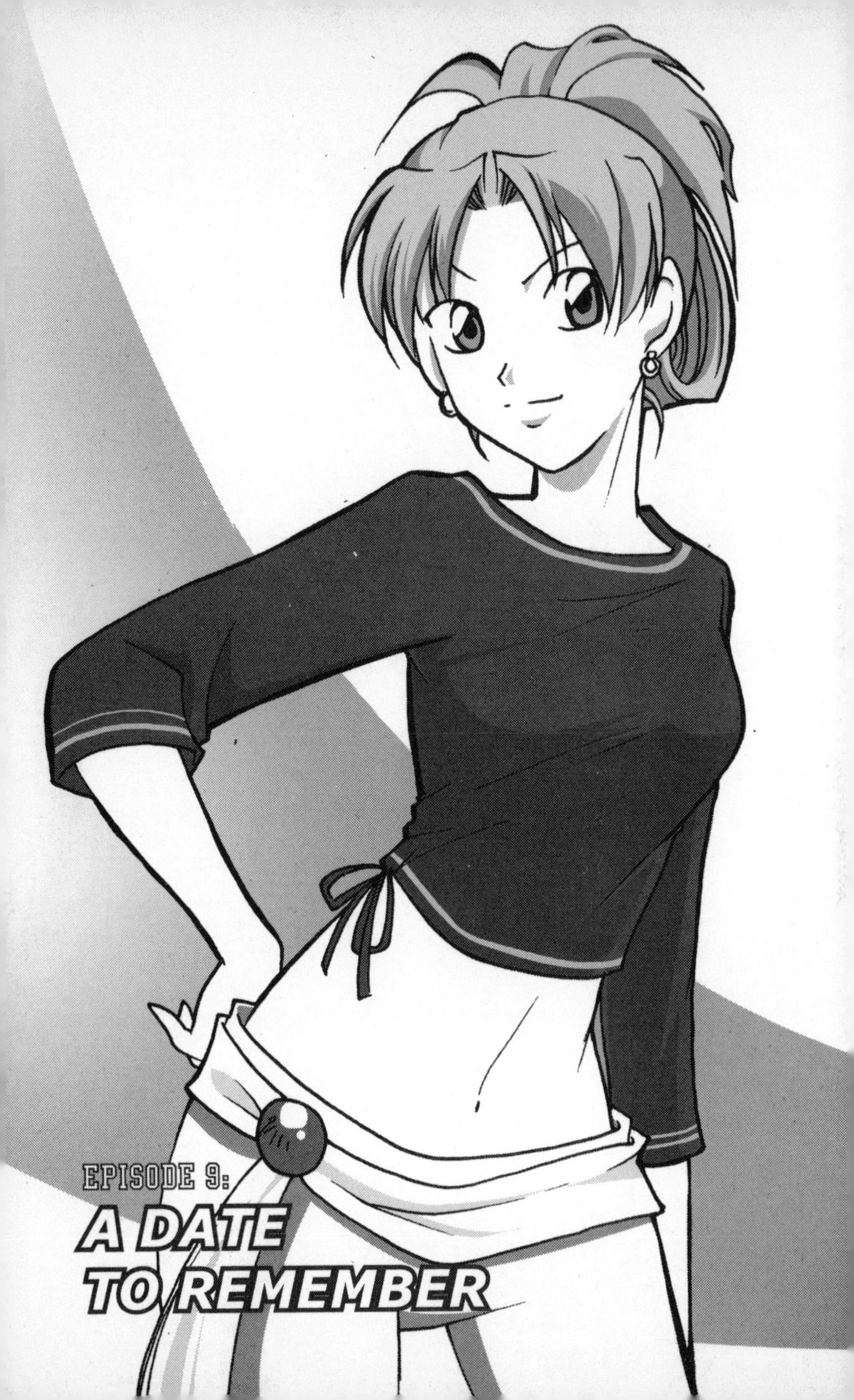
EPISODE 9:
A DATE
TO REMEMBER

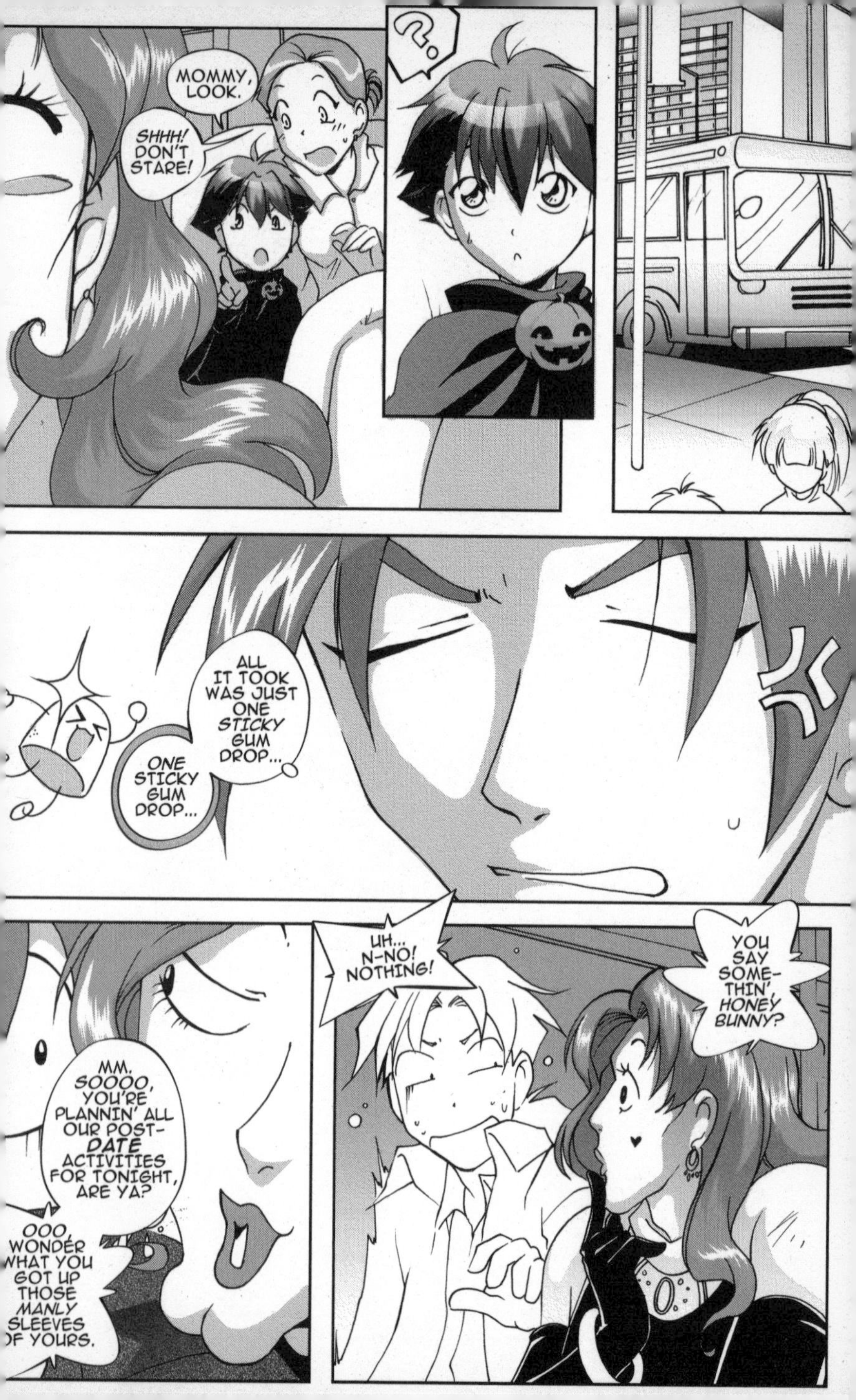
?
MOMMY, LOOK.
SHHH! DON'T STARE!
ALL IT TOOK WAS JUST ONE *STICKY* GUM DROP...
ONE STICKY GUM DROP...
YOU SAY SOMETHIN', HONEY BUNNY?
UH... N-NO! NOTHING!
MM. *SOOOO*, YOU'RE PLANNIN' ALL OUR POST-**DATE** ACTIVITIES FOR TONIGHT, ARE YA?
OOO, WONDER WHAT YOU GOT UP THOSE *MANLY* SLEEVES OF YOURS.

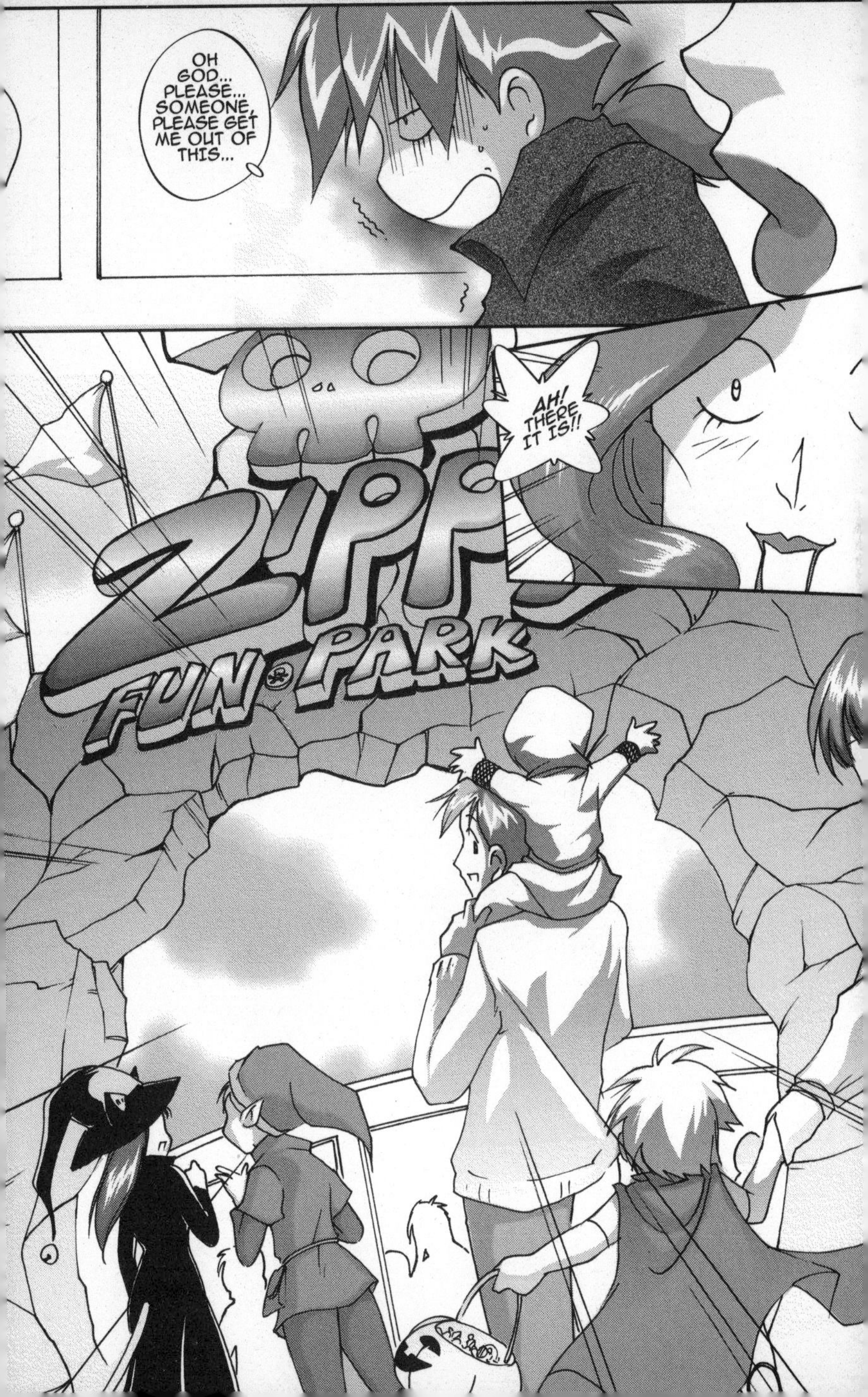
OH GOD... PLEASE... SOMEONE, PLEASE GET ME OUT OF THIS...
AH! THERE IT IS!!
FUN PARK

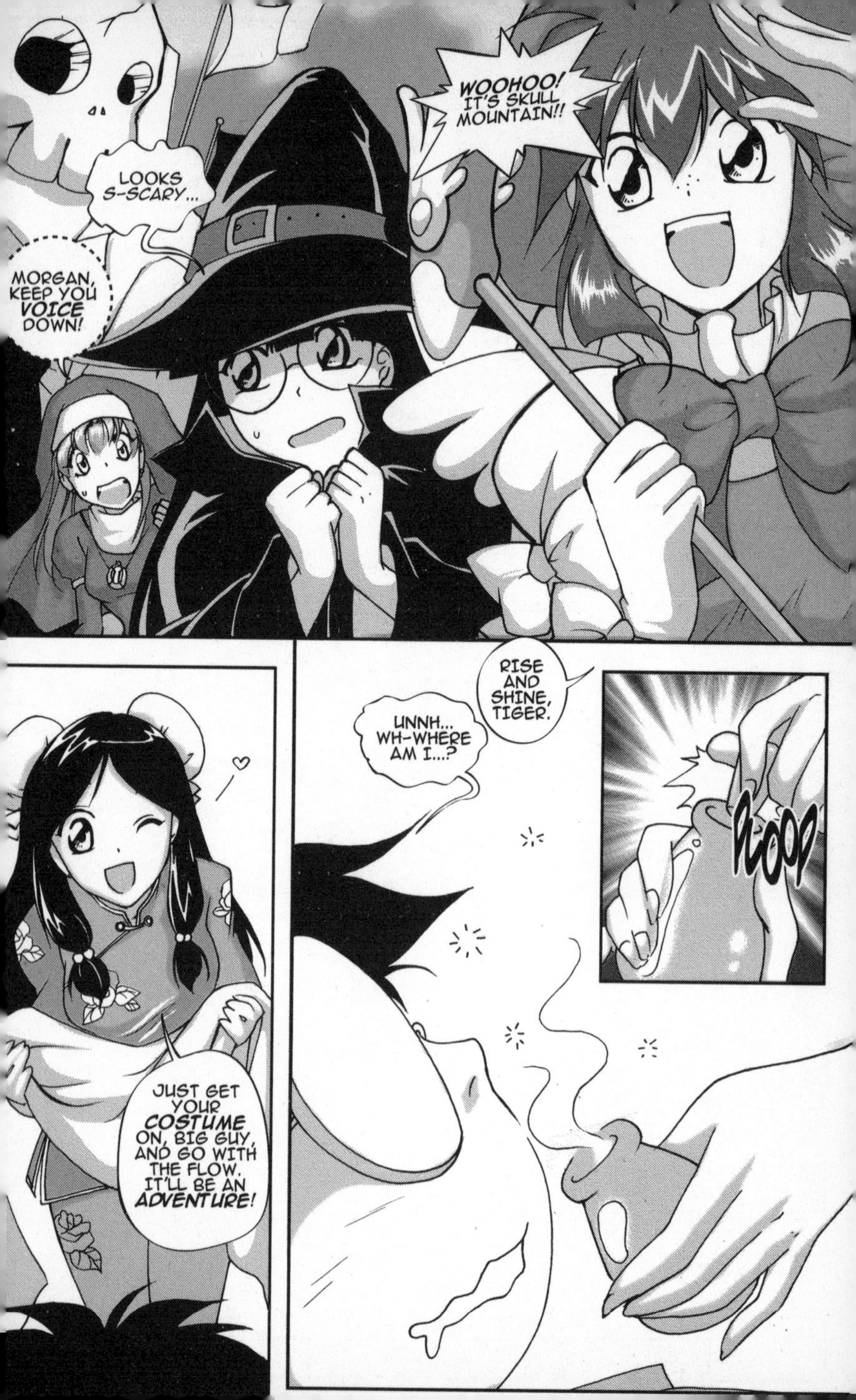
WOOHOO! IT'S SKULL MOUNTAIN!!
LOOKS S-SCARY...
MORGAN, KEEP YOU VOICE DOWN!
PLOOP
RISE AND SHINE, TIGER.
UNNH... WH-WHERE AM I...?
JUST GET YOUR COSTUME ON, BIG GUY, AND GO WITH THE FLOW. IT'LL BE AN ADVENTURE!

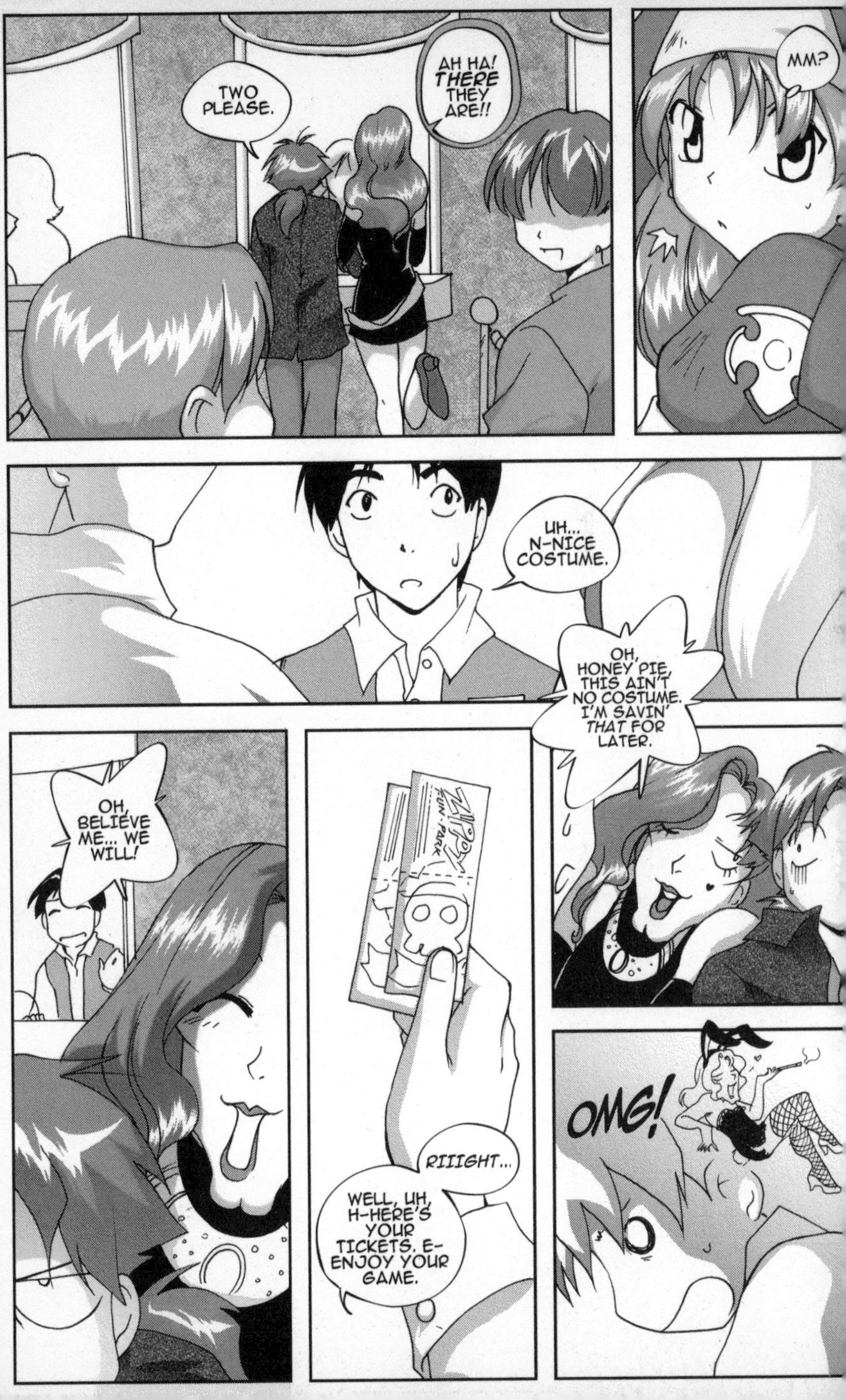
MM?
AH HA! *THERE* THEY ARE!!
TWO PLEASE.
UH... N-NICE COSTUME.
OH, HONEY PIE, THIS AIN'T NO COSTUME. I'M SAVIN' *THAT* FOR LATER.
OMG!
RIIIGHT...
WELL, UH, H-HERE'S YOUR TICKETS. E-ENJOY YOUR GAME.
OH, BELIEVE ME... WE WILL!

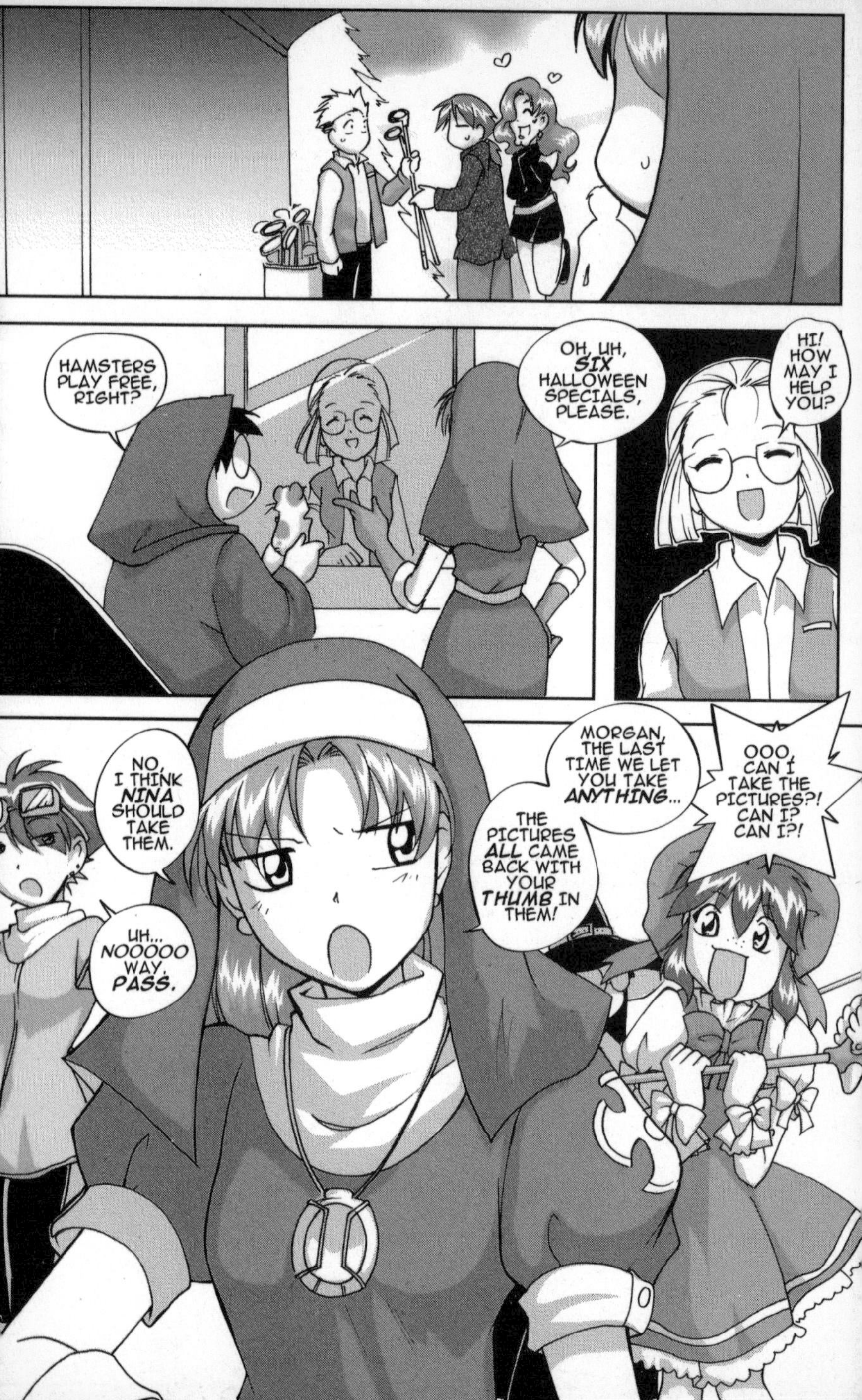
HI! HOW MAY I HELP YOU?
OH, UH, SIX HALLOWEEN SPECIALS, PLEASE.
HAMSTERS PLAY FREE, RIGHT?
OOO, CAN I TAKE THE PICTURES?! CAN I? CAN I?!
MORGAN, THE LAST TIME WE LET YOU TAKE ANYTHING...
THE PICTURES ALL CAME BACK WITH YOUR THUMB IN THEM!
NO, I THINK NINA SHOULD TAKE THEM.
UH... NOOOOO WAY. PASS.

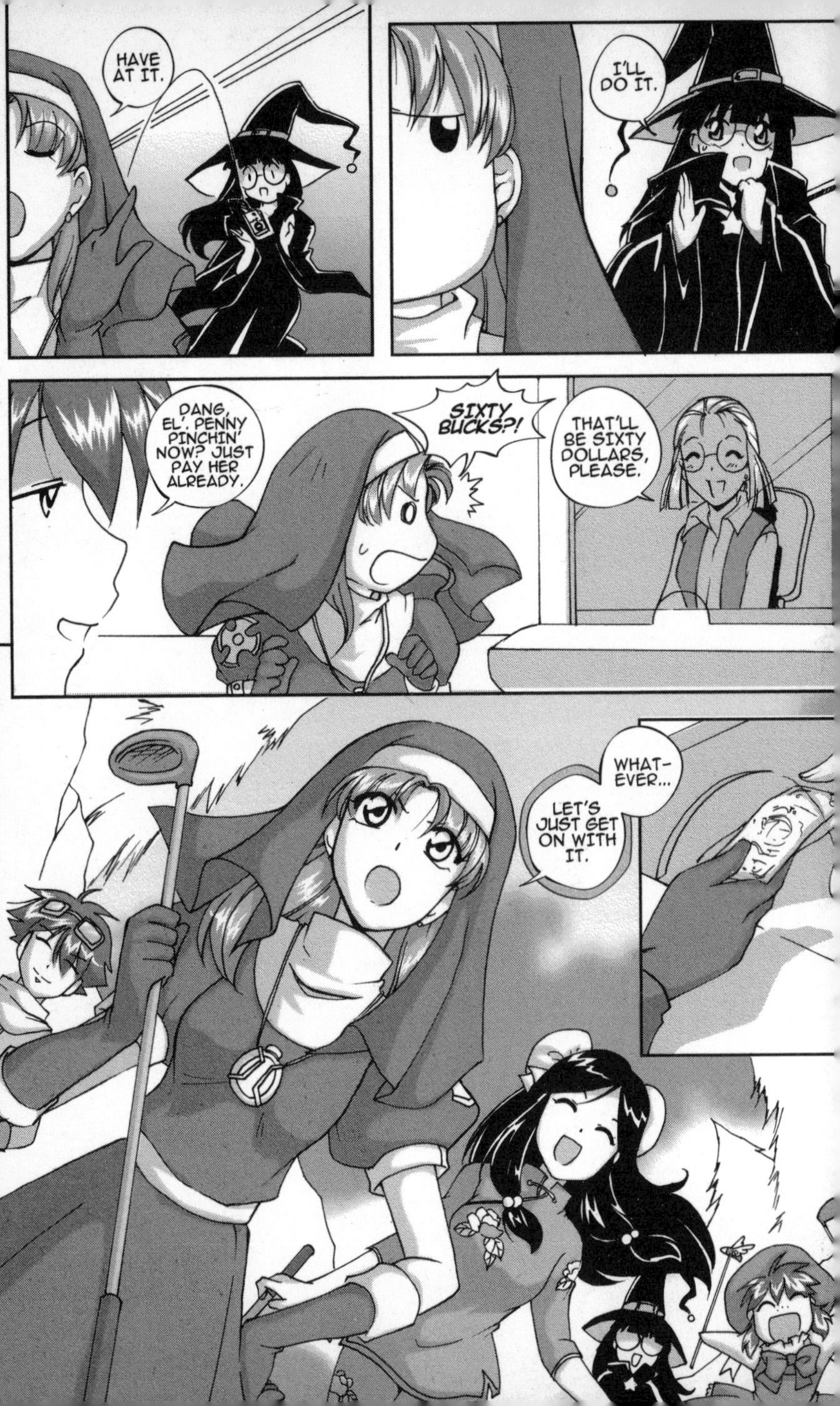
I'LL DO IT.
HAVE AT IT.
THAT'LL BE SIXTY DOLLARS, PLEASE.
SIXTY BUCKS?!
DANG, EL'. PENNY PINCHIN' NOW? JUST PAY HER ALREADY.
WHAT-EVER... LET'S JUST GET ON WITH IT.

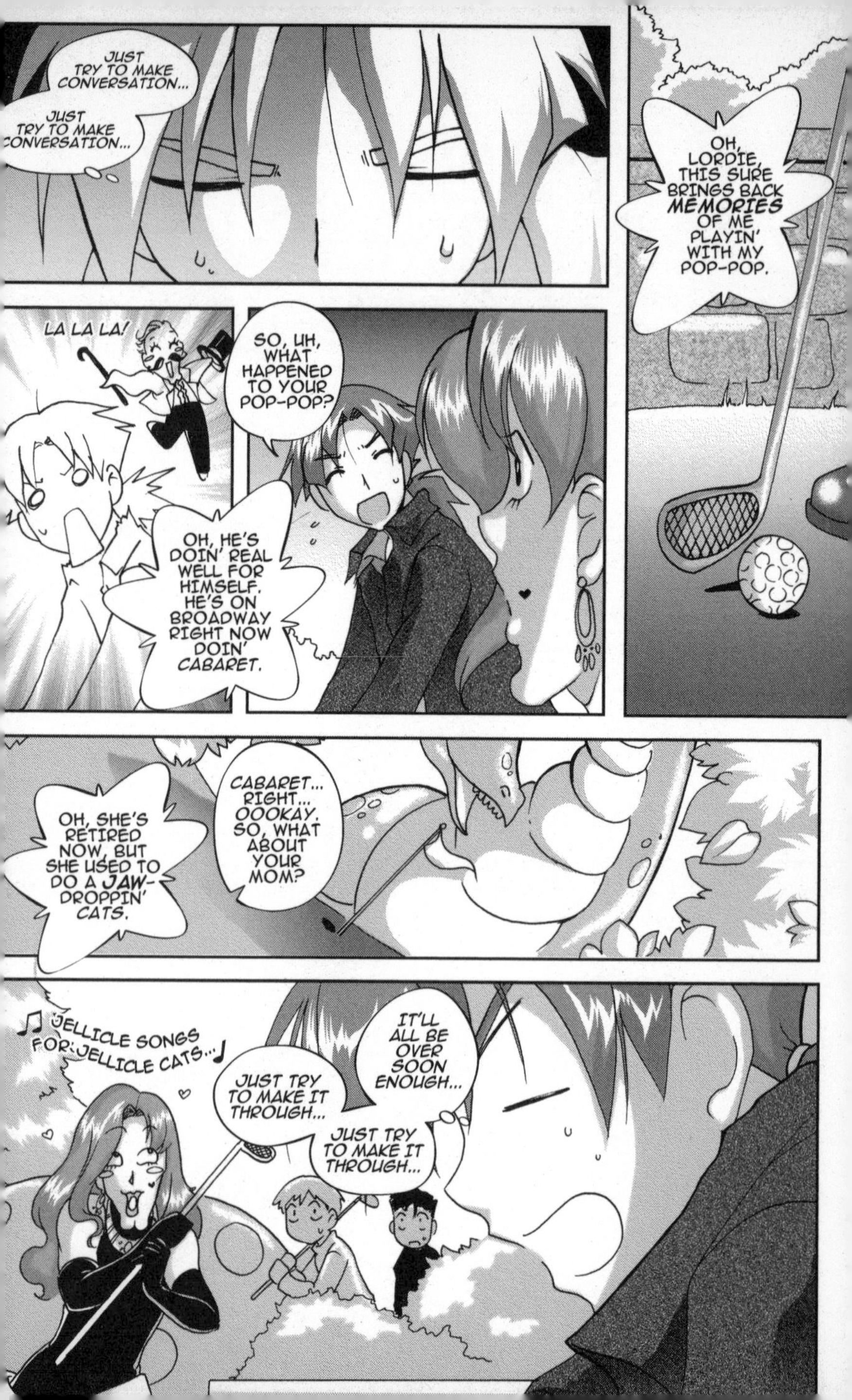
OH, LORDIE, THIS SURE BRINGS BACK *MEMORIES* OF ME PLAYIN' WITH MY POP-POP.
JUST TRY TO MAKE CONVERSATION...
JUST TRY TO MAKE CONVERSATION...
SO, UH, WHAT HAPPENED TO YOUR POP-POP?
OH, HE'S DOIN' REAL WELL FOR HIMSELF. HE'S ON BROADWAY RIGHT NOW DOIN' *CABARET*.
LA LA LA!
CABARET... RIGHT... OOOKAY. SO, WHAT ABOUT YOUR MOM?
OH, SHE'S RETIRED NOW, BUT SHE USED TO DO A *JAW*-DROPPIN' *CATS*.
IT'LL ALL BE OVER SOON ENOUGH...
JUST TRY TO MAKE IT THROUGH...
JUST TRY TO MAKE IT THROUGH...
♫ JELLICLE SONGS FOR JELLICLE CATS... ♩

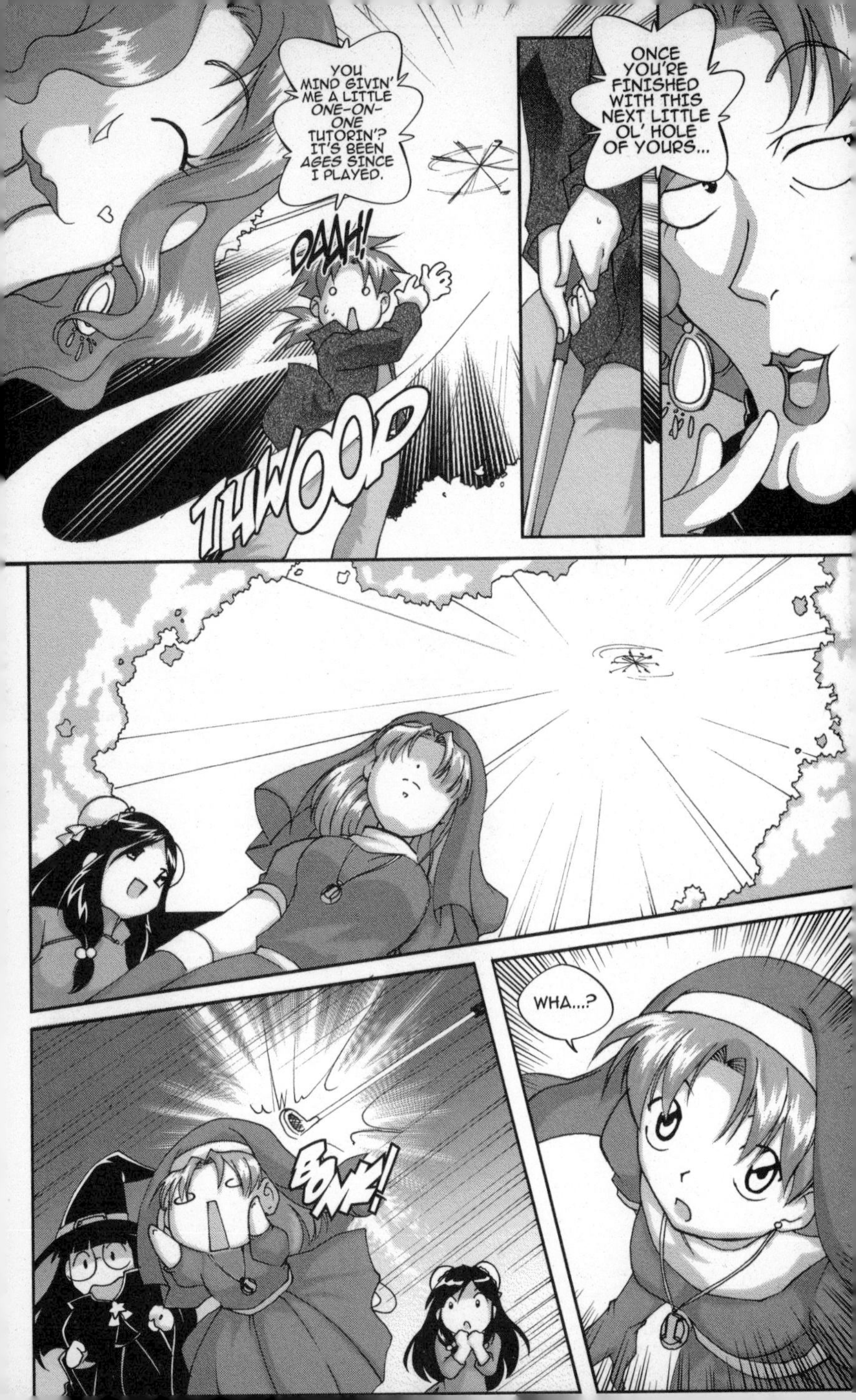
ONCE YOU'RE FINISHED WITH THIS NEXT LITTLE OL' HOLE OF YOURS...
YOU MIND GIVIN' ME A LITTLE ONE-ON-ONE TUTORIN'? IT'S BEEN AGES SINCE I PLAYED.
DAAH!
THWOOP
WHA...?
BONK!

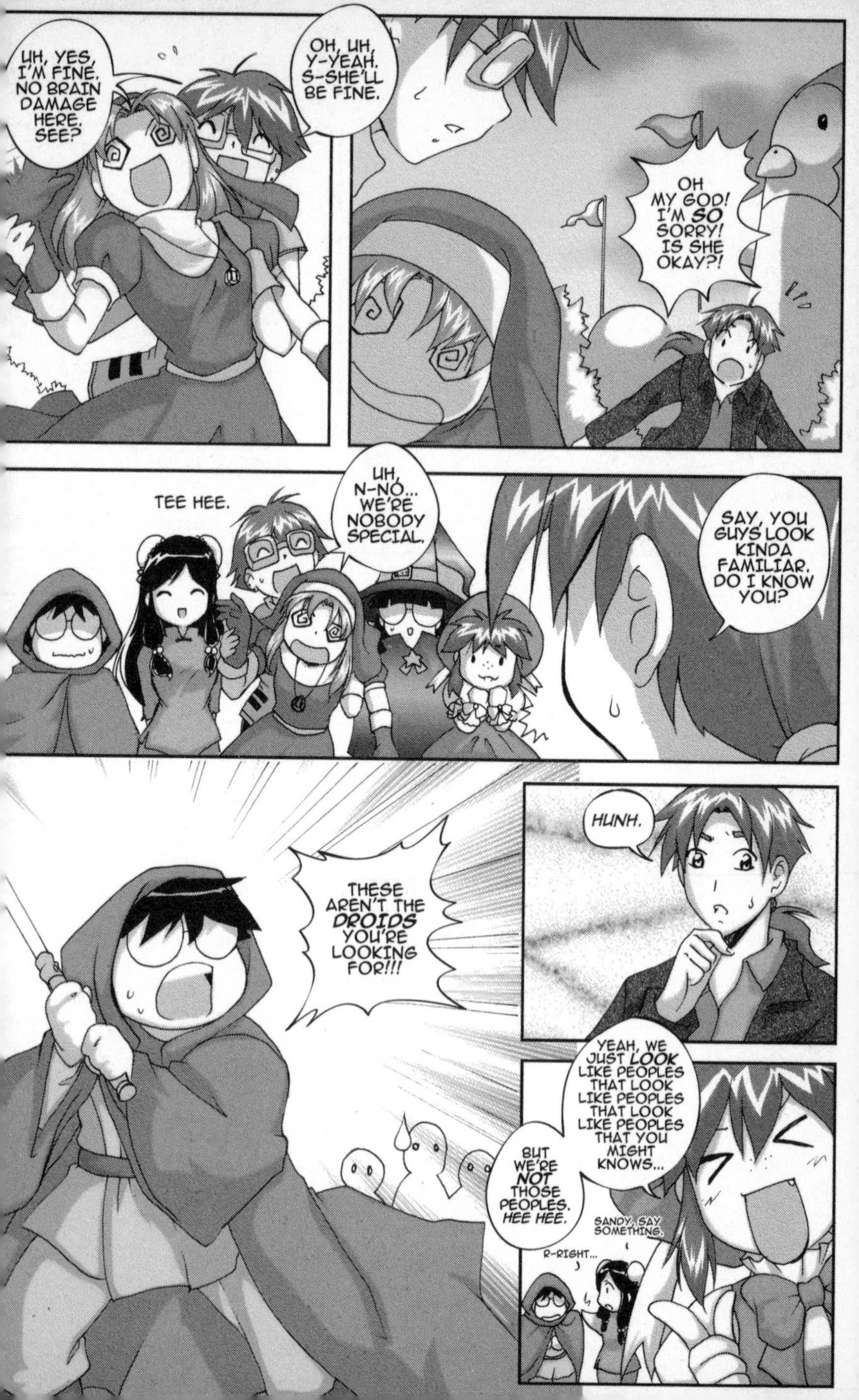

OH MY GOD! I'M SO SORRY! IS SHE OKAY?!
OH, UH, Y-YEAH. S-SHE'LL BE FINE.
UH, YES, I'M FINE. NO BRAIN DAMAGE HERE. SEE?
SAY, YOU GUYS LOOK KINDA FAMILIAR. DO I KNOW YOU?
UH, N-NO... WE'RE NOBODY SPECIAL.
TEE HEE.
HUNH.
YEAH, WE JUST LOOK LIKE PEOPLES THAT LOOK LIKE PEOPLES THAT LOOK LIKE PEOPLES THAT YOU MIGHT KNOWS...
BUT WE'RE NOT THOSE PEOPLES. HEE HEE.
SANDY, SAY SOMETHING.
R-RIGHT...
THESE AREN'T THE DROIDS YOU'RE LOOKING FOR!!!

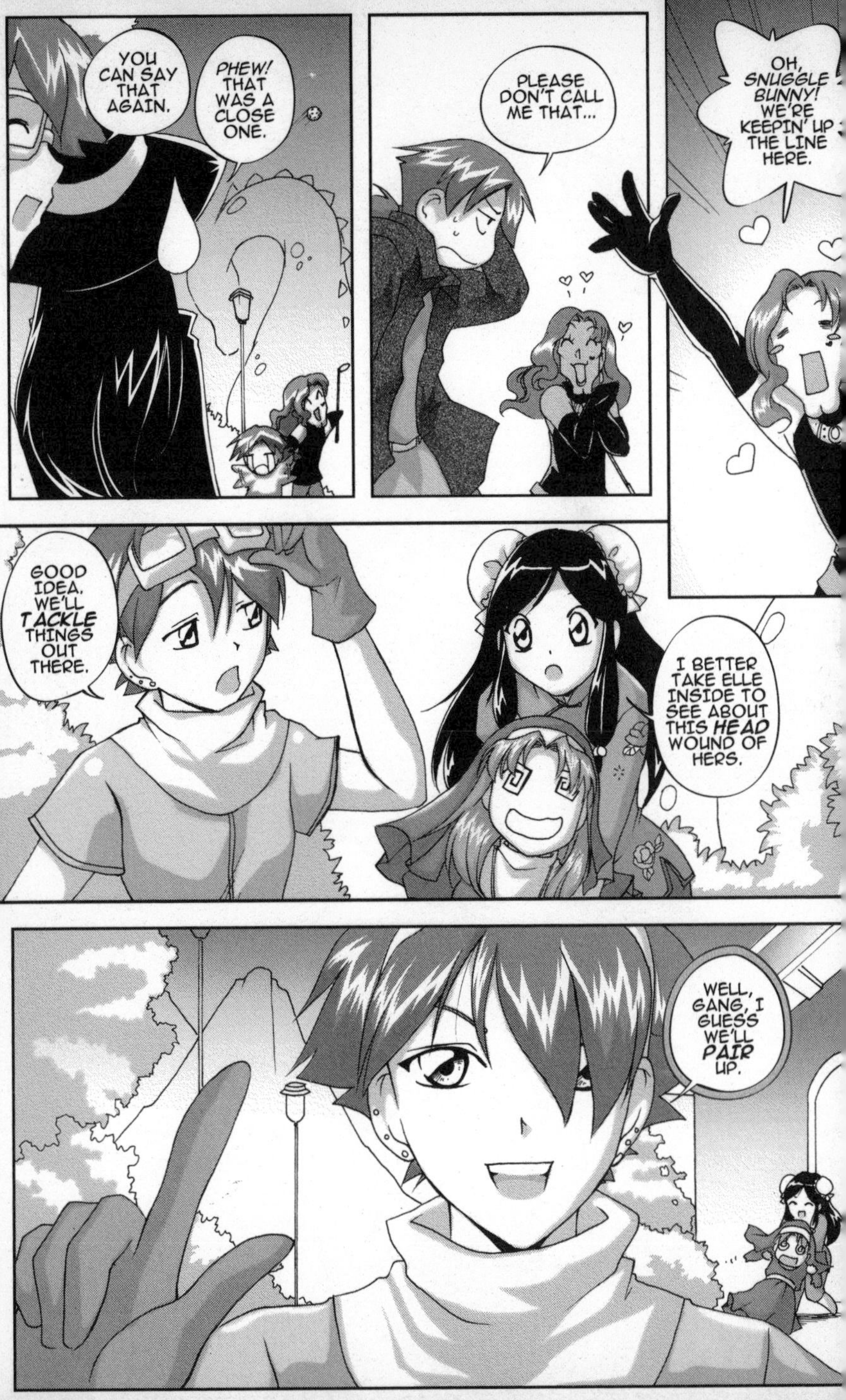
OH, SNUGGLE BUNNY! WE'RE KEEPIN' UP THE LINE HERE.
PLEASE DON'T CALL ME THAT...
PHEW! THAT WAS A CLOSE ONE.
YOU CAN SAY THAT AGAIN.
I BETTER TAKE ELLE INSIDE TO SEE ABOUT THIS HEAD WOUND OF HERS.
GOOD IDEA. WE'LL TACKLE THINGS OUT THERE.
WELL, GANG, I GUESS WE'LL PAIR UP.

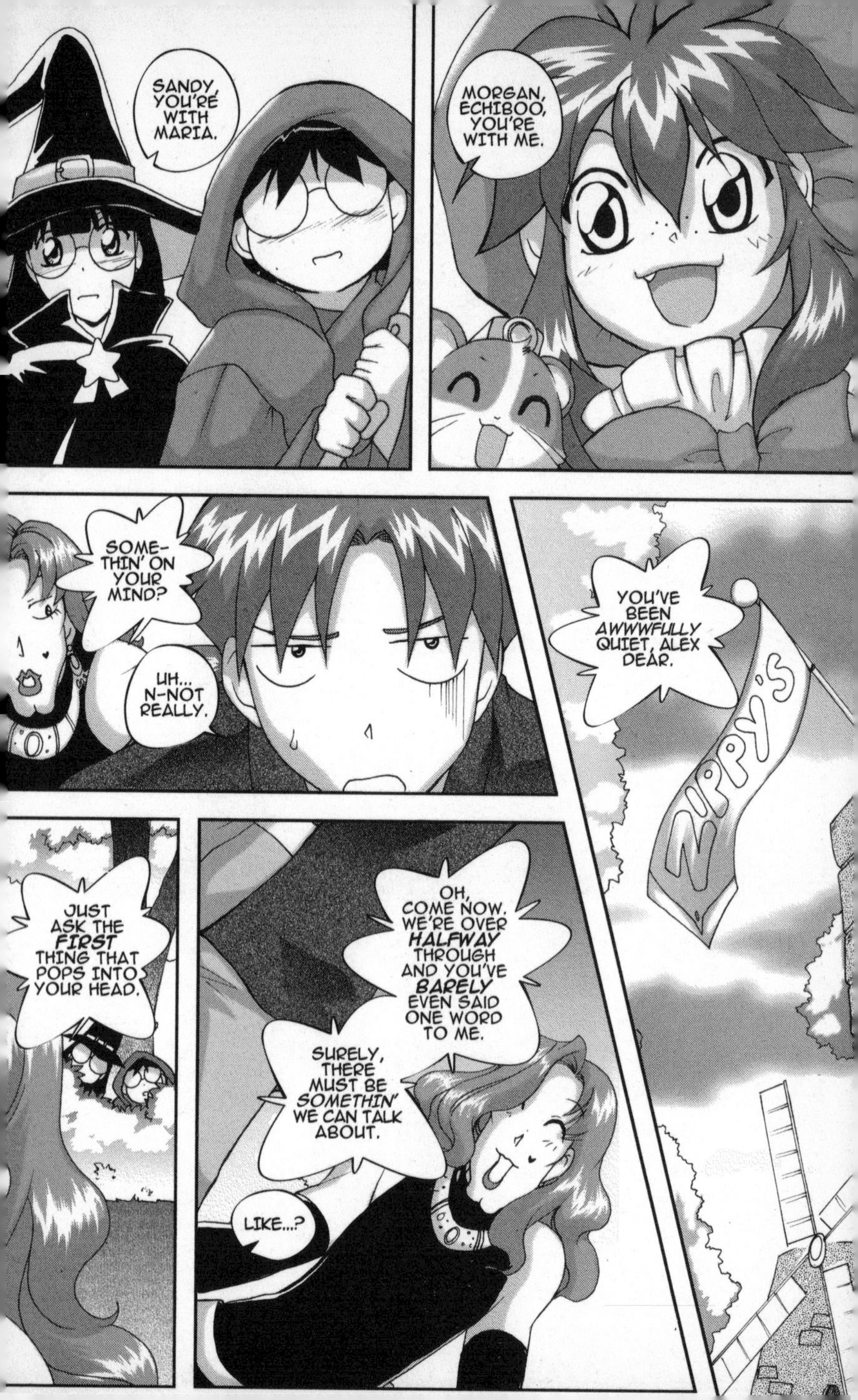
MORGAN, ECHIBOO, YOU'RE WITH ME.
SANDY, YOU'RE WITH MARIA.
YOU'VE BEEN AWWWFULLY QUIET, ALEX DEAR.
ZIPPY'S
SOME-THIN' ON YOUR MIND?
UH... N-NOT REALLY.
OH, COME NOW. WE'RE OVER HALFWAY THROUGH AND YOU'VE BARELY EVEN SAID ONE WORD TO ME.
SURELY, THERE MUST BE SOMETHIN' WE CAN TALK ABOUT.
LIKE...?
JUST ASK THE FIRST THING THAT POPS INTO YOUR HEAD.

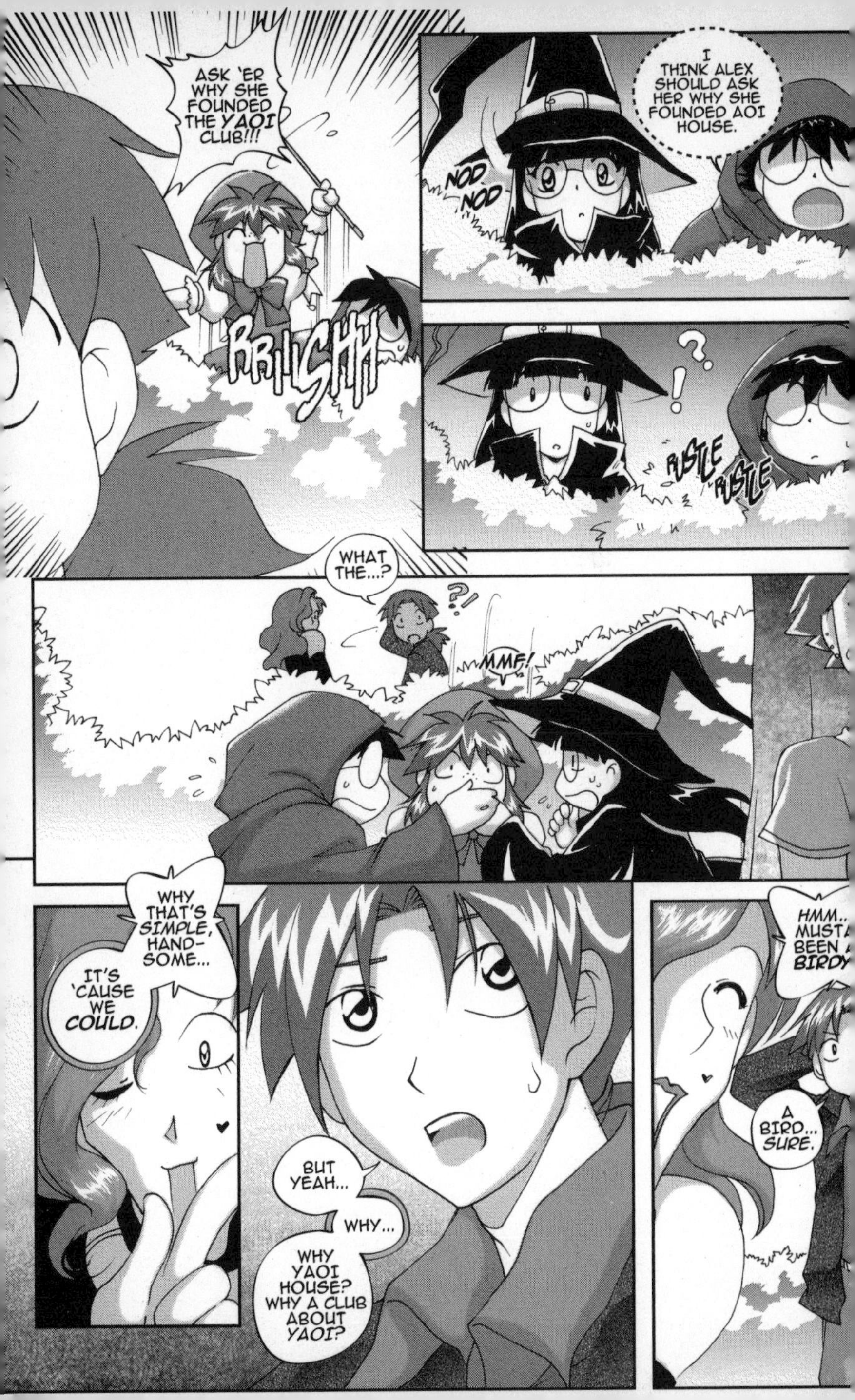
I THINK ALEX SHOULD ASK HER WHY SHE FOUNDED AOI HOUSE.
NOD NOD
?
!
RUSTLE RUSTLE
ASK 'ER WHY SHE FOUNDED THE YAOI CLUB!!!
BRRUSHH
WHAT THE...?
?!
MMF!
HMM.. MUSTA BEEN BIRDY
A BIRD... SURE.
BUT YEAH...
WHY...
WHY YAOI HOUSE? WHY A CLUB ABOUT YAOI?
WHY THAT'S SIMPLE, HAND-SOME...
IT'S 'CAUSE WE COULD.

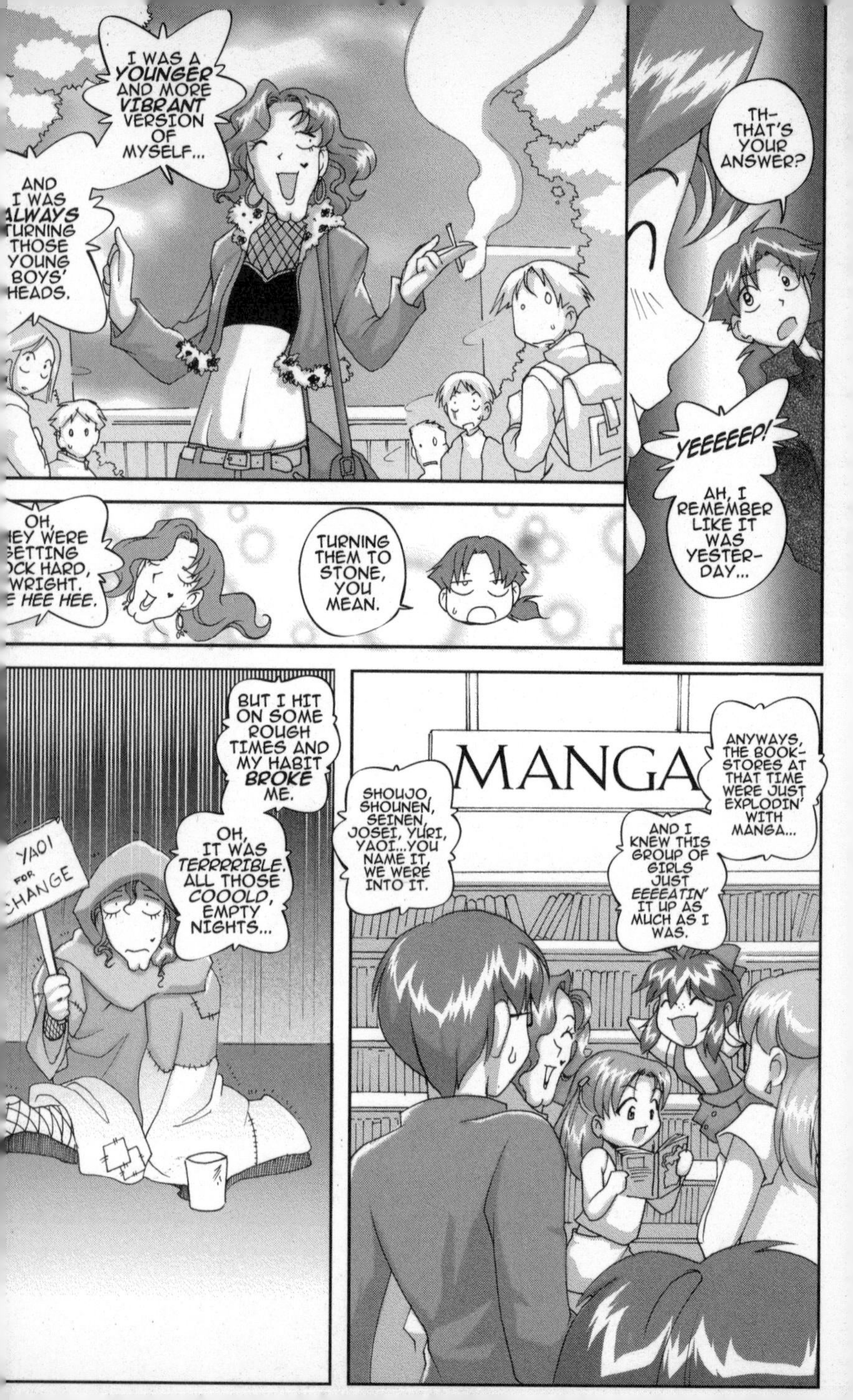
TH-THAT'S YOUR ANSWER?
YEEEEEP!
AH, I REMEMBER LIKE IT WAS YESTER-DAY...
I WAS A YOUNGER AND MORE VIBRANT VERSION OF MYSELF...
AND I WAS ALWAYS TURNING THOSE YOUNG BOYS' HEADS.
TURNING THEM TO STONE, YOU MEAN.
OH, HEY WERE GETTING OCK HARD, WRIGHT. E HEE HEE.
MANGA
ANYWAYS, THE BOOK-STORES AT THAT TIME WERE JUST EXPLODIN' WITH MANGA...
AND I KNEW THIS GROUP OF GIRLS JUST EEEEATIN' IT UP AS MUCH AS I WAS.
SHOUJO, SHOUNEN, SEINEN, JOSEI, YURI, YAOI...YOU NAME IT, WE WERE INTO IT.
BUT I HIT ON SOME ROUGH TIMES AND MY HABIT BROKE ME.
OH, IT WAS TERRRRIBLE. ALL THOSE COOOLD, EMPTY NIGHTS...
YAOI FOR CHANGE

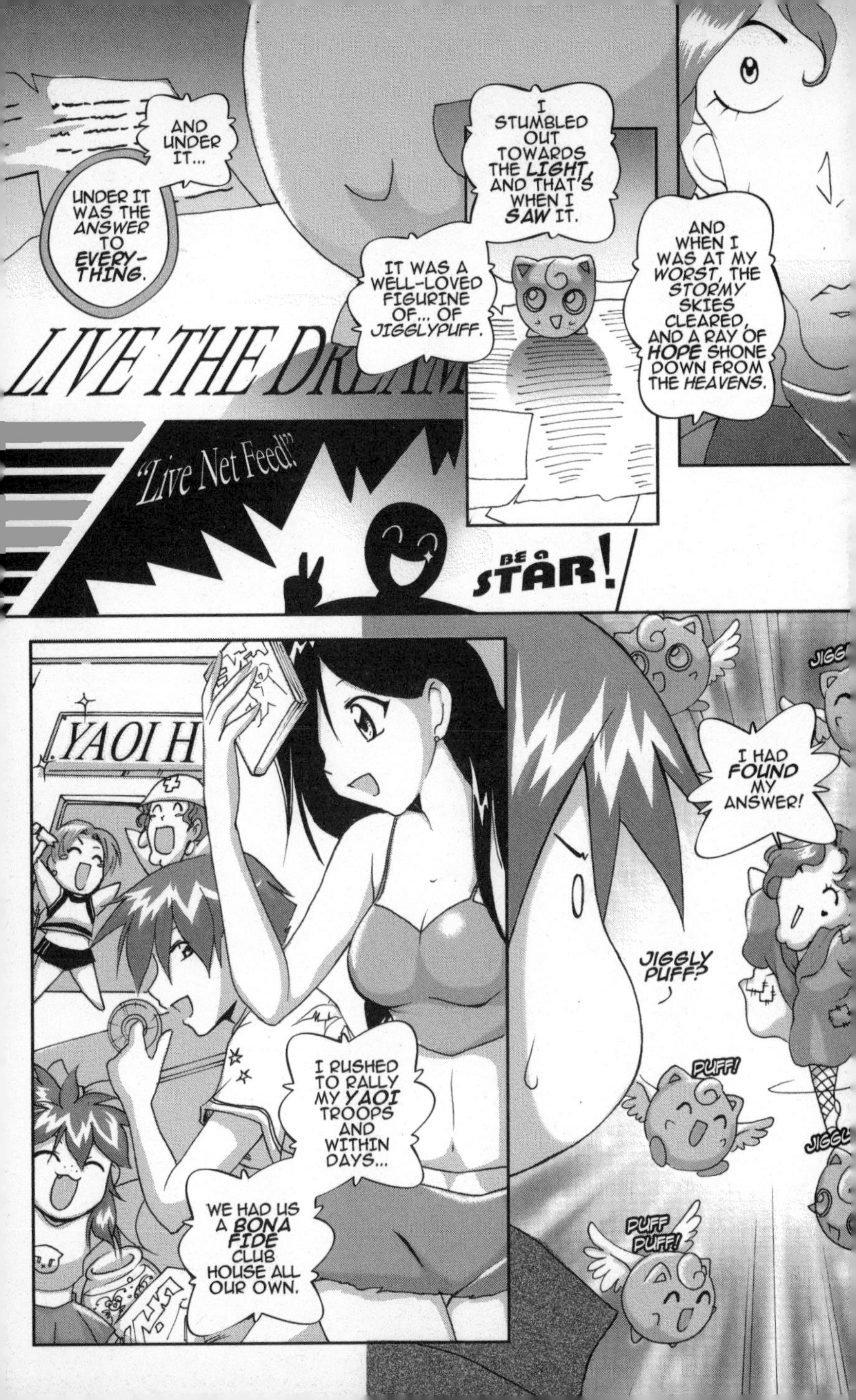
AND WHEN I WAS AT MY WORST, THE STORMY SKIES CLEARED, AND A RAY OF HOPE SHONE DOWN FROM THE HEAVENS.
I STUMBLED OUT TOWARDS THE LIGHT, AND THAT'S WHEN I SAW IT.
IT WAS A WELL-LOVED FIGURINE OF... OF JIGGLYPUFF.
AND UNDER IT...
UNDER IT WAS THE ANSWER TO EVERYTHING.
LIVE THE DREAM
"Live Net Feed!"
BE A STAR!
I HAD FOUND MY ANSWER!
JIGGLY PUFF?
PUFF!
PUFF PUFF!
YAOI H
I RUSHED TO RALLY MY YAOI TROOPS AND WITHIN DAYS...
WE HAD US A BONA FIDE CLUB HOUSE ALL OUR OWN.

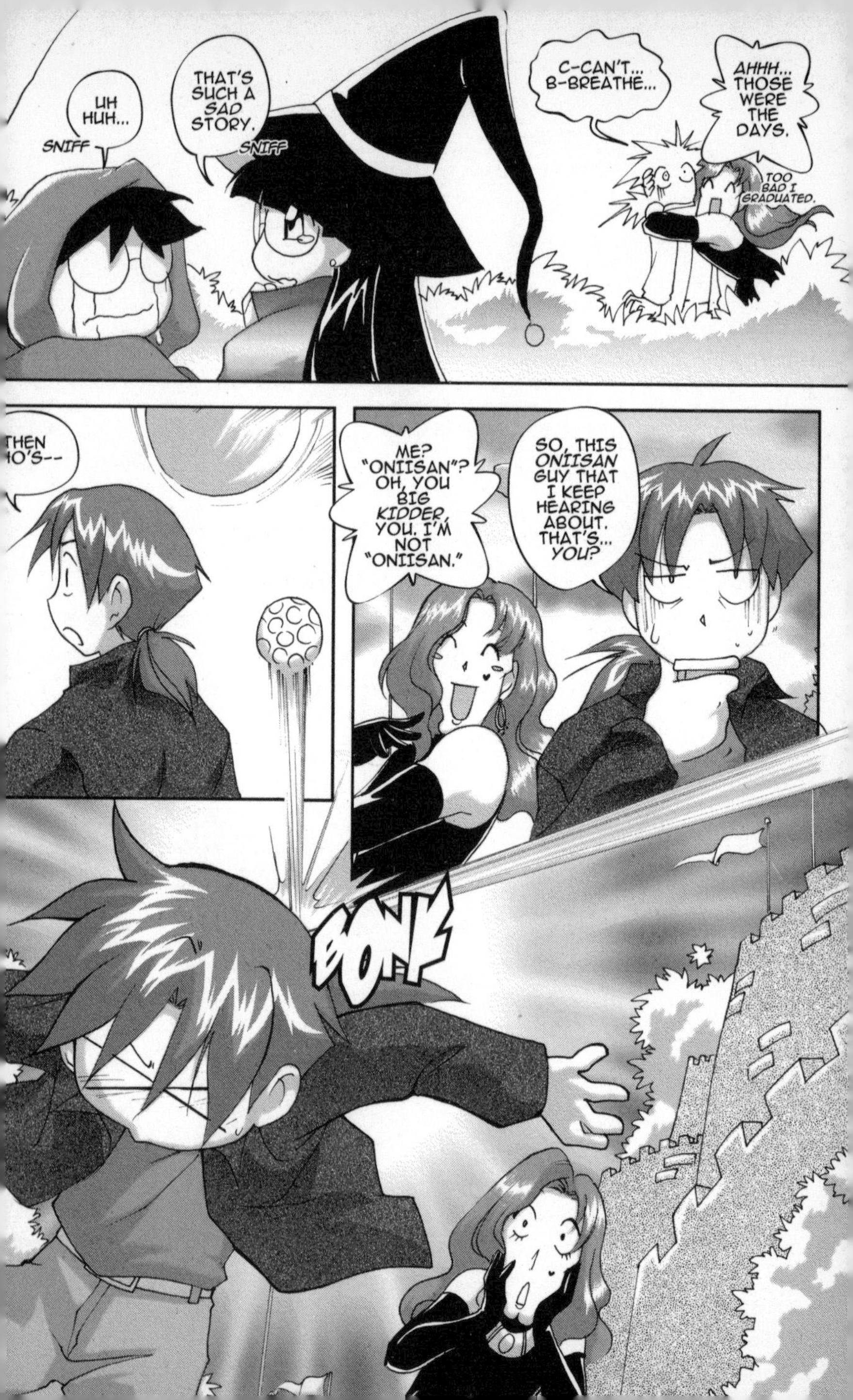
AHHH... THOSE WERE THE DAYS.
TOO BAD I GRADUATED.
C-CAN'T... B-BREATHE...
SNIFF
THAT'S SUCH A SAD STORY.
UH HUH...
SNIFF
SO, THIS ONIISAN GUY THAT I KEEP HEARING ABOUT. THAT'S... YOU?
ME? "ONIISAN"? OH, YOU BIG KIDDER, YOU. I'M NOT "ONIISAN."
THEN HO'S--
BONK

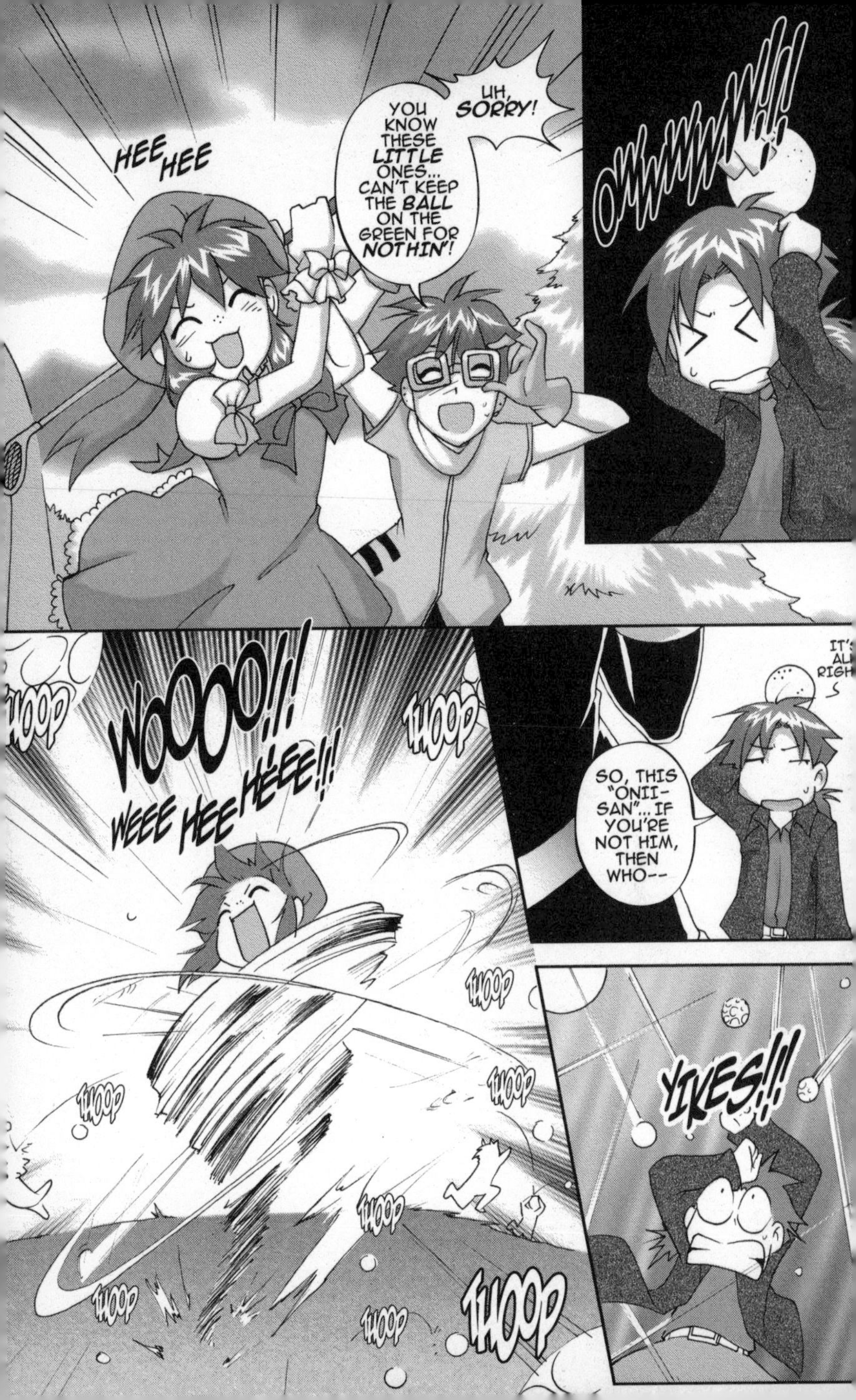
OWWWWW!!
UH, SORRY!
YOU KNOW THESE LITTLE ONES... CAN'T KEEP THE BALL ON THE GREEN FOR NOTHIN'!
HEE HEE
IT'S ALL RIGH
SO, THIS "ONII-SAN"... IF YOU'RE NOT HIM, THEN WHO--
YIKES!!
WOOOO!!
WEEE HEE HEEE!!
THOOP
THOOP
THOOP
THOOP
THOOP
THOOP
THOOP
THOOP

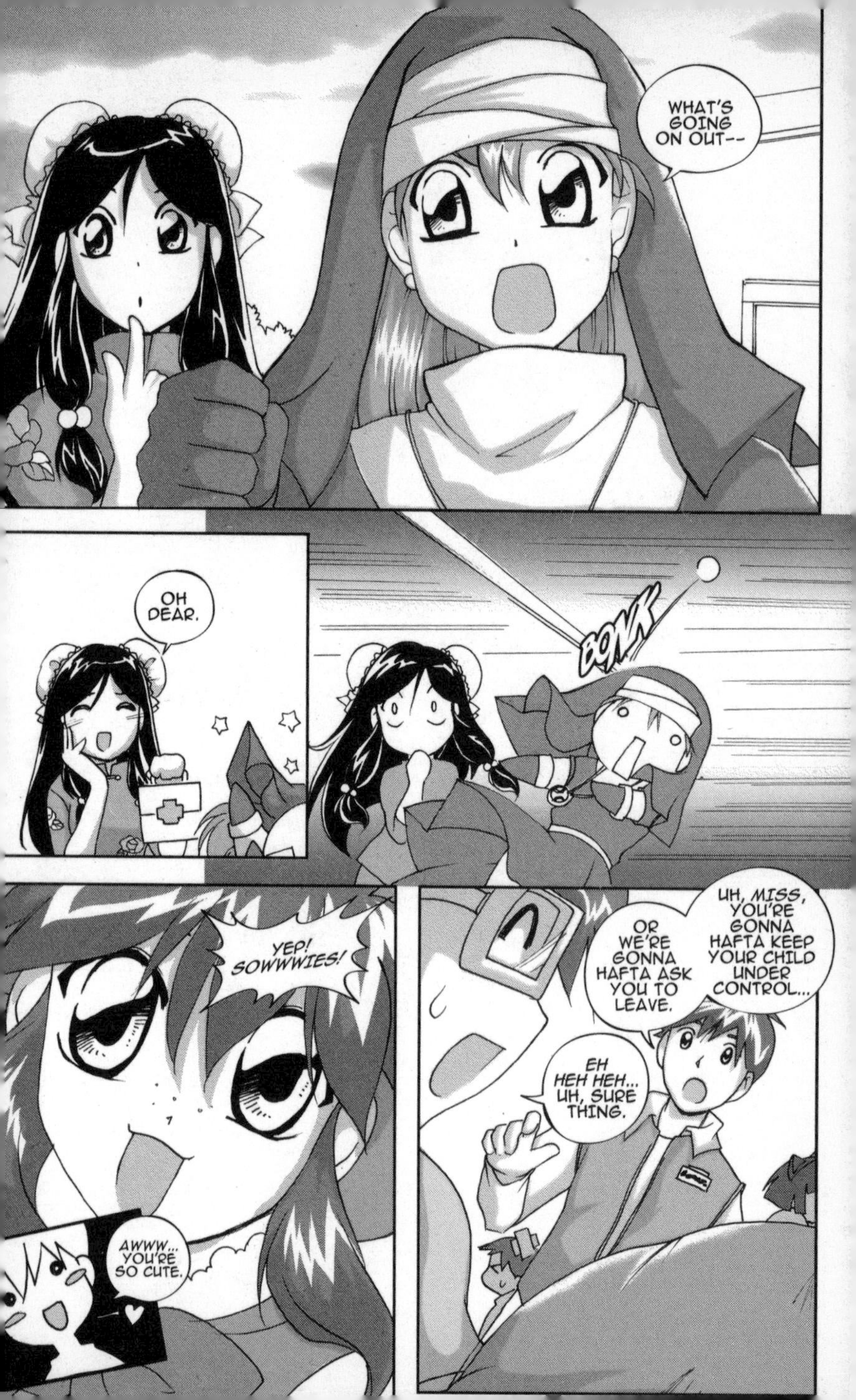
WHAT'S GOING ON OUT--
BONK
OH DEAR.
UH, MISS, YOU'RE GONNA HAFTA KEEP YOUR CHILD UNDER CONTROL...
OR WE'RE GONNA HAFTA ASK YOU TO LEAVE.
EH HEH HEH... UH, SURE THING.
YEP! SOWWWIES!
AWWW... YOU'RE SO CUTE.

WHOA.

THIS IS IT...

LAST HOLE OF THE NIGHT.

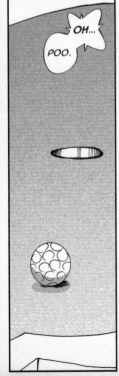

OH... POO.

KROONK

KROONK

WOOHOO!!!

HEY, GET DOWN FROM THERE!

THANK GOD IT'S ALMOST OVER.

THWAACK

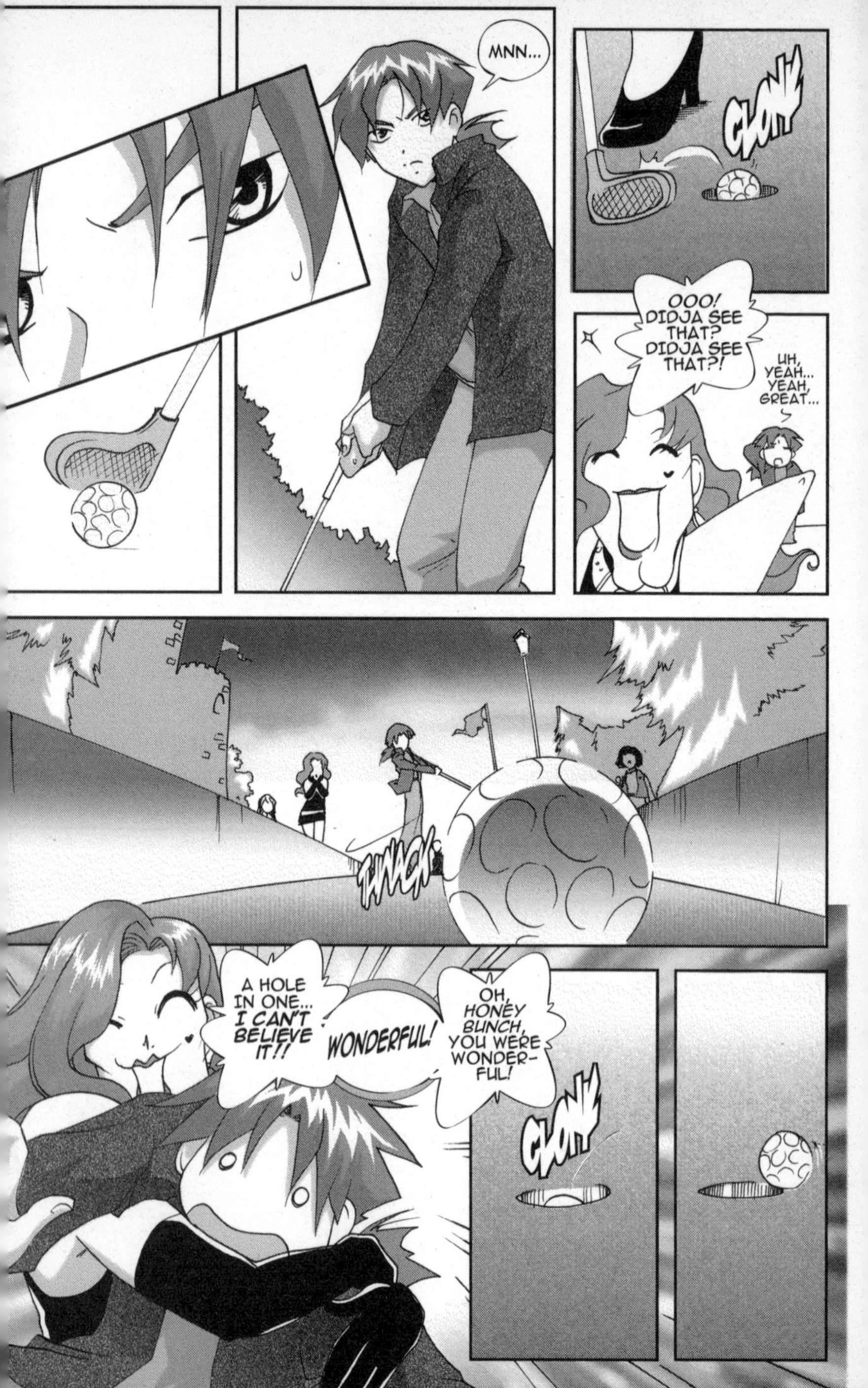
CLONK
OOO! DIDJA SEE THAT? DIDJA SEE THAT?!
UH, YEAH... YEAH, GREAT...
MNN...
TWACK
OH, HONEY BUNCH, YOU WERE WONDER-FUL!
WONDERFUL!
A HOLE IN ONE... I CAN'T BELIEVE IT!!
CLONK

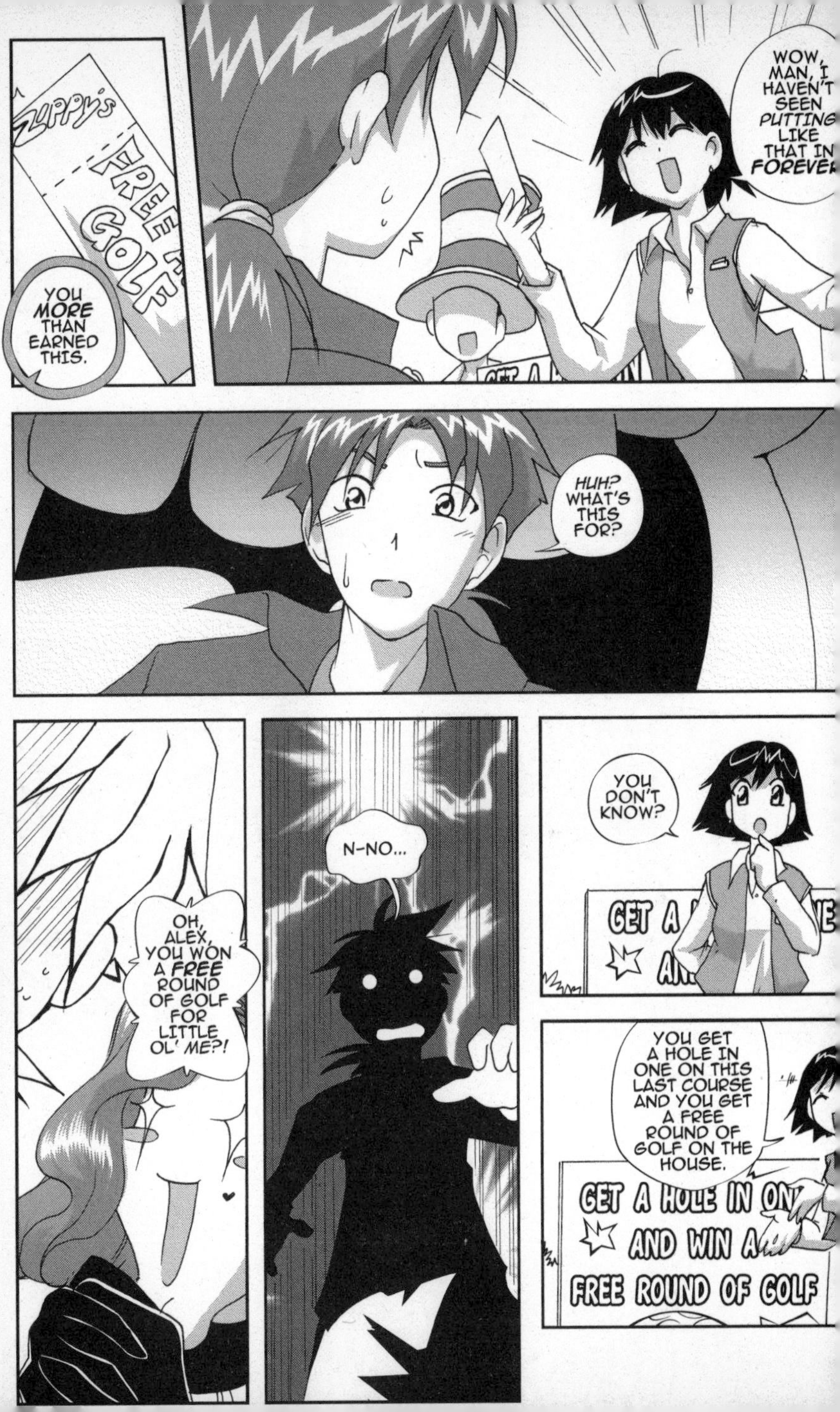
WOW, MAN, I HAVEN'T SEEN *PUTTING* LIKE THAT IN ***FOREVER***
ZIPPY's
FREE
GOLF
YOU ***MORE*** THAN EARNED THIS.
HUH? WHAT'S THIS FOR?
YOU DON'T KNOW?
YOU GET A HOLE IN ONE ON THIS LAST COURSE AND YOU GET A FREE ROUND OF GOLF ON THE HOUSE.
GET A HOLE IN ON
AND WIN A
FREE ROUND OF GOLF
N-NO...
OH, ALEX, YOU WON A ***FREE*** ROUND OF GOLF FOR LITTLE OL' *ME*?!

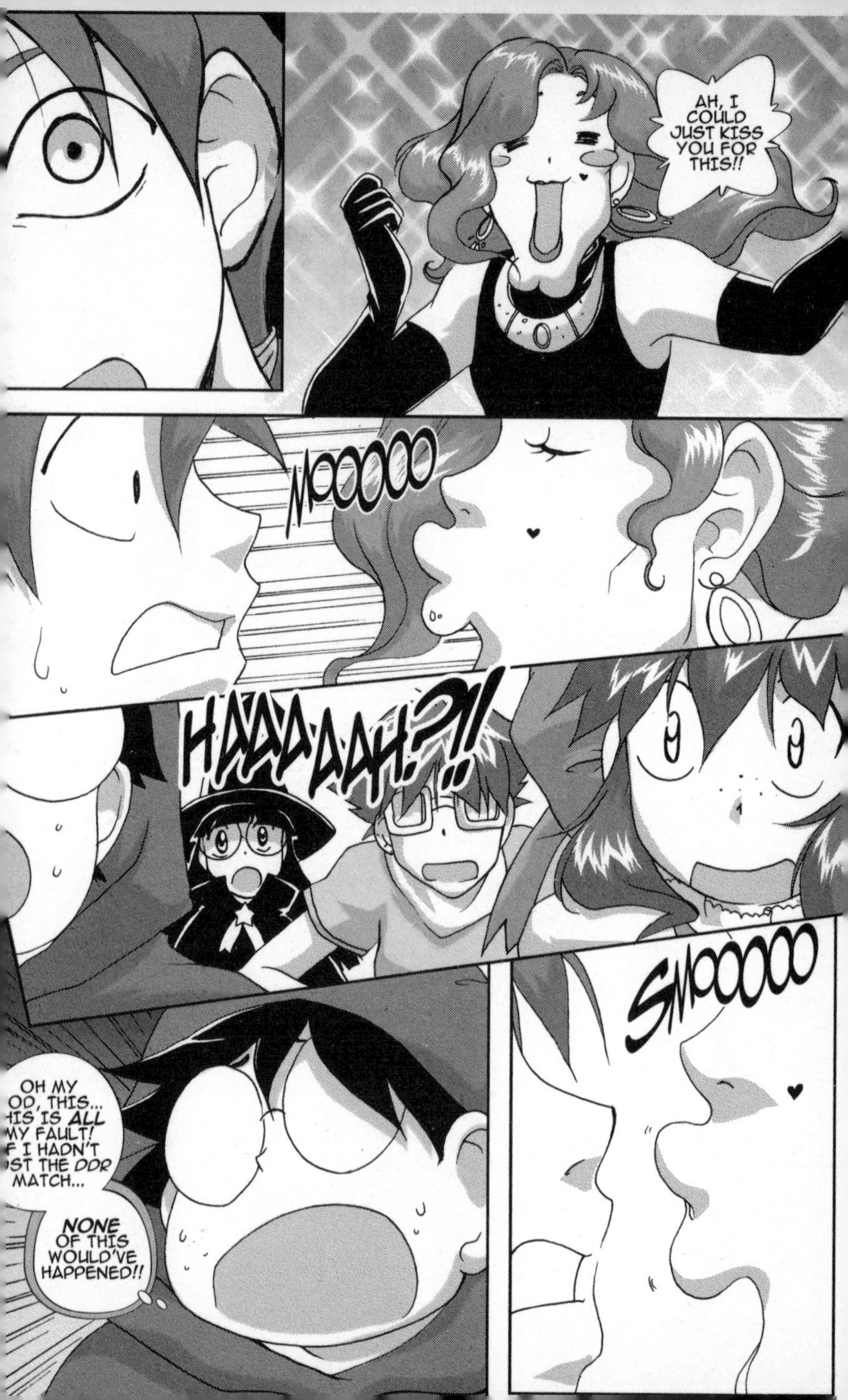

AH, I COULD JUST KISS YOU FOR THIS!!
MOOOOO
HAAAAAH?!!
SMOOOOO
OH MY
OD, THIS...
HIS IS *ALL*
MY FAULT!
F I HADN'T
ST THE *DDR*
MATCH...
NONE OF THIS WOULD'VE HAPPENED!!

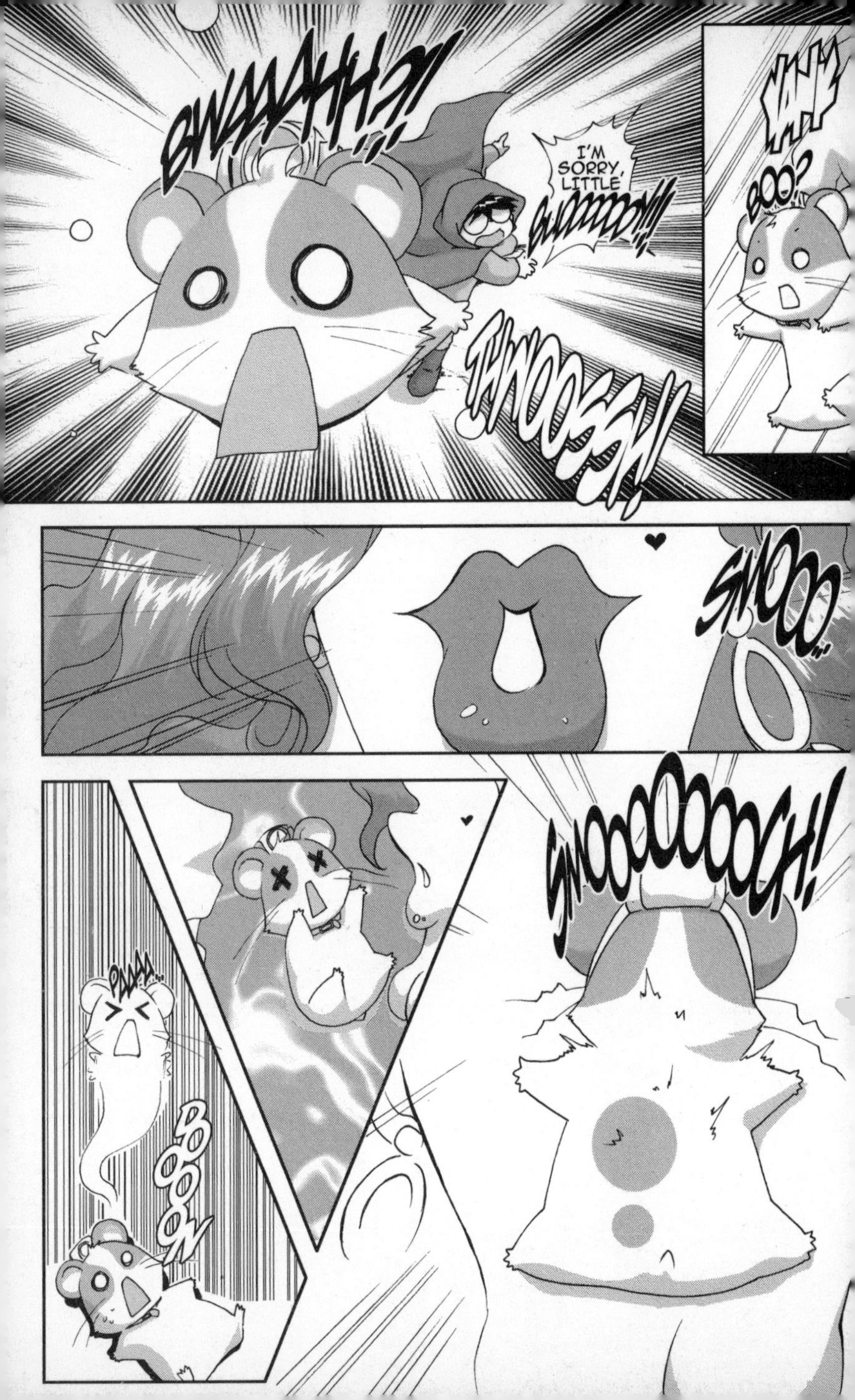
BOO?
BWAAAHH?!
I'M SORRY, LITTLE BLOOOOOOM!!!
TWOOOSH!!
SMOOO...
SMOOOOOOOOCH!
PAAAA...
BOOOOM

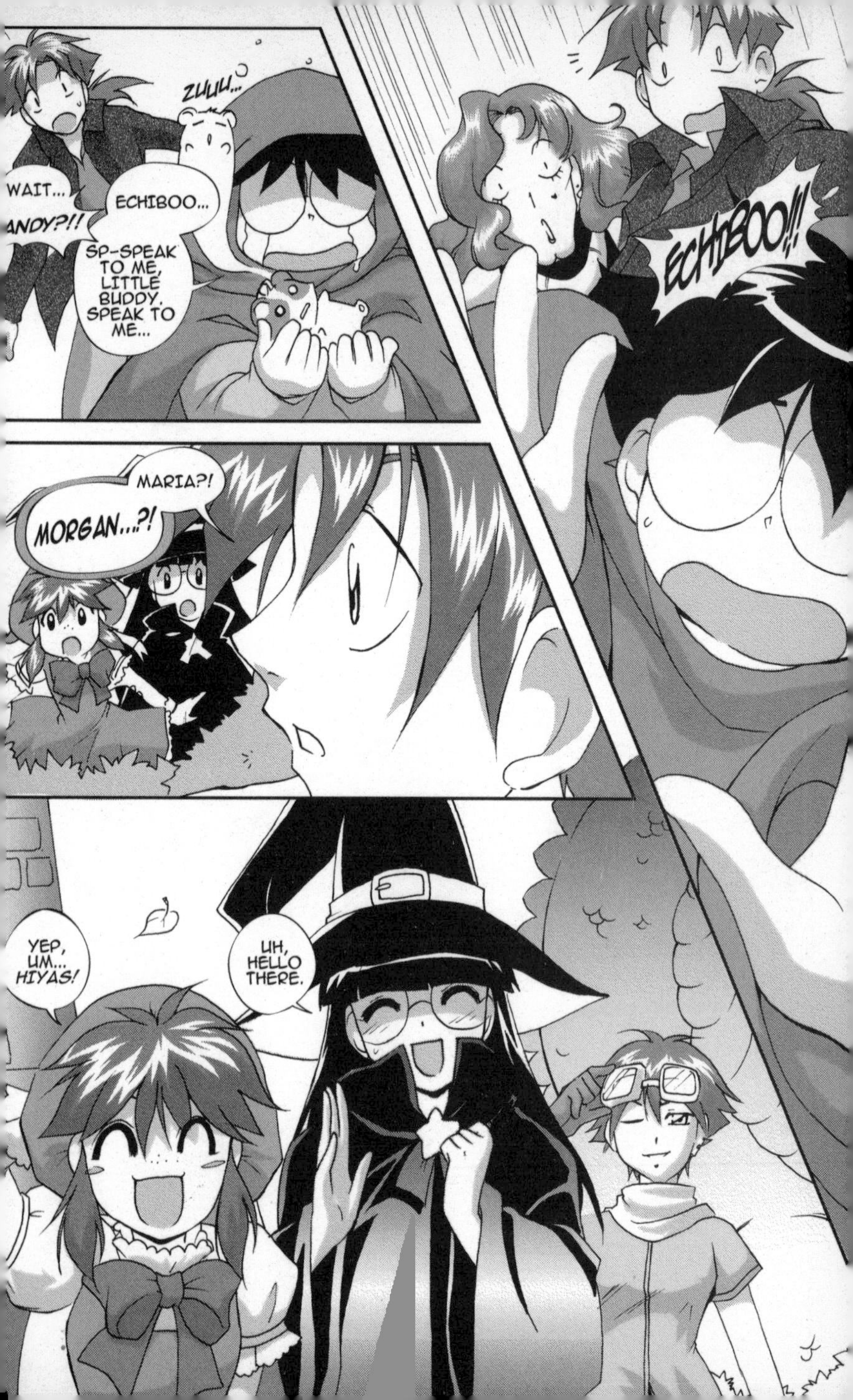
ECHIBOO!!!
ZUUU...
ECHIBOO...
SP-SPEAK TO ME, LITTLE BUDDY. SPEAK TO ME...
WAIT...
ANDY?!!
MARIA?!
MORGAN...?!
UH, HELLO THERE.
YEP, UM... HIYAS!

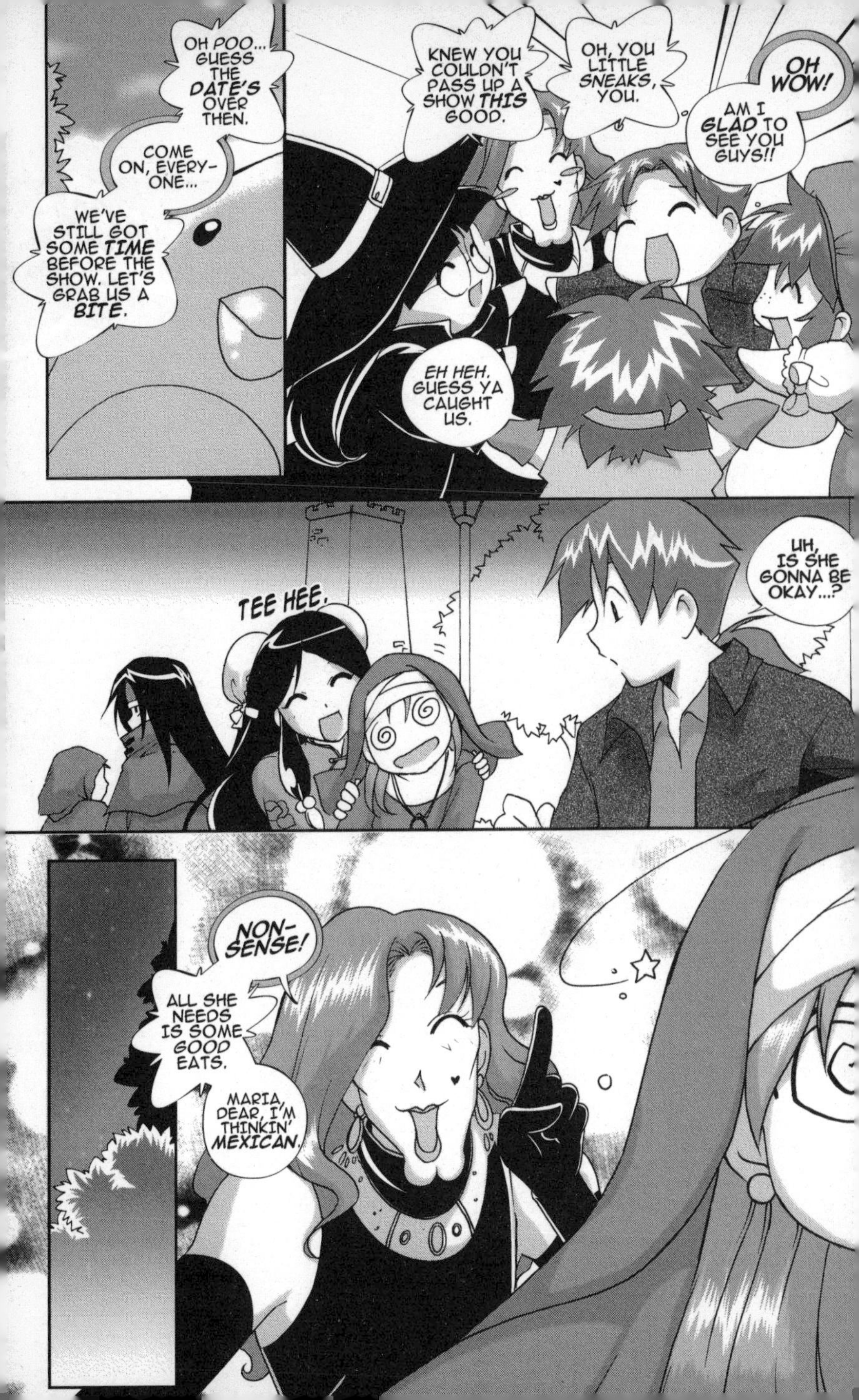
OH WOW!
AM I GLAD TO SEE YOU GUYS!!
OH, YOU LITTLE SNEAKS, YOU.
KNEW YOU COULDN'T PASS UP A SHOW THIS GOOD.
EH HEH. GUESS YA CAUGHT US.
OH POO... GUESS THE DATE'S OVER THEN.
COME ON, EVERY-ONE...
WE'VE STILL GOT SOME TIME BEFORE THE SHOW. LET'S GRAB US A BITE.
UH, IS SHE GONNA BE OKAY...?
TEE HEE.
NON-SENSE!
ALL SHE NEEDS IS SOME GOOD EATS.
MARIA, DEAR, I'M THINKIN' MEXICAN.

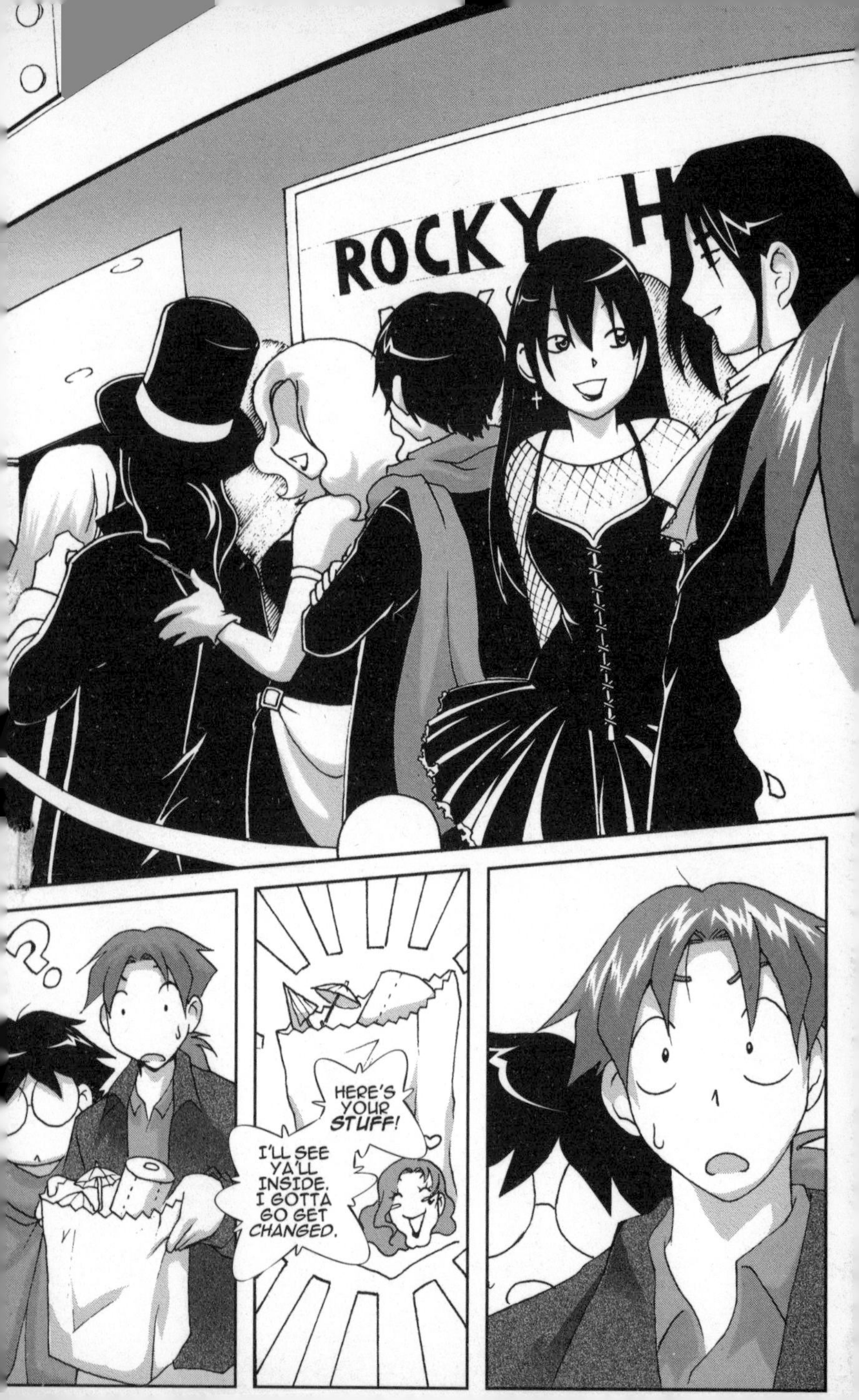
ROCKY H
HERE'S YOUR STUFF!
I'LL SEE YA'LL INSIDE. I GOTTA GO GET CHANGED.

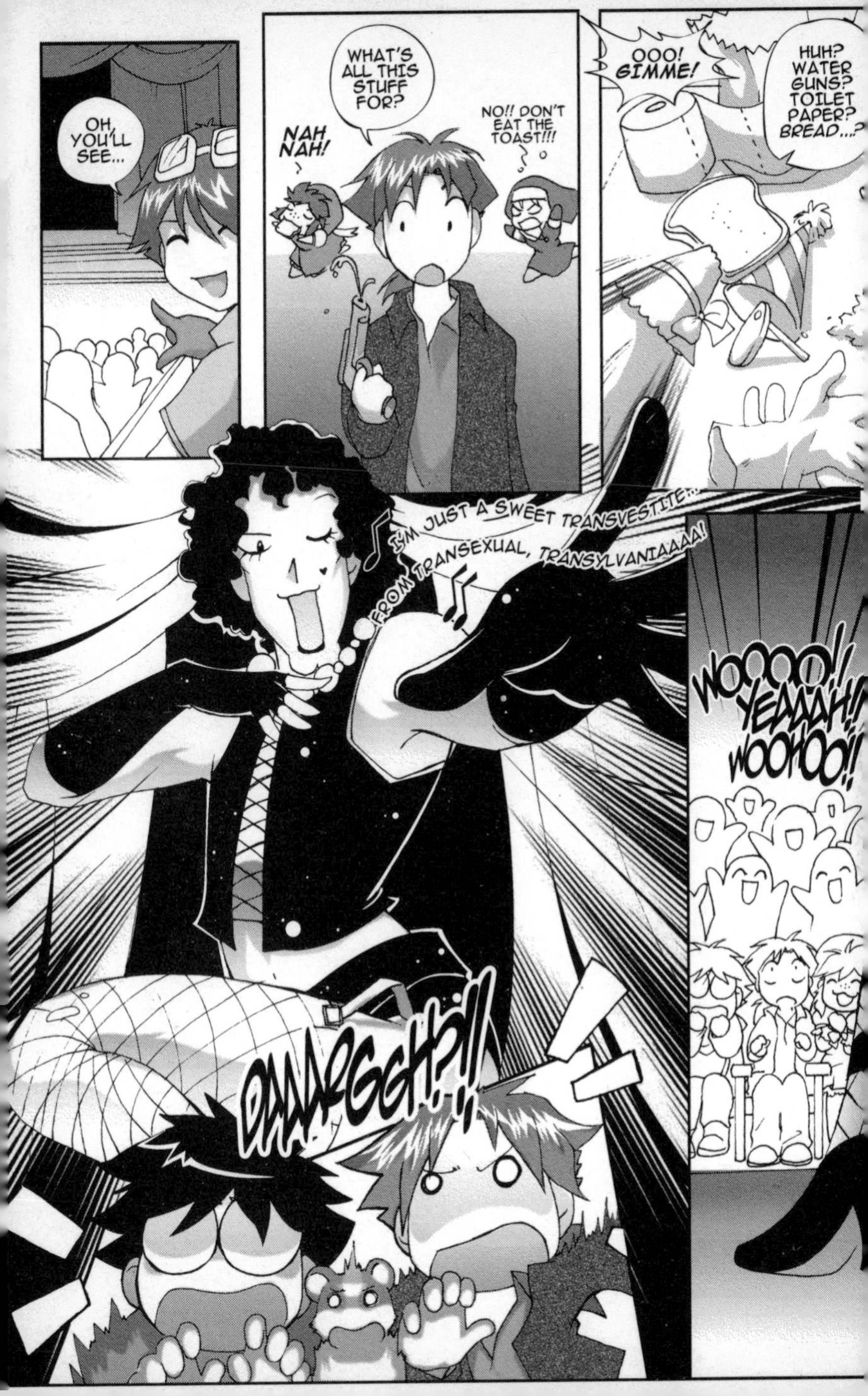
HUH? WATER GUNS? TOILET PAPER? BREAD...?
OOO! GIMME!
WHAT'S ALL THIS STUFF FOR?
NO!! DON'T EAT THE TOAST!!!
NAH NAH!
OH, YOU'LL SEE...
WOOOO!! YEAAAH!! WOOHOO!!
I'M JUST A SWEET TRANSVESTITE... FROM TRANSEXUAL, TRANSYLVANIAAAA!
DAAAGGH?!!

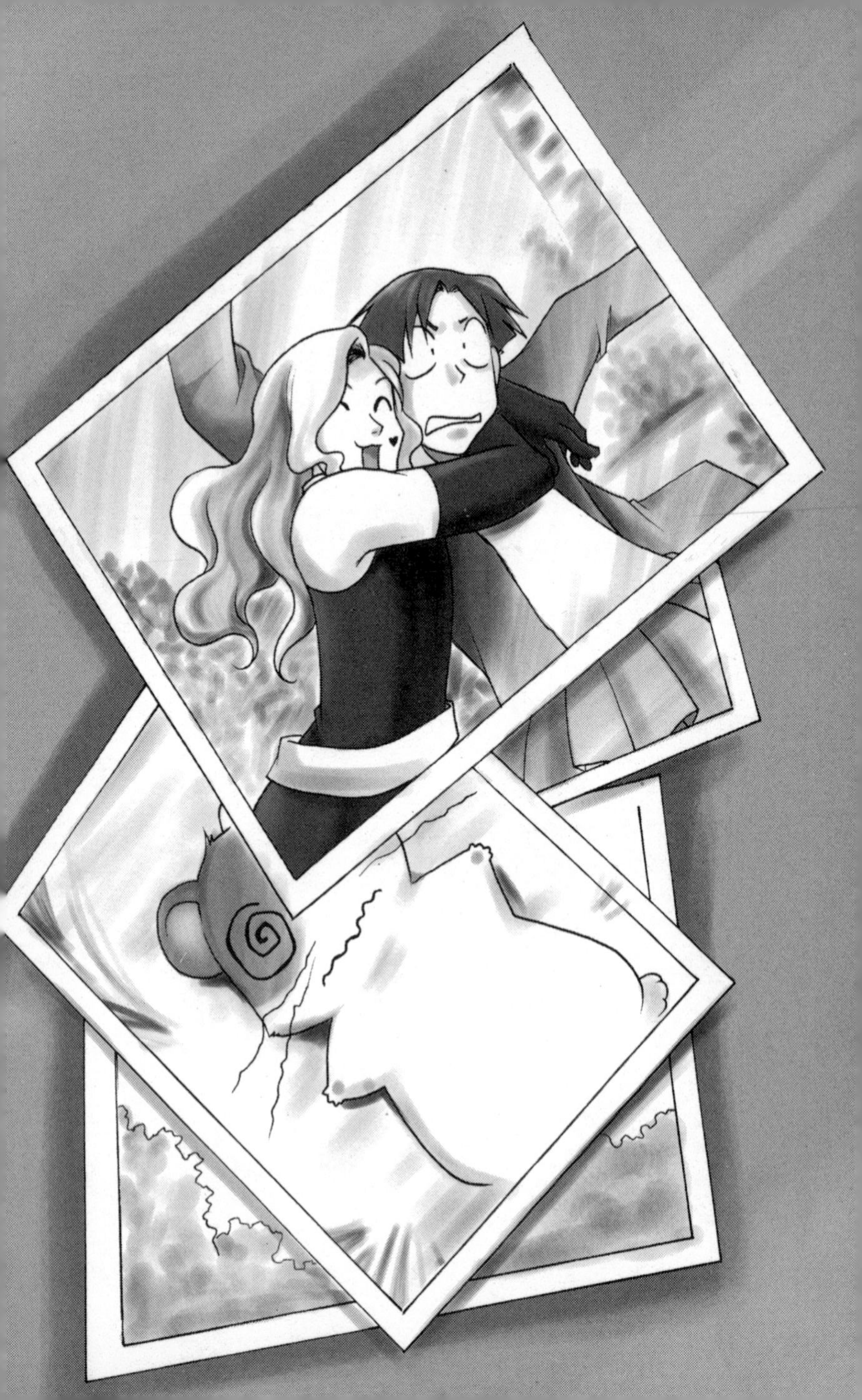

EPISODE 10:

CHARMED

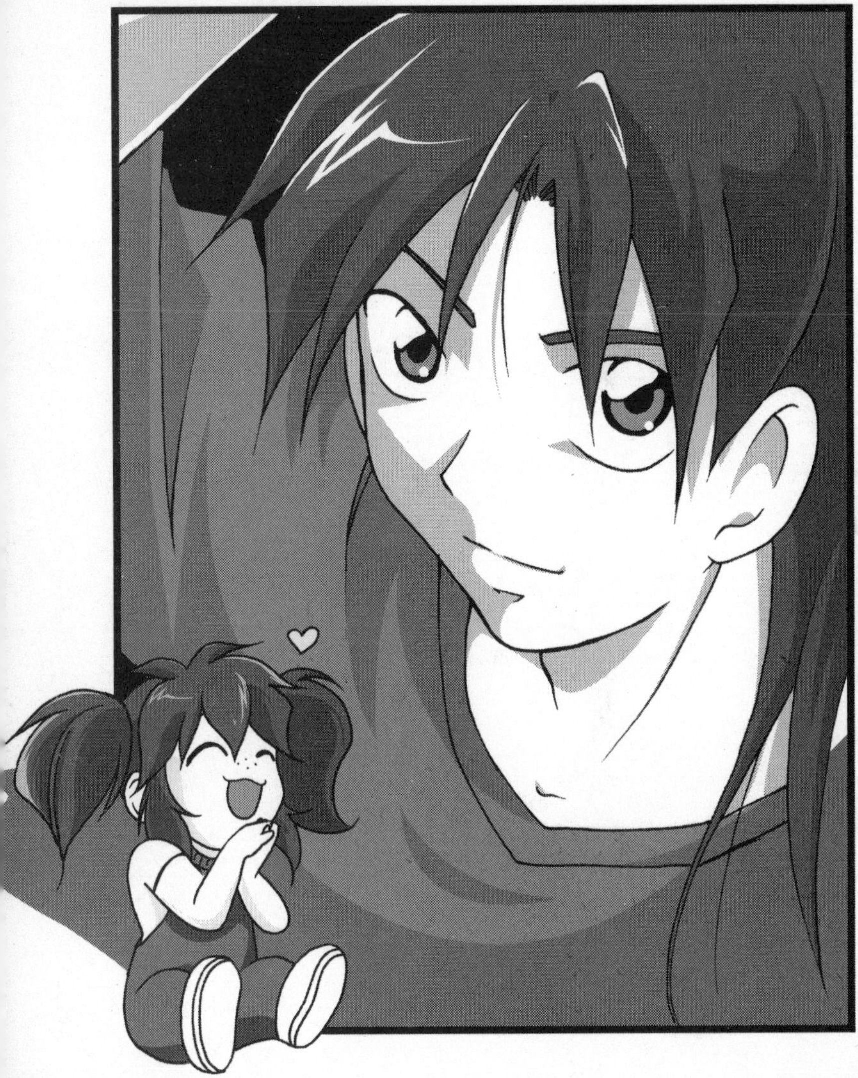

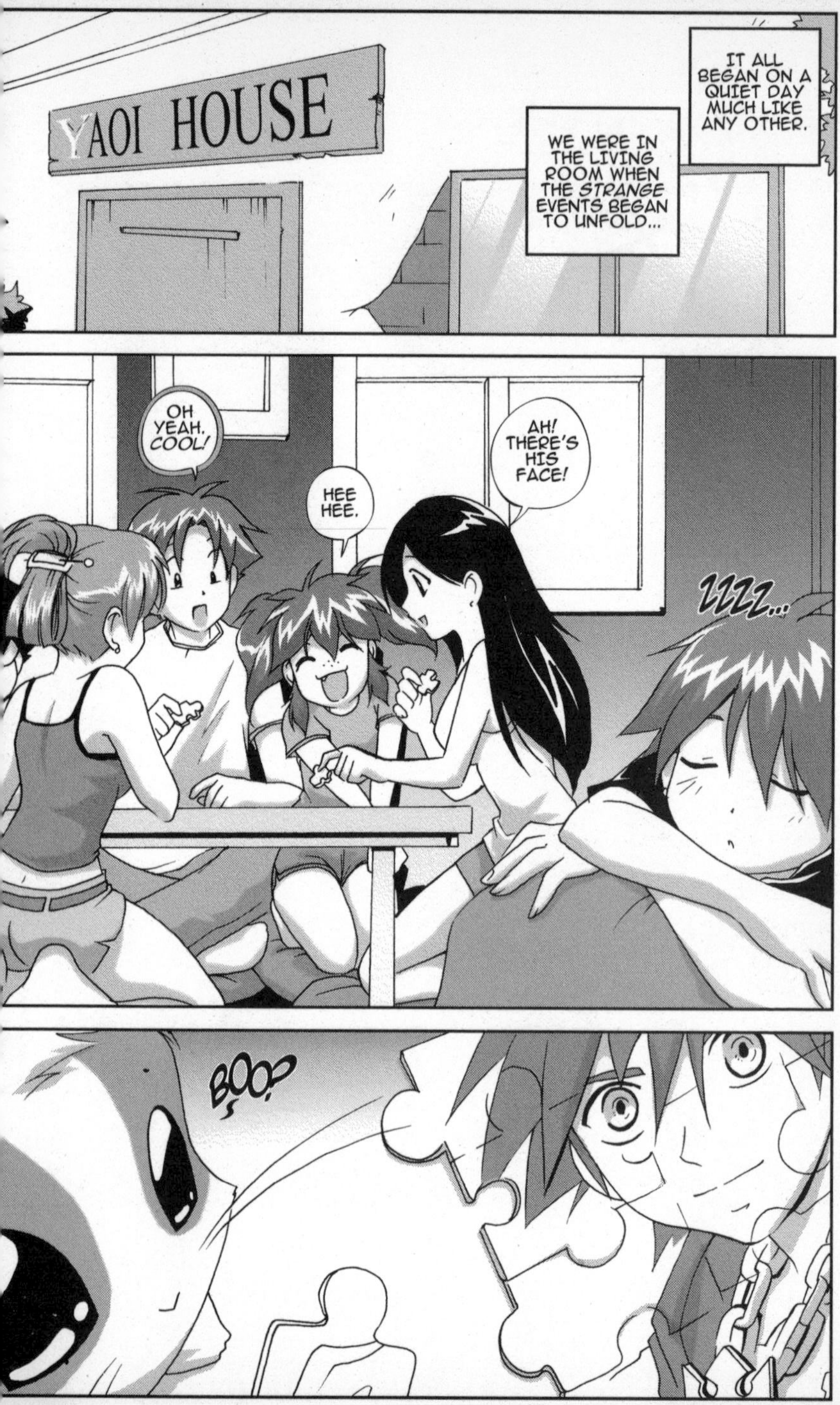
IT ALL BEGAN ON A QUIET DAY MUCH LIKE ANY OTHER.
WE WERE IN THE LIVING ROOM WHEN THE *STRANGE* EVENTS BEGAN TO UNFOLD...
YAOI HOUSE
ZZZZ...
AH! THERE'S HIS FACE!
HEE HEE.
OH YEAH, *COOL!*
BOOP

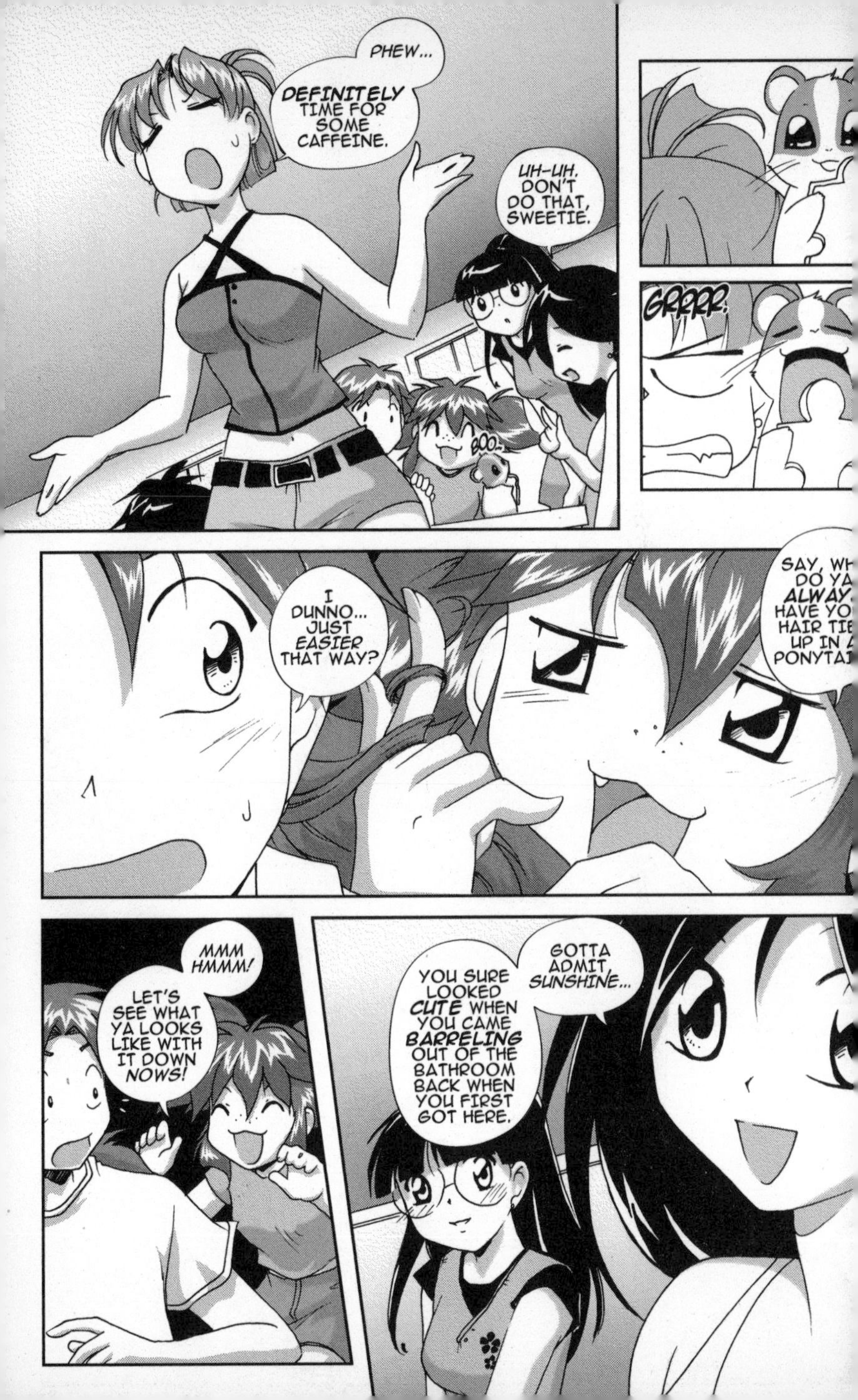
GRRRR.
PHEW...
DEFINITELY TIME FOR SOME CAFFEINE.
UH-UH. DON'T DO THAT, SWEETIE.
BOO..
SAY, WH DO YA ALWAY HAVE YO HAIR TIE UP IN A PONYTAI
I DUNNO... JUST EASIER THAT WAY?
GOTTA ADMIT, SUNSHINE...
YOU SURE LOOKED CUTE WHEN YOU CAME BARRELING OUT OF THE BATHROOM BACK WHEN YOU FIRST GOT HERE.
MMM HMMM!
LET'S SEE WHAT YA LOOKS LIKE WITH IT DOWN NOWS!

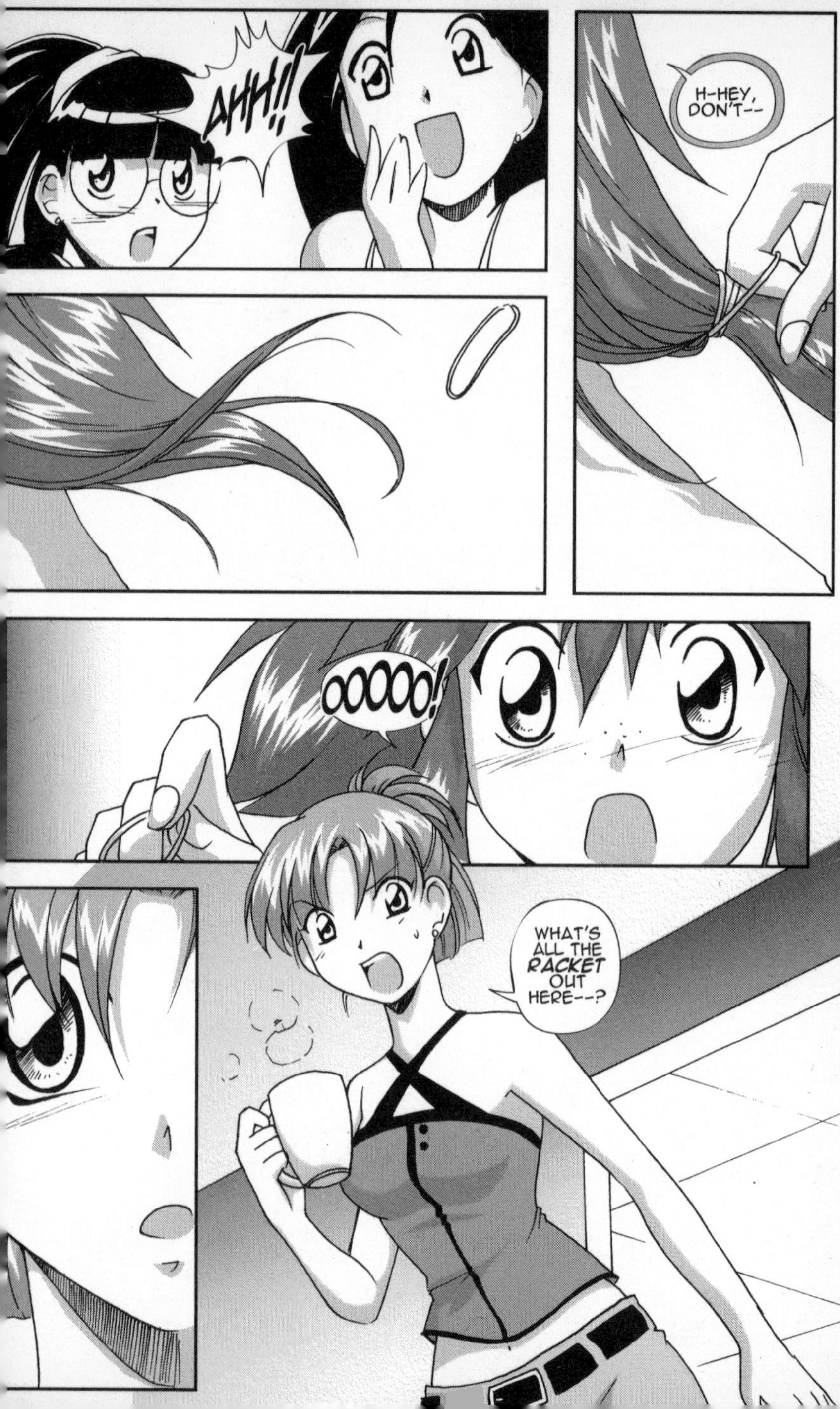
H-HEY, DON'T--
AHH!!
OOOOO!
WHAT'S ALL THE RACKET OUT HERE--?

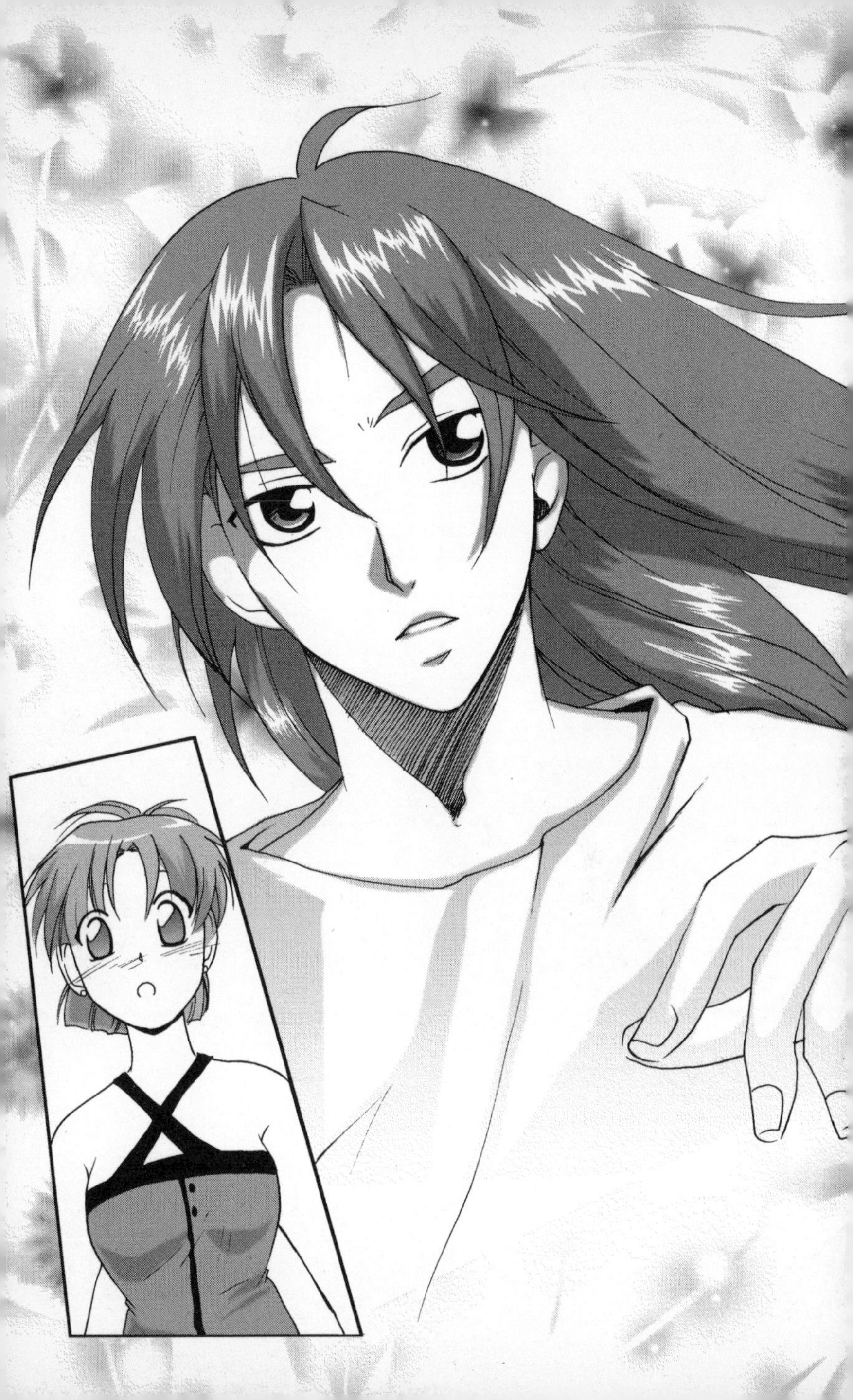

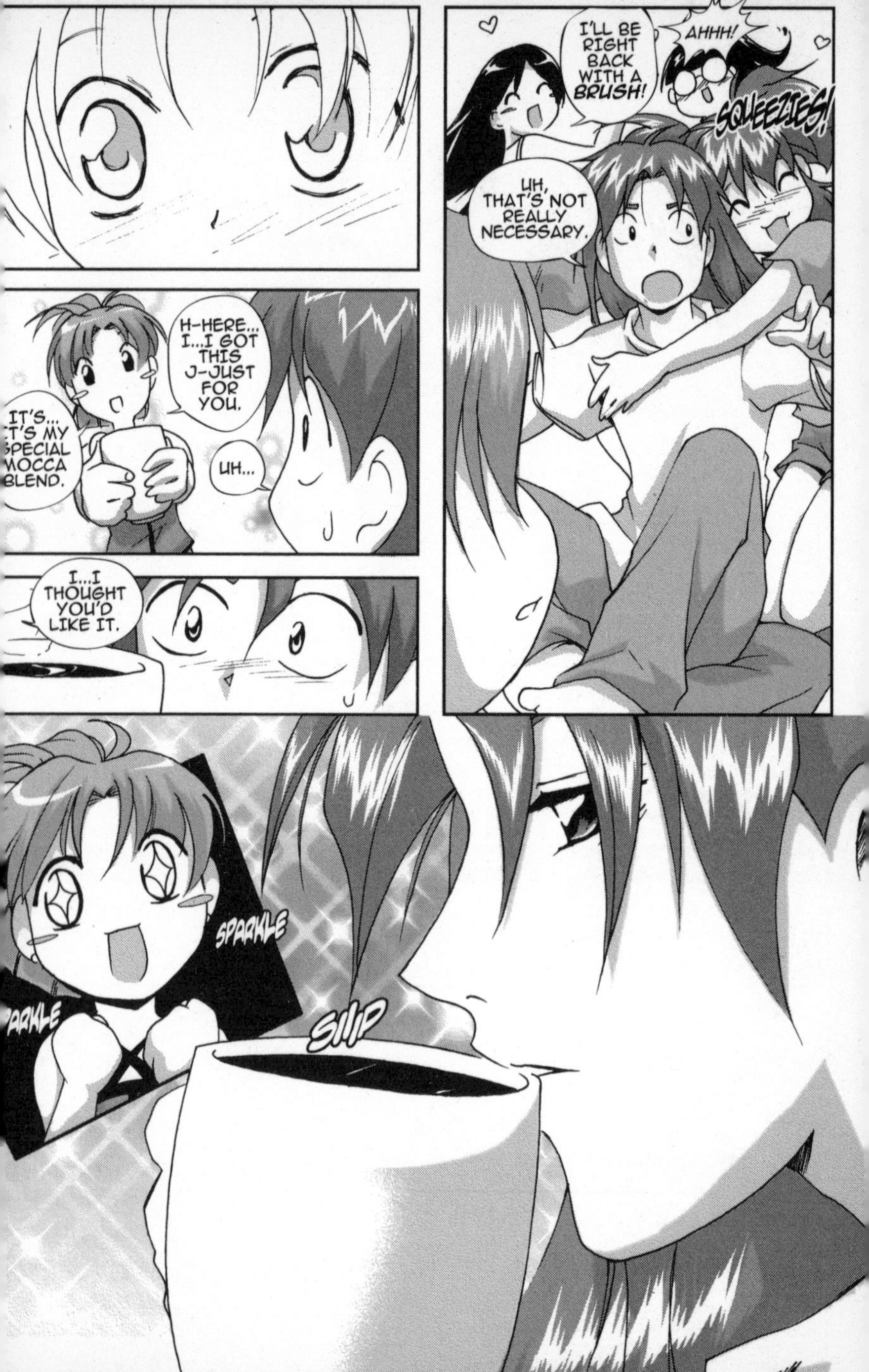
AHHH!
I'LL BE RIGHT BACK WITH A BRUSH!
SQUEEZIES!
UH, THAT'S NOT REALLY NECESSARY.
H-HERE... I...I GOT THIS J-JUST FOR YOU.
IT'S... IT'S MY SPECIAL MOCCA BLEND.
UH...
I...I THOUGHT YOU'D LIKE IT.
SPARKLE
SPARKLE
SIIP

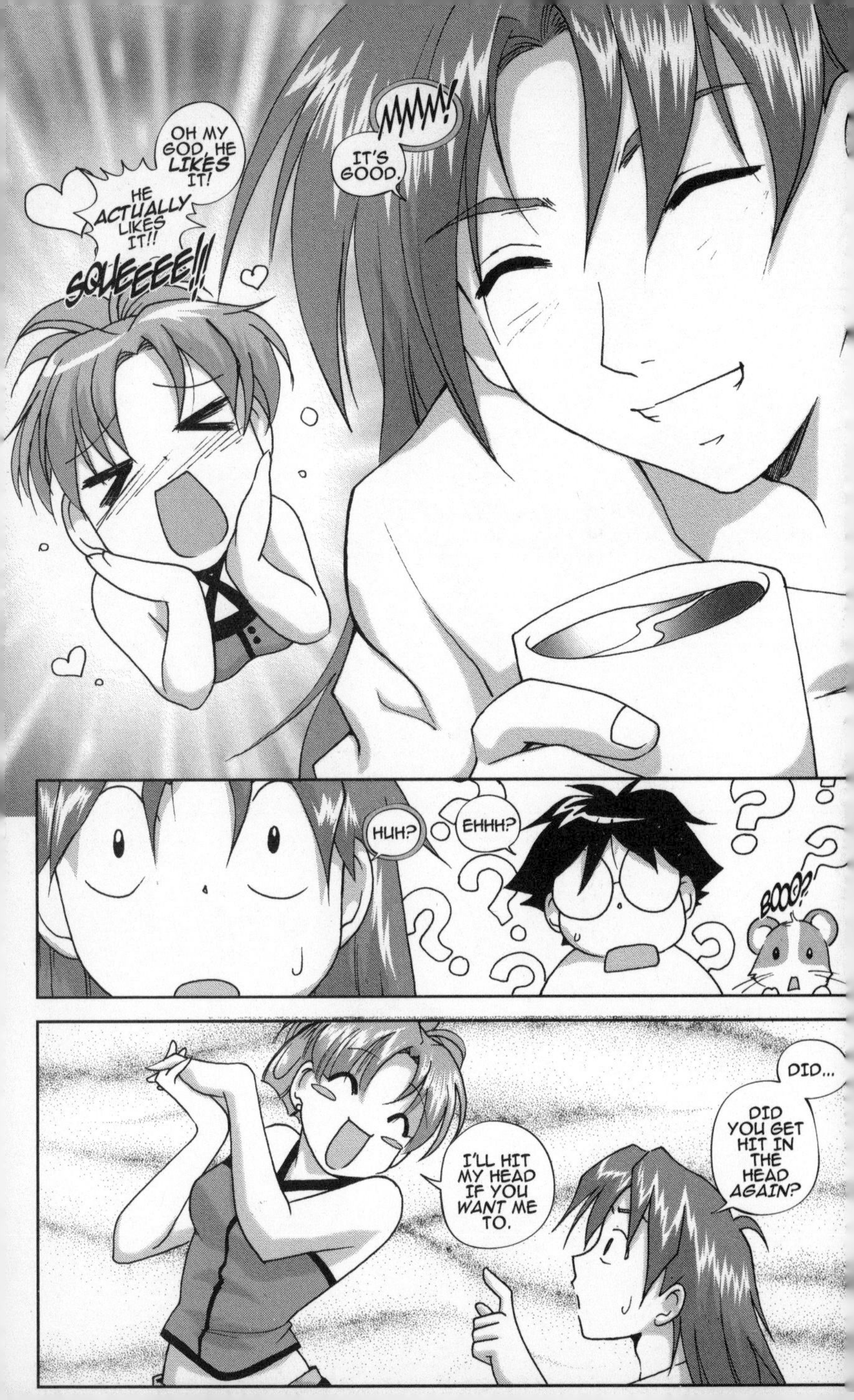
MMMM!
IT'S GOOD.
OH MY GOD, HE LIKES IT!
HE ACTUALLY LIKES IT!!
SQUEEEEE!!!
BOOO?
EHHH?
HUH?
DID...
DID YOU GET HIT IN THE HEAD AGAIN?
I'LL HIT MY HEAD IF YOU WANT ME TO.

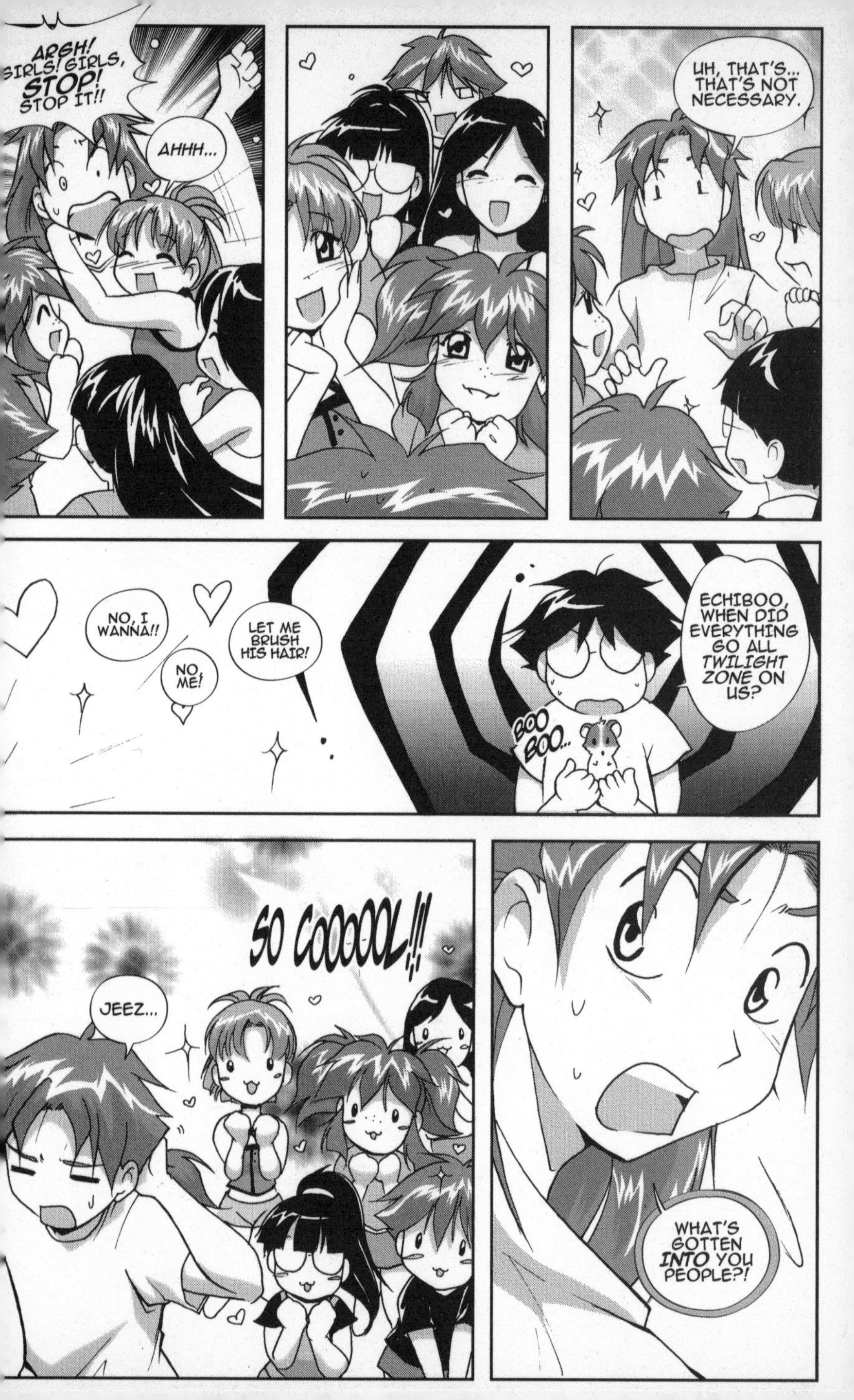
UH, THAT'S... THAT'S NOT NECESSARY.
ARGH! GIRLS! GIRLS, STOP! STOP IT!!
AHHH...
ECHIBOO, WHEN DID EVERYTHING GO ALL TWILIGHT ZONE ON US?
BOO BOO...
LET ME BRUSH HIS HAIR!
NO, I WANNA!!
NO, ME!
WHAT'S GOTTEN INTO YOU PEOPLE?!
SO COOOOOL!!!
JEEZ...

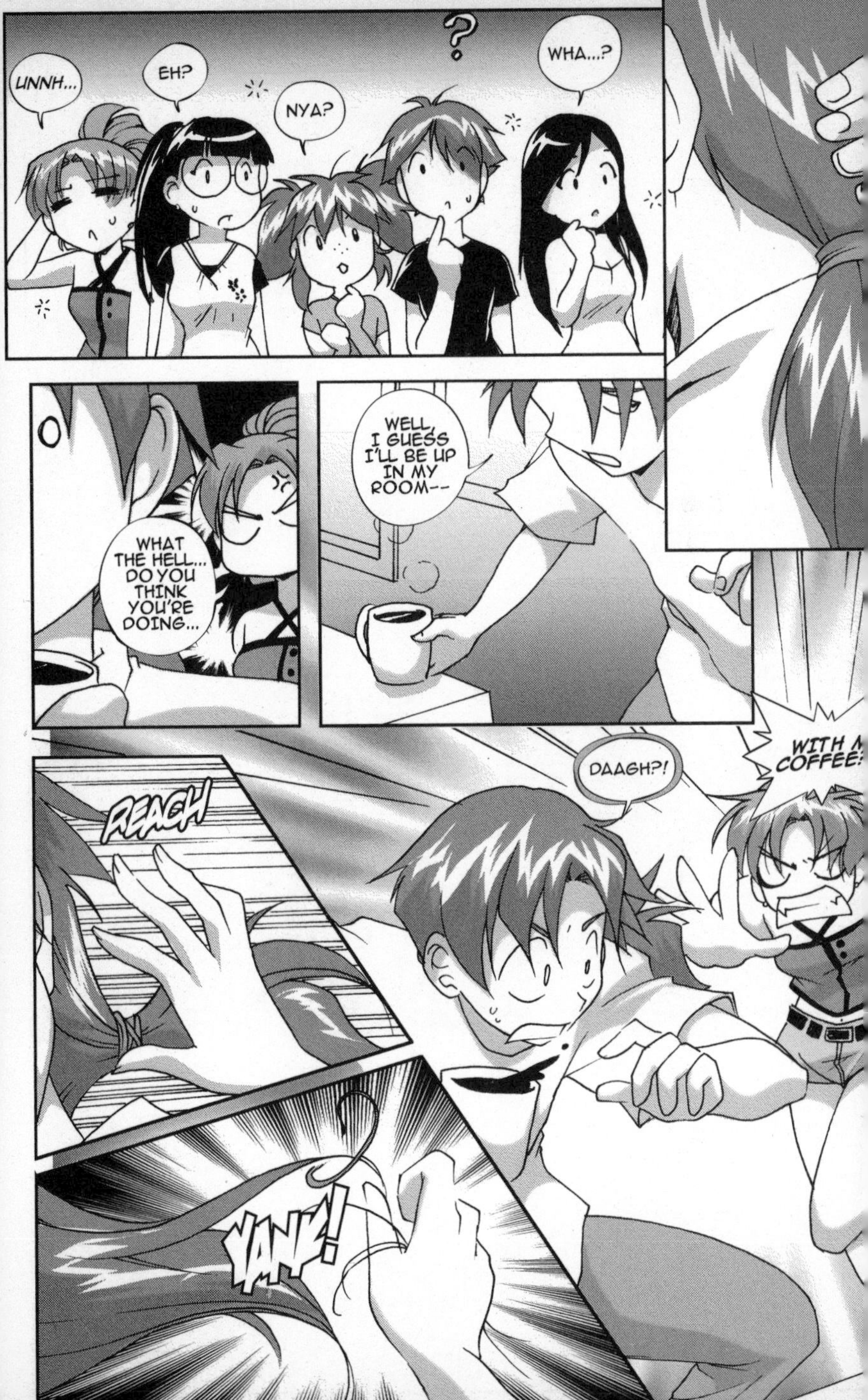
WHA...?
?
NYA?
EH?
UNNH...
WELL, I GUESS I'LL BE UP IN MY ROOM--
WHAT THE HELL... DO YOU THINK YOU'RE DOING...
WITH M COFFEE
DAAGH?!
REACH
YANK!

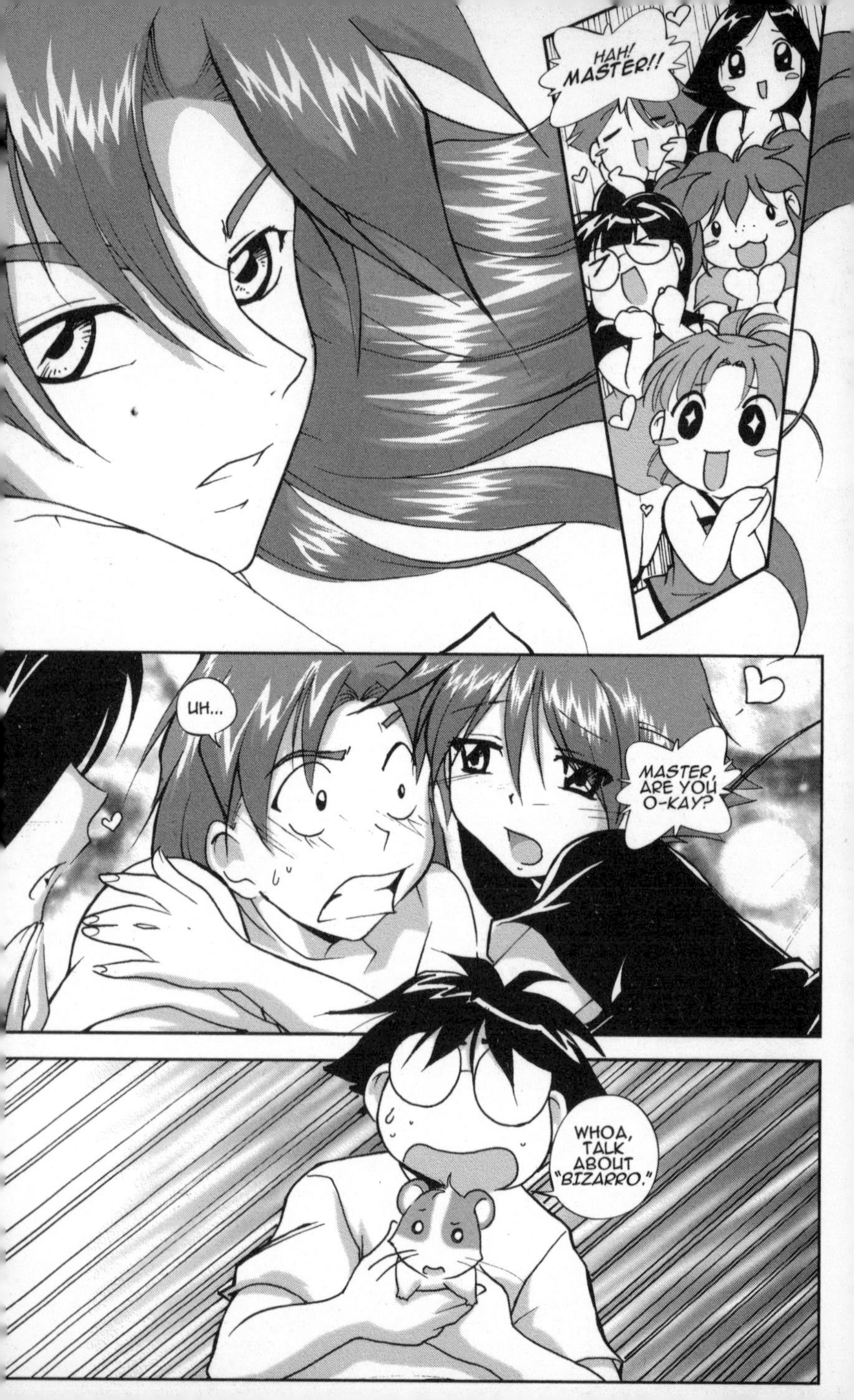
HAH! MASTER!!
MASTER, ARE YOU O-KAY?
UH...
WHOA, TALK ABOUT "BIZARRO."

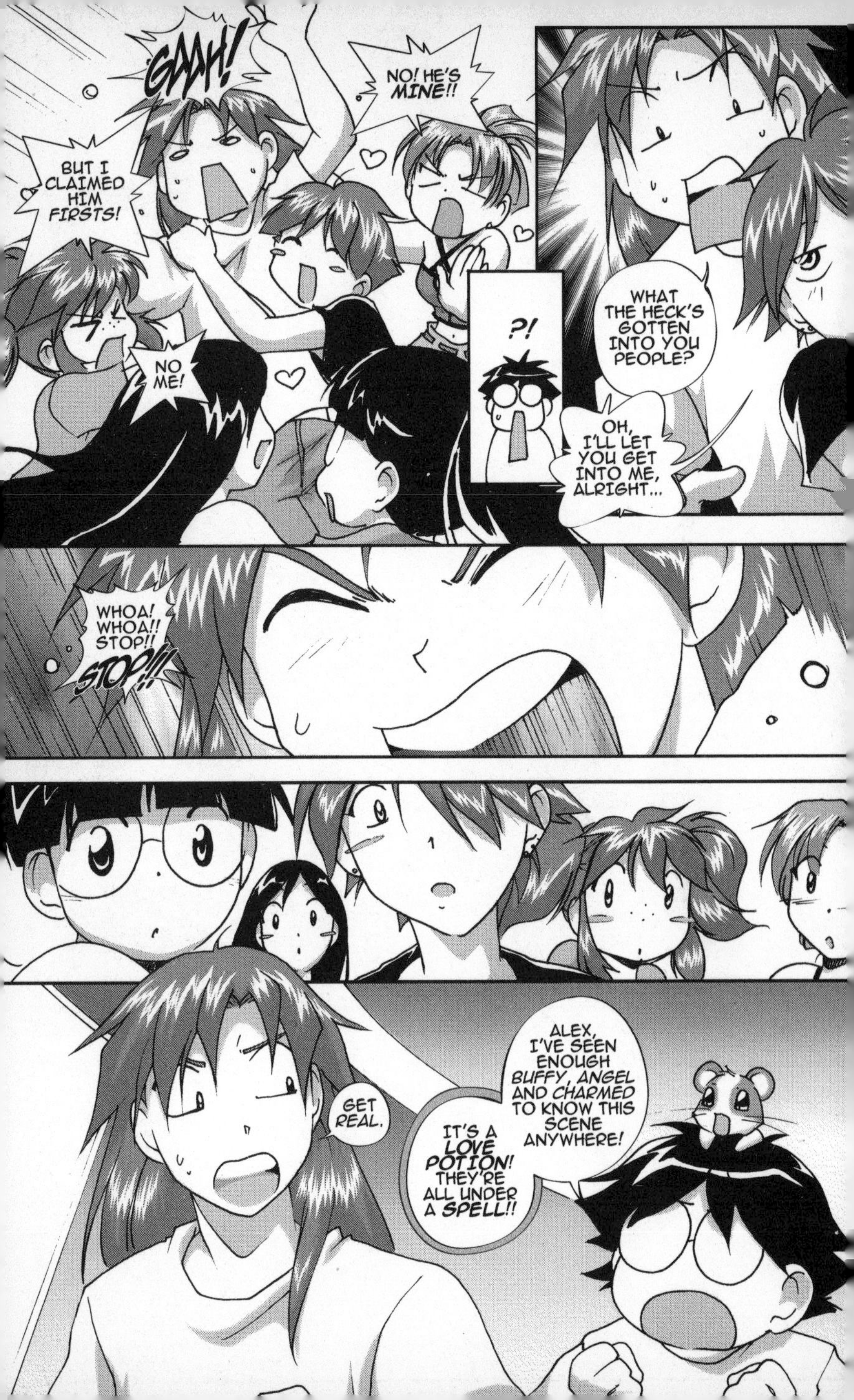
WHAT THE HECK'S GOTTEN INTO YOU PEOPLE?
OH, I'LL LET YOU GET INTO ME, ALRIGHT...
?!
NO! HE'S MINE!!
GAAH!
BUT I CLAIMED HIM FIRSTS!
NO ME!
WHOA! WHOA!! STOP!! STOP!!!
ALEX, I'VE SEEN ENOUGH BUFFY, ANGEL AND CHARMED TO KNOW THIS SCENE ANYWHERE!
IT'S A LOVE POTION! THEY'RE ALL UNDER A SPELL!!
GET REAL.

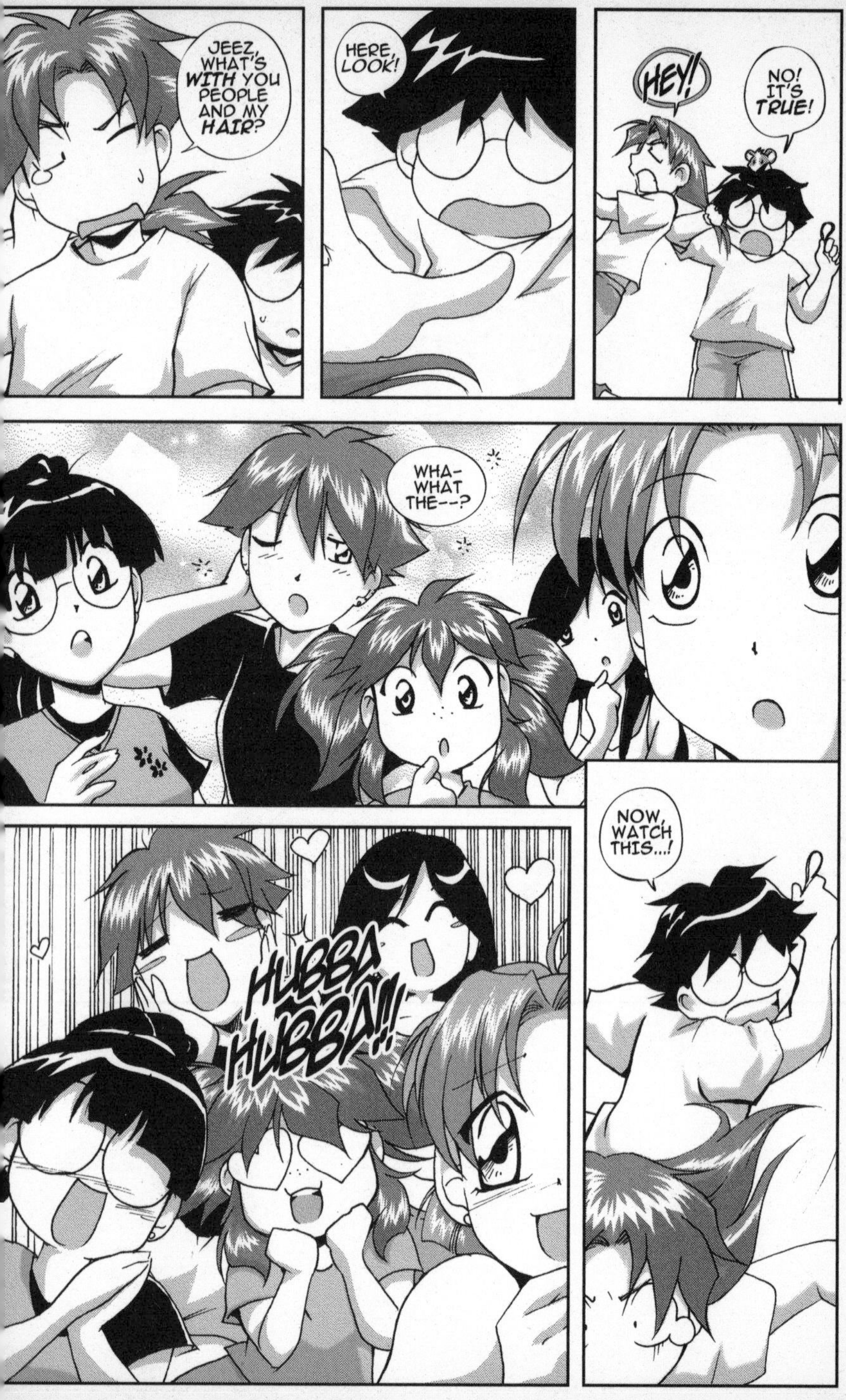
NO! IT'S TRUE!
HEY!
HERE, LOOK!
JEEZ, WHAT'S WITH YOU PEOPLE AND MY HAIR?
WHA-WHAT THE--?
NOW, WATCH THIS...!
HUBBA HUBBA!!

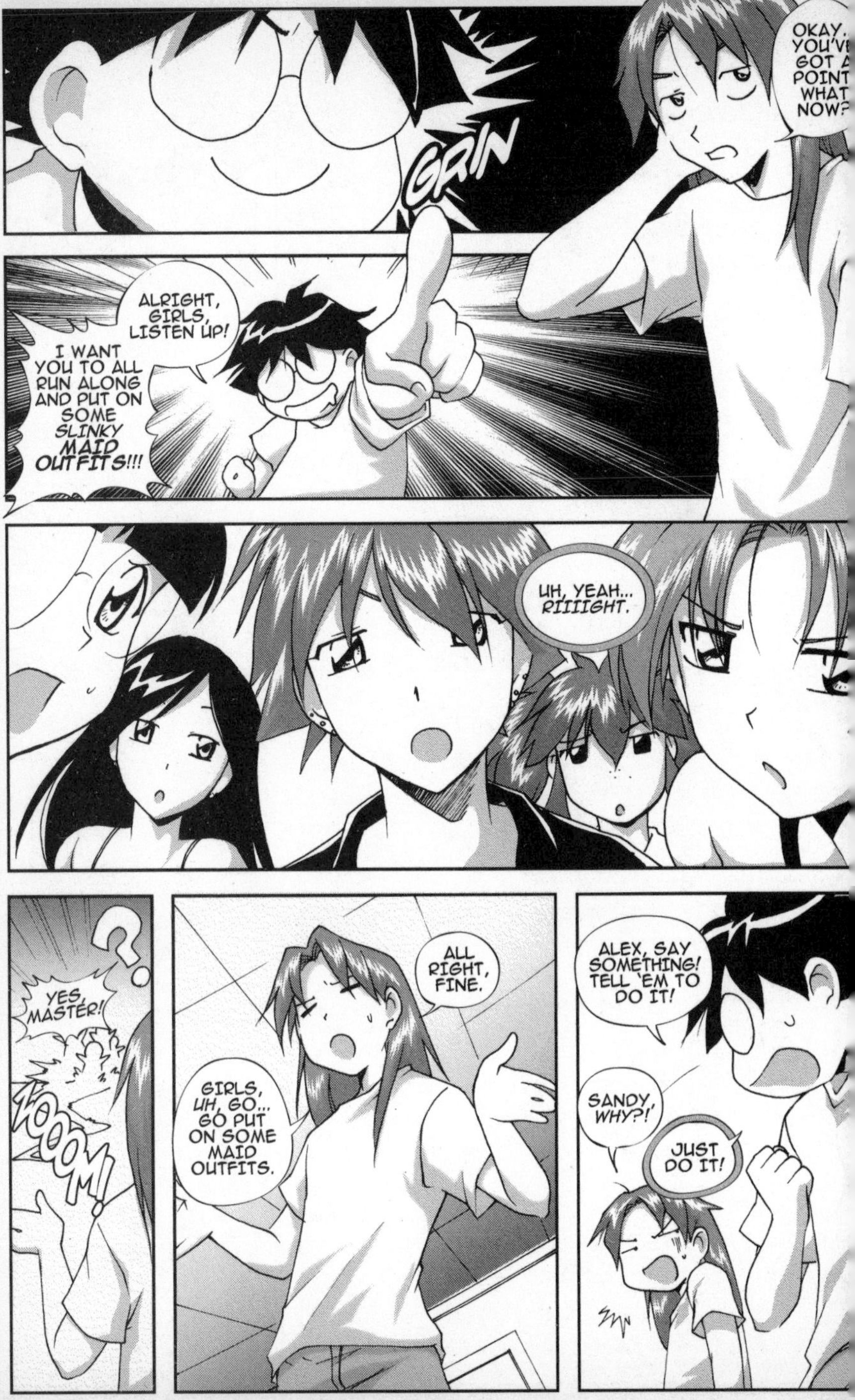
OKAY. YOU'VE GOT A POINT WHAT NOW?
GRIN
ALRIGHT, GIRLS, LISTEN UP!
I WANT YOU TO ALL RUN ALONG AND PUT ON SOME SLINKY MAID OUTFITS!!!
UH, YEAH... RIIIIGHT.
ALEX, SAY SOMETHING! TELL 'EM TO DO IT!
SANDY, WHY?!'
JUST DO IT!
ALL RIGHT, FINE.
GIRLS, UH, GO... GO PUT ON SOME MAID OUTFITS.
?
YES, MASTER!
VOOOOM!

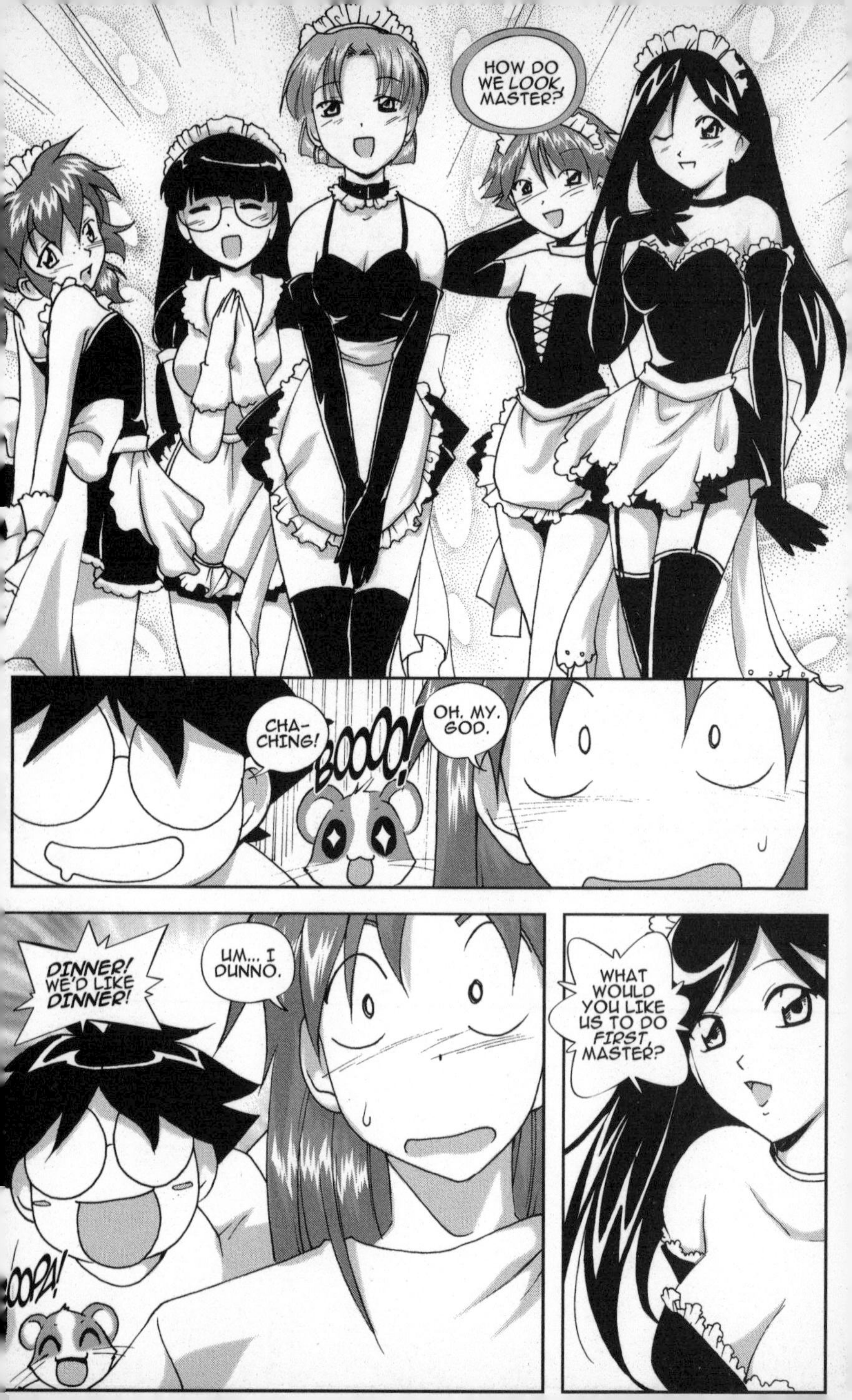
HOW DO WE LOOK, MASTER?
OH, MY. GOD.
CHA-CHING!
BOOOO!
WHAT WOULD YOU LIKE US TO DO FIRST, MASTER?
UM... I DUNNO.
DINNER! WE'D LIKE DINNER!

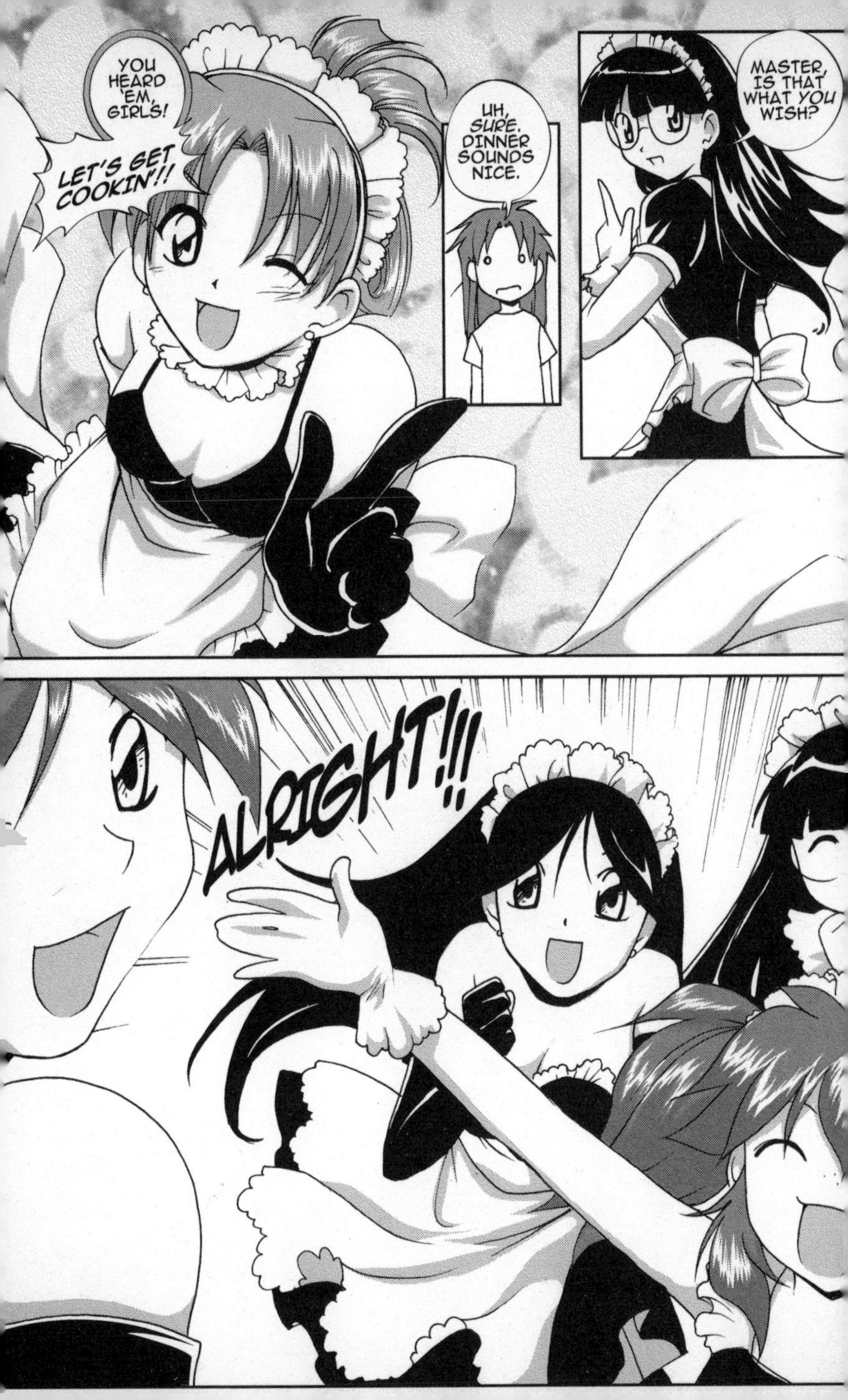
MASTER, IS THAT WHAT YOU WISH?
UH, SURE. DINNER SOUNDS NICE.
YOU HEARD 'EM, GIRLS!
LET'S GET COOKIN'!!
ALRIGHT!!!

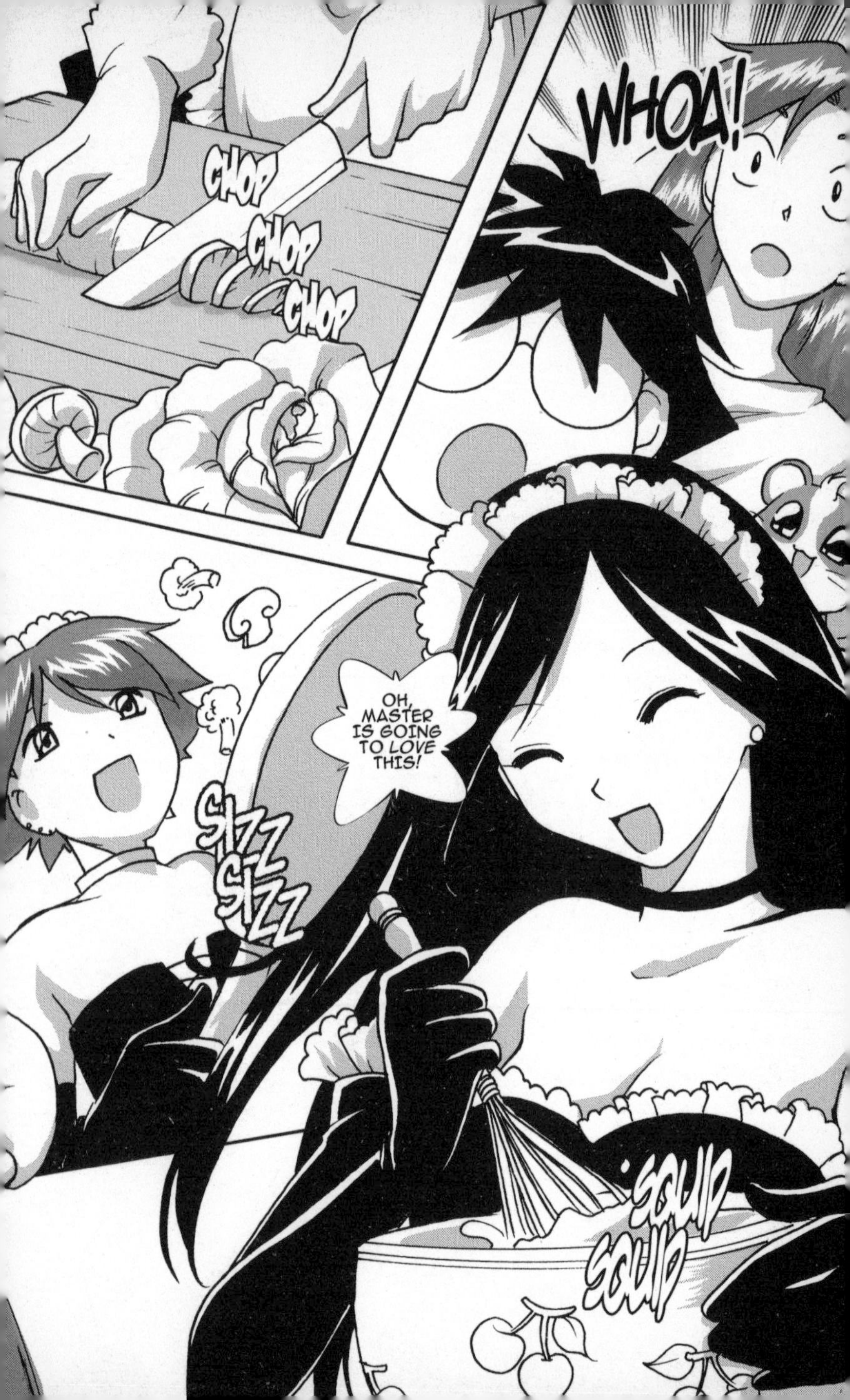
WHOA!
CHOP CHOP CHOP
OH, MASTER IS GOING TO LOVE THIS!
SIZZ SIZZ
SQUID SQUID

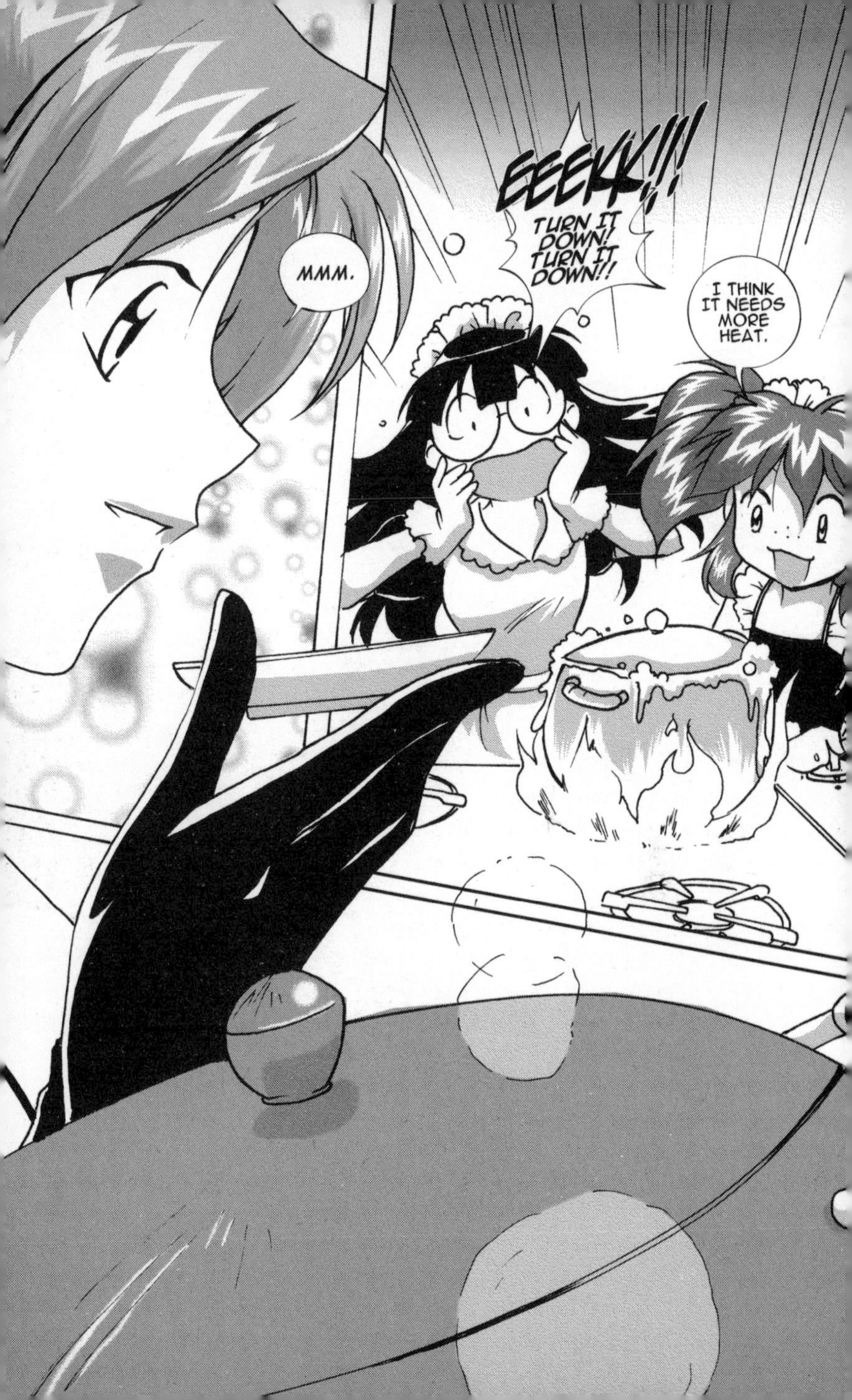
I THINK IT NEEDS MORE HEAT.
EEEKK!!!
TURN IT DOWN! TURN IT DOWN!!
MMM.

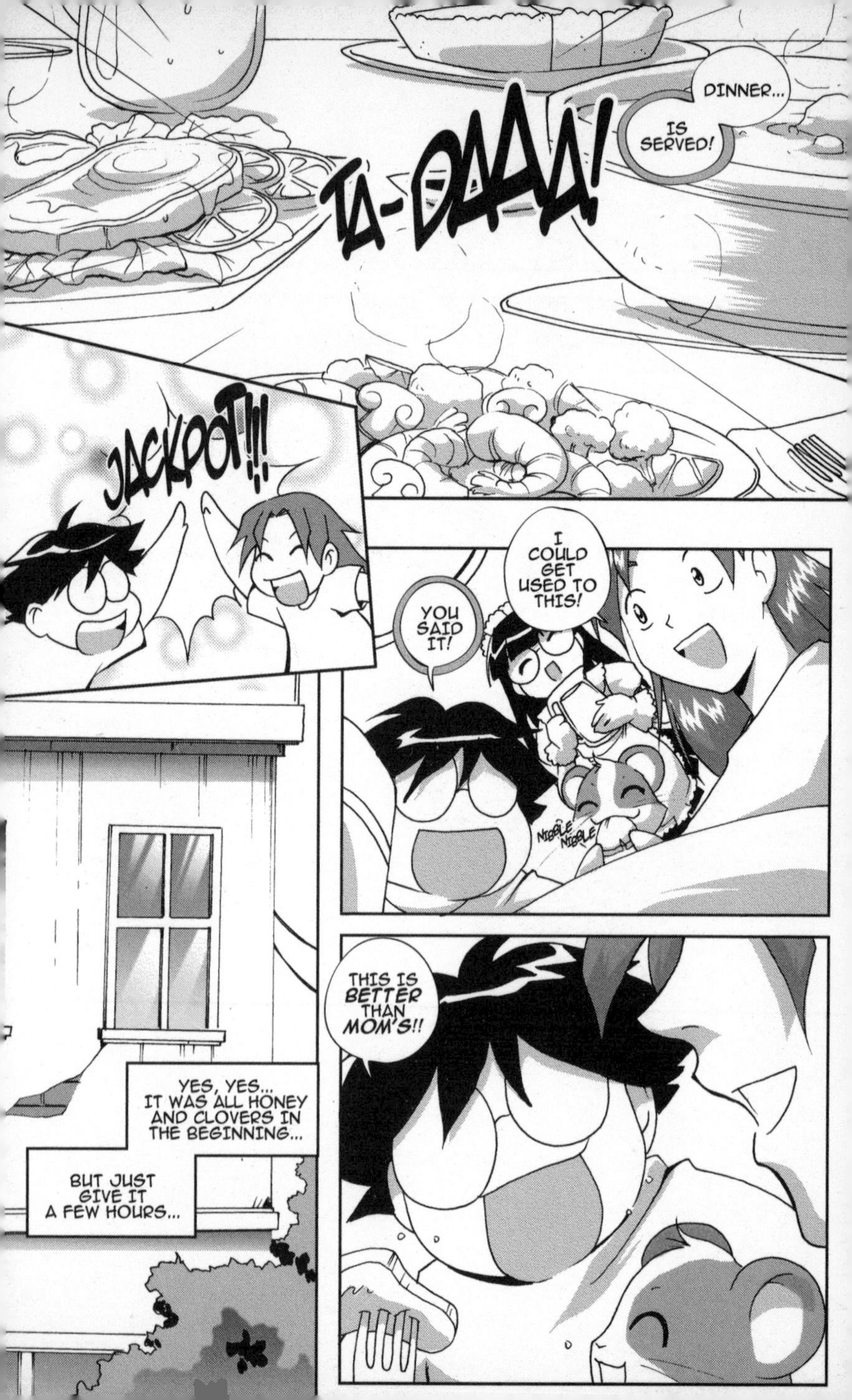
DINNER...
IS SERVED!
TA-DAAA!
JACKPOT!!!
I COULD GET USED TO THIS!
YOU SAID IT!
NIBBLE NIBBLE
THIS IS BETTER THAN MOM'S!!
YES, YES... IT WAS ALL HONEY AND CLOVERS IN THE BEGINNING...
BUT JUST GIVE IT A FEW HOURS...

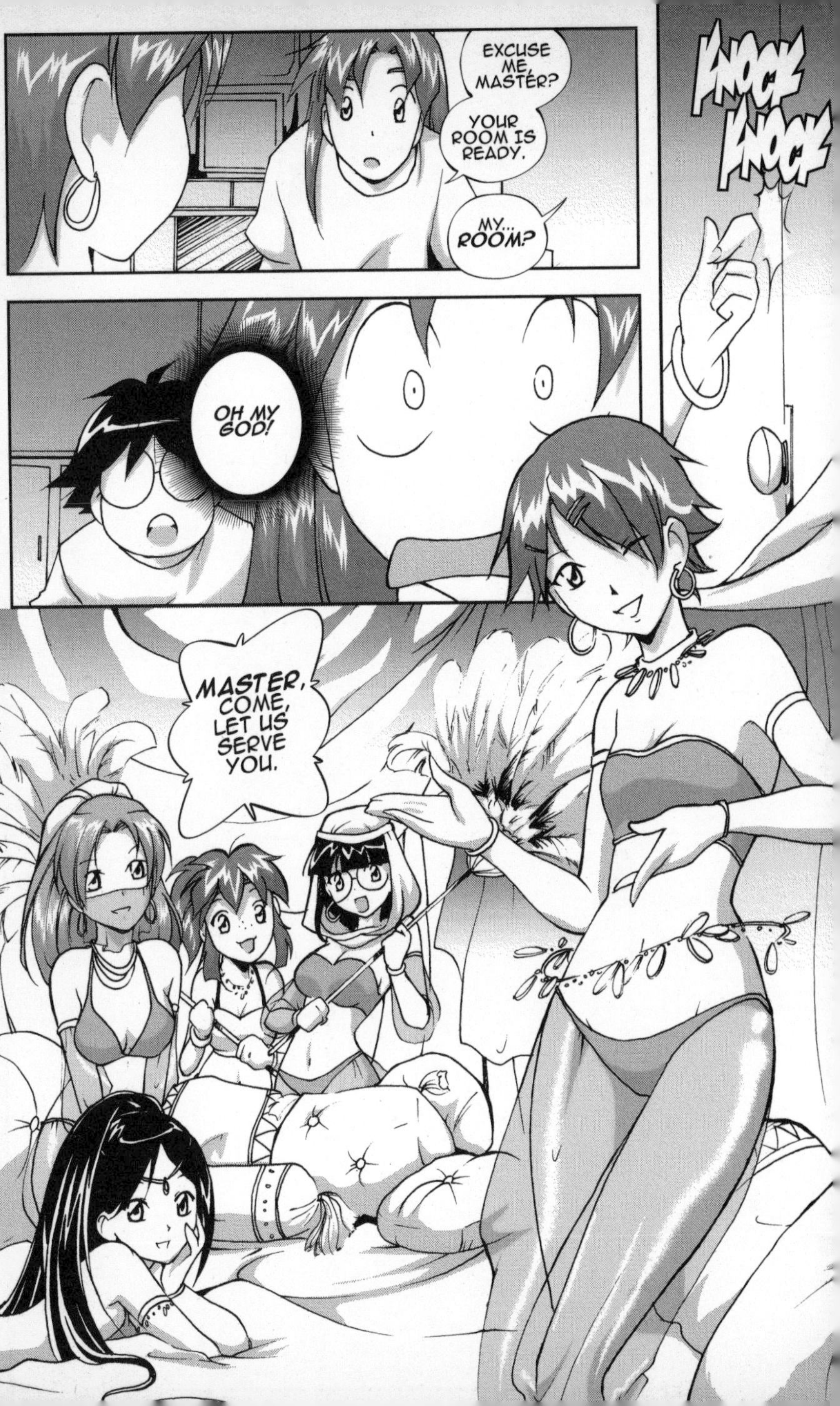
KNOCK KNOCK
EXCUSE ME, MASTER?
YOUR ROOM IS READY.
MY... ROOM?
OH MY GOD!
MASTER, COME, LET US SERVE YOU.

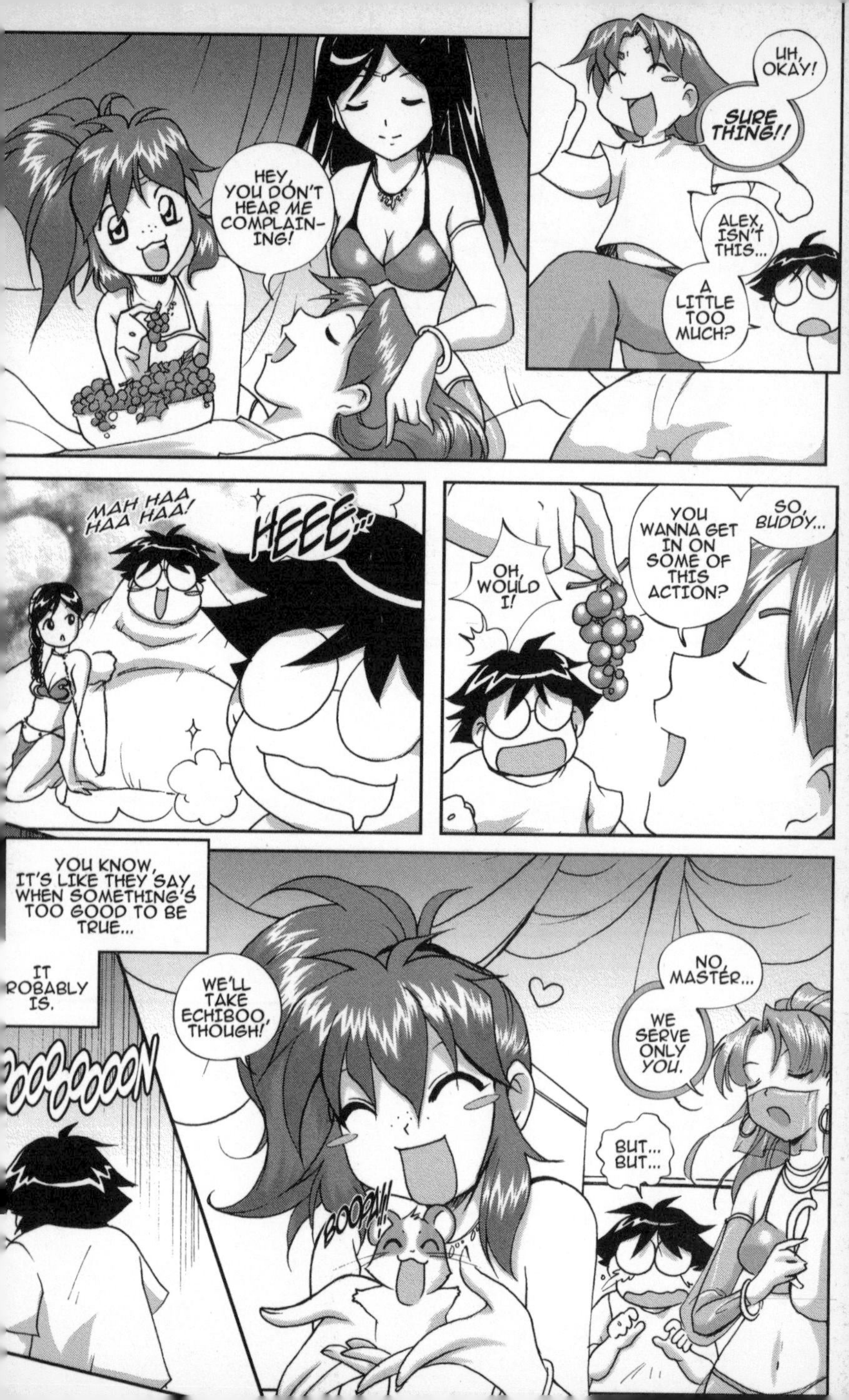
UH, OKAY!
SURE THING!!
ALEX, ISN'T THIS...
A LITTLE TOO MUCH?
HEY, YOU DON'T HEAR *ME* COMPLAINING!
SO, BUDDY...
YOU WANNA GET IN ON SOME OF THIS ACTION?
OH, WOULD I!
HEEE..!
MAH HAA HAA HAA!
NO, MASTER...
WE SERVE ONLY *YOU*.
BUT... BUT...
WE'LL TAKE ECHIBOO, THOUGH!
YOU KNOW, IT'S LIKE THEY SAY, WHEN SOMETHING'S TOO GOOD TO BE TRUE...
IT ROBABLY IS.

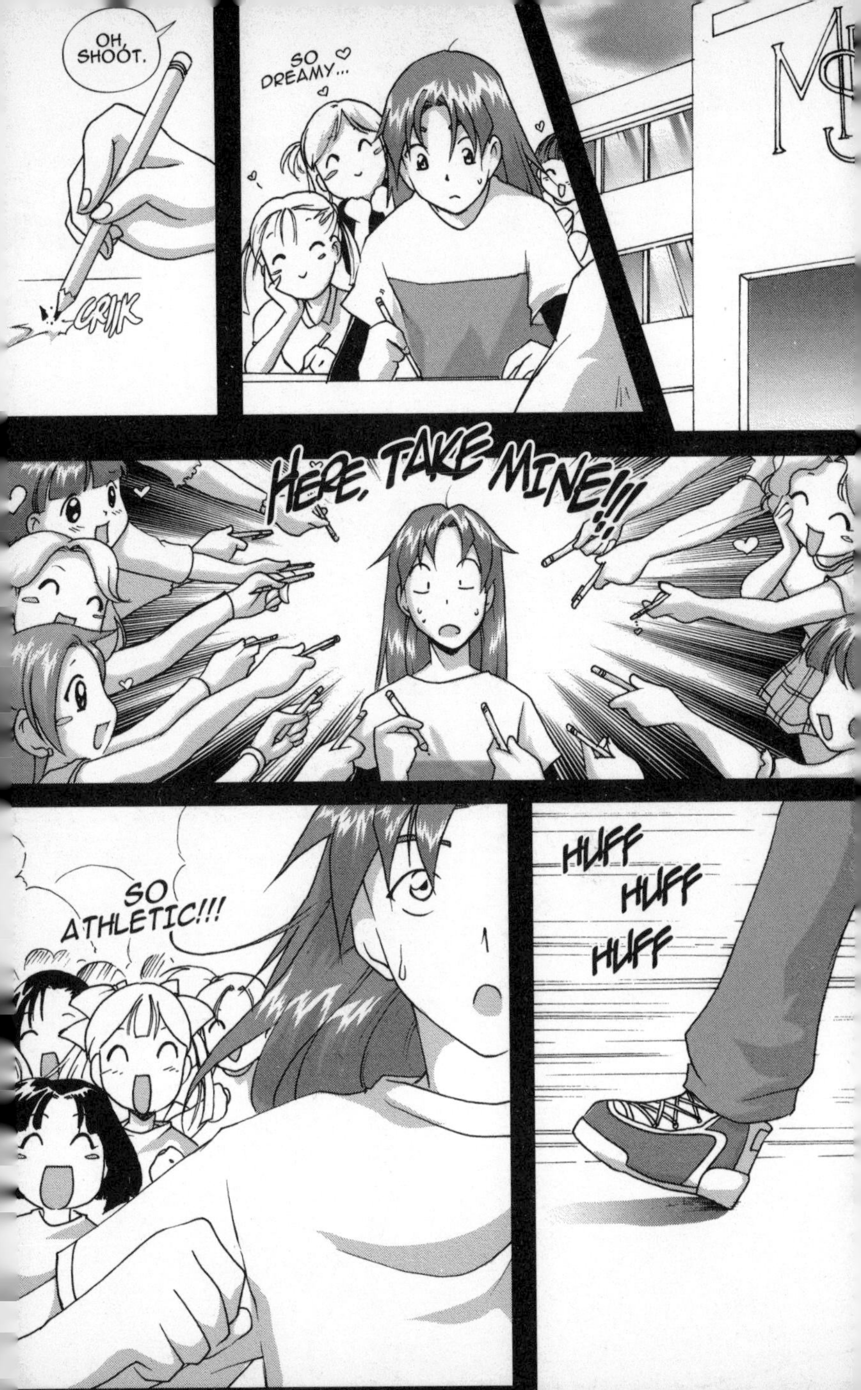
SO DREAMY...
OH, SHOOT.
CRIK
HERE, TAKE MINE!!!
HUFF
HUFF
HUFF
SO ATHLETIC!!!

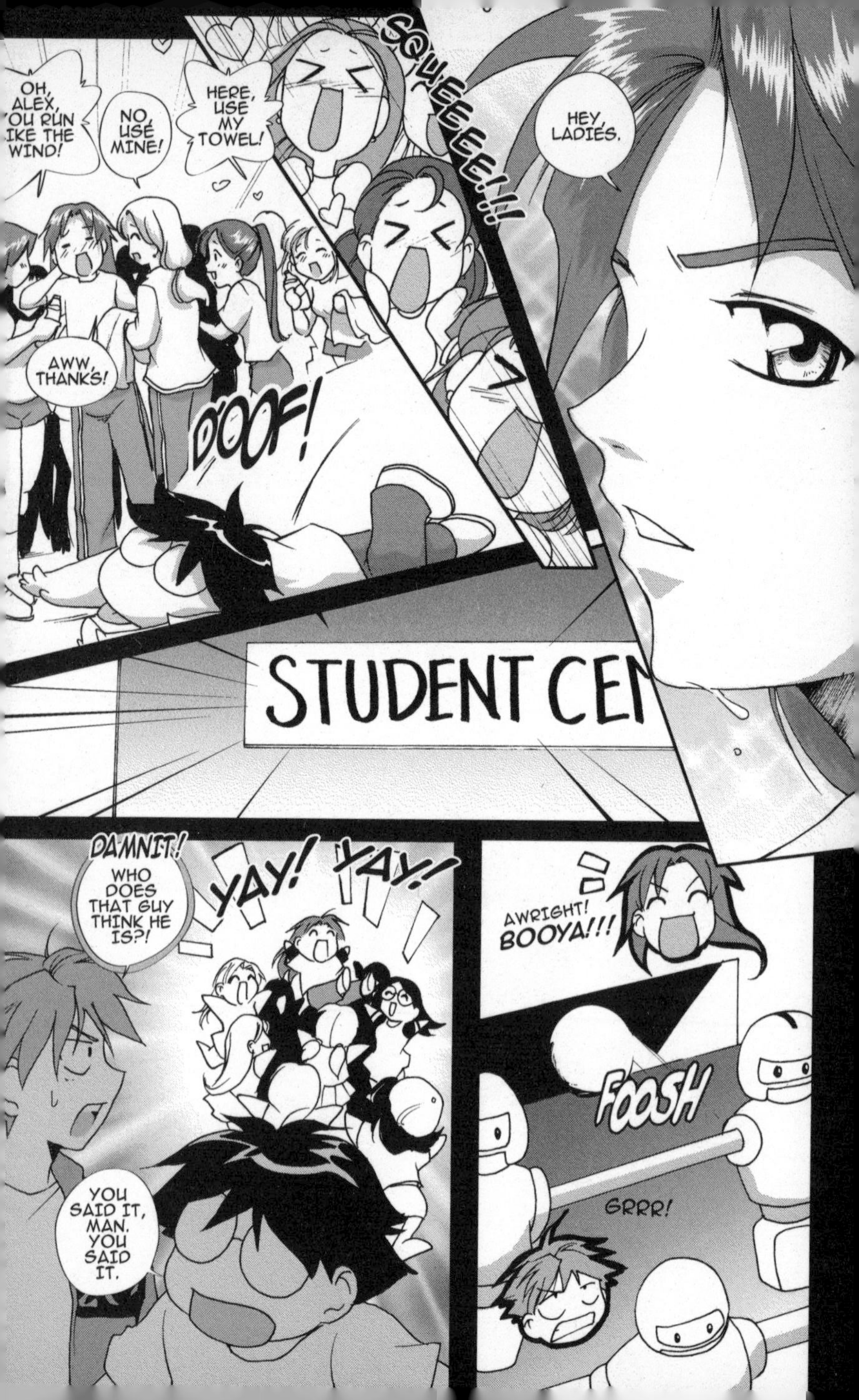
HEY, LADIES.
SQUEEEEE!!!
HERE, USE MY TOWEL!
NO, USE MINE!
OH, ALEX, OU RUN IKE THE WIND!
AWW, THANKS!
DOOF!
STUDENT CEN
AWRIGHT! BOOYA!!!
FOOSH
GRRR!
YAY! YAY!
DAMNIT! WHO DOES THAT GUY THINK HE IS?!
YOU SAID IT, MAN. YOU SAID IT.

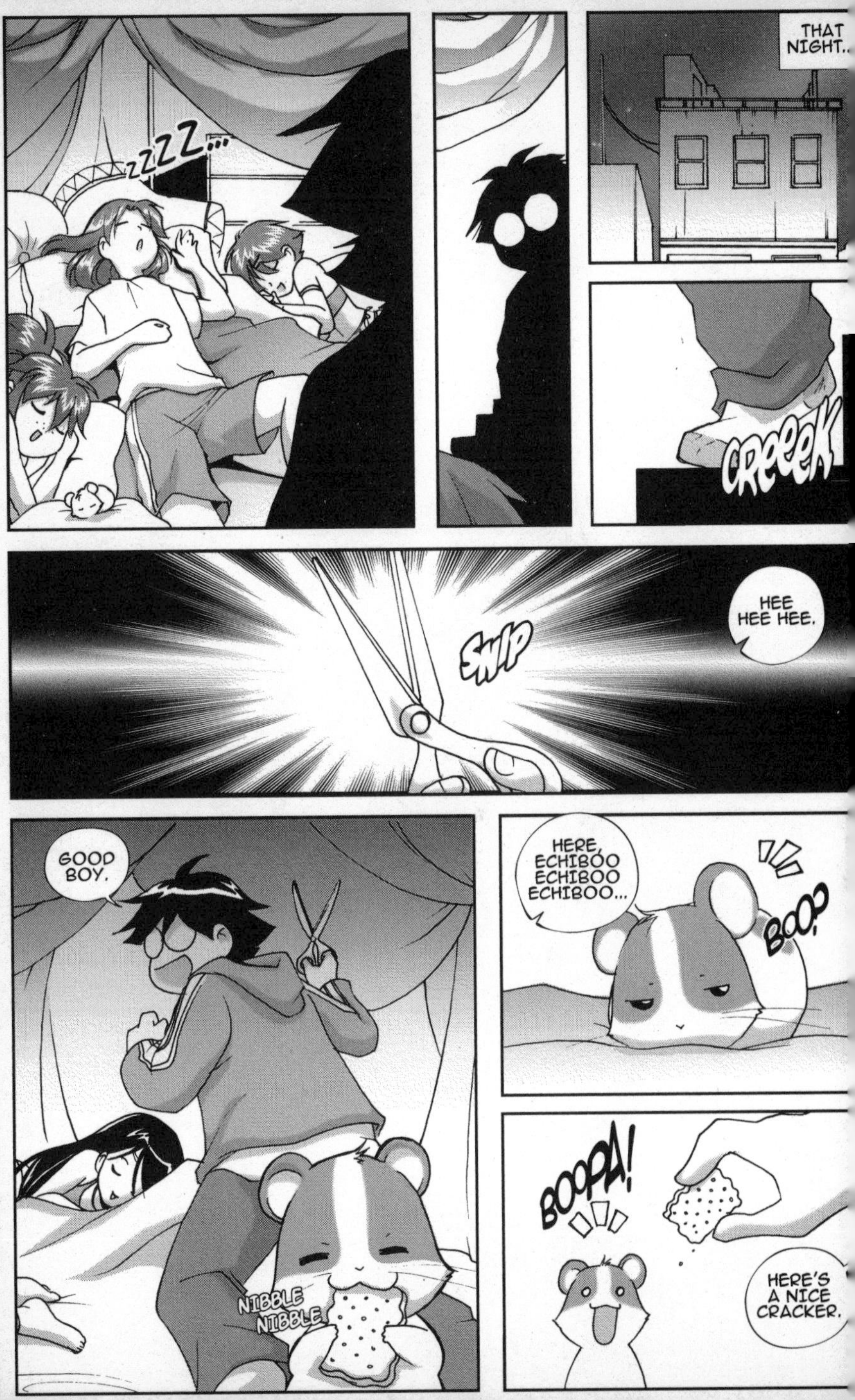
THAT NIGHT...
CREEEK
zzZZ...
HEE HEE HEE.
SNIP
HERE, ECHIBOO ECHIBOO ECHIBOO...
BOO?
HERE'S A NICE CRACKER.
BOOPA!
GOOD BOY.
NIBBLE NIBBLE

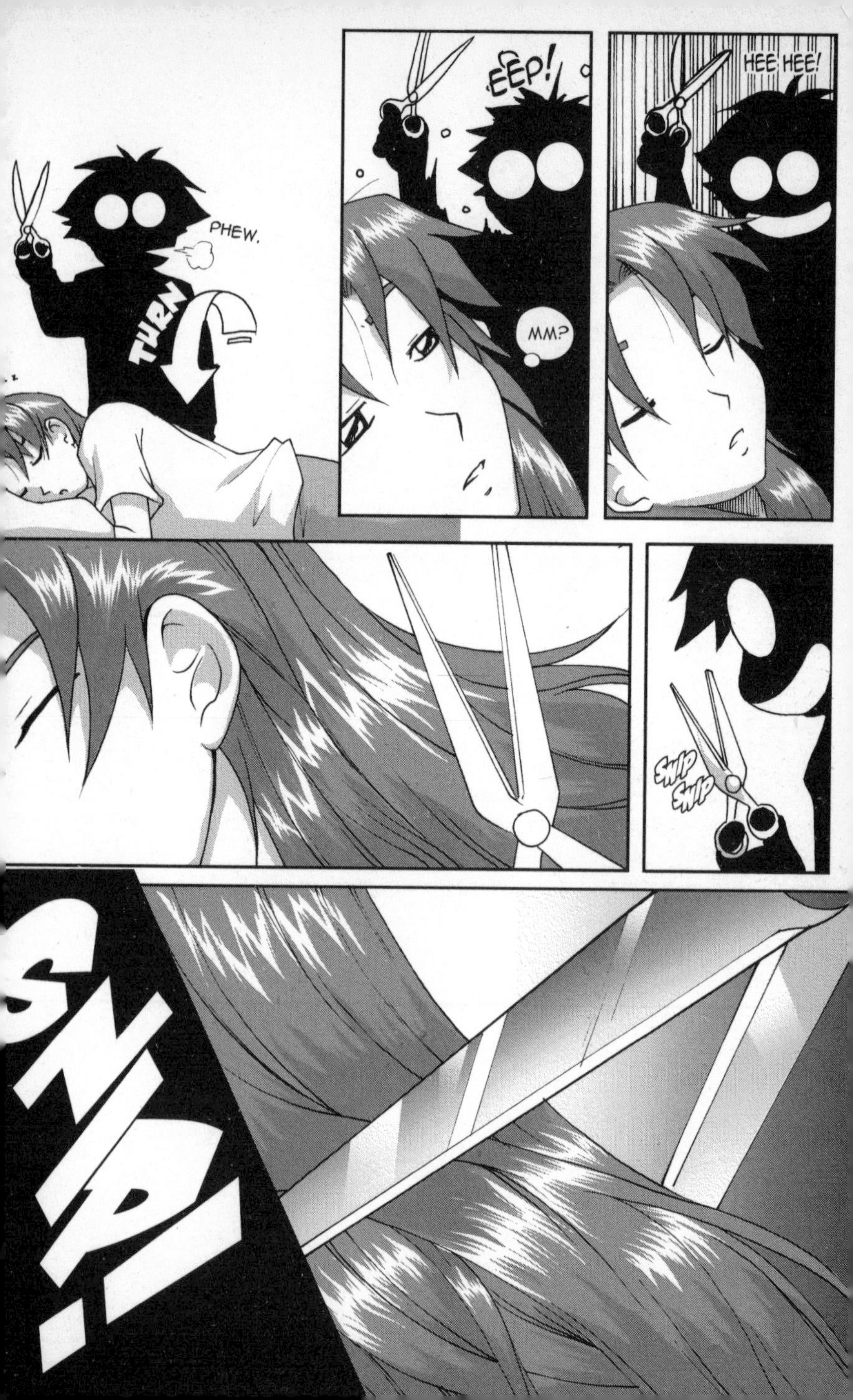
HEE HEE!
EEP!
MM?
PHEW.
TURN
SNIP SNIP
SNIP!

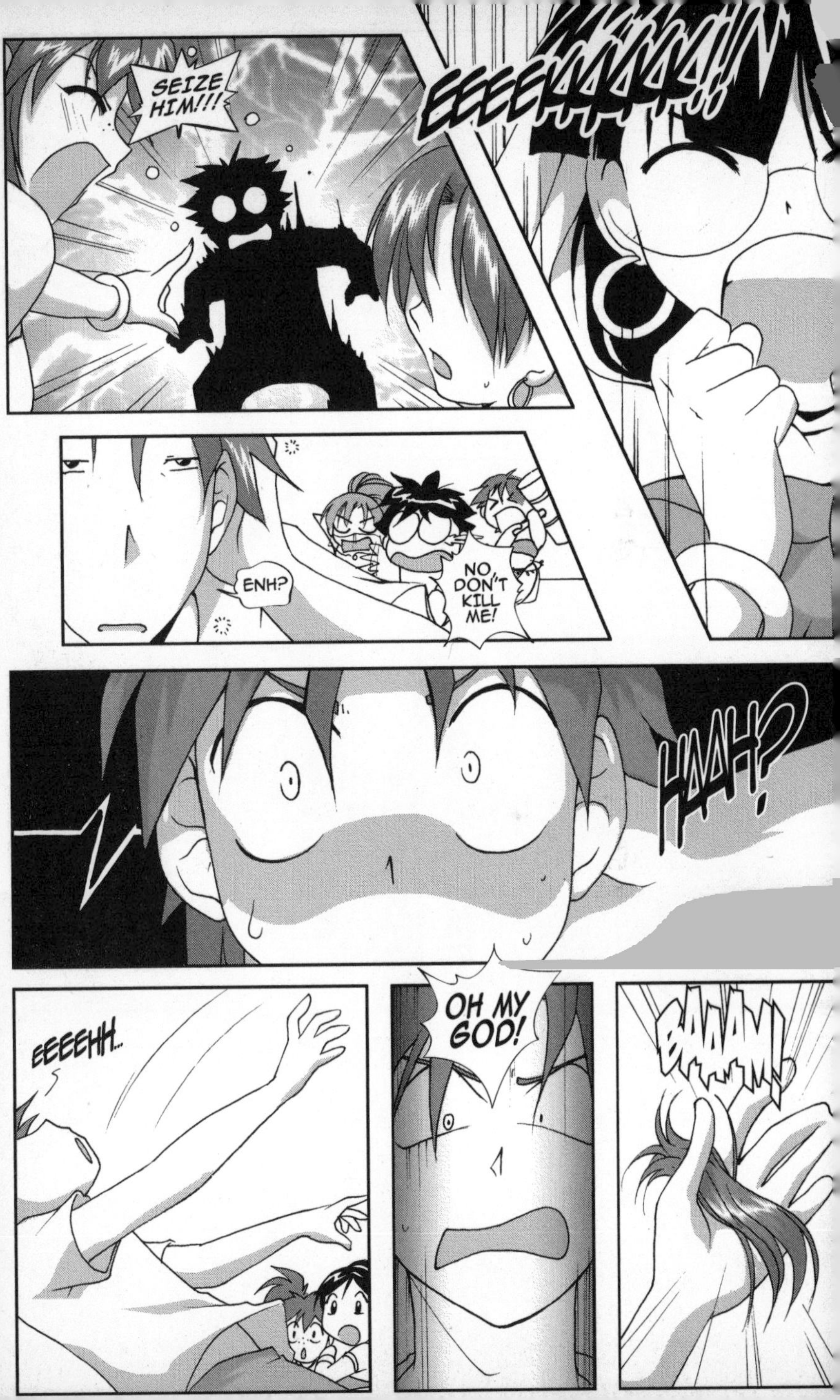
SEIZE HIM!!!
NO, DON'T KILL ME!
ENH?
HAAH?
BAAAM!
OH MY GOD!
EEEEHH..

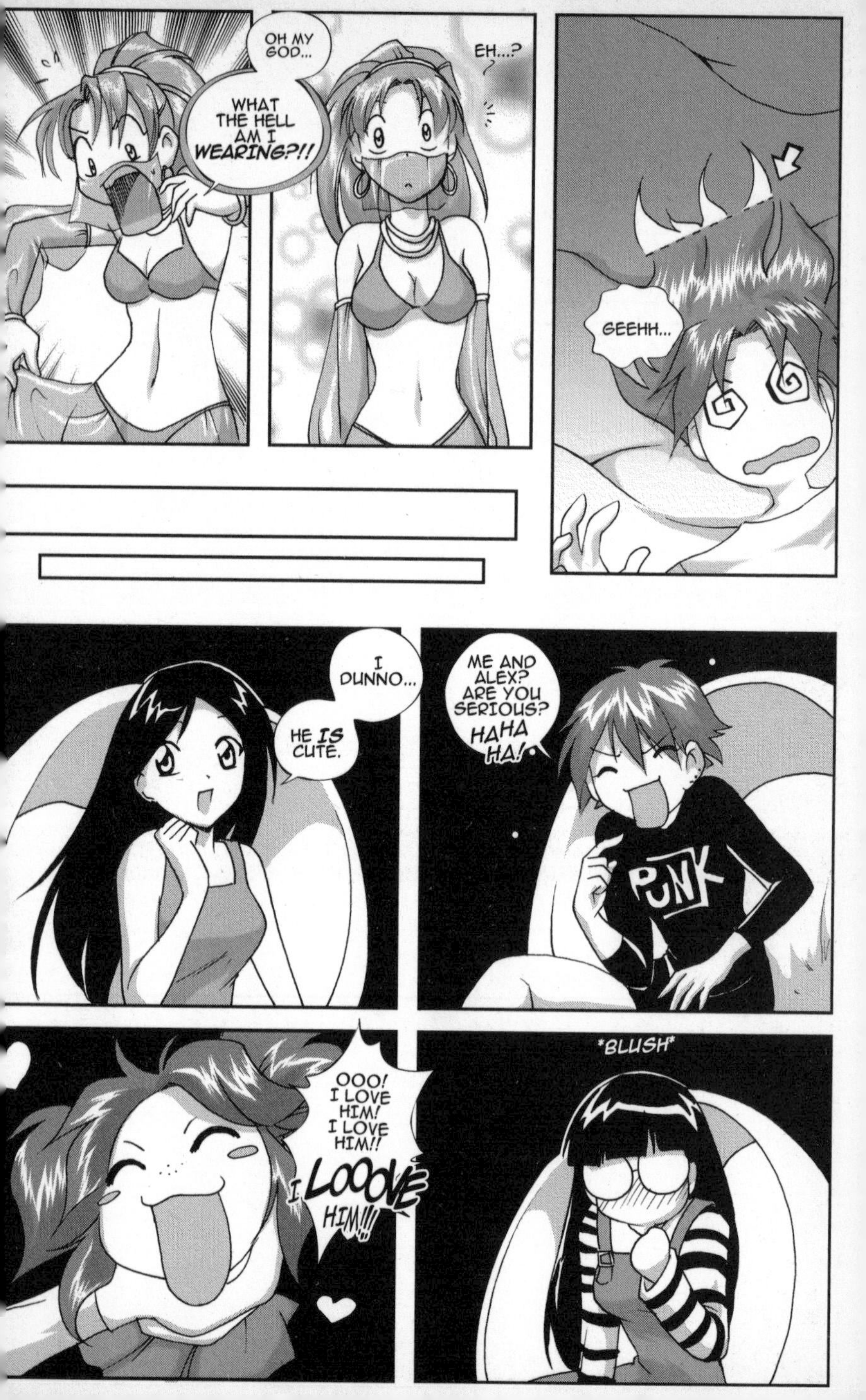
GEEHH...
EH...?
OH MY GOD...
WHAT THE HELL AM I WEARING?!!
ME AND ALEX? ARE YOU SERIOUS? HAHA HA!
PUNK
I DUNNO...
HE IS CUTE.
BLUSH
OOO! I LOVE HIM! I LOVE HIM!!
I LOOOVE HIM!!!

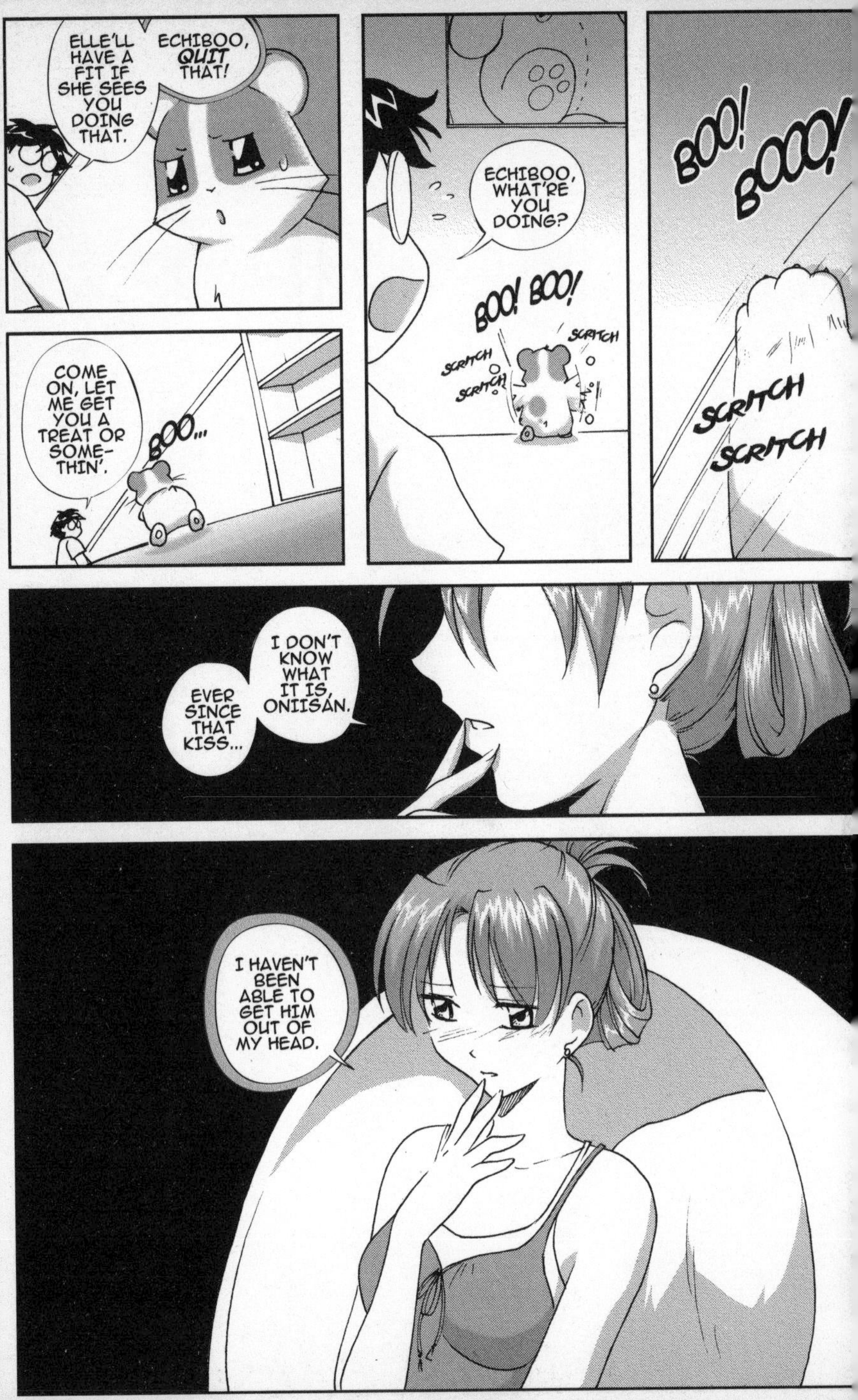
BOO! BOOO!
SCRITCH SCRITCH
ECHIBOO, WHAT'RE YOU DOING?
BOO! BOO!
SCRITCH SCRITCH SCRITCH
ECHIBOO, QUIT THAT!
ELLE'LL HAVE A FIT IF SHE SEES YOU DOING THAT.
BOO...
COME ON, LET ME GET YOU A TREAT OR SOME-THIN'.
I DON'T KNOW WHAT IT IS, ONIISAN.
EVER SINCE THAT KISS...
I HAVEN'T BEEN ABLE TO GET HIM OUT OF MY HEAD.

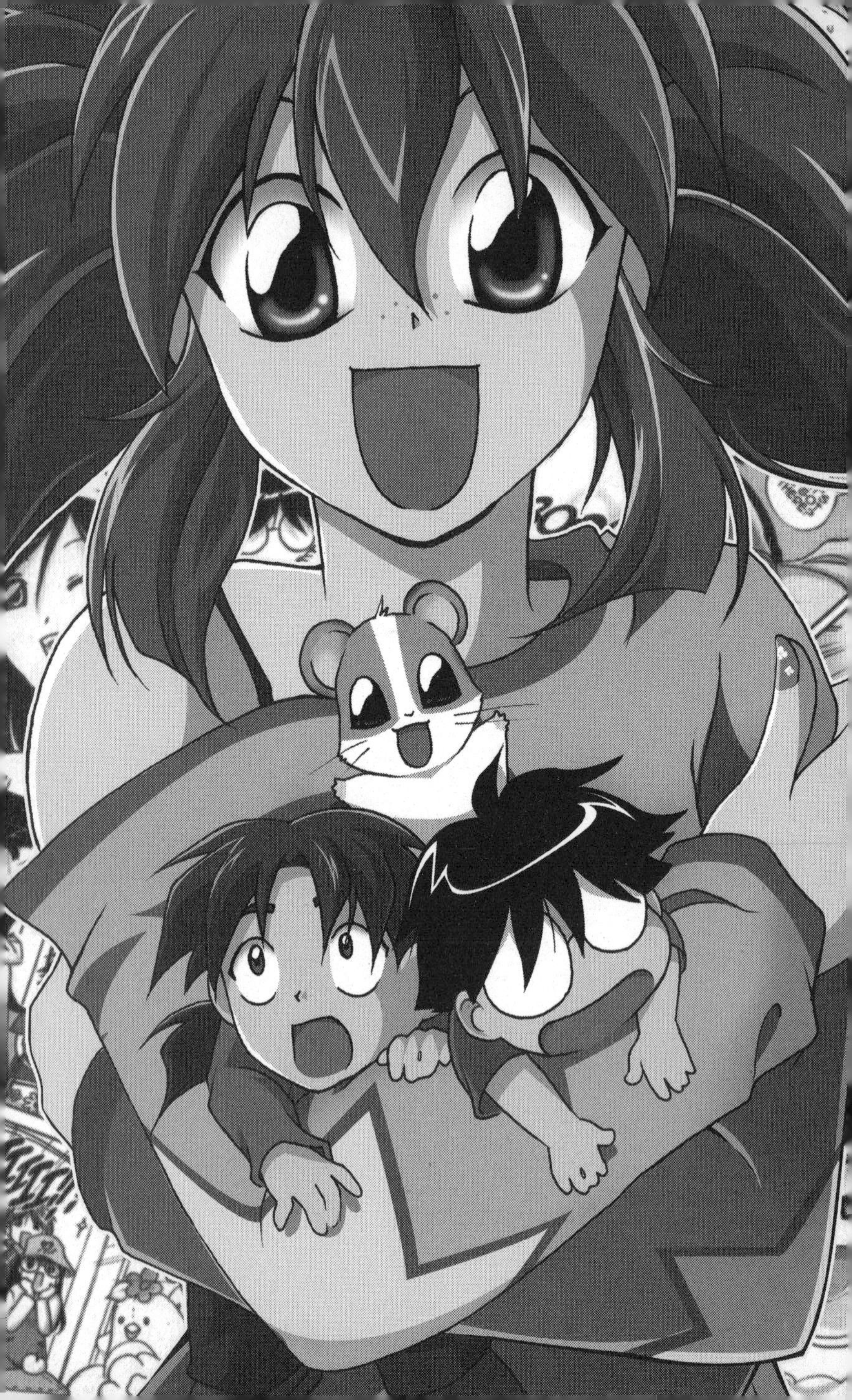

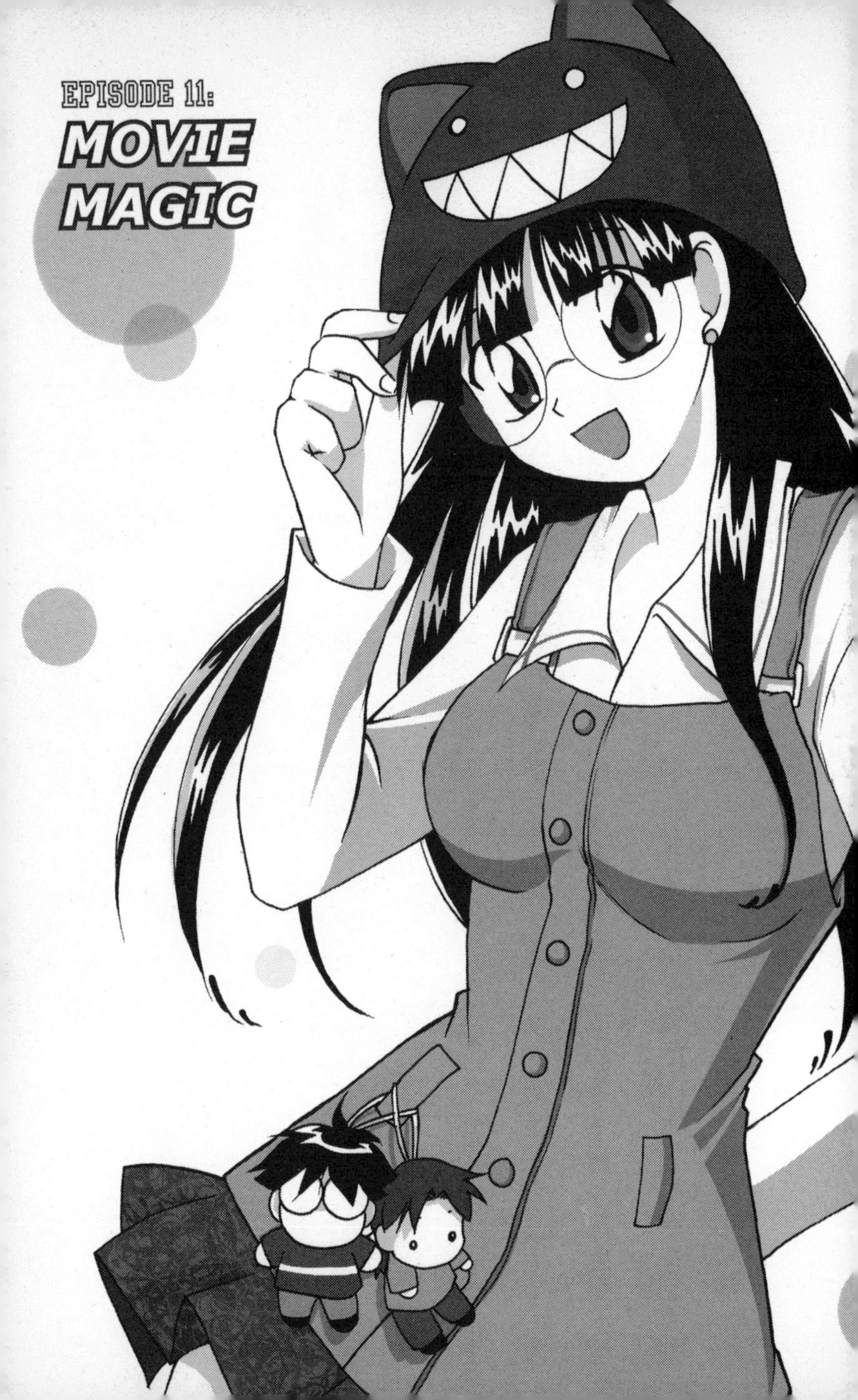
EPISODE 11:
MOVIE MAGIC

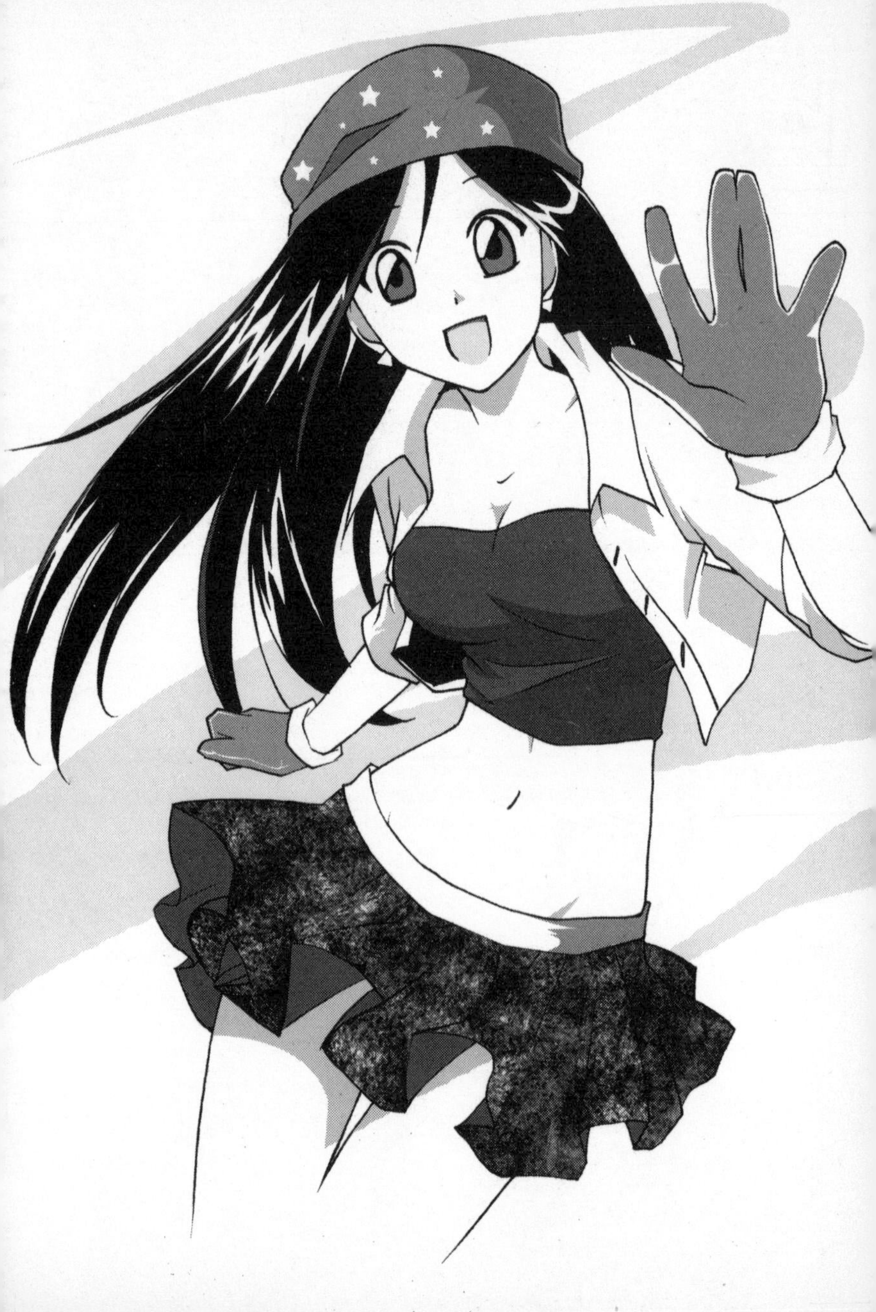

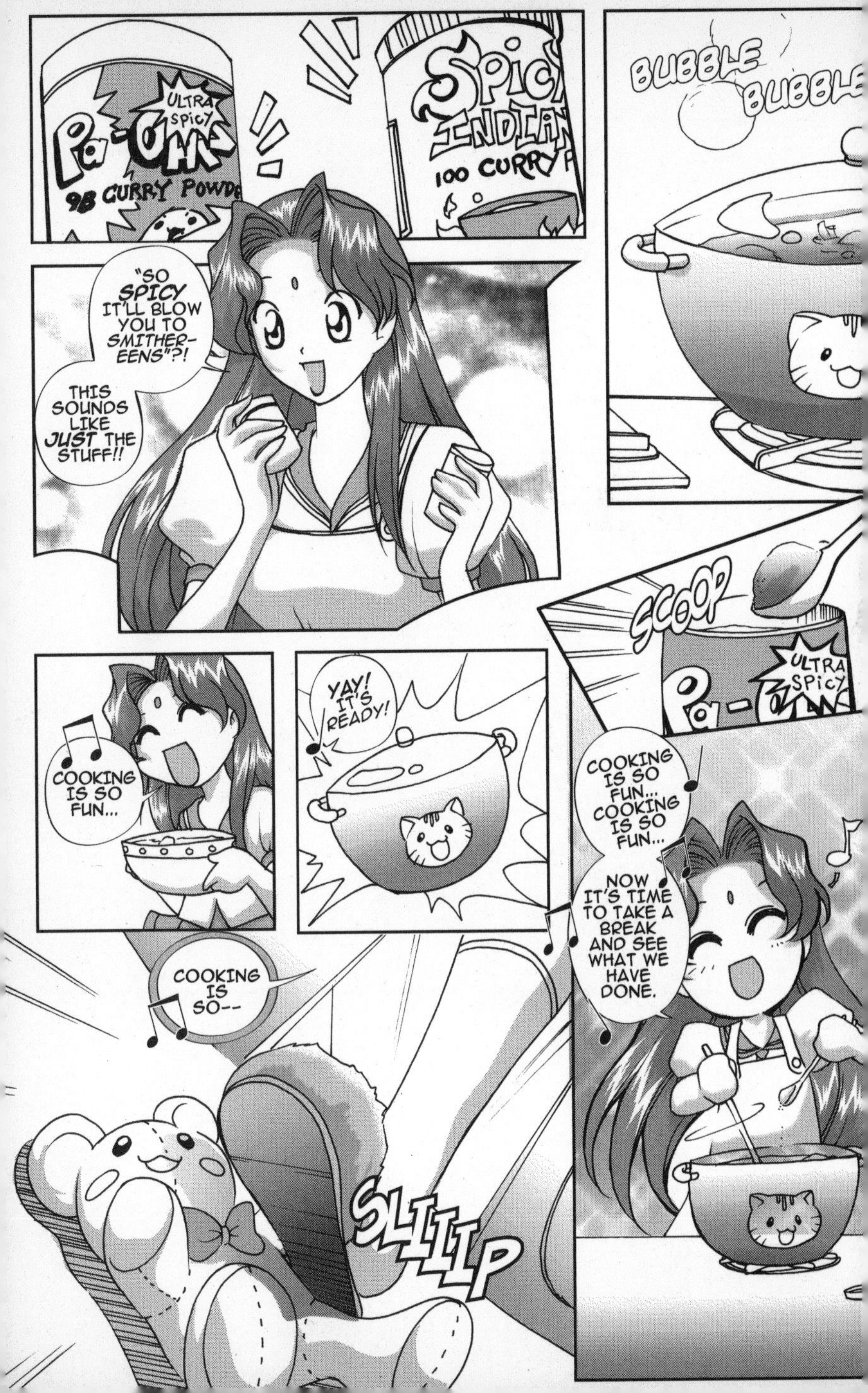
BUBBLE BUBBLE
ULTRA Spicy
98 CURRY POWDE
Spicy INDIAN
100 CURRY
"SO SPICY IT'LL BLOW YOU TO SMITHER-EENS"?!
THIS SOUNDS LIKE JUST THE STUFF!!
SCOOP
ULTRA Spicy
COOKING IS SO FUN... COOKING IS SO FUN...
NOW IT'S TIME TO TAKE A BREAK AND SEE WHAT WE HAVE DONE.
YAY! IT'S READY!
COOKING IS SO FUN...
COOKING IS SO--
SLIIIP

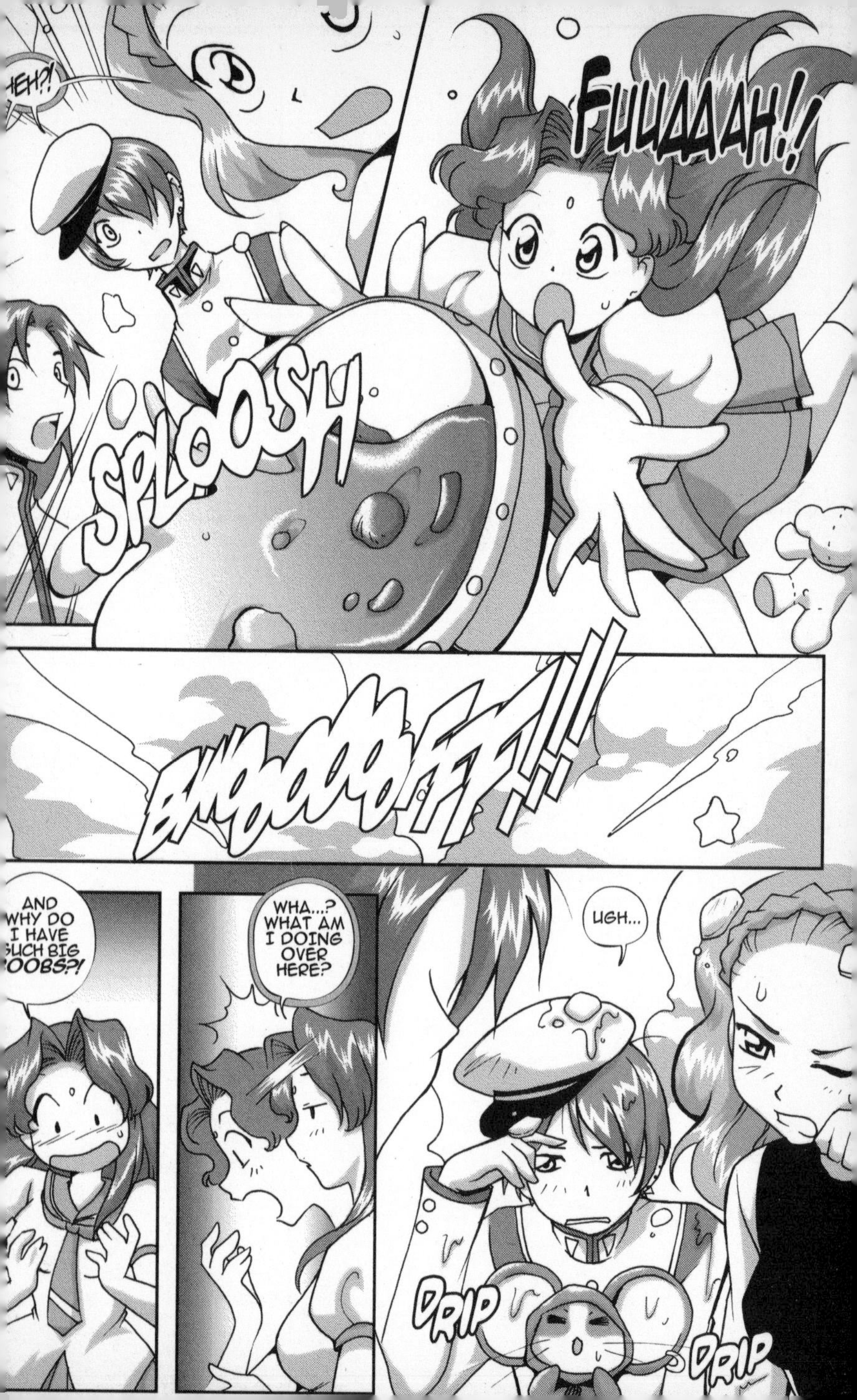
FUUAAAH!!
HEH?!
SPLOOSH
BHOOOOOFF!!!
UGH...
DRIP
DRIP
WHA...? WHAT AM I DOING OVER HERE?
AND WHY DO I HAVE SUCH BIG BOOBS?!

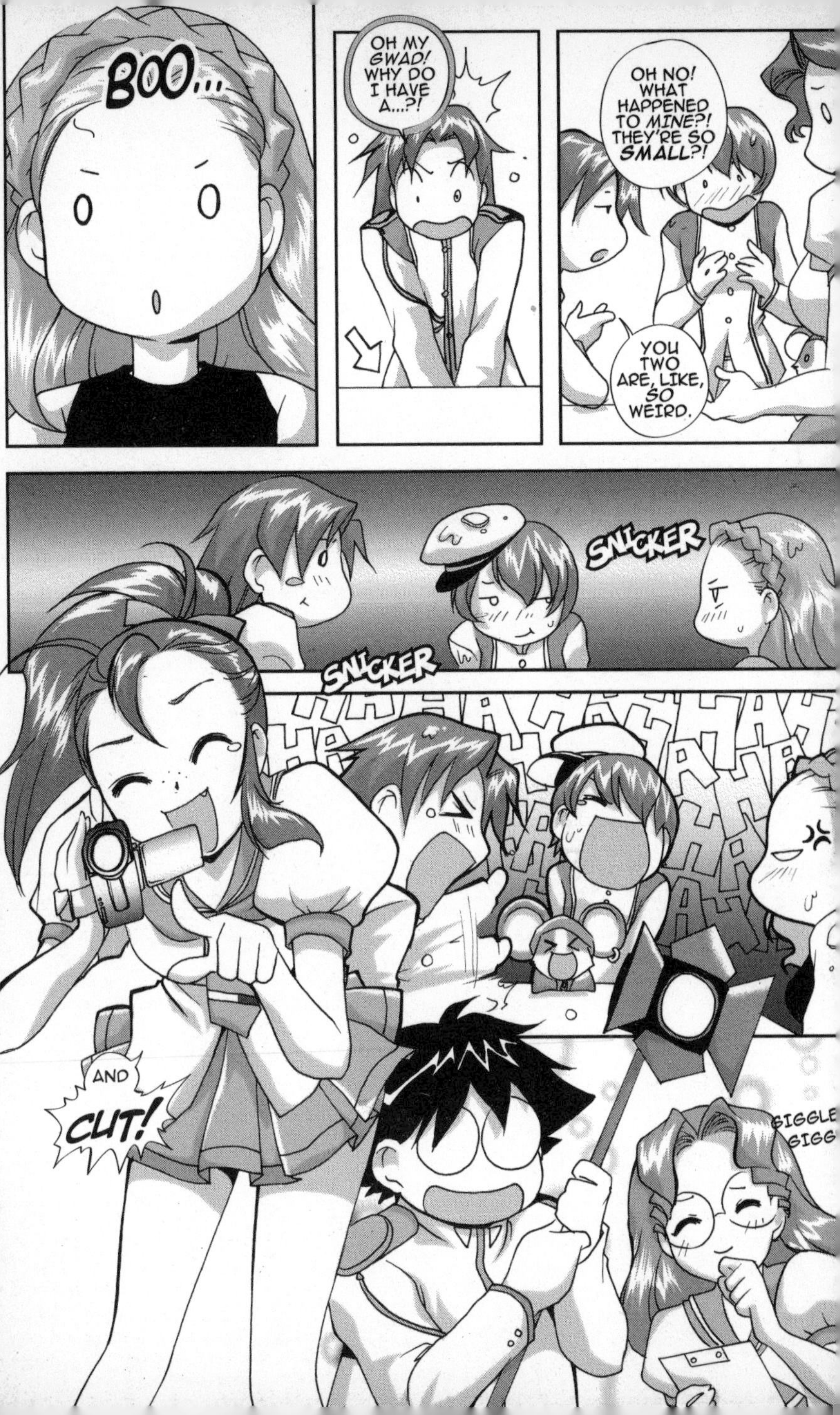
OH NO! WHAT HAPPENED TO MINE?! THEY'RE SO SMALL?!
YOU TWO ARE, LIKE, SO WEIRD.
OH MY GWAD! WHY DO I HAVE A...?!
BOO...
SNICKER
SNICKER
HA HA HA HA
AND CUT!
GIGGLE

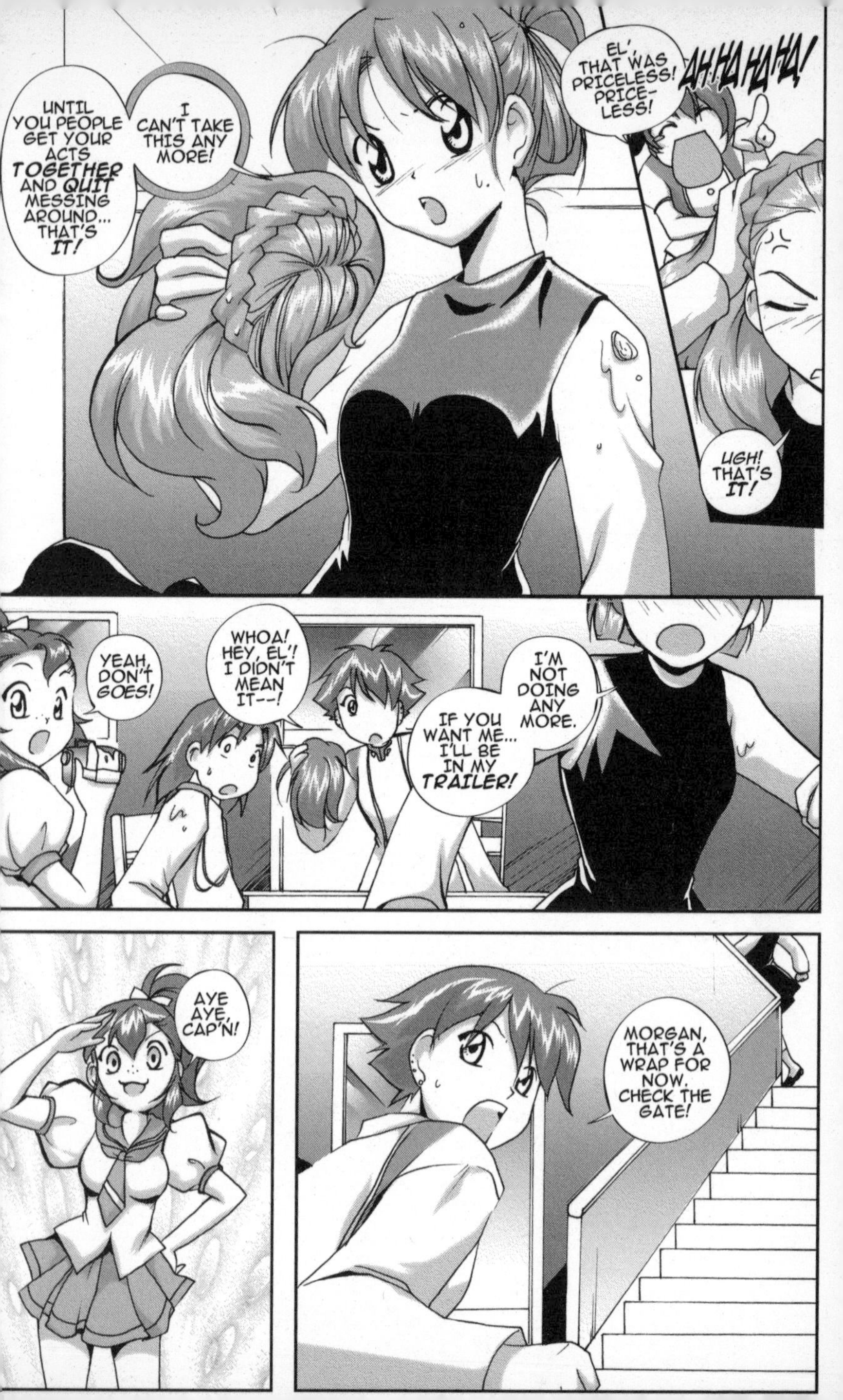
EL', THAT WAS PRICELESS! PRICE-LESS!
AH HA HA HA!
UGH! THAT'S IT!
I CAN'T TAKE THIS ANY MORE!
UNTIL YOU PEOPLE GET YOUR ACTS TOGETHER AND QUIT MESSING AROUND... THAT'S IT!
I'M NOT DOING ANY MORE.
IF YOU WANT ME... I'LL BE IN MY TRAILER!
WHOA! HEY, EL'! I DIDN'T MEAN IT--!
YEAH, DON'T GOES!
MORGAN, THAT'S A WRAP FOR NOW. CHECK THE GATE!
AYE AYE, CAP'N!

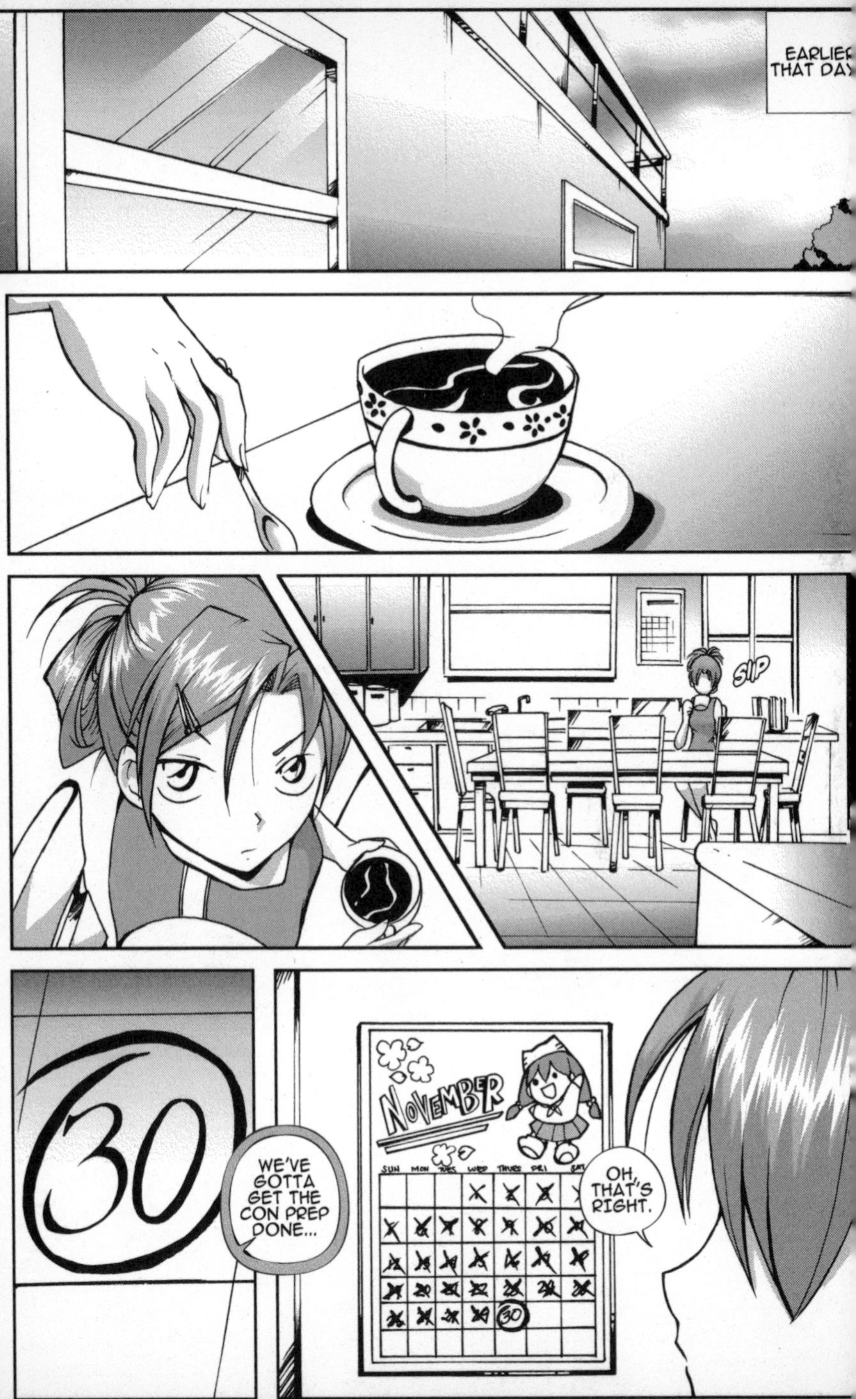
EARLIER THAT DAY
SIP
OH, THAT'S RIGHT.
NOVEMBER
WE'VE GOTTA GET THE CON PREP DONE...
30

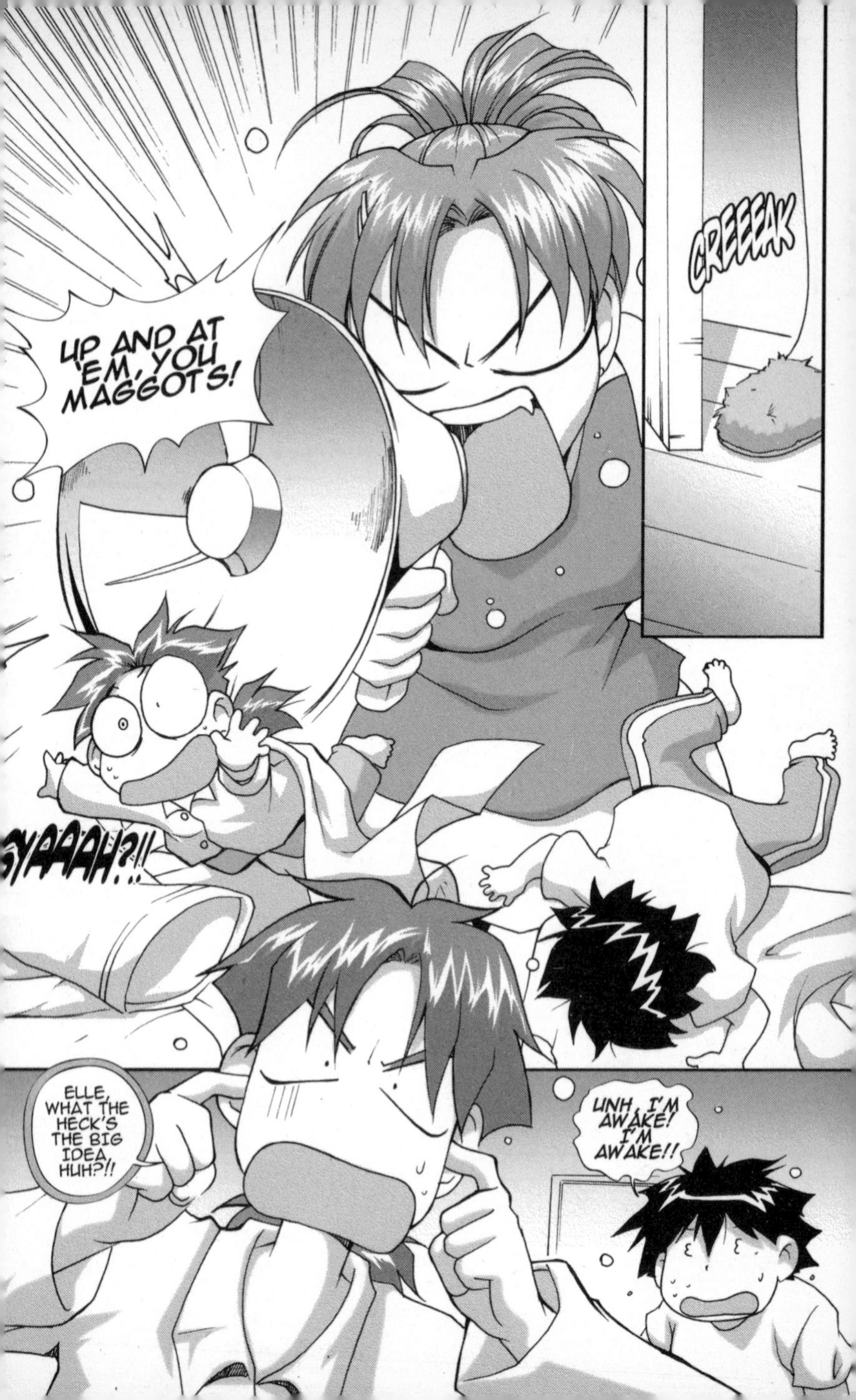
CREEEAK
UP AND AT 'EM, YOU MAGGOTS!
YAAAH?!!
UNH, I'M AWAKE! I'M AWAKE!!
ELLE, WHAT THE HECK'S THE BIG IDEA HUH?!!

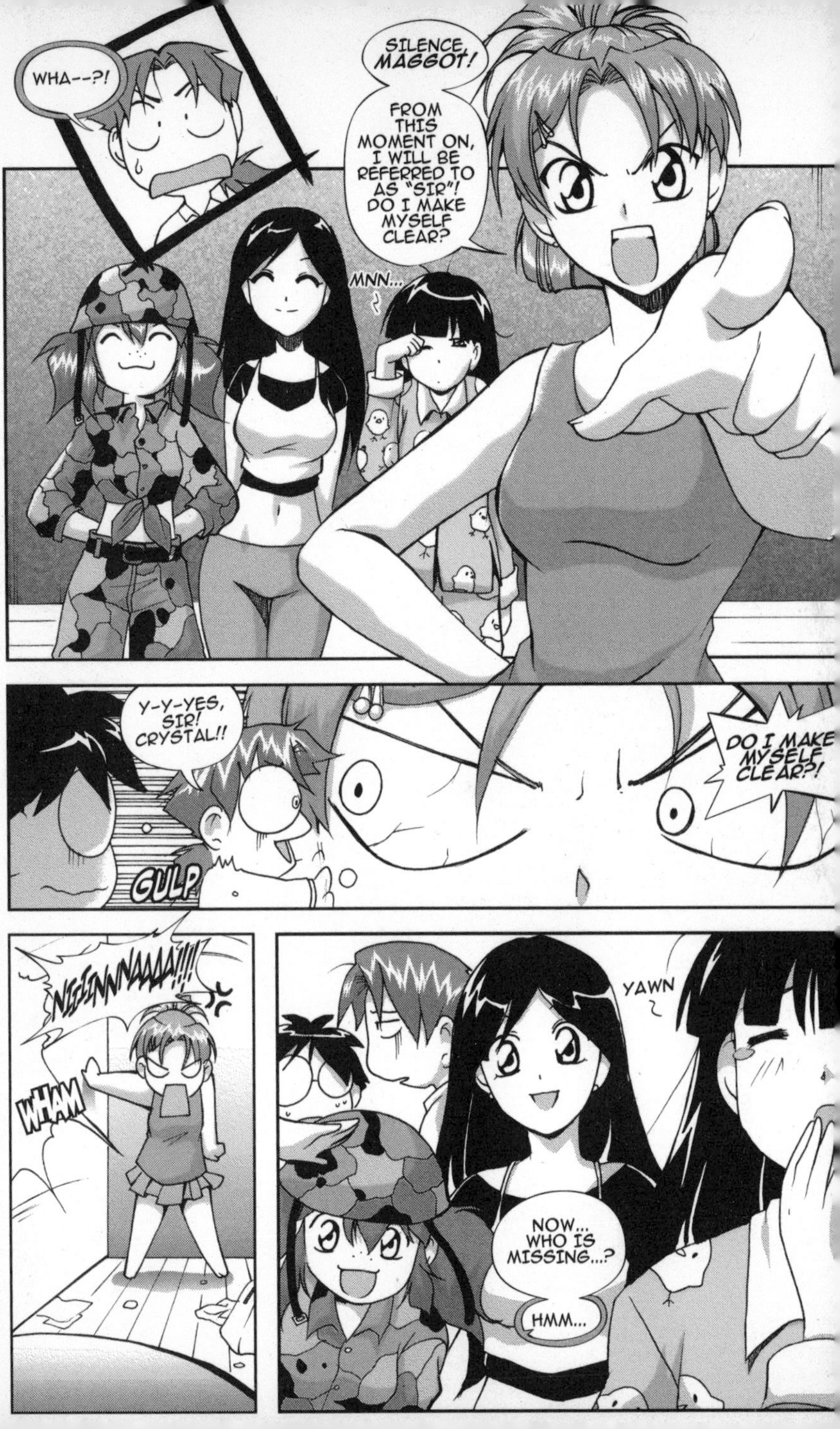
SILENCE, MAGGOT!
FROM THIS MOMENT ON, I WILL BE REFERRED TO AS "SIR"! DO I MAKE MYSELF CLEAR?
WHA--?!
MNN...
DO I MAKE MYSELF CLEAR?!
Y-Y-YES, SIR! CRYSTAL!!
GULP
YAWN
NOW... WHO IS MISSING...?
HMM...
NIIINNNAAAA!!!!
WHAM

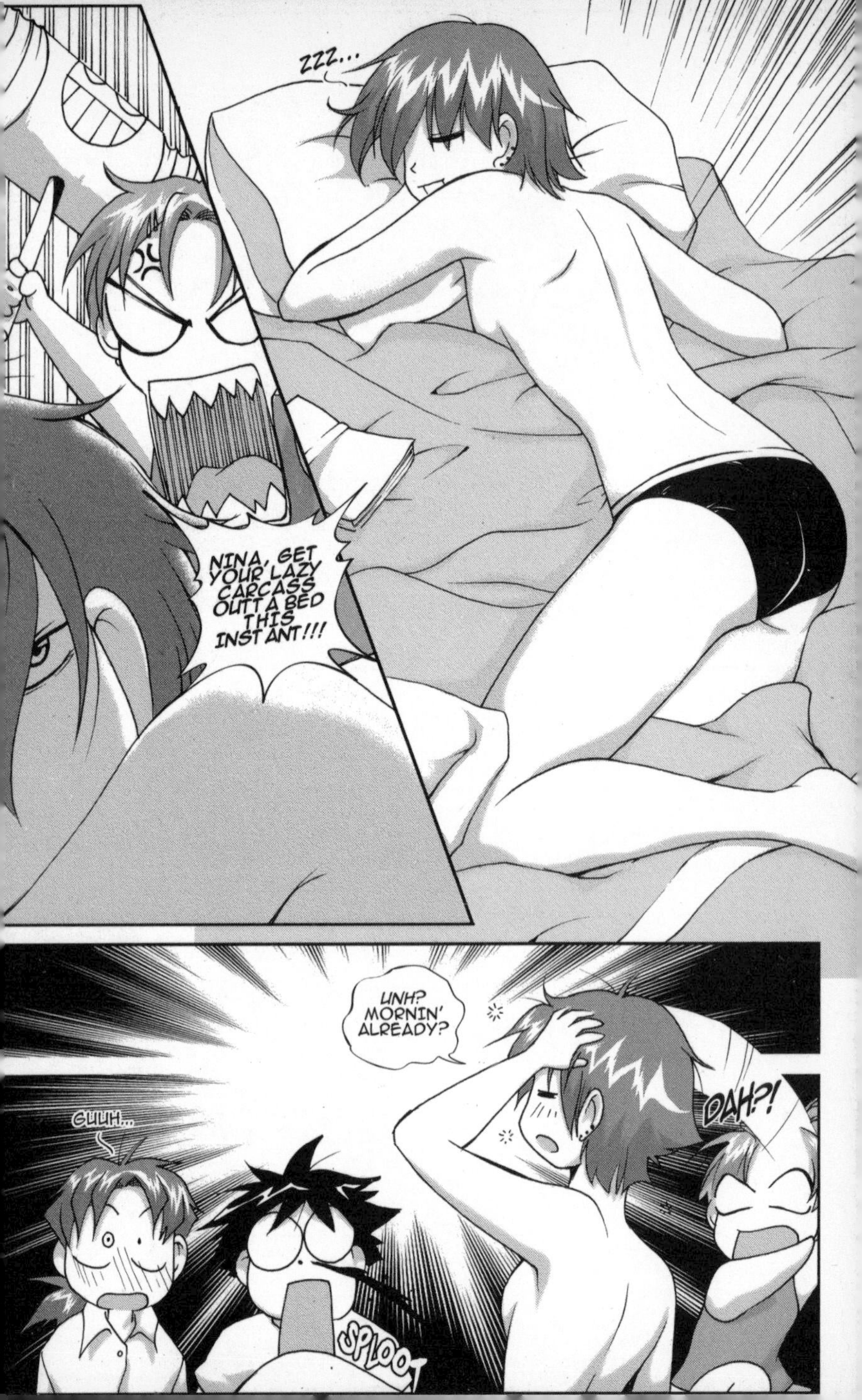
ZZZ...
NINA, GET YOUR LAZY CARCASS OUTTA BED THIS INSTANT!!!
UNH? MORNIN' ALREADY?
DAH?!
GULH...
SPLOOT

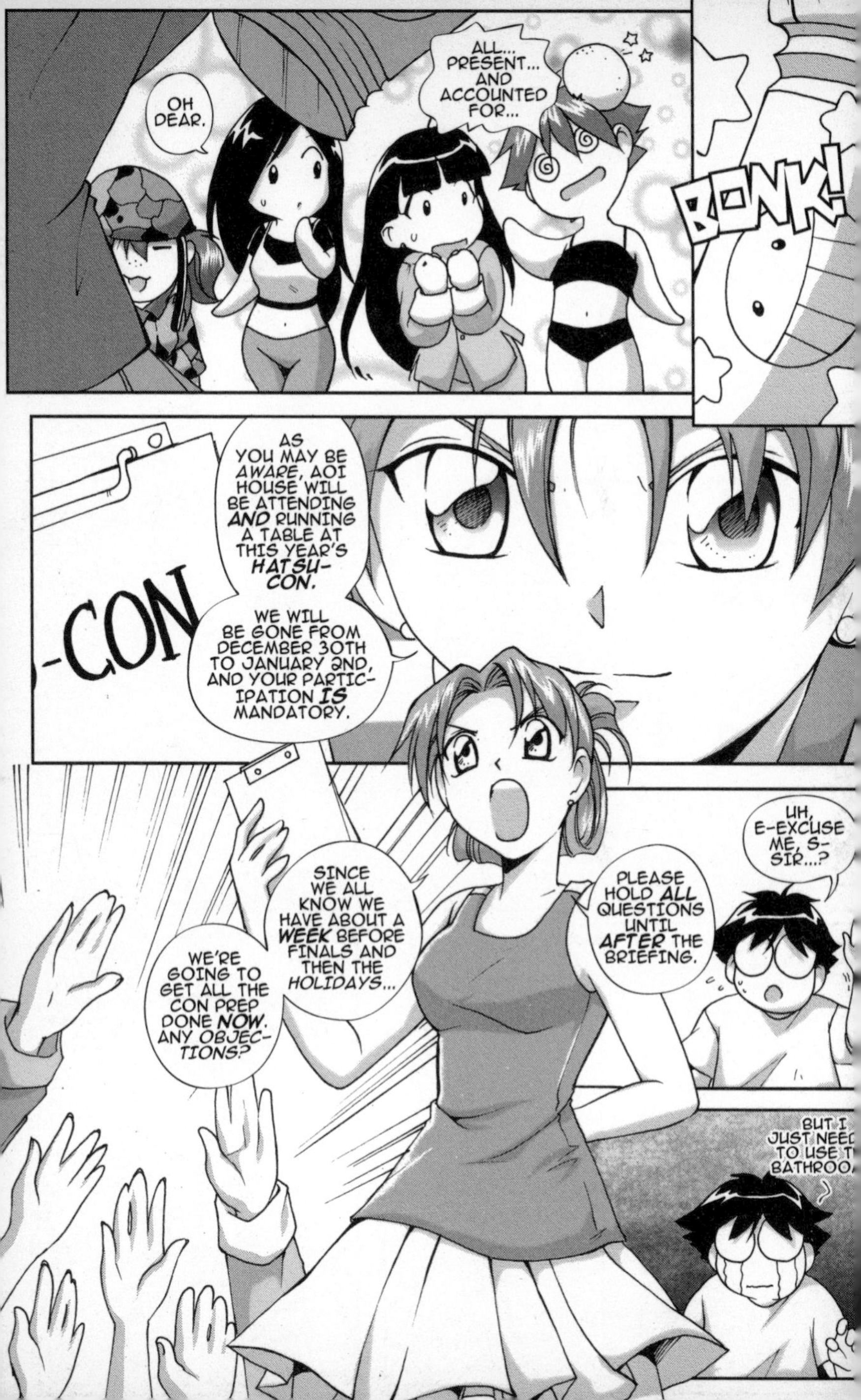
BONK!
ALL... PRESENT... AND ACCOUNTED FOR...
OH DEAR.
AS YOU MAY BE AWARE, AOI HOUSE WILL BE ATTENDING **AND** RUNNING A TABLE AT THIS YEAR'S ***HATSU-CON.***
WE WILL BE GONE FROM DECEMBER 30TH TO JANUARY 2ND, AND YOUR PARTICIPATION **IS** MANDATORY.
-CON
UH, E-EXCUSE ME, S-SIR...?
BUT I JUST NEED TO USE T BATHROO
PLEASE HOLD **ALL** QUESTIONS UNTIL ***AFTER*** THE BRIEFING.
SINCE WE ALL KNOW WE HAVE ABOUT A ***WEEK*** BEFORE FINALS AND THEN THE *HOLIDAYS...*
WE'RE GOING TO GET ALL THE CON PREP DONE **NOW**. ANY *OBJECTIONS?*

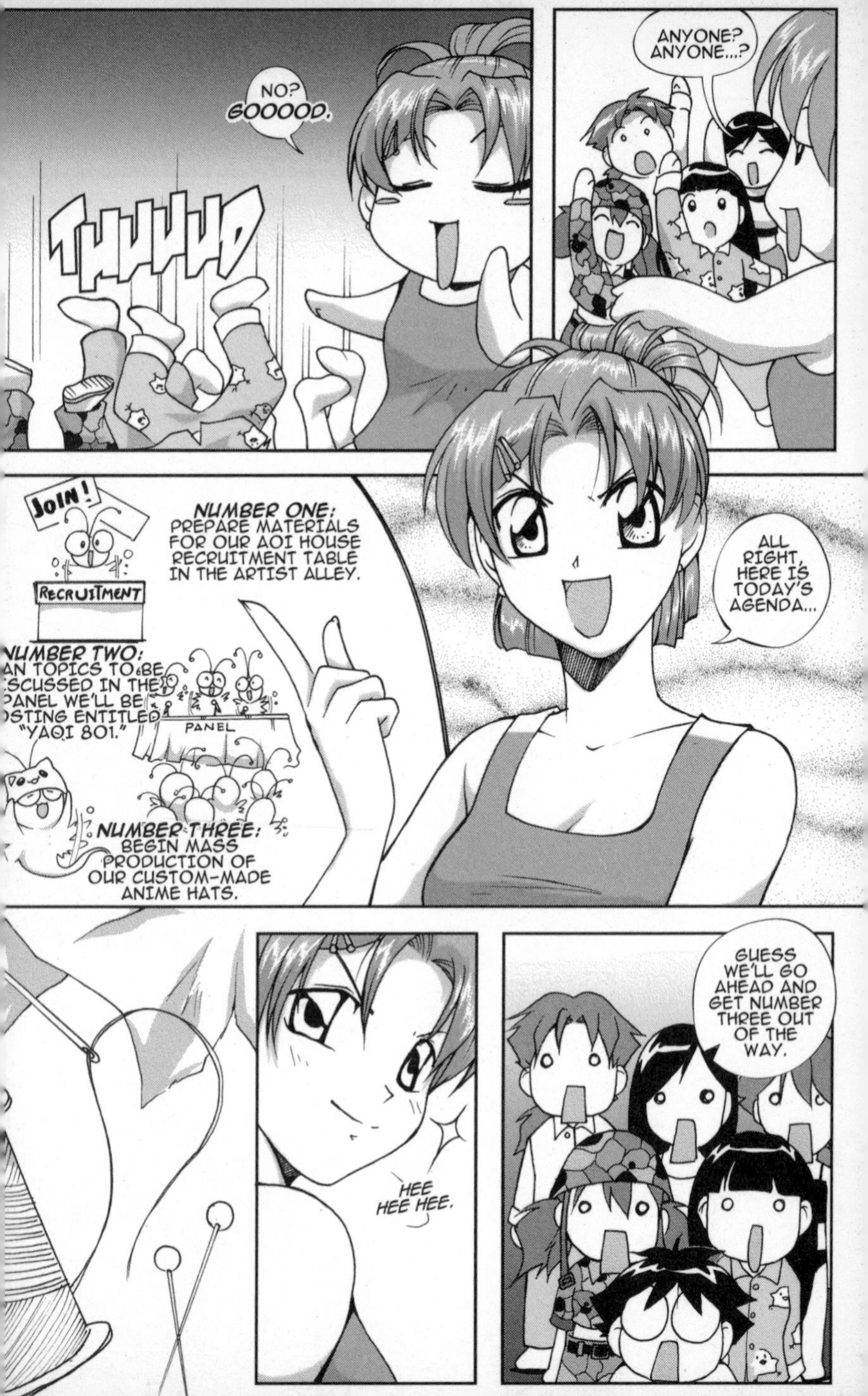
ANYONE? ANYONE...?
NO? GOOOOD.
THUUUD
ALL RIGHT, HERE IS TODAY'S AGENDA...
NUMBER ONE: PREPARE MATERIALS FOR OUR AOI HOUSE RECRUITMENT TABLE IN THE ARTIST ALLEY.
JOIN!
RECRUITMENT
NUMBER TWO: AN TOPICS TO BE SCUSSED IN THE PANEL WE'LL BE OSTING ENTITLED "YAOI 801."
PANEL
NUMBER THREE: BEGIN MASS PRODUCTION OF OUR CUSTOM-MADE ANIME HATS.
GUESS WE'LL GO AHEAD AND GET NUMBER THREE OUT OF THE WAY.
HEE HEE HEE.

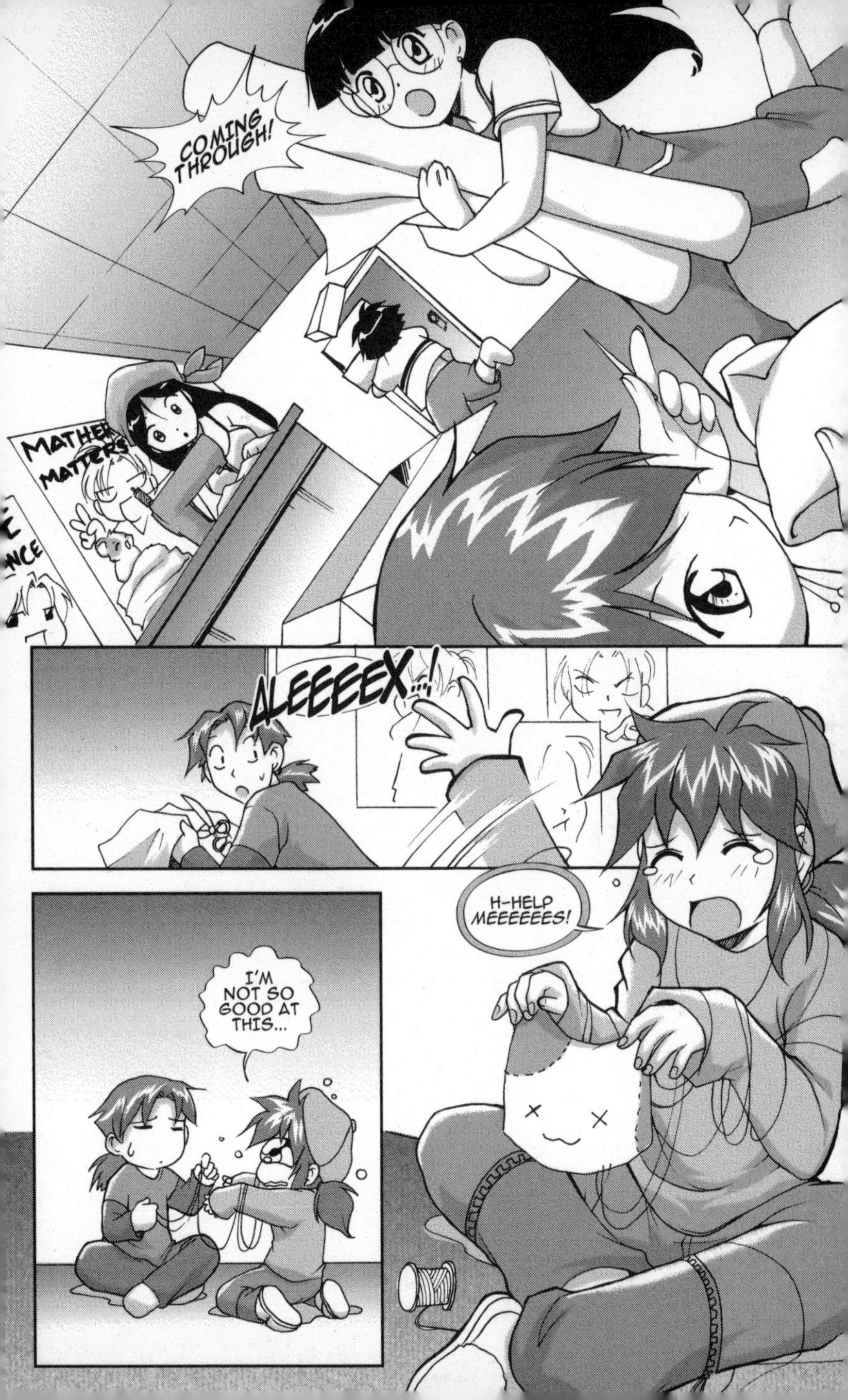
COMING THROUGH!
MATHER MATTERS
ALEEEEEX...!
H-HELP MEEEEEES!
I'M NOT SO GOOD AT THIS...

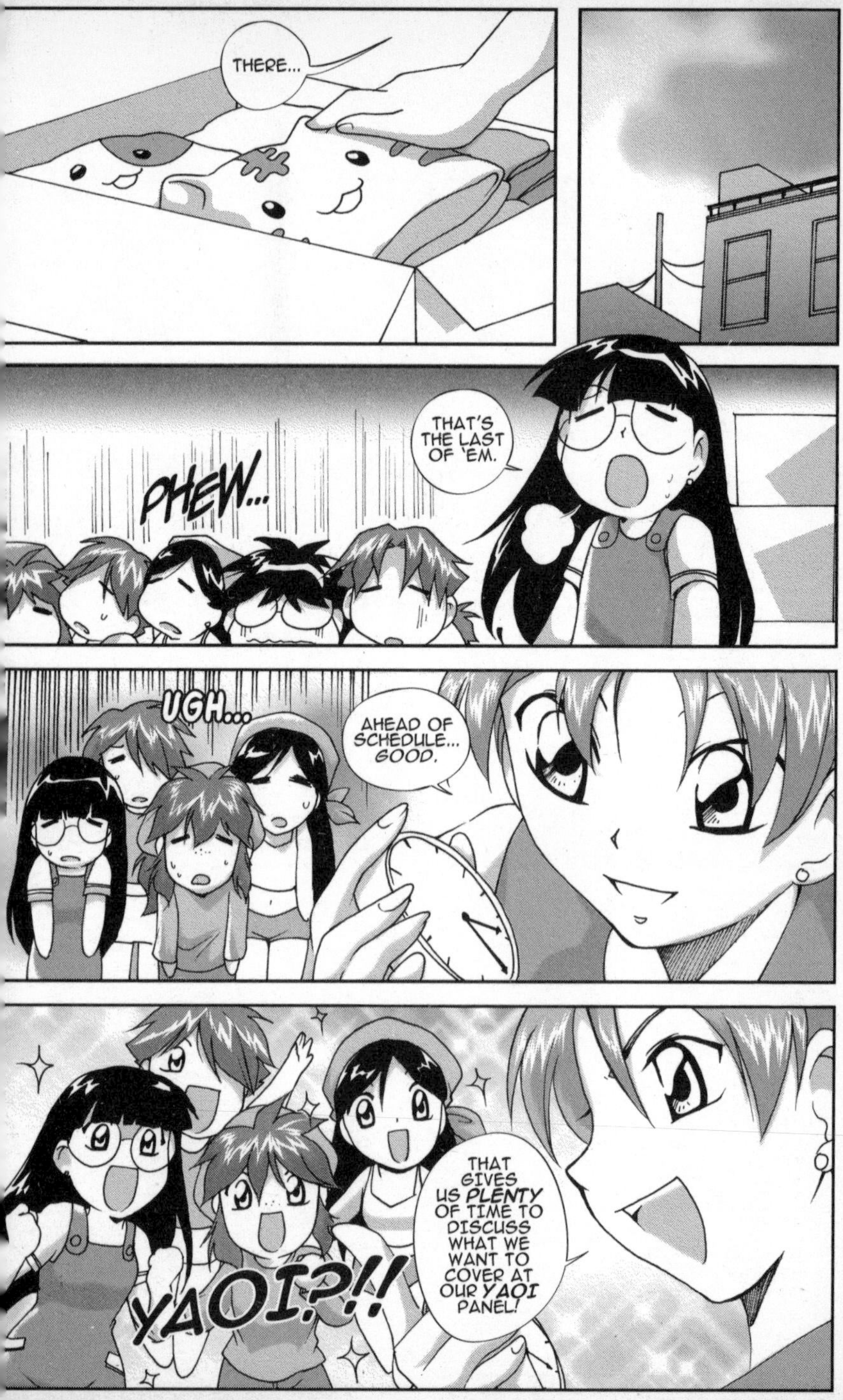
THERE...
THAT'S THE LAST OF 'EM.
PHEW...
AHEAD OF SCHEDULE... GOOD.
UGH...
THAT GIVES US PLENTY OF TIME TO DISCUSS WHAT WE WANT TO COVER AT OUR YAOI PANEL!
YAOI?!!

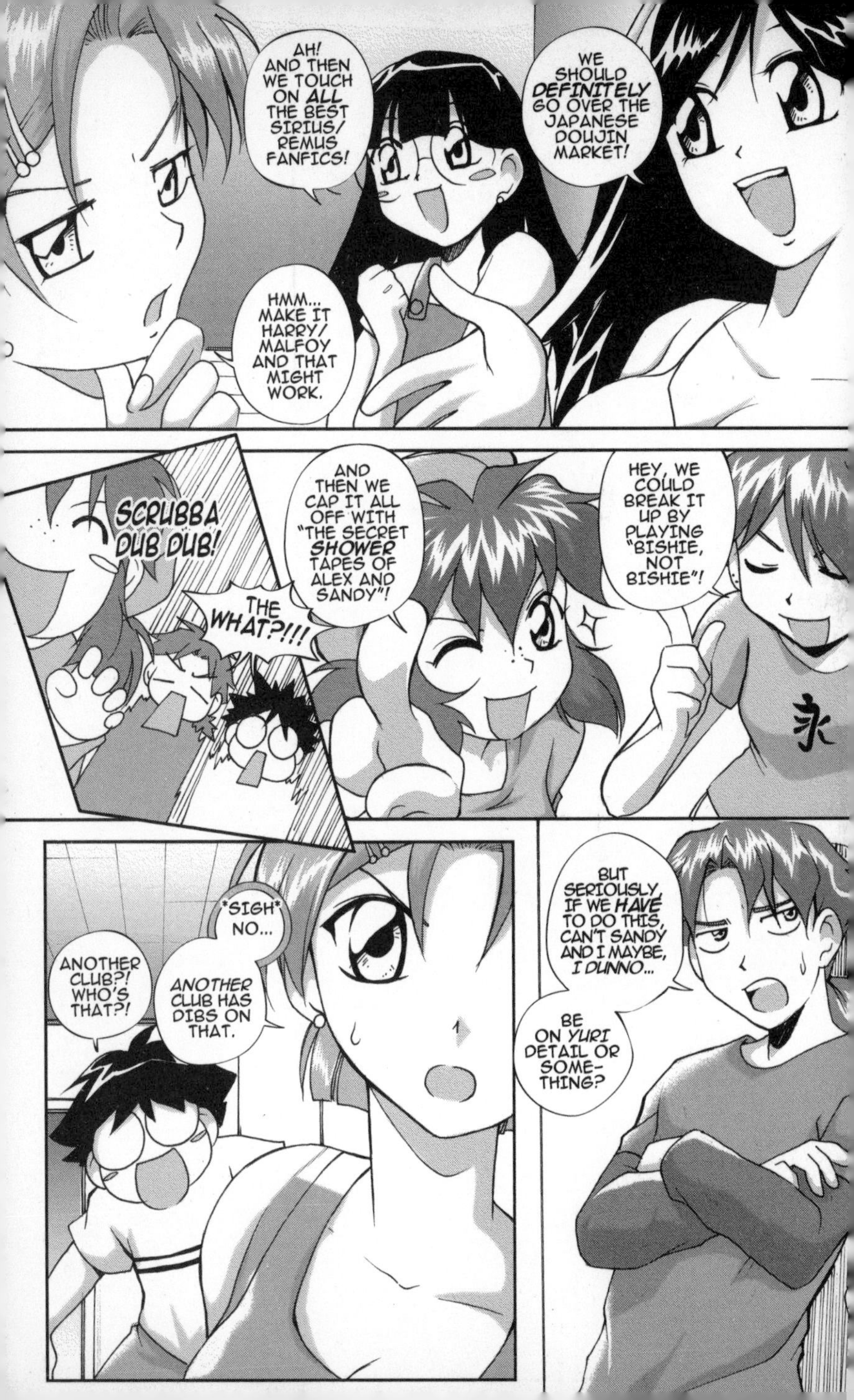
WE SHOULD DEFINITELY GO OVER THE JAPANESE DOUJIN MARKET!
AH! AND THEN WE TOUCH ON ALL THE BEST SIRIUS/REMUS FANFICS!
HMM... MAKE IT HARRY/MALFOY AND THAT MIGHT WORK.
HEY, WE COULD BREAK IT UP BY PLAYING "BISHIE, NOT BISHIE"!
AND THEN WE CAP IT ALL OFF WITH "THE SECRET SHOWER TAPES OF ALEX AND SANDY"!
THE WHAT?!!!
SCRUBBA DUB DUB!
BUT SERIOUSLY, IF WE HAVE TO DO THIS, CAN'T SANDY AND I MAYBE, I DUNNO...
BE ON YURI DETAIL OR SOME-THING?
SIGH NO...
ANOTHER CLUB HAS DIBS ON THAT.
ANOTHER CLUB?! WHO'S THAT?!

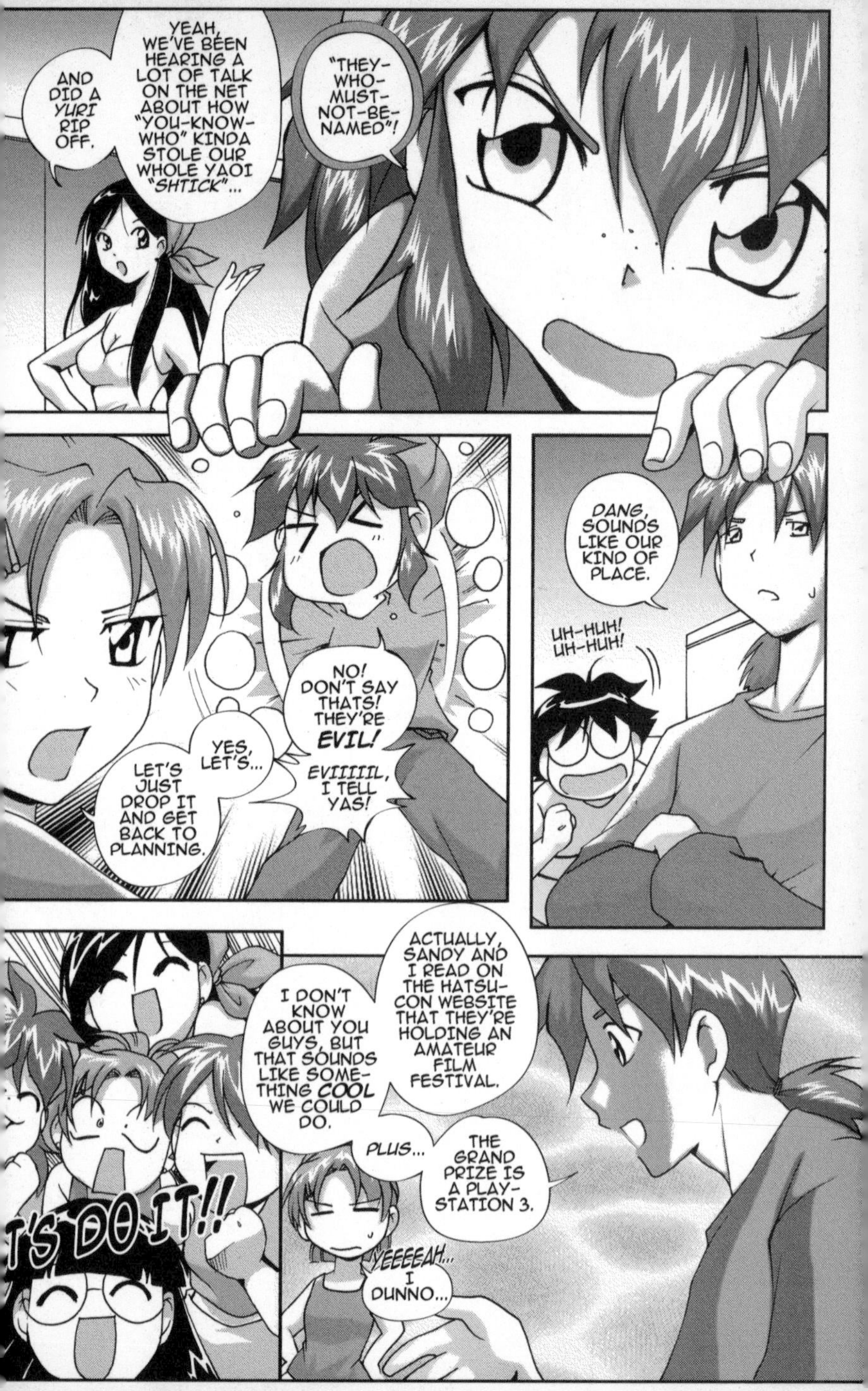
"THEY-WHO-MUST-NOT-BE-NAMED"!
YEAH, WE'VE BEEN HEARING A LOT OF TALK ON THE NET ABOUT HOW "YOU-KNOW-WHO" KINDA STOLE OUR WHOLE YAOI "SHTICK"...
AND DID A YURI RIP OFF.
DANG, SOUNDS LIKE OUR KIND OF PLACE.
UH-HUH! UH-HUH!
NO! DON'T SAY THATS! THEY'RE EVIL!
EVIIIIIL, I TELL YAS!
YES, LET'S...
LET'S JUST DROP IT AND GET BACK TO PLANNING.
ACTUALLY, SANDY AND I READ ON THE HATSU-CON WEBSITE THAT THEY'RE HOLDING AN AMATEUR FILM FESTIVAL.
I DON'T KNOW ABOUT YOU GUYS, BUT THAT SOUNDS LIKE SOME-THING COOL WE COULD DO.
PLUS...
THE GRAND PRIZE IS A PLAY-STATION 3.
YEEEEAH... I DUNNO...
T'S DO IT!!

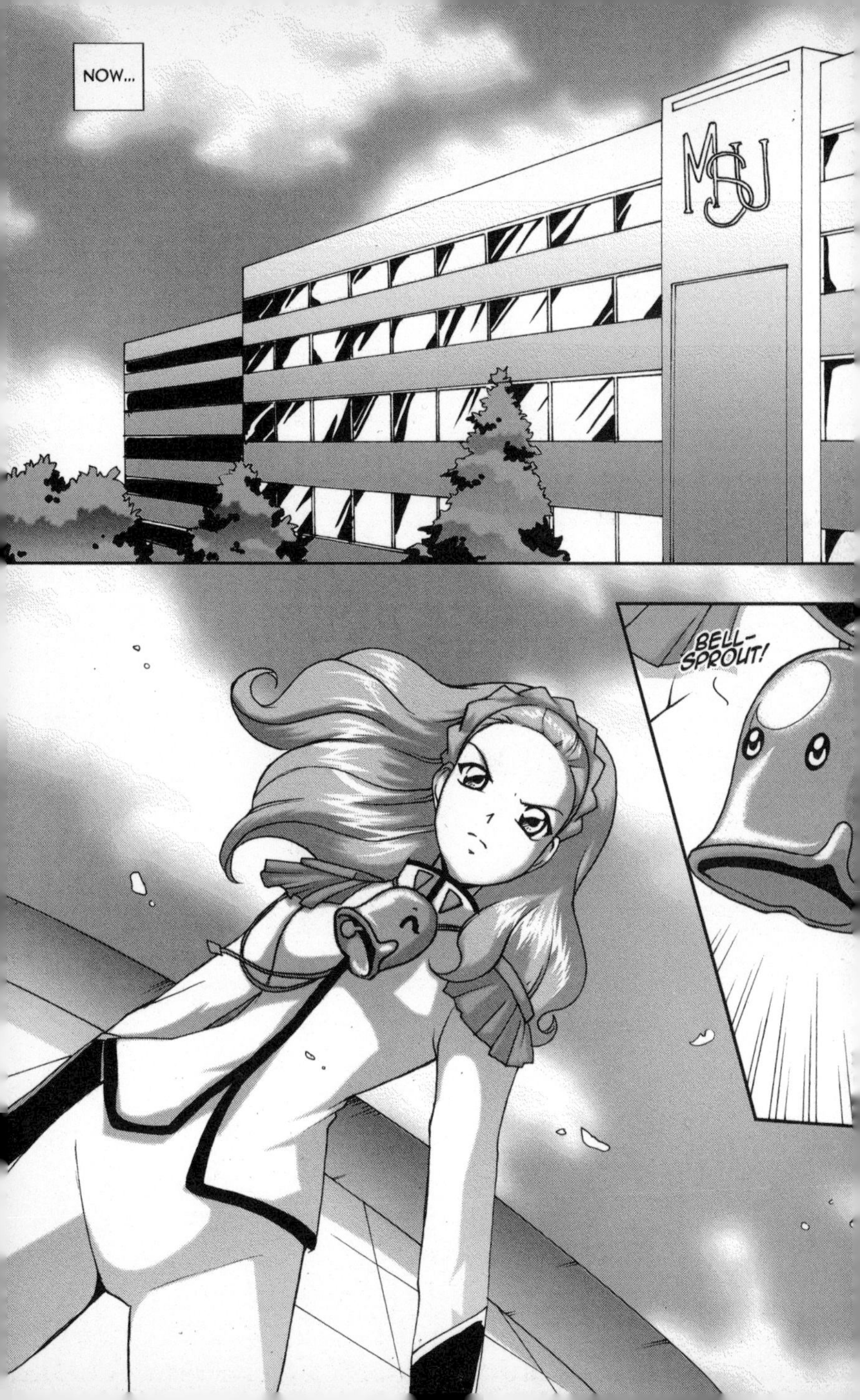
NOW...
MSU
BELL-SPROUT!

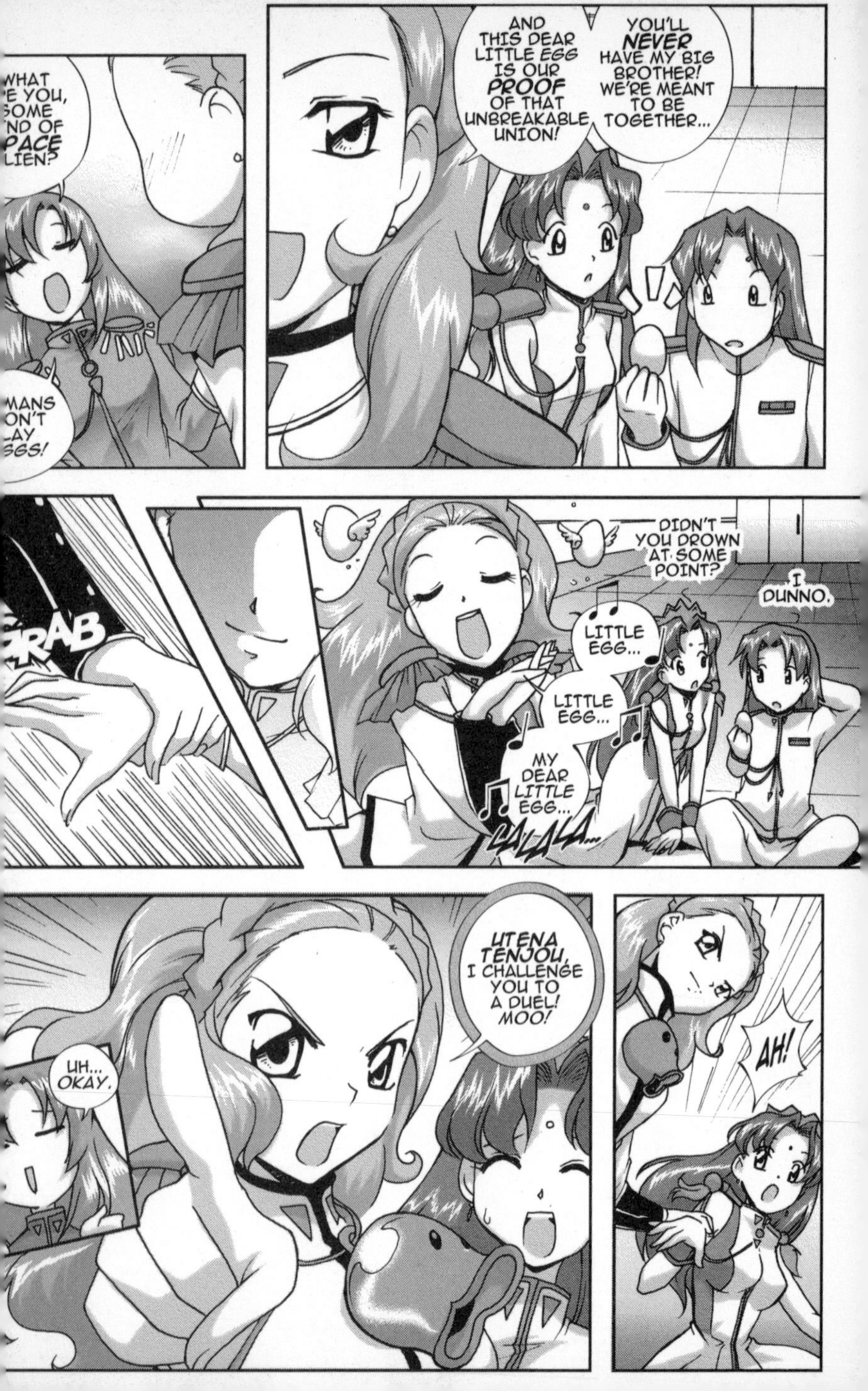
YOU'LL NEVER HAVE MY BIG BROTHER! WE'RE MEANT TO BE TOGETHER...
AND THIS DEAR LITTLE EGG IS OUR PROOF OF THAT UNBREAKABLE UNION!
WHAT 'E YOU, SOME ND OF PACE LIEN?
MANS ON'T LAY GGS!
DIDN'T YOU DROWN AT SOME POINT?
I DUNNO.
LITTLE EGG...
LITTLE EGG...
MY DEAR LITTLE EGG...
LA LA LA...
RAB
AH!
UTENA TENJOU, I CHALLENGE YOU TO A DUEL! MOO!
UH... OKAY.

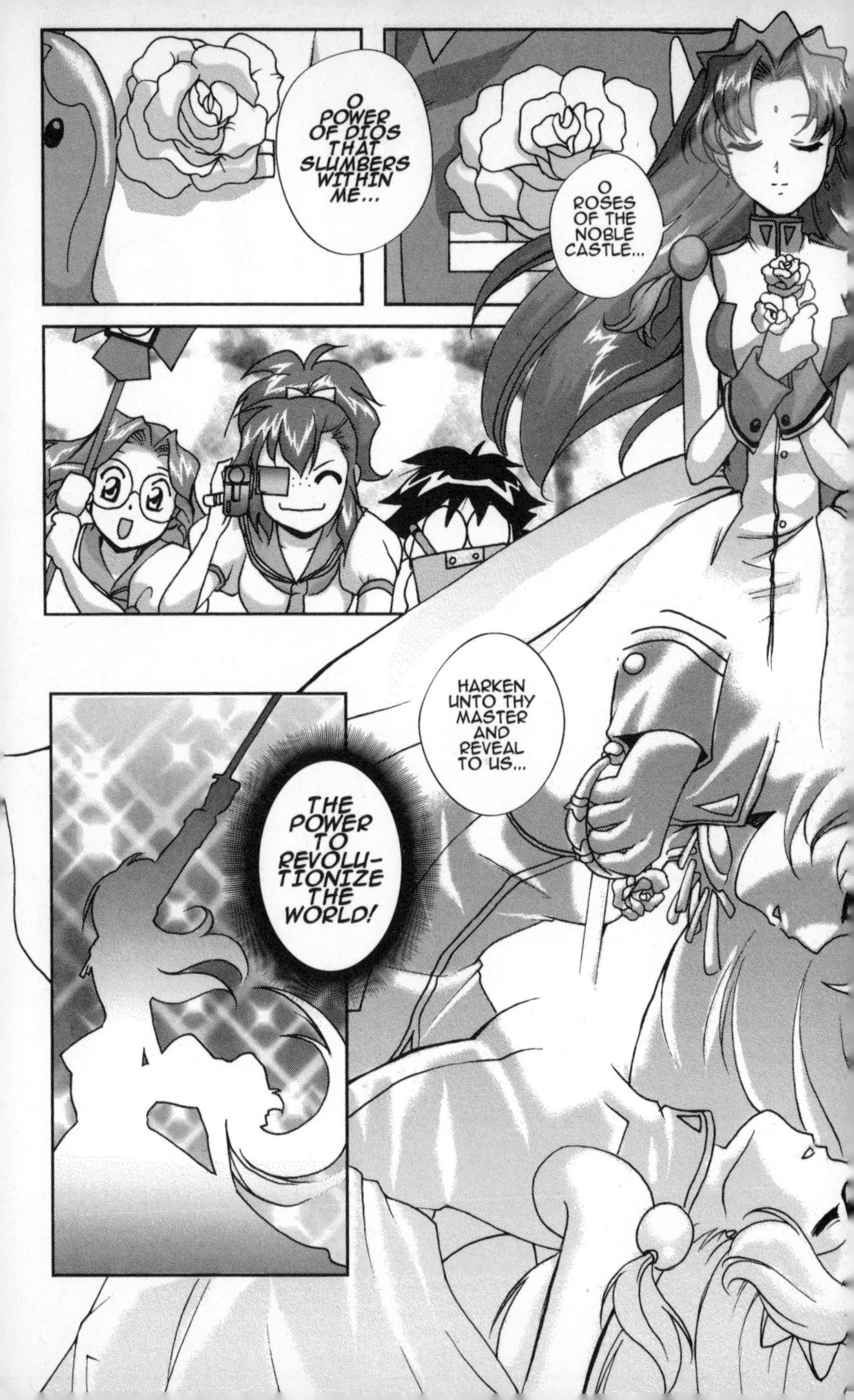
O ROSES OF THE NOBLE CASTLE...
O POWER OF DIOS THAT SLUMBERS WITHIN ME...
HARKEN UNTO THY MASTER AND REVEAL TO US...
THE POWER TO REVOLUTIONIZE THE WORLD!

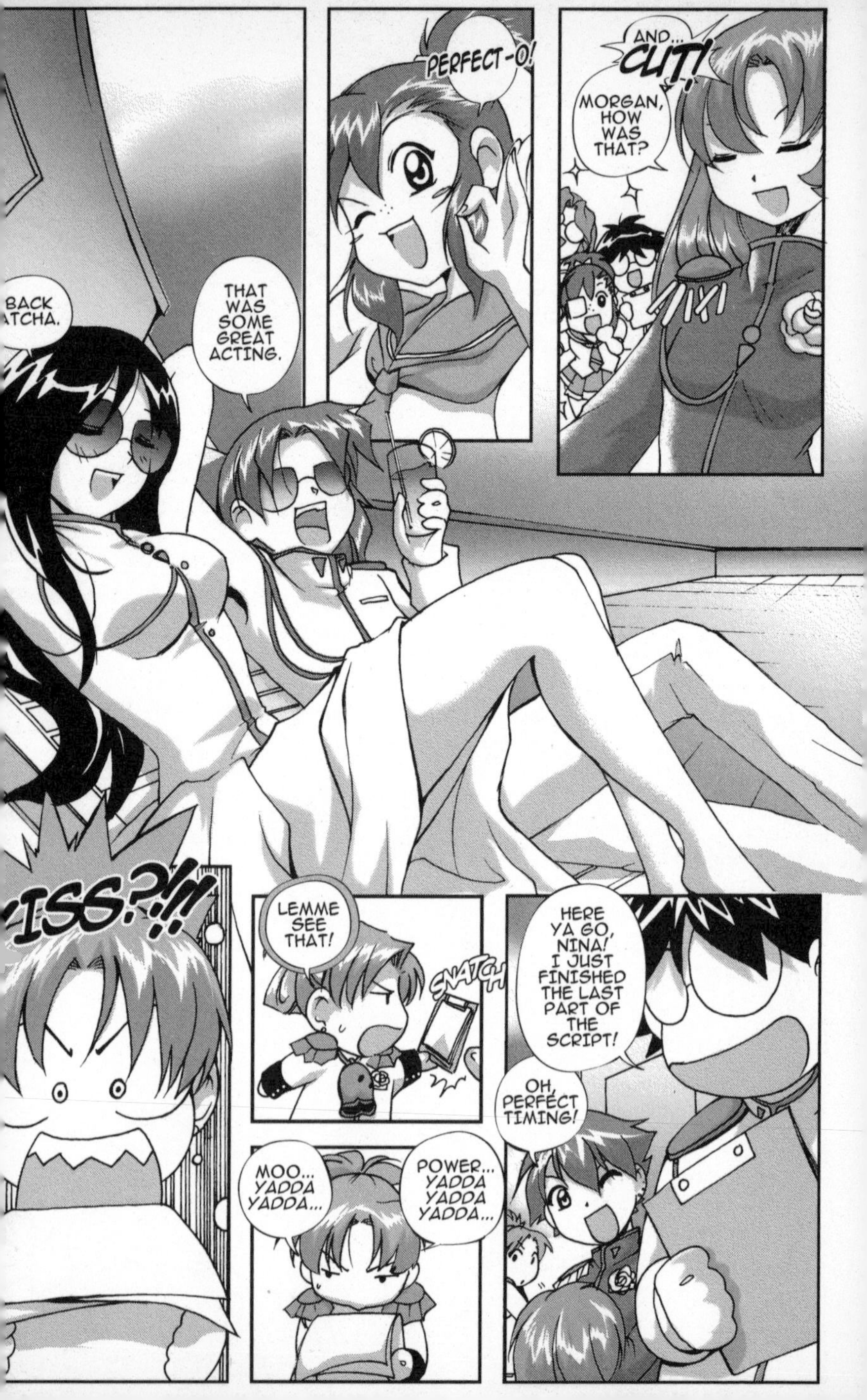
AND... CUT!
MORGAN, HOW WAS THAT?
PERFECT-O!
THAT WAS SOME GREAT ACTING.
BACK ATCHA.
HERE YA GO, NINA! I JUST FINISHED THE LAST PART OF THE SCRIPT!
OH, PERFECT TIMING!
LEMME SEE THAT!
SNATCH
POWER... YADDA YADDA YADDA...
MOO... YADDA YADDA...
ISS?!!!

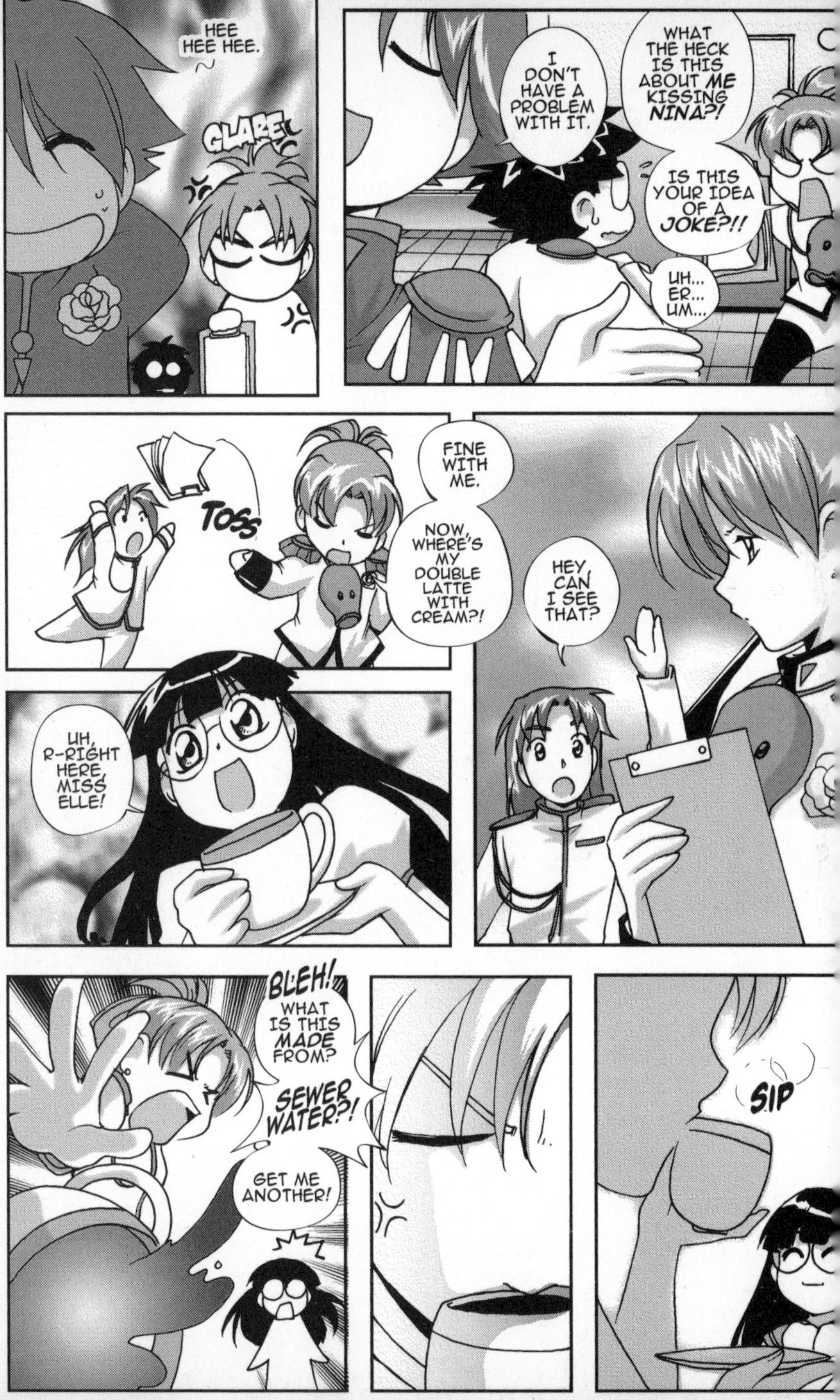
WHAT THE HECK IS THIS ABOUT ME KISSING NINA?!
I DON'T HAVE A PROBLEM WITH IT.
IS THIS YOUR IDEA OF A JOKE?!!
UH... ER... UM...
HEE HEE HEE.
GLARE
HEY, CAN I SEE THAT?
FINE WITH ME.
NOW, WHERE'S MY DOUBLE LATTE WITH CREAM?!
TOSS
UH, R-RIGHT HERE, MISS ELLE!
SIP
BLEH!
WHAT IS THIS MADE FROM?
SEWER WATER?!
GET ME ANOTHER!

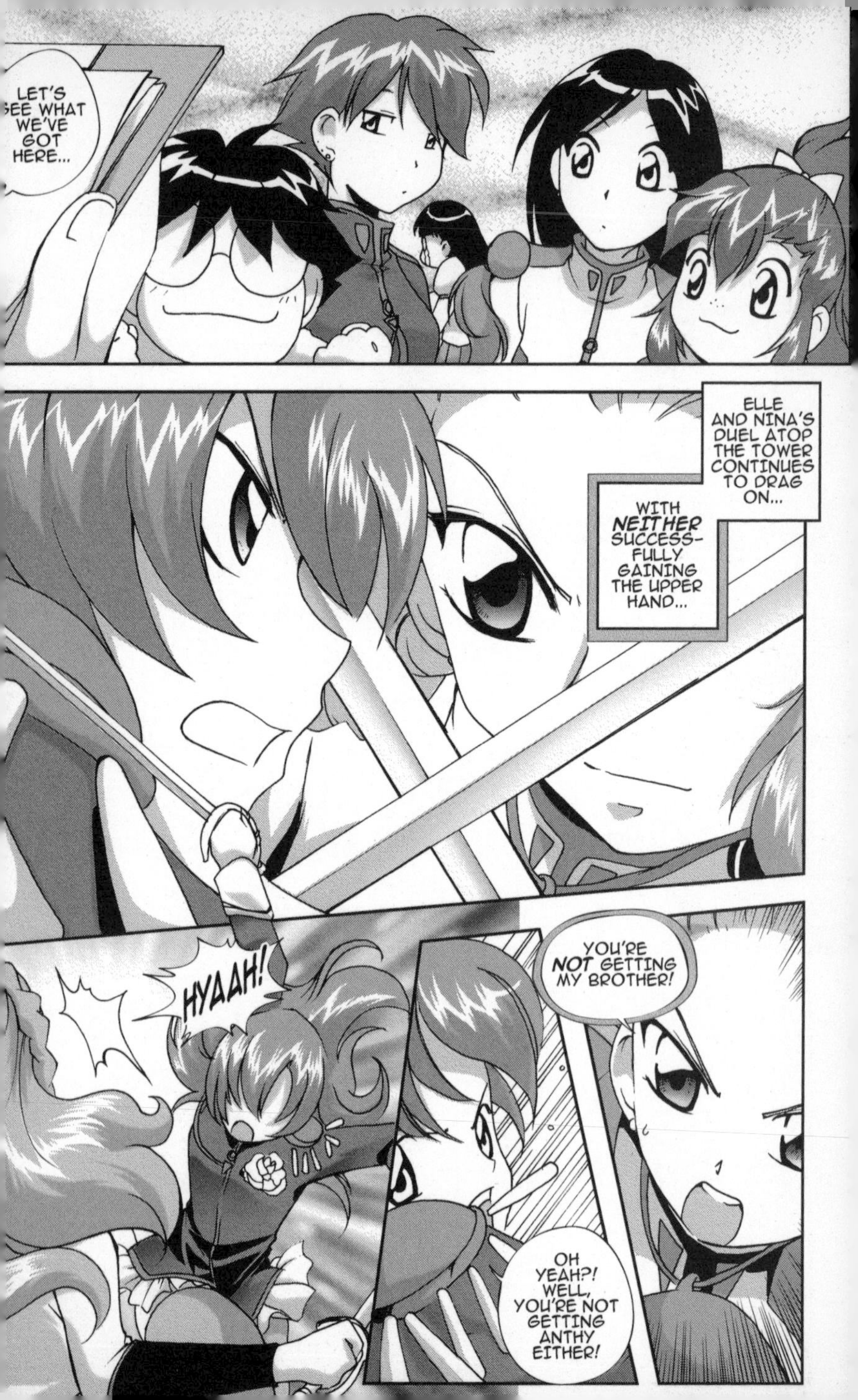
LET'S SEE WHAT WE'VE GOT HERE...
ELLE AND NINA'S DUEL ATOP THE TOWER CONTINUES TO DRAG ON...
WITH NEITHER SUCCESSFULLY GAINING THE UPPER HAND...
YOU'RE NOT GETTING MY BROTHER!
OH YEAH?! WELL, YOU'RE NOT GETTING ANTHY EITHER!
HYAAH!

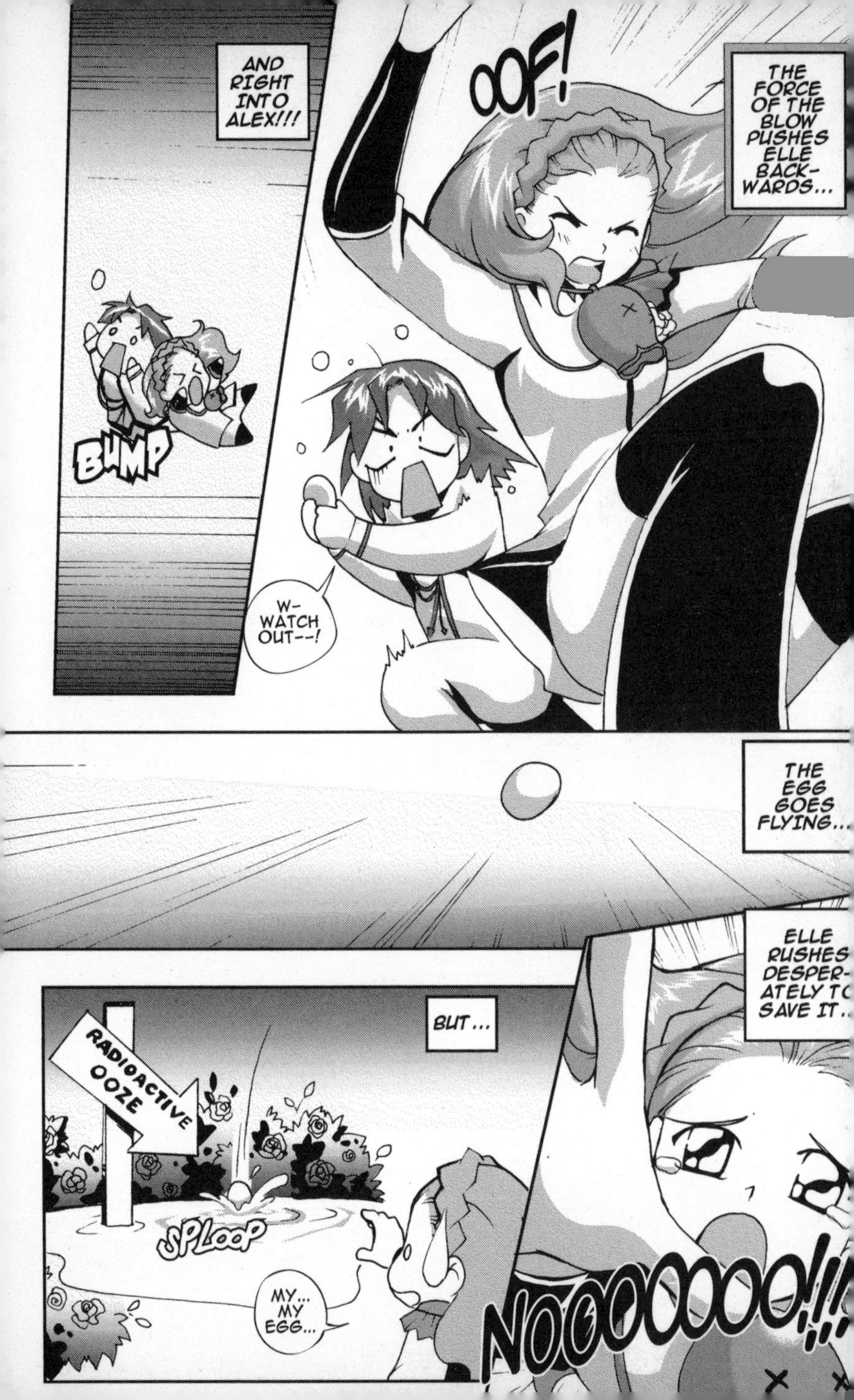
OOF!
THE FORCE OF THE BLOW PUSHES ELLE BACK-WARDS...
W-WATCH OUT--!
AND RIGHT INTO ALEX!!!
BUMP
THE EGG GOES FLYING...
ELLE RUSHES DESPER-ATELY TO SAVE IT...
NOOOOOOO!!!
BUT...
RADIOACTIVE OOZE
SPLOOP
MY... MY EGG...

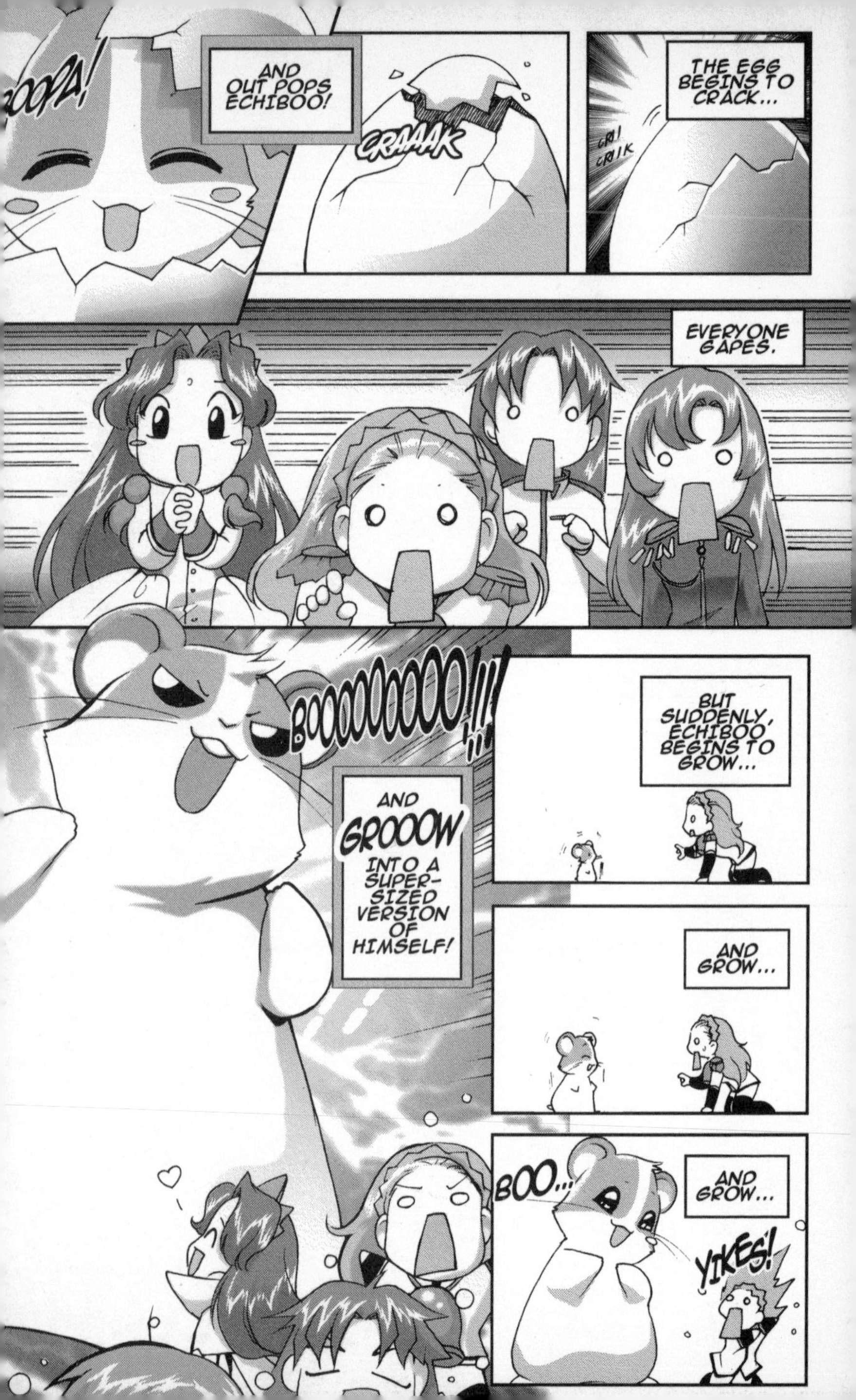
THE EGG BEGINS TO CRACK...
CRI CRIK
AND OUT POPS ECHIBOO!
CRAAAK
OOPA!
EVERYONE GAPES.
BUT SUDDENLY, ECHIBOO BEGINS TO GROW...
AND GROW...
AND GROW...
BOO...
YIKES!
BOOOOOOOOOO!!!
AND GROOOW INTO A SUPER-SIZED VERSION OF HIMSELF!

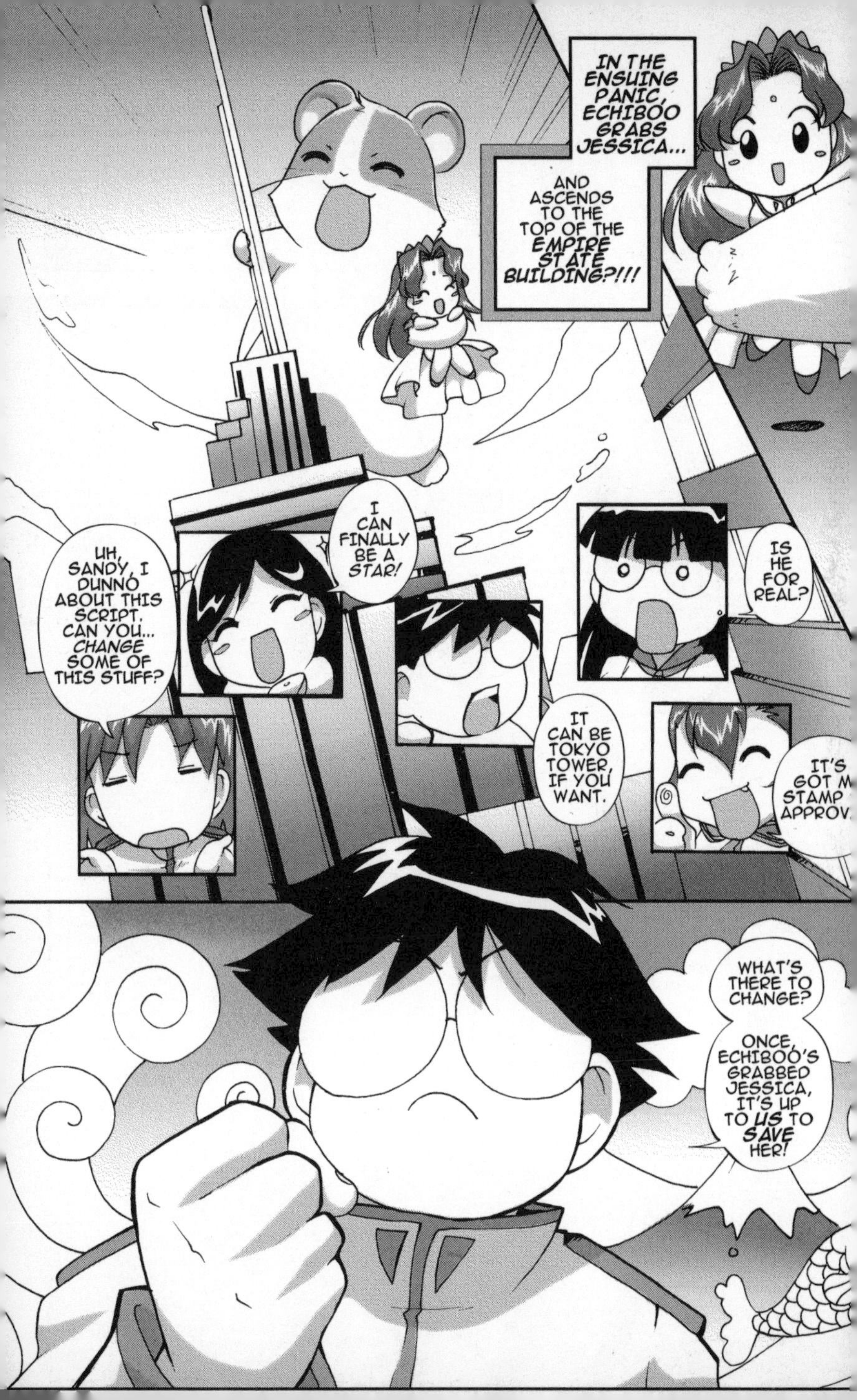
IN THE ENSUING PANIC, ECHIBOO GRABS JESSICA...
AND ASCENDS TO THE TOP OF THE EMPIRE STATE BUILDING?!!!
IS HE FOR REAL?
I CAN FINALLY BE A STAR!
IT'S GOT M STAMP APPROV
IT CAN BE TOKYO TOWER, IF YOU WANT.
UH, SANDY, I DUNNO ABOUT THIS SCRIPT. CAN YOU... CHANGE SOME OF THIS STUFF?
WHAT'S THERE TO CHANGE?
ONCE, ECHIBOO'S GRABBED JESSICA, IT'S UP TO US TO SAVE HER!

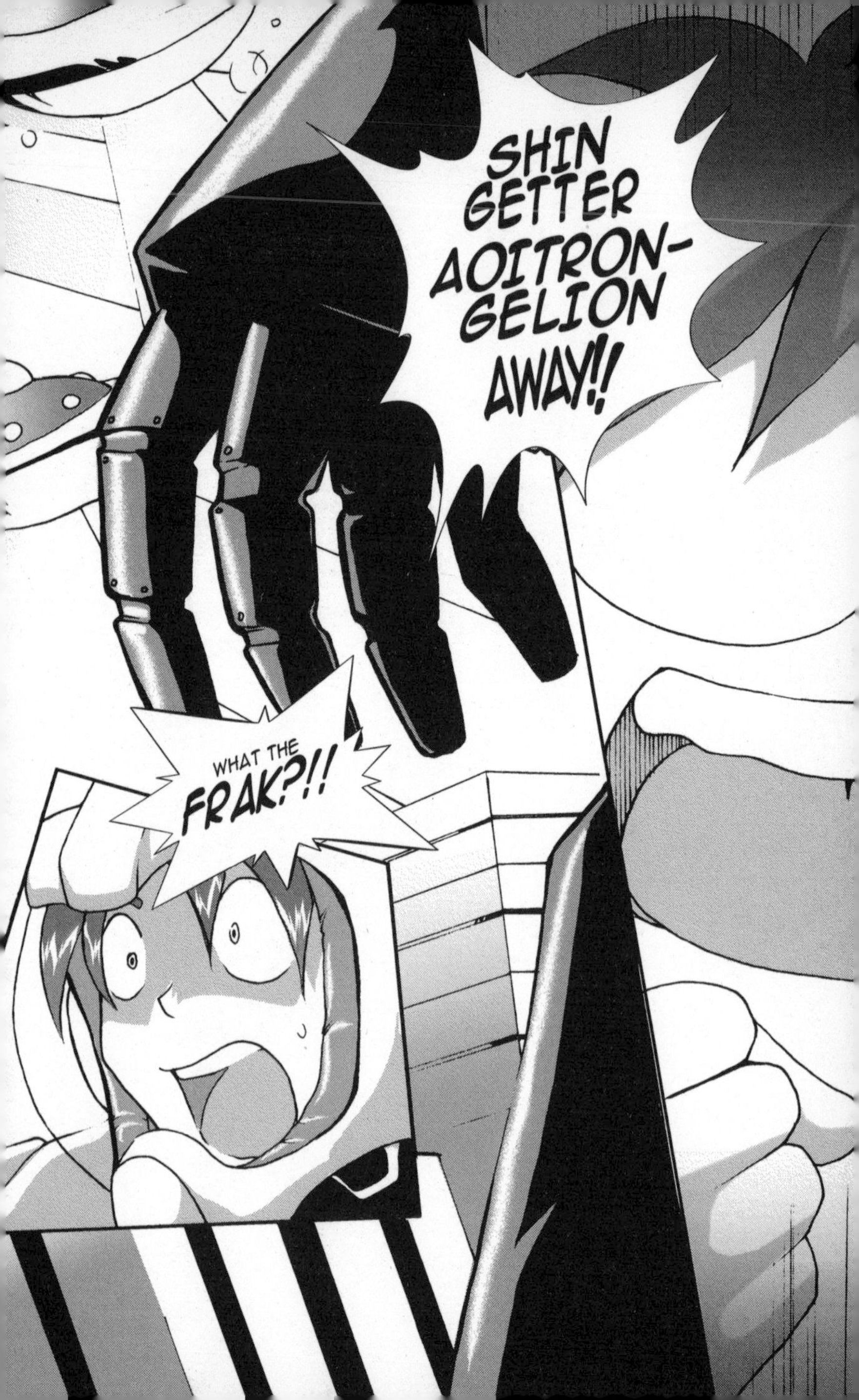
SHIN GETTER AOITRON-GELION AWAY!!
WHAT THE FRAK?!!

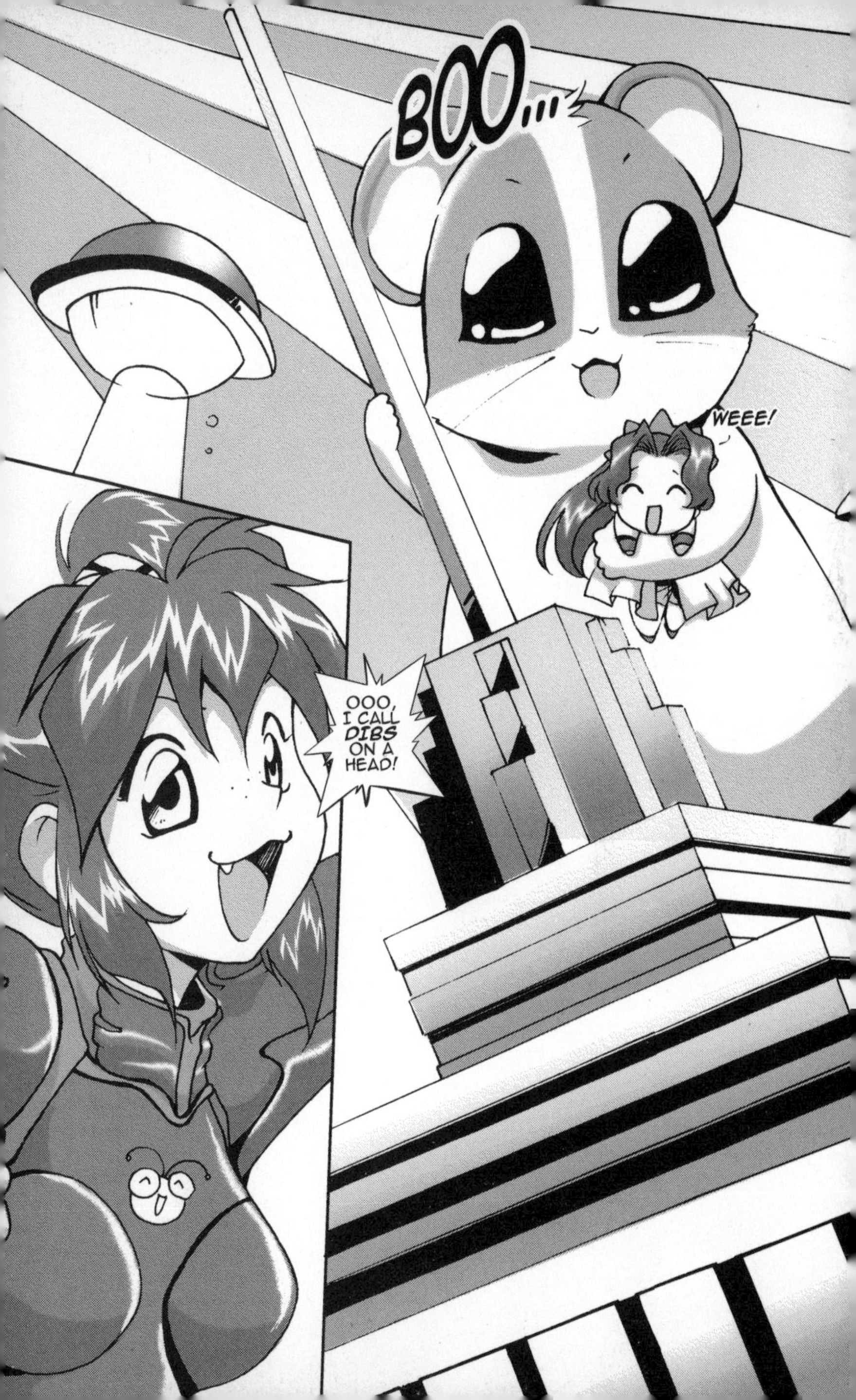
BOO...
WEEE!
OOO, I CALL DIBS ON A HEAD!

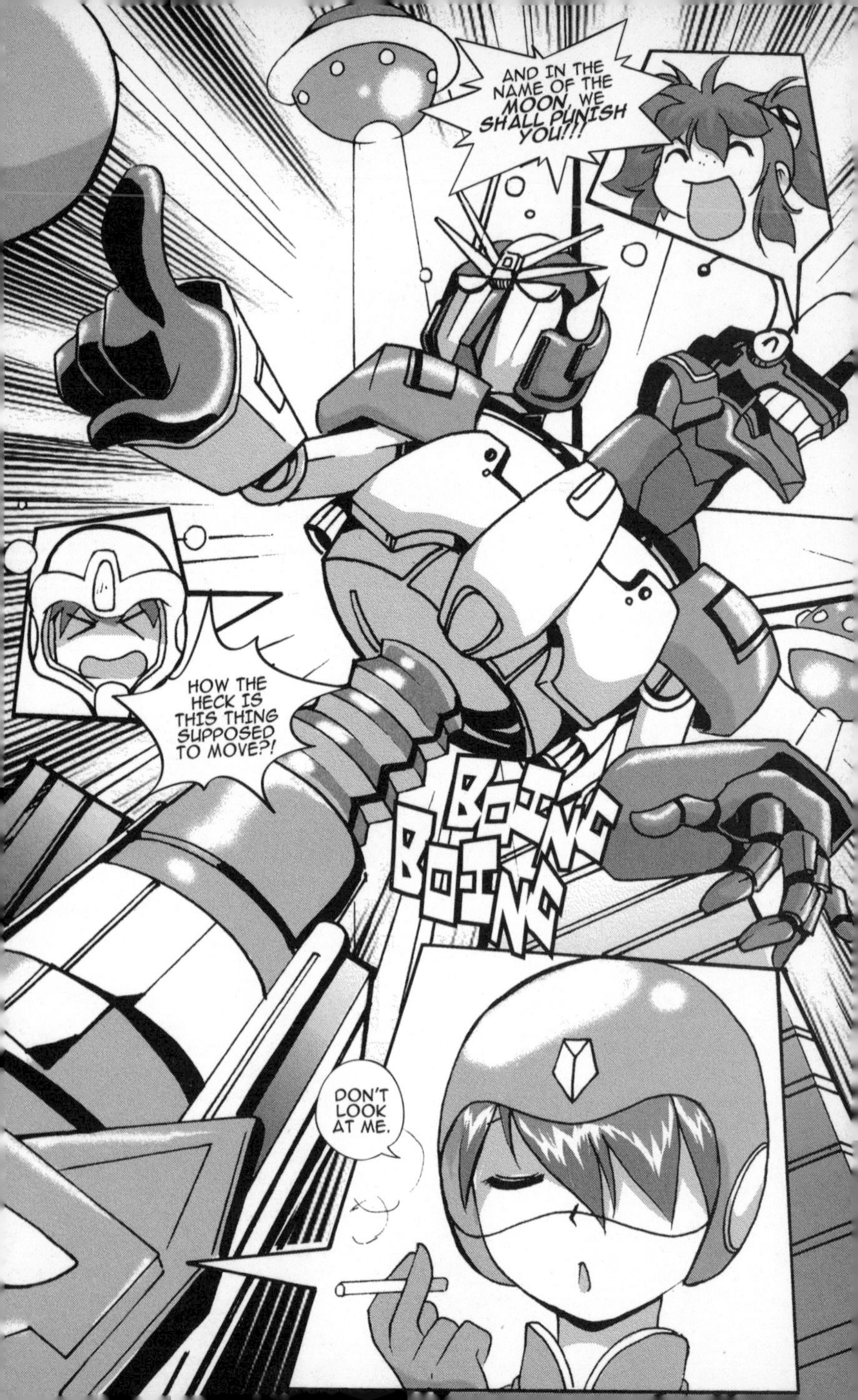
AND IN THE NAME OF THE MOON, WE SHALL PUNISH YOU!!!
HOW THE HECK IS THIS THING SUPPOSED TO MOVE?!
BOING
BOING
DON'T LOOK AT ME.

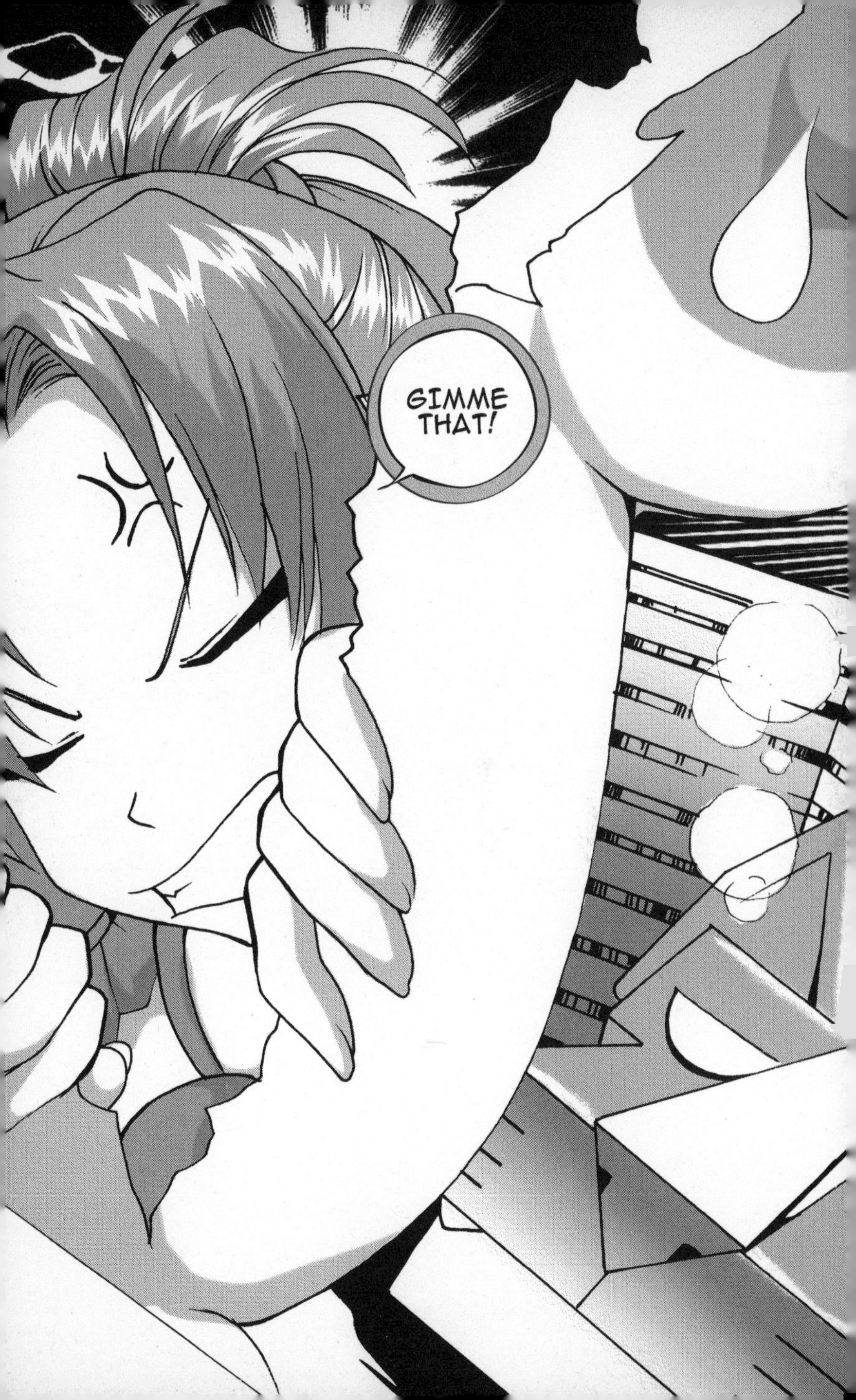
GIMME THAT!

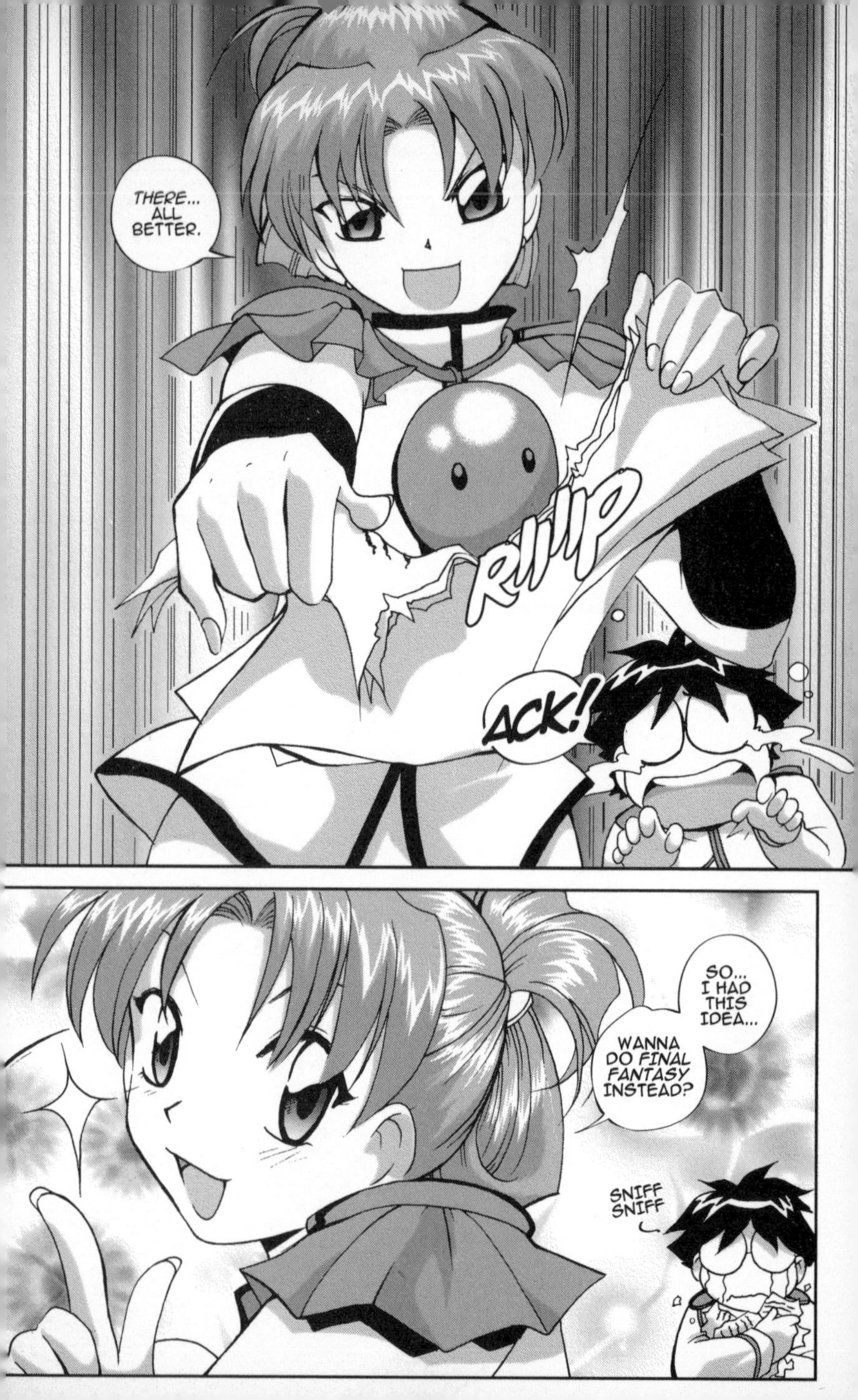
THERE... ALL BETTER.
RIIIP
ACK!
SO... I HAD THIS IDEA...
WANNA DO FINAL FANTASY INSTEAD?
SNIFF SNIFF

SIDE STORY—AOI HOUSE PRESENTS:

FRUIT CAKE FANTASY

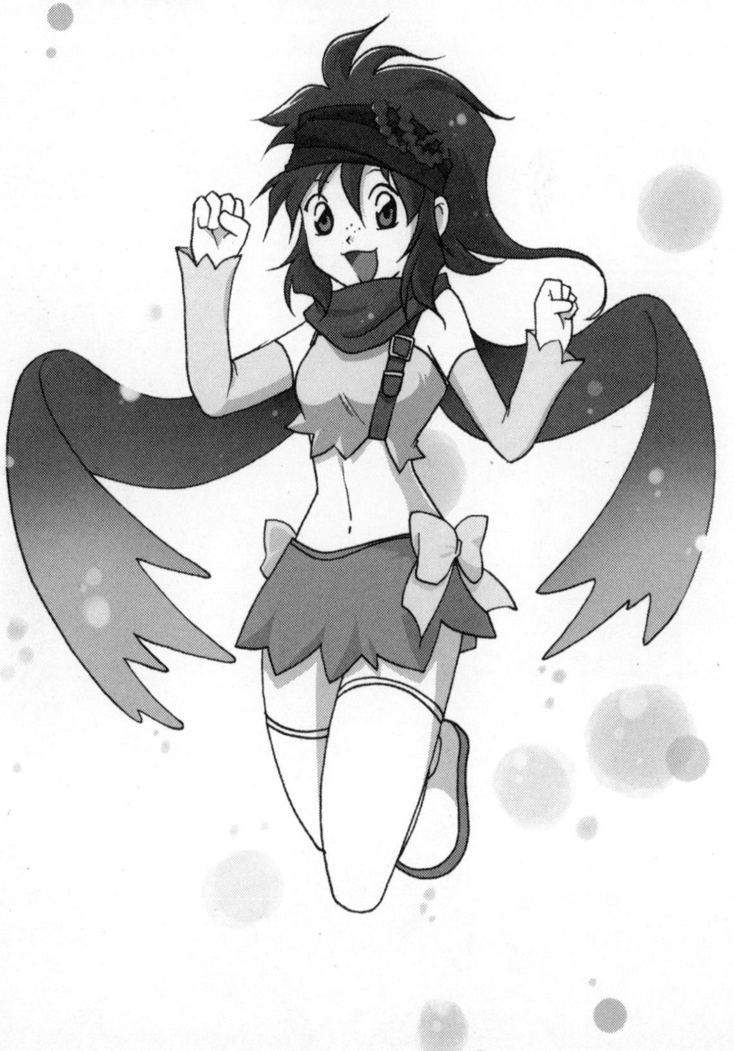

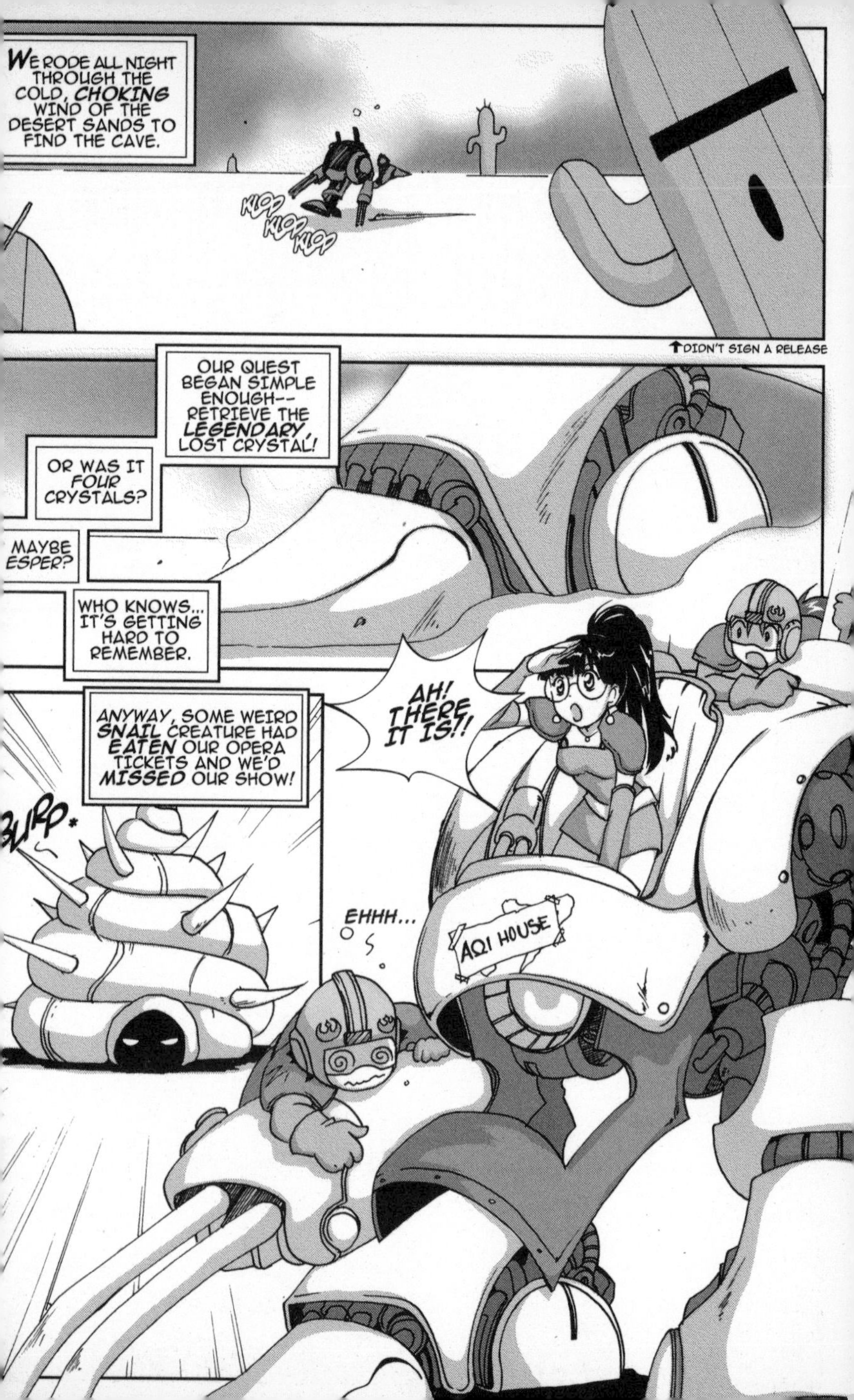
WE RODE ALL NIGHT THROUGH THE COLD, CHOKING WIND OF THE DESERT SANDS TO FIND THE CAVE.
KLOP KLOP KLOP
↑DIDN'T SIGN A RELEASE
OUR QUEST BEGAN SIMPLE ENOUGH-- RETRIEVE THE LEGENDARY, LOST CRYSTAL!
OR WAS IT FOUR CRYSTALS?
MAYBE ESPER?
WHO KNOWS... IT'S GETTING HARD TO REMEMBER.
AH! THERE IT IS!!
ANYWAY, SOME WEIRD SNAIL CREATURE HAD EATEN OUR OPERA TICKETS AND WE'D MISSED OUR SHOW!
BURP*
EHHH...
AQI HOUSE

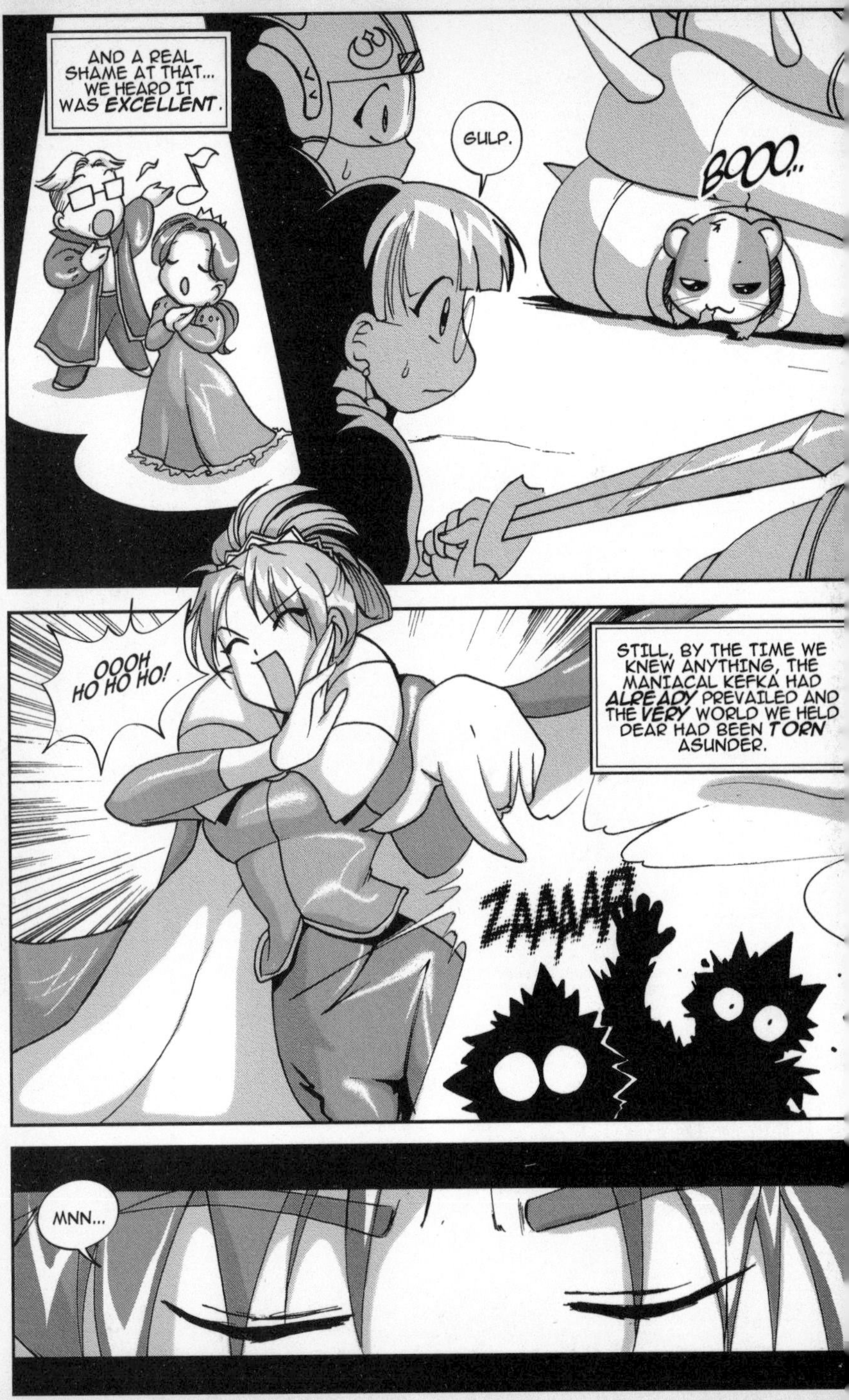
AND A REAL SHAME AT THAT... WE HEARD IT WAS EXCELLENT.
GULP.
BOOO...
STILL, BY THE TIME WE KNEW ANYTHING, THE MANIACAL KEFKA HAD ALREADY PREVAILED AND THE VERY WORLD WE HELD DEAR HAD BEEN TORN ASUNDER.
OOOH HO HO HO!
ZAAAAR
MNN...

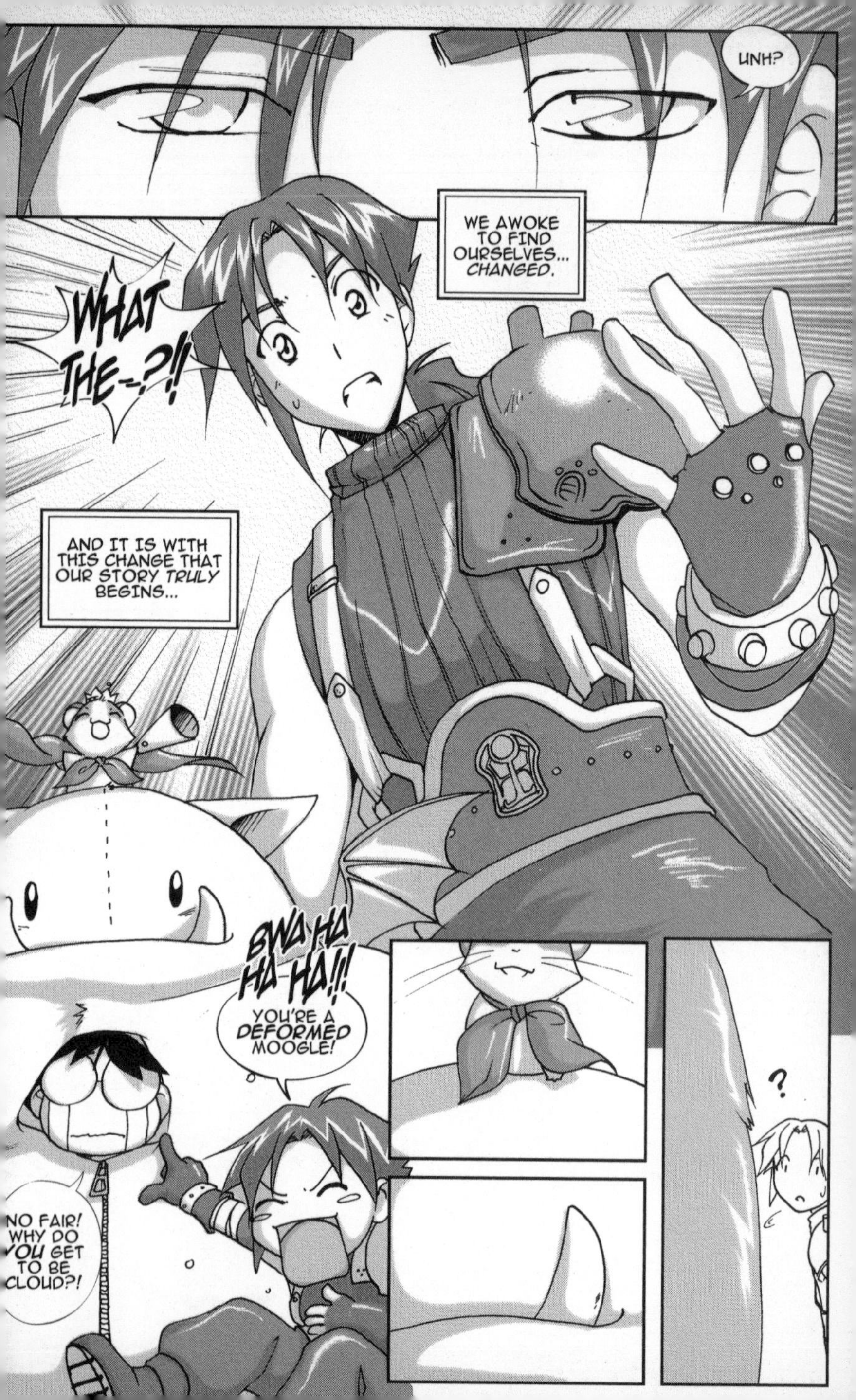
UNH?
WE AWOKE TO FIND OURSELVES... *CHANGED.*
WHAT THE--?!!
AND IT IS WITH THIS CHANGE THAT OUR STORY *TRULY* BEGINS...
?
BWA HA HA-HA!!!
YOU'RE A *DEFORMED* MOOGLE!
NO FAIR! WHY DO *YOU* GET TO BE CLOUD?!

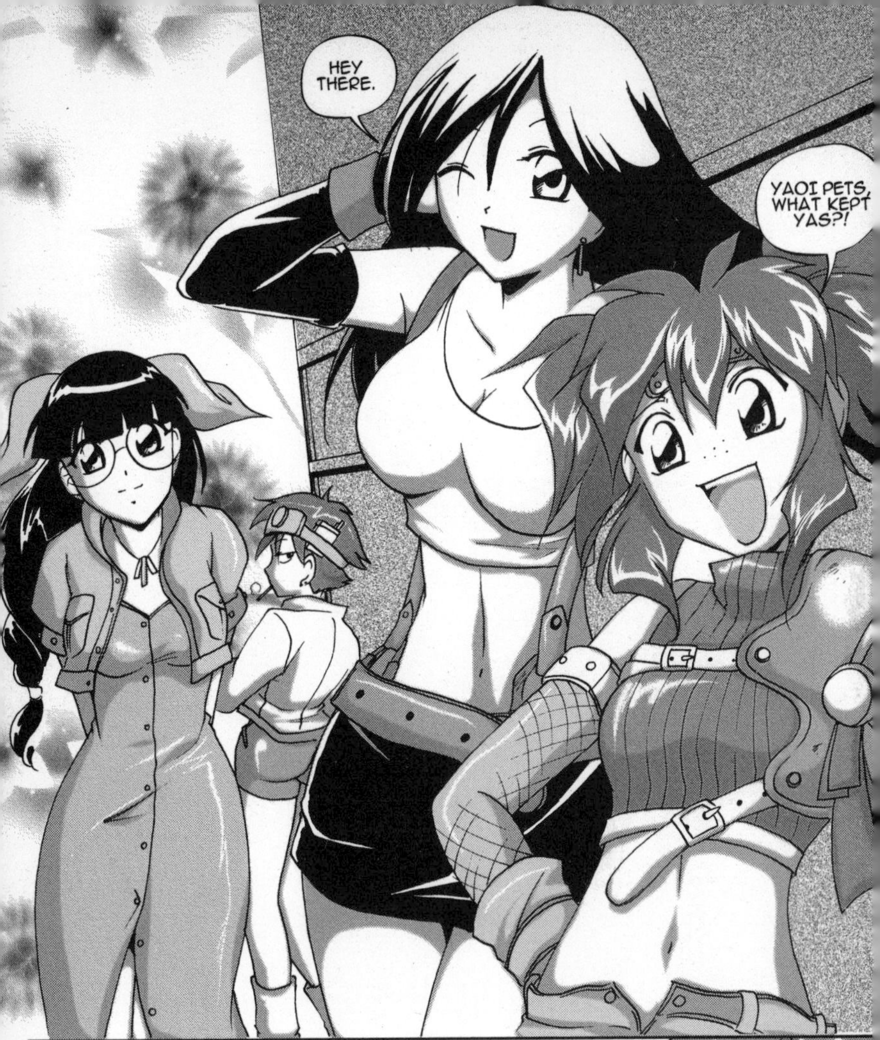
HEY THERE.
YAOI PETS, WHAT KEPT YAS?!
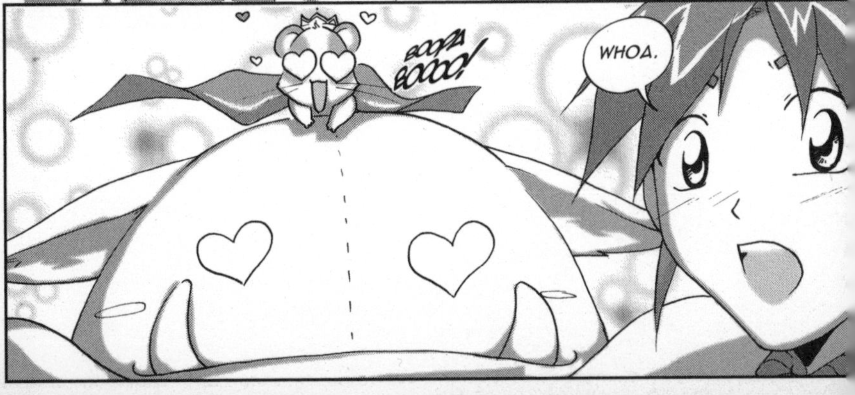
WHOA.
BOOPA BOOOO!

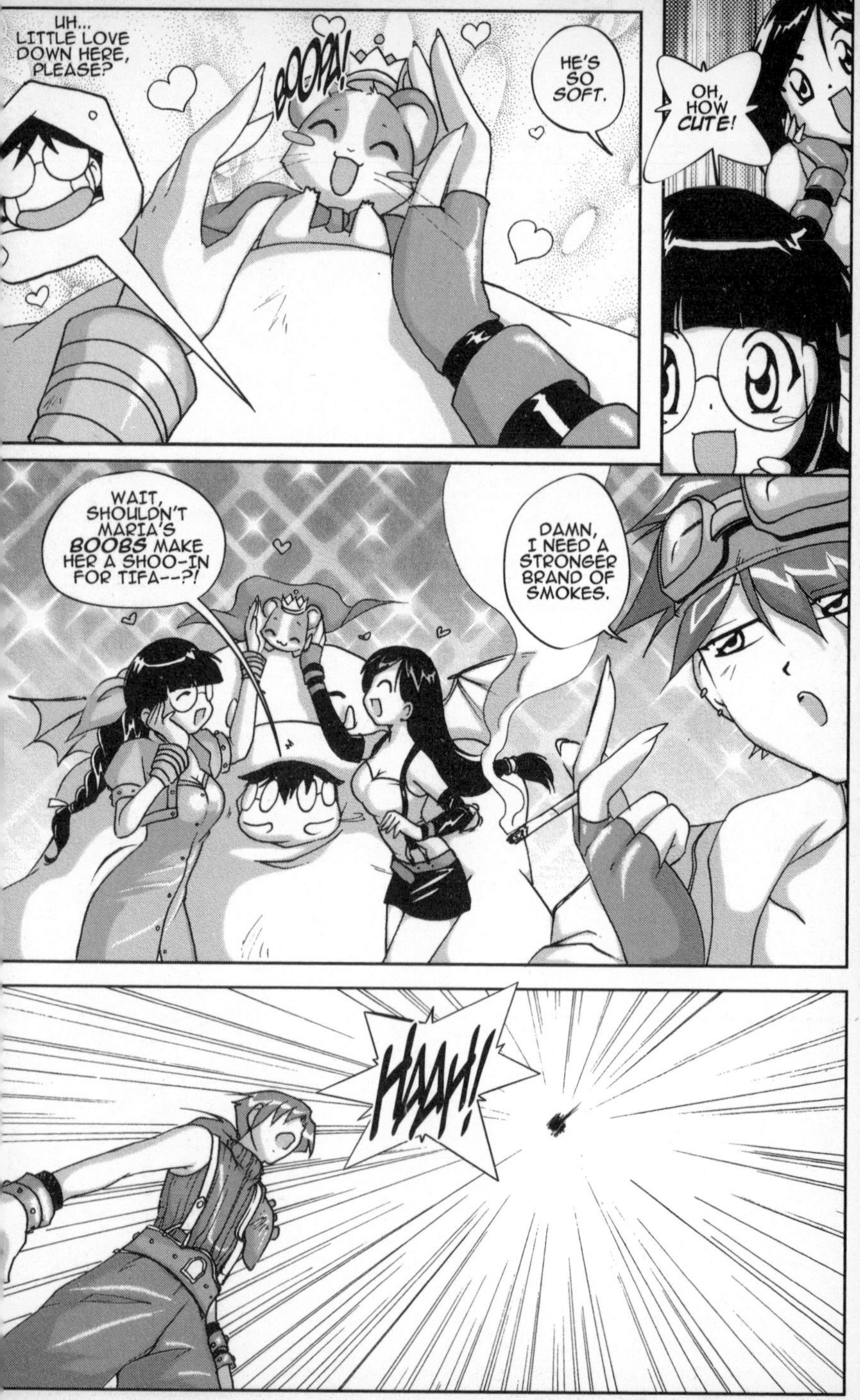
OH, HOW CUTE!
HE'S SO SOFT.
BOOPA!
UH... LITTLE LOVE DOWN HERE, PLEASE?
DAMN, I NEED A STRONGER BRAND OF SMOKES.
WAIT, SHOULDN'T MARIA'S BOOBS MAKE HER A SHOO-IN FOR TIFA--?!
HAAH!

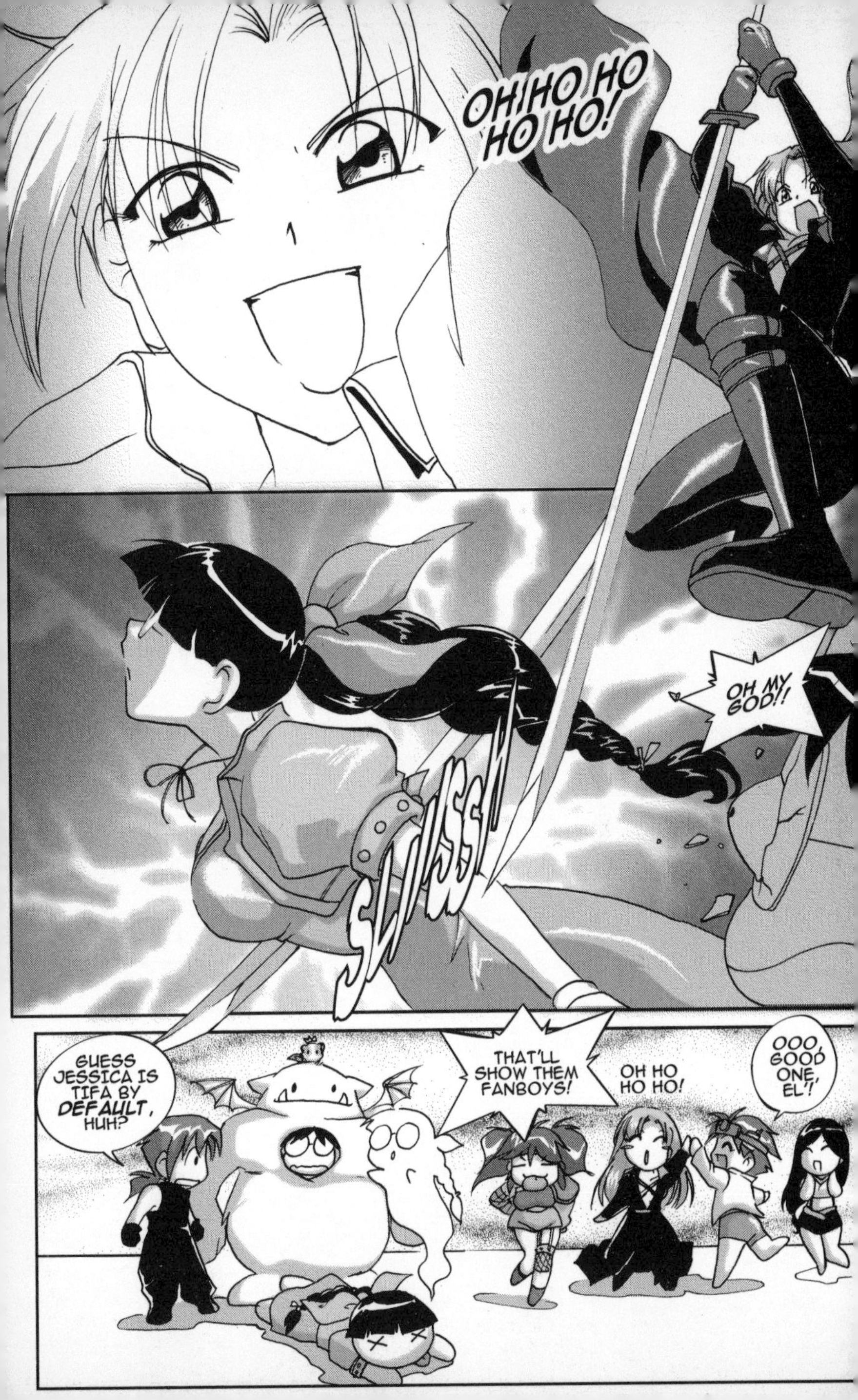
OH HO HO HO HO HO!
OH MY GOD!!
SLISSS
OOO, GOOD ONE, EL!
OH HO HO HO!
THAT'LL SHOW THEM FANBOYS!
GUESS JESSICA IS TIFA BY **DEFAULT**, HUH?

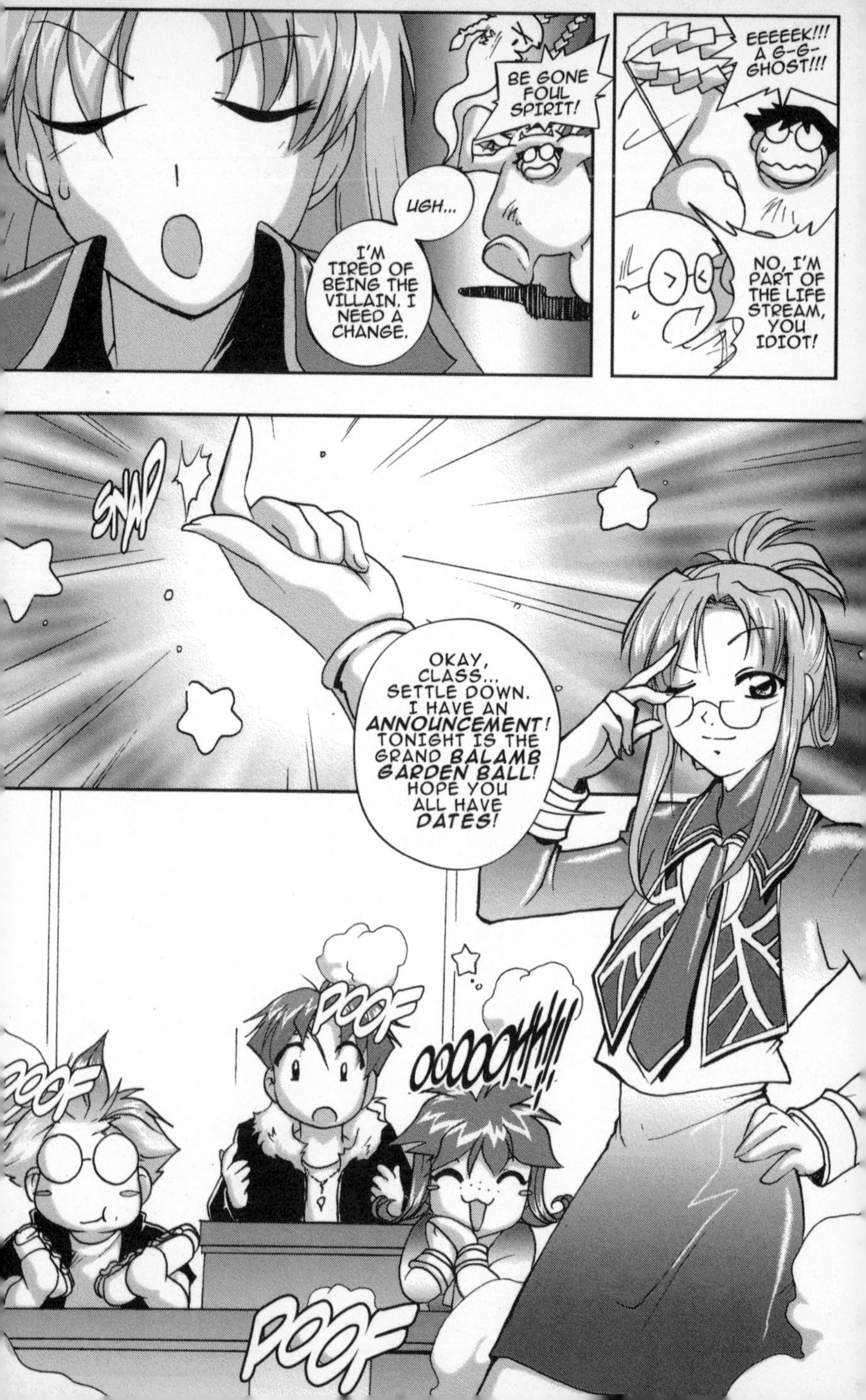
EEEEEK!!! A G-G-GHOST!!!
NO, I'M PART OF THE LIFE STREAM, YOU IDIOT!
BE GONE FOUL SPIRIT!
UGH...
I'M TIRED OF BEING THE VILLAIN. I NEED A CHANGE.
SNAP
OKAY, CLASS... SETTLE DOWN. I HAVE AN ANNOUNCEMENT! TONIGHT IS THE GRAND BALAMB GARDEN BALL! HOPE YOU ALL HAVE DATES!
POOF
OOOOOH!!!
POOF
POOF

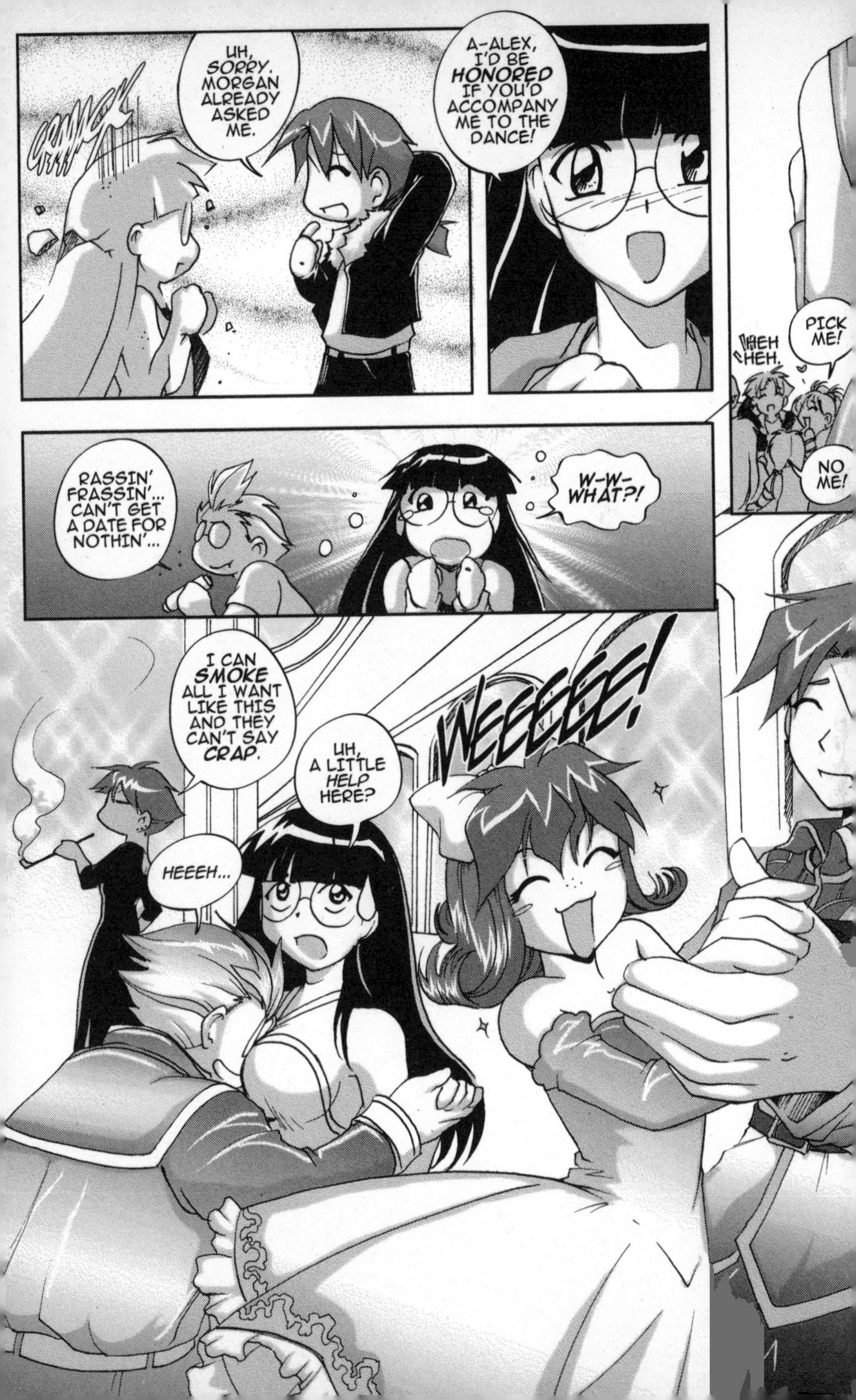
PICK ME!
HEHEH HEH.
NO ME!
A-ALEX, I'D BE **HONORED** IF YOU'D ACCOMPANY ME TO THE DANCE!
UH, SORRY. MORGAN ALREADY ASKED ME.
W-W-WHAT?!
RASSIN' FRASSIN'... CAN'T GET A DATE FOR NOTHIN'...
WEEEEEE!
UH, A LITTLE *HELP* HERE?
I CAN **SMOKE** ALL I WANT LIKE THIS AND THEY CAN'T SAY **CRAP**.
HEEEH...

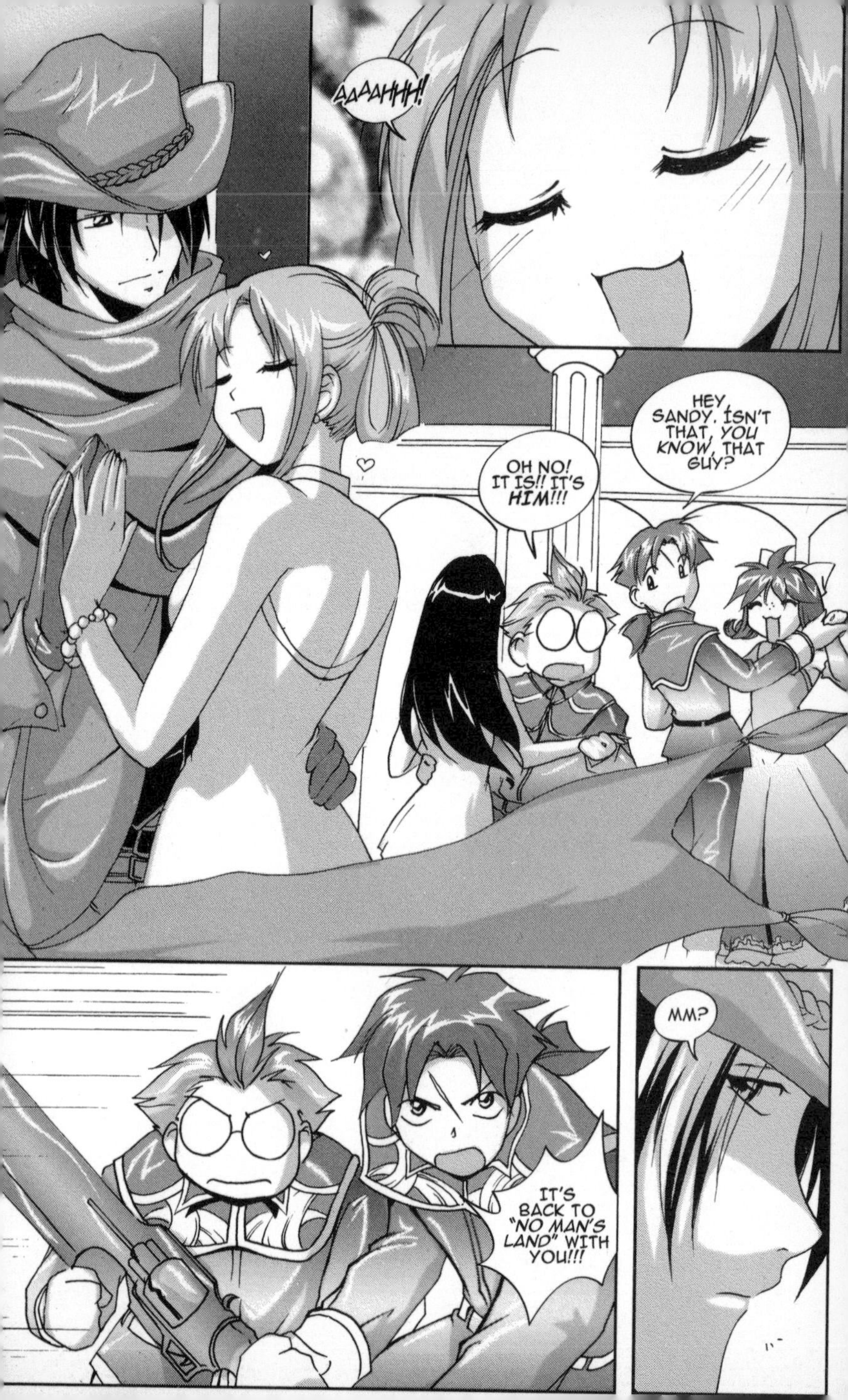
AAAAHHH!
HEY SANDY. ISN'T THAT, YOU KNOW, THAT GUY?
OH NO! IT IS!! IT'S HIM!!!
MM?
IT'S BACK TO "NO MAN'S LAND" WITH YOU!!!

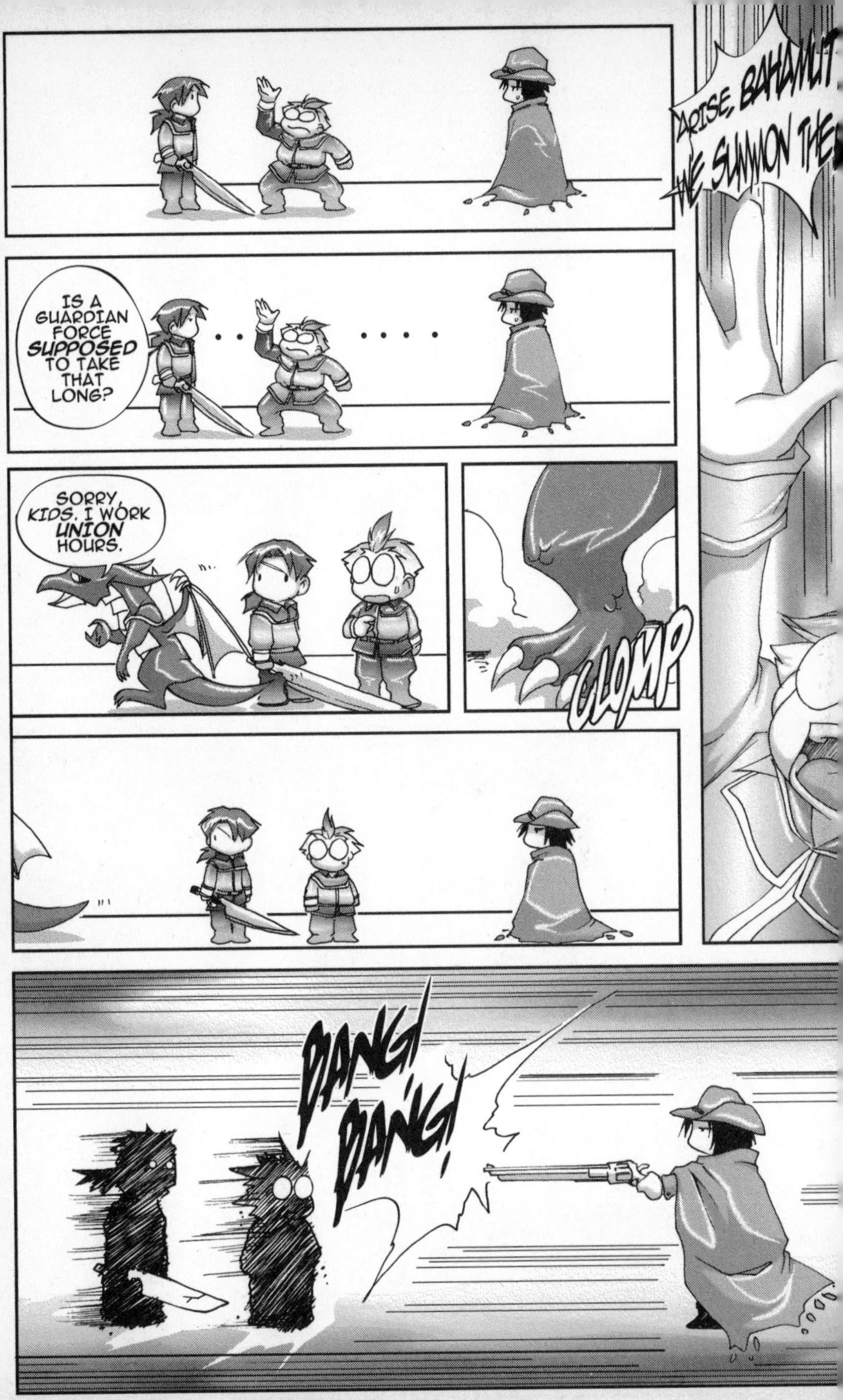
ARISE, BAHAMUT!
WE SUMMON THE
IS A GUARDIAN FORCE SUPPOSED TO TAKE THAT LONG?
CLOMP
SORRY, KIDS. I WORK UNION HOURS.
BANG! BANG!

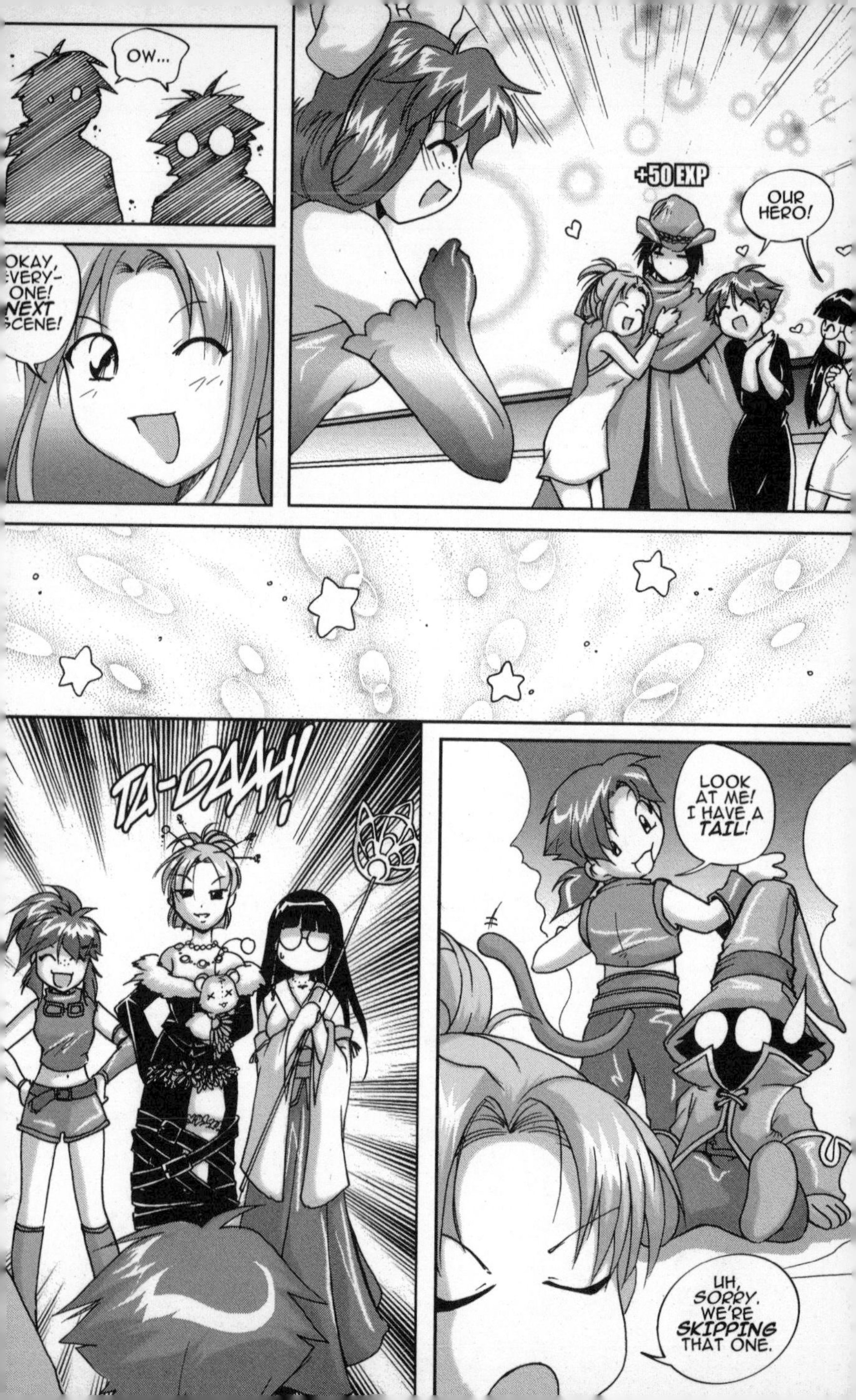
+50 EXP
OUR HERO!
OW...
OKAY, EVERY-ONE! NEXT SCENE!
LOOK AT ME! I HAVE A TAIL!
UH, SORRY. WE'RE SKIPPING THAT ONE.
TA-DAAH!

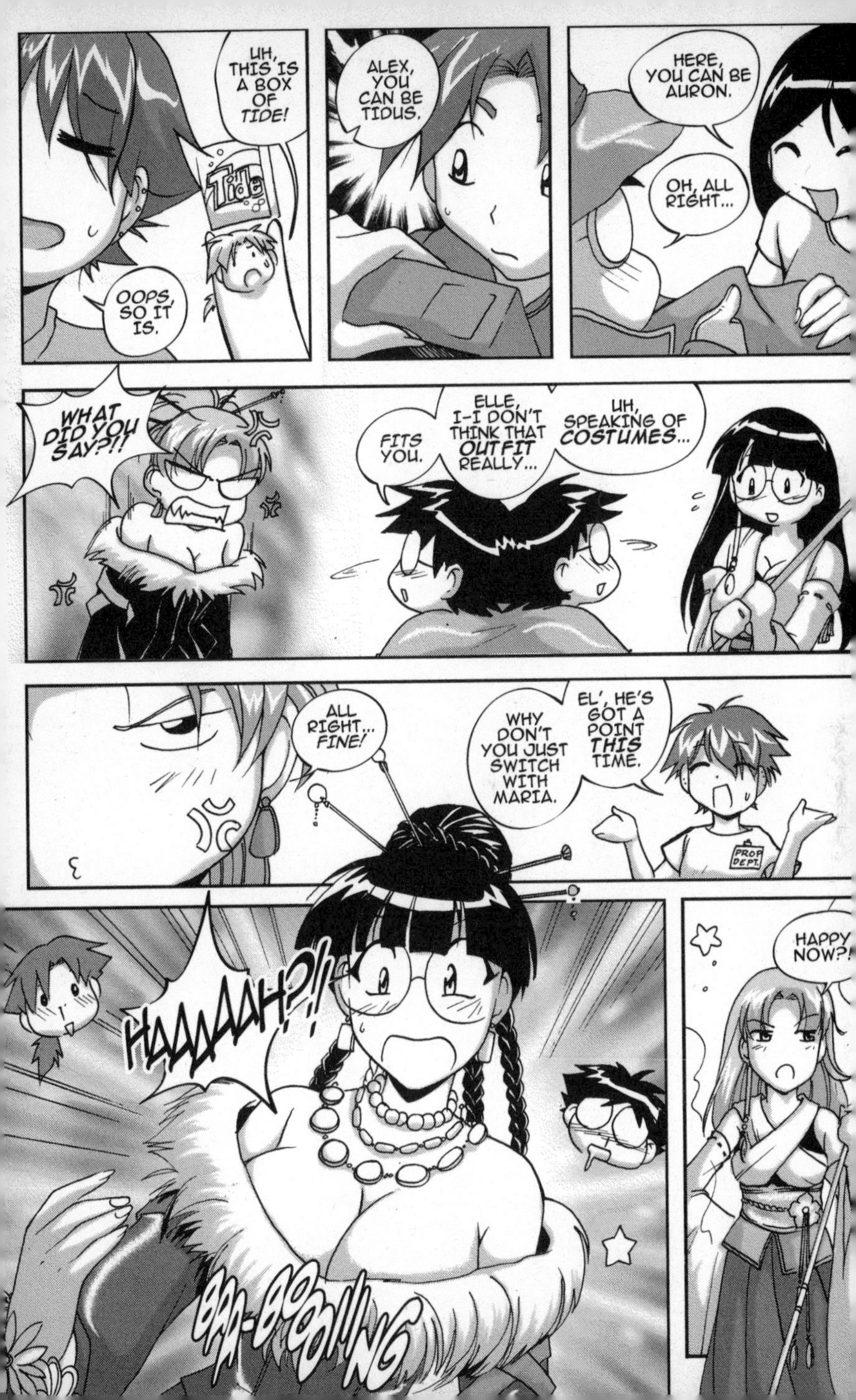

HERE, YOU CAN BE AURON.
OH, ALL RIGHT...
ALEX, YOU CAN BE TIDUS.
UH, THIS IS A BOX OF *TIDE*!
Tide
OOPS, SO IT IS.
UH, SPEAKING OF *COSTUMES*...
ELLE, I-I DON'T THINK THAT *OUTFIT* REALLY...
FITS YOU.
WHAT DID YOU SAY?!!
EL', HE'S GOT A POINT *THIS* TIME.
WHY DON'T YOU JUST SWITCH WITH MARIA.
PROP DEPT.
ALL RIGHT... *FINE!*
HAPPY NOW?!
HAAAAAH?!!
BA-BOOIING

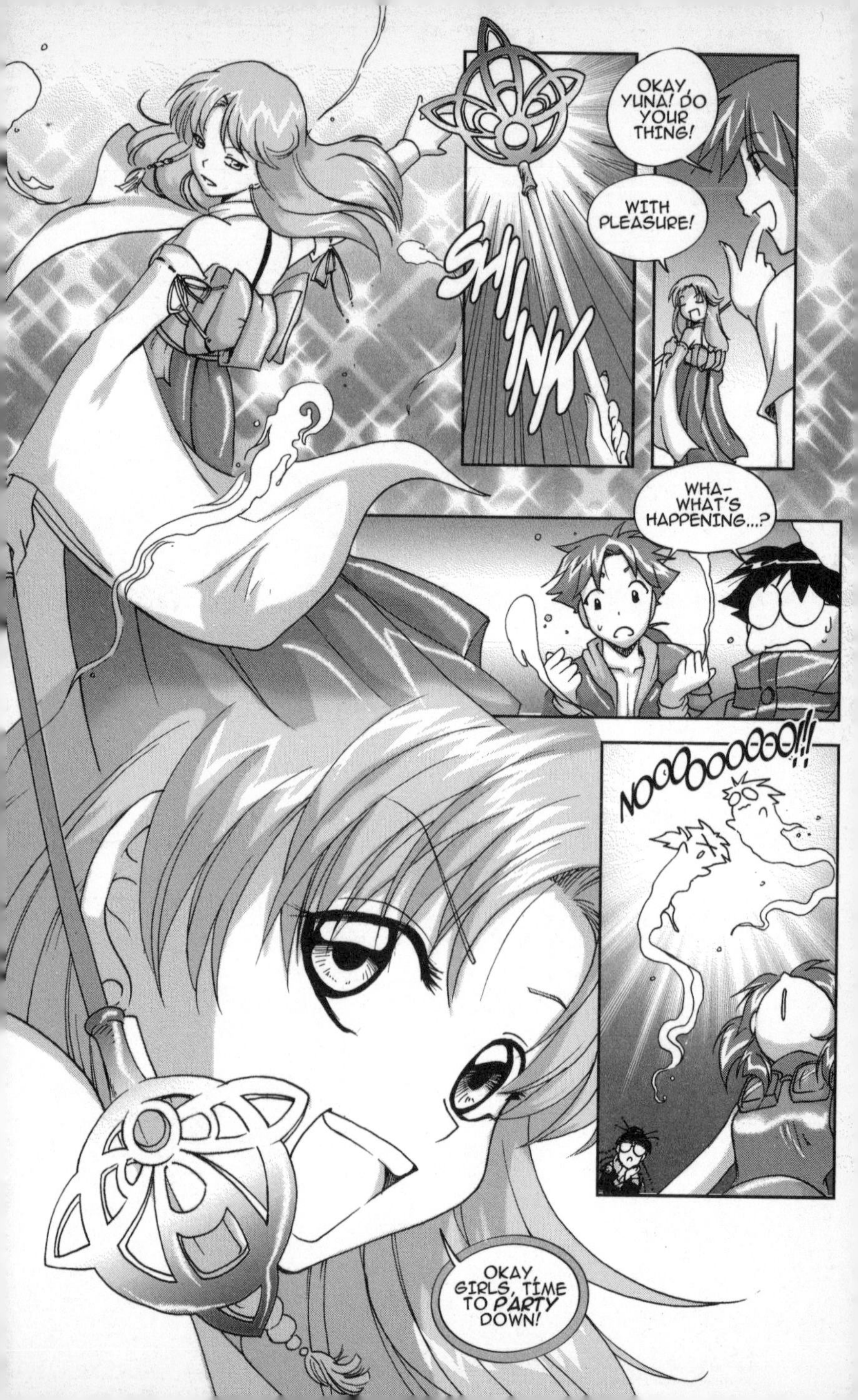
OKAY, YUNA! DO YOUR THING!
WITH PLEASURE!
SHIIINK
WHA- WHAT'S HAPPENING...?
NOOOOOOOOOO!!!
OKAY, GIRLS, TIME TO PARTY DOWN!

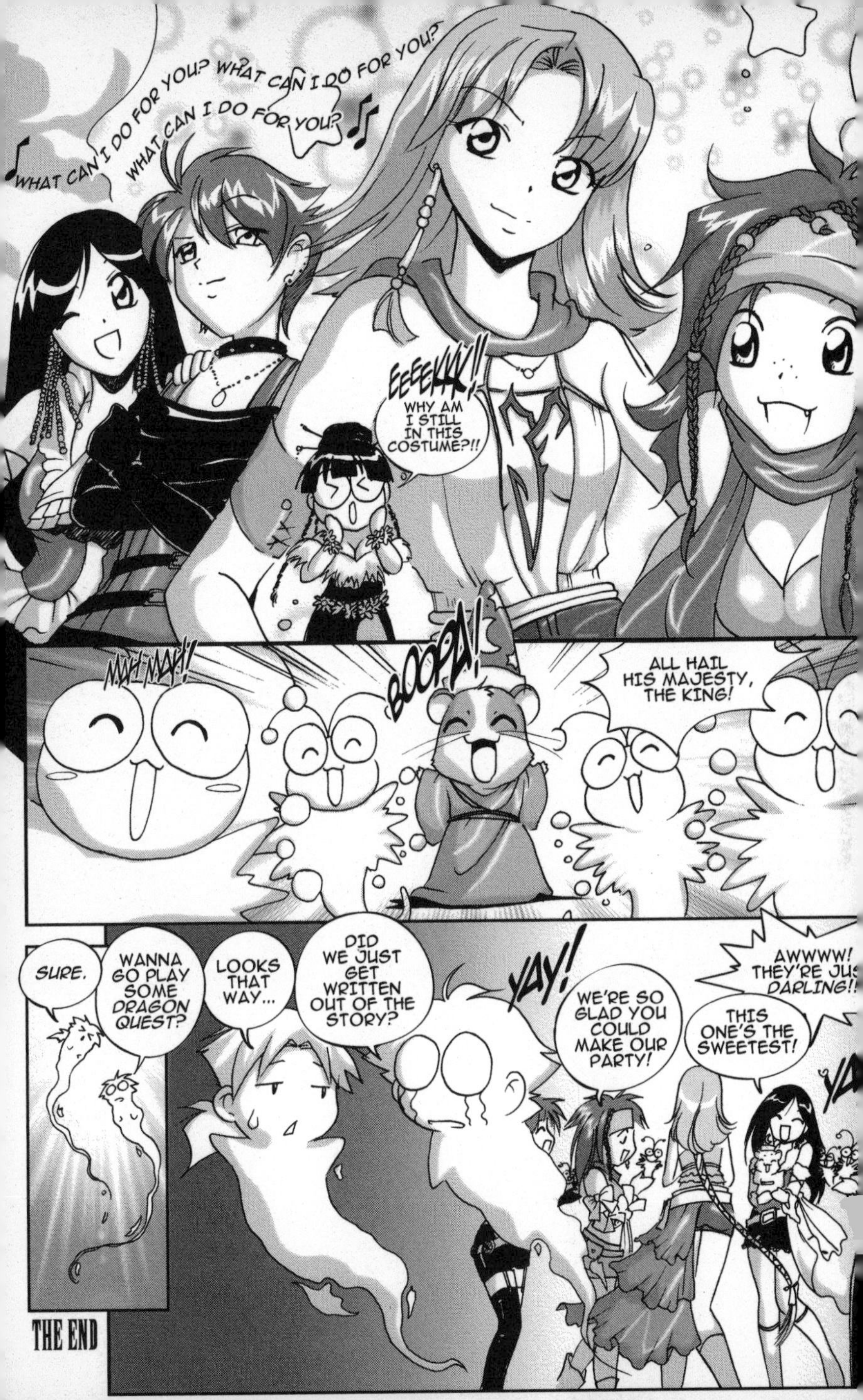
WHAT CAN I DO FOR YOU? WHAT CAN I DO FOR YOU?
WHAT CAN I DO FOR YOU?
WHAT CAN I DO FOR YOU?
EEEEKKK! WHY AM I STILL IN THIS COSTUME?!!
ALL HAIL HIS MAJESTY, THE KING!
BOOPA!
MAY! MAY!
AWWWW! THEY'RE JUS DARLING!!
THIS ONE'S THE SWEETEST!
WE'RE SO GLAD YOU COULD MAKE OUR PARTY!
YAY!
DID WE JUST GET WRITTEN OUT OF THE STORY?
LOOKS THAT WAY...
WANNA GO PLAY SOME DRAGON QUEST?
SURE.
THE END

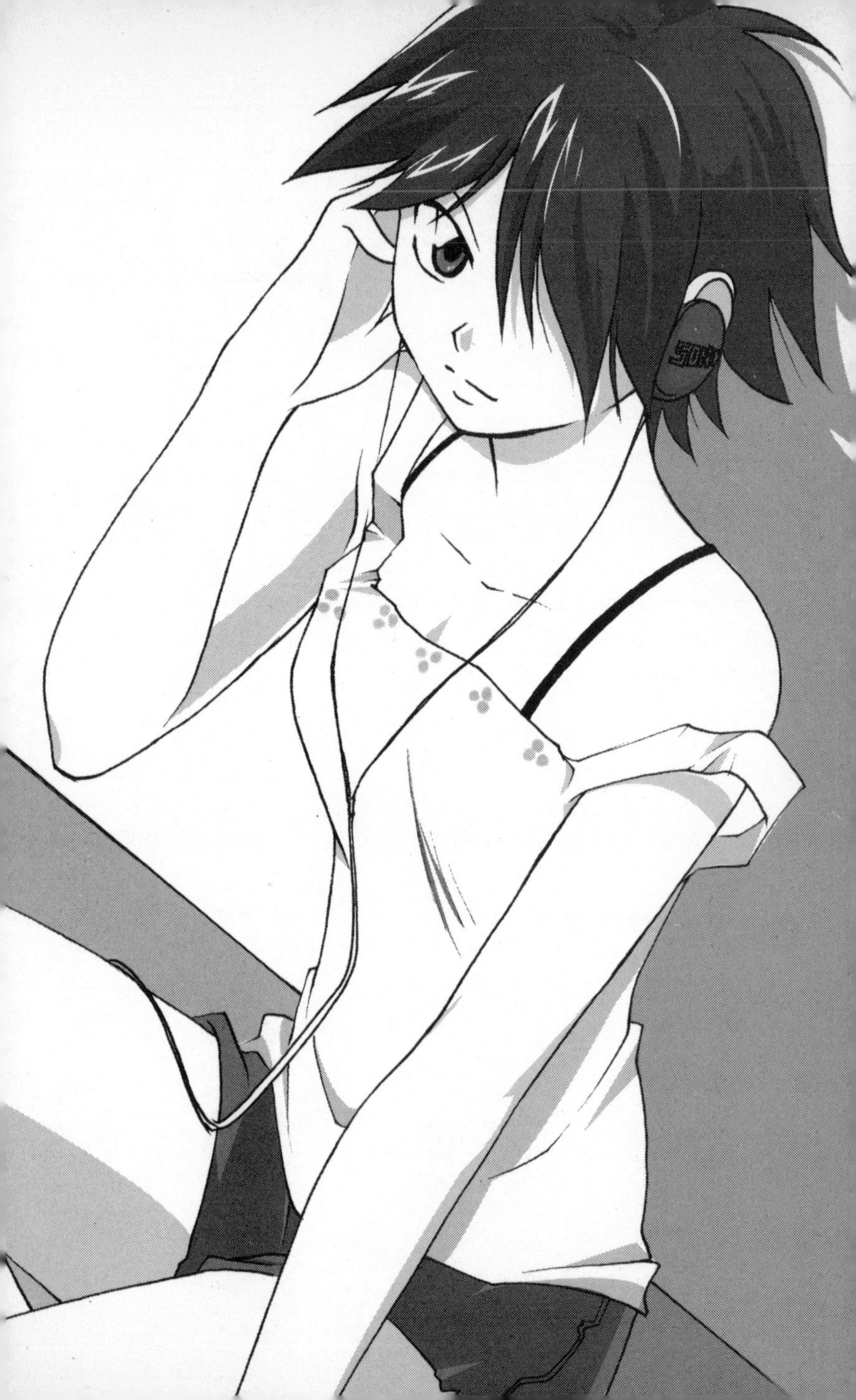

EPISODE 12:

THE NIGHTMARE BEFORE CHRISTMAS

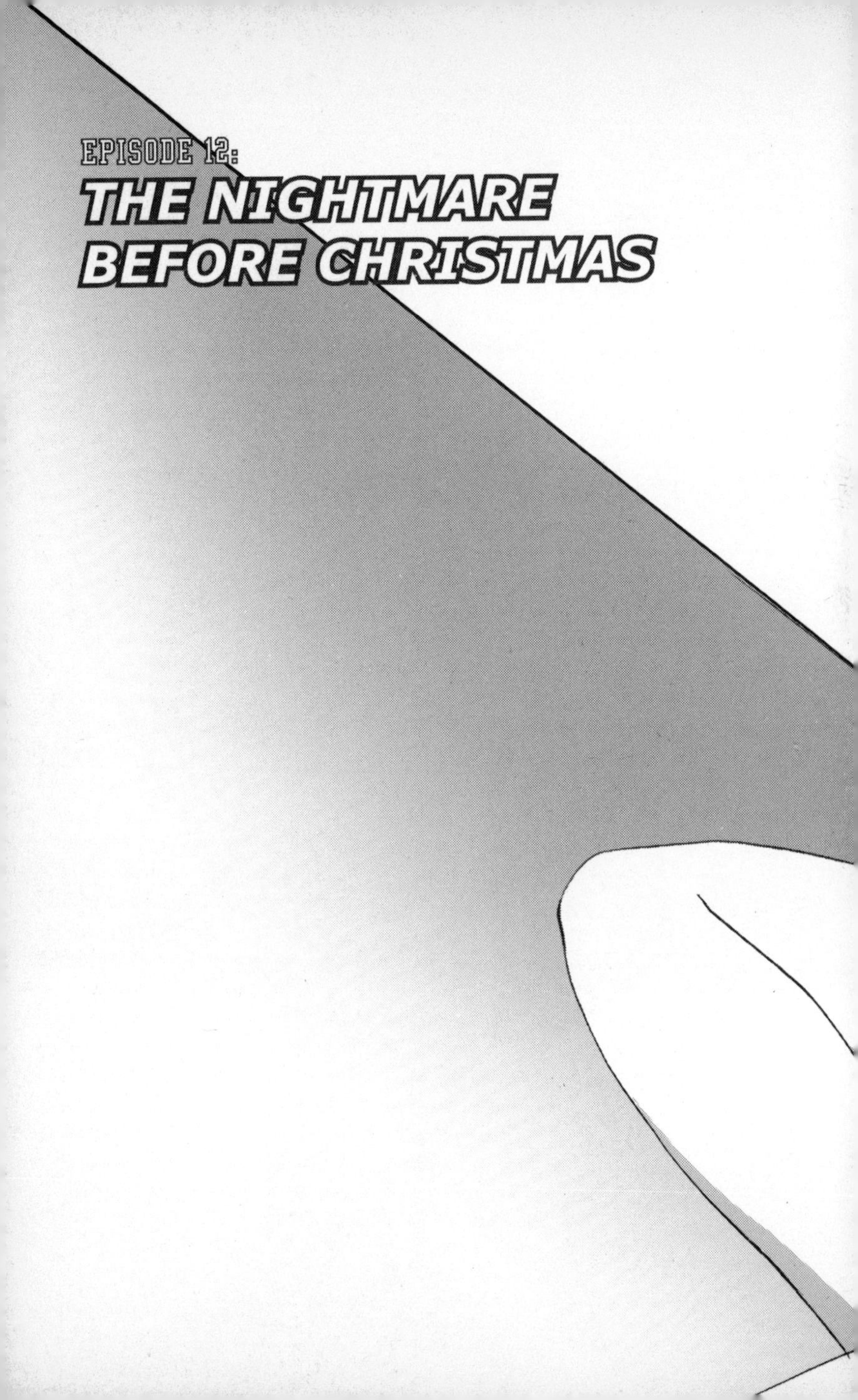

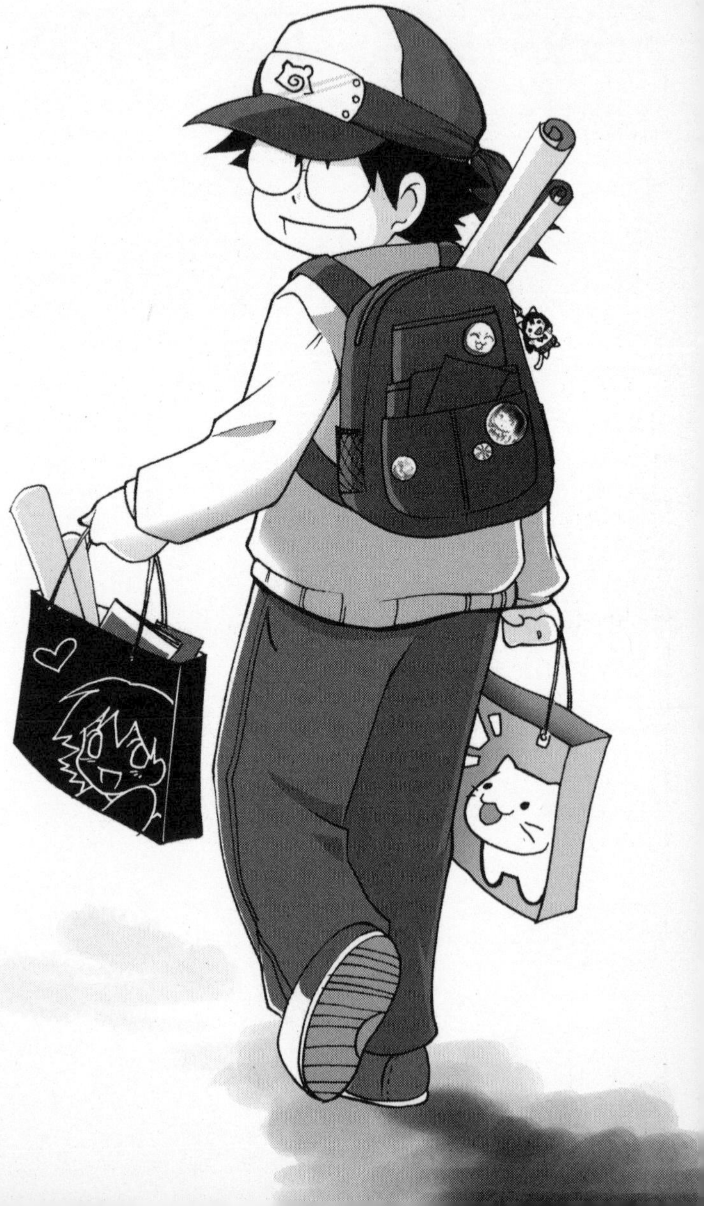

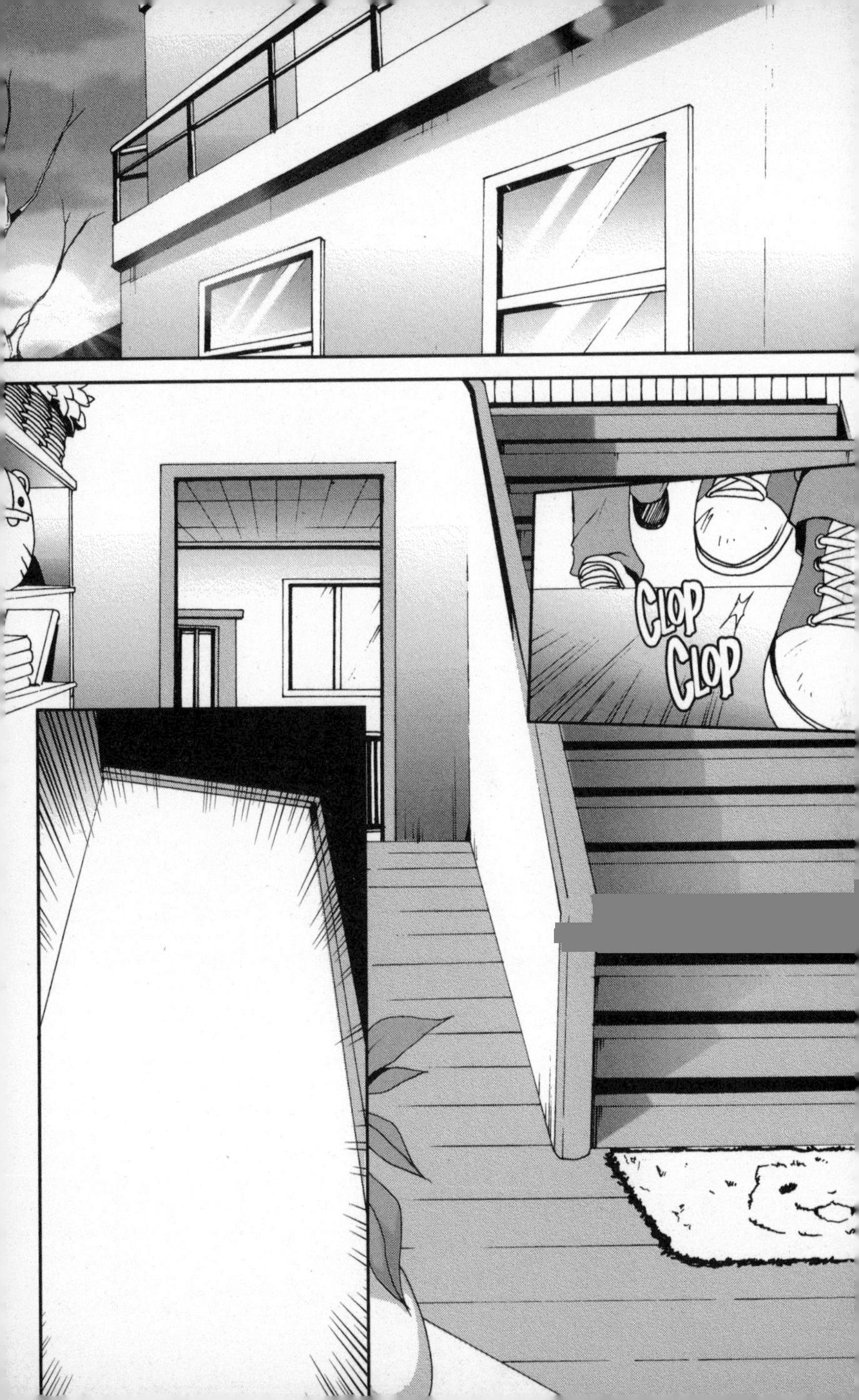
CLOP CLOP

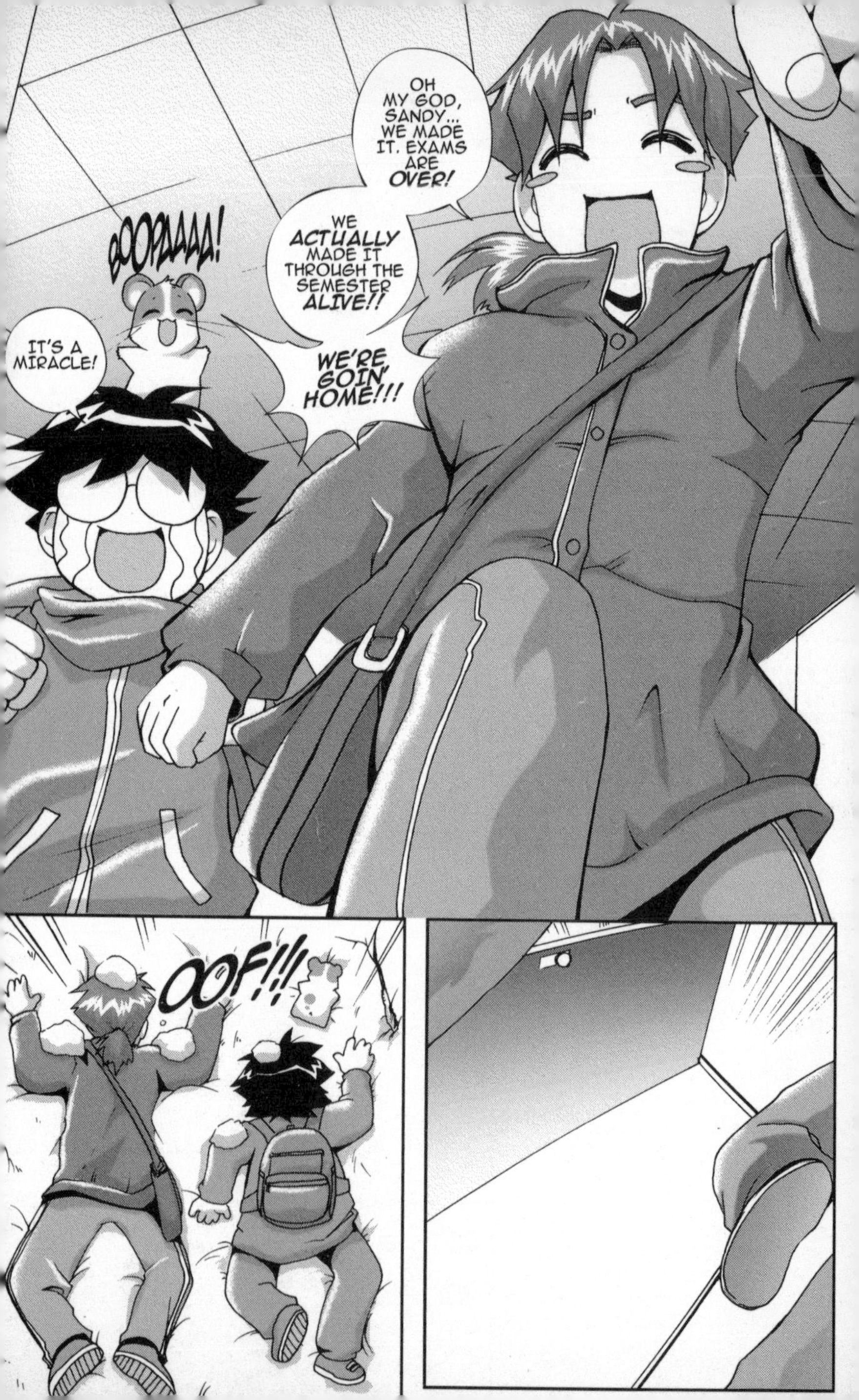
OH MY GOD, SANDY... WE MADE IT. EXAMS ARE OVER!
WE ACTUALLY MADE IT THROUGH THE SEMESTER ALIVE!!
WE'RE GOIN' HOME!!!
IT'S A MIRACLE!
OOF!!!

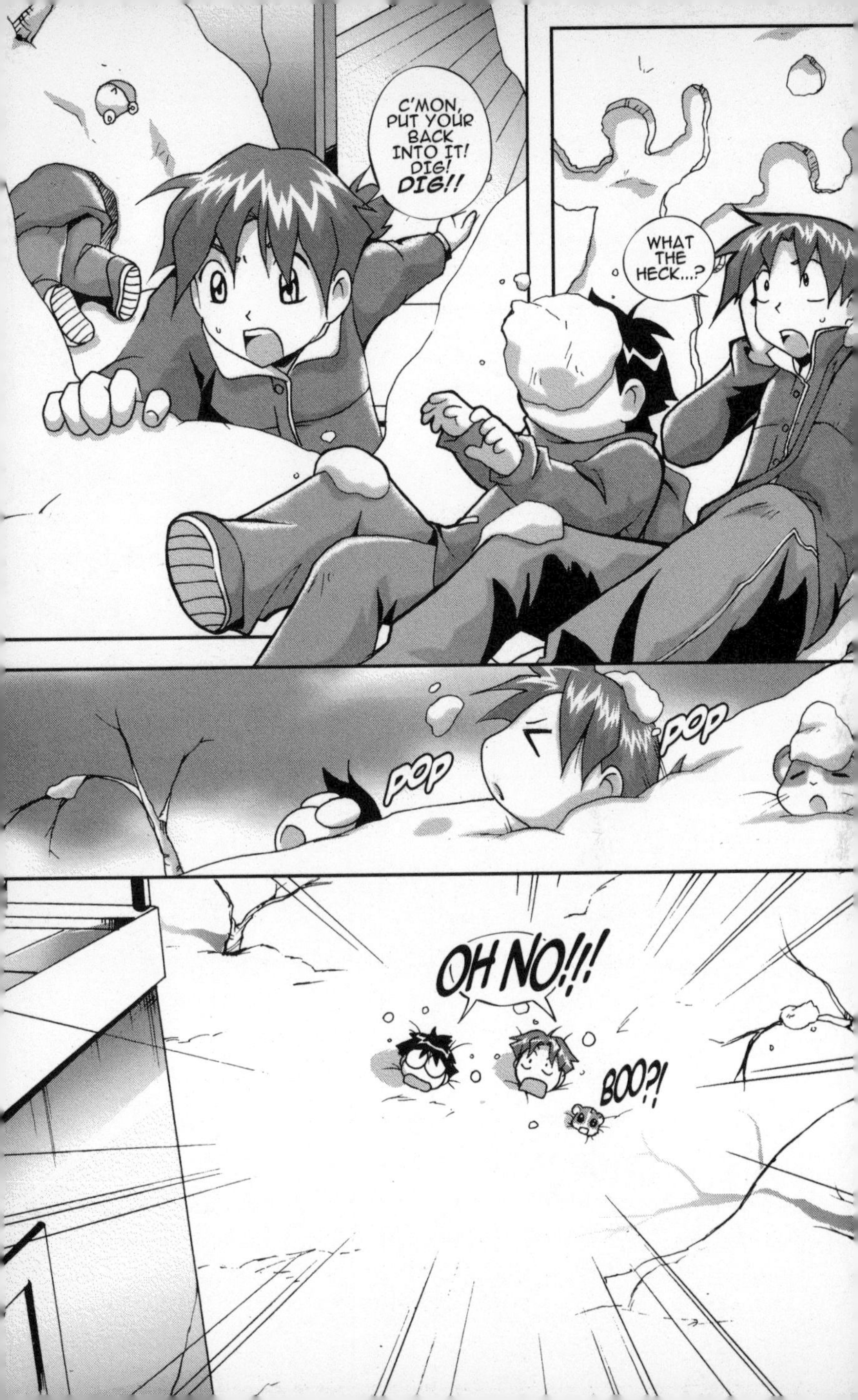
WHAT THE HECK...?
C'MON, PUT YOUR BACK INTO IT! DIG! DIG!!
POP
POP
OH NO!!!
BOO?!

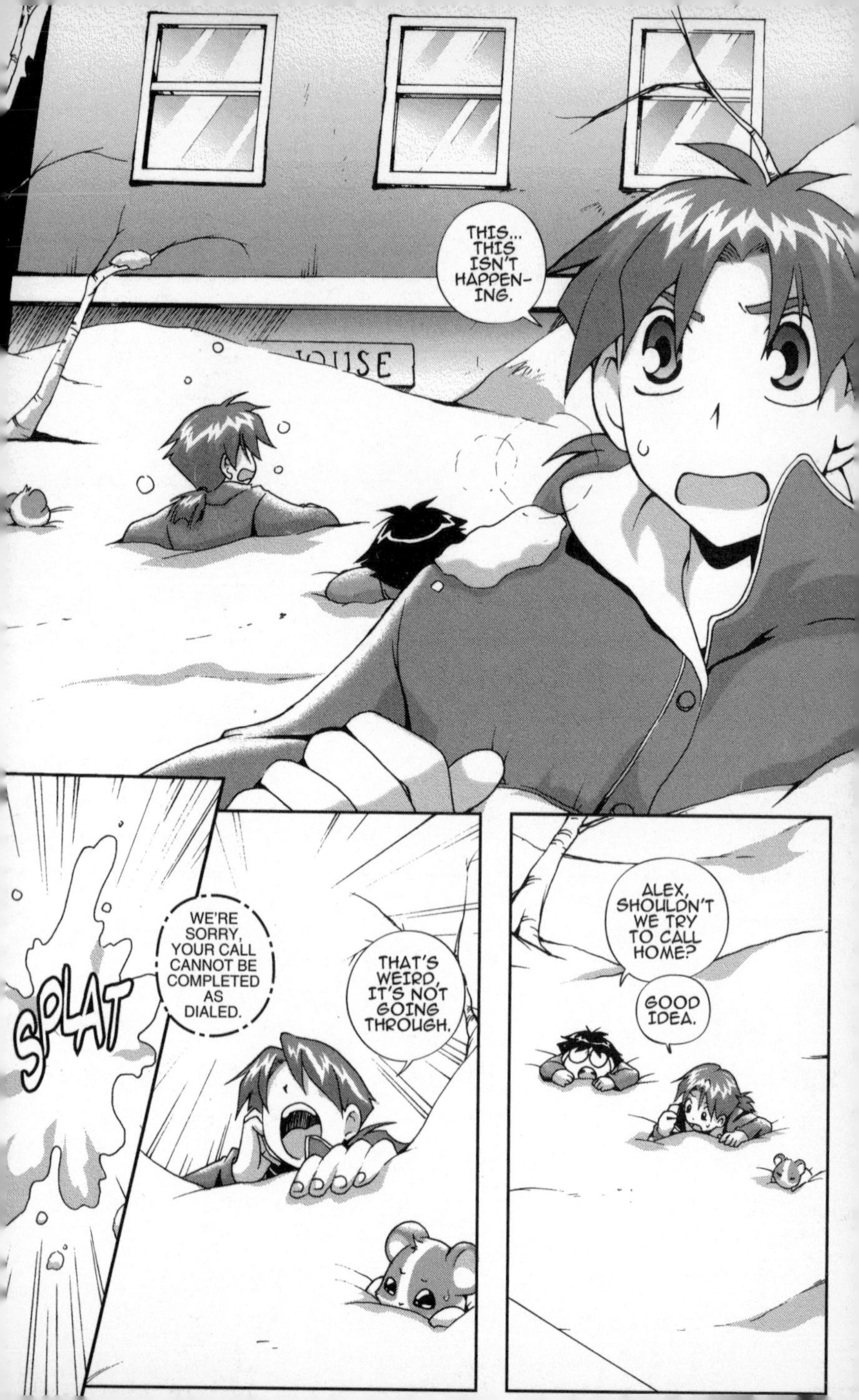
THIS... THIS ISN'T HAPPEN-ING.
ALEX, SHOULDN'T WE TRY TO CALL HOME?
GOOD IDEA.
THAT'S WEIRD, IT'S NOT GOING THROUGH.
WE'RE SORRY, YOUR CALL CANNOT BE COMPLETED AS DIALED.
SPLAT

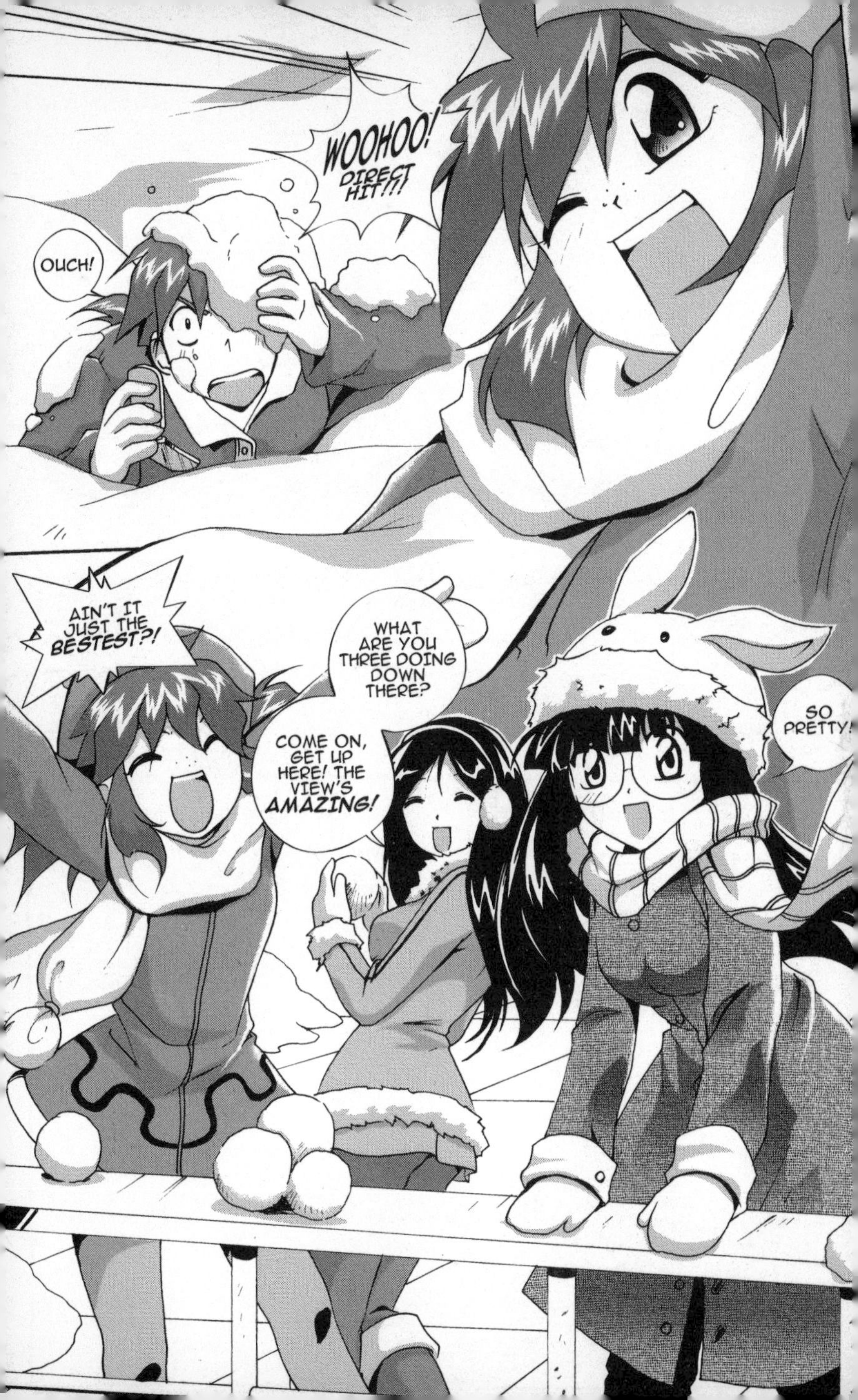
WOOHOO! DIRECT HIT!?!
OUCH!
SO PRETTY!
WHAT ARE YOU THREE DOING DOWN THERE?
COME ON, GET UP HERE! THE VIEW'S AMAZING!
AIN'T IT JUST THE BESTEST?!

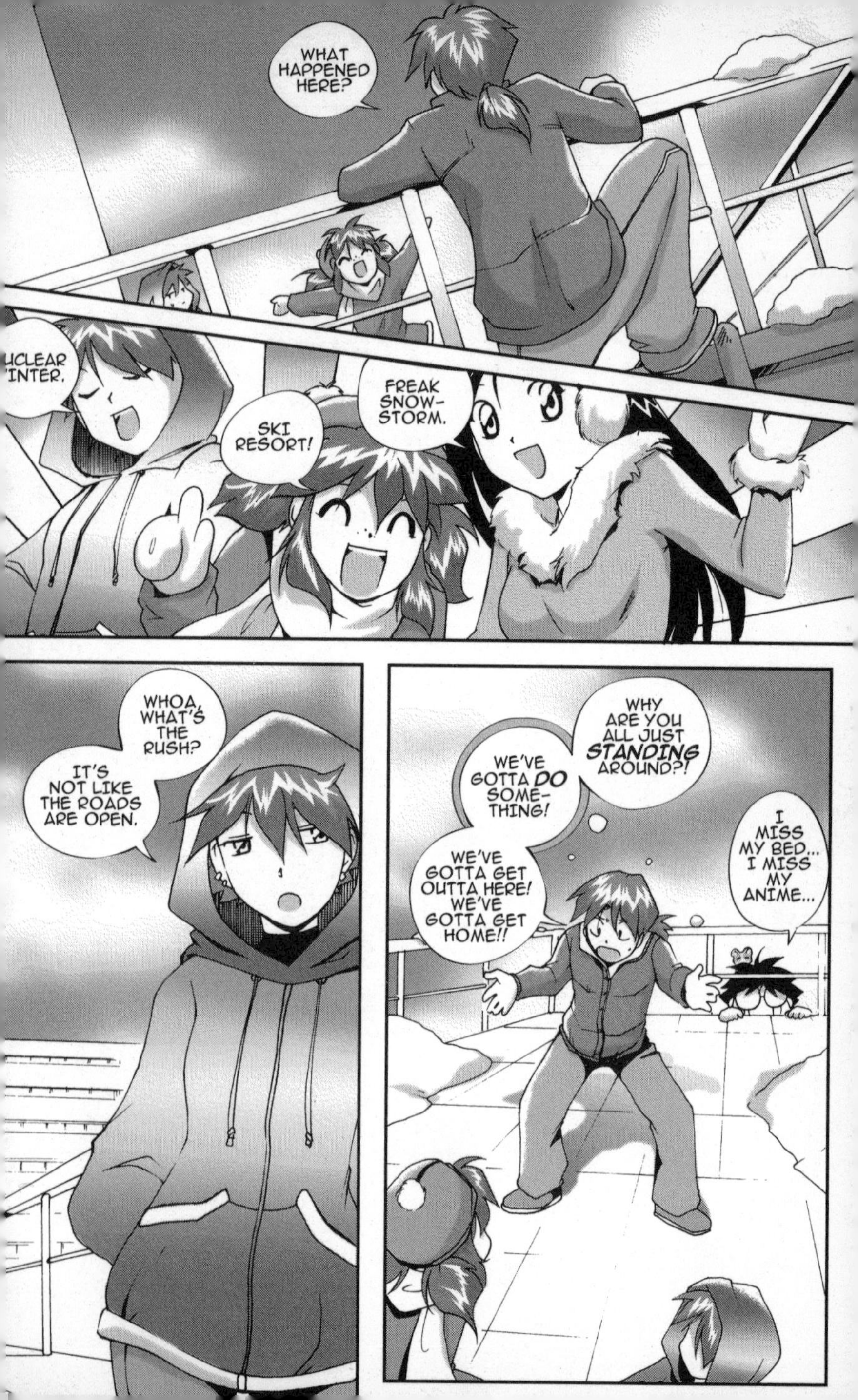
WHAT HAPPENED HERE?
FREAK SNOW-STORM.
SKI RESORT!
UCLEAR 'INTER.
WHY ARE YOU ALL JUST STANDING AROUND?!
WE'VE GOTTA DO SOME-THING!
WE'VE GOTTA GET OUTTA HERE! WE'VE GOTTA GET HOME!!
I MISS MY BED... I MISS MY ANIME...
WHOA, WHAT'S THE RUSH?
IT'S NOT LIKE THE ROADS ARE OPEN.

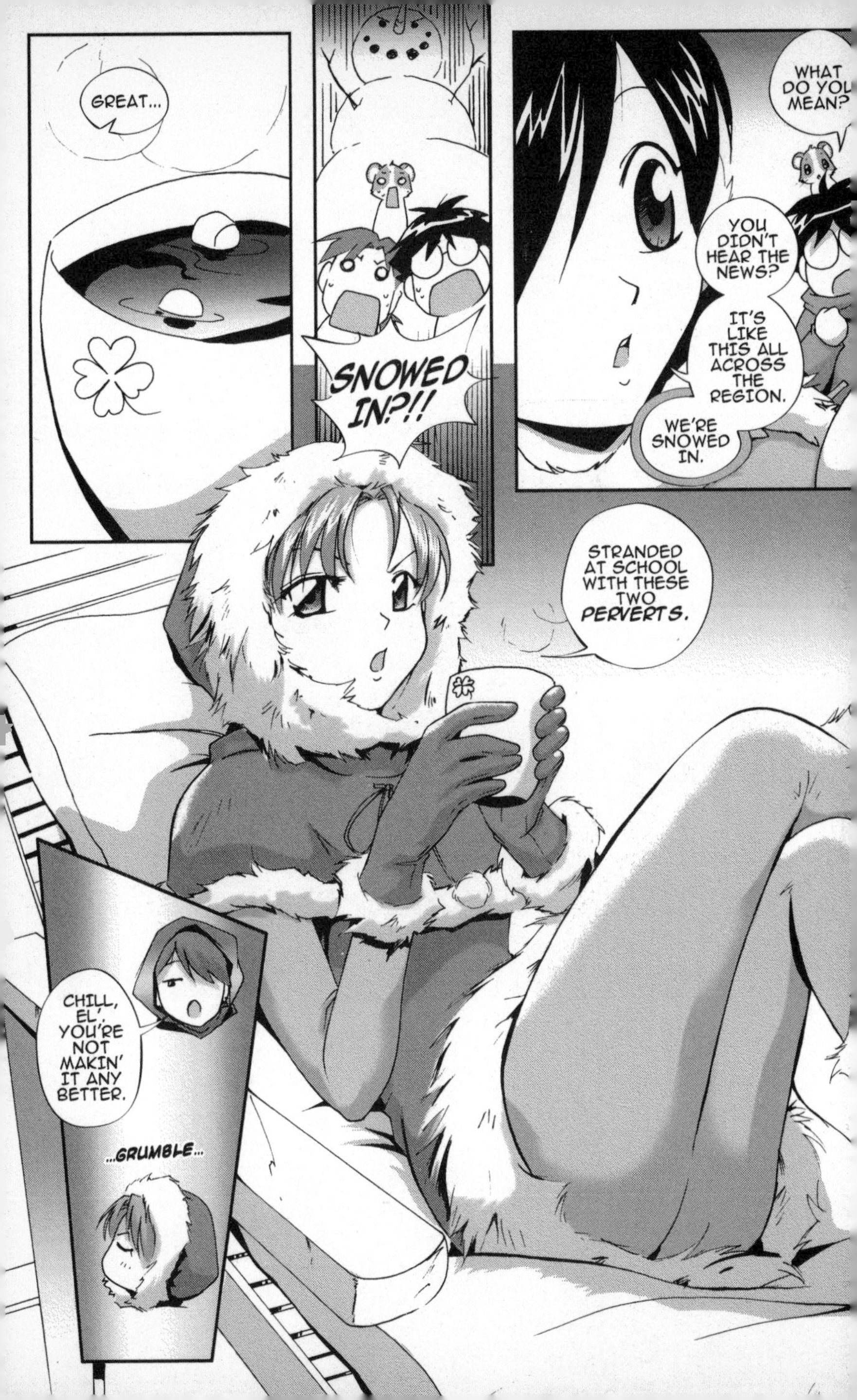
WHAT DO YOU MEAN?
YOU DIDN'T HEAR THE NEWS?
IT'S LIKE THIS ALL ACROSS THE REGION.
WE'RE SNOWED IN.
SNOWED IN?!!
GREAT...
STRANDED AT SCHOOL WITH THESE TWO PERVERTS.
CHILL, EL', YOU'RE NOT MAKIN' IT ANY BETTER.
...GRUMBLE...

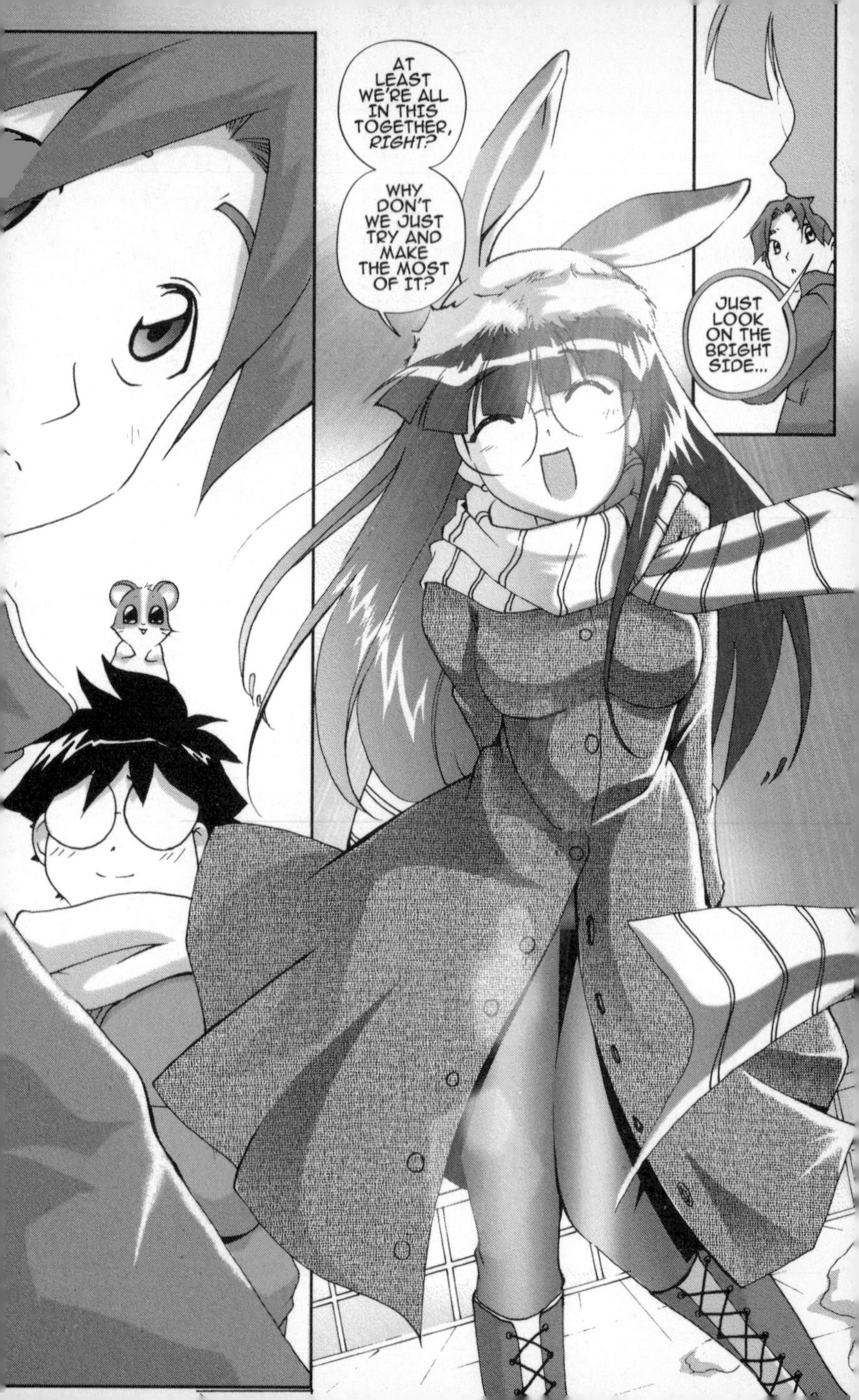
JUST LOOK ON THE BRIGHT SIDE...
AT LEAST WE'RE ALL IN THIS TOGETHER, *RIGHT?*
WHY DON'T WE JUST TRY AND MAKE THE MOST OF IT?

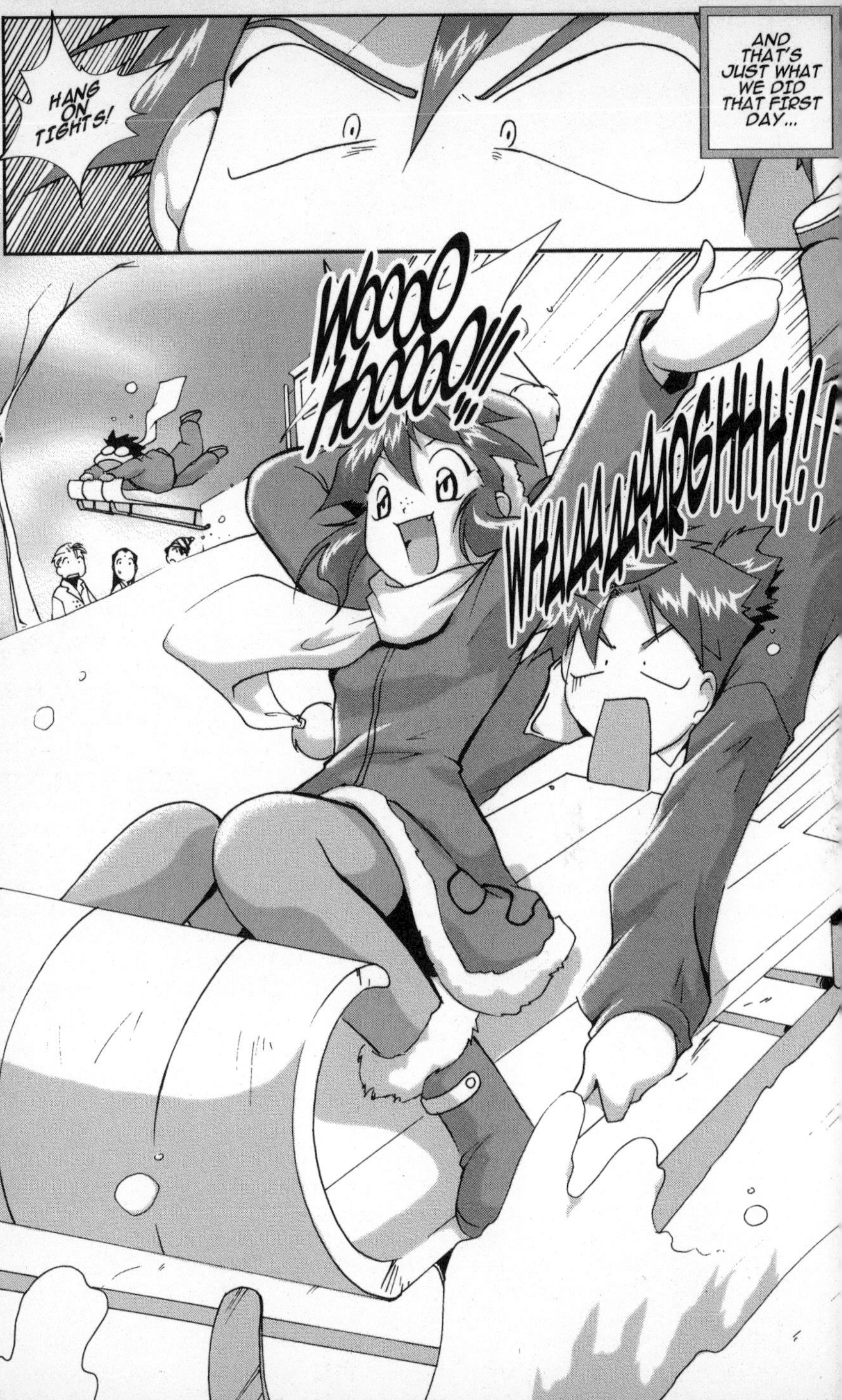
AND THAT'S JUST WHAT WE DID THAT FIRST DAY...
HANG ON TIGHTS!
WOOOO HOOOOO!!!
WHAAAAAAGHHH!!!

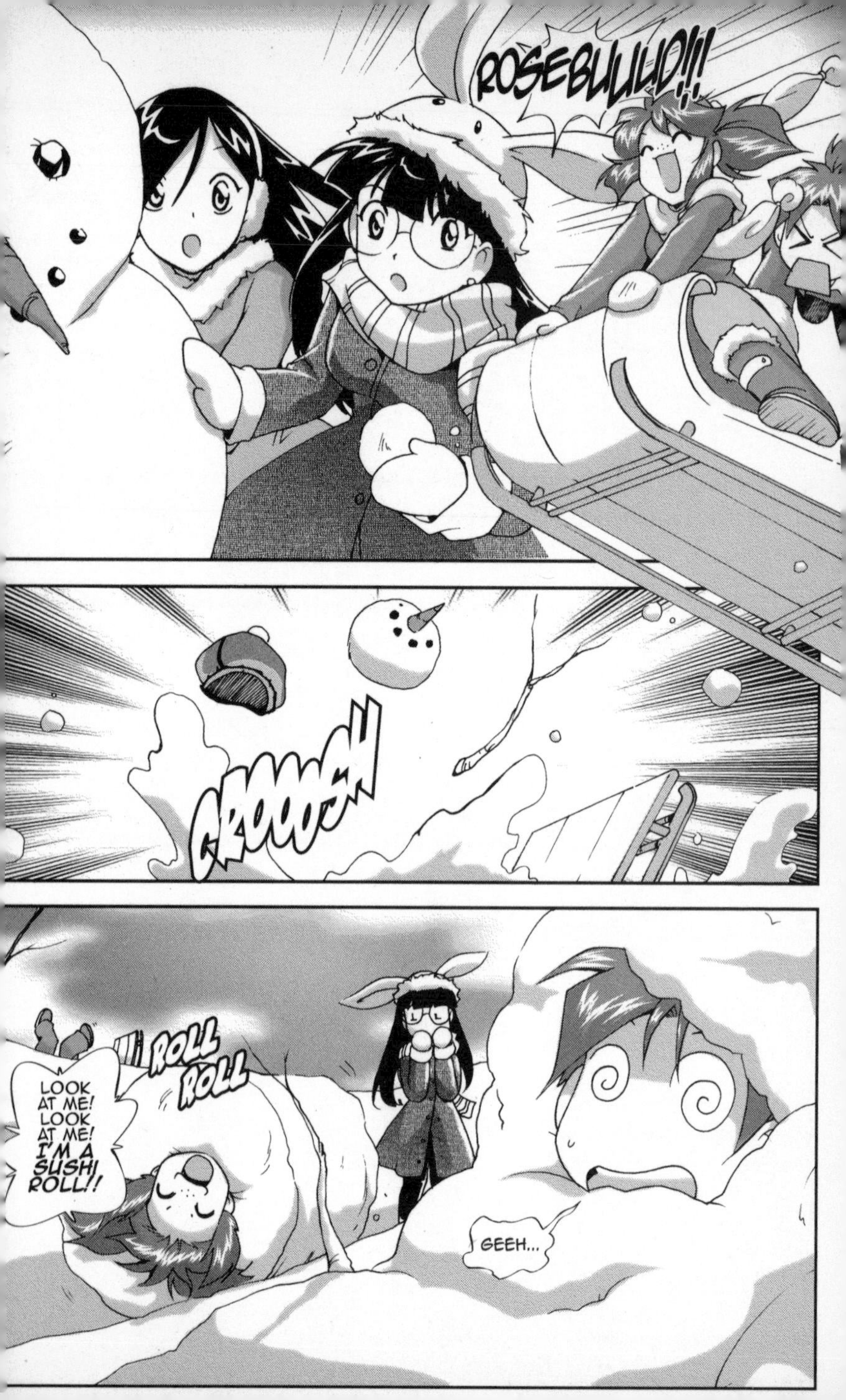
ROSEBUUUD!!!
CROOOOSH
ROLL ROLL
GEEH...
LOOK AT ME! LOOK AT ME! I'M A SUSHI ROLL!!

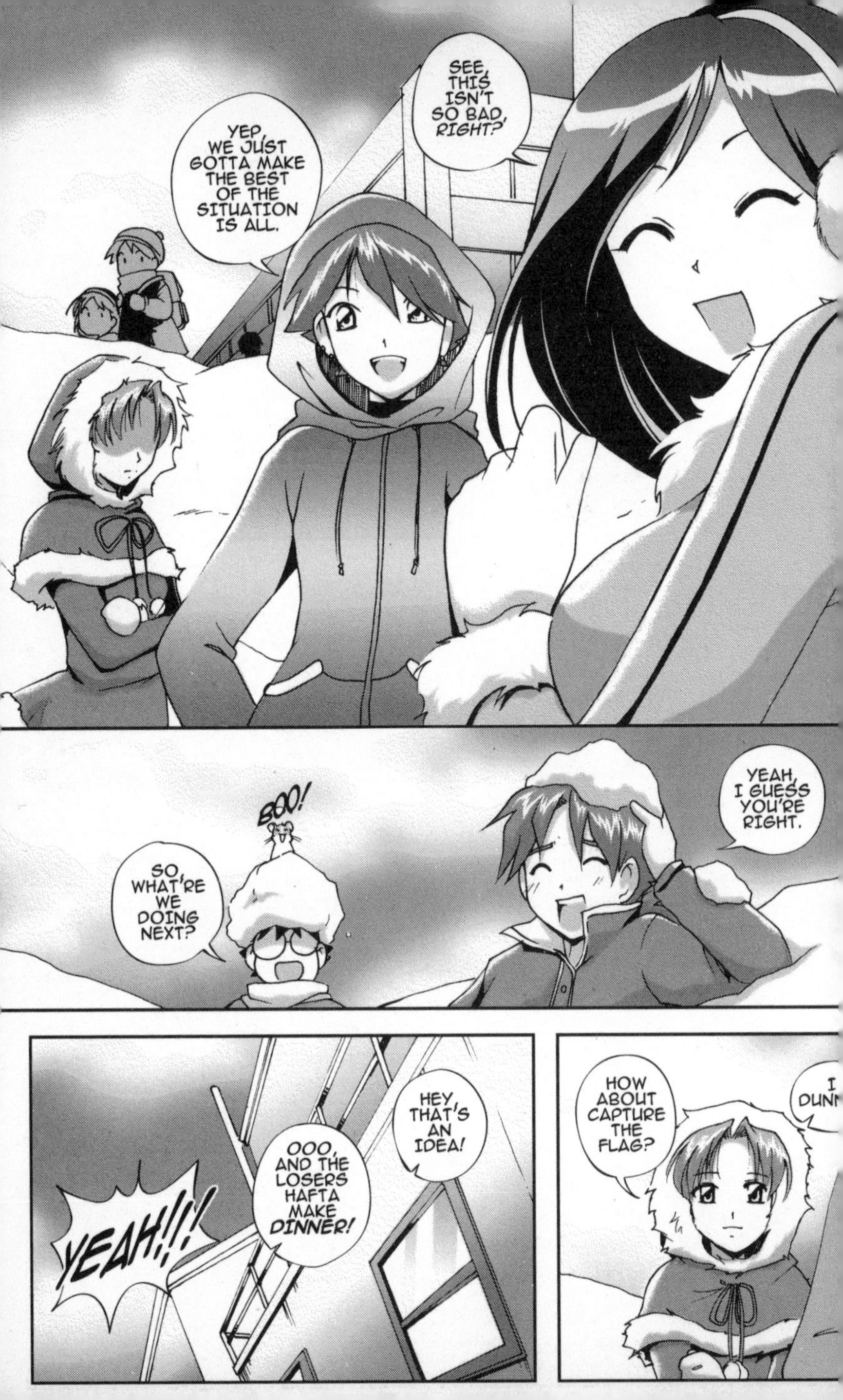
SEE, THIS ISN'T SO BAD, RIGHT?
YEP, WE JUST GOTTA MAKE THE BEST OF THE SITUATION IS ALL.
YEAH, I GUESS YOU'RE RIGHT.
BOO!
SO, WHAT'RE WE DOING NEXT?
I DUNN
HOW ABOUT CAPTURE THE FLAG?
HEY, THAT'S AN IDEA!
OOO, AND THE LOSERS HAFTA MAKE DINNER!
YEAH!!!

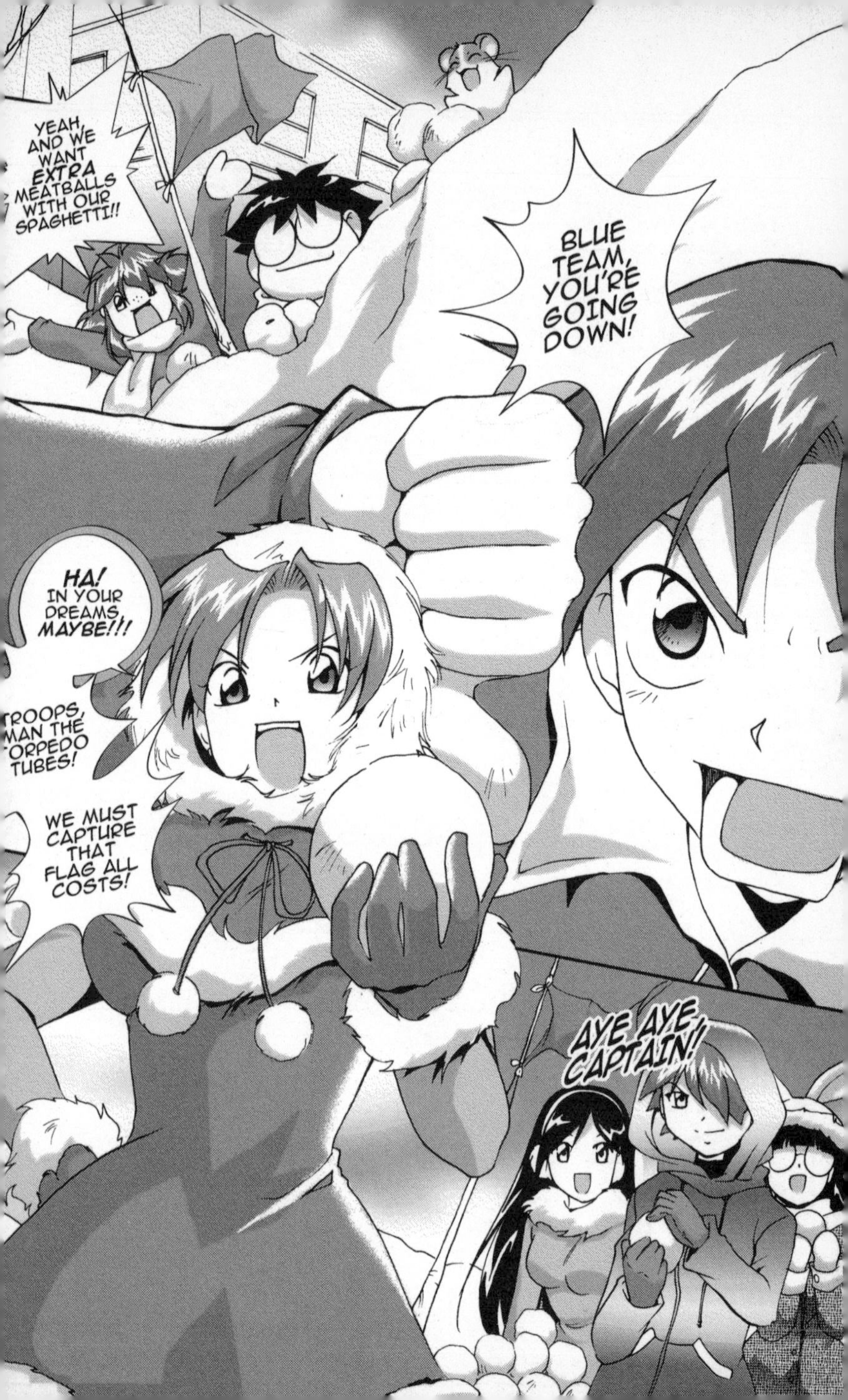
BLUE TEAM, YOU'RE GOING DOWN!
YEAH, AND WE WANT EXTRA MEATBALLS WITH OUR SPAGHETTI!!
HA! IN YOUR DREAMS MAYBE!!!
TROOPS, MAN THE TORPEDO TUBES!
WE MUST CAPTURE THAT FLAG ALL COSTS!
AYE AYE CAPTAIN!

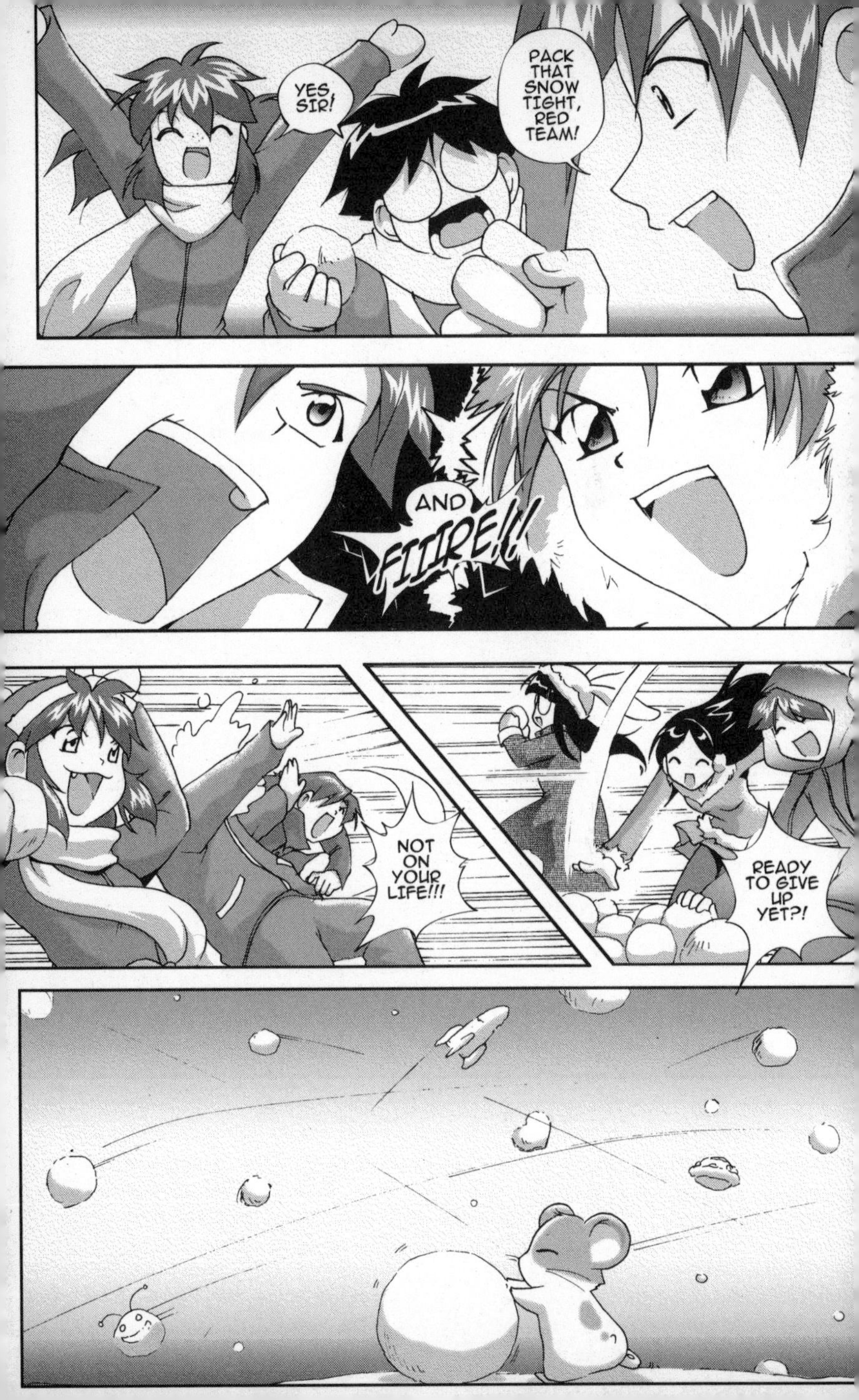
PACK THAT SNOW TIGHT, RED TEAM!
YES, SIR!
AND FIIIRE!!!
READY TO GIVE UP YET?!
NOT ON YOUR LIFE!!!

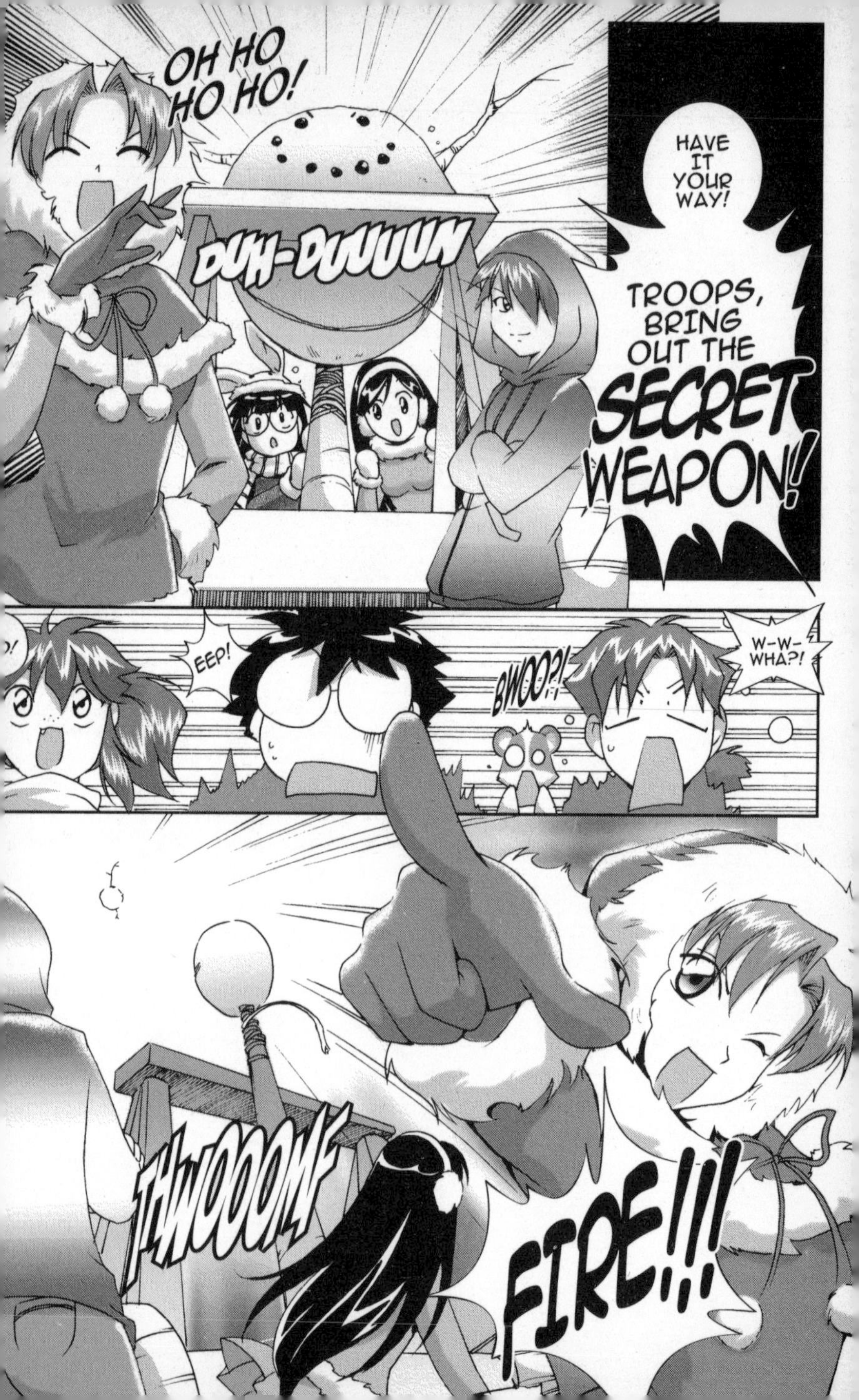
HAVE IT YOUR WAY!
TROOPS, BRING OUT THE SECRET WEAPON!!
OH HO HO HO!
DUH-DUUUUN
W-W-WHA?!
BWOO?!
EEP!
FIRE!!!
THWOOOM

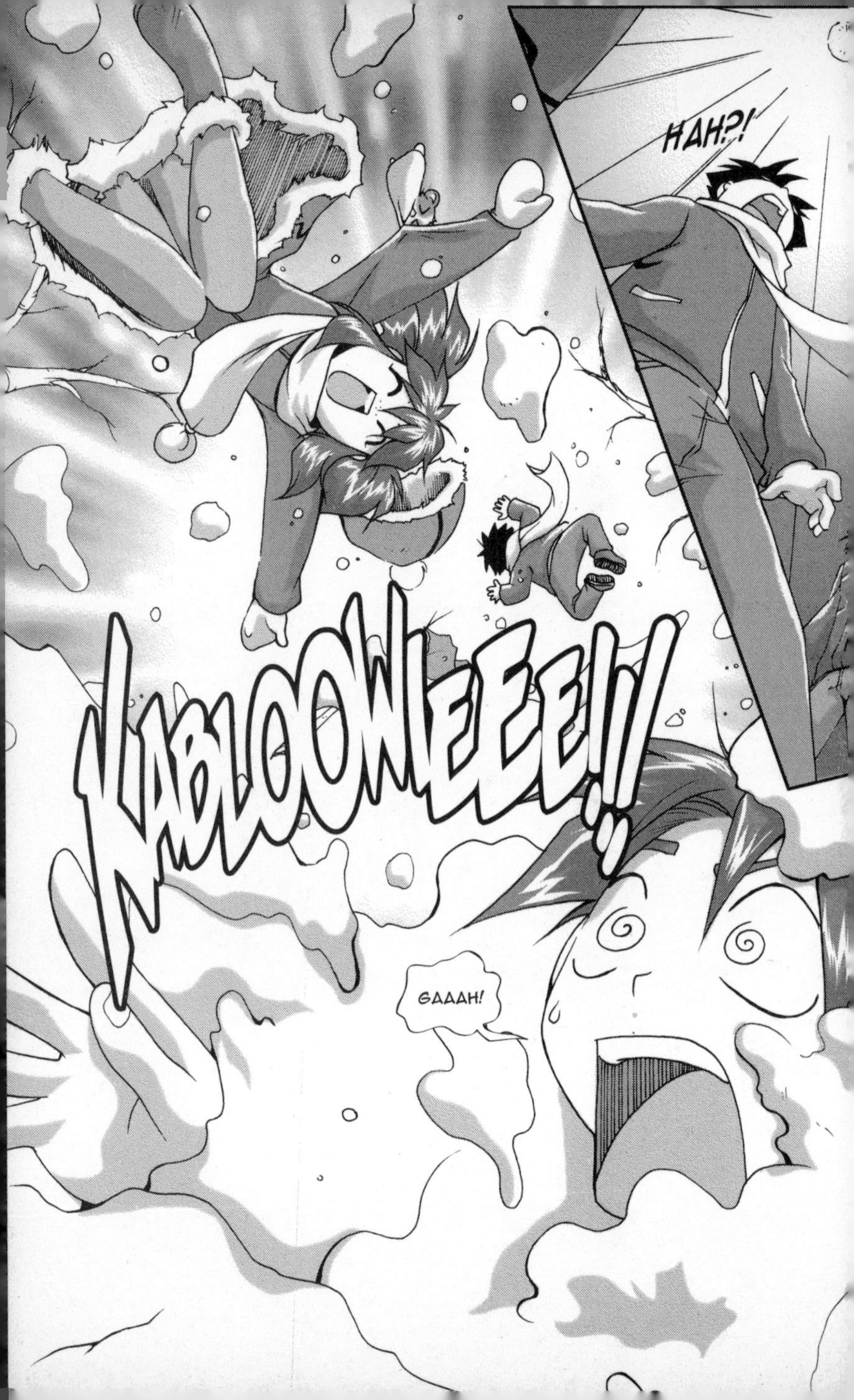
HAH?!
KABLOOWIEEE!!!
GAAAH!

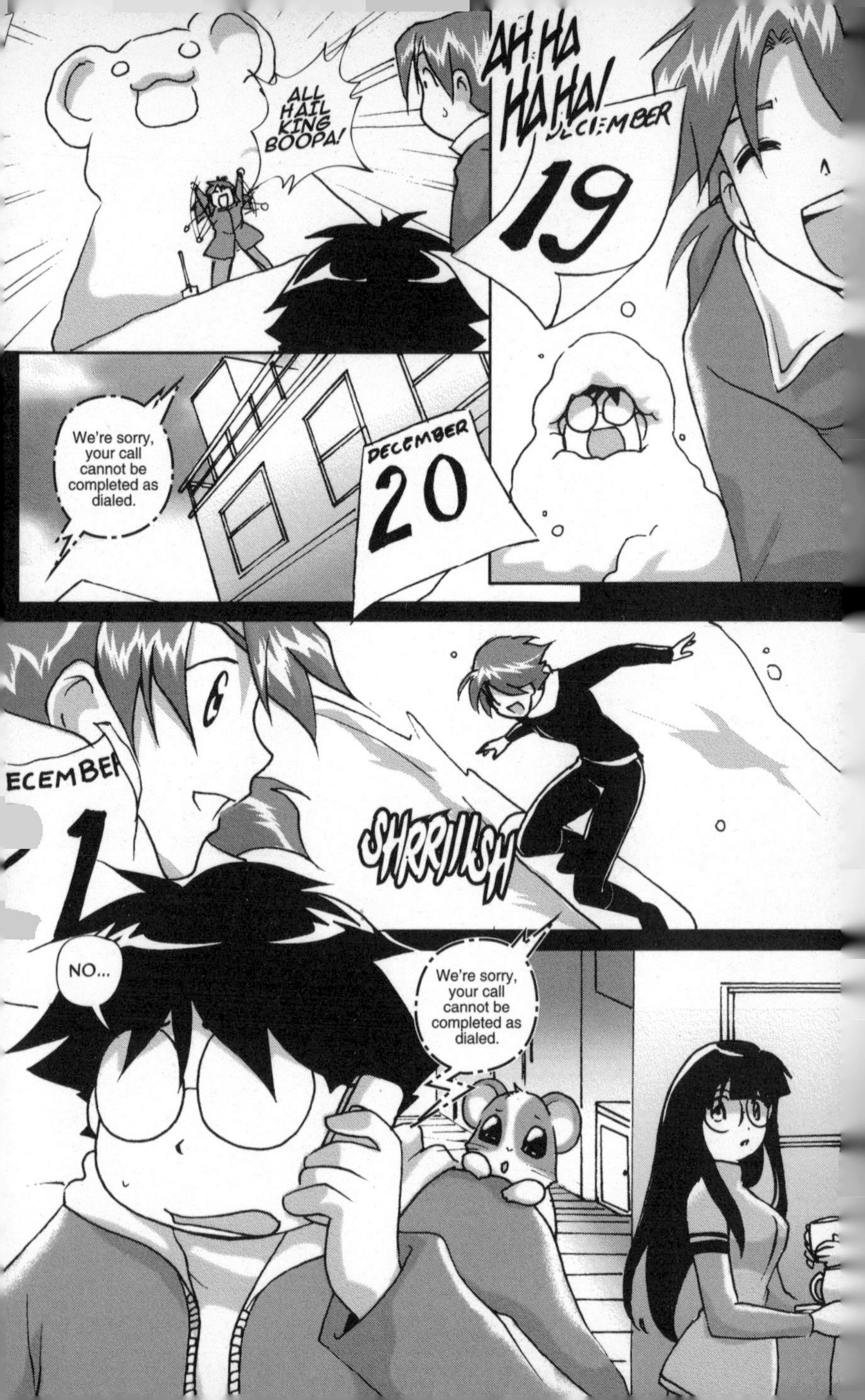
AH HA HA HA!
19
ALL HAIL KING BOOPA!
We're sorry, your call cannot be completed as dialed.
DECEMBER
20
SHRIIISH
ECEMBER
We're sorry, your call cannot be completed as dialed.
NO...

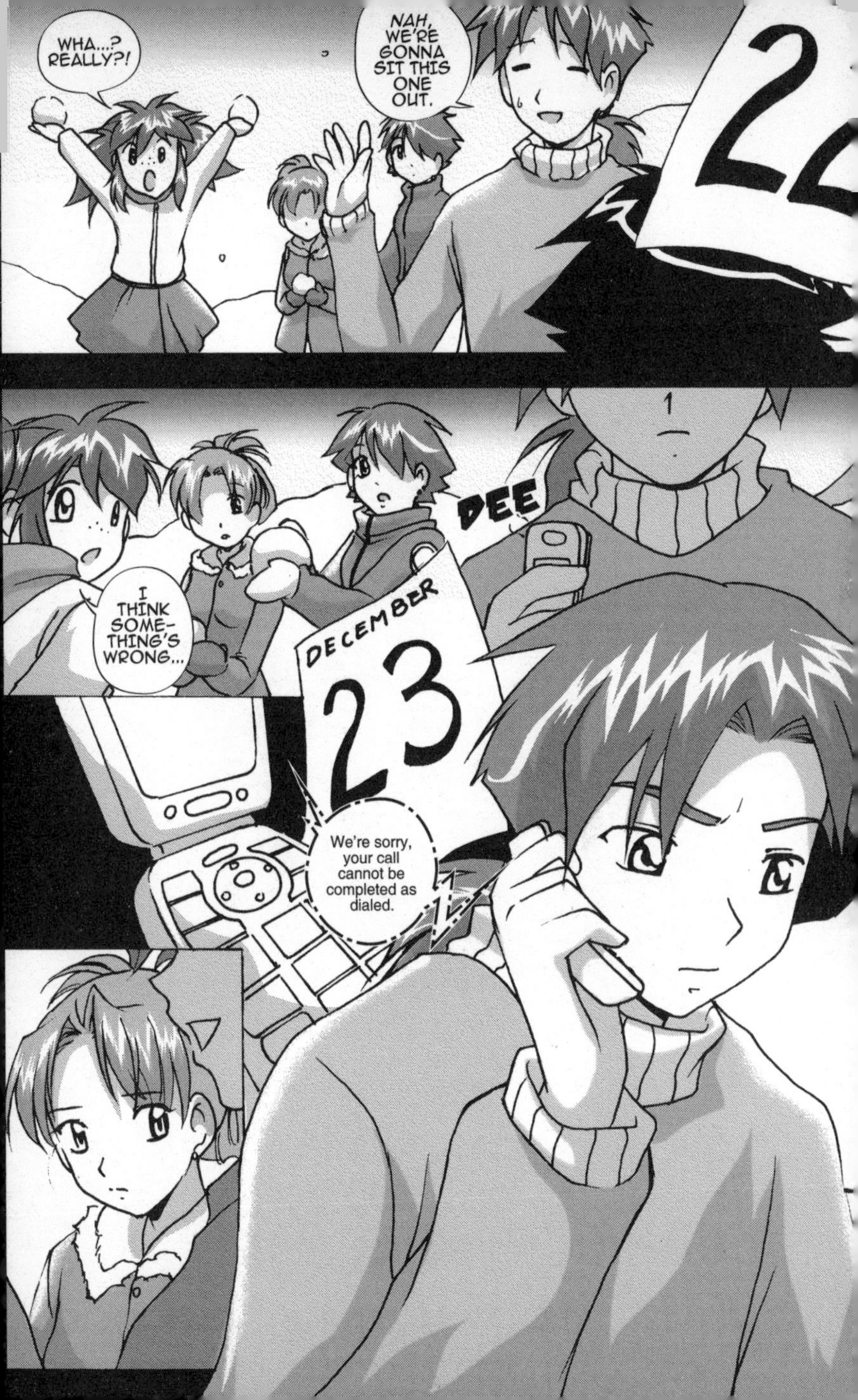
22
NAH, WE'RE GONNA SIT THIS ONE OUT.
WHA...? REALLY?!
DEE
I THINK SOMETHING'S WRONG...
DECEMBER 23
We're sorry, your call cannot be completed as dialed.

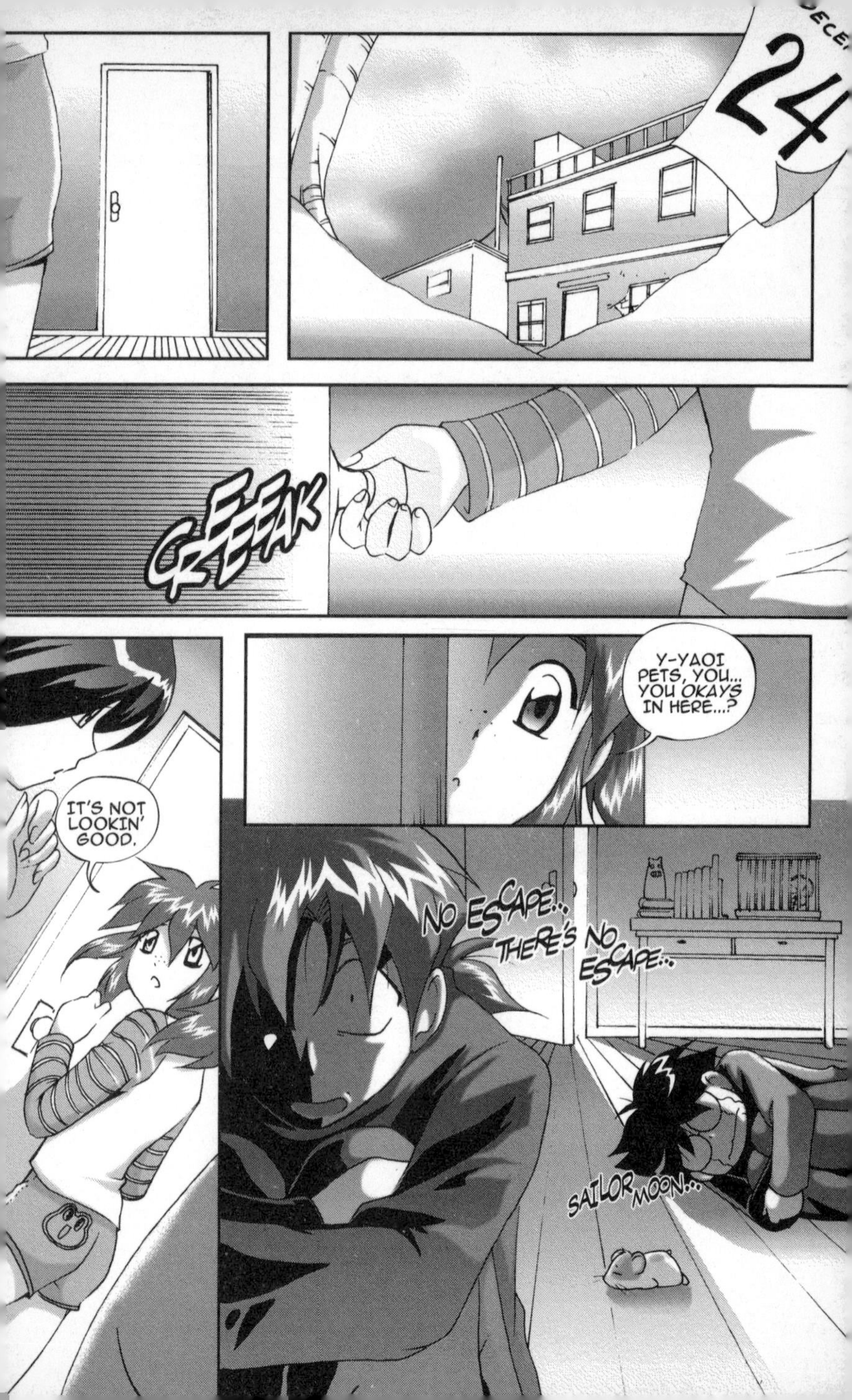
24
CREEEAK
Y-YAOI PETS, YOU... YOU OKAYS IN HERE...?
NO ESCAPE... THERE'S NO ESCAPE...
SAILOR MOON...
IT'S NOT LOOKIN' GOOD.

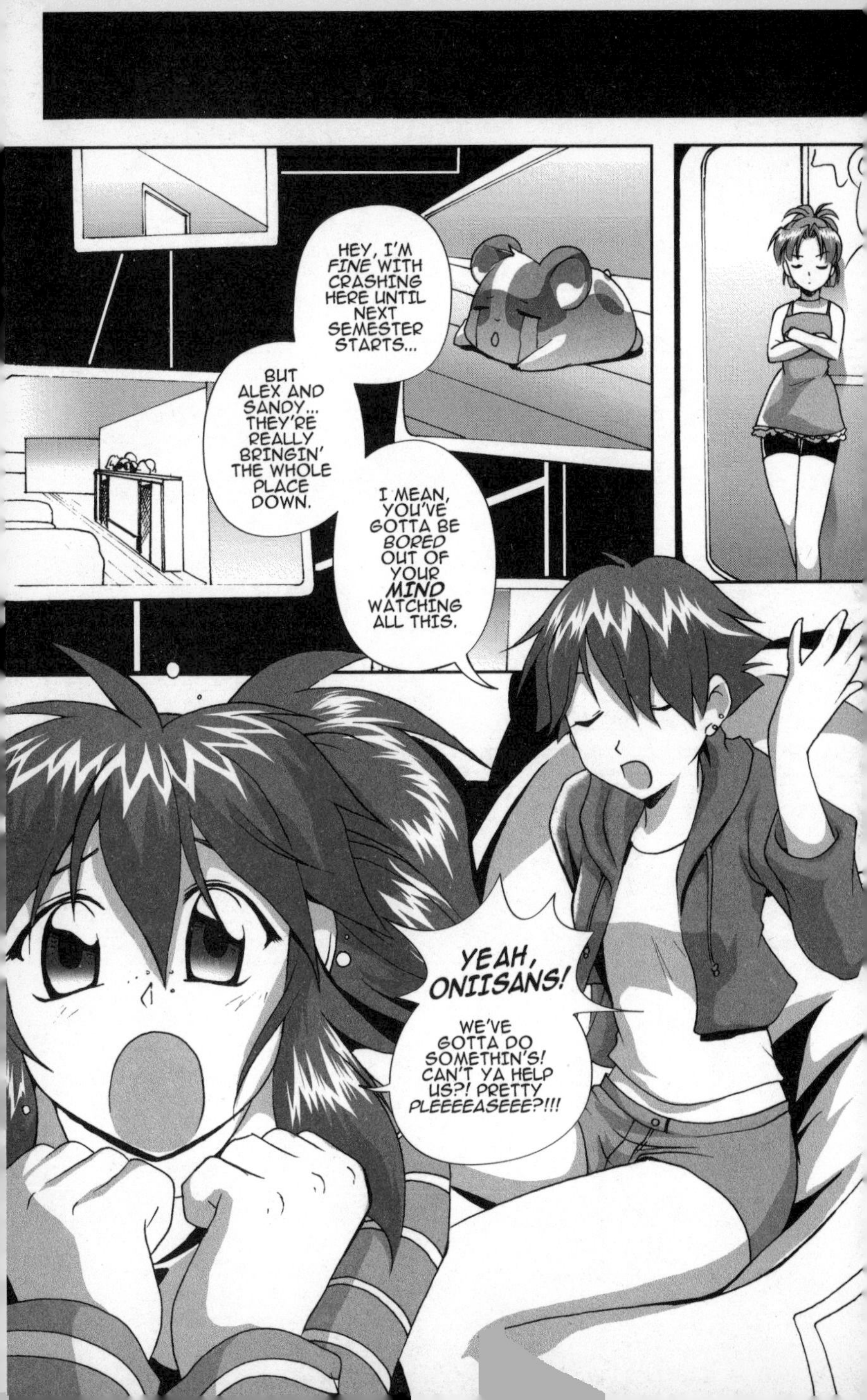
HEY, I'M *FINE* WITH CRASHING HERE UNTIL NEXT SEMESTER STARTS...
BUT ALEX AND SANDY... THEY'RE REALLY BRINGIN' THE WHOLE PLACE DOWN.
I MEAN, YOU'VE GOTTA BE *BORED* OUT OF YOUR ***MIND*** WATCHING ALL THIS.
YEAH, ONIISANS!
WE'VE GOTTA DO SOMETHIN'S! CAN'T YA HELP US?! PRETTY PLEEEEASEEE?!!!

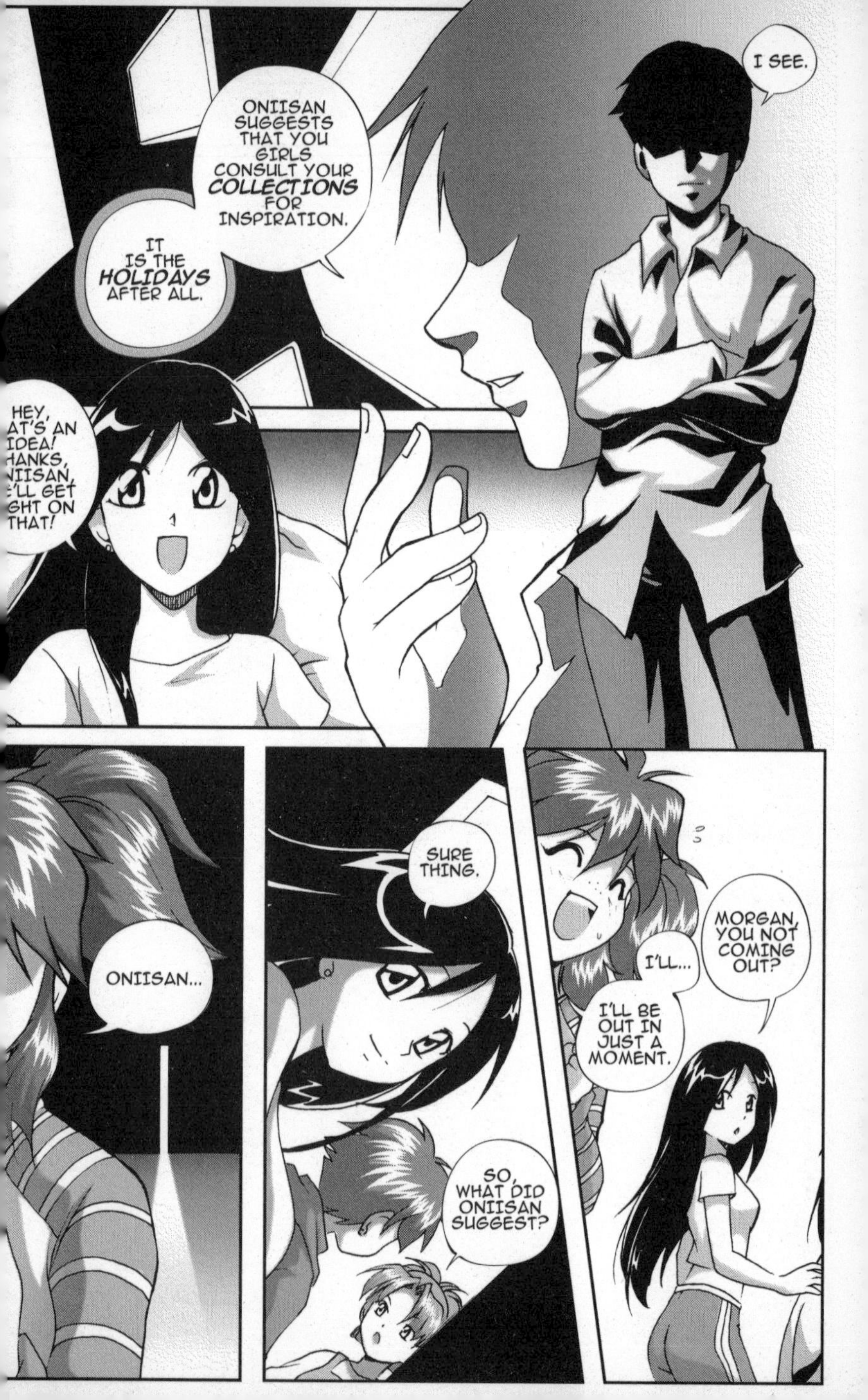
I SEE.
ONIISAN SUGGESTS THAT YOU GIRLS CONSULT YOUR ***COLLECTIONS*** FOR INSPIRATION.
IT IS THE ***HOLIDAYS*** AFTER ALL.
HEY, AT'S AN IDEA! HANKS, NIISAN, E'LL GET GHT ON THAT!
MORGAN, YOU NOT COMING OUT?
I'LL...
I'LL BE OUT IN JUST A MOMENT.
SURE THING.
SO, WHAT DID ONIISAN SUGGEST?
ONIISAN...

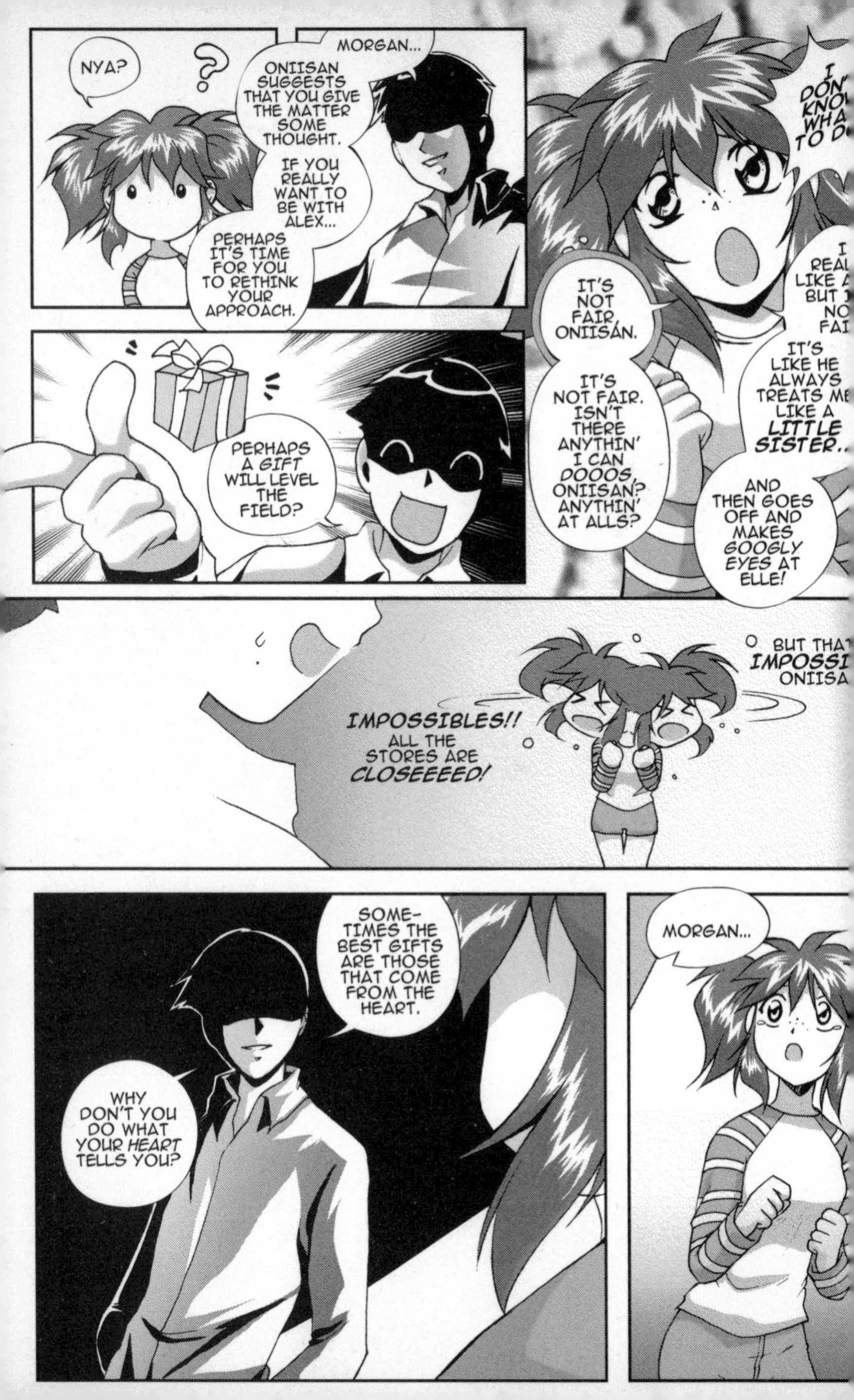
I DON' KNOW WHA TO D
I REAL LIKE A BUT I NO FAI
IT'S NOT FAIR, ONIISAN.
IT'S LIKE HE ALWAYS TREATS ME LIKE A LITTLE SISTER..
AND THEN GOES OFF AND MAKES GOOGLY EYES AT ELLE!
IT'S NOT FAIR. ISN'T THERE ANYTHIN' I CAN DOOOS, ONIISAN? ANYTHIN' AT ALLS?
MORGAN...
ONIISAN SUGGESTS THAT YOU GIVE THE MATTER SOME THOUGHT.
IF YOU REALLY WANT TO BE WITH ALEX...
PERHAPS IT'S TIME FOR YOU TO RETHINK YOUR APPROACH.
NYA?
PERHAPS A GIFT WILL LEVEL THE FIELD?
BUT THA IMPOSSI ONIISA
IMPOSSIBLES!! ALL THE STORES ARE CLOSEEEED!
MORGAN...
SOME-TIMES THE BEST GIFTS ARE THOSE THAT COME FROM THE HEART.
WHY DON'T YOU DO WHAT YOUR HEART TELLS YOU?

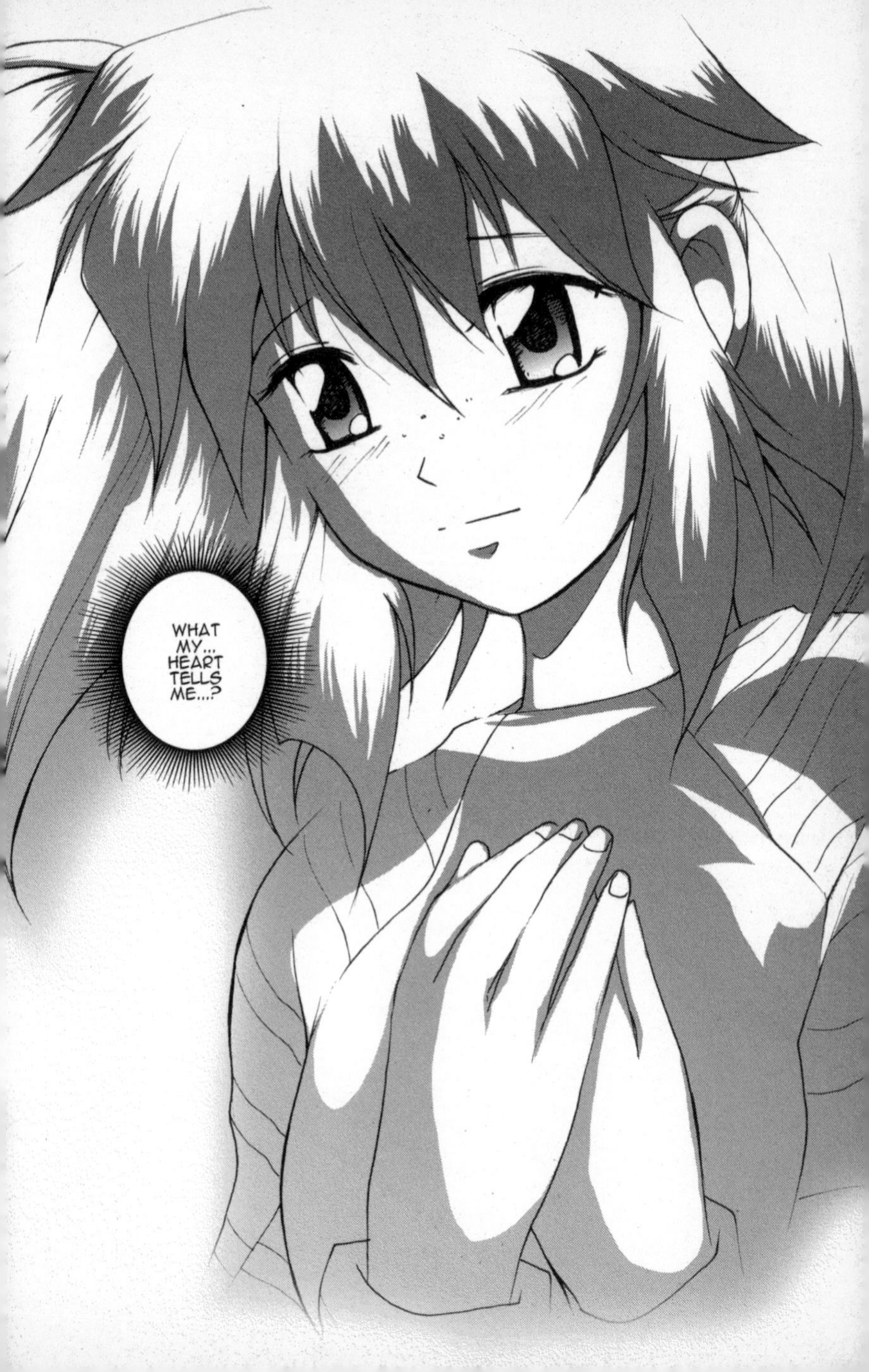
WHAT MY... HEART TELLS ME...?

EPISODE 13:
EVERGREEN PARTY NIGHT

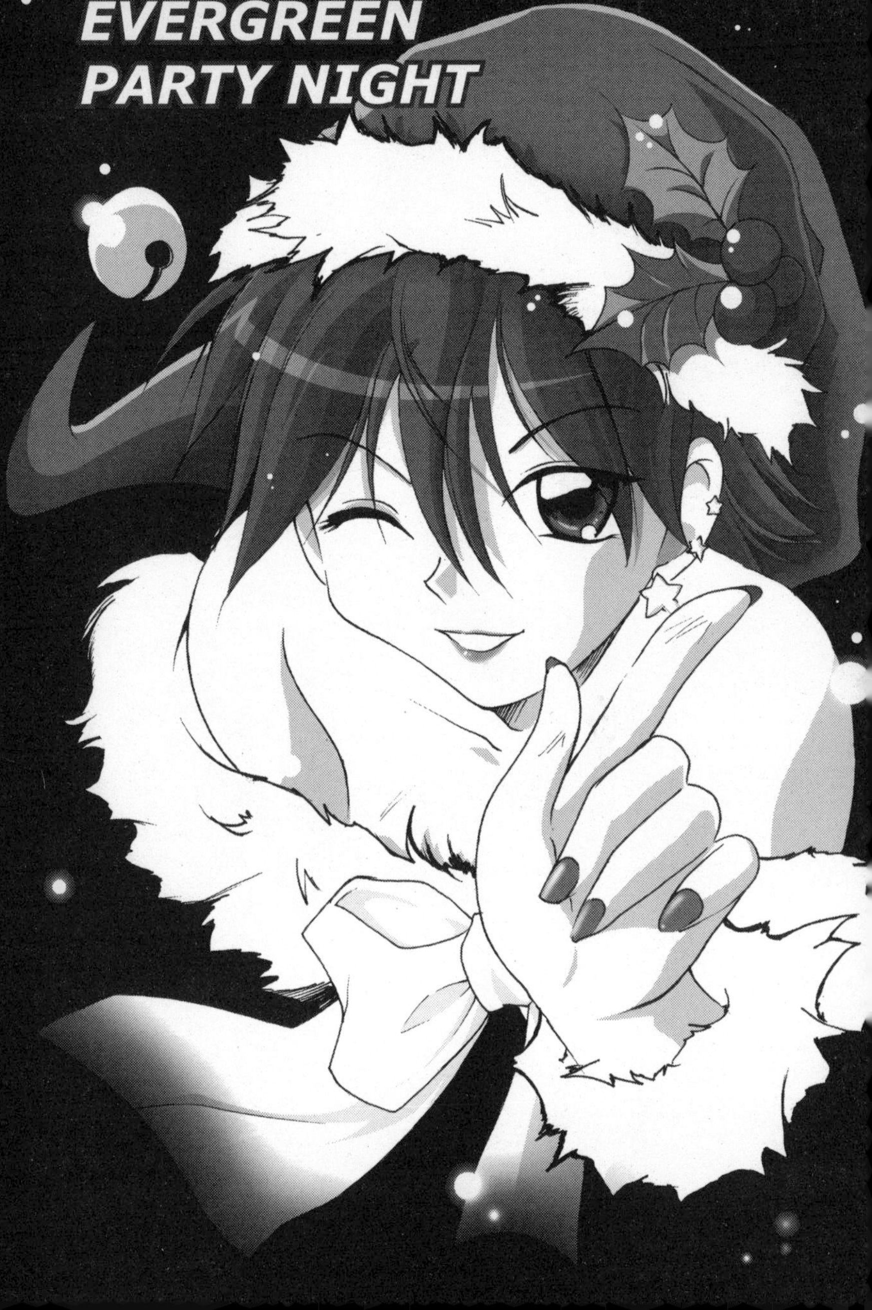

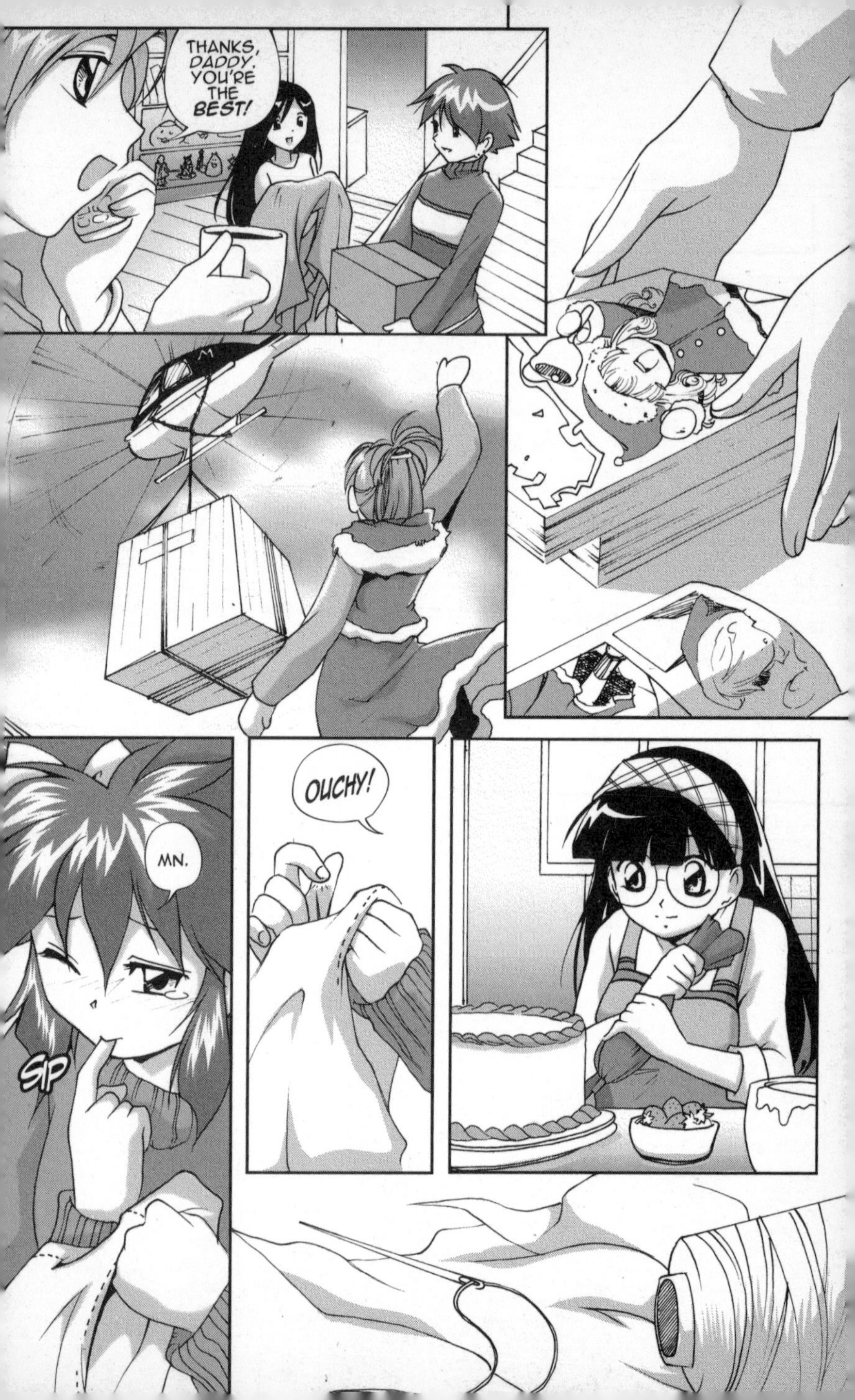
THANKS, DADDY. YOU'RE THE BEST!
OUCHY!
MN.
SIP

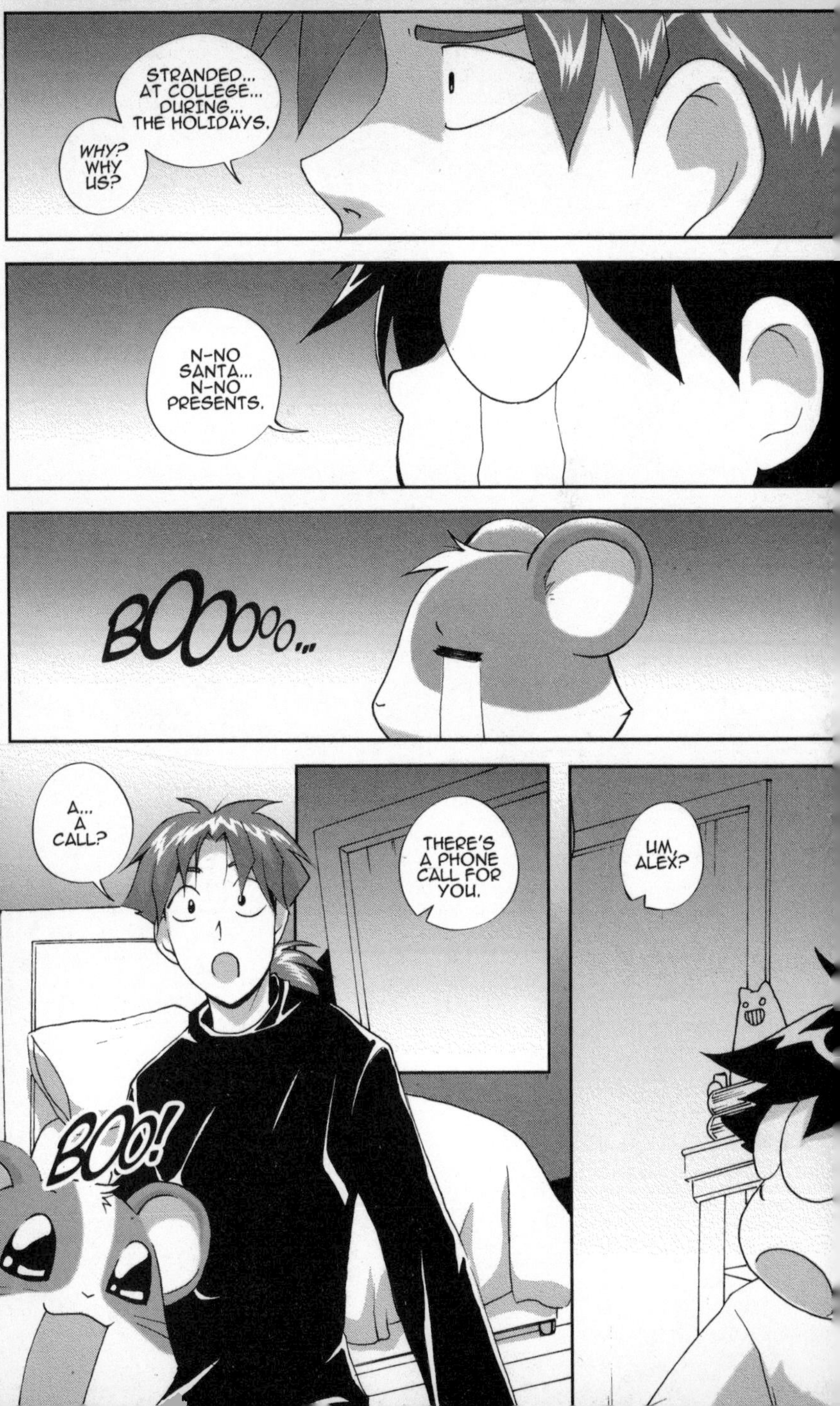
STRANDED... AT COLLEGE... DURING... THE HOLIDAYS.
WHY? WHY US?
N-NO SANTA... N-NO PRESENTS.
BOOOOO...
UM, ALEX?
THERE'S A PHONE CALL FOR YOU.
A... A CALL?
BOO!

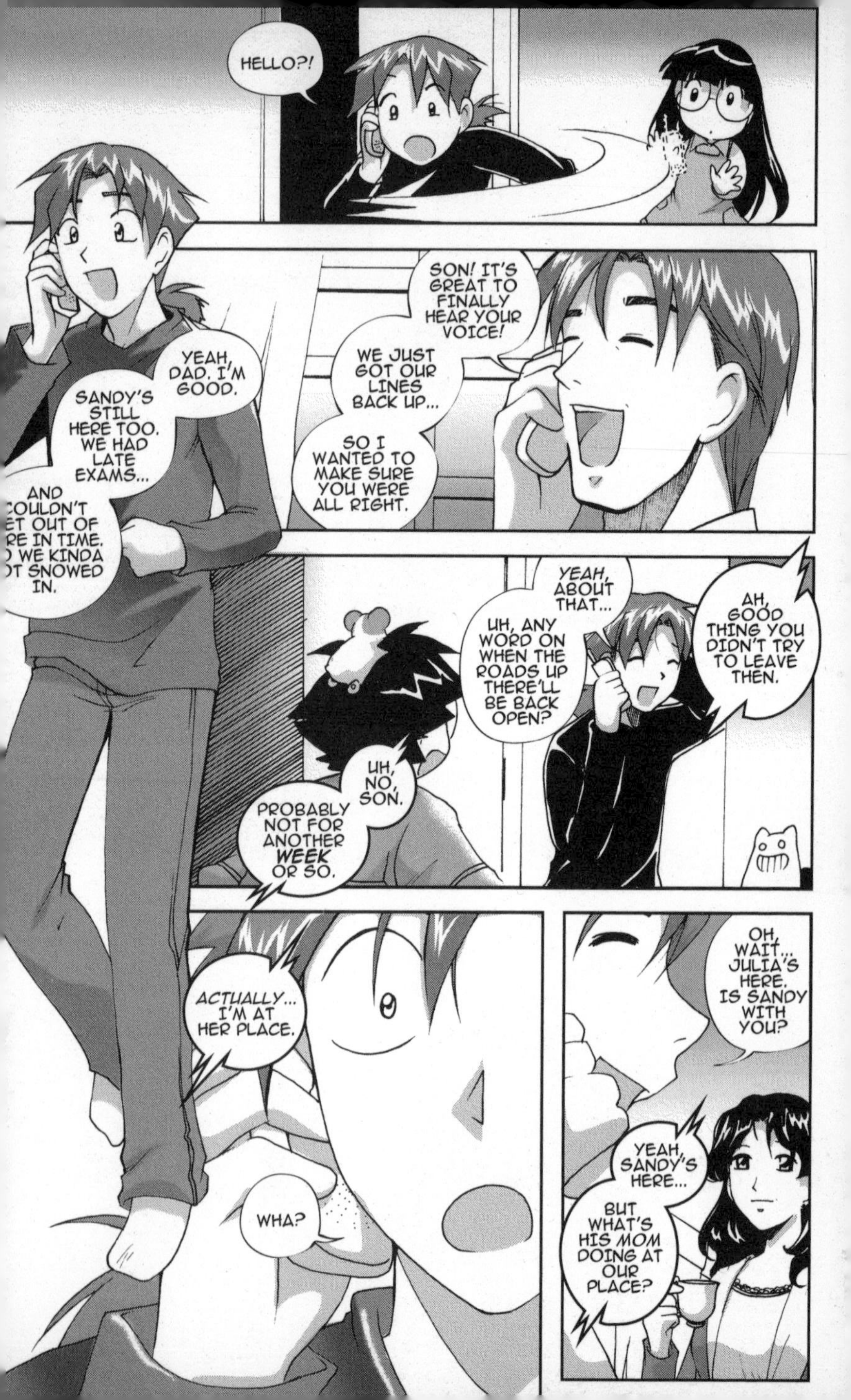
HELLO?!
SON! IT'S GREAT TO FINALLY HEAR YOUR VOICE!
WE JUST GOT OUR LINES BACK UP...
SO I WANTED TO MAKE SURE YOU WERE ALL RIGHT.
YEAH, DAD. I'M GOOD.
SANDY'S STILL HERE TOO. WE HAD LATE EXAMS...
AND COULDN'T ET OUT OF RE IN TIME. D WE KINDA OT SNOWED IN.
AH, GOOD THING YOU DIDN'T TRY TO LEAVE THEN.
YEAH, ABOUT THAT...
UH, ANY WORD ON WHEN THE ROADS UP THERE'LL BE BACK OPEN?
UH, NO, SON.
PROBABLY NOT FOR ANOTHER WEEK OR SO.
OH, WAIT... JULIA'S HERE. IS SANDY WITH YOU?
YEAH, SANDY'S HERE...
BUT WHAT'S HIS MOM DOING AT OUR PLACE?
ACTUALLY... I'M AT HER PLACE.
WHA?

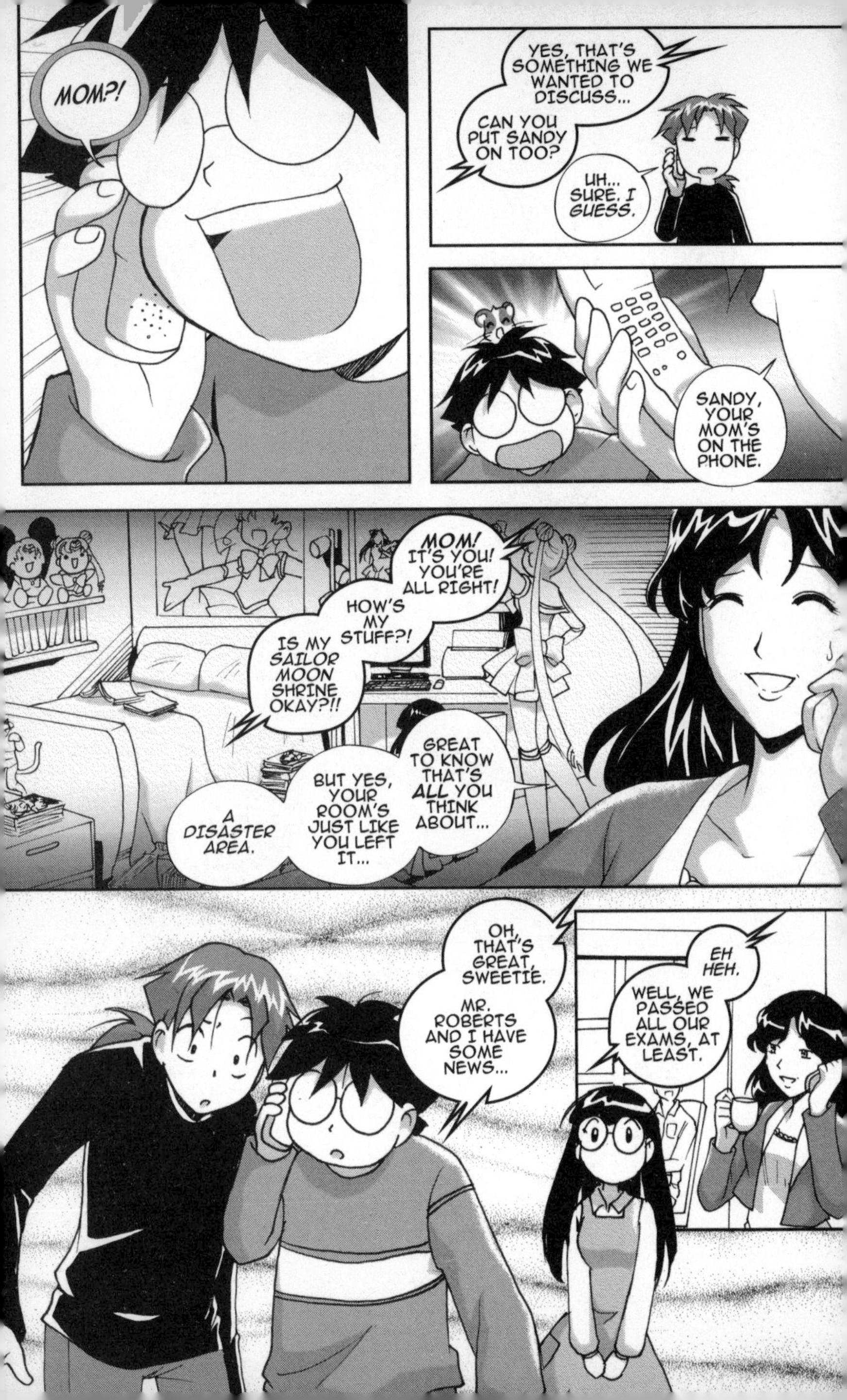
YES, THAT'S SOMETHING WE WANTED TO DISCUSS...
CAN YOU PUT SANDY ON TOO?
UH... SURE. I GUESS.
SANDY, YOUR MOM'S ON THE PHONE.
MOM?!
MOM! IT'S YOU! YOU'RE ALL RIGHT!
HOW'S MY STUFF?!
IS MY SAILOR MOON SHRINE OKAY?!!
GREAT TO KNOW THAT'S ALL YOU THINK ABOUT...
BUT YES, YOUR ROOM'S JUST LIKE YOU LEFT IT...
A DISASTER AREA.
EH HEH.
WELL, WE PASSED ALL OUR EXAMS, AT LEAST.
OH, THAT'S GREAT, SWEETIE.
MR. ROBERTS AND I HAVE SOME NEWS...

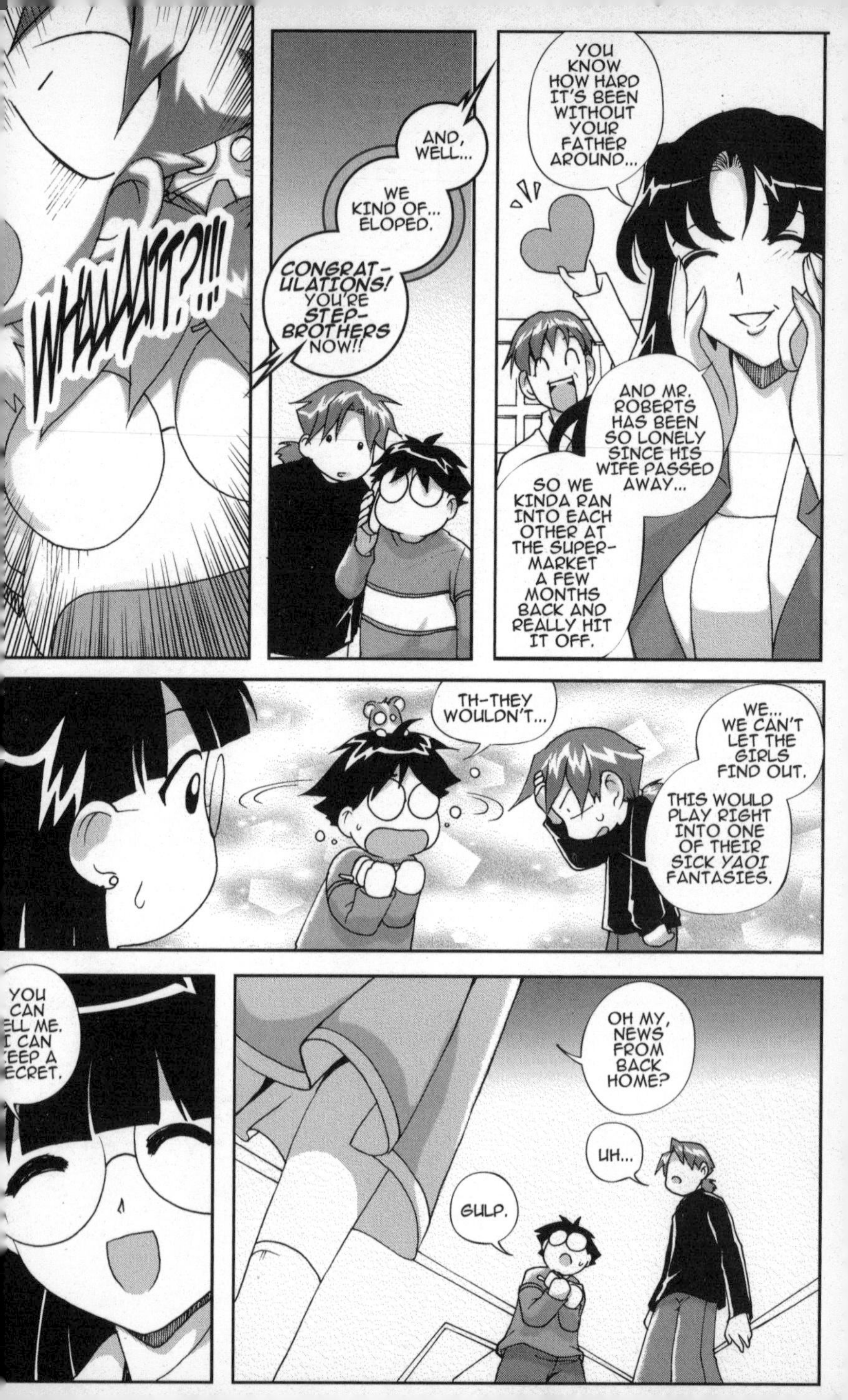
YOU KNOW HOW HARD IT'S BEEN WITHOUT YOUR FATHER AROUND...
AND MR. ROBERTS HAS BEEN SO LONELY SINCE HIS WIFE PASSED AWAY...
SO WE KINDA RAN INTO EACH OTHER AT THE SUPER-MARKET A FEW MONTHS BACK AND REALLY HIT IT OFF.
AND, WELL...
WE KIND OF... ELOPED.
CONGRATULATIONS! YOU'RE STEP-BROTHERS NOW!!
WHAAAT?!!!
WE... WE CAN'T LET THE GIRLS FIND OUT.
THIS WOULD PLAY RIGHT INTO ONE OF THEIR SICK YAOI FANTASIES.
TH-THEY WOULDN'T...
OH MY, NEWS FROM BACK HOME?
UH...
GULP.
YOU CAN ELL ME. I CAN EEP A ECRET.

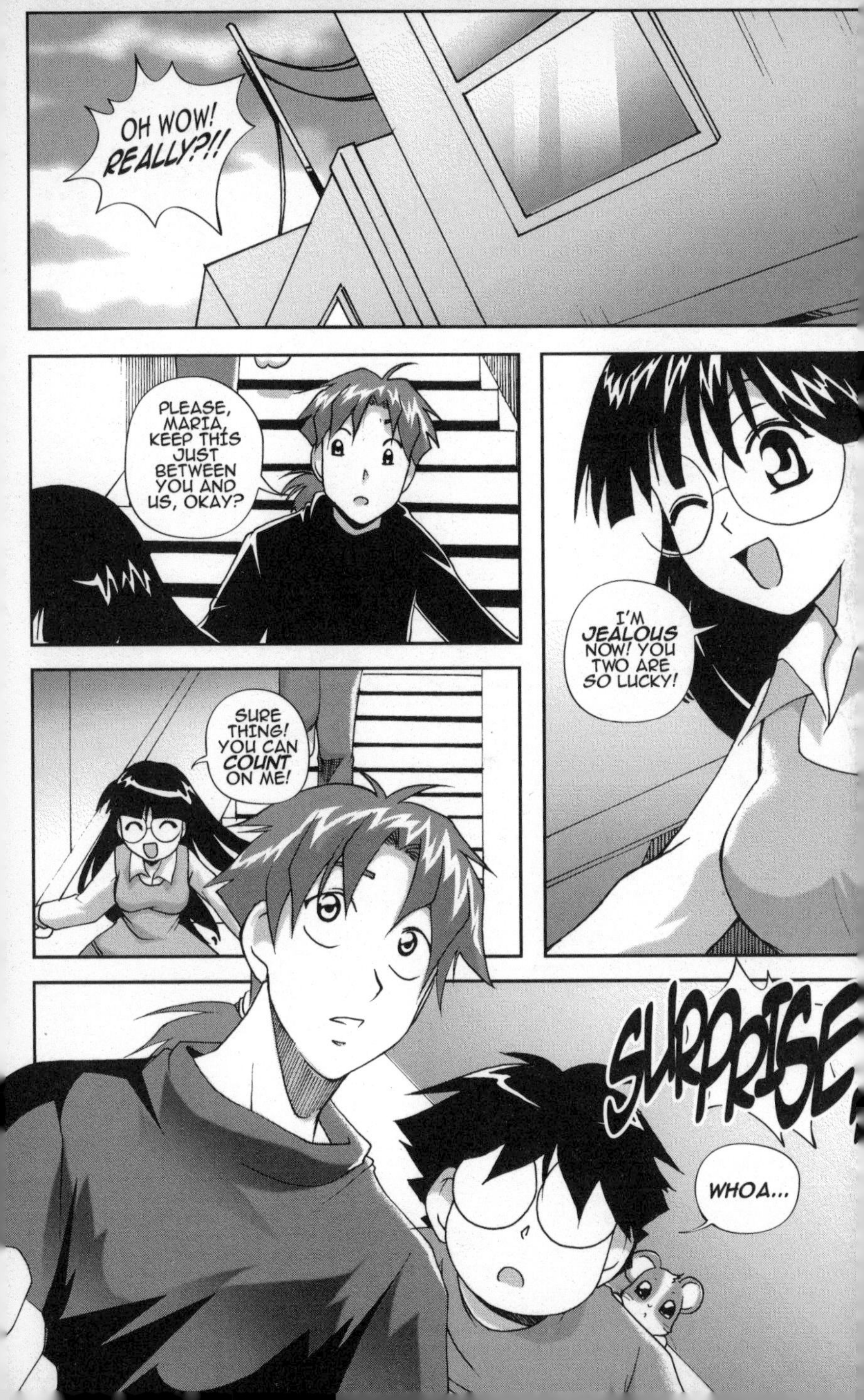
OH WOW! REALLY?!!
I'M JEALOUS NOW! YOU TWO ARE SO LUCKY!
PLEASE, MARIA, KEEP THIS JUST BETWEEN YOU AND US, OKAY?
SURE THING! YOU CAN COUNT ON ME!
SURPRISE
WHOA...

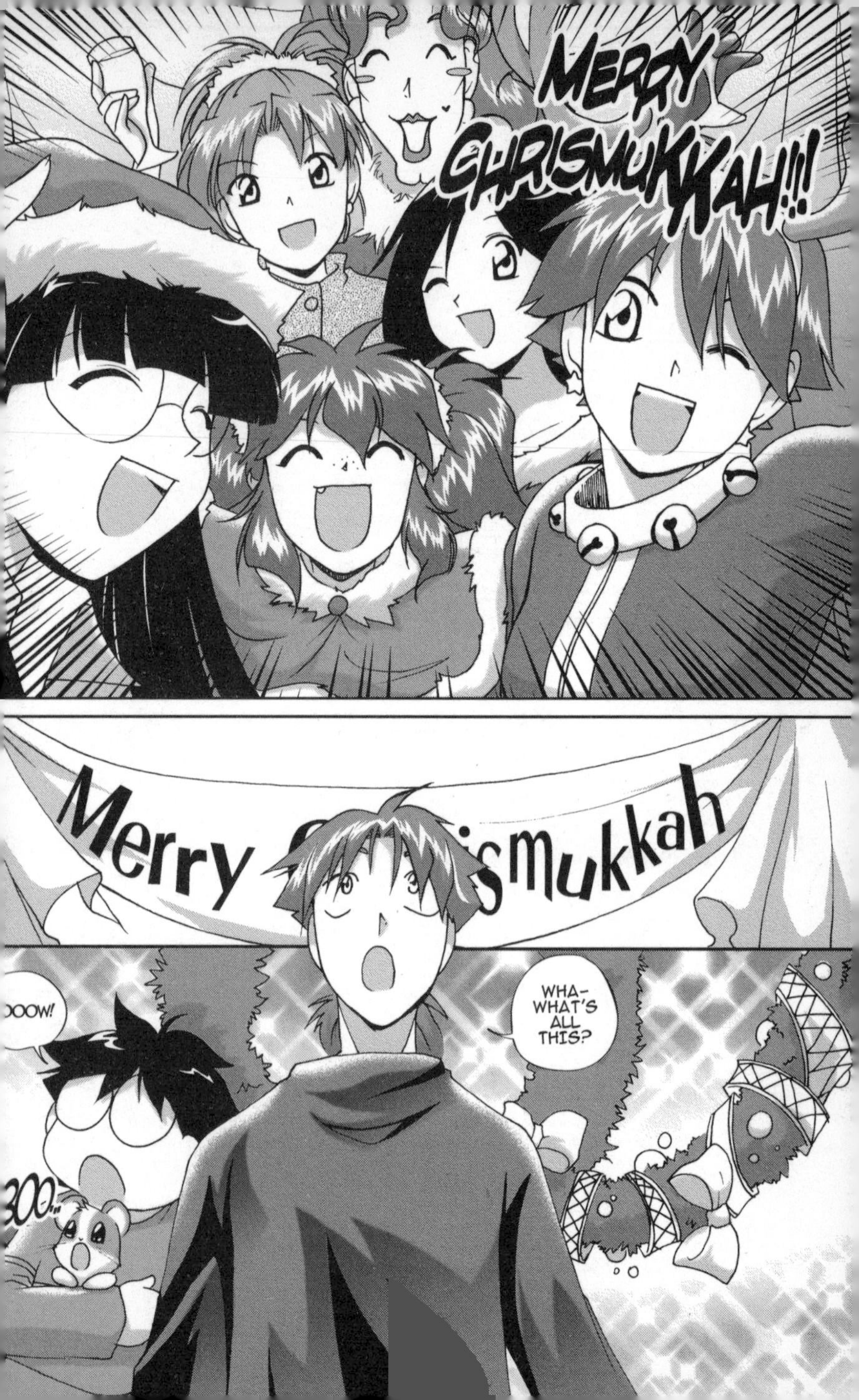
MERRY CHRISMUKKAH!!!
Merry
ismukkah
WHA-WHAT'S ALL THIS?
OOOW!

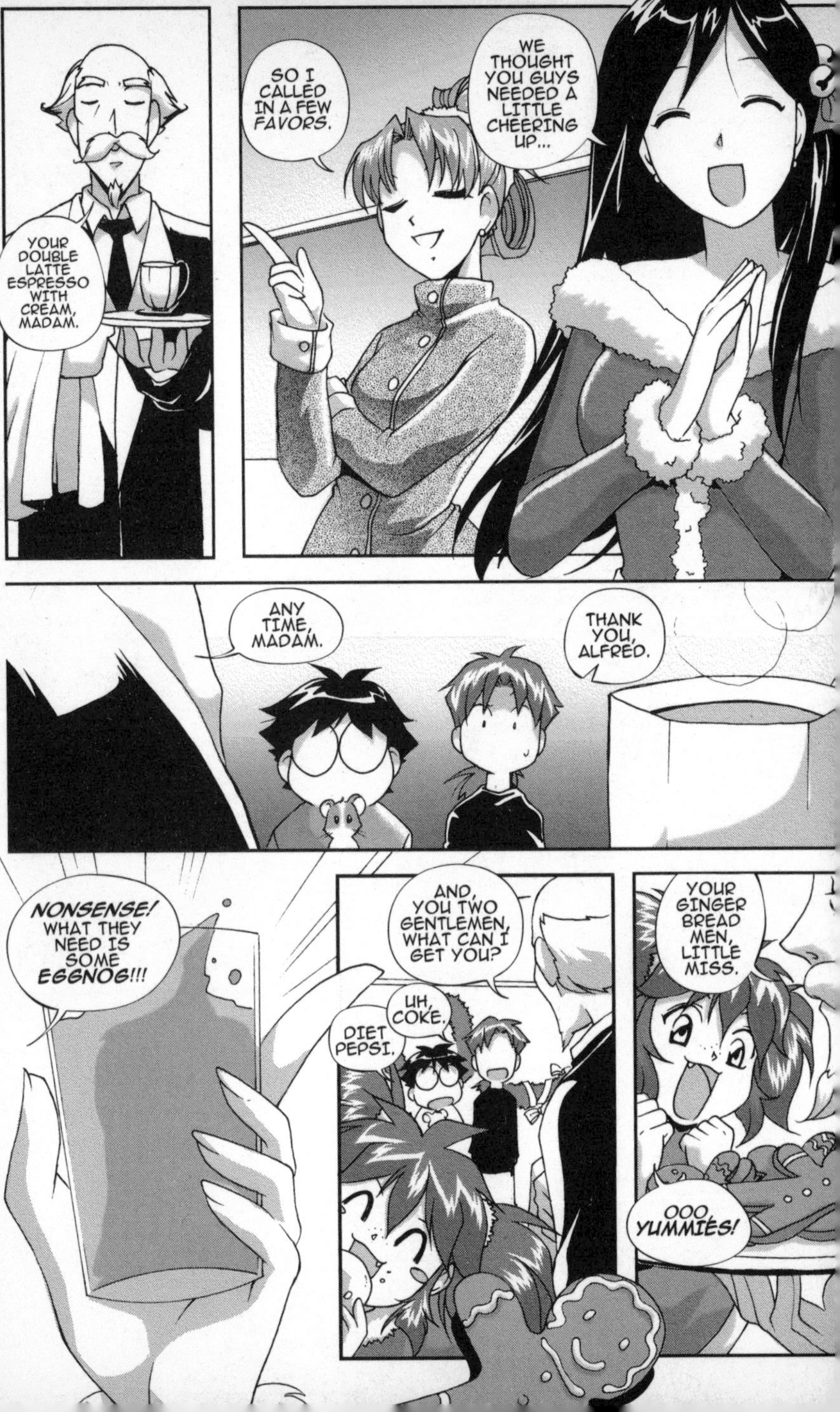
WE THOUGHT YOU GUYS NEEDED A LITTLE CHEERING UP...
SO I CALLED IN A FEW FAVORS.
YOUR DOUBLE LATTE ESPRESSO WITH CREAM, MADAM.
THANK YOU, ALFRED.
ANY TIME, MADAM.
YOUR GINGER BREAD MEN, LITTLE MISS.
OOO YUMMIES!
AND, YOU TWO GENTLEMEN, WHAT CAN I GET YOU?
UH, COKE.
DIET PEPSI.
NONSENSE! WHAT THEY NEED IS SOME EGGNOG!!!

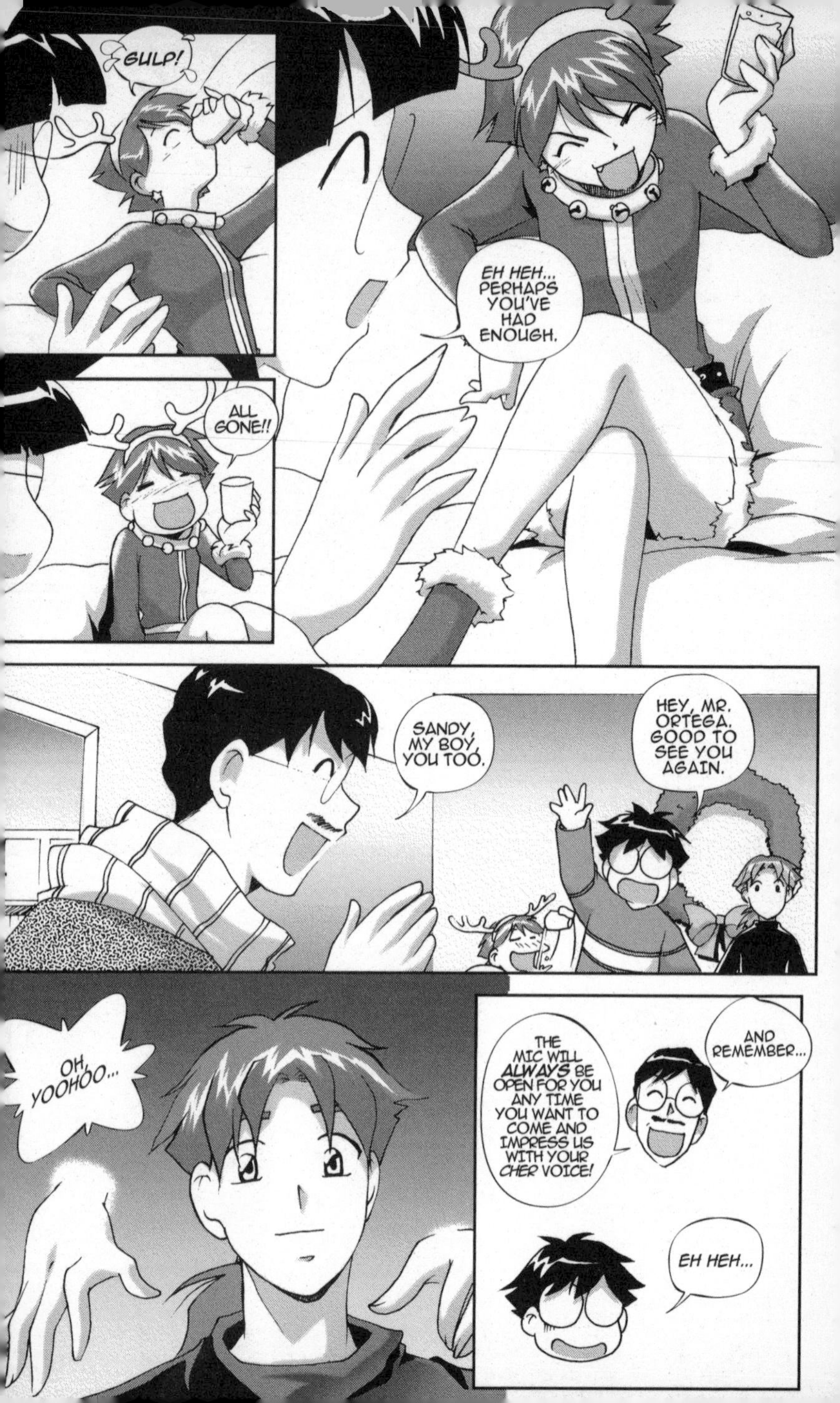
EH HEH... PERHAPS YOU'VE HAD ENOUGH.
GULP!
ALL GONE!!
HEY, MR. ORTEGA. GOOD TO SEE YOU AGAIN.
SANDY, MY BOY, YOU TOO.
AND REMEMBER...
THE MIC WILL *ALWAYS* BE OPEN FOR YOU ANY TIME YOU WANT TO COME AND IMPRESS US WITH YOUR *CHER* VOICE!
EH HEH...
OH, YOOHOO...

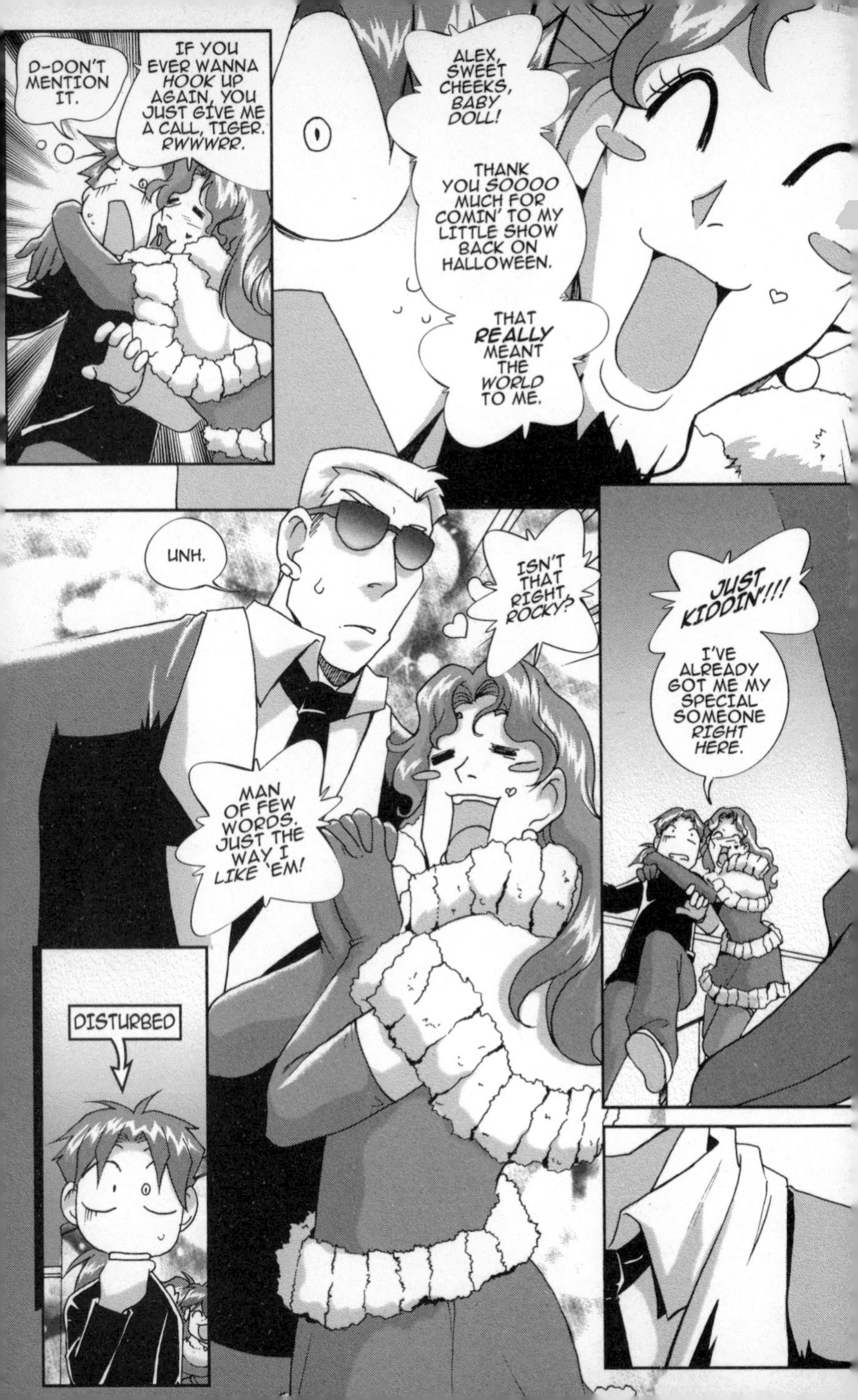
ALEX, SWEET CHEEKS, BABY DOLL!
THANK YOU SOOOO MUCH FOR COMIN' TO MY LITTLE SHOW BACK ON HALLOWEEN.
THAT REALLY MEANT THE WORLD TO ME.
IF YOU EVER WANNA HOOK UP AGAIN, YOU JUST GIVE ME A CALL, TIGER. RWWWRR.
D-DON'T MENTION IT.
JUST KIDDIN'!!!
I'VE ALREADY GOT ME MY SPECIAL SOMEONE RIGHT HERE.
ISN'T THAT RIGHT, ROCKY?
UNH.
MAN OF FEW WORDS. JUST THE WAY I LIKE 'EM!
DISTURBED

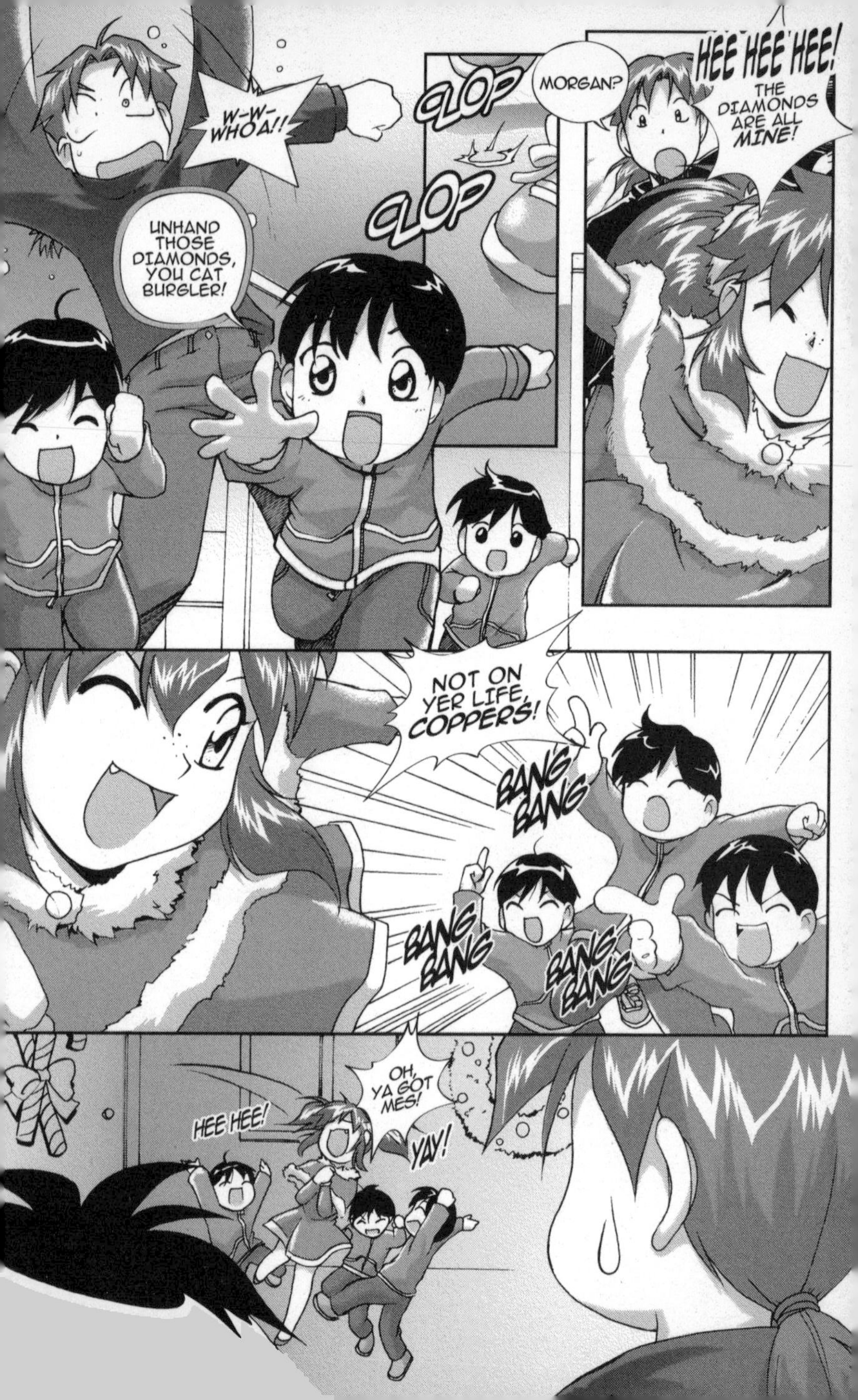
HEE HEE HEE!
THE DIAMONDS ARE ALL MINE!
MORGAN?
CLOP
CLOP
W-W-WHOA!!
UNHAND THOSE DIAMONDS, YOU CAT BURGLER!
NOT ON YER LIFE, COPPERS!
BANG BANG
BANG BANG
BANG BANG
OH, YA GOT MES!
YAY!
HEE HEE!

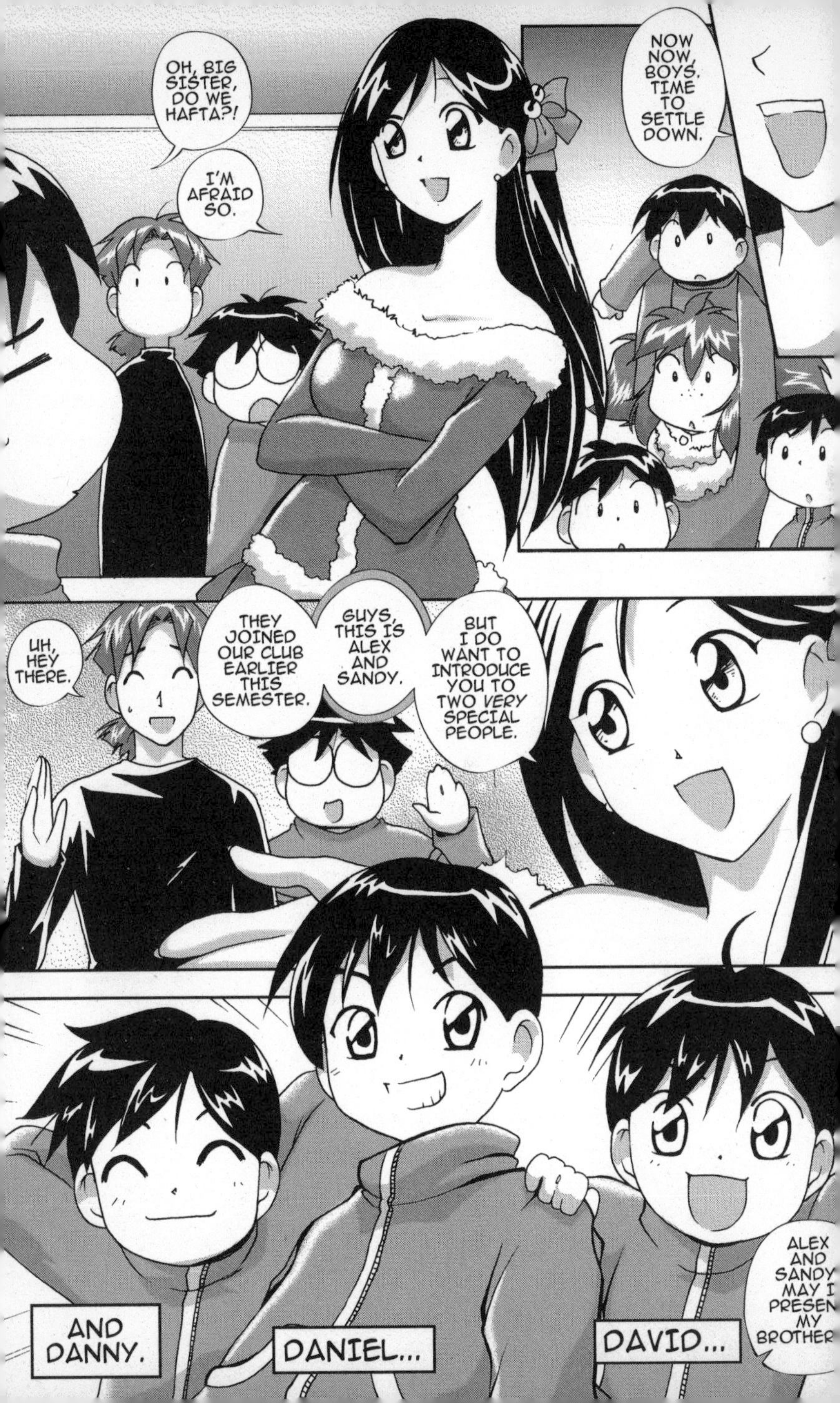
NOW NOW, BOYS. TIME TO SETTLE DOWN.
OH, BIG SISTER, DO WE HAFTA?!
I'M AFRAID SO.
BUT I DO WANT TO INTRODUCE YOU TO TWO *VERY* SPECIAL PEOPLE.
GUYS, THIS IS ALEX AND SANDY.
THEY JOINED OUR CLUB EARLIER THIS SEMESTER.
UH, HEY THERE.
ALEX AND SANDY MAY I PRESEN MY BROTHER
DAVID...
DANIEL...
AND DANNY.

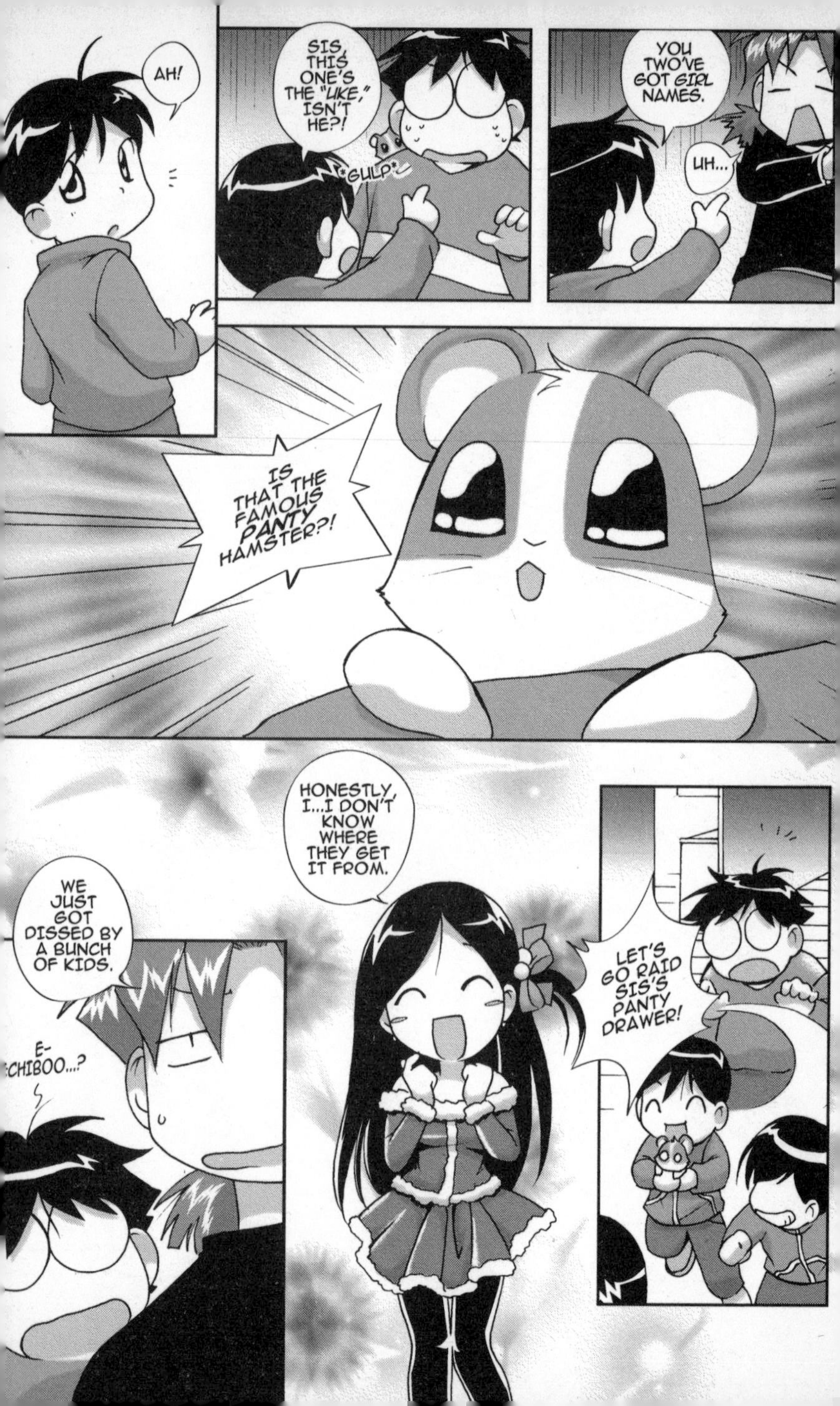
YOU TWO'VE GOT GIRL NAMES.
UH...
SIS, THIS ONE'S THE "UKE," ISN'T HE?!
GULP
AH!
IS THAT THE FAMOUS PANTY HAMSTER?!
LET'S GO RAID SIS'S PANTY DRAWER!
HONESTLY, I...I DON'T KNOW WHERE THEY GET IT FROM.
WE JUST GOT DISSED BY A BUNCH OF KIDS.
E-ECHIBOO...?

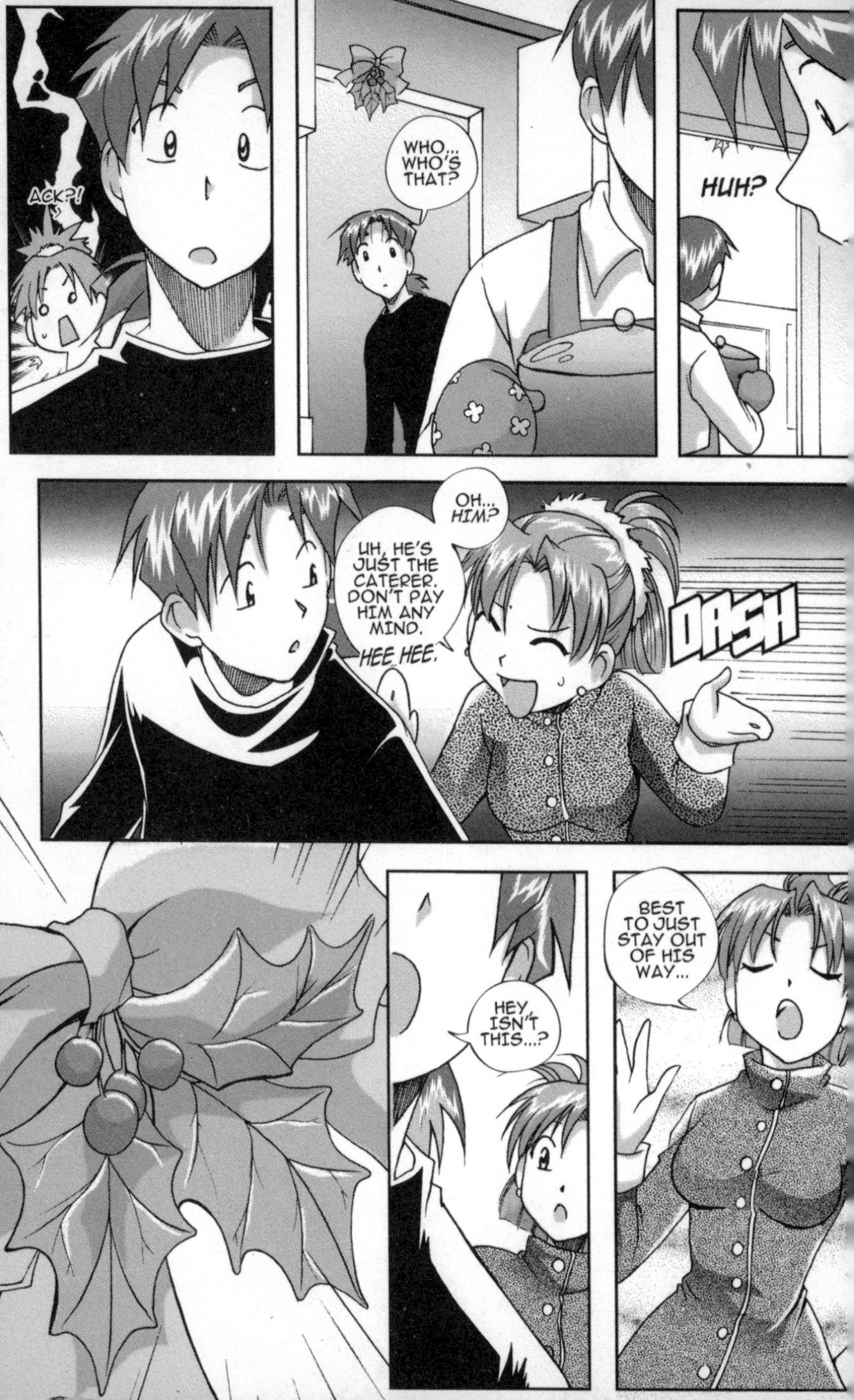
HUH?
WHO... WHO'S THAT?
ACK?!
OH... HIM?
DASH
UH, HE'S JUST THE CATERER. DON'T PAY HIM ANY MIND.
HEE HEE.
BEST TO JUST STAY OUT OF HIS WAY...
HEY, ISN'T THIS...?

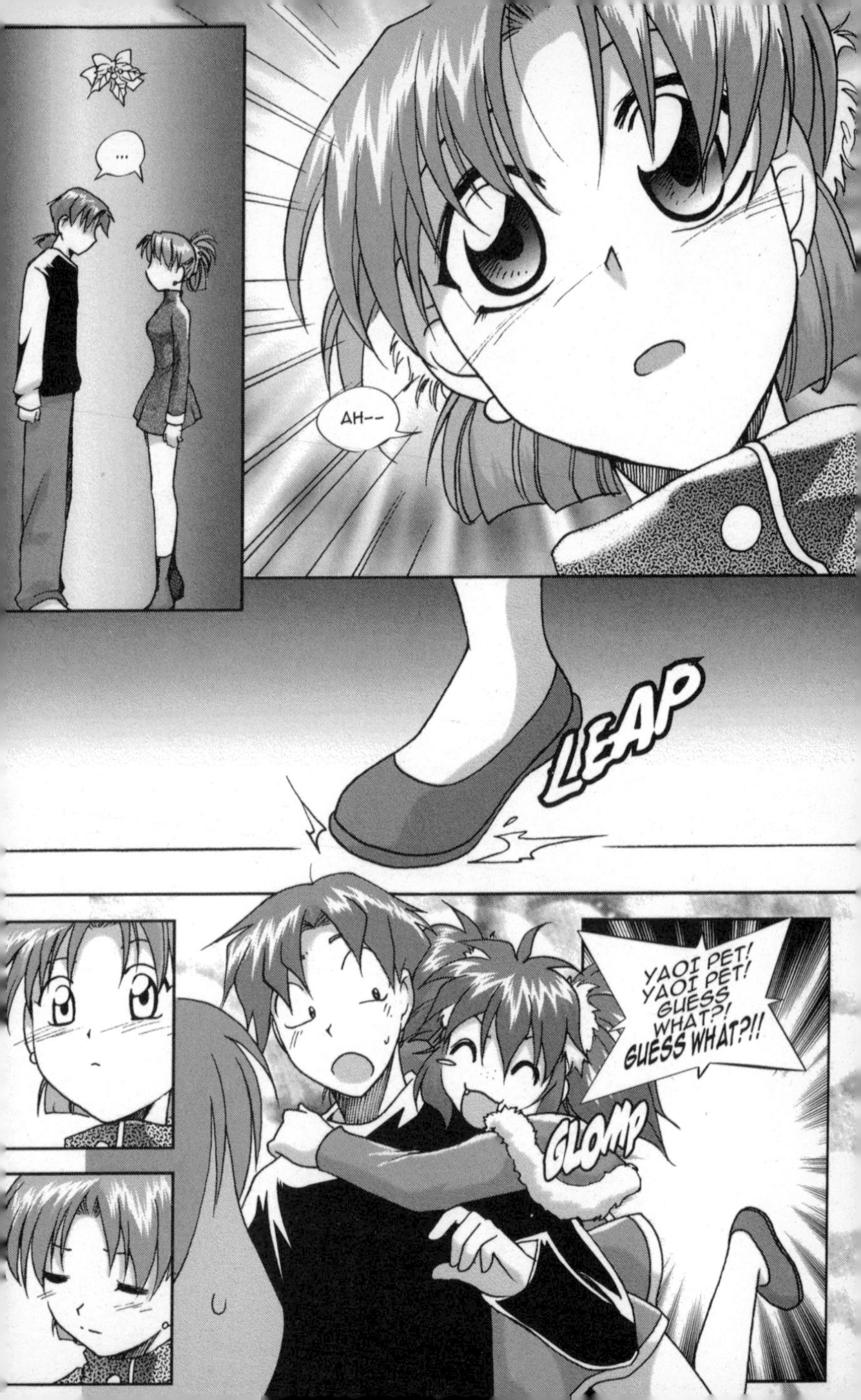
AH--
...
LEAP
YAOI PET! YAOI PET! GUESS WHAT?! GUESS WHAT?!!
GLOMP

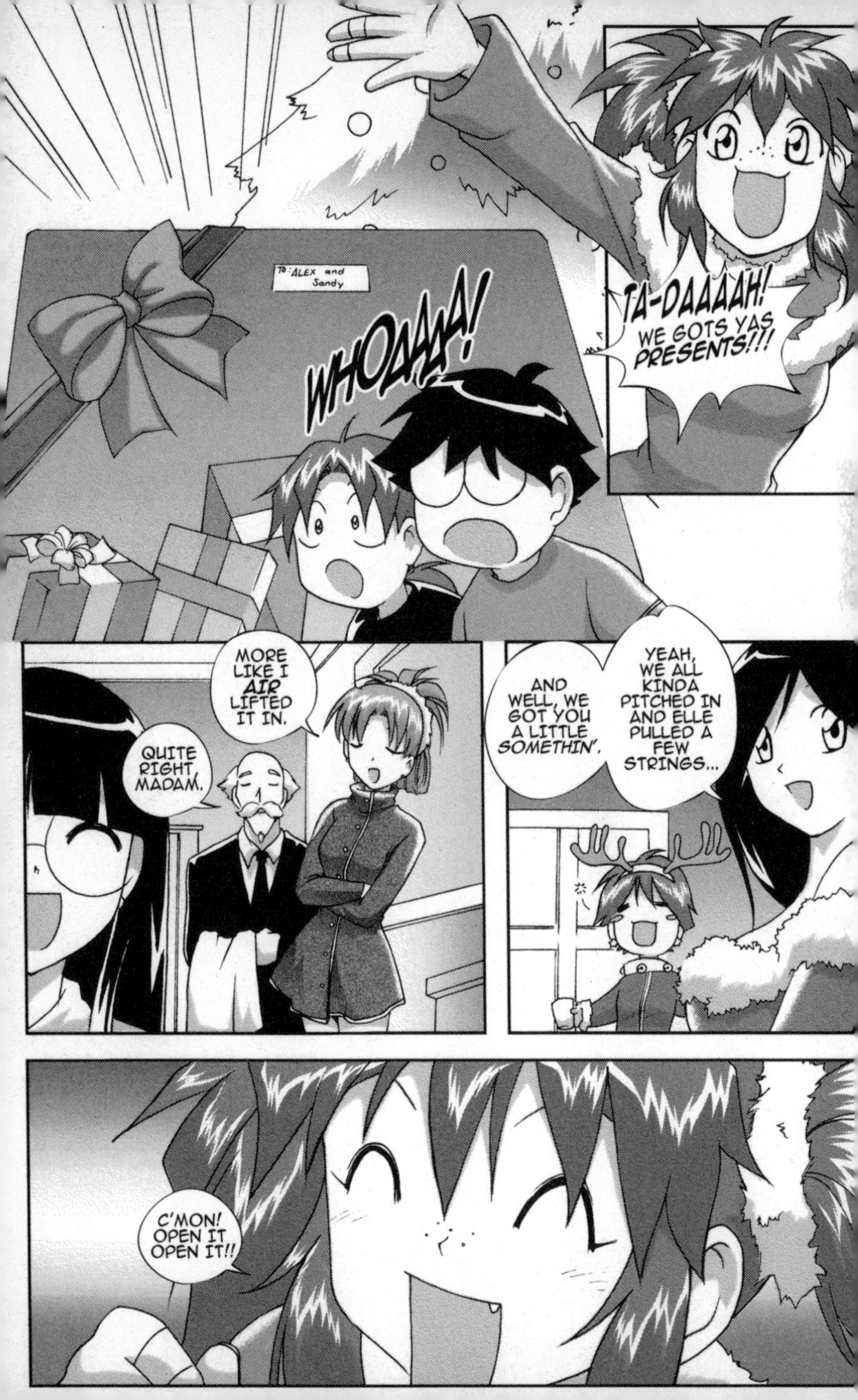
TA-DAAAAH! WE GOTS YAS PRESENTS!!!
TO: ALEX and Sandy
WHOAAAA!
YEAH, WE ALL KINDA PITCHED IN AND ELLE PULLED A FEW STRINGS...
AND WELL, WE GOT YOU A LITTLE SOMETHIN'.
MORE LIKE I AIR LIFTED IT IN.
QUITE RIGHT MADAM.
C'MON! OPEN IT OPEN IT!!

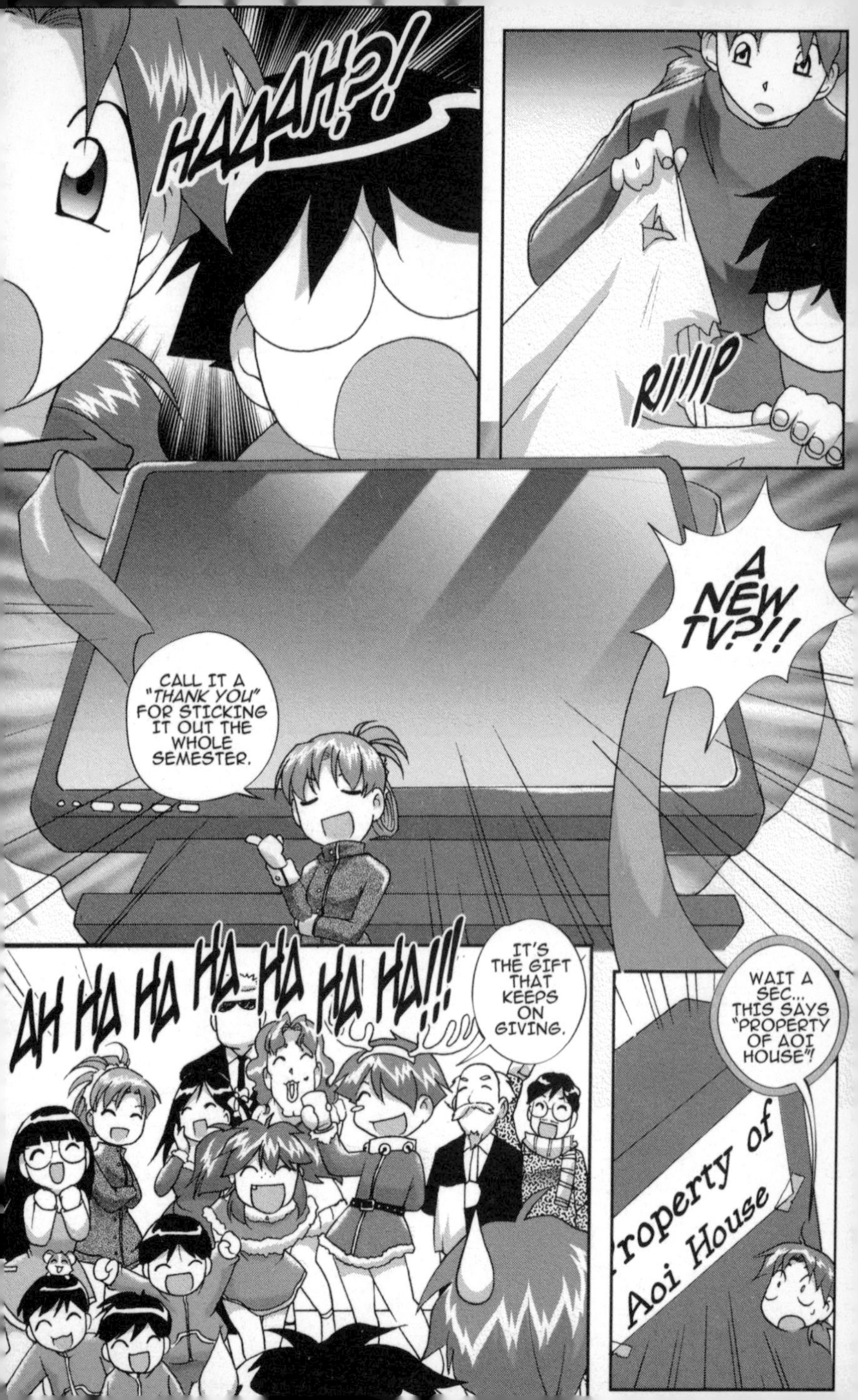
RIIIIP
HAAAH?!
A NEW TV?!!
CALL IT A "THANK YOU" FOR STICKING IT OUT THE WHOLE SEMESTER.
WAIT A SEC... THIS SAYS "PROPERTY OF AOI HOUSE"!
Property of Aoi House
IT'S THE GIFT THAT KEEPS ON GIVING.
AH HA HA HA HA HA HA!!!

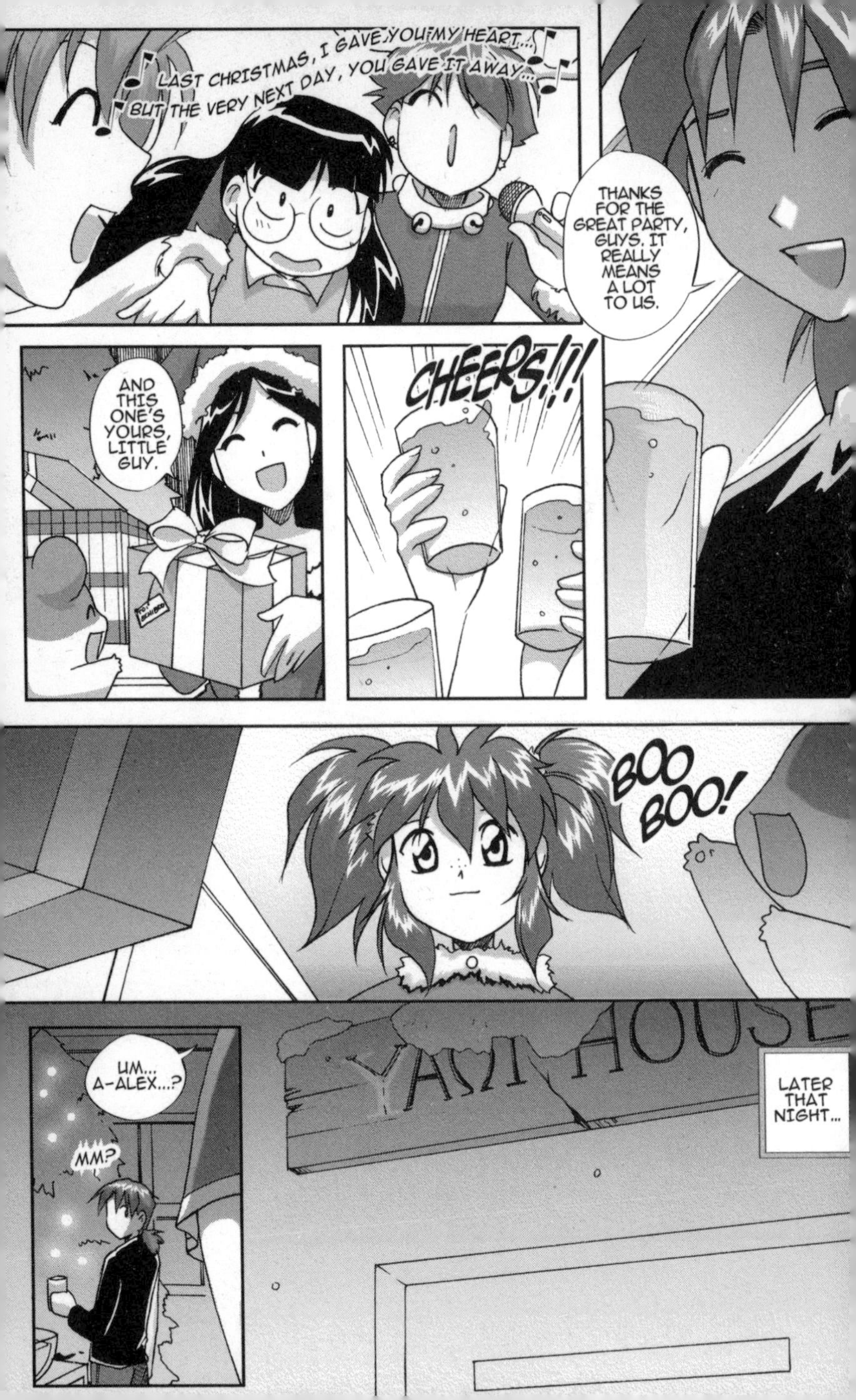
THANKS FOR THE GREAT PARTY, GUYS. IT REALLY MEANS A LOT TO US.
LAST CHRISTMAS, I GAVE YOU MY HEART...
BUT THE VERY NEXT DAY, YOU GAVE IT AWAY...
CHEERS!!!
AND THIS ONE'S YOURS, LITTLE GUY.
BOO BOO!
LATER THAT NIGHT...
UM... A-ALEX...?
MM?

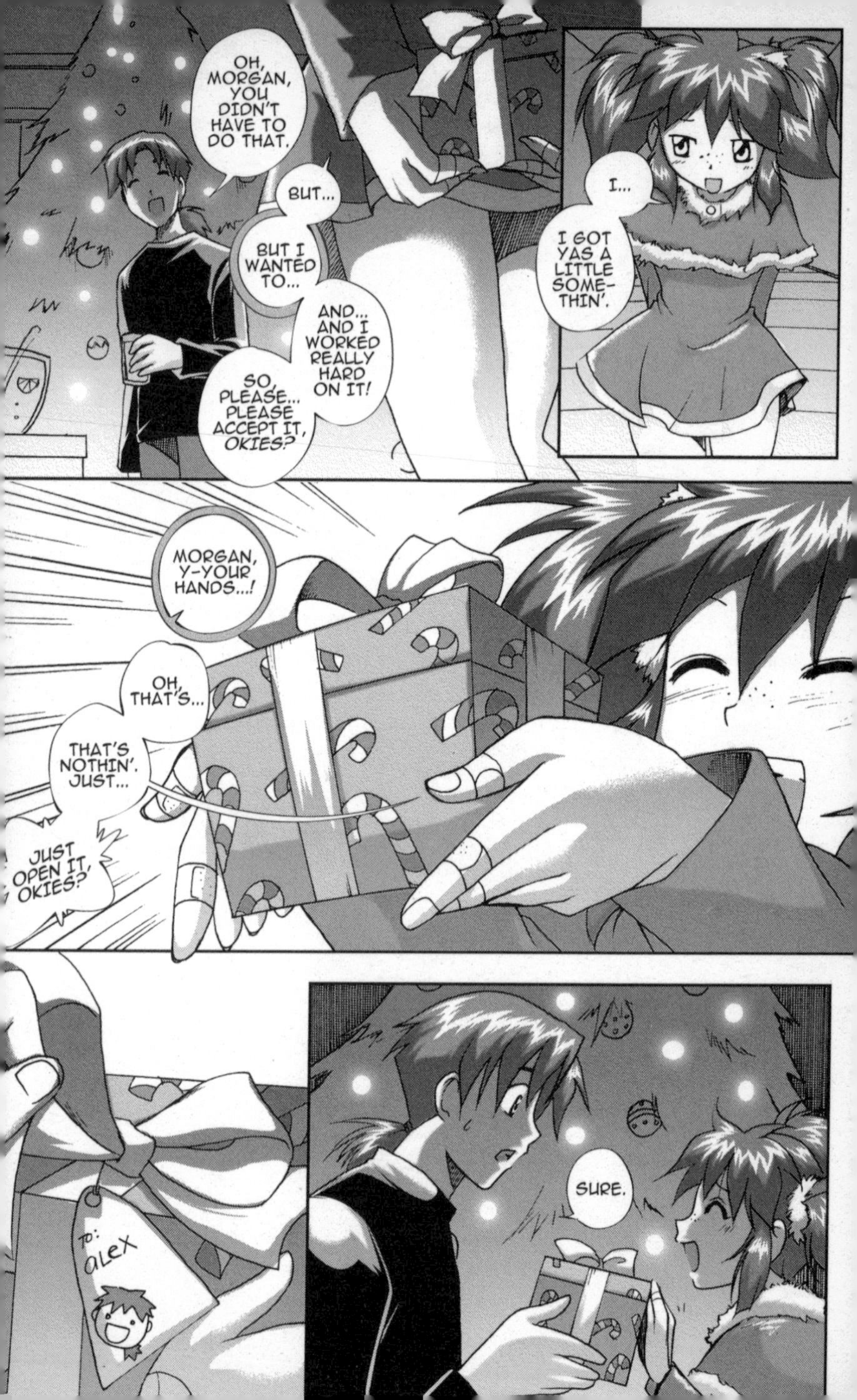
I...
I GOT YAS A LITTLE SOME-THIN'.
OH, MORGAN, YOU DIDN'T HAVE TO DO THAT.
BUT...
BUT I WANTED TO...
AND... AND I WORKED REALLY HARD ON IT!
SO, PLEASE... PLEASE ACCEPT IT, OKIES?
MORGAN, Y-YOUR HANDS...!
OH, THAT'S...
THAT'S NOTHIN'. JUST...
JUST OPEN IT, OKIES?
SURE.
To: alex

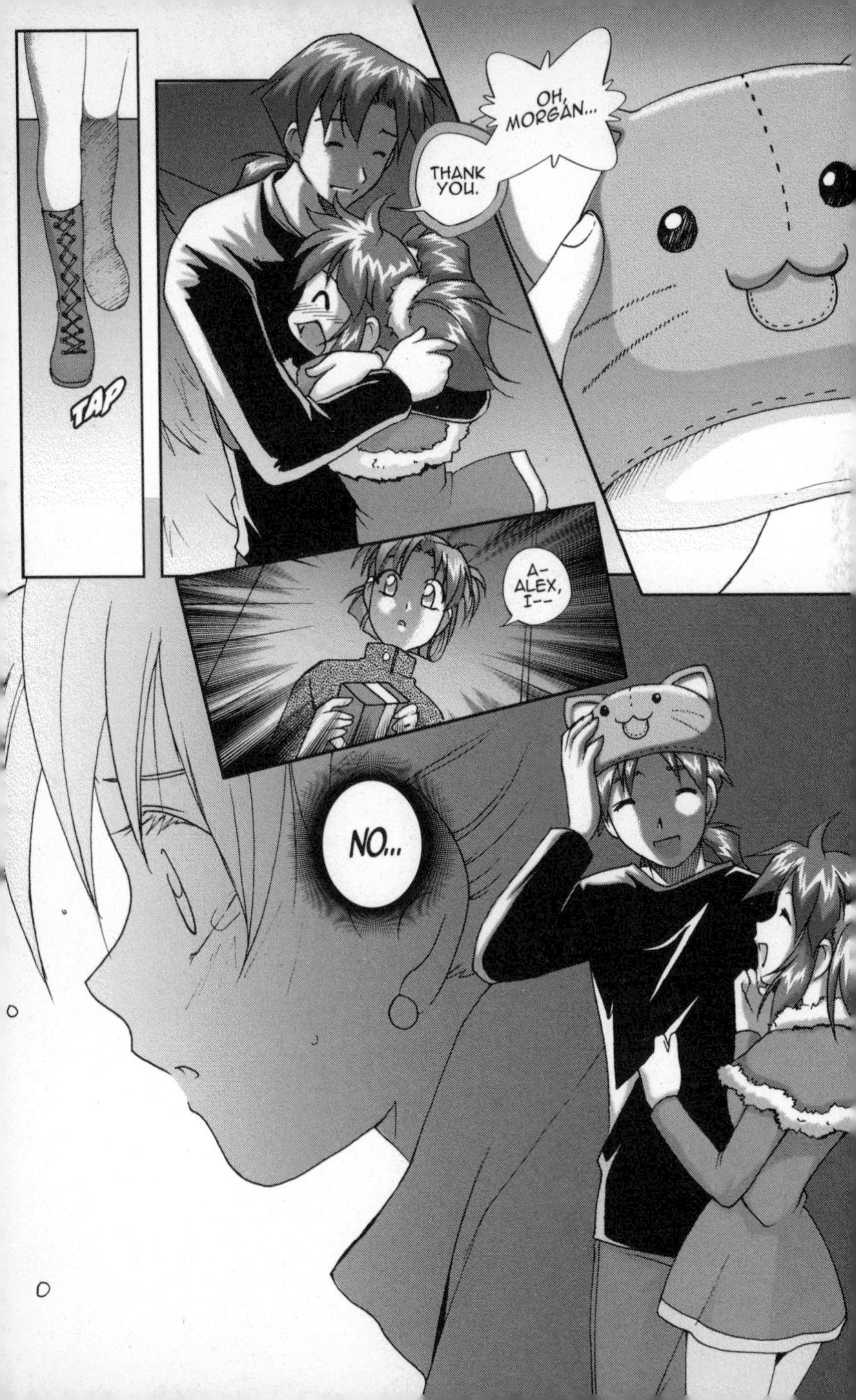
OH, MORGAN...
THANK YOU.
TAP
A-ALEX, I--
NO...

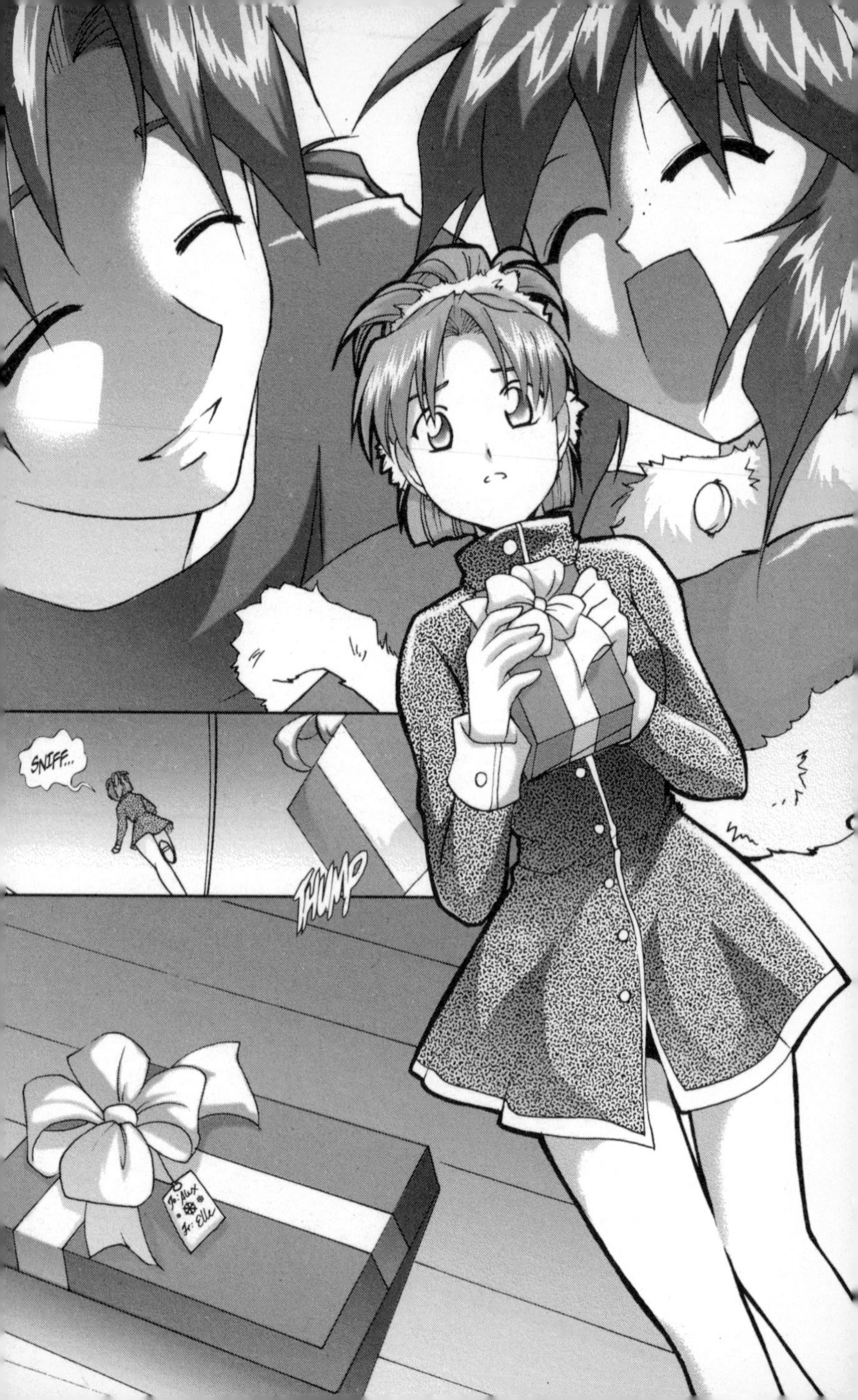
SNIFF...
THUMP
To: Alex
Fr: Elle

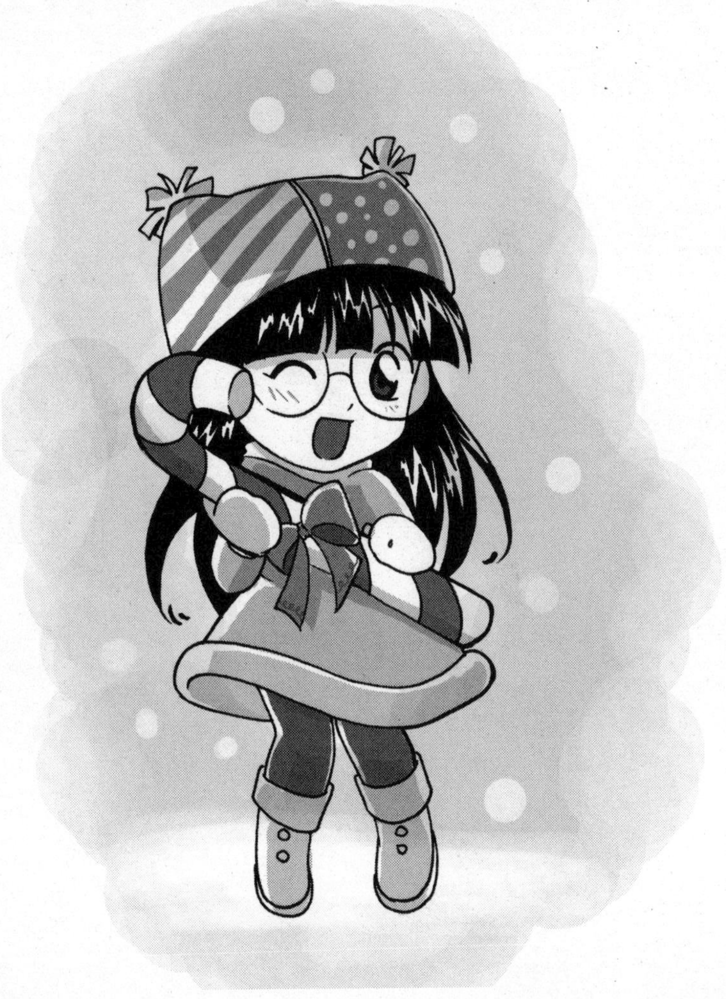

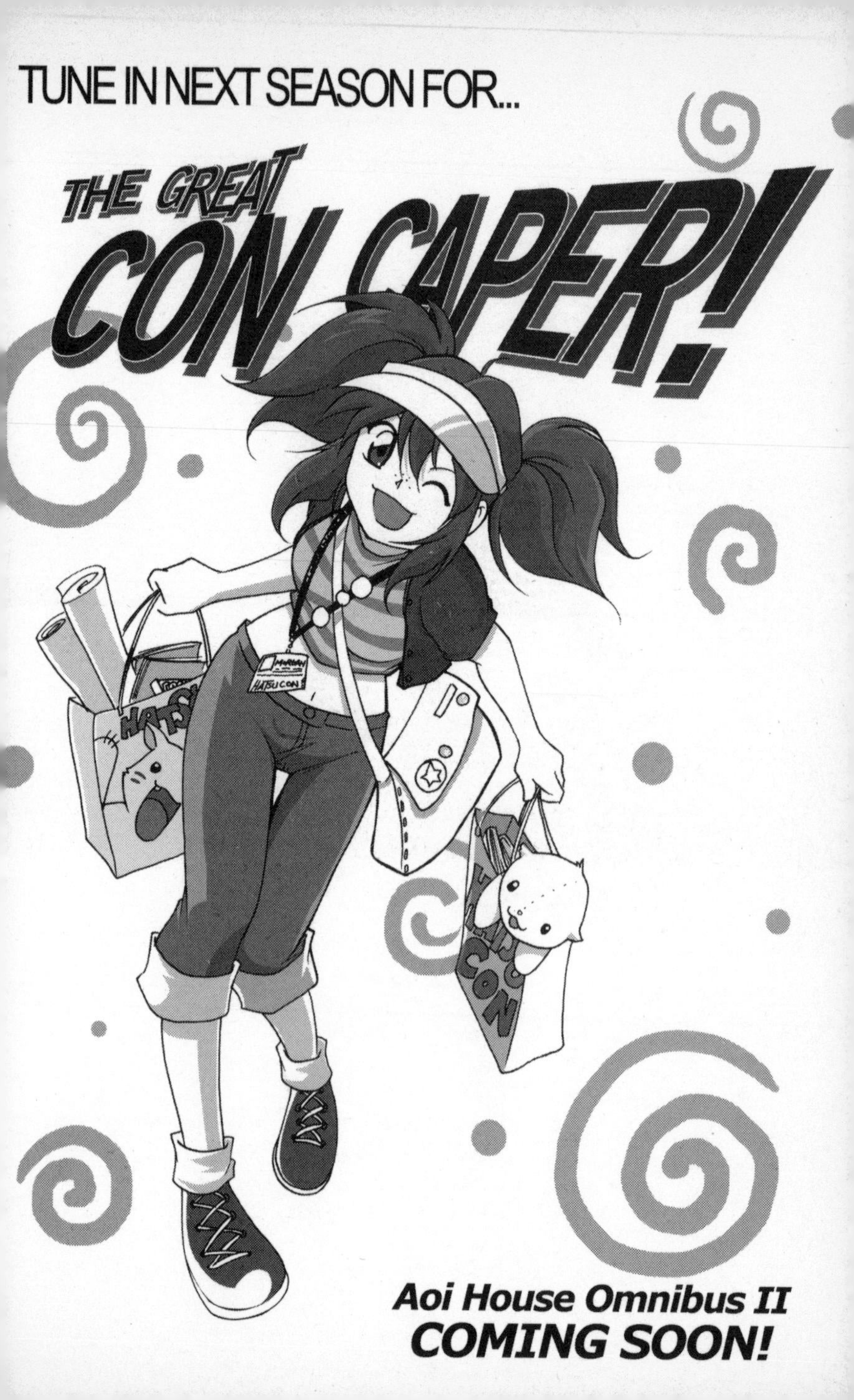
TUNE IN NEXT SEASON FOR...
THE GREAT
CON CAPER!
Aoi House Omnibus II
COMING SOON!

STUDENT RECORDS

ALEX

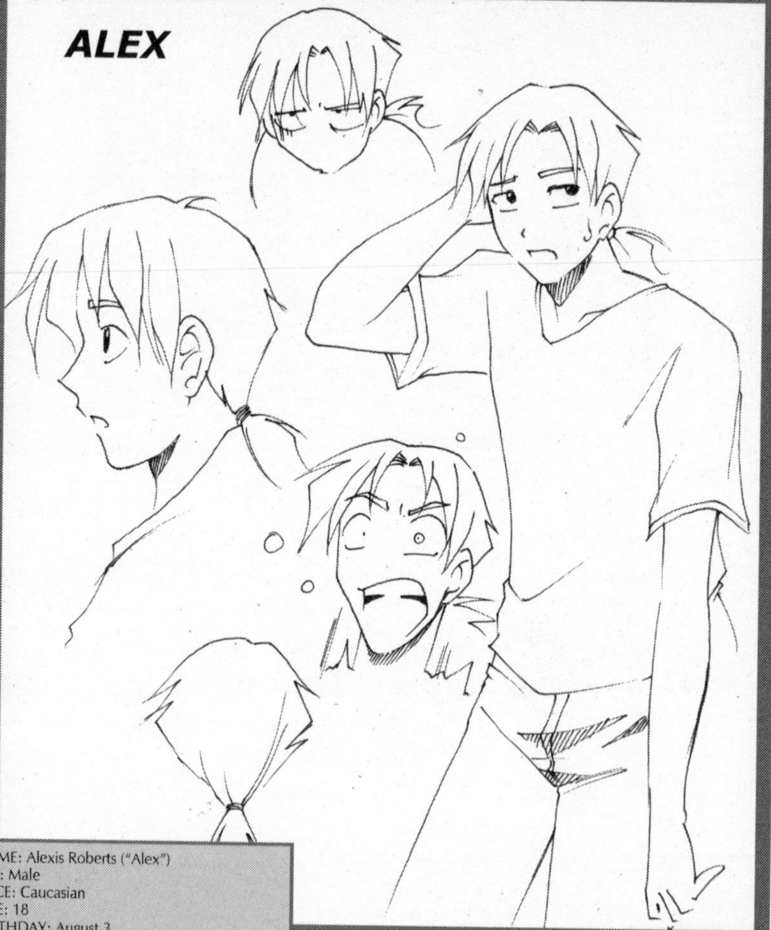

NAME: Alexis Roberts ("Alex")
SEX: Male
RACE: Caucasian
AGE: 18
BIRTHDAY: August 3
HAIR COLOR: Brown (long)
EYE COLOR: Green
OCCUPATION: Student
MAJOR: Graphic Design
HOBBIES: AMV Editing, Drawing
FAVORITE VIDEO GAME: Dance Dance Revolution, Tekken
FAVORITE SERIES: Neon Genesis Evangelion, Cowboy Bebop
ROOMS WITH: Sandy
ROOM CHARACTERISTICS: Has a computer smaller than Sandy's, a stereo and normal guy stuff.
PERSONALITY: The Slightly-With-It-But-Not-Quite-Hip-But-Would-Make-A-Nice-Boyfriend Type.

MAJOR CHARACTERISTICS: Alex is the Everyman. Not gym crazy, but quasi-athletic. He keeps his hair long, but in a ponytail that he patterned after Highlander character Duncan MacLeod. He is neither too preppy nor too grungy. Alex tries to at least keep up with the latest fashion trends as much as he can, though. He's the clean cut, regular guy type. Alex is not a complete otaku type; he's one part regular guy and one part otaku, and relies on his pal Sandy for his anime fix. Between the two of them, Alex is the ringleader, and the one who is more sociable and presentable in public. But when it comes to otaku-related pursuits, he defers to Sandy's obsessive expertise.

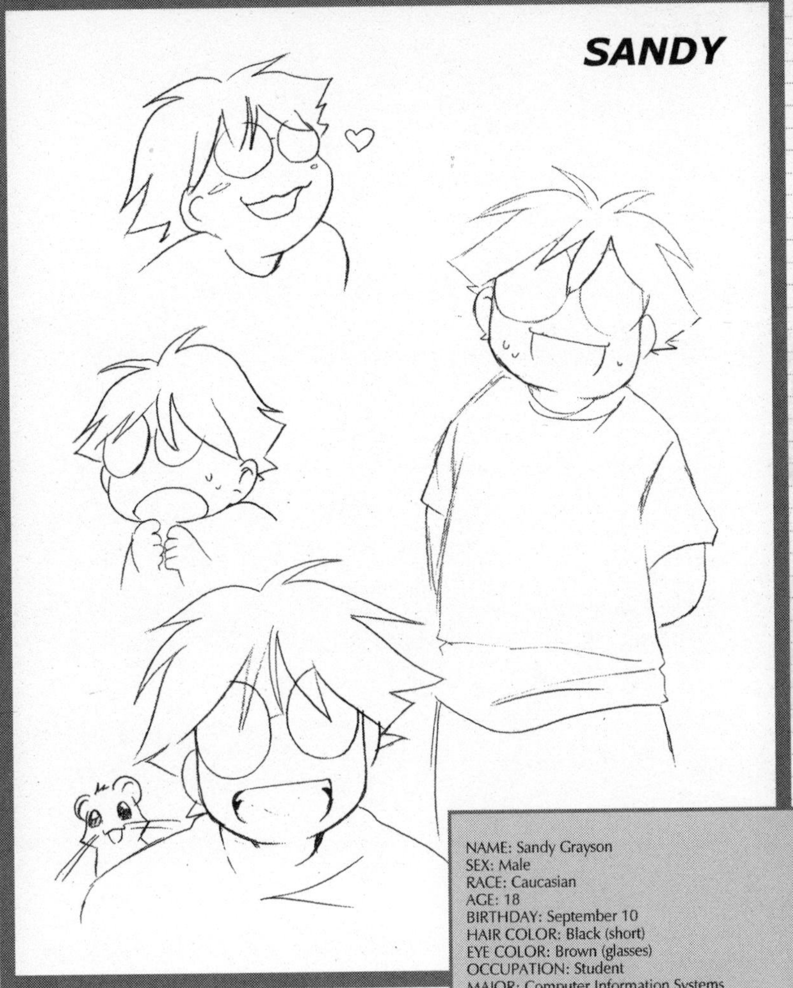
SANDY

NAME: Sandy Grayson
SEX: Male
RACE: Caucasian
AGE: 18
BIRTHDAY: September 10
HAIR COLOR: Black (short)
EYE COLOR: Brown (glasses)
OCCUPATION: Student
MAJOR: Computer Information Systems
HOBBIES: Chatting on the Internet
FAVORITE VIDEO GAME: Pretty much anything
FAVORITE SERIES: Ai Yori Aoshi, Bubblegum Crisis, Cardcaptor Sakura, Chobits, Fushigi Yugi, Inu-Yasha, Love Hina, Lupin III, Macross, Neon Genesis Evangelion, Noir, Rurouni Kenshin, Sailor Moon, Samurai Deeper Kyo, Tenchi Muyo... the list goes on and on and on.
ROOMS WITH: Alex
ROOM CHARACTERISTICS: Video game consoles, massive computer to die for and a hamster cage.
PERSONALITY: The Slightly-Overweight Obsessive Otaku Collector Type; Hentai

MAJOR CHARACTERISTICS: Sandy is the absolute epitome of an obsessed otaku. His hair is always slightly unkempt and he dresses in various anime, comic book and sci-fi themed T-shirts. While not grossly overweight, Sandy is chubby and pale skinned. He sunburns very easily, but does enjoy the beach (because of the girls). Sandy gets easily worked up over things that a sane person would not, and tends to drool and sweat profusely.

ELLE

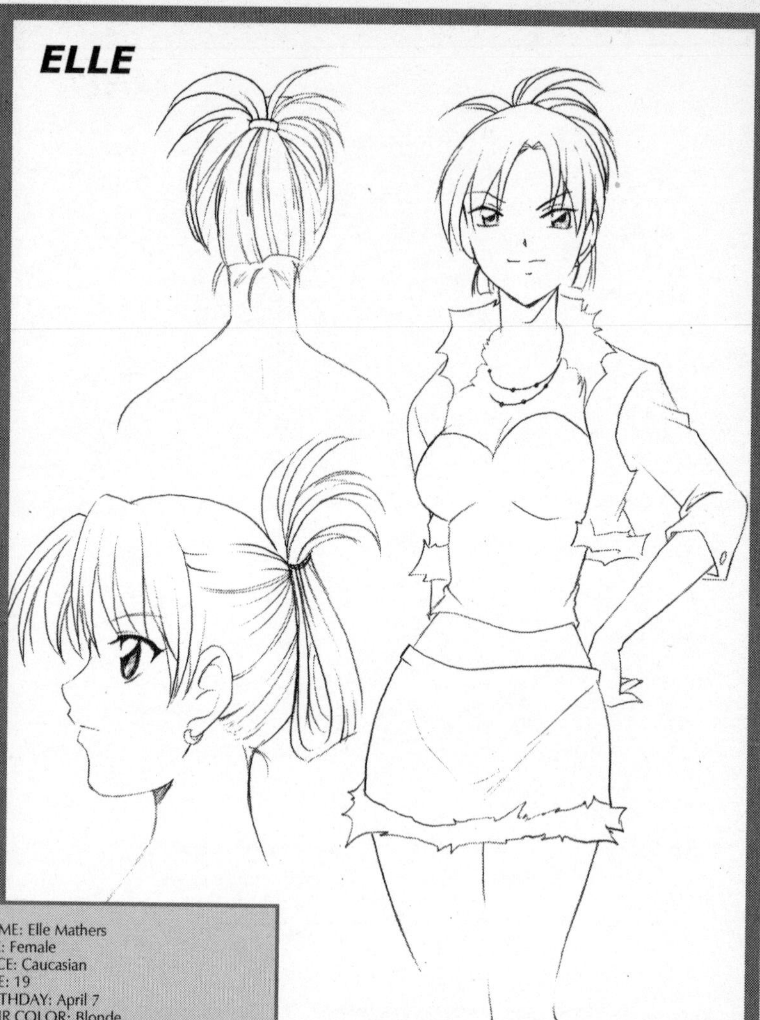

NAME: Elle Mathers
SEX: Female
RACE: Caucasian
AGE: 19
BIRTHDAY: April 7
HAIR COLOR: Blonde
EYE COLOR: Blue (contacts)
OCCUPATION: Student
MAJOR: Interior Design
HOBBIES: Fashion, Music, Tennis, Collecting/Making Dolls
FAVORITE VIDEO GAME: The Sims
FAVORITE SERIES: Super Gals, Cardcaptor Sakura, Kodocha
ROOMS WITH: Jessica
ROOM CHARACTERISTICS: Extensive doll collection. Lots of plushies.
PERSONALITY: The Bitchy-Fashion Model-Rich-Girl Type

MAJOR CHARACTERISTICS: Drop-dead gorgeous with a fashion sense to match. Elle always stands out in the crowd and her parents are loaded. She is high-strung, demanding and dominating, but is a natural-born leader. She can spring into dominatrix mode at the drop of a pin.

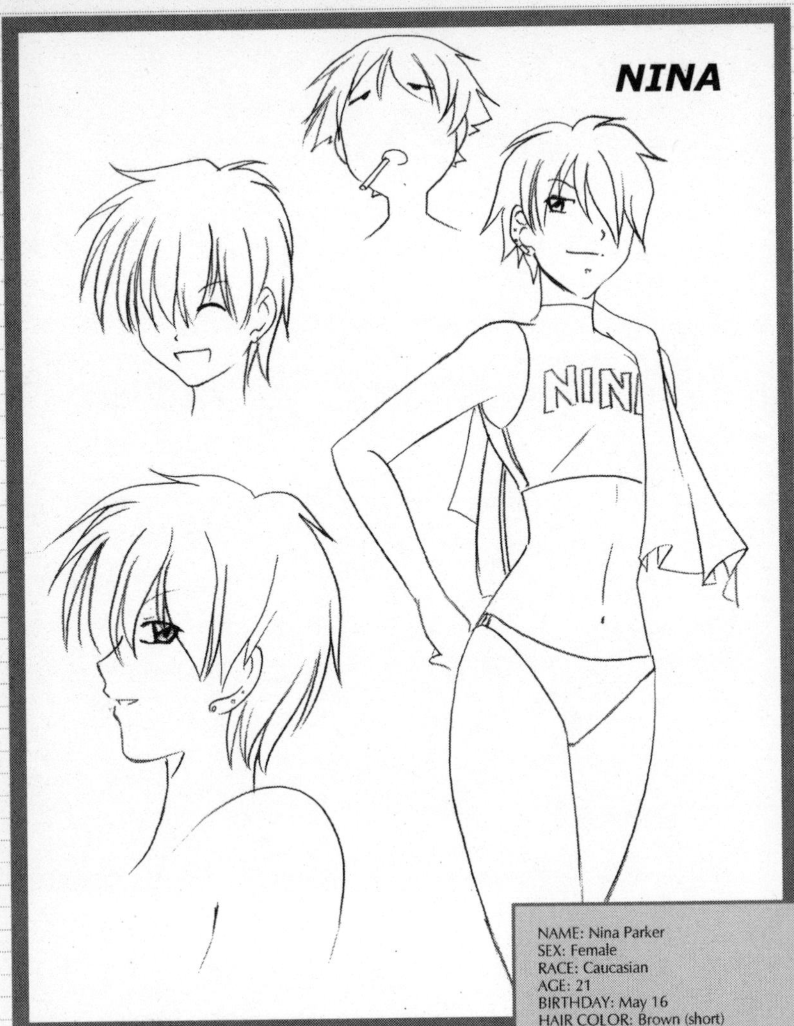
NINA
NINA

NAME: Nina Parker
SEX: Female
RACE: Caucasian
AGE: 21
BIRTHDAY: May 16
HAIR COLOR: Brown (short)
EYE COLOR: Green
OCCUPATION: Student
MAJOR: Art
HOBBIES: Synchronized Swimming, Drawing
FAVORITE VIDEO GAME: Final Fantasy VII, VIII, X, X-2
FAVORITE SERIES: Fake, Gravitation
ROOMS WITH: Morgan
ROOM CHARACTERISTICS: Totally messy with piles of clothes and food everywhere. The stereotypical college room.
PERSONALITY: Macho, indifferent type

MAJOR CHARACTERISTICS: Stunning legs that are quite muscular due to being a Synchronized Swimmer. Inversely her bust size is smaller than average. Often comes back dressed in her swimming suit. Nina likes to keep her hair short and thus gives off a rather tomboyish appearance that matches her feminist ways. But she's not a feminist in the political sense; she's just completely convinced of female supremacy. Unlike Elle, she is not hostile to the boys, but is mostly indifferent to them. She thinks that they're whining wimps, and non-entities, and has no qualms about walking around naked in front of them, since they are not the objects of her affection. Nina is also a habitual smoker, which irritates Elle to no end. The rule is that Nina is supposed to only smoke in the room she shares with Morgan which is a disaster zone, with mounds of clothes on the floor, clouds of cigarette smoke in the air, and flies a-buzzing.

MORGAN

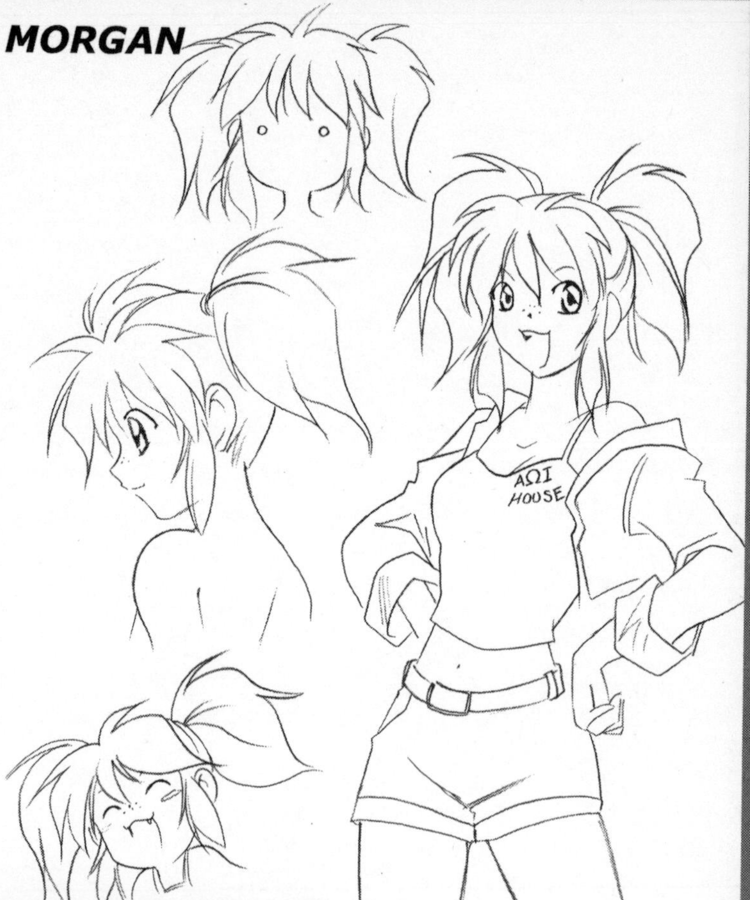
AΩI
HOUSE

NAME: Morgan McKnight
SEX: Female
RACE: Caucasian
AGE: 18
BIRTHDAY: July 10
HAIR COLOR: Red
EYE COLOR: Green
OCCUPATION: Student
MAJOR: Undecided
HOBBIES: Pestering Others, Eating Japanese Snacks
FAVORITE VIDEO GAME: Anything fun
FAVORITE SERIES: Anything you put in front of her as long as there are snacks involved.
ROOMS WITH: Nina
ROOM CHARACTERISTICS: Totally messy with piles of clothes and food everywhere. The stereotypical college room.
PERSONALITY: The Spunky Type

MAJOR CHARACTERISTICS: Shorter than all the other girls and constantly cheerful. Has freckles. Total troublemaker, but is truly endearing and loveable in all her over-the-top antics. Other than that, she's pretty much indescribable.

JESSICA

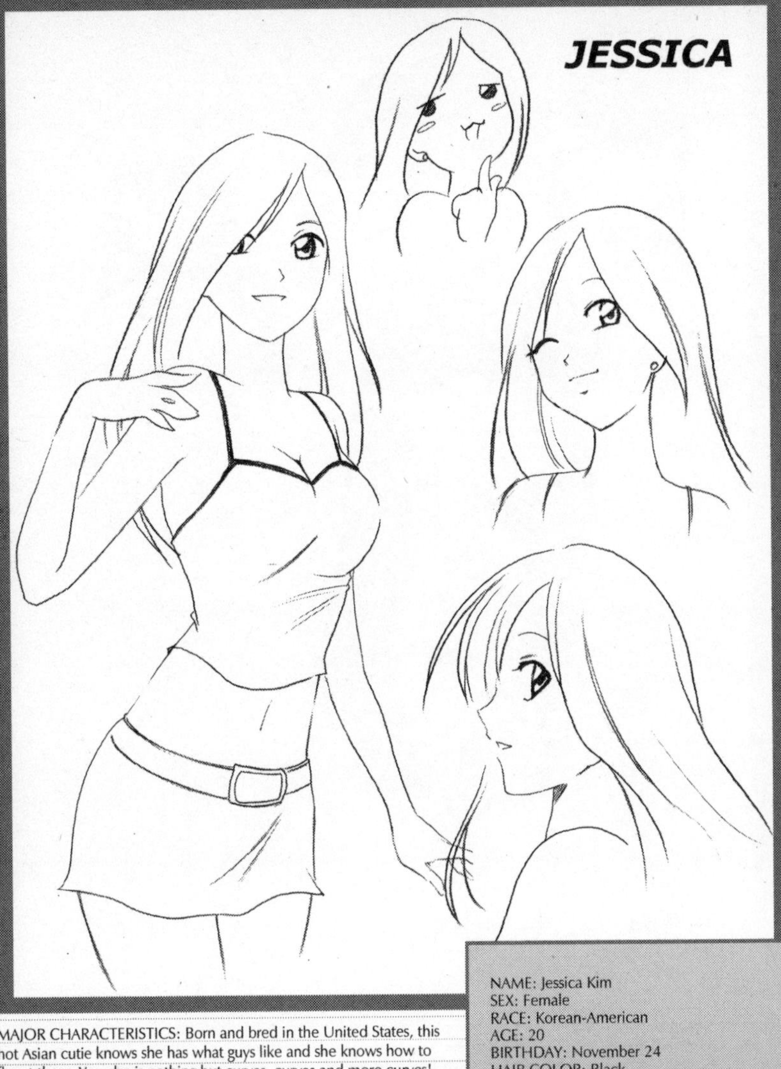

NAME: Jessica Kim
SEX: Female
RACE: Korean-American
AGE: 20
BIRTHDAY: November 24
HAIR COLOR: Black
EYE COLOR: Brown
OCCUPATION: Student
MAJOR: Nursing
HOBBIES: Shopping, Fandubbing
FAVORITE VIDEO GAME: Gran Turismo, Halo
FAVORITE SERIES: Tenchi Muyo!, Chobits, Love Hina, Ah! My Goddess
PERSONALITY: The Nurturing, Motherly Type

MAJOR CHARACTERISTICS: Born and bred in the United States, this hot Asian cutie knows she has what guys like and she knows how to flaunt them. Yes, she is nothing but curves, curves and more curves! Her radiant beauty and shapeliness is to die for and her fashion sense is casual, but always seems to highlight her most prominent features (her J-LO booty). She is the kind of person that once she latches on to someone, loves to mother them or tease them—whichever suits her mood at the moment, but she is a genuinely kind person. She loves brushing other people's hair, helping out with any chores someone might have, shopping for new clothes and gifts and even tutoring. Jessica even has her nursing outfit already and has more than a couple of times come back to the clubhouse decked out in it.

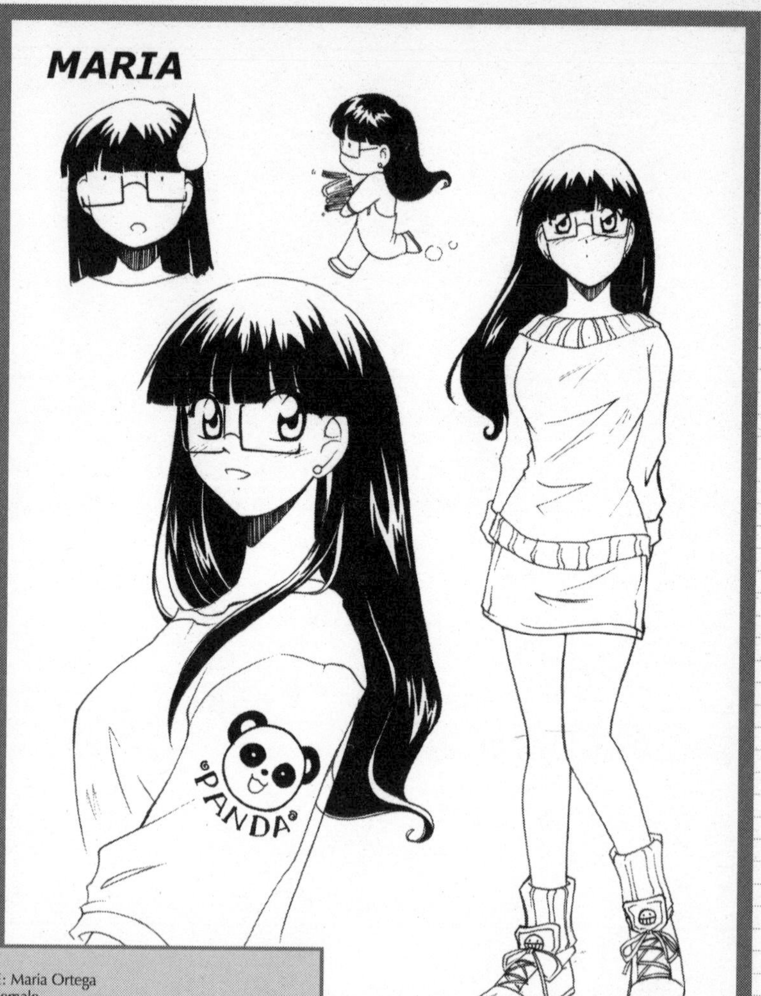
MARIA
PANDA

NAME: Maria Ortega
SEX: Female
RACE: Hispanic
AGE: 18
BIRTHDAY: September 14
HAIR COLOR: Brownish-Black
EYE COLOR: Brown (glasses)
OCCUPATION: Student, helps at family restaurant when she can
MAJOR: Business Administration
HOBBIES: Writing
FAVORITE VIDEO GAME: Dance Dance Revolution (the one thing that brings her out of her shell)
FAVORITE SERIES: Sailor Moon, Fruits Basket, Kare Kano
PERSONALITY: The Shy and Insecure Brainiac Type

MAJOR CHARACTERISTICS: Maria is very smart and can easily excel in school; unfortunately, she is very shy and often does not stand out in a crowd. You might not notice it by glancing at her, but she has very large breasts—even larger than Jessica's! She tries to keep her huge breasts a secret by wearing unflattering clothes and keeping her arms crossed a lot—but she's not always successful in hiding them; they seem to have a mind of their own, much to Maria's supreme embarrassment. Like Sandy and Alex, Maria just joined the same day and has a long way to go before she can truly emerge from her shell. Maria can also speak Spanish in addition to English.

CARLO

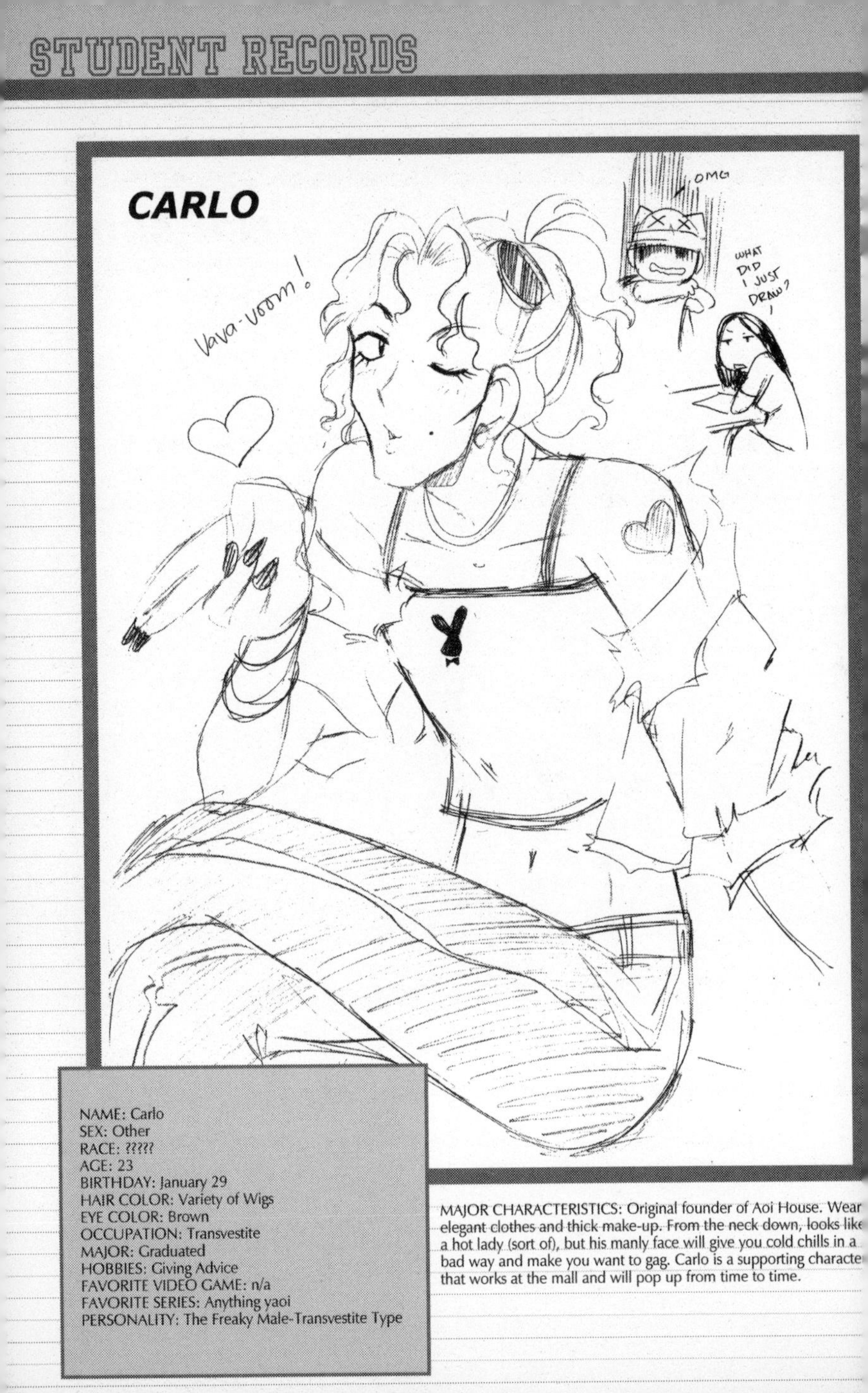
Vava-voom!
OMG
WHAT DID I JUST DRAW?

NAME: Carlo
SEX: Other
RACE: ?????
AGE: 23
BIRTHDAY: January 29
HAIR COLOR: Variety of Wigs
EYE COLOR: Brown
OCCUPATION: Transvestite
MAJOR: Graduated
HOBBIES: Giving Advice
FAVORITE VIDEO GAME: n/a
FAVORITE SERIES: Anything yaoi
PERSONALITY: The Freaky Male-Transvestite Type

MAJOR CHARACTERISTICS: Original founder of Aoi House. Wear elegant clothes and thick make-up. From the neck down, looks like a hot lady (sort of), but his manly face will give you cold chills in a bad way and make you want to gag. Carlo is a supporting characte that works at the mall and will pop up from time to time.

ECHIBOO

He looks like a bean.

I WANNA HUG HIM!

MAJOR CHARACTERISTICS: Echiboo is a pet. He shall squeak from time to time, but never talks. The spots on the little rascal's head are slightly reminiscent of those found on the character of Ebichu, but have other unique patterns elsewhere on its body. Whenever not in his cage, Echiboo loves exploring his new surroundings in his uber-cute hamster ball. However, Echiboo is a troublemaker to the core and can't help but eating holes in the girl's tennis shorts and dragging out panties whenever he gets on the loose.

NAME: Echiboo
SEX: Male
RACE: Hamster
BIRTHDAY: Unknown
HAIR COLOR: Brown and White
PERSONALITY: Hyperactive
FAVORITE ACTIVITY: Rolling around in his hamster ball

HEY, KIDS, IT'S TIME FOR SOME FUN!

FUN ZONE

FIND-A-WORD

O	P	O	L	R	A	C	I	S	S	E	J	W
T	M	A	R	I	A	D	A	M	E	H	E	V
A	C	O	N	A	G	R	O	M	I	I	K	M
K	O	O	A	T	E	S	U	O	H	I	O	A
U	S	O	N	S	I	Y	W	O	S	A	A	C
T	P	B	I	V	X	E	C	R	U	O	R	I
A	L	I	M	H	E	K	S	Y	L	N	A	H
G	A	H	E	L	L	N	A	R	P	I	K	C
N	Y	C	L	I	A	O	T	A	N	I	N	C
A	N	E	G	N	I	M	M	I	W	S	G	E
M	O	O	R	E	L	A	N	D	O	A	W	R
O	Y	K	C	O	P	E	R	K	I	N	S	D
K	H	Y	D	N	A	S	H	I	E	I	O	D

ADAM
ALEX
AMV
ANIME
AOIHOUSE
CARLO
CONVENTION
COSPLAY
DDR
DIARYROOM
ECCHICAM
ECHIBOO
ELLE
JESSICA
KARAOKE
KOMA

MANGA
MARIA
MOORELAND
MORGAN
NINA
ONIISAN
OTAKU
PANTIES
PERKINS
PLUSHIES
POCKY
SANDY
SEAMONKEY
SHIEI
SWIMMING
YAOI

COMPLETE THE PUZZLE FOR A HIDDEN MESSAGE!

PRESENTING YOUR VERY OWN AOI HOUSE MEMBERSHIP CARD!
CUT THIS BABY OUT AND PUT IT IN YOUR WALLET!

YAΩI HOUSE
OFFICIAL CLUB MEMBER

MEMBER NAME

AOI
House
SEAL OF APPROVAL

JOIN DATE

SEE REVERSE SIDE FOR CLUB RULES AND DISCOUNTS!

(P.S. YOU COULD ALSO JUST COPY THIS PAGE IF YOU DON'T WANT TO MESS UP YOUR BOOK!)

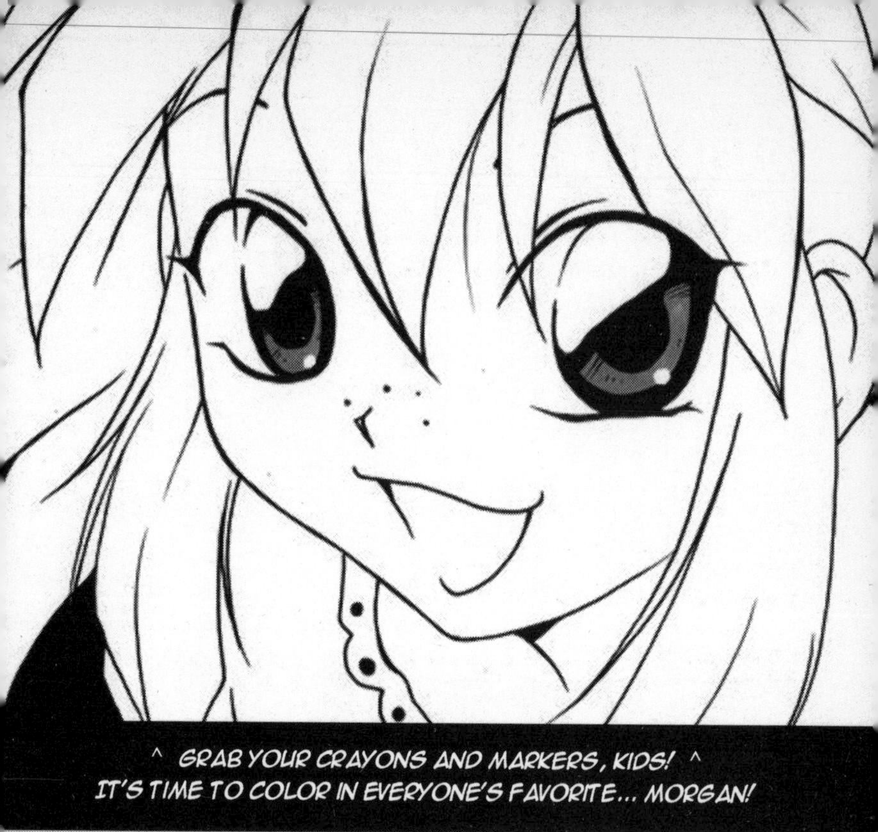
^ GRAB YOUR CRAYONS AND MARKERS, KIDS! ^
IT'S TIME TO COLOR IN EVERYONE'S FAVORITE... MORGAN!

CLUB RULES

1. Thou shalt embrace shonen-ai and yaoi with all your heart.
2. Your undying devotion shall be pledged to all things GACKT.
3. Participation in all club-related activities is mandatory!
4. We have a strict no locked doors policy -- follow it!
5. If you scratch our DVDs... you're dead!
6. Always smile. ^_^

MEMBER'S SIGNATURE

www.aoihouse.net

CLUB DISCOUNTS

- 20% off manga at BOOKS ETC
- 10% off candy at SWEET SHACK
- 10% off used games at GAME STOPPERS
- 5% off at CAPPUCCINO WORLD

Present your membership card at any of these fine area merchants and get a special, uber-cool discount!

THE LOST SCENE

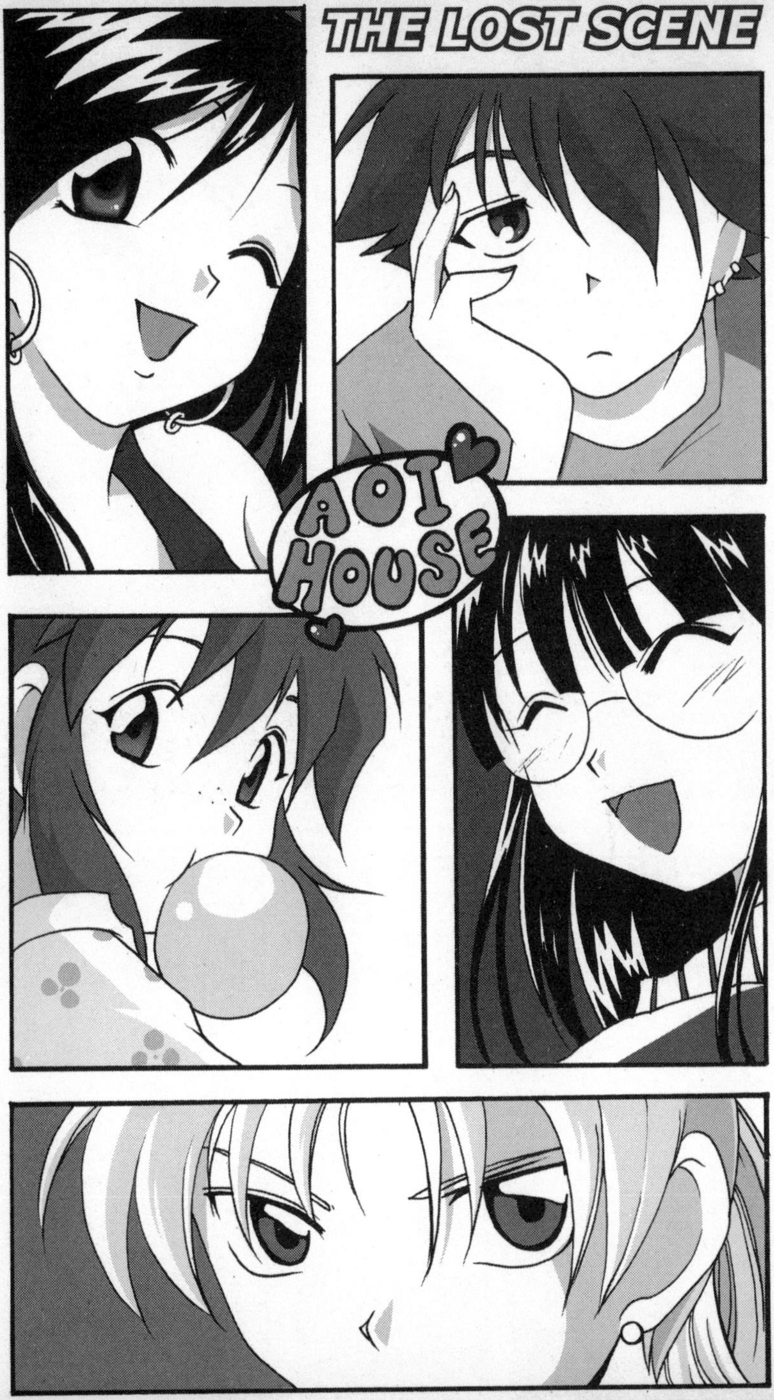
AOI HOUSE

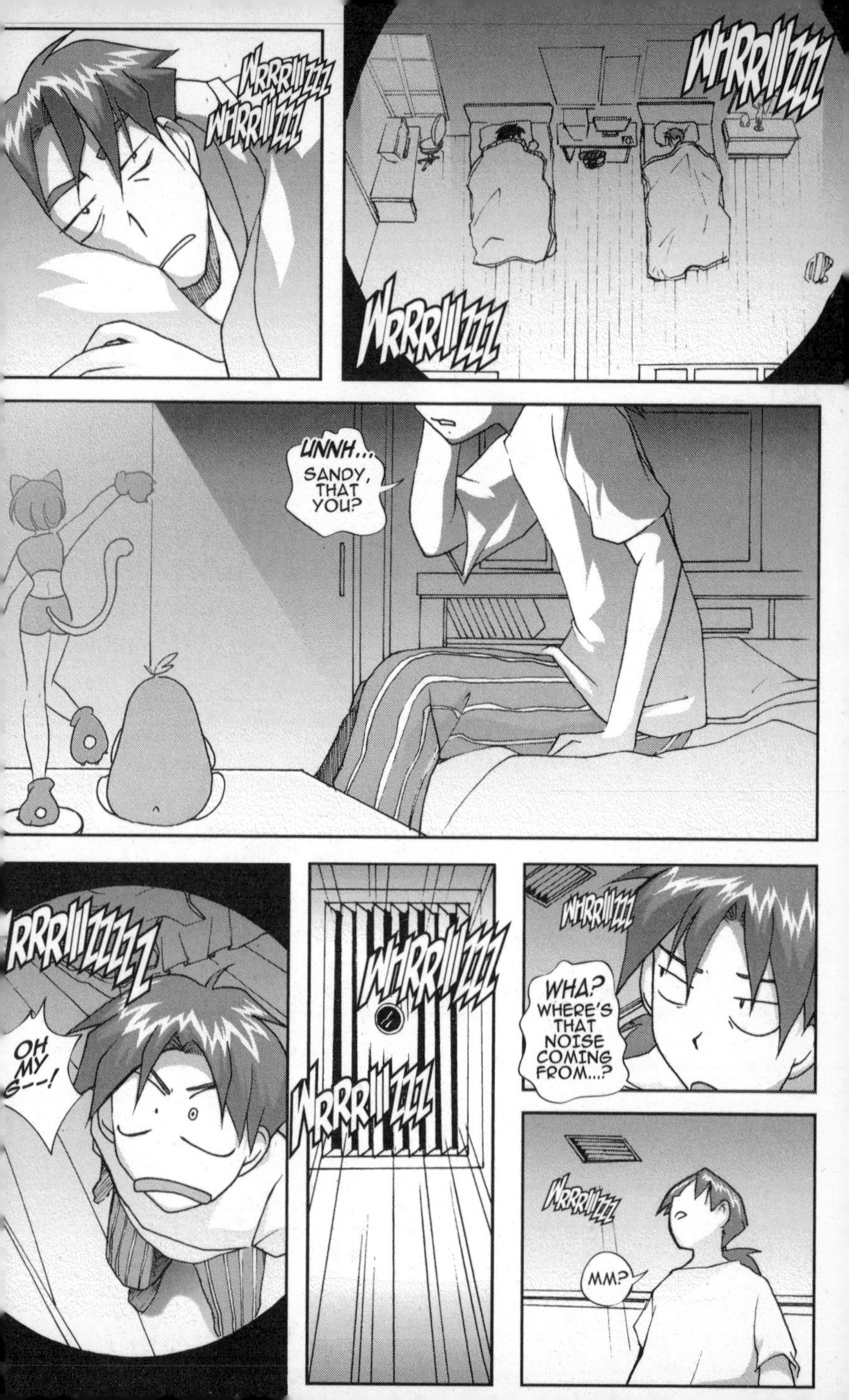
WHRRIIIZZZ
WRRRIIIZZZ
WRRRIIIZZZ
WHRRIIIZZZ
UNNH... SANDY, THAT YOU?
WHRRIIIZZZ
WHA? WHERE'S THAT NOISE COMING FROM...?
WRRRIIIZZZ
MM?
WHRRIIIZZZ
WRRRIIIZZZ
RRRIIIZZZZZ
OH MY G--!

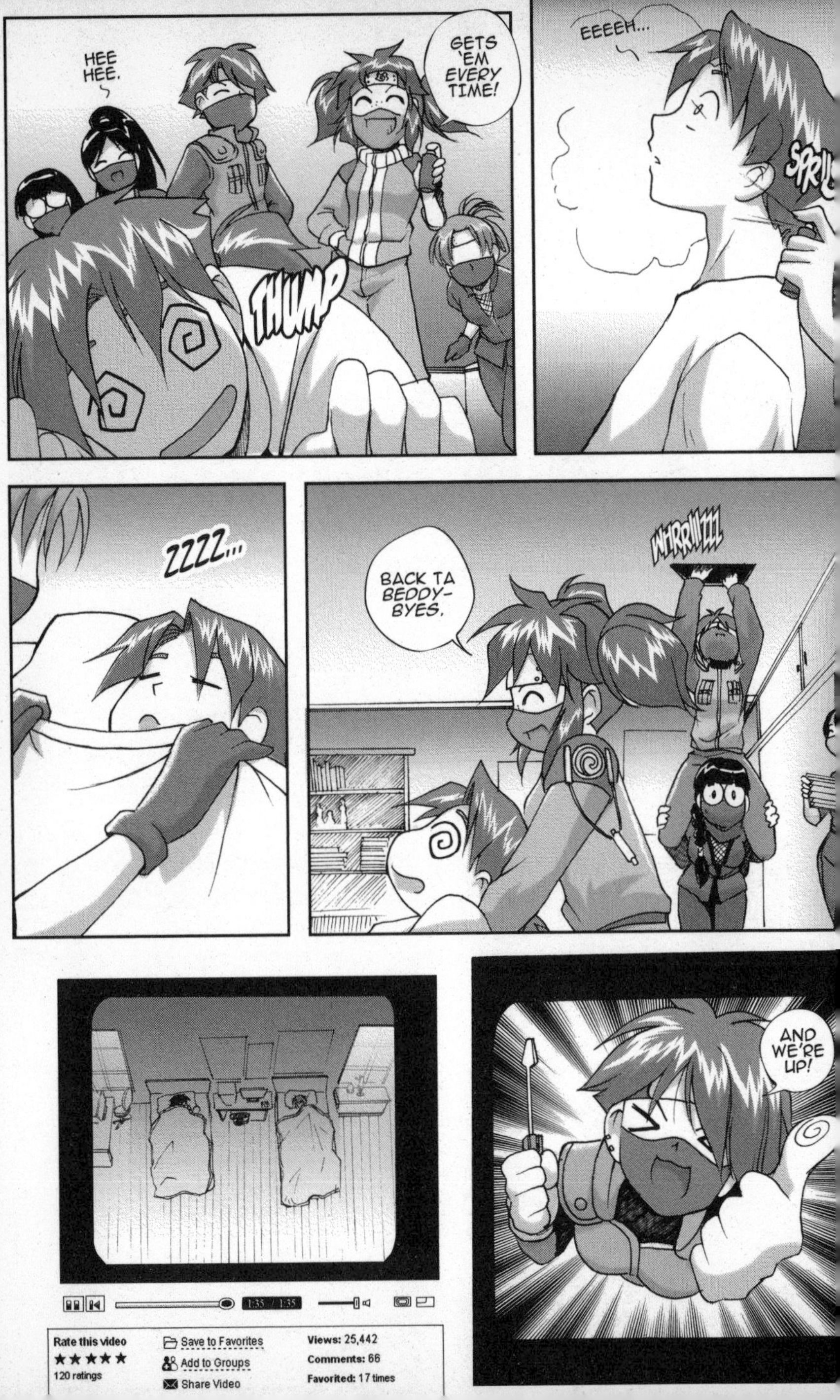
EEEEH...
SPRI
GETS 'EM EVERY TIME!
HEE HEE.
THUMP
WHRRIIIZZZ
BACK TA BEDDY-BYES.
ZZZZ...
AND WE'RE UP!
1:35 / 1:35
Rate this video
★★★★★
120 ratings
Save to Favorites
Add to Groups
Share Video
Views: 25,442
Comments: 66
Favorited: 17 times

THE END

YOU'RE READING THE WRONG WAY

This is the last page of
Aoi House Omnibus Collection I

This book reads from right to left, Japanese style. To read from the beginning, flip the book over to the other side, start with the top right panel, and take it from there.

If this is your first time reading manga, just follow the diagram. It may seem backwards at first, but you'll get used to it! Have fun!